GODLY PEOPLE

Sir Edward and Lady Susan Lewkenor

The Lewkenors are represented on their tomb in the parish church of Denham, Suffolk. Lewkenor, an exemplary godly magistrate and parliament man, succumbed to smallpox on 6 October 1605, the day after his wife. (*By courtesy of the Reverend John Bridgen and the Parochial Church Council of St Mary's church, Denham, Suffolk.*)

GODLY PEOPLE
Essays on English Protestantism and Puritanism

Patrick Collinson

THE HAMBLEDON
PRESS

Published by The Hambledon Press
35 Gloucester Avenue, London NW1 7AX

ISBN 0 907628 15 X

History Series 23

British Library Cataloguing in Publication Data

Collinson, Patrick
     Godly people: essays in English Puritanism and
     Protestantism – (History series; 23)
     1. Protestantism – History   2. Puritans – England –
     History   3. England – Church history – 16th century
     4. England – Church history – 17th century
     5. England – Church history – 18th century
     I. Title   II. Series
     280'. 4'0942   BR756

Printed and bound in Great Britain by
Robert Hartnoll Ltd., Bodmin, Cornwall

CONTENTS

ACKNOWLEDGEMENTS

The articles collected here were originally published in the following places and are reprinted by the kind permission of the original publishers.

This chapter appears here for the first time.

Journal of Religious History, Vol. 6 (1971), 305-30.

Bulletin of the Institute of Historical Research,
Special Supplement No. 5 (1960).

Journal of Ecclesiastical History, Vol. 30 (1979), 205-29.

Historical Journal, Vol. 23 (1980), 255-73.

Studies in Church History Vol. 3, ed. G.J. Cuming
(E.J. Brill, Leiden, 1966), 91-125.

Journal of Ecclesiastical History, Vol. IX (1958), 188-208.

Reform and Reformation: England and the Continent c. 1500- c. 1750.
Studies in Church History Subsidia 2, ed. D. Baker (Oxford, 1979),
71-102.

Proceedings of the Huguenot Society of London, Vol. 20 (1964), 528-55.

0   *Studies in Church History*, Vol. 2, ed. G. J. Cuming (1965), 258-72.

1   Friends of Dr. Williams's Library Annual Lecture 1965.

2   *Journal of Ecclesiastical History*, Vol. 15 (1964), 192-200.

3   *Elizabethan Government and Society: Essays Presented to*
Sir John Neale, ed. S.T. Bindoff, J. Hurstfield and
C.H. Williams (Athone Press, London, 1961), 127-62.

4   *The English Commonwealth 1547-1640: Essays in Politics and*
Society Presented to Joel Hurstfield, ed. P. Clark, A.G.T. Smith
and N. Tyacke (Leicester University Press, 1979), 39-57, 219-27.

5   *Reformation Principle and Practice: Essays Presented to*
A.G. Dickens, ed. P.N. Brooks (Scolar Press, London, 1980), 173-202.

6   *Studies in Church History* Vol. 1, ed. C.W. Dugmore and
C. Duggan (1964), 207-21.

viii

17   *Reformation, Conformity and Dissent: Essays in Honour of
      Geoffrey Nuttall*, ed. R.B. Knox (Epworth Press, London, 1977), 77-91.

18   *Bulletin of the Institute of Historical Research*, Vol. 48 (1975), 181-213

19   *Renaissance and Renewal in Christian History.
      Studies in Church History*, Vol. 14, ed. D. Baker (Blackwells,
      Oxford, 1977), 223-49.

20   *The Dissenting Tradition: Essays for Leland H. Carlson*,
      ed. C. Robert Cole and Michael E. Moody (Ohio University Press,
      Athens, Ohio, 1975), 3-38.

LIST OF ILLUSTRATIONS

Dedicated to the memory and lasting inspiration
of my mentors in Elizabethan Studies,
S.T. Bindoff, Joel Hurstfield and, *primus inter pares*, J.E. Neale

PREFACE

The articles and essays retrieved in this volume are the casual litter strewn in the wake of half a lifetime of research devoted to the second and third generations of English Protestantism. They make a companion volume, however unworthy, for the first generation *Reformation Studies* already published in this series by my friend, sometime colleague and esteemed mentor, Professor A.G. Dickens. Some of the sons and grandsons of the English Reformation, the 'hotter sort', were known to their contemporaries as 'puritans', but they called themselves 'the godly'. Hence the title, *Godly People*. When my supervisor, Sir John Neale, suggested to me in October 1952 that I should work on the Elizabethan puritans I had scarcely heard of these people. Two years later he said: 'Collinson, I like to think of you spending the rest of your life on this subject'. I laughed inwardly at the thought, having firm plans to escape into other centuries and research topics. But Neale was right and almost thirty years later I am still where I was then, an unsuccessful escapologist, striving to understand the religious culture of post-Reformation England and its implications for the politics, mentality and social relations of the Elizabethans and Jacobeans. When I started there were no more than two or three other researchers with kindred interests in the whole country and it seemed in no way absurd to select the Elizabethan puritan movement in something like its entirety as the subject of the doctoral thesis which I presented in 1957. Marshall Moon Knappen had published in 1939 a magisterial book called *Tudor Puritanism*, but nothing of much consequence had been done since. The task which I set myself was to complement and perhaps even in some respects improve upon Knappen. Whether I succeeded in any measure readers and reviewers were able to judge when my book *The Elizabethan Puritan Movement* appeared in 1967.

The situation by then was altered. The number of historians interested in post-Reformation religious history in all its aspects had multiplied, and it has continued to increase almost exponentially, in spite of the discouragement meted out by academic retrenchment. Of the making of theses, articles and books on Puritanism there appears to be no end, a living reminder of the wisdom of King Solomon in Ecclesiastes 11.12. In the seventies, a biennial colloquium devoted to

English Reformation studies regularly brought together fifty or more of the younger researchers, who between them have left scarcely a stone unturned on the broad strand of sixteenth and seventeenth-century ecclesiastical history.

Meanwhile a giant of a book had appeared, Keith Thomas's *Religion and the Decline of Magic* (1974), reducing the efforts of Mr. Thomas's contemporaries to pygmy proportions. The scope of the religious history of the early modern period, increasingly reclassified as the history of 'mentalities', was at once vastly extended. Religious historians of an earlier vintage were forced to stumble out of the narrow confines of conventional studies into a more brilliant day, blinking and rubbing their eyes as they strove to absorb new images and entities: witchcraft, magic, astrology, healing, divination, dreams, hopes of the Millennium, paranoid fears of the Jesuits, witches and the threatening, feckless poor. Christopher Hill announced that religious historians were no longer interested in what people were supposed to believe but in what they in fact believed, and even more with the uses to which their beliefs were put, the profoundly difficult problem of function.

In the early eighties the agenda has shifted again, away from the 'hotter' religious minorities and the more exotic forms of alternative or surrogate religion towards the conformable social majority. Now at last we may discover that the bulk of our Elizabethan and Jacobean ancestors were neither spiritual supermen nor pagan folklorists but humdrum, conventional christian believers of the kind we encounter two centuries later in the novels of Eliot and Trollope: as careful in the practice of their religion as in the drafting of a will or the making of a marriage contract. I suppose that we always knew that but thirsted for a little excitement. Scholarly interest in Puritanism may now have outlived its capacity to arouse an excited response. Gone are the days when Professor Neale punctuated his Monday evening seminar with the eager question: 'Was he a puritan? Was he a radical?' In a routine undergraduate lecture I attended in Oxford in the summer of 1981, Dr. Christopher Haigh confessed that he was heartily sick of the godly, and he seemed to strike an answering chord. It is time for me to tuck up my articles and occasional pieces in this stout volume and to utter no more on the subject, unless compelled to do so by main force.

No attempt has been made to correct the essays or to bring them up to date, although they are doubtless pitted with the pock-marks of error and often quaintly old-fashioned in their perspectives. When I wrote 'The Role of Women in the English Reformation Illustrated by the Life and Friendships of Anne Locke' feminist history was scarcely visible, a cloud on the horizon the size of a man's (or rather a person's) hand. And it was felt necessary to apologise for the term 'grass roots' as an exotic Americanism. Some will see it as a distortion of the true position for the earlier articles to have assumed a measure of coherence and purposeful political integration in Elizabethan Puritanism which some historians (among them Professor G.R. Elton) have since come to doubt. However it has seemed best to make no concessions to recent 'revisionism' but to publish the articles without alteration, as the record of one historian's developing perceptions. And revisionism will have gone too far if it forgets the existence of John Field and ignores the militant and genuinely revolutionary programme of the extreme wing of Elizabethan Puritanism. The point of my early studies, and one which still stands, was to demonstrate that if extreme Puritanism was the ideology of a minority within a minority, its methodology of propaganda and political agitation was all the more impressive.

In my recent book *The Religion of Protestants* (1982) I acknowledged many debts to friends and fellow workers. On this occasion it is only necessary to add my thanks to Martin Sheppard of the Hambledon Press for the remarkable speed and efficiency with which he has brought this enterprise to fruition, a shining example to larger publishing houses. And for help with the illustrations I acknowledge with gratitude the invaluable assistance of John and Mary Todd of St. Bees, Cumbria; of the Reverend John Bridgen and the Parochial Church Council of St. Mary's church, Denham, Suffolk; and of Dr. Christopher Haigh of Christ Church, Oxford.

PATRICK COLLINSON

THE GODLY: ASPECTS OF POPULAR PROTESTANTISM

"The godly" was the appellation preferred by those sixteenth-century Englishmen whose unsympathetic neighbours called them "puritans", "precisians", and, with an equally derogatory intent, "saints" and "scripture men". The same people knew themselves as "gospellers" (and even as "hot gospellers") and as sincere "professors" of true religion. Evidently, what is called puritanism in many of the sources cannot be readily distinguished in the field from mere protestantism, the protestantism, that is, of the convinced, the instructed and the zealous. To define "puritanism" with respect to the actual conditions obtaining in the local community, it may not be necessary to refer to the issues of conscience which in learned circles divided puritans from those we are bound, for want of a less anachronistic label, to call Anglicans. One must, however, exercise some appreciation of the peculiarities in behaviour and ethos which distinguished those individuals and households whose protestantism was more than a formality. As for those who pursued a more conventional way of life, it hardly assists our understanding of the realities of the Elizabethan religious situation to describe them, as R.G. Usher did, as "loyal Anglicans"![1]

The isolation of the practising protestant element in society was not as complete as it would have been in a wholly alien, catholic environment. Yet it is clear that "puritan", no less than "lollard" in the past, and "huguenot" across the Channel, was a social stigma, expressing distaste for a singular way of life, and popular rather than polite in its origins, as these stereotyped complaints will show: "I perceive you are a puritan outright, you are one of these new men that would have nothing but preaching. It was never merry world since that sect came first amongst us". "A shame take all professors, for they are all dissemblers and liars". "'Oh', say the scorning railers, 'now this holy man will go to heaven in a hay-barn, now these puritans flock together' ":[2] Clearly, the discussion of the early puritan movement

1 R.G. Usher, "The People and the Puritan Movement", *Church Quarterly Review*, lviii (1904), pp. 103-18; and in his *The Reconstruction of the English Church* (New York, 1910), i, pp. 244-81.
2 I.B., *A dialogue between a vertuous gentleman and a popish priest*, (1581), Sig. Bviii[v]; words attributed to John Huckford of Elmstead in proceedings in the Archdeaconry Court of Colchester 1591, Essex Record Office, D/ACA/19, fo. 226[r]; Bartimaeus Andrewes, *Certaine verie worthie godlie and profitable sermons*, (1583), p. 185.

must be given a sociological reference. A recent study of the theological difference between Anglicanism and puritanism has exposed the superficiality of some of the classical accounts of English church history in this period. But one may question the claim to have uncovered "the basis" of the conflict in theology alone.[3]

The progressive protestant cause in Elizabethan England can be compared to a tripod, consisting of puritan preachers, adherents and sympathizers among the nobility and gentry, and the popular element which contemporaries normally had in mind when they spoke substantively of "the godly". Much remains to be learned of the structure of the puritan movement in each of these areas of support, and the points of interdependence and incompatibility between them will repay closer attention. Clerical puritanism is the most adequately explored: for "puritan" in much of the literature, read "puritan minister". A more recent discovery has been the reliance of progressive protestantism on the patronage of the landed classes, a dependence less complete than that of the catholic recusant community, but probably the key to the fluctuations in its local and national fortunes. By comparison, the contribution of the lower orders remains an unknown quantity. A general awareness of the disposition towards protestantism of the middling and "industrious sort of people" has sustained the work of sociologists and social historians, and most recently has guided Dr. Christopher Hill's penetrating studies of the non-theological motives and implications of puritanism.[4] In this sense, there has been no lack of sociological interpretation. But concern with the end-products (or by-products?) of the puritan ethic has not always assisted the social study of religion itself, which should have as one of its main objects in this period precise knowledge of the structures of protestantism and puritanism. On the other hand, reformation studies as pursued by the church historians have as yet made little use of the techniques of religious sociology perfected elsewhere.

This paper will contain three elementary contentions: that the preaching and assimilation of the primary protestant doctrines in Elizabethan conditions set up processes which were calculated to divide and even to dissolve the parish as the essential unit of ecclesiastical organization; that the popular protestant element in Elizabethan society was not subordinate to the preachers, but possessed of a mind and a will of its own, to which the conduct of the puritan minister, including his own nonconformity, was partly a response; and that the

3   J.F.H. New, *Anglican and Puritan: The Basis of their Opposition, 1558-1640*, (London, 1964).

4   *Economic Problems of the Church from Archbishop Whitgift to the Long Parliament*, (Oxford, 1956); *Society and Puritanism in Pre- Revolutionary England*, (London, 1964).

character of popular protestantism inevitably tended towards congregational independency. Little claim of originality can be made for
observations which for the most part have occurred, some of them in
developed form, in Christopher Hill's *Society and Puritanism in Pre-
Revolutionary England*. The object of this essay is to continue the
exploration of these themes, and to provide illustrative material from
the county of Essex, a locality already deeply penetrated by protestant
influences in the Elizabethan period.

This discussion will lack foundations which, in an age of scientific
history, may be thought indispensable for the serious treatment of
popular religion. There are as yet no local studies of the kind which
would allow us to estimate the numerical strength of the godly element
in Elizabethan society, or to give an exact account of its geographical
distribution. It may be that the lack of any formal criterion by which
to identify convinced and active protestants will exclude a statistical
treatment of these problems. One is left with the general impressions
built up from the literature of the period, ecclesiastical visitation and
court records, and the documents accumulated by the puritans themselves.[5] "Professors" were a minority group, perhaps even a small
minority if we accept the gloomy assessment of the observer who wrote
in the year of the St. Bartholomew massacres in France that "it is
terrible to consider that not every fortieth person in England is a good
and devout gospeller (unless it be in London)".[6] The godly were thinly
distributed and even totally absent in those dark corners where there
was little or no preaching; more or less strongly represented in London,
Essex, and East Anglia, as well as in the weald of Kent and Sussex,
much of the east and central midlands, parts of Lincolnshire and the
west country, and in market and port towns elsewhere.

This paper also evades any attempt at a sociological or occupational
analysis of Elizabethan protestantism. Precise knowledge of this kind
must support any but the most speculative attempt to link religious and
and ethical with social aspirations. But the argument to be developed
here hardly depends upon it, and can take refuge in crude social
categories. Puritan preachers often spoke of "the people", as when that
gifted organizer and propagandist John Field remarked that if constitutional methods should fail to establish the presbyterian discipline,
"it is the multitude and people that must bring the discipline to pass

5 Especially the collection of papers originally made by John Field and calendared by A. Peel
   as *The Seconde Parte of a Register*, 2 vols., (Cambridge, 1915). The provenance of the
   documents in the collection is itself an indication of the distribution of the puritan
   movement. Hereafter quoted as *Seconde Parte*.
6 Quoted, H. N. Birt, *The Elizabethan Religious Settlement*, (London, 1907) p. 435.

which we desire".[7] Differences of rank were scrupulously observed in the seating and other arrangements at sermons and other puritan assemblies. Yet as the preachers used the expression, "the people" embraced all except the clergy and persons of quality, a concept as classless as that of the Christian *laos* to which it was related, but often restricted by implication to those of proven godliness. In practice, this element in the puritan parish can hardly have been representative of what, since the industrial revolution, has been understood by "the common people". Christopher Hill must be right to locate puritanism in the ranks of the economically independent. It is significant that almost the only specific reference to poverty in the minutes of the Dedham *classis*, a conference of preachers which met in the clothing towns of the Essex-Suffolk border, concerned some "froward poor men" of the village of Wenham, who were "every way disordered". In Dedham itself, the vicar and lecturer, together with the headboroughs, undertook a quarterly inspection of the depressed and "suspected" places of the town, with an eye to relieving those in want and correcting "the naughty disposition of disordered persons". This was evidently a slumming operation, conducted among those living below the median line of decency, and in all probability excluded by their extreme poverty from active membership of the congregation.[8] No doubt "the people" who were caught up in the absorbing round of puritan "exercises" were for the most part householders and their wives, together with the more receptive of the servants who were catechized at home and, at Dedham as in many other towns, were required to accompany their masters to sermons and lectures. And to quote Dr. Hill: "There is little doubt that when sixteenth and seventeenth century Puritans spoke of 'the people' in connection with church government, they excluded the very poor".[9]

The godly might enjoy dominance, if they included persons of substance, or they might find themselves in a relatively unfavourable position. But most places exposed to puritan preaching were likely to experience a cleavage at some point in the community. It was a stock argument of anti-puritan invective that the preachers set their towns at variance, whereas the non-preachers they affected to despise were past-masters at the art of reconciling their quarreling parishioners at the ale-bench. Of the puritan ministers of the Kentish weald it was said:

7   P.R.O., Star Chamber 5 A 49/34, deposition of Thomas Edmunds.
8   *The Presbyterian Movement in the Reign of Queen Elizabeth, as Illustrated by the Minute Book of the Dedham Classis, 1582-1589*, ed. R.G. Usher (Camden Soc., 3rd ser., viii, 1905), pp. 71, 100. Hereafter quoted as *P.M.*
9   Hill, *Society and Puritanism*, pp. 474, and 124-44, 443-81, *passim*.

> Hath not Minge brought Ashford from being the quietest town of Kent to be at deadly hatred and bitter division? What hath Casslocke done at Chart? ...

> Hath not Eelie set Tenterden, his parish, together by the ears, which before was quiet? What broil and contention hath Fenner made in Cranbrook, and all the rest likewise in their several cures?

The more uncompromising of puritan spokesmen scarcely troubled to deny the charge, but fell back on those New Testament passages which emphasized the divisive action of the Gospel. "Can ye put fire and water together, but there will be a rumble?"[10]

Yet few ministers with a settled cure or preaching charge desired to exercise their ministry on any other basis than that of the parish. The reformed theology to which they subscribed sustained a high doctrine of the visible church, which was constituted by the sincere adminstration of word and sacraments, not by the quality of discipleship displayed by its members. The church in an ideal sense might be limited to God's elect, but there was no question of identifying those who had received a true inward calling, or of organizing them into an exclusive church. Rather the belief that the elect were scattered throughout the church visible was a powerful incentive to labour for the general provision of a godly preaching ministry and of an all-embracing parochial discipline. When John More, the "apostle of Norwich", called for a supply of preachers for those who had never heard in Norfolk, it was "the people of the Lord" whose salvation he desired.[11] If the puritan clergy had been free to employ the discipline which they believed to be an integral part of the pastoral ministry, obedience to the gospel would have been impressed on the whole parish. None of their parishioners could have voluntarily excluded themselves from participation in the Lord's supper, still less from the systematic instruction and the searching examination which would have preceded it. The famous Richard Greenham of Dry Drayton could recommend that at the first commencement of a preaching ministry, there should be no ministration of the communion until a period of intensive teaching followed by "some requisite trial" could ensure that the sacrament would not be abused. Yet a London minister who claimed to reserve the sacraments to such as he knew to be "faithful" could insist that all his parishioners were "faithful, holy, free people", with the exception of a single household. The separatist Henry

10 *Seconde Parte*, 1, p. 238; *A dialogue concerning the strife of our church*, (1584).
11 John More, *Three godly and fruitful sermons*, (Cambridge, 1594) pp. 66-9.

Barrow, the recipient of this information, was to conclude with disgust that "these men still would have the whole land to be the church, and every parish therein a particular congregation of the same".[12]

As a theological conviction, the reformed ecclesiology sustained the prophetic ministry to the whole of society to which the puritan preacher believed himself called. But his pastoral experience was likely to lead to quite contradictory notions of the church, if, like many members of the Dedham *classis*, his ministry was withstood by "untoward", "disordered" and "negligent" persons,[13] and if its most conspicuous success consisted in evoking the voluntary response of a select group within the parish. In effect, the successful preacher made converts, who were lifted out of their background into a new experience. In France or the Netherlands they would have formed the nucleus of wholly separated reformed churches, which would have acquired the institutions of the Calvinist ministry and discipline. Writing to his friends in north Devon in 1562, a Somerset preacher could refer to an individual "lately turned to the Lord". In Northamptonshire, twelve years later, where protestant preaching was still an innovation, the ministers spoke of those who were "going forward" and of "the number of those that have been won by preachers", variously estimated at twelve or twenty persons in one parish. At Lawshall, in Suffolk, ten years later still, the first three years of regular preaching had led to "a stirring of many ... to seek the Lord in his word". Those stirred to be seekers were about fifty strong.[14]

Inevitably, those who found themselves using this language tended to regard their "forward" people as constituting the church of God in a special sense. "If God have any church or people in the land", it could be said, "no doubt the title is given them". Such expressions as "the brethren" and "the godly brotherhood" could acquire a narrow exclusiveness, "denying in very deed the name of a brother to be proper unto any, but unto such as are of their own faction and opinion".[15] Calvin's doctrine of the church and its relation to the Christian state could not be held indefinitely in its original form apart from the effective practice of a church order of the type which Calvin himself had laboured to establish in Geneva. Nor, for that matter, was any part of Calvin's theology separable from his practical achievement. It was

12 John Rylands Library, Rylands English MS. 524, fo. 2ʳ; *Writings of John Greenwood, 1587-1590*. ed. L. H. Carlson, (Elizabethan Nonconformist Texts, iv, 1962), pp. 183-5; *Writings of Henry Barrow, 1587-1590*, ed. L. H. Carlson, (Elizabethan Nonconformist Texts, iii, 1962), p. 558.

13 *P.M., passim.*

14 Brit. Mus., MS. Lansdowne 377, fo. 27; *Seconde Parte*, i, p. 122; Brit. Mus., MS. Additional 38492, fo. 107.

15 *A dialogue, concerning the strife of our church*, p. 49; P.R.O., Star Chamber 5 A 49/34, deposition of John Johnson.

applied rather than pure theology, not an abstraction which could be easily assimilated in a church and society of a radically different type. By the end of the century, the English divines were altering the balance of Calvin's original synthesis, placing novel emphases on experience and assurance, piety and ethics, enlarging the concept of covenant. These developments, which amounted to the emergence of a distinct system of English puritan divinity, can be interpreted as the domestication of Calvinist doctrine to fit the needs of voluntary societies of the godly whose godliness enjoyed an independence of the ordered, sacramental life of the church which Calvin, for one, would have found undesirable. It was a domestication in the most literal sense, for, as Christopher Hill has amply shown, the household had become the essential unit of puritan religion rather than the parish.[16]

Initially, the society of the godly was not introverted. On the contrary, its *raison d'être* was thought to be general and complete reformation. "I pray you neighbour", the puritan was encouraged to say, "Let us go together to such a sermon or such a godly exercise, and *I will go with you*".[17] Yet the vivid experience of integration and fellowship within the minority group necessarily had its exclusive aspects. The local historian must tell us, if he can, how far an incipient separatism was carried into marital, commercial and general social dealings. Thomas Edmunds, a London parson with experience of the *classis* led by John Field, gave evidence that the godly, "as much as they might conveniently, refrained to buy or sell or usually to eat or drink with any person or persons which are not of their faction and opinions, or inclining that way".[18] But this was said in pursuit of a line of reasoning suggested to him by counsel for the attorney general in Star Chamber proceedings. Presumably the godly-minded shunned ale-houses — "a little hell" according to one writer[19] — and avoided bowling-alleys and the more sophisticated forms of recreation provided in Southwark and other London suburbs. Leisure time which might otherwise have been spent in idle pastimes was assiduously devoted to public religious "exercises", which in rural areas at least were voluntary and brought together a regular clientele of "gadders to sermons" from a wide circle of parishes. "I could like the better", complained one Essex critic, "if the preaching might be only upon the sabbath day; but now they run in the week-days and leave their business and beggar themselves. They go to other towns also, which is a pity that it is suffered. It is a great disorder". "If you can trot to sermons", a group of Essex men

16 Hill, *Society and Puritanism*, pp. 443-81.
17 Andrewes, *Certaine verie worthie sermons*, p. 186. The italics are in the original.
18 P.R.O., Star Chamber 5 A 49/34, deposition of Thomas Edmunds.
19 *A dialogue concerning the strife of our church*, p. 6.

were told by the archdeacon's official, "we will make you trot to the courts".[20]

Areas which were well-served with godly learned ministers could furnish a number of Sunday afternoon and weekday lectures, and, in the earlier years of Elizabeth, the gatherings of preaching clergy for public conference known as "prophesyings". In Essex, for example, these took place at Colchester, Chelmsford, Horndon-on-the-Hill, Maldon, Brentwood and Rochford. When the prophesyings were officially suppressed in the southern province in 1577, they were replaced in many centres by "exercises", which differed from the earlier institution only in the restriction of the public part of the proceedings to a single sermon. On the frequent occasions when calamitous or challenging events prompted the unauthorized pro-clamation of a day of public fasting, several hours would be spent in preaching, and more than one speaker would take part. Some fasts served as "preparations" for solemn administrations of the communion, which drew communicants from many parishes, and were sometimes held in gentlemen's houses or in the open air. Those who "gadded" to sermons met in their homes in the evenings in what were potentially conventicles, often to take part in formal "repetition", a kind of catechizing in which the doctrine delivered earlier in the day was rehearsed, on other occasions for more or less spontaneous reading and prayer.[21] These forms of religious activity, none of which was parochial, provided the basic pattern of life for the godly, the fixed events around which other things must have had to take their place. For the puritan exorcist, John Darrell, in the last decade of the century, they provided the frame or reference in which to recollect his movements. Monday, for example, was "the day of the common exercise" at Burton-on-Trent.[22] So familiar and well-established were these habits by the early seventeenth century that the so-called non-separating congregationalists could justify their somewhat perverse adherence to the established church by pointing to the effective toleration of such assemblies, "wherein none are present by constraint, and where the service-book doth not so much as appear". William Ames wrote with good reason of the "thousands in England" whose views were almost indistinguishable from those of the separatists, but who

20 George Gifford, *A briefe discourse of ... the countrie divinitie*, (1582), fo. 43ᵛ; Brit. Mus., MS. Additional 48064, fo. 79ᵛ.

21 For the prophesyings, see S.E. Lehmberg, "Archbishop Grindal and the Prophesyings", *Historical Magazine of the Prot. Episcopal Church*, xxxiv, (1965), pp. 87-145; and for all these practices, P. Collinson, "The Puritan Classical Movement in the Reign of Elizabeth I" (London Univ. Ph.D. thesis, 1957), esp. chaps. 3, 4, 7 vi, 8 i.

22 Samuel Harsnet, *A discovery of the fraudulent practises of John Darrel*, (1599), pp. 270-1.

23 *A manudiction for M. Robinson*, (1614), Sigs P4ᵛ, Q1ʳ; 4ʳ; cf. Perry Miller, *Orthodoxy in Massachusetts, 1630-50; A Genetic Study*, (Cambridge Mass., 1933), pp. 75-101.

remained members of the ordinary parishes there".[23]

That these patterns of behaviour were socially disturbing needs no further emphasis. They were also a solvent of the ecclesiastical parish, and, ultimately, of the national church grounded on the parochial principle. The process can be closely observed in Essex, where the local records, and especially the act books of the archdeaconry courts of Essex and Colchester, are exceptionally informative.[24] A large number of entries in the act books confirm that the godly of Essex were assured that a church service was "no service, unless there be a sermon",[25] and that those who were saddled with a non-preaching or otherwise unacceptable incumbent made a practice of travelling elsewhere on Sundays. (Their gadding on other days was never a matter of presentment or enquiry in the archdeacons' courts.) For example, Thomas Woodham of Purleigh, one of six parishioners cited in 1585, admitted "that he goeth to other places, viz., sometimes to Maldon, sometimes to Danbury, sometimes to Langford, where the word is more purely preached". Three parishioners of St. Nicholas's, Colchester, swore "flatly that they will not come because of the simplicity of our minister, Mr. Shilbury. Howbeit, they go to other places for instructions".[26] Similar cases occur from other Colchester parishes, and from East Donyland, Greenstead by Colchester, Fering, Ramsey, Tendring, Hatfield Peverel, Goldhanger, Great Sampford and Nessing, all in the archdeaconry of Colchester, and all between 1582 and 1587;[27] And in the archdeaconry of Essex, from Great Burstead, Cold Norton, Woodham Mortimer, Woodham Ferrers, Doddinghurst, Steeple, Great Sutton, Sandon, Stock, Shopland, Canewdon, East Tilbury, Bobbingworth, Chignal, Little Leighs, Ramsden Bellhouse, Stow Maries and Nazeing, all between 1583 and 1591.[28]

In some of these places there were parishioners who refused to receive the communion at the hands of their own minister, and who communicated elsewhere, like one Cold Norton man who, in a revealing phrase, spoke of receiving "with Mr. Gifford, vicar of Maldon".[29] The

24 Essex Record Office, D/AEA, D/ACA. This paper makes use of AEA 9-15 (1575-92) and ACA 10-19 (1581-93). Hereafter quoted as AEA, ACA. I am indebted to Mr. F. G. Emmison, sometime County Archivist of Essex, and to his colleagues of the Essex Record Office, for the facilities granted to consult these valuable act books, and for many incidental courtesies.

25 Statement by Richard Yawlinge of Woodham Mortimer in proceedings in the Archdeaconry Court of Essex, 15 April 1584, AEA/12, fo. 90^v.

26 AEA/12, proceedings of 12 Sept. 1585; ACA/14, fo. 50^r.

27 ACA/14, fos. 18^v, 19^r, ACA/10, fos. 46^v, 51^v, 66^r, 75^r, 107^v, ACA/12, fos. 60^r, 112^v, ACA/16, fo.8^v.

28 AEA/12, fos. 40^r, 89^r, 90^v, 131^v, and proceedings of 22 July 1584, 25 May 1585, AEA/13, proceedings of 19. Jan., 20 Jan., 14 Sept. 1587, and fo. 190, AEA/14, fos. 10^r, 55^v, AEA/15, fo. 193^r.

29 AEA/12, fo. 89^r.

same prejudice would lead the godly to import an acceptable minister for the baptism of their children.[30] So ineradicable were these habits that in 1587 eight parishioners of Shopland were licensed to go elsewhere when there was no sermon in their own church, provided that not more than two absented themselves on any one occasion. In the following year, six men of Canewdon applied for a similar dispensation.[31] It would, of course, be an oversimplification to say that parish boundaries were only broken by those starved of nourishment at home. The godly ministers themselves stood in danger of losing their auditory if a rival attraction proved too strong. This was the fate of Robert Lewis, a Colchester minister who failed to compete with the popular town preacher, George Northey, and asked his brethren of the Dedham *classis* for a ruling "that a pastor should have his own people". In London the same problem, internal to the puritan movement itself, prompted the publication of a dialogue "persuading the people to reverence and attend the ordinance of God in the ministry of their own pastors".[32]

There is valuable evidence in the Essex archdeaconry records, supported from other sources, of the analogue of "gadding": the gathering of the godly in house-meetings of the kind which Bishop Aylmer called "night conventicles".[33] These took place typically on Sunday evenings, a time which is set aside for such "exercises" by Nicholas Bownd, John Udall and other puritan writers in their discussion of the proper use of the sabbath.[34] But in Maldon there seem to have been very few evenings when George Gifford failed to be in company with some of the godly of the town in one or other of their houses.[35] We have evidence, most of it from the 1580s, of night conventicles in the following Essex communities: Strethall, (an early occurrence, in 1574), Aythorp Roding, Maldon, Wethersfield (upwards of twenty persons), East Hanningfield (twelve men and eleven women named, three of them from other parishes), Great Wakering (seven men named), Cold Norton, Laindon Hills, Rayleigh and Hornchurch (a very heterodox group with marked separatist and even anabaptist leanings, and so in a rather different category).[36]

30 ACA/18, fo. 132, AEA/12, fos. 93ᵛ, 94ʳ.
31 AEA/13, proceedings of 19 Jan. 1587; AEA/14, fo. 19ʳ.
32 *P.M.*, pp. 30, 62; *Sophronistes. A dialogue, perswading the people* (etc.), (1589).
33 John Strype, *Life of Aylmer*, (Oxford, 1821), p. 71.
34 Bownd, *The doctrine of the sabbath*, (1595), pp. 210-22, 235-46; Udall, *Two sermons of obedience to the gospell*, in *Certaine sermons*, (1596), Sig. I i iiijʳ.
35 Essex Record Office, Maldon Borough Records, D/B/3/3/178, D/B/3/3/442/2.
36 Inner Temple Library, MS. Petyt 538/47, fos. 492-3; Brit. Mus., MS. Lansdowne 157, fo. 186; evidence for Maldon cited in previous note; Richard Rogers, *Seaven treatises*, (1605), pp. 497-8; AEA/12, fos. 103-4ʳ, 115ᵛ-16ʳ, 266ʳ-7ᵛ, and Brit. Mus., MS. Additional 48064, fos. 85ᵛ-6ʳ; AEA/12, fo. 92ᵛ; *ibid.*, fo. 89ʳ; *ibid.*, fo. 199ʳ; AEA/13, proceedings of 21 Febr. 1587; AEA/12, fo. 112ᵛ, AEA/14, fo. 85.

At Aythorp Roding, on a typical occasion, the godly met in the house of one Davies, "to the number of ten persons or thereabouts of his kindred and neighbours, being invited thither to supper". Over the meal, "they then conferred together of such profitable lessons as they had learned that day at a public catechizing". After supper, some "attended to one that read in the Book of Martyrs", and the rest to John Huckle, the vicar, then under suspension, who was "in company with them, and was reading by the fireside a piece of a catechism ... which he had then in his hand." Finally they all sang a psalm and prayed, "and so departed about ten o'clock at night". A similar procedure seems to have been followed at Great Wakering, except that there was no resident preaching minister to offer leadership. The godly met "sometimes ... at one neighbour's house, sometimes at another's, that are well-given", and "only on the Lord's days or holidays".[37] At East Hanningfield, a village almost evenly divided between those who took part in these assemblies and allegedly "irreligious" persons, the church had virtually ceased to be parochial. Besides joining in "secret conventicles and meetings", the puritan rector, William Seridge, in effect reserved the sacraments for the godly. As many as nineteen male parishioners, some of them with wives, were repelled from the communion on a single occasion, on grounds of disorderly conduct or insufficient knowledge. The archdeacon and his official took the side of the "irreligious" and licensed them to receive at West Hanningfield, content that they had not called their opponents "saints and scripture men in contempt of their profession, but in respect of their abuse".[38]

For all their personal dependence on the preachers, it would be wrong to suppose that the godly were in all places and circumstances amenable to clerical leadership. Preaching and the other offices of the pastoral ministry played a large part in bringing such people to a lively faith, but these were not the only means of acquiring knowledge, and many lay protestants were urgent proselytizers in their own right. When the Brownist schism occurred in Norfolk, Robert Harrison told the puritan preachers that though it might appear that the "children" were "forwarder than their father", the truth was that they were begotten not so much by the ministers as by the people themselves, "by fruitful edifying of gracious speech and godly conference". At Cranbrook, in the weald, many protestants attributed their conversion to the energetic apostolate of Richard Fletcher, father of a bishop of London and grandfather of the dramatist. Yet when Fletcher retracted his earlier

37 Brit. Mus., MS. Lansdowne 157, fo. 186; AEA/12, fo. 92^v.
38 AEA/12, fos. 10^r, 49^v, 103-4^r, 115^v-17, 226-7; Brit. Mus., MS. Additional 48064, fos. 85-7.

teaching by commending the ceremonies, it was said that " those very parties do now also affirm that [he] hath run headlong, to the eversion of many consciences". There followed "open challenges in the midst of preaching in the congregation, libelling, ... pens walking at sermons".[39]

Once the inner momentum of popular protestantism is recognized, the puritan movement and its vicissitudes take on a new dimension. It becomes clear that the preachers were not only perplexed by the conflict of conscience and the demands of their ecclesiastical superiors. They were troubled perhaps even more by threats of schism and heterodoxy among their own people. The two problems were not unconnected, in that the preacher who was obliged to choose between conformity and suspension or deprivation was likely to lose control of his congregation in either eventuality. In Norfolk, at the time of Archbishop Whitgift's demand for subscription to the three articles, the preachers complained that they had "much ado" to keep the people clear of Brownism even when there was "reasonable plenty of preaching". But if the preachers were replaced with idle ministers, "we fear the unruly sort will make that rent in the church, which we had rather be dead (if God so please) than live to behold".[40]

Sectarianism and doctrinal idiosynocracies appear to have persisted obstinately in districts with an old dissenting tradition, such as the weald of Kent and parts of Essex.[41] Bocking was an area torn with conflicting opinions in Edward's reign, and again in the early years of Elizabeth.[42] Not all the "disordered" persons who vexed the Dedham *classis* and its members were irreligious: some were a ready prey to sheep-stealers like Edward Glover, or hardened sectaries like the men of East Bergholt "who did single themselves from the church", one of them telling a member of the *classis* who ministered in Bergholt that he counted him "no minister, nor their church no church".[43] At Ramsey there was a preaching-place in the woods, with straw and moss for seating, "and the ground trodden bare with much treading". On midsummer day, 1581, a Sunday, a dozen villagers, most of them women, gathered in this clearing to eat roast beef and goose while

39 *The Writings of Robert Harrison and Robert Browne*, ed. A. Peel and L.H. Carlson, (Elizabethan Nonconformist Texts, ii, 1953), pp. 52-3; Dr. Williams's Library, MS. Morrice B II, fos. 11^v, 18^v.

40 *Seconde Parte*, i, p. 224.

41 J. A. F. Thompson, *The Later Lollards, 1414-1520*, (Oxford, 1965), pp. 173-91, 117-38; J. E. Oxley, *The Reformation in Essex to the Death of Mary*, (Manchester, 1965), pp. 3-16; Harold Smith, *The Ecclesiastical History of Essex under the Long Parliament and Commonwealth*, (Colchester, n.d.), pp. 6-8. There are implications of old lollard traditions in the papers relating to troubles at Cranbrook in John Field's collections (Dr. Williams's Library, MS. Morrice B II, fos. 6-25), calendared, *Seconde Parte*, i, pp. 116-23.

42 Oxley, *Reformation in Essex*, pp. 164-6, 191-3; Richard Kitchen to Mr. Pearson, 3 July 1564, Inner Temple Library, MS. Petyt 538/47, fos. 526-7.

43 *P.M.*, pp. 54-5, 56, 60.

listening to one William Collett who expounded St. John's Gospel from a ladder. At Hornchurch, at the opposite extremity of the county, a sizable conventicle clustered around John Leach, the schoolmaster. Its members kept their children without baptism, and on at least one occasion participated in a novel form of funeral in which all present threw earth over the corpse.[44] Anglicans might occasionally consider what they may owe to the puritan clergy for striving to reduce such spiritual anarchy to a coherent and orderly Calvinism.

Contrary to the impression conveyed by some of the authorities,[45] the strongest prejudices against the most concrete and symbolic of popish survivals in the Church of England, the surplice, resided not in the puritan clergy but among "simple gospellers". When some people of Nayland descended with their preacher on neighbouring Boxted, on the Essex bank of the Stour, the vicar prudently left off the offending garment, knowing that "some that came out of Suffolk side would have liked him the worse if he had worn it". Edmund Grindal as bishop of London licensed Thomas Upcher, rector of Fordham, to minister without the surplice in recognition of the strength of feeling in his congregation, but asked him "privately to exhort the godly so to frame their judgments that they conceive no offence if it be altered hereafter by authority". (Upcher as a some-time weaver of Bocking, and an Aarau exile in Mary's reign, was a man with a past. He had belonged to the protestant underworld himself). A similar situation was known to prevail in protestant areas of the north of England. When the puritans of south-east Lancashire were required to adopt the surplice in 1590, many of them for the first time, Dr. John Reynolds of Oxford advised them to comply, but admitted that "the godly would mislike thereof, and would depart (divers of them) from their public ministration". Archbishop Parker knew better than Roland Green Usher or Canon Dixon when he blamed the preachers for their responsiveness to "the folly of the people, calling it charity to feed their fond humour".[46]

An investigation of the tendencies and pressures contained within the popular protestantism of the later sixteenth century, such as this

44 ACA/10, fos. 66-7ʳ, AEA/15, fos. 273ᵛ-4ᵛ , AEA/14, fo. 148.
45 Canon R. W. Dixon described Elizabethan nonconformity as "of ministerial origin", and not likely in itself to arouse partisan feelings in the community". (*History of the Church of England from the Abolition of Roman Jurisdiction*. (London and Oxford, 1884-1902), vi, p. 42.) Cf. R. G. Usher, in *Church Quarterly Review*, lviii (1904), pp. 103-18, and in *Reconstruction of the English Church*, i, pp. 244-81.
46 Greater London Record Office, London Division, Consistory Court of London Records, DL/C/213, depositions relating to Philip Gilgate, vicar of Boxted, 3 Nov. 1589; Bishop Grindal to Archdeacon Pulleyn of Colchester, 5 June 1560, Corpus Christi College Oxford, MS. 297, fo. 17; Oxley, *Reformation in Essex*, pp. 165-6, 192-3, 195, 204; John Reynolds to Edward Fleetwood, rector of Wigan, 30 Nov., n.y., Queen's College Oxford, MS. 280, fos. 174-5ʳ; *Correspondence of Matthew Parker*, ed. J. Bruce, (Parker Socy., Cambridge, 1853), p. 149.

paper has attempted, suggests that its habits and embryonic forms were those of "the congregational way", as this would be defined in the third quarter of the seventeenth century. The origins of congregationalism, as indeed of the remaining denominations of the old dissent, has often been *une question mal posée*. Those puritans (*scil*. puritan ministers) who retained a foothold in the established church have been classified as presbyterians; while the credentials of a succession of Elizabethan separatist leaders, Fitz, Browne and Harrison, Barrow and Greenwood, have been examined to determine which should be accorded recognition as the founding-father of independency. This enterprise has not been without its point, but to make the problem of denominational origins one of simple genealogy is to face difficulties in the period 1604-40, where it is hard to trace much continuity of either leadership or ideas. It is at least equally desirable to conduct the search in the half-formed attitudes and positions adopted in the inchoate groups of the godly-minded which never acquired a label through separation, and which flourished as a church within the church in so many Elizabethan and Jacobean parishes.

Some of the earliest congregational churches, properly so- called, which date from the 1640s, grew out of a background of circumstances closely analagous to those which have been described in this paper. The decision to separate was made not by individuals but by groups, which already enjoyed an identity before their separation.[47] This may have been equally true of the decision to emigrate. Among "Mr. Hooker's company" which left Essex for New England in 1632 were a number of Braintree and Bocking families which were partly interrelated and closely allied in business and testamentary dealings. Samuel Collins, the vicar of Braintree, vouched for the strength of the tradition out of which these emigrants came when he wrote in the same year that his congregation had been disorderly "these fifty years", which would appear to have been a conservative estimate.[48] Dr. Geoffrey Nuttall, in describing the emergence of the first congregational churches in his *Visible Saints*, suggests that it was not until the mid-seventeenth century that the long exposure of lay Englishmen to the vernacular Bible could be expected to bear this kind of fruit.[49] This one may doubt. If the role of the clerical leaders is not exaggerated, a number of earlier movements of separation, as far back as the London sects of the

---

47 G. F. Nuttall, *Visible Saints: The Congregational Way*, 1640-1660, (Oxford, 1957), pp. 43-69.

48 I owe this information to Mr. A. G. E. Jones of Tunbridge Wells who kindly allowed me to read his unpublished paper, "Braintree, Bocking and New England, 1620-1650"; see Smith, *Ecclesiastical History of Essex*, pp. 29-35.

49 Nuttall, *Visible Saints*, pp. 43-5.

late 1560s, may be found open to a similar interpretation. The potential separatism of the godly became actual through some external pressure or alteration in circumstances, such as the loss of a preaching minister and the intrusion of a "hireling". As Robert Harrison told a Norfolk minister, apropos of the Brownist schism: "Also, you are placed and displaced by the bishops; therefore when we have most need of you, you are gone".[50]

Dr. Nuttall distinguishes four main principles as distinctive of those who adopted the congregational way: separation, fellowship (implied in the name 'congregational'), freedom, (implied in "independent") and fitness, (implied in the conviction that church membership should be restricted to "visible saints"). Enough has already been said to establish that the impulse towards the separation of "saints and scripture men" and their integration in sectarian fellowship existed widely, and was uneasily accomodated within the Elizabethan church. William Ames would argue that the covenant constituting a separatist church had been virtually concluded wherever a group of Christians were accustomed to hold regular, voluntary meetings. Membership of the Essex "night conventicles" cannot have been wholly spontaneous and casual, and at least one of these groups went so far as to be bound by a form of written covenant. At Wethersfield, the town where Richard Rogers, the puritan diarist, was lecturer, "certain well-minded persons" were accustomed to meet "for the continuance of love, and for the edifying of one another, after some bodily repast and refreshing". In 1588 this company of "well-nigh twenty persons" subscribed a covenant in which they confessed the unprofitableness of their Christian profession, resolved to "turn to the Lord in all sincerity", and were bound to a common rule of life and the regular practice of mutual conference about their spiritual estate. This document had nothing to do with separation from, or, for that matter, with adherence to the parish church. But its pietism, like that of Roger's *Seven Treatises* in which the covenant is printed, was in the long run no less subversive of the parish than the principles of Robert Browne.[51]

It remains to consider whether the Elizabethan godly were impelled by the as yet undefined principles of congregational independency. There can be little doubt that in the conferences of puritan ministers which arose more or less spontaneously in some parts of the country in

---

50 *Writings of Harrison and Browne*, p. 60.
51 Miller, *Orthodoxy in Massachusetts*, p. 87; Rogers, *Seaven treatises*, pp. 497-8.

the late 1570s and 1580s, the "godly discipline", a form of presbyteriansim, was the current orthodoxy. But one is entitled to suspect that in what one member of the Dedham *classis* called those "confused days" in which there was "no discipline nor good order",[52] the actual state of the parishes under puritan control was likely to be one of effective independency, tempered by a measure of presbyterian and, of course, episcopal intervention from outside. This suggestion can be substantiated in detail from only one area, and that admittedly in the most prosperous and socially advanced part of East Anglia. The eastern counties were not only a stronghold of congregationalism in the mid-seventeenth century, but the home of an idiosyncratic congregationalism in which many of the ministers combined their pastorates with livings in the established church.[53]

The minutes and correspondence of the Dedham *classis* suggest that for all their interest in manuals and schemes of "discipline", where their personal interests or those of their congregations were touched, the members were unlikely to be bound by the advice of the conference, still less to concede that it possessed a jurisdiction in their affairs. The conference assumed the power to place and displace its members, and generally to regulate the life of the churches within its orbit. It could record as a general principle that a pastor ought not to leave his people, "they being unwilling of his departure". Yet on two occasions members of the *classis* left their cures and migrated elsewhere, even after the conference had consulted with their parishioners, debated the case, in the one instance by convening an extraordinary meeting, and had made clear recommendations to the contrary.[54] On the other hand, the congregation at East Bergholt[55] could take the law into its own hands in expelling its pastor, John Tilney, in spite of the intervention of six members of the *classis* as arbiters of a dispute between them. Critical but impotent words were spoken in the *classis* "of the people's course in rejecting and receiving their pastors without counsel of others". When the godly of East Bergholt secured as their new pastor another member of the *classis* and a doctor of divinity, Richard Crick, feelings ran so high that for some time Crick could find no-one willing to preach at his induction. Finally, when scarcely on speaking terms with his brethren, Crick addressed a letter to the *classis* which contained a

52 *P. M.*, p. 45.
53 Nuttall, *Visible Saints*, pp. 22-4.
54 *P.M.*, pp. 42-9.
55 Not, it would seem, the congregation of the parish church. East Bergholt contrived to support two masters of arts, John Tilney and Thomas Stoughton, and a doctor of divinity, Richard Crick (both before and after his call to the pastorate), none of whom was the incumbent. When the *classis* was convened at Bergholt, it met "at Hog Lane".

conscientious defence of the liberty of the local church, "being become now at the length as jealous for the honour of the church as any of you are for your own, or for his whom she hath most worthily thrown out". If the congregation knew the facts, they would satisfy their need of advice by fetching it "from as far beyond London as London is hence, rather than from you, though ye would beg to be of counsel with them". In its dealing with other presbyterian assemblies, claiming provincial authority, the *classis* itself could display the same instincts. When a synod meeting in London attempted to redistribute some of its swollen membership, the brethren paid lip-service to the "gracious advices" of London, but claimed to be "best privy in our conference" of the inconveniences of the proposal.[56]

Congregationalism was only one of the tendencies of the reformation, and not necessarily the most dominant. But it is hard to see how the movements generated within popular protestantism, left to themselves, can have had any other end. By the mid-seventeenth century, it was certain that they would frustrate any attempt to conserve intact the national and parochial church, whether episcopal or presbyterian in its consitution. This paper has provided grounds for supposing that this development was implicit in the processes of the English reformation, and not merely of the English revolution.

56 *P. M.*, pp. 63, 67, 69, 98; John Rylands Library, Rylands English MS. 874 (original MS. of the Dedham *classis* papers), fos. 55[r], 37.

NOTE

Since this paper was composed in 1966 for a conference of the Past and Present Society there have been some shifts in my own thinking about the questions to which it is addressed and considerable advances in the microscopic investigation of religion, morality and culture in the social context of the late sixteenth and early-seventeenth-century village community. The reader may refer to the studies of three Cambridgeshire villages in Margaret Spufford, *Contrasting Communities. English Villagers in the Sixteenth and Seventeenth Centuries* (Cambridge, 1974); of the Essex parishes of Terling and Kelvedon Easterford in Keith Wrightson and David Levine, *Poverty and Piety in an English Village 1525-1700* (1979) and J.A. Sharpe, 'Crime and Delinquency in an Essex Parish 1600-1640', in J.S. Cockburn ed., *Crime in England 1550-1800* (1977), pp. 90-109; of the Wealden communities of Warbleton (Sussex) and Cranbrook (Kent) in N.R.N. Tyacke, 'Popular Puritan Mentality in Late Elizabethan England', in *The English Commonwealth 1547-1640*, ed. Peter Clark, A.G.R. Smith and Nicholas Tyacke (Leicester, 1979), pp. 77-92 and Patrick Collinson, 'Cranbrook and the Fletchers: Popular and Unpopular Religion in the Kentish Weald', in P.N. Brooks, ed., *Reformation Principle and Practice. Essays in Honour of A.G. Dickens* (1980), pp. 173-202, see below Chapter 15, pp. 399 ff.; and in a forthcoming study of Wiltshire by Dr. Martin Ingram. Comparison of this paper with the final chapter of my *The Religion of Protestants: The Church in English Society 1559-1625. The Ford Lectures 1979* (Oxford, 1982) will suggest that I am less inclined than I once was to regard protestantism/puritanism as a solvent of parochial religion and as congregationalist in potential. The corrosive, divisive effects of these religious tendencies are not to be denied and they will be further explored in the published version of my 1981 Birkbeck Lectures, *The Roots of Nonconformity*. But they were mitigated and to some extent kept in check by a profound and widespread aversion for separatism and a conscientious respect for religious institutions which the twentieth century may find hard to understand or even to accept, but which was analogous to the modern sense of civic responsibility.

The 1574 conventicle at Strethall, mentioned on p. 10, is now known from the work of Dr. Felicity Heal, Mr. Nicholas Penrhys-Evans and others to have been held by a group of adherents of the sect known as the Family of Love, and so by no means as innocent in character as its adherents pretended. If I was deceived, in 1965, so was Dr. Andrew Perne of Peterhouse and other commissioners in 1574. Indeed, such deception was the speciality of Familism.

2

THE REFORMER AND THE ARCHBISHOP
MARTIN BUCER AND AN ENGLISH BUCERIAN

In 1970 Martin Bucer was still, granted some literary licence, 'the
neglected reformer', 'little more than a footnote in the history of the
Reformation'.[2] In spite of a modest revival of Bucer studies in this
century,[3] the publication of the Latin *Opera* lags sadly behind the
German *Schriften*, themselves incomplete.[4] The definitive biographical
study is lacking in any language[5] and could not be written without the
assimilation of much intractable manuscript material.[6]

Yet the theme of Bucer and the English Reformation is hardly
virginal. Sixty-five years have elapsed since A. E. Harvey submitted
a Marburg thesis on *Martin Bucer in England*,[7] and twenty-five since
Dr Constantin Hope (then Hopf) published a monograph with the
same title—a learned book, if downright eccentric in its structure.[8]
August Lang,[9] Wilhelm Pauck[10] and, most recently, Herbert Vogt[11]

1. This article arises from a paper read at the Conference in Reformation Studies held at Ormond College, University of Melbourne, in May 1970.
2. Stephens, W. P., *The Holy Spirit in the Theology of Martin Bucer*, Cambridge, 1970, p. vii.
3. Thompson, Bard, 'Bucer Study since 1918', *Church History*, XXVI, 1950, 63-82.
4. Only vol. XV of the *Opera Latina* (hereafter *OL*) has been published, ed. François Wendel, Paris, 1956, containing *De Regno Christi* (together with vol. XV *bis* which provides the French text of the same work). Vols I, II, III and VII of the *Deutsche Schriften* have so far appeared, with Robert Stupperich as general editor, Gütersloh, 1960. Both series are sponsored by the same international committee. Professor Stupperich is the author of the standard bibliography of Bucer's works, 'Bibliographa Bucerana' in Bornkamm, Heinrich, *Martin Bucers Bedeutung für die europäische Reformationsgeschichte*, Gütersloh, 1952, pp. 39-96.
5. This is not to disparage the best available biography, Eells, Hastings, *Martin Bucer*, New Haven, 1931.
6. See the remarks of Pollet, J. V., *Martin Bucer: Etudes sur la correspondance*, I, Paris, 1958, p. v; II, Paris, 1962, pp. 23ff.; and in *Archiv für Reformationsgeschichte*, XLVI, 1955, pp. 213ff. Fr Pollet's two volumes of *Etudes* have opened up major tracts of Bucer's correspondence. 1,406 letters are extant from Bucer and 641 from his correspondents (Pollet, op. cit., II, p. 16, n. 5). Compare with the almost 12,000 known letters of Bullinger who, unlike Bucer, retained copies of his own letters.
7. Harvey, A. E., *Martin Bucer in England*, Marburg, 1906.
8. Hopf, Constantin, *Martin Bucer in England*, Oxford, 1946.
9. 'Butzer in England', *Archiv für Reformationsgeschichte*, XXXVIII, 1941; *Puritanismus und Pietismus. Studien zu ihren Entwickelung von M. Butzer bis zum Methodismus*, Neukirchen, 1941. Lang was the author of the seminal study of the Bucer renascence, *Der Evangelienkommentar Martin Butzers und die Grundzüge seiner Theologie*, Leipzig, 1900.
10. *Das Reich Gottes auf Erden. Utopie und Wirklichkeit. Eine Untersuchung zu Butzers De Regno Christi und der englischen Staatskirchen des 16 Jahrhunderts*, Berlin, 1928; and the introduction to his English translation of *De Regno Christi*, Library of Christian Classics (hereafter LCC), XIX, London, 1969.
11. *Martin Bucer und die Kirche von England*, Inaugural Dissertation, Westfälischen Wilhelm-Universität zu Münster, 1966; published in typescript 1968. I am indebted to Hr Dr Vogt who so kindly sent me a copy of his dissertation.

from the side of German scholarship, C. H. Smyth from within the Anglican tradition,[12] and François Wendel from Strasbourg[13] have added to the short but solid bibliography which has been erected on the slender basis of the twenty-two months which the Alsatian reformer spent in England, from April 1549 until February 1551, for much of that time and until his death regius professor of divinity at Cambridge. Bucer's influential review of the first Prayer Book and his connection with the English Ordinal have aroused the particular interest of Anglican scholars and their confessional opponents. On these matters, and on Bucer's part in the Edwardian dispute over vestments, a role which he continued to play posthumously in the early Elizabethan period,[14] there is not very much more to be said. But in M. Jean Rott's very exact elucidation of what survives of Bucer's papers in English archives,[15] and in Hr Vogt's catalogue of Bucer's English correspondence,[16] the terrain is mapped out for any further investigations which may be undertaken.

Liturgy and ceremonies, bones of contention for so many writers on the English Reformation, were not for Bucer the heart of the matter. Pauck's study of *De Regno Christi* and Wendel's magisterial introduction to the definitive edition of the same work suggest that Tudor Church historians should have in mind the impression which may have been made on the English scene by Bucer's more fundamental theological insights; and in particular by the characteristically corporate social understanding of the Christian life which resounds through his writings in the repeated use of such expressions as community and kingdom, *Gemeinde, Liebesgemeinschaft, regnum Christi, respublica Christiana*, and by his firm directions on the practicalities of church organization. The deficiencies in performance of the English Church were a constant cause of complaint in Bucer's correspondence with the continent.[17] Wendel has remarked that

> seul parmi les reformateurs du XVIe siècle, Bucer a eu le courage ou la témérité de vouloir tirer de l'Ecriture non seulement son organisation ecclésiastique ou ses préceptes moraux, mais jusqu'à des institutions politiques et aux règles d'une bonne administration.[18]

12. *Cranmer and the Reformation under Edward VI*, Cambridge, 1926.
13. In his introduction to Vol. XV of *Opera Latina* and in his article 'Un document inédit sur le séjour de Bucer en Angleterre', *Revue d'histoire et de philosophie religieuses*, XXXIV, 1954, pp. 223-33, which is informative on the subject of Bucer's Cambridge *ménage*.
14. In addition to Hopf, op. cit., see Primus, John H., *The Vestments Controversy*, Kampen, 1960, pp. 43-55, 134-43; and the documents gathered by Gorham, G. C., *Gleanings of a Few Scattered Ears during the Period of the Reformation in England*, 1857.
15. 'Le sort des papiers et de la bibliothèque de Bucer en Angleterre', *Revue d'histoire et de philosophie religieuses*, XLVI, 1966, pp. 346-67.
16. Vogt (op. cit.) lists every known copy and publication of 326 letters to or from Bucer, or bearing upon his English experience. This forms one section of an elaborate and scholarly bibliography which occupies sixty pages of his dissertation.
17. *Original Letters Relative to the English Reformation*, ed. Robinson, Hastings, II, Parker Society, Cambridge, 1847, pp. 534-51.
18. *OL*, XV, p. xl.

The subject is too extensive in its implications to be dealt with definitively in a single article, and these pages can only offer to treat it suggestively, and with reference to a particular churchman of the Elizabethan period, Archbishop Edmund Grindal.

I

Bucer's richly social doctrine of the Church was one of the focal points of his theology. In the strictest sense of the word he was a churchman.[19] Another related point of emphasis (the underlying presupposition according to Dr Stephens[20]) was the doctrine of election, and another the operation of the Holy Spirit within the elect community, working the fruits of the Spirit, principally love ('for faith shows its power through love'[21]) which demonstrated itself in fulfilment of the divine law and conspicuously in mutual care and charity, the behaviour of responsible citizens of the divine kingdom.[22] By the power of the Spirit, 'we who formerly sought only our own advantage in everything, having denied ourselves, seek the advantage of others, and in sincere love dedicate ourselves as slaves to all men, but especially to those who are of the household of faith.'[23] To be a Christian was to be made 'again useful to all creatures',[24] the theme of his earliest publication, *Das ym selbs niemant, sonder anderen leben soll* (1523),[25] which regards the functions of ministers and magistrates as supreme examples of living for others.

If Bucer moved, so to speak, in the same orbit as Calvin in many of his theological concerns, there remains a sense in which he was divided from Geneva by a difference of Copernican immensity. If Calvin's theology was in the fullest sense theocentric, Bucer's mind revolved around the wellbeing of the people of God. 'Butzer thought of religion first of all as ministering to man's salvation, while Calvin related it primarily to the eternal God.'[26] Consequently the best summary of the high-notes of his theology is to be looked for in the definition of the Kingdom which opens the fifth chapter of Book I of *De Regno Christi*:

Regnum servatoris nostri Iesu Christi administratio est et procuratio

19. Bucer is characterized as 'un homme d'Eglise' by Jaques Courvoisier, *La notion d'Eglise chez Bucer dans son développement historique*, Etudes d'histoire et de philosophie publiées par la faculté de théologie protestante de l'université de Strasbourg, no. 28, Paris, 1933. See also Torrance, T. F., *Kingdom and Church*, Edinburgh, 1956.
20. Stephens, op. cit., p. 24.
21. *De Regno Christi*, I.iii (LCC, XIX, p. 196).
22. Hence Bucer's high evaluation of baptism and the emphasis (novel among the reformers) on confirmation. See much relevant material in Fisher, J. D. C., *Christian Initiation in the Reformation Period*, Alcuin Club Collections LI, London, 1970.
23. Quoted Stephens, op. cit., p. 76.
24. Ibid., p. 49.
25. *Deutsche Schriften*, I, pp. 29-67, French edn. Strohl, Henri (Ed.), *De l'amour du prochain*, Paris, 1949. Courvoisier provides a synopsis, op. cit., pp. 43-50. The theme of love of neighbour is detectable in such traces as remain of Bucer's earliest ministry: see the *Summary* of his preaching at Wissembourg, *Deutsche Schriften*, I, pp. 69-147.
26. Pauck, Wilhelm, *The Heritage of the Reformation*, rev. edn, Oxford, 1966, p. 99.

salutis aeternae electorum Dei, qua hic ipse Dominus et rex coelorum,
doctrina et disciplina sua per idoneos et ab ipso delectos ad hoc
ipsum ministros administratis, electos suos, quos habet in mundo
dispersos et vult nihilominus mundi potestatibus esse subiectos,
colligit ad se, sibique et Ecclesiae suae incorporat atque in ea sic
gubernat, ut purgati indies plenius peccatis bene beateque vivant et
hic et in futuro.[27]

Partly as a consequence of controversy with the Anabaptists who
congregated in Strasbourg in great numbers, Bucer (to a greater extent
than his colleagues) came to identify the elect, loving community with
the entire multitudinous society of the city. According to Professor
Bernd Moeller, he was equipped to lay the ecclesiological foundations
for a Protestant politics and social policy by his own thorough
socialization in the civic life. His theology was 'typically urban', even
'bourgeois', itself a social product and distinguished from Lutheranism
by the affinity which it enjoyed with the civic notion of *publica utilitas*
and by the strong measure of civic humanism which it had absorbed.[28]
Is this more or less perceptive than Mrs Chrisman's suggestion (following Professor Kohls) that 'the concept of the common good,
gemeynen nutz, was a new and original contribution of the Strasbourg
reformers and probably originated with Bucer himself'?[29] To let this
pass: if we accept any form of sociological analysis of the Bucerian
Reformation, it may seem incongruous that a society so retarded by
comparison with the great German imperial cities as Tudor England
should have taken Bucer for a mentor, and that this essay should argue
the point that the example of the Strasbourg reformer was of particular
importance for an archbishop who could scarcely have been less of a
bourgeois, hailing as he did from the western part of Cumberland.[30]
But however we may speculate about its other than theological
sources, Bucer's copious discussion of the spiritual economy of the
Christian society, drawn from scripture and from Plato and Cicero
read through scriptural spectacles, was calculated to appeal to protestant
intellectuals and clerics regardless of social background. Amidst the
practical business of church organization, especially in the struggle
against the Anabaptists in Strasbourg, but also in Cologne, Hesse,

27. *De Regno Christi*, I.v (*OL*, XV, p. 54; LCC, XIX, p. 225).
28. *Villes d'empire et Réformation* (tr. from *Reichsstadt und Reformation*), Travaux
d'histoire éthico-politique, Geneva, 1966, Chs 3, 4. Cf. Pollet's remark (op. cit., I, p. 1)
that Bucer's 'théologie participe en quelque sorte de la position géopolitique de son
église'; and Baron, Hans, 'Calvinist Republicanism and its Historical Roots', *Church
History*, VIII, 1939. On Bucer's humanism see Strohl, Henri, *Bucer, humaniste chrétien*,
Etudes d'histoire et de philosophie religieuses, no. 29, 1939.
29. Chrisman, M. U., *Strasbourg and the Reform: A Study in the Process of Change*,
Yale Historical Pubns Misc. 87, New Haven, 1967, p. 262, following Ernst-Wilhelm
Kohls, *Die Schule bei Martin Bucer in ihren Verhältnis zu Kirche und Obrigkeit*,
Heidelberg, 1963. Wendel has derived the expression 'communis utilitas' from Jacques
Lefèvre d'Etaples's translation of Aristotle's *Politics* (*OL*, XV, p. 11 n. 6).
30. Edmund Grindal was born in the parish of St Bees. Edwin Sandys, equally a
confidant of Bucer in Edwardian Cambridge and Grindal's successor in both London
and York, was possibly a native of the same place and was certainly brought up
with Grindal.

Hamburg, Ulm, Augsburg and Constance,[31] and finally in England, it was natural that Bucer's vision of Christian discipleship within a loving, responsible *respublica* should receive a firm ecclesiastical expression. This occurred as Bucer defined the fourfold ministry derived from the Pauline texts and dwelt upon the necessity of church discipline, always accommodated to the rights and interests of the magistracy as local circumstances dictated. In the last year of his life he wrote:

> Disciplina vitae et morum in eo sita est, ut non publici modo Ecclesiarum ministri (quamquam hi praecipue), sed singuli etiam Christiani curam proximorum suorum gerant, ac quisque proximos suos ex authoritate et magisterio Domini nostri Iesu Christi, tamquam eius discipulos in fide et cognitione eius, ubi ubi possit, confirmet et provehat, atque ad progrediendum in vita Dei adhortetur . . . Etenim Christus, magister et gubernator noster, vivit agitque in Christianis singulis. In singulis igitur et per singulorum ministeria quaerit, quod periit, et salvum facit.[32]

Quamquam hi praecipue! The foreshadowing of twentieth-century theological fashions is partly deceptive. For all the quite deliberate concessions made in this passage to lay sentiment, Bucer often describes the exercise of discipline by the clergy ('une des pièces maîtresses de sa conception de royaume du Christ'[33]) as if it were equivalent to the work of the Holy Spirit in the Church. Before Calvin (or should one say before Beza?) Bucer had written with his own unmistakable bias: 'Wo kein Zucht und Bann ist, ist auch kein Gemein.'[34] When the Dutch congregation in Edwardian London desired a pastor, Bucer suggested to his old friend Albert Hardenberg that he might supply from Bremen a preacher 'doctum ad regnum Dei et disciplinae Christi studiosum'.[35]

If Bucer never tired of pastoral discourses, occasions were seldom lacking to provoke them. The incessant voice carries on through the German of *Von der waren Seelsorge und dem rechten Hirtendienst* (1538),[36] Bucer's principal treatise on ecclesiastical discipline and a monument to the struggle to establish it in Strasbourg; in the Latin of *De vera animarum cura*;[37] in such a document as the programme for the rehabilitation of the chapter of St Thomas in Strasbourg;[38] in the 1539 scheme for the reform of Hesse, the pioneering 'Ziegenhaimer Zuchtordnungen', which in Courvoisier's words provided for 'une dis-

31. See much relevant material in Pollet, op. cit., II; and the discussion in Courvoisier, op. cit., pp. 81-134.
32. *De Regno Christi*, I.viii (*OL*, XV, pp. 70-1; LCC, XIX, pp. 240-1).
33. *OL*, XV, p. xlviii.
34. Courvoisier, op. cit., p. 23; *Scripta Anglicana*, p. 863.
35. Pollet, op. cit., I, p. 216.
36. *Deutsche Schriften*, VII, pp. 67-245; discussed, Courvoisier, op. cit., pp. 97-115, who describes it as 'le premier traité de théologie pastorale de l'Eglise réformée' and as sufficient in itself to convey Bucer's ecclesiology.
37. *Scripta Anglicana*, pp. 260-356.
38. *De reformatione collegii canonici scriptum Martini Buceri*, in *Scripta Anglicana*, pp. 192-214.

cipline strictement et complètement ecclésiastique';[39] in *De legitima
ordinatione ministrorum*,[40] written in England and connected, to say no
more, with the English Ordinal; in the Lectures on Ephesians delivered
in Cambridge in 1550 and of particular interest for the impression they
may be presumed to have made on their English hearers;[41] in *De vi et
usu sacri ministerii explicatio*,[42] a document referred to by Elizabethan
controversialists, which was no more than an abstract from the Ephe-
sians lectures;[43] and above all in his swansong, *De Regno Christi*.

It is almost superfluous to remark that Bucer's ecclesiology was
closely connected to his understanding of the Lord's Supper, a topic
which necessarily absorbed his attention in his most public role as an
ecumenical protestant leader. In England he linked the total repudiation
of any doctrine of the real presence with the reluctance of powerful
men to allow religion to have anything to do with matters of public
and social policy. Those who confined the body of Christ 'to a certain
limited place in heaven' were also prone 'to reduce the whole of the
sacred ministry into a narrow compass'.[44] But here we must exclude
consideration of Bucer's eucharistic doctrine, great though its importance was in the general history of the Reformation.

The discussion must also be confined to what concerns Bucer's direct
and personal impact on English protestantism. Anyone who has
followed the argument over how Bucer and Calvin are to be related,
and has been told by Lang that Bucer was Calvin's 'geistlich Vater',[45]
by Pauck that Calvin was Bucer's 'strong and brilliant executive',[46]
and by Hyma that 'Bucer . . . made Calvin a Calvinist',[47] must be
conscious of the difficulties involved in accurately circumscribing
Bucer's influence. Anyone who has ever compared Bucer's prolixity
with Calvin's clarity and economy of utterance will not find it surprising
that Bucer, who died in 1551, was superseded as counsellor of the
Reformed churches by Calvin, who survived until 1564. Nevertheless,
without stumbling among the logical fallacies which invariably surround
the attribution of 'influence'[48] (and which have not been absent from

39. Diehl, W., *Martin Butzers Bedeutung für das kirchliche Leben in Hessen*, Schriften
des Vereins für Reformationsgeschichte, Halle, 1904; Courvoisier, op. cit., p. 39.

40. *Scripta Anglicana*, pp. 238-59.

41. *Praelectiones doctissimi in Epistolam D.P. ad Ephesios . . . habitae Cantabrigiae in
Anglia Anno MDL et LI*, Basle, 1562; dedicated by the editor, Tremellius, to Sir
Nicholas Throckmorton; see also *Explicatio Martini Buceri in illud apostoli Ephes. IIII*,
Scripta Anglicana, pp. 504-38.

42. Ibid., pp. 553-610.

43. Hopf, op. cit., pp. 19-20.

44. *Original Letters*, II, p. 544.

45. *Zwingli und Calvin*, Bielefeld and Leipzig, 1913.

46. *The Heritage of the Reformation*, p. 91.

47. Hyma, Albert, *Renaissance to Reformation*, Grand Rapids, 1951, p. 389. Cf. the
more balanced view of Wendel, *Calvin: The Origin and Development of his Religious
Thought*, tr. Mairet, London, 1963, pp. 137-44; and of Jacques Pannier, 'Bucer et
Calvin étaient biens faits pour se comprendre', *Calvin à Strasbourg*, Strasbourg, 1925.

48. Skinner, Quentin, 'Meaning and Understanding in the History of Ideas', *History
and Theory*, VII, 1969, pp. 3-53. For an example, close to home, of methodological
naïveté in this respect, see Cremeans, C. D., *The Reception of Calvinistic Thought in
England*, Illinois Studies in Social Sciences, XXXI, no. 1, Urbana, 1949.

attempts to trace the pedigree of Bucer's own ideas[49]) this much will be suggested, with proper caution: that what was distinctive in Bucer's teaching on the Church and its polity and in its formulation lent itself to English conditions and was one of the sources of inspiration for what was attempted by some of the leaders of the Church of England in the reign of Elizabeth I. In view of all that subsequently transpired in Strasbourg, it could be argued that it was in England that the echo of Bucer's voice resounded longest.[50]

II

No doubt the name of Bucer was long held in reverence in scholarly and devout circles. When Thomas Cartwright wrote of certain 'gross absurdities' in Bucer's writings (a reference to his views on the dissolution of marriages), John Whitgift exclaimed that he was the first protestant he had known to abuse 'so reverent, so learned, so painful, so sound a father.'[51] But meaningful ascriptions of influence should at least depend upon concrete proof of literary indebtedness. Evidence of this kind is not freely available in support of the present argument. The tally of Buceriana translated into English in the period covered by Pollard and Redgrave's *Short-title Catalogue* is so trifling as almost to suggest deliberate neglect.[52] On this showing Pauck is entitled to remark that 'there is very little evidence to show that Bucer's total program made a deep impression upon any churchmen in either the Anglican or the Puritan party.'[53]

The great book *De Regno Christi*, containing amongst much else Bucer's mature reflections on the Church's polity and ministry, was admittedly written in England and presented to the young king himself as a New Year's gift. The ms. prepared for the purpose reposes in

49. In *Zwingli A Reformed Theologian*, London, 1963, Jaques Courvoisier suggests that in their definition of the ministry 'Bucer and Calvin merely gave precision and clarity to what Zwingli had already said' (p. 59).

50. Thomas Blaurer wrote to Conrad Hubert in 1564: 'Sed translata est fortasse illorum (Buceri scil., Capitonis, Hedionis, Zellii) atque talium opera ad alias gentes, certe Anglia id sensit, ad quam fuit delatus Bucerus, et sentit haud dubie Christo nunc adolescens Galliae regnum.' (Quoted, Pollet, op. cit., II, p. 23 n. 4.)

51. Whitgift, John, *Works*, II, Ayre, John (Ed.), Parker Society, Cambridge, 1852, pp. 533-4.

52. *STC*, nos 3962-3966. Of these, 3962 (*A briefe examination of a certaine declaration*, 1566) and 3964 (*The mynd and exposition of M. Bucer uppon these wordes of S. Mathew: Woe be to the Wordle (sic)*, Emden, 1566) together with *STC* 1040 (*The fortresse of fathers*) are pamphlets from the Vestments Controversy which exploit Bucer for polemical purposes. 3963 (*The gratulation of the most famous clerk Master Martin Bucer unto the Churche of Englande*, 1549, translated by Sir Thomas Hoby and largely an attack on an old enemy, Stephen Gardiner, on the subject of clerical marriage) and 3966 (*A briefe treatise concerning the burnyng of Bucer and Phagius at Cambrydge*, translated by Arthur Golding from *Historia vera de vita, obitu, sepultra* (etc.), Basle, 1562) correspond to material in *Scripta Anglicana*. 3965 (*A treatise how by the word of God Christian mens almose ought to be distributed*, n.d.) is a translated extract from *De Regno Christi*. John Bradford's *Restoration of all things*, printed in 1564 in Coverdale's *Letters of the martyrs* (pp. 478-89) was a pastiche of Bucer's commentaries. (*Writings of John Bradford*, Townsend, A. (Ed.), Parker Society, Cambridge, 1848, p. 350.)

53. LCC, XIX, p. 172.

the British Museum.[54] Yet while two distinct French editions, which were in part distinct translations, appeared in 1558 (from presses in Geneva and Lausanne), and German editions in 1563 and 1568,[55] it was only the other day that the greater part of *De Regno Christi* was published for the first time in an English version.[56] There is no evidence that the book was widely known to the post-Edwardian generation. It is true it was published at Basle in 1577 as the most substantial part of a volume called *Scripta Anglicana*, which also contained many more occasional pieces from Bucer's English period. But *De Regno Christi* had been separately published by Oporinus at Basle in 1557 from a ms. which Bucer's widow had carried back to Germany, and Conrad Hubert, editor of the *tomus anglicanus*, was not dependent upon an English source for the text.[57]

While there is so little evidence of the currency of *De Regno Christi* under Elizabeth, it is pleasant to record the presence in Australia, in the Broughton Library of Moore Theological College in Sydney, of a copy of *Seripta Anglicana*[58] which was once the property of the Francis Place of Elizabethan Puritanism, John Field.[59] Field's signature appears on the title-page, together with the information that the book cost him 8s. 8d. Below this occurs the signature of Thomas Coleman, perhaps the Thomas Coleman who was a member of the Westminster Assembly until his death in 1647. Either Field or Coleman—most probably Field —has underscored some passages in the text and many isolated phrases, and it is noticeable that these marks occur most frequently where matters of church polity are under discussion. Their tendency, as one would expect of Field, was to enlist Bucer in a cause which in truth he would have deplored, as in the following passage:

Regni Christi restitutionem, ab Episcopis nullo modo esse expectandam; dum adeo pauci inter eos sunt, qui vim huius regni et propria munia plane ipsi cognoscant; plerique autem eorum illud etiam quibus possunt et audent modis, vel oppugnent, vel differant atque remorentur.[60]

54. Ms. Royal 8 B VII; described, *OL*, XV, pp. liv-lv.

55. Ibid., pp. lx-lxiv.

56. Pauck's edition, LCC, XIX. This excludes chapters xxii-xlvi of Lib. II, containing much of the '*Tractatus de conjugio*'. Some of this material was translated and published by Milton in his *Judgment of Martin Bucer concerning divorce* (1644) and is reproduced in various editions of the prose works.

57. *OL*, XV, pp. lvi-lix.

58. I am informed by the Librarian, Rev. Noel Pollard, that the volume was an acquisition of the last decade, and that its previous provenance was the Library of the London College of Divinity. I am most grateful to Mr Pollard and to the Principal of Moore College for enabling me to work in the Broughton Library. With a most curious symmetry the library of another Sydney seminary—St Patrick's College, Manly —contains a book which was once in the possession of Field's offsider, Thomas Wilcox. A copy of *Ethices philosophiae compendium*, printed at Heidelberg by the university printer in 1561, bears among other inscriptions the signature 'T. Wilcox', a motto in his hand 'Vivit post funero virtus' and the information that it cost him 6d.

59. See my 'John Field & Elizabethan Puritanism' in *Elizabethan Government & Society*, Bindoff, Hurstfield and Williams (Eds), London. 1960, pp. 127-62; and *The Elizabethan Puritan Movement*, London, 1967, *passim. See below*, pp. 335-70.

60. Lib. II, cap. i.

No 'influence' here! Only a hard and unsusceptible mind gathering ammunition in the arsenal of Bucer's writings.

If we are to find disciples of Bucer it will be by looking in another direction, towards the Elizabethan episcopate which Field rejected, or rather towards the younger scholars and junior reformers of Edwardian days from whom both the Elizabethan bishops and their earliest opponents were mostly recruited, and who had sat at Bucer's feet in Cambridge and with Peter Martyr Vermigli in Oxford. What Bucer had to say about the ministry was apt for reception in the Church of England. Although he was primarily responsible for the adaptation of Paul's description of the fourfold ministry in the Epistle to the Ephe-sians,[61] in practice Bucer did not set out to erect a novel-antique church order without connection with the immediate past, but rather to transform inherited institutions. With as much patristic as biblical reference,[62] he assumed the persistence of an hierarchically ordered ministry, but justified it functionally, not on grounds of succession. In naming bishops Bucer was inclined to reach for some form of words which would escape the conditioned response to a term overlaid with the accretions of centuries. Such expressions were 'consul in senatu',[63] 'superintendens, id est, episcopus',[64] 'episcopi, hoc est, inspectores',[65] 'dux et quasi antistes'.[66] Here was 'Protestant Catholicity', attractive to this present ecumenical century in which French-speaking Protestants have been glad to trace their churchmanship from Strasbourg rather than too exclusively from Geneva.[67]

Bucer recognized no difference of order between bishops and inferior clergy. Elizabethan controversialists would follow him in adapting St Jerome to the effect that 'presbyterorum atque episcoporum unum, idemque officium ac munus esse'.[68] The bishop was not to govern monarchically, 'sine reliquorum presbyterorum consilio'.[69] But a bishop was a bishop, and when he was ordained 'omnia aliquanto pluribus et gravius gerantur et perficiantur quam cum ordinatur presbyter secundi ac tertii ordinis'.[70] Bucer's ideal structure for the ministry was a chal-lenge to the English polity, but unlike later Calvinism it was not a defiance of it and might be expected to mould the thinking of those who became bishops in the English Church.

Another aspect of Bucer's thinking of minor interest to modern

61. See Strohl, Henri, 'La théorie et la pratique des quatre ministres à Strasbourg avant l'arrivée de Calvin', *Etudes sur Calvin*, Paris, 1935, pp. 122-44.
62. The most concrete evidence of Bucer's reliance on the Fathers is in the ms. patristic *Florilegium* still preserved in the Library of Corpus Christi College, Cam-bridge. (Wendel, loc. cit., p. 224; Rott, loc. cit., p. 354.)
63. *Scripta Anglicana*, p. 194.
64. Ibid., p. 259.
65. Ibid., p. 280.
66. Ibid.
67. See, for example, Pannier, Jacques, *Calvin et l'episcopat*, Paris, 1927.
68. *Scripta Anglicana*, p. 280. Cf. Sykes, Norman, *Old Priest, New Presbyter*, Cam-bridge, 1957, pp. 26-8.
69. *De Regno Christi*, II.xii (*OL*, XV, p. 118; LCC, XIX, p. 284).
70. *Scripta Anglicana*, p. 259.

ecumenists, but no less pertinent in the sixteenth century, was the
positive but respectful attitude which he adopted towards the role in
church affairs of the secular magistracy. The function of government
was in itself a gift of the Spirit and intended for the good of the
Church and for the maintenance of religion. Kings and princes were to
'humbly hear the voice of Christ from the ministers and respect in
them the majesty of the Son of God', and there was a sense in which
they were to 'yield fully not only to the public ministers of Christ and
to the pastors of the churches, but also to the churches in their entirety,
and nourish and adorn them with ardent zeal . . .'[71] But Bucer neither
suggested that secular government should give way to spiritual authority
in this area of its responsibilities, nor that it should ordinarily be subordinate to the Church's officers, and in Strasbourg it would have been
idle to have entertained such pretensions. In Courvoisier's words, the
Church was 'institution divine, tout à la fois unie à l'Etat independante
mais inspiratrice'.[72] A superficial reading of Bucer might suggest that
he was not far out of sympathy with the English polity, of which he
was an observant student from the early days of the Henrician Reformation. In 1536 he published a German version of Stephen Gardiner's
De vera obedientia.[73] But that he later fell out with Gardiner on the
matter is a further indication of the difference between his principles
and official thinking in England.[74] Once again the differences were not
so profound as to deny him a hearing.

There was no barrier to the reception in England of doctrine which
emphasized the retention and renewal of the episcopal office and which
assumed a harmonious and constructive association of ministers and
secular magistrates. Dare we say that there was an equal affinity
between Bucer's teaching and certain characteristic emphases in English
protestantism, not to speak of that less substantial entity, the 'English
religious tradition'? Since for Bucer it was almost the ultimate purpose
of religion to minister to salvation, it follows that the whole thrust of
his argument, when church polity was under discussion, was ethical
and practical, relating to the implementation of the gospel. So it was
for the most part in England. Although the Elizabethan presbyterians
were to demand a total reconstruction of the Church's outward structures in accordance with certain New Testament texts as the only
reformation worth discussion, much of the pressure for continuing
reform in England arose not out of legalistic respect for every letter of
scripture or for fine details of polity but from a concern to restore the
divine order and to build the Church on its proper foundations, in words
recently used of Bucer himself, 'to let the biblical word take body

71. *De Regno Christi*, I.ii (LCC, XIX, p. 188; *OL*, XV, pp. 16-17).
72. Op. cit., p. 40; and see Pauck, *Das Reich Gottes auf Erden*, esp. pp. 64ff.
73. Hopf, op. cit., pp. 195ff.; *Obedience in Church and State*, Janelle, Pierre (Ed.),
Cambridge, 1930, p. xxiv; and references in *OL*, XV, p. 16 n. 2.
74. Janelle, Pierre, 'La controverse entre Etienne Gardiner et Martin Bucer sur la
discipline ecclésiastique (1541-1548)', *Revue des sciences religieuses*, VII, 1927,
pp. 452-66.

both in the life of men and in the structure of society'.[75] The desire
was disturbing in its implications, but it did not threaten a total disruption of the Church's inherited structures.

By the end of the century, even this relatively pragmatic programme
tended to be less typical of the evolving puritan tradition in England
than the cultivation of godliness among individuals and in only loosely
associational groups. If with Dr Stoeffler in his study *The Rise of
Evangelical Pietism* we are prepared to derive the piety of Greenham,
Perkins and Rogers from an Edwardian source (Hooper and Bradford)
then we may go a step further with Stoeffler and with Professor Trinterud[76] and connect this tradition with the persistent influence in
England of the practical, refining programme of Christian Humanism,
mediated through the Rhineland reformers and by way of Bucer in
particular, who was once known somewhat disparagingly (and very
misleadingly) as 'the pietist among the Reformers'.[77] Bucer was too
committed a churchman and citizen to be usefully described as a pietist.
Yet for him, too, godliness was to be pursued, if necessary, at all costs.
The provision for its cultivation in the pietistic cells of Bucer's later
Strasbourg years, the *Christlichen Gemeinschaften* within the greater
Gemeinde,[78] were not unlike the brotherhoods and societies for mutual
edification and discipline which were an escape for the Elizabethan
puritans from the indifference of the official Church.[79]

Finally, in this survey of the points of natural affinity between Bucer
and English protestantism, we cannot ignore the social dimension.
Great though the social differences between Strasbourg and England
were, it was characteristic of the Edwardian reformers to erect on
partly new and evangelical foundations a conservative (in the fullest
and best sense) and paternalistic social programme such as Bucer
himself might have devised.[80] 'Commonwealth' coalesced with 'gemeynen
nutz' as Bucer strove in *De Regno Christi* to adapt his social philosophy
to English conditions. It may even be argued that in some chapters of
the book (although not in the interminable and in places deviant treatise
on marriage which it incorporates) Bucer acted as the spokesman for

75. Stephens, op. cit., p. 10. This is the theme of a recent study by Coolidge, J. S., *The Pauline Renaissance in England: Puritanism and the Bible*, Oxford, 1970.

76. Stoeffler, Ernst, *The Rise of Evangelical Pietism*, Leiden, 1965, following in the steps of Lang, *Puritanismus und Pietismus* (op. cit.); Trinterud, Leonard, Jr, 'The Origins of Puritanism', *Church History*, XX, 1951, repr. in *The Role of Religion in Modern European History*, Burrell, Sidney A. (Ed.), London, 1964. See also *Elizabethan Puritanism*, Trinterud (Ed.), A Library of Protestant Thought, New York, 1971, pp. 3-10.

77. See, e.g., Lang, *Der Evangelienkommentar Martin Butzers* (op. cit.), p. 14; Troeltsch, Ernst, *The Social Teaching of the Christian Churches*, trans. Wyon, O., London, 1931, II, p. 677. The question was reopened by Gerard Itti in a Strasbourg thesis of 1936, *Dans quelle mésure Bucer est-il piétiste?*

78. The standard account is Bellardi, Werner, *Geschichte der 'Christlichen Gemeinschaften' in Strasbourg (1546-1550)*, Leipzig, 1934, who is followed by Bullock, F. W., *Voluntary Religious Societies, 1520-1799*, St Leonards on Sea, 1963. See also Anrich, Gustav, in *Festschrift für Hans von Schubert*, Leipzig, 1929.

79. Collinson, *Elizabethan Puritan Movement*, pp. 372-82.

80. See, most recently, Jones, W. R. D., *The Tudor Commonwealth, 1529-1559*, London, 1970.

some of the 'commonwealth men' who were without easy access to court in the days of Northumberland's ascendancy.[81]

III

The text for what has been hinted at in these pages is furnished in a letter written to Lord Burghley in 1573[82] by Thomas Sampson, the early Elizabethan nonconformist leader, and as Latimer's nephew a link with the Edwardian past.[83] Sampson commended to the Lord Treasurer a further reform of the state of the Church ('the government of the Church appointed in the gospel yet wanteth here') but implicitly condemned the manner of urging reform chosen by the youthful authors of *An admonition to the Parliament*, published not long before. To dissociate the cause from this embarrassment, he reminded Burghley that 'this matter of reforming the state of the government of the Church was in hand in the days of King Edward'. It was then that 'that learned Martin Bucer' had written the book *De Regno Christi* which Sampson had brought to Burghley's attention on an earlier occasion. He now sent a digest of the book, urging him to read it and to 'take the matter to heart'. 'True and diligent ministers of the word . . . are means to make God a holy people, and to the queen's majesty, good subjects.' Moreover—and this surely was the punchline: 'He that concludes that to have the Church governed by meet pastors and ministers taketh away the authority of Christian magistrates is by Bucer sufficiently confuted.'[84]

Speaking about the composition of *De Regno Christi*, Sampson tells us that Bucer supplied his ignorance of England 'by report of his familiars in Cambridge'.

And they were the same which are now archbishops of York and Canterbury, bishop of London [Edmund Grindal, Matthew Parker, Edwin Sandys], Bradford and such like. I know not what conference they had with him when he made the book; but I am sure that since his death, in private talk, they have much approved his book.

From sources such as Bradford's letters and Bucer's own correspondence it is possible to reconstruct the circle of 'familiars' which, if we except the large German stove which he received as a present from

---

81. Suggested by Wendel, *OL*, XV, pp. xxxv, lii-liii; and by Pauck, LCC, XIX, pp. 161-3. According to Wendel (*OL*, XV, p. liii) 'l'accord entre le *De Regno Christi* et les écrits anglais est trop constant pour être du à des rencontres fortuites'.

82. Strype, John, *Annals of the Reformation*, Oxford, 1824, II, i, pp. 392-5, following B.M., ms. Lansdowne 18, fols 55-6.

83. Sampson admired Bucer enough to make a Latin translation of his very verbose *Verwantwortung* to Gropper's *Antididagma*, an attack on the scheme for the reform of the archdiocese of Cologne (Rott, loc. cit., pp. 356 n. 51, 362 n. 83; Hopf, op. cit., pp. 53-4). Rott has suggested that the original copy of Bucer's *Censura* of the 1549 Prayer Book (New College, Oxford, ms. 317) was preserved by Sampson. If so it is odd that the *Censura* were known to Whitgift, but not to Cartwright. (Whitgift, *Works*, II, pp. 533-4; III, pp. 346-7.)

84. In the same year (1574) Sampson made a more general appeal to much the same effect in his Preface to *Two notable sermons made by . . . John Bradford*, *Writings of Bradford*, I, p. 31.

the king, must have been Bucer's chief comfort in a chilly environment which knew how to resist his moral exhortations.[85] Parker was at this time Master of Corpus Christi and Sandys of St Catherine's. It is well known that Bucer was the friend of the notable English philologists and educationists, Cheke, Ascham and Walter Haddon. Apart from these, a significant number of his university friends seem to have been members of Pembroke Hall (a college which lies across the street from Corpus) and it is in Pembroke that we may imagine him spending much of his time, perhaps in that orchard where Ridley, Master of the college, learned 'without book' almost all the canonical epistles, and which was stocked with plants by the pioneer naturalist William Turner, fellow of the college, Latimer's disciple and the Thomas Huxley of his age.[86] The place of Pembroke in the Edwardian Reformation has never been duly acknowledged. It is appropriate that one of the two copies of De Regno Christi which was prepared under Bucer's personal supervision, apparently the copy which was in his study at the time of his death, should be found in the college library,[87] the gift of Lancelot Andrewes in his time as Master.[88]

The fellows of Pembroke when Bucer was in Cambridge included Sampson himself and that arresting figure John Bradford, whose conversion Sampson had engineered by taking him to hear his uncle Latimer preach. There was also Bradford's 'godly companion'[89] Thomas Horton, to whom we owe an account of Bucer denouncing the perennial sins of academic life 'non cessans', 'etiam ad nauseam et fastidium'.[90] Bradford was Bucer's acolyte, 'right familiar and dear unto him' as Sampson puts it.[91] According to Foxe it was by Bucer's persuasion that Bradford submitted to ordination. Bradford called him 'my father in the Lord' and addressed his letters to 'patri ac domino suo observandissimo'. He accompanied Bucer on a summer jaunt to Oxford, sat up with him day and night in his last illness, studied his writings in prison, and in his 'Farewell to Cambridge' cried: 'Remember the readings and preachings of God's true prophet and true preacher, Martin Bucer!'[92] John Whitgift, a scholar of Pembroke at this time, was Bradford's pupil, which, as Pauck suggests, may account for the frequency with which

85. Peter Martyr's Oxford household was the hub of a similar circle (anticipating the holy clubs of later generations?) which included John Jewel and Jewel's future biographer and Sampson's later companion in nonconformity, Laurence Humphrey, and which in Mary's reign transferred itself to the establishments maintained by Peter Martyr in Strasbourg and later in Zürich. (Southgate, W. M., John Jewel and the Problem of Doctrinal Authority, Cambridge, Mass., 1962, pp. 8-23.)

86. Raven, C. E., English Naturalists from Neckham to Ray, Cambridge, 1947, pp. 48-137.

87. Ms. 217.

88. OL, XV, p. lv; Rott, loc. cit., p. 361.

89. Sampson's Preface; Writings of Bradford, I, p. 31.

90. In a letter to Dryander, 15 May 1550, quoted Vogt, op. cit., p. 47; and in translation, Smyth, op. cit., pp. 163-4.

91. Writings of Bradford, I, p. 31.

92. Ibid., I, pp. 31, 355, 445; II, Townsend, A. (Ed.), Parker Society, Cambridge, 1853, pp. 352-4; Foxe, John, Acts and Monuments, Townsend, G. (Ed.), VII, 1847, pp. 143-4.

Bucer is quoted in Whitgift's controversial writings.[93] Yet another fellow, Nicholas Carr, the regius professor of Greek, composed an account of Bucer's last days and deathbed speeches,[94] although after reverting to the old religion under Mary, Carr would later testify against him at the posthumous heresy trial.

It remains to mention the President of Pembroke Hall at this time, *de facto* head of the house in the absence of Ridley: the future Bishop of London, Archbishop of York and Archbishop of Canterbury, Edmund Grindal.

IV

Grindal has been roughly handled by historians. According to an entrenched tradition, he was an incompetent and spineless administrator, over-indulgent to puritanism,[95] whose choice to succeed Parker as Archbishop of Canterbury can only be attributed to a grave lapse of Queen Elizabeth's judgment, 'a mistake',[96] attributable to 'some passing turn of policy'.[97] Repenting of her momentary lapse, the queen allowed Grindal to incur her profound displeasure, with the consequence that within less than twelve months of his elevation he slipped into a limbo where he remained for the last six years of his life.[98] It is hardly surprising that his primacy was marked by 'ineffectiveness',[99] for its effective duration was little more than a year. Grindal was neither the first nor the last Archbishop of Canterbury to have outlived the circumstances of his appointment, but his was the most immediate and irrevocable of disasters.

Grindal's disgrace seems to have been procured by his enemies as a blow against everything for which he was known to stand,[100] but the formal offence for which he suffered suspension was his refusal to transmit to his suffragans a royal order for the suppression of the preaching conferences known as 'prophesyings' and, less specifically, for the 'abridging' of the number of preaching ministers. This act of conscience, announced in a celebrated letter to the queen[101] of 8 Decem-

93. LCC, XIX, p. 172 n. 24.

94. *De obitu doctissimi et sanctissimi theologi Doctoris Martini Buceri*, Basle, 1551; and in *Scripta Anglicana*, pp. 867-82.

95. See, e.g., Frere, W. H., *A History of the English Church in the Reigns of Elizabeth and James I*, London, 1904, p. 192; Kennedy, W. P. M., *Studies in Tudor History*, London, 1916, p. 260. According to Sir Sidney Lee he 'feebly temporised with dissent' (*Cambridge Modern History*, III, Cambridge, 1907, p. 341).

96. Welsby, P. A., *George Abbot, the Unwanted Archbishop*, London, 1962, p. 1.

97. Gwatkin, H. M., *Church and State in England to the Death of Queen Anne*, London, 1917, p. 255.

98. Many of the documents connected with Grindal's disgrace are separately gathered in *The Remains of Edmund Grindal*, Nicholson, W. (Ed.), Parker Society, Cambridge, 1843, pp. 372-403.

99. Frere, op. cit., p. 192.

100. Collinson, *Elizabethan Puritan Movement*, pp. 159-67, 193-201; Trinterud, *Elizabethan Puritanism*, pp. 193-7.

101. *Remains*, pp. 376-90. For a better text (from Grindal's papers in the Laud-Selden-Fairhurst mss, Lambeth Palace Library) see Lehmberg, S. E., 'Archbishop Grindal and the Prophesyings', *Historical Magazine of the Protestant Episcopal Church*, XXXIV, 1965, pp. 87-145.

ber 1576,[102] made Grindal an admired figure in the eyes of those in the
seventeenth century who favoured 'moderation', and in due course a
hero for nonconformist historians.[103] By the same token he became an
odious symbol for Tory high flyers, the 'perfidious prelate' of Dr
Sacheverell's sermon of 5 November 1709.[104] By this time all memory
was lost of Grindal's real qualities and contemporary reputation. Even
Strype, whose friendly *Life of Grindal* was hastened to the press by
the Sacheverell affair,[105] as an annalist lacked the insight and the
motive to set Grindal in his proper context. This is not the place to
argue the case that Grindal, far from displaying weakness and incom-
petence in government, was an effective bishop, a lawyer by instinct
if not by formal training who is likely to have appreciated the positive
evaluation of Christian law, including the law of the Christian Empire,
which we find in Bucer's writings;[106] nor to assert that he was a natural
choice for each of the three sees which he occupied.[107] Enough to
quote the opinion of Sir John Hayward, who remembered him as

> a man famous, whilst he lived, for his deep judgment, both in learning
> and affairs of the world; famous also for his industry and gift in
> preaching; but chiefly he was famous for his magnanimous courage;
> in that it was no less easy to divert the sun from his proper course
> than to pervert him to indirect actions.[108]

That Grindal should have been so gravely misrepresented by posterity
implies a certain discontinuity between his churchmanship and that of
later generations in the Church of England, or for that matter outside
it. The Anglicanism of Grindal was without a direct succession: it was
the victim of divisions which later became permanent but which were
held in tension in his time. Similarly, the distinctive aspects of Bucer's
achievement failed to survive his own epoch, least of all in the Strasbourg of Lutheran reaction, and were not transmitted in an enduring
tradition.[109] It may be that these two facts are connected, like sub-
terranean caves. The recognition that a stream of inspiration passed

102. For the correct date, often wrongly given as 20 December, *Remains*, p. 391.

103. Milton, John, *Of reformation, touching church-discipline in England*, 1641, p. 15;
Prynne, William, *The antipathie of the English lordly prelacie*, 1641, pp. 147-9; Neal,
Daniel, *The History of the Puritans*, 1793 edn, I, pp. 346-7.

104. Sacheverell, Henry, *The perils of false brethren, both in Church and State*, 1709;
The tryal of Dr. Henry Sacheverell, 1710; cf. Scudi, A. T., *The Sacheverell Affair*,
New York, 1939.

105. Evidence in Strype's correspondence in the Cambridge University Library, Baumgartner ms. 6, and in William Cole's transcripts, with comments, B.M., ms. Add. 5853;
in Strype's letters to Ralph Thoresby, *Letters of Eminent Men addressed to Ralph
Thoresby*, II, 1832; and in the list of subscribers printed with the *Life of Grindal*,
1710.

106. *OL*, XV, pp. xlvi-xlvii.

107. I hope to substantiate these assertions in my biography of Grindal, to be published in the series 'Leaders of Religion'.

108. *Annals of Queen Elizabeth*, Bruce (Ed.), Camden Society, 1840, p. 89.

109. Cf. Joseph L. McLelland's suggestion that the doctrine of Peter Martyr failed
to receive 'definite expression by any group in the subsequent history of the Church of
England', while 'its influence is evident throughout the history of the Church of
England' (*The Visible Words of God: A Study in the Theology of Peter Martyr*,
Edinburgh, 1957, p. 39).

from Bucer to Grindal may help us to reach a more just assessment
of that maligned prelate and also to award Bucer a more creative role
in the formation of Elizabethan Anglicanism than he has yet been
credited with.

Any intimacy which may have existed between Bucer and Grindal
is concealed rather than disclosed by the documents. Grindal was not
among the seventy-seven scholars whose *epigrammata* and *encomiastica*
adorned Bucer's memorial volume,[110] nor does his name appear among
the surviving letters to Bucer from English correspondents.[111] Not by
any stretch of an elastic term can Grindal be called a humanist, and
he was not given to effusion. But when Bucer felt threatened by
Dr John Young and other theological adversaries it was to 'doctissime
et carissime Grindalle' that he appealed for help in representing his
case to Ridley.[112] And Grindal was one of those who bore the coffin
at his funeral.[113]

At that time Matthew Parker had the stronger claim to be regarded
as Bucer's legatee.[114] Parker thought it worth preserving their ephemeral
correspondence, including a note in which Bucer had touched him for
a loan. He sponsored Bucer's candidature for the DD *honoris causa*,
preached the English sermon at the funeral and with Walter Haddon,
who delivered the Latin oration on the same occasion, served as Bucer's
executor. In this last capacity Parker was involved in complex negotiations with the much-widowed Wibrandis Bucer over disposal of her
late husband's effects, including books and papers. Although these were
supposedly conveyed to three parties, the young king himself, the
Duchess of Suffolk and Archbishop Cranmer, M. Jean Rott has shown
that some at least of the papers were in Parker's hands as early as
1551. In his library, preserved in Corpus Christi College, much of the
contents of Bucer's study are still to be found, with evidence that
Parker examined the papers from time to time with the assistance of
Bucer's *famulus* in Cambridge, Martin Brem.[115] Parker knew the value
for learning and also for controversy of letters and treatises exchanged
with the most famous scholars and divines of the age on the great
issues of the age. In Elizabeth's reign he would turn some of the
material to polemical account against the puritans. But Bucer was
Parker's colleague, not his spiritual father, and he addressed him as
'clarissimus', not 'carissimus'. On Parker's side there is no evidence of
the filial devotion which Bradford and Grindal expressed, no sug-

110. *Historia vera de vita, obitu, sepultura* (etc.), Hubert, Conrad (Ed.), Basle, 1562;
and in *Scripta Anglicana*, pp. 902-14, 946-58. The authors included the young Duke
of Suffolk and Charles Brandon, his brother, John Cheke, Anthony Cooke, John Cul-
pepper, Thomas Wilson, Nicholas Carr, Walter Haddon, Thomas Lever, Alexander
Nowell, Bartholomew Traheron, Nicholas Udall, Thomas Penny and William Day.
Theodore Beza was the only foreign name to appear in the collection.
111. Pollet, op. cit., *passim*; Rott, loc. cit., pp. 358-61; Vogt, op. cit., pp. 167-204.
112. *Scripta Anglicana*, pp. 803-4; Gorham, op. cit., pp. 163-7.
113. *Scripta Anglicana*, p. 936.
114. This paragraph is based on Rott, loc. cit.; and on Parker's *Correspondence*,
Bruce, J. (Ed.), Parker Society, Cambridge, 1853, pp. 41-5, 46-8.
115. For Brem, see Wendel, loc. cit., pp. 225-6.

gestion of a theological response. He stayed in England under Mary, corresponded with the continent hardly at all, and as Archbishop of Canterbury was to find more to inspire him in the antiquities of the British Church than in the current practice of what others knew as 'the best reformed churches overseas'. He would offend a fellow-bishop with disparaging talk of 'Germanical natures'.[116]

Grindal's was the Germanical nature *par excellence*. The only circumstance of his exile recorded by Foxe is that 'he went into the country to learn the Dutch tongue' and fifteen years later as Archbishop of York he could still read German.[117] As Bishop of London he employed a German secretary, who was none other than Diethelm Blaurer, son of a famous pastor and a name intimately linked with Bucer. He also read Luther, critically, in the original.[118] In exile he had lived in Strasbourg where he became friends with Conrad Hubert, Bucer's secretary and the tutor of his youngest surviving son. Hubert was a devoted collector of Bucer's correspondence and literary remains and his would-be biographer.[119] With other Englishmen Grindal attended the lectures of Peter Martyr, who had been so close in spirit to Bucer: 'a very notable father' as he assured Ridley.[120] Grindal loved Strasbourg and always spoke warmly of it.[121]

Back in England, he made it his business to supply Hubert with such of the treatises and disputations as were later to appear in *Scripta Anglicana*, the *tomus anglicanus* which was intended as the first instalment of that complete edition of Bucer which we still lack. In the late 1550s Hubert hoped that his master's later writings could be used to heal the bitter 'supper strife' then convulsing South Germany. Recently Grindal, as a resident of Strasbourg, had collected the 'acts' of the Marian martyrs with a similar motive.[122] But the *Scripta Anglicana* manuscripts (which are still preserved in Strasbourg) reached Hubert very slowly, and for reasons which are far from clear he was never to know the extent of the literary remains of Bucer which had survived the persecution. To be sure these were the legal property of those who had done business with Bucer's widow and of their heirs.[123]

In May 1559, when Grindal sent over the records of Bucer's doctoral disputation and of his controversy with Young, he told Hubert that Parker had written of other 'fragmenta' in his possession which after being hidden were 'corrosa a scoribus et prorsus corrupta'. This was

116. *Parker Correspondence*, p. 125.
117. Foxe, op. cit., VIII, p. 598; *Zurich Letters*, I, Robinson, Hastings (Ed.), Parker Society, Cambridge, 1842, p. 224.
118. *Zurich Letters*, II, Robinson (Ed.), Parker Society, Cambridge, 1845, pp. 22-4, 74, 107.
119. Rott, loc. cit.; Pollet, op. cit., II, p. 18. Pollet prints (ibid., II, pp. 30-1) Hubert's preface (c. 1556) to an intended edition of Bucer's letters.
120. *Remains*, p. 239.
121. See his remarks to Cecil after entertaining a diplomat who had been a civil law student in Strasbourg in his time: B.M., ms. Lansdowne 7, fol. 133; and his assurances to Hubert, *Zurich Letters*, II, p. 52.
122. Pollet, op. cit., II, pp. 18-23; *Remains*, pp. 219-38.
123. Hubert's problems were not all in England (Pollet, op. cit., II, pp. 21-3).

perhaps disingenuous on Parker's part, and Hubert's letters to Grindal and to Diethelm Blaurer show that he was not satisfied.[124] In October 1560 Grindal was able to send some other writings 'quae hactenus inter reverendissimi D. Cantuensis schedas delituerant, ab ipsomet mihi in hunc fidem tradita'. He found it hard to cope with Bucer's notorious script[125] and was not well-informed about the contents of the papers which passed through his hands. As the intermediary between Parker and Strasbourg there is no reason to suspect Grindal of any intention other than to further Hubert's plans for publication.[126] On his own initiative he 'caused to be carefully drawn up' an account of the macabre proceedings of February 1557, when the bones of Bucer and of his colleague Paul Fagius had been exhumed and burned after a process for heresy. This was forwarded to Strasbourg only when he could attach a description of the Elizabethan ceremony of rehabilitation.[127] He resisted the preferment of the turncoat, Andrew Perne, who as vice-chancellor in 1557 and again in 1561 presided on both these occasions, arguing that to encourage Perne, 'his apostasie beinge so notorious', would 'moche comforthe all dissemblers and neutralles and discorage the zealouse and syncere'.[128] It was not inappropriate that when *Scripta Anglicana* appeared belatedly from a Basle press in 1577, Hubert should have dedicated the volume to Grindal as Archbishop of Canterbury.

'As Master Bucer used to say' was a phrase which Grindal used, and in correspondence with Hubert he speaks of 'Buceri manes, communis praeceptoris nostri'.[129] With the Strasbourg authorities displaying an aggressive gnesio-Lutheranism, he wrote: 'Tu vero, Conrade doctissime, perge in Buceri fama tuenda, ac veritate propugnanda.'[130] Evidently Grindal was a Bucerian.

Why (aside from Grindal's extreme obscurity outside his own country, and even inside it) has this not attracted earlier comment? Why in 1969 does Professor Pauck say so little about Grindal in assessing Bucer's impact upon England, which in general he believes to have been slight?[131] Pauck's suggestion in *Das Reich Gottes auf Erden* that *De Regno Christi* should be read as a Protestant *Utopia*[132] is presumably linked with his low evaluation of its effect in the real world. Another reason may be found in the obsession of historians with puritan-Anglican divisions, so that Bucer's influence has been

124. Ibid., II, p. 19.
125. On the subject of Bucer's handwriting, see Pollet, op. cit., II, pp. 24 n. 5, 27 n. 1.
126. This follows closely Rott, loc. cit.; and Grindal to Hubert in *Epistolae Tigurinae* (bound with translations in *Zurich Letters*, II), pp. 10-11, 30-1.
127. Ibid., pp. 30-1, 45.
128. Grindal to Sir William Cecil, 3 August 1564; B.M., ms. Add. 35831, fol. 184.
129. *Zurich Letters*, II, p. 24; *Epistolae Tigurinae*, p. 44.
130. Ibid., p. 45.
131. LCC, XIX, pp. 170-3.
132. Pauck renews a disagreement with Wendel on this point in LCC, XIX, p. 164 n. 16. And see Vogt's criticism of the comparison with *Utopia*, op. cit., pp. 91-3.

looked for in relation to Elizabethan conflicts rather than in the
ordinary conduct of affairs by the earlier Elizabethan bishops.[133] Moreover Bucer's traces have been sought in the evidence of the *writings* of
English divines that they were familiar with Bucer's *writings*. To bring
these two observations together, the most obvious evidence of a continuing debt to Bucer is to be found in the pamphlets exchanged
between the opponents and upholders of uniformity in the 1560s, and
in Whitgift's controversy with Cartwright in the 1570s.[134] But Bucer
appeared to his contemporaries not as a theologian, in the modern
sense of an academic specialist and writer, but as a Christian of mag-
netic quality, a religious genius whose grasp on the heart of the matter
never relaxed, the head of a model household, a type and example
of the godly bishop.[135] Only in relation to all these qualities was he
respected as a controversialist. Bucer made an impression in Cambridge through his life and conversation, and by the example of an
orderly and studious family where no one was tolerated 'quis non amat
vere Dominum Iesum' and where no detail of the quotidian routine
escaped careful regulation.[136] It is very likely that the mark of his
influence is to be found in the conduct of his friends who later became
bishops.

Finally, and here the argument is somewhat at variance, the impediments to the effective implementation in the early Elizabethan Church
of Bucer's pastoral ideals were so insuperable that we have to look
for the hand of Bucer in the intention rather than in the deed. A
general rehabilitation of the pastoral ministry was prevented by the
depleted state of the universities, the insufficient numbers and quality
of ordinands, the poverty of most livings, and the difficulties associated
with the collection of tithes. The bishop was almost obliged to institute
to livings the persons whom the patrons presented, unless he chose to
invite action in the courts. And to displace any but the most flagrantly
unfit of the incumbent clergy was not feasible. Taking account of all
these circumstances, as every bishop was obliged to do, it would be
naive to seek in the Elizabethan Church for an extensive application
of Bucer's doctrine of perfection. This is not to mention the even more
irremovable obstacles to the erection, in Protestant England, of clerical

133. See Pauck, *The Heritage of the Reformation*, p. 74: 'Anglicanism and Puritanism
alike could rightly claim him as their godfather.'

134. For Bucer's posthumous role in the Elizabethan vestments controversy, see Hopf
and Primus, op. cit., and Trinterud, *Elizabeth Puritanism*, pp. 89-95; for the use of
Bucer by both Whitgift and Cartwright, *Works of Whitgift*, Ayre, J. (Ed.), Parker
Society, Cambridge, 1851-3, *passim*.

135. In 1543 Peter Martyr wrote from Bucer's house in Strasbourg: 'Behold, well-
beloved brethren, in our age, bishops upon the earth, or rather in the Church of
Christ, which be truly holy. This is the office of a pastor, this is that bishop-like
dignity described by Paul in the Epistles unto Timothy and Titus. It delighteth me
much to read this kind of description in those Epistles, but it pleaseth me a great
deal more to see with the eyes the patterns themselves.' (Gorham, op. cit., pp. 21-2.)

136. See the curious 'Formula vivendi prescripta familiae sue A.M. Bucero et propria
manu revisa', in the hand of Martin Brem, printed by Wendel, loc. cit., pp. 231-2
(cf. Vogt, op. cit., pp. 57-8). Wendel remarks (p. 227): 'Sa propre maison ne devait
pas plus y échapper que l'Etat, les relations sociales et économiques ou les institutions
ecclésiastiques.'

power. And to put it in crude terms, clerical power was what Bucer's *Zucht* amounted to in lay eyes.

In spite of all this, we may still hope to find the legacy of Bucer not so much in literary statements of indebtedness as in the whole conduct of Grindal's episcopate, and most of all in his own persistent discontent with the practical deficiencies of the Church. As late as 1569 he advised the Scottish Earl of Murray that if he intended 'the continuance of the Gospell, as I know you doo', he must 'labor that sufficient and certaine stipendis be appointed for the ministers of the word'. Scotland should not follow 'our example' and divert church possessions to private gain while appointing 'readers in stede of teachers, as we do in most places to the decaye of religion and learn-inge'.[137] But this is not a venture to launch out on in the closing pages of an already congested article. What follows are no more than suggestions, which a forthcoming study of Grindal will pursue at greater leisure.

In three areas of his episcopal conduct Grindal appears to have acted, consciously, as a Bucerian: in his evaluation of the pastoral ministry and in the spirit and mode of the pastoral care which he himself exercised; in his understanding of the proper relationship of spiritual to secular authority; and in his handling of the puritans.

To take first the question of church-state relations: Bucer, as we have seen, held in balance his insistence on discipline and his recog-nition of the magistrate's role in church affairs, pursuing a *via media* between Erastianism of the English type and the resurgent clericalism which would later develop within Calvinism. That Grindal sought for a *modus vivendi* along these very lines is suggested by the excellent relationship which as Archbishop of York he maintained with the Earl of Huntingdon as Lord President of the Council in the North, con-trasting with the total discord which later prevailed between Huntingdon and Grindal's successor.[138] It is implicit in another context in Grindal's celebrated letter to the queen of December 1576, where the archbishop (quoting St Ambrose) asks that she should refer 'all those ecclesiastical matters which touch religion, or the doctrine and discipline of the Church' to her bishops and divines, to be adjudged '*in ecclesia, seu synodo, non in palatio*'; yet where he also offers to restore the authority which he has received from the Crown:

> If it be your majesty's pleasure, for this or any other cause, to remove me out of this place, I will with all humility yield thereunto, and render again to your Majesty that I received of the same.[139]

Grindal did not disobey a royal order, nor did he even challenge the right of the queen to make it. Rather he questioned the wisdom and propriety of such an order and declined to forward it to the other

137. Grindal to Murray, 17 Jan. 1569; B.M., ms. Royal 18, B. VI, fol. 288v.
138. Cross, Claire, *The Puritan Earl*, London, 1966, pp. 226-69.
139. *Remains*, pp. 376-90 and esp. pp. 387-90.

bishops.[140] Fine distinctions were drawn very much as they were drawn by the Strasbourg ministers in their defence of ecclesiastical discipline, and by Bucer in resisting Jacob Sturm at the time of the Imperial Interim. The underlying presumptions were Bucerian rather than Calvinist.[141]

The major difficulty confronting a biographer of Grindal is to place him in the right relation to the puritans. Here too Bucer seems to hold the key. Much of his teaching was an anticipation of aspects of what would later be recognized as points of puritanism, generously defined: the prominence of the doctrine of election, the high estimation of the preaching ministry, the sense of Reformation as a creative, ongoing, refining process of purification and of the English Church as in these respects 'eine junge Kirche',[142] the practical concern with abuses, the high moral tone of his utterances. In all of these respects Grindal too was a puritan. Yet Bucer was conspicuously unsympathetic to those puritan attitudes which contemporaries regarded as 'precise': extreme scrupulosity with respect to surplices, square caps and other sartorial vestiges of the old order, and other expressions of a narrow legalism and of literal scripturalism. As part of the innocent creation, such objects were not in themselves an abuse. The fault was in 'the impurity of those minds which abuse them'. The godly ought not to be so obsessed with 'the marks and signs' of Antichrist as to lose sight of 'the nerves and joints'. To be sure Bucer was no promoter of empty ceremonies. The unity of the Church consisted 'not in garments, not in ceremonies', but 'in the unity of the spirit, of charity, of the word of God, of Christ, of the sacraments, and in the communion of gifts'. And it was possible for the Elizabethan puritans to quote harsher judgments on 'Antichrist's relics' than these.[143] But just as Bucer could not equate Reformation with the mere erasure of the past, so he could not accept it as the hallmark of a godly conscience to set such store by externals that matters of real importance were obstructed. In Bucer's view John Hooper, as bishop-elect of Gloucester the original vestiarian nonconformist, was excessively concerned with his own rectitude in these respects. He wrote to Hooper in November 1550: 'This controversy afflicts me exceedingly, since it places such an impediment in the way of the ministry of yourself and others.'[144] And to John à Lasco he wrote of 'Satan's accustomed slights, whereby he leadeth us away from the care of necessary things to carefulness about those things which may be well let pass'.[145]

Grindal's attitude to the *adiaphora* and his handling of the problem of conscientious nonconformity in the Elizabethan Church were so

140. Head, R. E., *The Royal Supremacy and the Trials of Bishops, 1558-1725*, London, 1962, p. 17.
141. The Bucerian undertones of Grindal's protest are noted by Vogt, op. cit., pp. 84-8.
142. Letter to Catherine Zell, 13 May 1549; Pollet, op. cit., I, p. 254.
143. Primus, op. cit., pp. 43-53; Trinterud, *Elizabethan Puritanism*, pp. 89-95.
144. Gorham, op. cit., pp. 200, 208; translated from *Scripta Anglicana*, pp. 705, 707.
145. Quoted Hopf, op. cit., p. 152.

closely in line with these values that they are very likely to have been directly influenced by Bucer's example. With the other émigré bishops he hoped to see the consciences of his puritan brethren relieved by further parliamentary action to remove ceremonies for which he held no brief whatsoever.[146] Nevertheless, as a bishop he did not ordinarily evade his responsibility to enforce existing laws relating to ceremonies. But where there were valid pastoral reasons for a local suspension of these laws (for example, a risk that by wearing the surplice a minister would grievously wound the consciences of his flock and even provoke schism) Grindal was prepared to be lenient, and even to license a temporary measure of nonconformity.[147] Consistently he sought, and can be seen in the major vestiarian crisis in London in 1566 to be seeking, a pastorally defensible solution to the problem posed by the present state of the law, the lawlessness which it served to expose, and the queen's determination to have the statute enforced.[148] On the other hand, where he considered that an arrogant scrupulosity threatened not only the unity of the Church but the preaching of the gospel itself, the puritans had no more resolute an opponent. This may explain what might otherwise appear strange: that this 'puritan' sometimes had harsher things to say about puritanism than other bishops whose interest in the matter did not extend beyond their role as 'superior officers' under the queen for the policing of the Church.[149]

The refusal to lose sight of pastoral and evangelical priorities in the performance of functions which in the Church of England were still as a rule formalized as matters of administrative routine may be illustrated from the policies pursued by Grindal as Archbishop of York. There is perhaps no need to emphasize that for Grindal preaching was the prime function of the ministry and of the essence of the Church. As he told the queen, who had suggested that two or three preachers might be sufficient for a shire: 'Public and continual preaching of God's word is the ordinary mean and instrument of the salvation of mankind.'[150] One could hardly claim Bucer as the source of a notion which was integral to the Reformation itself, although De Regno Christi specifically rebutted 'those who want the holy preaching of the gospel restricted to fewer evangelists' or even omitted altogether 'because by this preaching, as they falsely say, controversies and disturbances are stirred up among the people'.[151] But we may note in passing these uncompromising statements from De Regno Christi: 'Frustra itaque illi se gloriantur esse Christi Ecclesiam, apud quos clara Evangelii et

146. Collinson, Elizabethan Puritan Movement, pp. 46-8, 64-7; Owen, G. H., 'The London Parish Clergy in the Reign of Elizabeth I', University of London PhD thesis, 1957.

147. His letter to Archdeacon Pulleyn of Colchester, 5 June 1560; Corpus Christi College, Oxford, ms. 297, fol. 17.

148. Collinson, Elizabethan Puritan Movement, pp. 74-6; Owen, op. cit., pp. 468-514.

149. For evidence of his total lack of sympathy for Thomas Cartwright, see Remains, pp. 323-4.

150. Ibid., p. 379.

151. De Regno Christi, I.xv (LCC, XIX, p. 260; OL, XV, p. 91).

assidua praedicatio non summo studio et cum primis exhibetur Christi populo, . . .'. The Kingdom of Christ being 'regnum praedicationis', 'ubi silet Domini nostri ista praedicatio, ibi nec ipsum, nec regnum eius adesse'.[152]

With more confidence we may call Bucerian the conviction that the renewal of the ministry was the key to the general rehabilitation of society. As a northerner himself and the son of a poor 'statesman' in a backward 'little angle'[153] of Cumberland, Grindal brought personal experience to a not very profound analysis of the ills of Tudor society which regarded lack of instruction as the chief cause of social distress and even of rebellion. His native country he described as 'the ignorantest part in religion, and most oppressed of covetous landlords, of any one part of this realm, to my knowledge'.[154] After his primary visitation as Archbishop of York he wrote to the Earl of Leicester about the gross insufficiency of the clergy, which, though 'a general inconvenience throughout the whole realm', was 'more common in these parts. The redress whereof were a good parliament matter.' If the clergy were incompetent, then 'by a necessary consequence the people cannot be well instructed'.[155] And as he assured the queen, with suitable examples to make his point, 'where preaching wanteth, obedience faileth'.[156]

For reasons already noted, Grindal could not hope to reform the clergy of Yorkshire[157] in one year, or even in the five years which he spent in York. He could neither deprive a majority of the incumbent clergy,[158] nor easily persuade them to mend their ways, nor lightly refuse to institute the clergy presented to him for institution. There was hardly space to wield a new broom. Yet there is some evidence in the act books of the Ecclesiastical Commission for the northern province[159] of a sharp campaign against the more openly scandalous clergy.[160] And the Institution Books record that the archbishop sometimes personally examined clergy applying for institution, and that on five occasions

152. *De Regno Christi*, I.iii, iv (*OL*, XV, pp. 26, 45-6; LCC, XIX, pp. 197, 216-17).

153. *Remains*, p. 256.

154. Ibid., pp. 256-7.

155. B.M., ms. 32091, fol. 242.

156. *Remains*, p. 379.

157. For much material on the Elizabethan clergy of Yorkshire, see Purvis, J. S., *Tudor Parish Documents of the Diocese of York*, Cambridge, 1948, and Tyler, P., 'The Status of the Elizabethan Parochial Clergy', *Studies in Church History*, IV, Cuming, G. J. (Ed.), Leiden, 1968.

158. The suggestion of Neville Williams (*Elizabeth Queen of England*, London, 1967, p. 170) that the Northern Rebellion was followed by the deprivation of hundreds of clergy is pure fantasy.

159. Borthwick Institute of Historical Research, University of York, R. VII HCAB. These voluminous and unique sources are described by Dr Philip Tyler, 'The Ecclesiastical Commission for the Province of York, 1561-1641', University of Oxford DPhil. thesis, 1965; and in his article 'The Significance of the Ecclesiastical Commission at York', in *Journal of Northern History*, II, 1967.

160. More especially in the backward archdeaconry of Richmond (diocese of Chester) and in those parts of it which lay closest to his native country of West Cumberland. (Borthwick Institute, R. VII. HCAB 6, fols 63v-4v, 65v, 81ff., 107v, 109v, 121v.)

institution was refused on grounds of insufficient learning.[161] (One of these who failed his examination was asked who had led Israel out of Egypt: 'Responduit, Rex Saul.') This is more remarkable than it may seem. Very few other instances of refusal to institute have come to light in the institution records of Elizabethan bishops.[162]

Grindal placed his hopes for the progressive reform of a backward diocese on the importation of a clerical élite. He would later inform the queen that he had 'procured above forty learned preachers and graduates, within less than six years, to be placed within the diocese of York'.[163] Grindal's York Ordination Registers show how such a policy was reconciled with the need to provide for the continuation of some kind of ministry in hundreds of Yorkshire and Nottingham-shire parishes. According to the custom of the diocese, Grindal con-ducted two kinds of ordinations: *ordines generales* which were conferred on large numbers of candidates for the diaconate and priesthood at the normal seasons; and *ordines speciales* which were conferred on very few candidates, or even on a single ordinand, privately, on as many as a dozen occasions in the course of the year.[164] It was at these times that the hand-picked men, graduates and *literati*, were admitted to the ministry. Bucer had recommended the strategic deployment of such able and adequate ministers.[165] What stung Grindal into open protest against the queen's conduct of church affairs was her declared opposition to preaching on the scale which Grindal (and Bucer) regarded as minimally necessary.

In nothing was Grindal so patently a Bucerian as in the exercise of his own pastoral functions. Bucer (himself regularly and familiarly described as bishop of Strasbourg) accepted the continuation of dio-cesan bishops, while insisting that their way of life should exclude worldly preoccupations, 'however helpful to mankind',[166] and that the work should occupy the bishop in person, but should be carried out in consultation with other presbyters, 'qui et ipsi, propter hanc communem Ecclesiarum administrationem, episcopi in scripturis vocantur'.[167] Bucer's consideration of the administration of discipline was marked by a continual return to first principles. Discipline was to be restorative, curative, personal, pastoral care in no merely formal sense. Politically,

161. Borthwick Institute, RIAB 2, fol. 126r, 3, fols 4v, 6, 8v, 10r, 21v, 23v-4r, 46v-7r, 81.

162. There are no examples from the archepiscopates of Grindal's predecessor at York, Young, nor from the time of his successor, Sandys. The late Dr H. G. Owen knew of only one example from the Elizabethan records of the diocese of London ('The London Parish Clergy in the Reign of Elizabeth I', unpublished London PhD thesis, 1957, pp. 115-16). My sometime research pupil Mrs M. R. O'Day informs me that she has not found institution refused in the Elizabethan and early Stuart records of the diocese of Coventry and Lichfield.

163. *Remains*, p. 380.

164. Borthwick Institute, Grindal's Register, R.I. 30; Institution Act Books, RIAB 2, 3.

165. In chapters 1-8, 12 of Lib. II of *De Regno Christi*. Unlike the Elizabethan puritans, he condoned the reading of homilies where preaching was not to be had. The text is in the *Censura* and was disputed between Cartwright and Whitgift (Whit-gift, *Works*, III, pp. 346-7).

166. *De Regno Christi*, II.xii (LCC, XIX, p. 290; *OL*, XV, p. 125).

167. *De Regno Christi*, II.xix (*OL*, XV, p. 118; LCC, XIX, p. 284).

Bucer described church government in the classical terms of what the sixteenth century knew as a 'mixed polity': the bishop 'as if he were a kind of consul' was to have 'attached' to him 'senators and subordinates' from the ranks of presbyters and deacons.[168]

Grindal's episcopal career embraces many episodes which suggest that it was in the light of this instruction that he interpreted his role. As superintendent of the foreign churches of protestant refugees in London, a position he occupied *ex officio* as Bishop of London, he was free to act as a senior pastor exactly according to the Bucerian model, patiently sorting out thorny problems of heretical doctrine and strained personal relationships, relinquishing all prelatical dignity in his dealings with French, Dutch and Spanish ministers, elders and church members.[169] As a bishop and archbishop it was not so easy to penetrate with genuine pastoral concern the formal processes of the church courts, or to associate the inferior clergy in a role from which they were excluded both by tradition and according to the new formularies. Nevertheless, as I have argued extensively elsewhere, the prophesyings which Grindal so obstinately defended contained the potential and even some of the present means for an association of the more competent clergy in pastoral oversight.[170]

When he himself presided in the courts, Grindal seems to have borne it in mind that these were pastoral institutions, set up to follow procedures which Christ himself had explained to the Apostles, not ecclesiastical versions of secular tribunals. Restoration of erring sinners was the objective, and persuasion was direct and personal. Grindal's arrival at York coincided with the more extensive use of English in the Act Books of the Ecclesiastical Commissioners,[171] and Grindal himself is to be found 'condescending to confer' with Catholic recusants before the court, and generally displaying the 'good will and considerable tact' which an episcopal historian, Creighton, once recognized as his outstanding qualities.[172]

A particular example of Grindal's pastoral conduct from an earlier period in his career will serve to bring an exploratory discussion to an end. As Bishop of London more than two years were spent in reasoning, listening, persuading with a colourful minor canon of St Paul's, a certain Sebastian Westcott, a papist who made a truculent display of his aberrance. Eventually Grindal resolved to excommunicate him 'who', as he commented, 'in doings had excommunicated himself'.

168. *De Regno Christi*, II.xii (LCC, XIX, p. 288; *OL*, XV, pp. 122-3).

169. Much of the documentation is in *Ecclesiae Londino-Batavae Archivum*, Hessels, C. H. (Ed.), II, Cambridge, 1889, III.i, Cambridge, 1897; and in *Remains*, pp. 242-4, 247-52, 254-6, 286-7, 309-14. Cf. Schickler, Baron F. de, *Les Eglises du réfuge en Angleterre*, Paris, 1892, I, Chs 3, 4. See my article 'The Elizabethan Puritans and the Foreign Reformed Churches in London', *Procs of the Huguenot Society of London*, XX, pp. 528-55; and much relevant material in Hauben, Paul J., *Three Spanish Heretics and the Reformation*, Geneva, 1967. *See below*, pp. 245-72.

170. Collinson, *Elizabethan Puritan Movement*, pp. 170-90; and my 'Episcopacy and Reform in England in the Later Sixteenth Century', *Studies in Church History*, III, Cuming, G. J. (Ed.), Leiden, 1967. *See below*, pp. 155-89.

171. Borthwick Institute, R. VII. HCAB 5.

172. Ibid., R. VII. HCAB 6, fols 13r, 51v, 8, fol. 4r; Tyler, op. cit., pp. 235-42.

He wrote: 'I seek herein his reformation: for excommunication in such disobedient persons is the ordinary mean taught by the Holy Ghost to reduce men to God.' In case this protracted affair may be taken as further evidence of Grindal's alleged weakness and indecision, it must be said that he withstood pressure from no less a personage than Robert Dudley, Earl of Leicester, who had asked him to handle Westcott with greater leniency. Grindal wrote to the earl:

> If Sebastian will acknowledge his fault and amend, I am ready most willingly to receive him. If no, I dare not absolve an impenitent sinner; for that were to loose him whom God bindeth, and to abuse the keys of the Church.[173]

Westcott was not vilified by Grindal as Calvin sometimes vilified the theologically or morally deviant. On the other hand he was not exposed to official indifference, as a mere case. There are distinct signs in Grindal's handling of the matter of what even a modern might recognize as affection and concern. But Grindal was not to be deterred by fear or favour from a course of action described in its essentials in the New Testament. This was pastoral care, very much as Bucer had conceived of it, active in the episcopal leadership of the Elizabethan Church.[174]

---

173. *Remains*, pp. 261-4.
174. 'Haec dicta sint de disciplina poenitentiae, quam, qui non restitui per omnia iuxta Christi praecepta, quae commemoravimus, summo studio elaborant, hi expetere se Christi regnum in veritate dicere non possunt. Qui itaque amant Dominum Iesum, et beatum eius regnum apud se vere cupiunt obtinere, hos [?] necesse est, ut, quae de summe salutari poenitentiae disciplina attulimus, et ex ipsis Domini verbis probe cognoscant, atque in usum revocare maximopere studeant.' (*De Regno Christi*, I.ix; *OL*, XV, p. 78.)

3

LETTERS OF THOMAS WOOD,
PURITAN, 1566-1577

Introduction

I. AMBROSE WOOD'S COMMONPLACE BOOK (MS. GORHAMBURY B/VIII/143, DEPOSITED IN THE HERTFORDSHIRE RECORD OFFICE, HERTFORD)

ONE OF THE more consequential members of Sir Francis Bacon's household was a certain Ambrose Wood,[1] a puritan and the son of a puritan of the first generation. His father, Thomas Wood, was an elder in the congregation of Marian exiles at Geneva and in Elizabeth's reign an active member of the organized presbyterian movement. More than forty years after his father's death,[2] and as an act of filial piety, Ambrose transcribed a number of Thomas Wood's letters into a small notebook where he also copied other puritan papers —letters, petitions and apophthegms—from the reign of Elizabeth and the early years of James I.[3] This commonplace book survives among the few Bacon MSS. which have been preserved at Gorhambury. The late earl of Verulam kindly gave permission to print the letters and thanks are due to the Hertford-shire County Archivist, Colonel Le Hardy, and his staff for their co-operation in enabling me to transcribe them.[4]

Thomas Wood's letters are an important source for the history of Elizabethan puritanism. They deepen our understanding of the internal discipline by which the militant wing of this movement was stiffened to resist the demands of authority and to agitate effectively for 'further reformation'; and they contain evidence of the connexions between the puritans and their friends at Court. These two factors, organization and patronage, largely account for the strength and vociferousness of the puritan movement. But they remain the two aspects of Elizabethan puritanism about which we are least informed, and where additional evidence is of especial value. The collection includes a correspondence

[1] Bacon left him £330 by his will. With one exception this was the largest legacy he gave to any of his servants. (James Spedding, *Letters and Life of Francis Bacon* (1861–72), vii. 543.)

[2] Ambrose Wood's commonplace book contains a copy of Francis Bacon's submission to the house of lords, 22 Apr. 1622.

[3] The notebook is 24·5 × 17·5 centimetres, bound in plain parchment and the pages ruled with two red lines. Some pages have been cut out of the centre of the book, but before the transcripts were made. The letters of Thomas Wood occupy 27 numbered folios. The other material begins at the other end of the book and occupies 38 unnumbered folios. The two sections are separated by 6 blank folios. Most of the other documents transcribed by Ambrose Wood are known from other copies: they include such familiar items as Archbishop Grindal's letter to the queen of 20 Dec. 1576 and Walter Travers' appeal to the privy council. There are two letters which I have not encountered in any other collection: a letter from John Morton to 'Mr. Walton now Archdeacon of Derby 1584' (John Walton, archdeacon of Derby 1590–1603), relating to the subscription to Archbishop Whitgift's articles; and 'a letter written by Mr. Warde preacher at Haverill to a servant who robbed his master and consumed parte thereof on weomen'.

[4] I also owe a debt of gratitude to Miss Norah M. Fuidge who first brought Ambrose Wood's commonplace book to my notice; and to Professor Sir John E. Neale for encouraging me to print Thomas Wood's letters.

between Wood and the earls of Leicester and Warwick which throws much light on Leicester's religious views and on his relationship to the puritan movement. Among these letters is one from Leicester himself which is the most personal document of his authorship to come to light since Professor Conyers Read printed his letter to Lady Douglas Sheffield twenty-five years ago.[1]

II. Thomas Wood

Little is known of Thomas Wood before 1554. His origins were either in Leicestershire or Yorkshire.[2] He apparently studied at Cambridge around 1530,[3] but there is no record of his college or that he took a degree. At his reception as a resident of Geneva in 1555 he was described as 'of London'.[4] Possibly he was the Thomas Wood, mercer and 'servant'—factor or agent?—to Henry Locke, who was examined by the privy council on 12 November 1553 for his 'lewde reportes' that Edward VI was still alive.[5] An association with the husband of John Knox's soul-mate Anne Locke would place Wood in the inner circle of London Protestantism on the eve of the Marian exile.[6] In his will he testifies to his conversion, thanking God 'especiallie for that it hath pleased hym to call me, his poore creature, from the bottomles pitt of papisticall idolatrie and superstition to the lighte of his gospell'.[7] He left England early in Mary's reign[8] and in June 1554 arrived in Frankfort in company with William Whittingham, Edmund Sutton and William Williams, 'the first Englishmen that there

[1] Conyers Read, 'A letter from Robert, Earl of Leicester to a lady', *Huntington Library Bull.*, ix (1936), 15–26. The original letter (among the Egerton papers in the Huntington Library) bears neither address nor endorsement, but Professor Read thought that Douglas was 'almost certainly' the recipient.

[2] In a letter to Anthony Gilby (see Appendix, pp. 24–5 below) Wood speaks of Robert Beaumont, Master of Trinity and vice-chancellor of Cambridge as 'my countryman'. Beaumont was probably of Leicestershire (J. and J. A. Venn, *Alumni Cantabrigienses*, I, i (Cambridge, 1922), p. 119) but may have belonged to the Yorkshire branch of his family (*D.N.B.*, *s.v.* Beaumont). Wood was in correspondence with a Yorkshire Beaumont in 1573, had a cousin resident in Yorkshire and claimed to have access to 'the best in Yorksheir' (see pp. 87–8 below). On the other hand in a letter to Thomas Cave of Bagrave, Leics., he claimed to have known of a certain local matter 'before yow were borne'. (See p. 86 below.)

[3] In his letter to Anthony Gilby, Wood speaks of the vice-chancellor's manner of riding to church as 'not used in our tyme as you knowe'. Gilby commenced B.A. from Christ's 1531–2. (Venn, ii. 215.)

[4] C. H. Garrett, *Marian Exiles* (Cambridge, 1938), p. 343.

[5] *Ibid.*; *Acts of the Privy Council*, ed. J. R. Dasent, iv. 368.

[6] The Clerk to the Worshipful Company of Mercers informs me that there is no record of Thomas Wood as a member of the Company. Yet Wood certainly had connexions with the Mercers. His nephew Roger Dransfelde, a close friend of Wood and an overseer of his will, was a mercer. Most of Dransfelde's other friends and associates were of the Company. (Principal Probate Registry, Somerset House; wills proved in the Prerogative Court of Canterbury; will of Thomas Wood, 16 Daughtrey (1577); will of Roger Dransfelde, 29 Bakon (1579).)

[7] Wood's will, P.C.C., 16 Daughtrey.

[8] I can find no evidence in the *Acts of the Privy Council* to support Garrett's assertion that Wood 'fled' from the proceedings against him.

arrived to remain and abide'.[1] Williams was Wood's brother-in-law,[2] but whether they became related in this way before or during the exile is not known.[3] How Wood and Whittingham first came together is equally uncertain, but Wood later reminded Whittingham that it was he who first taught him to reject the ceremonies of the 1552 Prayer Book.[4] Consequently Wood was a staunch member of Whittingham's faction at Frankfort in the struggle against those who 'would have the face of an English Church'.[5] His signature stands to the invitation to other English colonies to unite with Frankfort; to the call to Knox to become pastor; to Frankfort's refusal to be bound by the Prayer Book; and finally to the announcement of the Knoxites' intended secession from Frankfort.[6] With his wife Anne and the daughter who had been born to them in Frankfort,[7] he arrived in Geneva in October 1555.[8] On 16 December 1557 he was elected an elder of the Geneva congregation, sharing office with his brother-in-law William Williams,[9] and there is evidence that he was clerk and archivist to the congregation, if only in its later and more depleted days.[10] Like Whittingham, he remained in Geneva long after Elizabeth's accession and was still there in September 1559, when Knox told Anne Locke that he had sent news of events in Scotland to Wood 'asking him to communicate the sam with yow and with other brethrein at Geneva'.[11] He probably left with Whittingham and Williams at the end of May 1560.[12]

Wood at first returned to London[13] where he may have remarried at about this time.[14] In October 1562 he left England with the English expeditionary

[1] *A Brief Discourse of the Troubles Begun at Frankfort*, ed. E. Arber (1908), p. 23.

[2] Wood's will, P.C.C., 16 Daughtrey. In the *Jour. Eccles. Hist.*, ix (1958), 202 I stated that Williams was Wood's son-in-law. This mistake arose from supplying a comma in the wrong position in the text of Wood's will.

[3] Wood's nephew Roger Dransfelde speaks in his will of his 'uncle William Williams' and 'Aunt Jane Williams' which suggests that Williams married Wood's sister. (Dransfelde's will, P.C.C., 29 Bakon.)

[4] See Wood's letter to Whittingham, p. 89 below.

[5] *Brief Discourse*, p. 54. [6] *Ibid.*, pp. 26–30, 36, 40–1, 81.

[7] The daughter—Debora—was still under age on 16 July 1576 when Wood made his will.

[8] Charles Martin, *Les Protestants Anglais Réfugiés à Genève au temps de Calvin, 1555–60* (Geneva, 1915), p. 331; Garrett, p. 343. Wood arrived in Geneva on 13 Oct. and was received as a 'resident' of the city on 24 Oct.

[9] Martin, p. 335. The other elders serving at that time were Anthony Gilby and John Bodley; the ministers, John Knox and Christopher Goodman.

[10] See Wood's letter to Whittingham, p. 89 below.

[11] John Knox, *Works*, ed. David Laing (Edinburgh, 1846–64), vi. 78. Wood's motive for lingering in Geneva may have been to assist in the production of the Geneva Bible, like his brother-in-law Williams (Martin, p. 70); Wood refers in his will to his 'old Bible printed at Geneva'. Or, like another member of the congregation, he may have been deterred from return by the luke-warmness of Elizabeth's reformation. (*The Seconde Parte of a Register, being a Calendar of Manuscripts under that title intended for publication by the Puritans about 1593 and now in Dr. Williams's Library, London*, ed. Albert Peel (Cambridge, 1915), ii. 57–8).

[12] Martin, p. 261.

[13] Wood to Sir William Cecil, 3 Aug. 1561, Public Record Office, S.P. 12/19/3.

[14] The suggestion is based on these facts: at the time of Wood's arrival in Geneva his wife's name was given as Anne, whereas at his death it was Agnes;

force for Newhaven (Le Havre) in Normandy where he was appointed clerk to the council of war and captain with command of a hundred Surrey men under the captain general, Ambrose Dudley, earl of Warwick.[1] This was a confidential post requiring, as Cecil noted, 'a man of gravitie and credite above a servante, whose conversation and feloweship shall not be with the lighte sorte'.[2] Most of the letters from the council at Newhaven to the privy council are in Wood's hand,[3] and he himself sent a number of reports to Cecil in which he vigorously represented Warwick's need of stronger support.[4] At Newhaven Wood was again in the company of William Whittingham who held the position of 'principal preacher' to the army.[5]

Wood sailed to Newhaven with Warwick and returned with him after the evacuation. On landing at Portsmouth he was the first to report to Lord Robert Dudley on his brother's sea-sickness and the state of his leg wound.[6] He named his eldest son after Warwick and later bequeathed him a target which Warwick had given him for a memento.[7] Wood may have been in the service of the Dudleys before 1562. This is suggested by the indulgence with which both the brothers later addressed him[8] and by Leicester's assumption that Wood would know what his religion had been 'from my cradle'.[9] In this event, Wood may have introduced Whittingham to Warwick. He was later to claim that it was he who had procured the letter from Warwick to Lord Robert Dudley which led to Whittingham's preferment to the deanery of Durham and that he had subsequently heard Warwick 'once or twise complaine' of Whittingham's ingratitude.[10] On the other hand Wood's letters from Newhaven suggest that Cecil rather than the Dudleys may have been his original patron.[11] He certainly had links with the Court before 1562. From Frankfort he had corresponded with Sir James Croft when Croft was a prisoner in the Tower,[12] and soon after his

in 1561 Wood petitioned Cecil for the wardship of the daughter of Bartholomew Pala, a leatherseller of Holborn, pleading his friendship with Pala's widow; Pala at the time of his death had an unmarried sister, Agnes. (Wood's will, P.C.C., 16 Daughtrey; P.R.O., S.P. 12/19/3; will of Bartholomew Pala, P.C.C., 26 Loftes.)

[1] Wood occurs on most of the extant lists for Newhaven as clerk to the council and captain. (P.R.O., S.P. 70/44/779, 45/895, 47/1082, 49/144, 58/790.) He gives details of his appointment to a captaincy in a letter to Cecil. (P.R.O., S.P. 70/48/48.)

[2] 'Memoires touchinge thestablishment of the garrison', P.R.O., S.P. 70/46/904.

[3] P.R.O., S.P. 70, vols. 43–61 passim.

[4] P.R.O., S.P. 70/44/771, 44/782, 45/823, 875, 46/946, 48/48, 53/491, 60/881. Wood suggested to both Cecil and Lord Robert Dudley that Sir James Croft should be appointed to assist Warwick. (S.P. 70/45/823.)

[5] P.R.O., S.P. 70/49/144.

[6] Wood to Dudley, 31 July 1563, P.R.O., S.P. 12/29/54.

[7] Wood's will, P.C.C., 16 Daughtrey.

[8] See the correspondence printed below, pp. 93–8,.

[9] See p. 95 below. Wood's second letter to Leicester in 1576 (see p.101 below) contains evidence that Wood was in correspondence with him as early as 1560.

[10] See Wood's letter to Whittingham and its enclosure, pp.88–91 below This claim is doubtful. Warwick had the highest opinion of Whittingham as his letters from Newhaven show. (P.R.O., S.P. 70/45/840, 46/992, 47/1077, 57/683.)

[11] Wood told Cecil of Warwick: 'A better naturall man dyd I never serve under.' The phrase also suggests that Wood may have seen military service on some earlier occasion. (Wood to Cecil, 26 Nov. 1562, P.R.O., S.P. 70/45/875.)

[12] P.R.O., S.P. 70/45/823.

return from Geneva he petitioned Cecil for a wardship and recalled his 'humble dutie' towards him.[1] In March 1563 Warwick licensed Wood to return to London to attend to a lawsuit in which he was 'lyke to sustaine great hinderaunce' from Lord Paget. He carried important despatches to the privy council and a warm testimonial from Warwick to Dudley and Cecil.[2] Two months later Paget was dead.[3] Wood had by then returned to Newhaven where he remained until the evacuation in late July. By that time the plague had reduced the active strength of his company to twenty-five.[4]

Wood returned to London,[5] where he may still have had business interests, but by 1570 he had settled as a farmer in Leicestershire. In June 1568 he lent £800 to the earl of Huntingdon on a security of 2,000 marks, a loan yielding an annual income of £80 derived from some of Huntingdon's Leicestershire lands, which Wood settled on his unmarried daughters at his death nine years later.[6] He purchased from a Mr. Henry Sekeford the lease of the demesne and manor-house of Groby, five miles from Leicester, and from Richard Martin, the goldsmith and warden of the Mint, the lease of the neighbouring farms of Stuarde Hayes and Whitemore Hayes.[7] He lived at Groby for the last four years of his life and died there after a long illness in 1577.[8] By then he ranked as a gentleman.[9] He seems to have served on the commission of the peace[10] and

[1] Wood to Cecil, 3 Aug. 1561, P.R.O., S.P. 12/19/3.

[2] P.R.O., S.P. 70/53/491, 54/523, 533, 641.　　　[3] D.N.B., s.v. Paget.

[4] P.R.O., S.P. 70/61/957. Cf. Wood to Cecil, 2 July 1563: 'There was never a town so besieged that had such want of provysone, for here are not lx able to serve.' (S.P. 70/60/881.)

[5] See letters on pp.83-4, 106-7 below.

[6] Wood's will, P.C.C., 16 Daughtrey; P.R.O., L.C. 4/191 (Recognisance Register), p. 41. I owe the second reference to M. Claire Cross, 'The Career of Henry Hastings, Third Earl of Huntingdon, 1536-1595' (unpublished Cambridge Ph.D. thesis, 1958), p. 393. Dr. Cross has shown (pp. 275-9) that most of Huntingdon's creditors forced him to pay his debts without long delay, although he sought long-term loans from relations and friends. The fact that Wood regarded his loan to the earl as a permanent investment argues a friendly connexion between them.

[7] Wood's will, P.C.C., 16 Daughtrey. The manor of Groby was leased from Sir Henry Grey, later 1st Baron Grey of Groby, son of Lord John Grey and cousin of the duke of Suffolk. (John Nichols, The History and Antiquities of the County of Leicester (1795-1815), iv. 633.) The farms of Stuarde Hayes and Whitemore Hayes seem to have been enclosed grazing-land, since Wood refers to Whitemore Hayes as 'alias Salisburye Closes' and speaks of 'the whole stock of cattle'.

[8] Wood's will (P.C.C., 16 Daughtrey) was made on 16 July 1576 and proved on 3 May 1577. See evidence of his illness in his correspondence.

[9] Wood's nephew Roger Dransfelde bequeathed to his cousin, Wood's son Thomas, a gold ring 'having his father's armes graven in yt'. (Dransfelde's will, P.C.C., 29 Bakon.)

[10] Wood does not occur as a J.P. in any of the three extant lists for these years. (List c. Nov. 1573, P.R.O., S.P. 12/93 ii; liber pacis c. 1573/4, British Museum, MS. Egerton 2345; liber pacis June 1575, P.R.O., S.P. 12/104.) But in about 1575 Nicholas Proctor petitioned Burghley that if his adversary Peach had a commission from the exchequer 'to Justices in Leycestershere' to value certain lands 'that I also may be admitted to joyne in the same Commission Mr Frauncis Hastinges, Mr Frauncis Brown and Mr Thomas Woodd for indifferencie sake'. (P.R.O., S.P. 12/106/21.)

with another puritan justice, Francis Browne of Wistowe, to have attached himself to Francis Hastings, in his brother the earl of Huntingdon's absence the dominant figure in the shire.[1] Hastings, Browne and the preacher Anthony Gilby were overseers of Wood's will and Henry Killigrew, brother-in-law to Burghley and a radical puritan, was an executor.[2]

III. Wood in the Puritan Movement

The letters published in this volume invest this versatile but otherwise obscure career with a significance which could hardly have been suspected from the formal *curriculum vitae* so far presented. They reveal that in Elizabeth's reign Wood played an important rôle in the small but effectively organized group of puritan activists who laboured to bring the English Reformation to what they conceived to be its logical conclusion. This movement[3] had its nucleus in the English colony at Geneva, a brotherhood not dissolved by the return of the exiles. In England Wood continued to exercise the functions of a ruling elder which had been his at Geneva: his concern was with the discovery of scandal and the exercise of corrective discipline in the cause of a godly reformation. His value to the movement lay in the access which he enjoyed to statesmen and courtiers of the stature of Cecil, Warwick, Leicester and Huntingdon; and in the unswerving puritan conscience which impelled him to threaten even them with the dire penalties of sin.

An intolerant zeal for the Word of God and a sense of solemn responsibility for his friends and acquaintances drives Wood to fearless and often uncharitable intervention whenever any of them is detected, or even rumoured to be at fault. He typically subscribes himself 'him that wisheth you well in the Lord' and constantly reminds his correspondents that 'this yow knowe is the expresse commandement of Christ'. In his letters to Leicestershire and Yorkshire country gentlemen we see him prying into disputes over landed property of a kind which furnished so much litigation in the sixteenth century, charging his correspondents with dereliction of trust and conspiracy to defraud. If Wood had no direct interest in such cases, they engaged his conscience and his concern was with the offence against the Law of God more than with any breach of the Common Law. 'For if it be not good and just before God, it is not the lawe of the realme that will dischardge yow in his presence.'

If these were the only letters in the collection, we might dismiss Wood as a Mr. Zeal-of-the-Land Busy whose convictions are instructive of the social morality of early Calvinism. Yet the remainder of the correspondence is concerned exclusively with the national puritan cause of a 'further Reformation' and reveals Thomas Wood in the thick of a succession of critical episodes in the

---

[1] Francis Hastings was dominant in Leicestershire during his brother's prolonged absences in the North in the 1570's. (Cross, 'Career of Huntingdon', p. 251.)

[2] Wood's will, P.C.C., 16 Daughtrey. Wood left two sons, Ambrose and Thomas; four unmarried daughters, Debora, Judith, Susan and Elizabeth (all under age in 1576); and a fifth daughter Ann, married before 1576 to Ralph Hetherington. (Wills of Thomas Wood and Roger Dransfelde, P.C.C., 16 Daughtrey, 29 Bakon.)

[3] P. Collinson, 'The Puritan Classical Movement in the Reign of Elizabeth I' (unpublished London Ph.D. thesis, 1957).

development of the movement: the struggle over the vestments in Cambridge in 1565 and in London in the following year; the 'inquisition' proceedings which endangered the early presbyterian movement in 1573; and the queen's suppression of the exercises of prophesying in 1576. In these crises, Wood pleads the cause of the puritan ministers with his patrons, exposes the agents or inspirers of reaction and threatens turncoats and backsliders with divine judgment and the social penalties of a general scandal. In so doing, he speaks for the general mind of 'the godly', as his correspondents seem to have understood very well. To Cecil he speaks of 'the pitifull complaint of all the godly' in London; Whittingham is told that his behaviour has been 'no small offence to the Church of God'; Warwick and Leicester are informed of what 'is commonly reported among the godly'. Although Wood assures Cecil that he has written 'without advice or consent of any' his very protestation is evidence of what might have been supposed to be the inspiration of all these letters. Leicester for one did not despise Wood's capacity to damage or redeem his credit. It was not for the sake of one family retainer that he wrote fifteen hundred words in his own hand in justification of his religion at a time when he was at the height of his power but in poor health.[1]

Wood's letters therefore provide an insight into that still mysterious sector of Elizabethan society, 'the godly'. Re-examining his career from 1559, it begins to look as if all Wood's movements were governed by the requirements of the godly cause. The Genevan émigrés were isolated almost as a distinct sect in the early Elizabethan Church both by the official disfavour which Knox and Goodman's political teachings had brought upon them and their consequent failure to find promotion, and by the exercise of tight internal discipline.[2] In September 1559, while those of 'the flock' who were already in London were concealing Goodman from the authorities, Wood, still in Geneva, was trying to pass on messages to him from Knox in Scotland.[3] In 1562 Wood was only one of several disaffected Genevans who found at Newhaven a cave of Adullam where they could escape the restraint of the Prayer Book and enjoy Calvinist worship and discipline.[4] Besides Whittingham, the preachers to the army included two other veterans of Knox's congregation, William Kethe[5] and Augustin Bradbridge, also a French Calvinist, Jean Veron.[6] After Bradbridge and Veron had left Newhaven, Warwick made repeated efforts to replace them with two more Geneva men, Percival Wiburn and Christopher Goodman himself.[7] The centre of the Genevan brotherhood was always in London, where Wood returned in 1563. From there he wrote to Anthony Gilby reporting that John Bodley and William Kethe 'and all the rest be in helthe and pray for you'.[8] As late as

[1] D.N.B., s.v. Leicester.
[2] Collinson, 'Classical Movement', pp. 17–33.
[3] Seconde Parte of a Register, ii. 59; Knox, Works, vi. 78; cf. D.N.B., s.v. Goodman.
[4] Evidence in 'Orders proclaymed in Newhaven' in Wood's hand and Wood's letter to Cecil on the subject (P.R.O., S.P. 70/44/782, 796); and Cecil's correspondence with Cuthbert Vaughan and Whittingham on the order of public prayer used at Newhaven. (S.P. 70/47/1022, 1027.)
[5] D.N.B., s.v. Kethe.
[6] P.R.O., S.P. 70/47/1077, 49/144.
[7] Warwick to Cecil, 17 Dec., 28 Dec. 1562, P.R.O., S.P. 70/46/992, 47/1077.
[8] See p.107below.

1573 and with reference to London, Wood could speak of the staunchest puritans to Whittingham as 'a remnant of your old acquaintance'.[1] As younger men came to London from the universities—among them John Field and Thomas Wilcox, the authors of *An Admonition to the Parliament*—and as others were driven from their parishes for nonconformity, the little flock of Geneva provided a focus for the development of a presbyterian movement in partial separation from the established Church.[2] Wood collaborated with the new leaders, especially in the preparation of printed propaganda. It was probably he who brought Field into the circle of Warwick's clients.[3] In 1571 he sent a Latin MS. of Anthony Gilby's authorship out of Leicestershire to Field in London, who at once took steps to have it translated and published.[4] In 1574, his son-in-law Ralph Hetherington acted as a messenger between Thomas Wilcox and Gilby.[5] At about the same time, Wood himself seems to have been collecting the materials which were soon afterwards printed in *A Brieff Discours off the Troubles Begonne at Franckford*.[6] With Field, Wood moved in these years into the full-flown presbyterian position: abandoning Calvin's distinction between 'godly bishops' and wealthy, idle, 'bastard bishops', he embraced Beza's doctrine of the necessity of consistorial discipline as a mark of the true Church.[7]

By settling in Leicestershire, Wood retreated to one of the safest localities for a puritan in all England. This was the country of the puritan earl of Huntingdon, 'our good Earl' to whom Wood had written on behalf of the nonconformists in 1565.[8] 'Father' Anthony Gilby, Huntingdon's lecturer at Ashby-de-la-Zouch, had been Wood's fellow-elder at Geneva and Wood had sponsored his daughter at her baptism.[9] Gilby had the standing almost of a bishop in Leicestershire and with Huntingdon's authority imposed a moderate puritan uniformity.[10] Furthermore, at Groby Wood was secure from the inconveniences of ordinary ecclesiastical surveillance. As a peculiar of the Court of Arches, Groby lay outside the bishop of Lincoln's jurisdiction and headed a group of parishes which were subject to visitation only by a lay commissary appointed by the lord of the manor.[11] In 1575 this official was William Stoughton, a civil lawyer of radical puritan views.[12]

---

[1] See p. 90 below.

[2] Collinson, 'Classical Movement', pp. 103–172; H. G. Owen, 'The London Parish Clergy in the Reign of Elizabeth I' (unpublished London Ph.D. thesis, 1957), pp. 515–40.

[3] Warwick was Field's patron from about 1565. (Collinson, 'Classical Movement', p. 41, n. 3.)

[4] Field to Gilby, 10 Jan. 1572, Cambridge Univ. Library, MS. Mm. 1. 43 (Baker 32), p. 447.

[5] Wilcox to Gilby, 2 Feb. 1574, *ibid.*, p. 439.

[6] P. Collinson, 'The authorship of *A Brieff Discours off the Troubles Begonne at Franckford*', *Jour. Eccles. Hist.*, ix (1958), 188–208. Here, pp. 191–211.

[7] See pp. 101, 103 below.

[8] See p. 106 below.

[9] Martin, p. 335.

[10] M. Claire Cross, 'Noble patronage in the Elizabethan Church', *The Historical Journal*, iii (1960), 1–16.

[11] Nichols, iv. 632.

[12] *Ibid.*; Simonds D'Ewes, *Journals of the House of Commons* (1682), p. 349; William Stoughton, *An Assertion for True and Christian Church-policie* (Middelburg, 1604).

Wood was not cut off from London in Leicestershire.[1] Indeed, he seems to have provided the link between the presbyterian organization in the capital and the strongly puritan country of the Midlands[2] and its three great patrons, Leicester, Warwick and Huntingdon. Enjoying the confidence of these noblemen and moving constantly among his friends, receiving and retailing reports, Thomas Wood makes it easier to understand how a handful of presbyterians made such a stir in Elizabethan society.

IV. Notes on the Correspondence

Wood to Sir William Cecil (29 March 1566) and Cecil to Wood (31 March 1566).

These letters are a commentary on the first serious crisis experienced by the puritan movement in London. On 26 March 1566, the whole London clergy were called[3] before the ecclesiastical commissioners at Lambeth and required to conform to the Book of Common Prayer and the prescribed vestments in accordance with the 'Advertisements' prepared by Archbishop Parker on the queen's orders.[4] Thirty-seven ministers[5] who refused were suspended and threatened with ultimate deprivation, while the fruits of their benefices were sequestered. This was done less than three weeks before Easter, and Wood echoes a common complaint when he tells Cecil that in some parishes there are no clergy to read the service, let alone to preach.[6] But Wood is concerned less with the suspension of beneficed clergy than with the silencing of most of the 'exercises of interpretacion of the scriptures' or parish lectureships. It has been shown that there were at least nine lecturers employed in city parishes by 1566 and that six or seven of them were among the nonconformists suspended on 26 March.[7] Wood is especially disturbed by the collapse of 'a most frutfull and comfortable exercise named prophesying used once a week at St. Peter's' and by the threatened downfall of a daily lecture at St. Antholin's. From his concern we can probably conclude that these two exercises were the main platform for Calvinist preaching in early Elizabethan London and the focal point of what was about to be singled out as a sectarian puritan faction.

[1] See the evidence of letters to Thomas Cave and William Whittingham, pp. 86, 88-90 below.

[2] Collinson, 'Classical Movement', Appendix. Map 3 plots the distribution of puritan ministers in the Midlands and demonstrates the strength of the movement in S. Northants., S.E. Warws., N. Oxon. and Leics.

[3] According to Owen (p. 498), curates and lecturers were summoned as well as beneficed clergy. Probably the only clergy not called were those with no kind of regular employment in the London churches.

[4] The fullest accounts of the vestments controversy in London are in R. W. Dixon, *History of the Church of England from the Abolition of the Roman Jurisdiction* (Oxford, 1878-1902), vi. 89-124; and in Owen, pp. 486-514.

[5] According to Wood, thirty-six, but he is allowing for one dissenter who had been released from suspension after subscribing on 28 Mar. (*Correspondence of Matthew Parker*, ed. John Bruce (Parker Soc., 1853), p. 272.)

[6] See Parker's correspondence with Cecil in the three weeks after 26 Mar. (*Parker Correspondence*, pp. 269-79.) Parker and Bishop Grindal of London had warned Cecil before 26 Mar. that some churches would probably be left unserved. (*Ibid.*, p. 268.)

[7] Owen, pp. 375-7.

The St. Antholin's lecture was the oldest of the endowed parish lectureships of London, and probably dated from the reign of Edward VI. From 1559 provision had been made for three lecturers to preach in turn on six days a week at six in the morning, the people gathering to sing psalms after the Geneva fashion for an hour before the sermon. In 1566 the lecturers were Robert Crowley, rector of St. Peter-le-Poor and vicar of St. Giles, Cripplegate, John Gough, rector of St. Peter Cornhill and John Philpot, rector of St. Michael Cornhill and of Stepney.[1] Not only were all three suspended on 26 March, but in the weeks that followed they emerged as the ring-leaders of a well-organized movement of protest among the suspended London ministers.[2]

The same group was probably responsible for maintaining the 'prophesying' to which Wood alludes, which must have been held in either Crowley's or Gough's church. This prophesying was not a monthly conference of preachers on the Zwinglian pattern.[3] Although widely established in Elizabethan market-towns, there is no evidence that this institution was ever seen in London.[4] The St. Peter's exercise was probably a form of congregational prophesying of the kind included (for example) in Jean à Lasco's orders for the stranger churches of Edwardian London, and in the *Forme of Prayers* of the English exiles in Geneva, in which the congregation met weekly to discuss doctrine with its pastor.[5] Assemblies of this kind were held in the foreign churches of Elizabethan London[6] which were envied by the puritans for their freedom to follow Reformed orders.[7] But Wood's letter is the only known evidence for the existence of such a practice in the Church of England. It suggests that even before the events of March 1566 the London puritans may have been making covert use of the *Forme of Prayers* in some of their assemblies, as they certainly did later in the semi-sectarian meetings at Plumbers Hall and elsewhere.[8]

It is not easy to know how far to credit the rumour that Cecil was chiefly responsible for the Lambeth proceedings of March 1566.[9] Like the queen herself, Mr. Secretary refused to be openly associated with the archbishop's

---

[1]Owen, pp. 370–5; *The Diary of Henry Machyn*, ed. J. G. Nichols (Camden Soc., lxii, 1848), p. 212; 'Stowe's Memoranda', *Three Fifteenth-Century Chronicles*, ed. James Gairdner (Camden Soc., n.s. xxviii, 1880), p. 139. In the early years of Charles I the society of 'feoffees for the purchase of impropriations' turned the St. Antholin's lecture into a school for the training of puritan preachers to be placed outside London by the society. (Isabel M. Calder, *Activities of the Puritan Faction of the Church of England, 1625–33* (1957), *passim*.)

[2]Collinson, 'Classical Movement', pp. 37–40; Owen, pp. 501–4.

[3]Collinson, 'Classical Movement', pp. 175–8; and pp. 59–60 below.

[4]Archdeacon Mullins to Bishop Sandys (July 1576), B.M., Add. MS. 29546, fo. 54v.

[5]Johannes à Lasco, *Opera*, ed. A. Kuyper (Amsterdam, 1866), ii. 101–2, 104–5; W. D. Maxwell, *John Knox's Genevan Service Book, 1556* (Edinburgh, 1931), p. 104.

[6]Nicolas Des Gallars, *Forme de police ecclésiastique instituée à Londres en l'église des François* (1561). A Latin version of these orders was in John Field's possession. (B.M., Add. MS. 48096 (Yelverton 105).)

[7]Notebook of Thomas Earl, rector of St. Mildred, Breadchurch St., Cambridge Univ. Library, MS. Mm. 1. 29, fo. 2v.

[8]Albert Peel, *The First Congregational Churches* (Cambridge, 1920), p. 7.

[9]Parker himself reported the rumour to Cecil on 12 Mar. (*Parker Correspondence*, pp. 262–3.)

efforts to impose uniformity and Parker repeatedly complained that he was not supported by Cecil and the council.[1] Yet these complaints were perhaps sharpened by the knowledge of Cecil's ultimate responsibility for the unpopular policy which Parker was forced to pursue. 'Your honour principally hath begun; it is for you to see that something be done.'[2] Cecil ignored Parker's invitation to take his place with the ecclesiastical commissioners at Lambeth.[3] Yet there is evidence that it was the queen who had ordered Parker to proceed against the London clergy[4] and Wood may not be far from the mark when he accuses Cecil of having had a hand in that order.[5] Nothing can be learned from Cecil's mild but equivocal reply. He refutes Wood's charges without commending the nonconformists, merely denying any intention 'to have ether the ministery of the word or of sacraments empayred'.

LETTERS FROM WOOD TO DR. FRANCIS CAVE, ESQ., LL.D., AND THOMAS CAVE, ESQ., OF BAGRAVE, LEICESTERSHIRE, c. 1573.[6]

The first of these three letters was written to Francis Cave of Bagrave, Leicestershire, a Doctor of Civil Laws and the fourth of the nine sons of Richard Cave of Stanford, Northamptonshire, by his second wife, Margaret Saxby. The remaining two were addressed to his son, Thomas Cave, who was knighted in 1603. Both Francis and Thomas Cave were justices of the peace for Leicestershire.[7] The relationship between the Caves and the other persons named or referred to in these letters is best shown by the genealogical tree[8] appended on p. xiv.

The circumstances behind the correspondence seem to have been as follows: Francis Cave, having married the widow of Edmund Ashton, probably soon after 1542,[9] continued with his wife to enjoy the use of the greater part of

[1] Dixon, vi. 44–102; Conyers Read, *Lord Burghley and Queen Elizabeth* (1960), pp. 111–12; *Parker Correspondence*, pp. 223–84.

[2] *Ibid.*, p. 234. Cecil certainly drafted the letter from the queen to Parker which began the whole action. (Dixon, vi. 44n.) In conference with the bishops in Mar. 1565, Cecil ordered them to enforce conformity or suffer the consequences. (De Silva to Philip II, 12 Mar. 1565, *Cal. S.P. Spanish, 1558–67*, p. 406.)

[3] Dixon, vi. 93-8.

[4] *Parker Correspondence*, p. 277.

[5] Parker was careful to warn Cecil in advance of the action he proposed. His pessimistic warning of the likely consequences suggests some anxiety to protect himself before embarking on a policy imposed on him by secular authority. (*Ibid.*, pp. 267–8.)

[6] I am grateful to Miss Sybil Thorpe of the History of Parliament Trust for help in identifying the recipients and persons named in these letters and in establishing the relationship between them.

[7] P.R.O., S.P. 12/104.

[8] Compiled from Nichols, iii. 290; *Visitation of Leicestershire, 1619* (Harleian Soc., ii, 1870), pp. 126–7; *Visitations of Surrey* (Harleian Soc., xliii, 1899), p. 68; *Miscellanea Genealogica et Heraldica*, i (1868), 7; emendations *ex inf.* Miss Thorpe. Persons named in the letters are printed in capitals and both they and others referred to in the text are identified by *.

[9] In June 1542 Cave was granted the wardship of Mary, the daughter of Edmund Ashton and his wife, Margaret Lisle. The daughter later married Wiat Wilde. (*Ex inf.* Miss Thorpe.)

certain woods in Cornwall which Wood alleges to be the lawful property of the heirs of Ashton's elder brother, William Ashton. Cave was now making arrangements to sell the property and Wood protests on behalf of Richard Dilkes of Kirkby Mallory, the husband of Ashton's daughter Elizabeth, who stands to inherit the property in his wife's name in the probable event of his brother-in-law's death.[1] The second letter, in reply to a retort from Thomas Cave, suggests

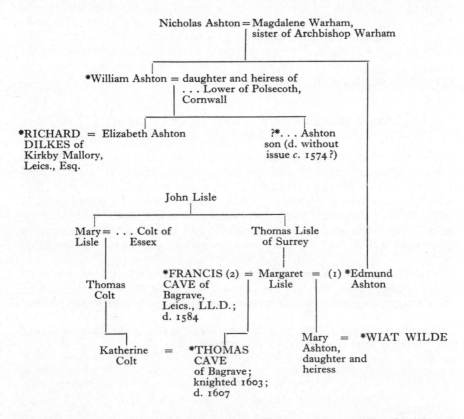

that Wood had made his allegations on insufficient evidence. The third letter apparently relates to a different dispute. Wood is here charging Thomas Cave with conspiring with his half-sister's husband, Wiat Wilde, to defraud a certain Mr. Randoll. This was probably Robert Randoll, a Leicestershire man who married Margaret Perwich, the daughter of John Perwich of Lubbenham, Leicestershire. Perwich married one Elizabeth Wood,[2] so that Randoll may have been distantly related to Thomas Wood.

[1] The genealogy of the Dilke family printed in *Miscellanea Genealogica* (i. 7) gives Elizabeth Ashton, Richard Dilkes' wife, as the only daughter and heir of William Ashton. But Wood refers to Ashton's 'children' and to Dilkes' brother-in-law. Since Dilkes was granted a crest to his arms in 1574 (*ibid.*, i. 9) and at this time quartered the Ashton arms with his own, it seems likely that William Ashton's son and heir died without issue between the date of Wood's letter and 1574.

[2] *The Visitations of Northamptonshire made in 1564 and 1615–18*, ed. Walter C. Metcalfe (1887), p. 42.

WOOD TO RICHARD BEAUMONT, ESQ., OF WHITLEY, YORKSHIRE, 12 DECEMBER 1573.[1]

The recipient of this letter was probably Richard Beaumont of Whitley in the West Riding, a member of the Yorkshire branch of the Leicestershire family of Beaumont and a justice of the peace. The letter concerns an alleged breach of trust committed by Beaumont as overseer of the will of the sister-in-law of Wood's cousin and namesake. Beaumont, it was said, had deprived the heirs of the lease of a farm called 'the Thorns' in order to please his wife by giving it to her brother-in-law Robert Nettleton.[2] Shortly afterwards, Nettleton had been forced to leave the farm and to flee the country, whether for debt or some other cause such as recusancy is not clear. Wood had now discovered that his recently deceased cousin, Thomas Wood, a man of simple wits, had named Beaumont as his overseer, although Beaumont and his wife and Nettleton had in the past been in league to defraud him in some small business transactions.

WOOD TO WILLIAM WHITTINGHAM, DEAN OF DURHAM, 15 FEBRUARY 1574.

This letter has been printed and discussed in the *Journal of Ecclesiastical History* and it will be sufficient to repeat briefly the arguments extended there.[3]

The presbyterian movement which was launched by Thomas Cartwright's Cambridge lectures of 1570 and the publication of *An Admonition to the Parliament* in 1572 at first enjoyed a relative immunity. But after July 1573 it was threatened by a demand for general subscription to the Prayer Book, enforced on the whole ministry[4] under pain of imprisonment by orders of the queen and privy council. Already under pressure, the movement was further embarrassed by the coldness—as the extremists viewed it, the defection—of almost all the older puritan leaders, amongst them William Whittingham.[5] Wood's letter reflects this emergency. Writing to Whittingham in the remoteness of Durham, he reports the events in London—confirming what we know from other sources[6]—and calls on him as he has done before, to repent of his backsliding. He encloses an old letter from Lord Robert Dudley to Warwick which shows that it was Warwick's testimonial alone which had secured Whittingham his deanery and adds the acid comment that 'if ever I did or thought yow harme, it was in procuring the lettre whereof this inclosed maketh mention'.

More specifically, Wood asks Whittingham to send a document which with

---

[1] I again acknowledge Miss Thorpe's assistance.

[2] Richard Beaumont married Jane Pilkington, daughter of Arthur Pilkington of Bradley, York, Esq.; Robert Nettleton married her sister Anne. (Nichols, iii. 662; Joseph Foster, *Visitation of Yorkshire, 1584* (1875), p. 557.)

[3] Collinson, 'The authorship of *A Brieff Discours*', *ubi supra*.

[4] And in London on some lay men and women known to be puritans. See p. 88 below.

[5] Details of Whittingham's conformity are given in the notes to M. A. E. Green's edition of the anonymous 'Life of Mr. William Whittingham', *Camden Miscellany*, vi (1871), 21–2.

[6] Especially Thomas Wilcox's letters to Anthony Gilby in Cambridge Univ. Library, MS. Mm. 1. 43 (Baker 32).

other Frankfort papers had been in his own possession until his departure from Geneva: Calvin's letter of 25 January 1555 in which the the Reformer commented on the quarrel of the English congregation at Frankfort and condemned as 'popish dregs' some parts of the 1552 Prayer Book which Whittingham had sent for his inspection. This, it was hoped, would invalidate the demand for subscription to the Book of 1559. Whether or not the letter was sent, within a few months it appeared in print in the context of *A Brieff Discours off the Troubles Begonne at Franckford*,[1] a tract which has been traditionally ascribed to Whittingham. The *Brieff Discours* told the story of the Knox and Cox disputes and of the later troubles at Frankfort by means of a tendentiously edited collection of original records. Its purpose was to prove that the puritan cause already had a long and reputable history, and it was printed at Heidelberg in 1574 as part of a co-ordinated literary apologia for English presbyterianism.

It is difficult in the light of Wood's letter to believe that Whittingham can have been the author of a work which clearly emanated from the 'central committee' of the presbyterian movement in London and which carried in its conclusion a round condemnation of conforming turncoats. If Wood's letter is that referred to in an anonymous life of Whittingham as from 'one that had bin with him at Geneva', the dean of Durham retorted with a justification of his conformity from Calvin's own teaching.[2] Although Whittingham later remembered some of his old Geneva friends in his will,[3] there is no evidence that he played any further part in the puritan movement.

John Field was probably behind the publication of the *Brieff Discours* as of many other anonymous tracts which seem to bear the imprimatur of the presbyterian organization. But the collector and editor of the documents which comprise the *Brieff Discours* may well have been Thomas Wood himself, in whose custody they apparently lay until the last exiles left Geneva.

WOOD'S CORRESPONDENCE WITH THE EARLS OF LEICESTER AND WARWICK, 1576–7.

This correspondence has to do with the events which led to the queen's suppression of the public conferences of preachers known as 'prophesyings'.[4] In June 1576 the exercise of prophesying at Southam in the south of Warwickshire, which Wood reckoned to be 'undoubtedly and without exception . . . the best exercise in this realme' had been put down by Bishop Bentham of Coventry and Lichfield and its moderators called before Archbishop Grindal, while the

---

[1] *A Brieff Discours off the Troubles Begonne at Franckford* (1575), pp. xxxiiii–xxxvi. Here the letter is acknowledged to be 'faithfully translated owte off Latten by Maister Whittingham', which suggests that the text may have been supplied by Whittingham in response to Wood's request. The Latin text of Calvin's letter was printed in Calvin's *Epistolae et Responsae* (Amsterdam, 1667), p. 98, and is accessible in Laing's edition of Knox's *Works*, iv. 51–3.

[2] 'Life of Mr William Whittingham', p. 22.

[3] He left tokens to Christopher Goodman, Anthony Gilby, Gilby's daughter who was his god-daughter and William Williams, Wood's brother-in-law. Wood predeceased Whittingham. (*Durham Wills and Inventories*, ed. W. Greenwell (Surtees Soc., xxxviii, 1860), p. 17.)

[4] This account of the prophesyings and their suppression is drawn from my 'Classical Movement', pp. 173–214.

justices who had supported it were discredited.[1] This was followed by the queen's command to Grindal to suppress all the prophesyings in his province, the archbishop's courageous but ineffective rearguard action in their defence, and his own sequestration in June 1577 which opened the way for a general reaction against the reformist tendencies in the Church which the evangelical Grindal had encouraged.[2]

To appreciate the despondency with which Wood faced the disappearance of the prophesyings, it must be understood that these market-town preaching exercises were probably the most effective means that had been found for propagating the Reformed religion in the rural areas of Elizabethan England. In some districts the bishops had been willing to enforce the attendance of the whole clergy, and to appoint as moderators over them the puritan preachers who in most cases were the initiators of the exercises. The unlearned ministers were indoctrinated and trained to be preachers by the performance of written tasks and later by taking their turn to speak in the assembly; while the whole company were subject to mutual 'censure' in private conferences following the public sermons which represented a reform of some importance in diocesan organization. In the Midlands, the prophesyings were linked together by travelling preachers, including Eusebius Paget, one of the Southam moderators, who went 'from shire to shire, from exercise to exercise, . . . accompanyed, countenanced and backed' by the puritan gentry.[3] Here the bishops had largely lost control of the movement. Bishop Bentham claimed ignorance of the very existence of the Southam exercise,[4] which had been set up by the puritan rector, John Oxenbridge,[5] and licensed by the gentlemen on the local

[1] Archbishop Grindal to Burghley, 10 June 1576, B.M., MS. Lansdowne 23, no. 4, fo. 7; and the evidence of these letters.

[2] Grindal's letter to the queen of 20 Dec. 1576 (*The Remains of Edmund Grindal*, ed. William Nicholson (Parker Soc., 1843), pp. 376–90 and transcribed (for example) in Ambrose Wood's commonplace book), has become famous, but the investigations which the archbishop undertook before writing it deserve to be better known. On receipt of the queen's order, he instructed all his suffragans to report on the conduct of the exercises in their dioceses. The bishops' letters are extant (St. Paul's Cathedral, Add. MS. VII; copies, B.M., Add. MS. 29546, fos. 40–56) and are mostly in favour of the continuance of the prophesyings subject to certain reforms and safeguards. Grindal accordingly drew up 'Orders for reformation of abuses abowte the learned exercises and conferences emonge ministers of the churche' (B.M., MS. Lansd. 109, no. 2, fos. 3 and 5) and prepared a learned defence of the exercises from the writings of the Church Fathers and Reformers (St. Paul's Cathedral, Add. MS. VII, no. 140). The queen by her own letters to the bishops ordered the suppression of the prophesyings on 7 May 1577 (John Strype, *The History of the Life and Acts of Edmund Grindal* (Oxford, 1822), app. x, pp. 574–6) and Grindal's sequestration followed in June. (*D.N.B.*, s.v. Grindal.)

[3] John Aylmer to Grindal, 28 Sept. 1576, B.M., Add. MS. 29546, fos. 56–7.
[4] Bentham to Grindal, 16 July 1576, *ibid.*, fo. 52.
[5] John Oxenbridge (*c.* 1525–1618); student of Christ Church 1550, B.A. 1553, M.A. 1556, B.D. sup. 1572; rector of Southam (1572) and Llanynis in the diocese of Bangor (1560) livings worth together £56 17s. 4d. in 1575; a moderator of Thomas Lever's prophesying at Coventry as well as at Southam in 1576; in trouble for nonconformity, 1576 and 1583–6; one of four preachers appointed by Bishop Overton of Coventry and Lichfield in 1584 to examine the ministry in Staffordshire; active member of the puritan classical movement in the 1580's and father-

ecclesiastical commission.[1] Where the prophesyings were public, they were a
demonstration of the strength of the Reformed faction in a sharply divided
society, especially when the local justices attended, as at Southam. Their
suppression was therefore, in Wood's eyes, the greatest imaginable disgrace
to the cause of the Gospel and an encouragement to its Catholic and irreligious
enemies.

The future of the prophesyings had been uncertain for at least two years
before the incident of Southam. In March 1574 the queen instructed Parker to
order their suppression, but his letters were countermanded by the privy council
and widely ignored.[2] In the following year, the exercises throughout the
diocese of Lincoln 'by little and little' ceased, after Elizabeth had conveyed her
displeasure to Bishop Cooper through Sir Thomas Smith.[3] The bishops of
Hereford and Gloucester took action against the exercises in their dioceses at
the same time.[4] Some months later, after both the judges of assize and some
bishops had complained of irregularities in the prophesyings,[5] the queen was
in particular 'most greveously informed' concerning the conduct of the preachers
and gentlemen at Southam. The queen mentioned these reports to Leicester
'first of any'; Warwickshire was his country.[6] But Grindal was informed of
the queen's complaints by Walsingham and Burghley as well as by Leicester.[7]
And several privy councillors made efforts to reform the remaining exercises
and so save them from the queen's displeasure.[8]

All that the puritans knew of these delicate negotiations was a bunch of tales
amounting to the persistent rumour that the overthrow of the Southam
prophesying was the earl of Leicester's 'only deed'. As Wood represents them
to Leicester and his brother, they were bewildered and scandalized. Small
wonder: they had counted Leicester to be their 'earnest favourer' and a noted
patron of the prophesyings which he now seemed bent to overthrow. To add to
the disillusionment of the godly, there were current 'other verie common brutes,

in-law of the leader of the movement in Oxford, Edward Gellibrand; 'eruditus sed
scismaticus' in a clergy return of 1592; in danger for not subscribing in 1605 when
he described himself as 'nearly fourscore years old'; apparently preaching in
Coventry in 1609; at the time of his death in 1618 'preacher in Coventry, late
minister of Southam, Co. Warwick'; grandfather of John Oxenbridge, celebrated
puritan divine. (*Seconde Parte of a Register*, ii. 174; Lambeth Palace MS. Carta
Miscellanea xiii (2), 32, 49; B.M., MS. Stowe 570, fo. 97v, Add. MS. 29546,
fo. 51v, MS. Eg. 1693, fo. 118; Benjamin Brook, *Lives of the Puritans* (1813), iii.
510; P.R.O., Star Chamber 5/A/49; Hist. MSS. Comm., *Hatfield MSS.*, xvii.
618; Thomas Sharp, *Illustrative Papers on the History and Antiquities of the City
of Coventry* (Birmingham, 1871), p. 136; P.C.C. Wills, 65 Meade; *D.N.B.*, s.v.
John Oxenbridge (the younger).)

[1] This is inferred from Wood's reference to the 'orders . . . which they receaved
from the High Commissioners'. It is unlikely that the High Commission in
London could have been meant.

[2] Collinson, 'Classical Movement', pp. 201–7.

[3] Cooper to Grindal, 22 July 1576, B.M., Add. MS. 29546, fos. 41v–42v.

[4] Bp. Scory to Grindal, 18 July 1576, *ibid.*, fos. 52v–53v; Bp. Cheyney to
Grindal, 16 Sept. 1576, *ibid.*, fo. 56r.

[5] *Remains of Edmund Grindal*, p. 471.

[6] See p. 96 below.

[7] Grindal to Burghley, 10 June 1576, B.M., MS. Lansd. 23, no. 4, fo. 7.

[8] See p. 93 below.

verie dishonorable and ungodly' touching Leicester's life, which Wood will not commit to writing. There can be little doubt of the nature of these rumours. They referred to Leicester's 'straying loves'[1] and perhaps implicated Lettice Knollys, the wife of Walter Devereux, earl of Essex.[2] Leicester's earlier liaison with Lady Douglas Sheffield was probably broken off by this time. In 1578 Leicester was to marry Lettice Knollys, whose first husband died in Ireland on 22 September 1576—seven weeks after Wood's cryptic reference to rumours of Leicester's 'ungodly life'.[3] *Leycesters Commonwealth*,[4] besides perpetuating the ill-founded report that Leicester's agents had poisoned Essex, asserted that there had been an adulterous association between Leicester and Lettice during her husband's absence.[5] A later tradition set the scene at Sir George Digby's house at Coleshill, twelve miles from Kenilworth where Leicester gave a famous entertainment for the queen in July 1575.[6] Lettice was probably present at the 'princely pleasures',[7] but then so were most people and there is no evidence of intimacy in her relations with Leicester before Essex's death.[8] But the rumours which Wood hints at must strengthen the charges of *Leycesters Commonwealth*, especially since Wood had intended to 'declare them particularly' to Leicester at Kenilworth in 1575 'if oportunity had served'. It is noteworthy that both Leicester and his brother seem aware of the nature of Wood's insinuations and that neither of them simply denies them. Warwick hopes that he will find them false, 'although I must needs confesse we be all flesh and blood and fraill of nature, therefore to be reformed'. Leicester confesses to being 'a sinner and flesh and blood as others be. And beside, I stand on the topp of the hill, where I knowe the smallest slipp semeth a fall. But I will not excuse my self; I may fall many wayes and have more witnesses thereof then many others who perhapps be no saintes nether, yet their faults lesse noted though somewayes greater then myne.'

[1] W. Camden, *Annales, or the history of the most renowned and victorious princesse, Elizabeth* (3rd edn., 1635), p. 191.

[2] Although if any credit is to be given to *Leycesters Commonwealth* Leicester was involved with many other 'such peeces of pleasure' besides Douglas Sheffield and Lettice Knollys. (*Copie of a leter*, pp. 38–9; *Leycesters Common-wealth* (1641), p. 71, marginal note.)

[3] Read, 'Letter from Robert, Earl of Leicester,' *ubi supra*; cf. Sir Sidney Lee in the *D.N.B.*, *s.v.* Leicester and Walter Devereux, earl of Essex.

[4] *The copie of a leter, wryten by a master of arte of Cambrige . . . concerning . . . the Erle of Leycester and his friendes in England*, printed, probably in Antwerp, in 1584; for long erroneously ascribed to Robert Parsons; attributed by Pollen (*Catholic Encyclopedia*) and Leo Hicks (*Studies*, xlvi (1957), 91–105) to Charles Arundell; reprinted in 1641 under the title *Leycesters Common-wealth* and by F. J. Burgoyne, 1904.

[5] *Copie of a leter*, pp. 19, 28–9.

[6] *Leycesters Commonwealth*, p. 71, marginal note.

[7] Walter Bourchier-Devereux, *Lives and Letters of the Devereux Earls of Essex* (1853), i. 118, 131–2.

[8] Read, 'Letter from Robert, Earl of Leicester', *ubi supra*, pp. 20–1; *D.N.B.*, *s.v.* Essex. The only piece of evidence, and that inferential, seems to be Leicester's anxiety to hasten Essex's return to Ireland in Mar. 1576, reported by Edward Waterhouse to Sir Henry Sidney. (Bourchier-Devereux, p. 131.) Richard Bagwell on the other hand thought that the facts 'tally very well with the common report that [Leicester] kept the Earl in Ireland while he made love to the Countess.' (*Ireland under the Tudors* (1885), ii. 327.)

The rumours current in the summer of 1576 might have disposed the puritans to agree with Leicester's defamer that 'beinge in dede of no religion' he had 'learned of his Mr Machvell to make a use of all religions', first emboldening the puritans against the bishops and then deserting them, 'soferinge the bishops to comitt them to prison' and yet 'streight tellinge the puritanes hee wilbe a meane to bringe Reformation and Discipline in the Church'.[1] The apparent ambivalence of Leicester's religious position, exploited so skilfully in *Leycesters Commonwealth*, has clung to him ever since. Both by his immediate posterity[2] and by modern historians[3] Leicester has been recognized as the 'Cherisher and Patron-General'[4] of the Elizabethan puritans but it has been generally supposed that his sympathy for the movement was devoid of religious conviction and assumed in mid-career for reasons of policy and self-interest. Robert Naunton, for example, thought him 'no good man', although for his letters and writings he 'never yet saw a style or phrase more seemingly religious, and fuller of the streams of devotion, and were they not sincere, I doubt much of his well-being, and I may fear that he was too well seen in the aphorisms and principles of Nicholas the Florentine, and in the reaches of Caesar Borgia'.[5] Conyers Read has succinctly stated the modern opinion: 'Leicester identified himself with the Puritans. But Leicester was for Leicester.'[6] Whether or not this will serve as an assessment of Leicester's character, there is a danger that it may divert attention from the attitudes and policies which he publicly adopted in matters of religion. These need have had little connexion with whatever religious element there may or may not have been in Leicester's personality[7] and they deserve a more serious examination than they have hitherto received,[8] as Miss Rosenberg's recent study of Leicester's literary patronage has already shown.[9] If Leicester exercised his ecclesiastical patronage and influence in the interest of the puritan party, that alone must have had a perceptible influence on the character of the Elizabethan Church. There is need to scrutinize Leicester's connexion with puritanism more closely and to attempt a definition of how far it went and for what motives.

[1] A MS. redaction of *Leycesters Commonwealth* in P.R.O., S.P. 15/28/113.

[2] See for example Izaak Walton in his *Life of Mr. Richard Hooker* (1670), p. 45.

[3] A. F. Scott Pearson, *Thomas Cartwright and Elizabethan Puritanism* (Cambridge, 1925), p. 266; J. E. Neale, *Elizabeth I and her Parliaments, 1559–1581* (1952), p. 292.

[4] Walton, p. 39.

[5] *Fragmenta Regalia*, in *Memoirs of Robert Cary* (Edinburgh, 1808), pp. 205–6. Cf. the views of John Harington, *A Briefe View of the State of the Church of England* (1653), p. 203. Lily B. Campbell has discussed the literary treatment of Leicester as the type of the English Machiavellian man. (*Shakespeare's 'Histories', Mirrors of Elizabethan Policy* (San Marino, 1947), pp. 326–32.)

[6] Read, *Burghley*, p. 237. Cf. the views of Sir Sidney Lee in the *D.N.B.*, *s.v.* Leicester, and M. M. Knappen, *Tudor Puritanism* (Chicago, 1939), p. 191.

[7] His father, the rapacious Northumberland, was lauded by Bishop Hooper as 'that most faithful and intrepid soldier of Christ'. (*Original Letters relative to the English Reformation*, ed. H. Robertson (Parker Soc., 1846–7), i. 82.)

[8] Few would now be prepared to state as categorically as Sir Sidney Lee that 'the general policy of Elizabeth was unaffected by [Leicester]'. (*D.N.B.*, *s.v.* Leicester.)

[9] Eleanor Rosenberg, *Leicester, Patron of Letters* (New York, 1955). See especially chapters 6 and 7 which examine Leicester's patronage of puritan and anti-Catholic writers and represent him as a serious-minded patriot.

Leicester's response to Wood's challenge is therefore of the greatest value, for in his letter he claims, with at least partial sincerity, to lay open his heart and mind on the religious question: 'Therefore for my religion I tell yow how it is.' His confession clarifies some of the apparent inconsistencies of his religious position and may be used to interpret other available evidence.

The letter is a reminder—as much for the modern student as for Leicester's puritan friends—of the extent of the ecclesiastical influence which he had exercised from the beginning of Elizabeth's reign:[1] 'Looke of all the bishops that can be supposed that I have commended to that dignity since my creditt any way served. . . . Looke of all the deanes . . . Looke into the University of Oxford lykewise whereof I am Chancelor.'[2] In these matters Leicester was indeed no lightweight. Of the first generation of Elizabethan bishops, at least six— Thomas Young of York,[3] Edmund Grindal of London,[4] Edwin Sandys of Worcester,[5] Robert Horne of Winchester,[6] Edmund Scambler of Peterborough[7]

---

[1] John Aylmer wrote to Dudley on 12 Aug. 1559: 'Good my Lord if the Deanery of Winchester be not already swallowed up, lett me amonge the rest of the small fishes have a snatche at the baite: if yt be gone, I besech your good Lordship cast a hooke for the Deanrie of Durham that when Mr Hoorn is spedd of a bishopprick I maie have that to serve God, my cuntrie and the Queene's Majestie in.' (B.M., Add. MS. 32091, fo. 172.)

[2] Cf. *Leycesters Commonwealth*: 'He that disposeth at his wil the Ecclesiastical livings of the Realm, maketh Bisshopes none, but such as wil do reason, or of his chapleines whome he listeth.' (*Copie of a leter*, pp. 68–9.)

[3] While still bishop of St. David's, Young used Dudley's mediation in a suit for the restoration of his temporalities. (P.R.O., S.P. 12/11/38.) In 1566, the Spanish ambassador reported that Young was 'a great friend of Lord Robert.' (*Cal. S.P. Spanish, 1558–67*, p. 553.) In 1565 Young conferred on Leicester the high stewardship and Mastership of the Game of the archbishopric at an annual fee of £40. (Information from the De L'Isle and Dudley papers at Longleat, kindly supplied to me by Miss Carolyn Merion.) Young leased to Leicester the manor of Southwell. (B.M., Add. MS. 32091, fo. 207.) Wood reminded Leicester that Young's promotion was 'your Lordship's doing'. (See p. 101 below.)

[4] Among several letters which establish the connexion, see Grindal to Leicester, 19 Jan. 1571 (as bishop of London) and 16 July 1571 (as archbishop of York), B.M., Add. MS. 32091, fos. 239–40, 242.

[5] Sandys to Dudley, 14 Apr. 1560: 'I thank you for commending me to your frends . . . and pray you to maintaine my honest and right cause as hitherto ye have done.' (De L'Isle and Dudley papers (Baskerville transcripts deposited with the National Registry of Archives), i. 139.) On 20 July 1566 Sandys wrote: 'Your Lordship nedith not to be a sueter unto me in reasonable and lawfull thinges, but rather to commande me.' (B.M., Add. MS. 32091, fo. 185.)

[6] Wood regarded Horne as one of Leicester's bishops. (See p. 102 below.) In 1568 Horne promised an advowson to one of Leicester's chaplains. (Hist. MSS. Comm., *Pepys MSS.*, p. 136.) In 1575 he granted him a rent-charge of £100 *per annum*. (Information from the De L'Isle and Dudley papers which I owe to Miss Merion.) This was still a charge on the revenues of the diocese in 1587. (John Strype, *Annals of the Reformation* (Oxford, 1824), III. ii. 263.)

[7] There is evidence of Scambler's dependence on Leicester in a number of letters between them. (Magdalene College, Pepys Library, MS. 'Papers of State', ii. 389–90, 647–8; De L'Isle and Dudley papers (Baskerville transcripts), ii. 160; P.R.O., S.P. 12/24/52 (2); B.M., MS. Harley 677, fos. 37–8.)

and James Pilkington of Durham[1]—seem to have owed their preferment at least partly to his influence. In 1569 Archbishop Parker informed Leicester before Cecil of his nominations for the vacant sees, and six years later felt bound to explain even to Burghley that his choice of a right-wing candidate for the bishopric of Norwich was not motivated by 'anye displeasure that I beare to my Lord of Leicester's chapleins'.[2] Leicester probably had a share in Grindal's ascent through York to Canterbury, and in Sandys' appointment to London.[3] Thomas Cooper of Lincoln and later of Winchester,[4] William Chaderton of Chester[5] and William Overton of Coventry and Lichfield[6] were his chaplains. John Bullingham of Gloucester was his sworn man.[7] As for deans, Leicester helped to promote Thomas Sampson to Christ Church, Oxford,[8] William Whittingham to Durham,[9] and, in later years, Ralph Griffin to Lincoln,[10] Matthew Hutton to York[11] and his chaplain Tobie Matthew to Durham.[12] At Leicester's suit George Gardiner was preferred in rapid succession to both the archdeaconry and the deanery of Norwich and to be the queen's chaplain.[13] With the exception of Young and Bullingham, all these men were Calvinists of a moderate puritan churchmanship and almost all of them had been exiles in Mary's reign.[14] Leicester was partly responsible for the ascendancy of radical Protestantism among the higher clergy in the first half

[1]Pilkington's appeal to Leicester of 25 Oct. 1565 on behalf of the nonconformists argues that he regarded him as his patron. (James Pilkington, *Works* (Parker Soc., 1842), pp. 658–62.) For a discussion of the interests of the Dudleys in the bishopric of Durham and its wealth, see H. R. Trevor-Roper, 'The bishopric of Durham and the capitalist reformation', *Durham Univ. Jour.*, xxxviii (1945), 45–58.

[2]*Parker Correspondence*, pp. 350, 477–8.

[3]Sandys as bishop of London gave Leicester the stewardship of his lands at an annual fee of £10. (Arthur Collins, *Letters and Memorialls of State* (1746), i. 45.)

[4]Rosenberg, pp. 124–8.

[5]Francis Peck, *Desiderata Curiosa* (1732–35), I. iii. 3–4.

[6]On 22 May 1571 Overton described himself to Leicester as 'your own chapleyne, or at least wise the Queen's Majestie's chapleyn by your only meanes put and preferred unto her.' (De L'Isle and Dudley papers (Baskerville transcripts), i. 237.) Cf. the status of George Gardiner, dean of Norwich, referred to below.) Leicester held the Mastership of the Game in the bishopric of Coventry and Lichfield. (Collins, i. 45.)

[7]P.R.O., Star Chamber 5 W 48/24. I am indebted for this reference to Miss N. M. Fuidge.

[8]Strype, *Annals*, I. ii. 148–9.

[9]See p.91 below.

[10]Collins, i. 45–6.

[11]B.M. Add. MS. 33207, fo. 1; *The Correspondence of Dr. Matthew Hutton* (Surtees Soc., 1843), p. 71.

[12]Harington, p. 204; Strype, *Annals*, III. i. 682.

[13]Leicester to Bp. Parkhurst of Norwich, 4 Dec. 1573, Cambridge Univ. Library, MS. Ee. 11. 34, no. 178, fo. 143; Strype, *Annals*, II. i. 443. Two months after Gardiner's installation, the high stewardship of the deanery was conferred on Leicester. (*Extracts from the Two Earliest Minute-Books of the Dean and Chapter of Norwich Cathedral, 1566–1849*, ed. J. F. Williams and B. Cozens-Hardy (Norfolk Record Soc., 1953), pp. 19, 31.)

[14]Edmund Scambler had remained in England, but as minister to a secret Protestant congregation. (*D.N.B.*, *s.v.* Scambler.)

of Elizabeth's reign, while the conservative reaction which set in after about 1580 was not unconnected with the decline of his influence. Most of the other prominent churchmen whom Leicester is known to have befriended were of the moderate puritan party. William Fulke, leader of the nonconformists in St. John's College in 1565 and later Master of Pembroke,[1] Robert Some, Master of Peterhouse,[2] Edmund Lillie, Master of Balliol,[3] and John Still, archdeacon of Sudbury and later bishop of Bath and Wells[4] were all his chaplains. James Calfhill,[5] Laurence Humphrey, President of Magdalen[6] and John Reynolds, President of Corpus Christi College, Oxford,[7] all looked upon Leicester as their friend at Court.

The consistent pattern of this patronage corresponds closely to Leicester's confession of his religion. He points to his long record of service to the Reformed religion and its preachers, but he condemns the schismatic tendencies of Wood's faction, denies that he is 'fantastically perswaded' in religion, and finds himself well satisfied with what is already established in 'this Universall Church of England.' He admits his moral failings, but professes that he has always held the Protestant faith in sincerity.[8] 'I take Almighty God to my record, I never altered my mind or thought from my youth touching my religion, and yow knowe I was ever from my cradle brought up in it.'

While a specious facility is detectable in Leicester's professions of faith,[9] there is no reason to doubt that the son of Northumberland had always been formally a Protestant. The Dudleys were allied by close ties of interrelationship to a group of families—Grey, Russel, Sidney, Hastings—whose fortunes were identified with the Reformation. Leicester's alleged instability in religion[10] in the early years of Elizabeth's reign appeared mainly in the field of state policy, where admittedly it is hard to find any consistency, unless in his ambition to marry the queen.[11] In domestic affairs of the Church, he seems to have been

[1] Rosenberg, pp. 40–2; H. C. Porter, *Reformation and Reaction in Tudor Cambridge* (Cambridge, 1958), p. 135.
[2] *M. Some laid open in his coulers* (1589), p. 1.
[3] P.R.O., S.P. 15/25/119, fo. 282v.
[4] Still to Leicester, 20 Feb. 1577, B.M., MS. Cotton Titus B. vii, fo. 42; Gabriel Harvey to Leicester, 24 Apr. 1579, De L'Isle and Dudley papers (Baskerville transcripts), ii. 207.
[5] Calfhill to Cecil, Feb. 1570, B.M., MS. Lansd. 12, no. 38, fo. 88.
[6] Rosenberg, pp. 260–3.   [7] *Ibid.*, pp. 240–1.
[8] Cf. his letter to Lady Douglas Sheffield: 'For albeyt I have byn and yet am a man frayll, yet am I not voyd of conscience toward God. . . .' (*Huntington Library Bull.*, ix. 24.)
[9] See a letter to Lord North (who according to *Leycesters Commonwealth* was responsible for drawing Leicester into the puritan faction): 'But yet I trust we do take the handy worke of the Lord as we ought, even as his crosse and punyshment for our synnes, for so and xx tymes more, yf yt may be, have we deserved.' (Bodleian Library, MS. Douce 393, fo. 24.) North reported that Leicester 'did sundry times by many good and godlie speeches both acknowledge and also humbly thank the Lord God for his infinite mercy and goodness, still devising and studying how he might walk in those ways that might be most pleasing to his mercifull God.' (Frances Bushby, *Three Men of the Tudor Time* (1911), pp. 91–2.)
[10] Conyers Read, *Mr. Secretary Cecil and Queen Elizabeth* (1955), p. 264.
[11] *Ibid.*, p. 303. Even so, Sir Sidney Lee in the *D.N.B.* made too much of Leicester's attempts to persuade De Quadra in 1561 and De Silva in 1564 that he

always known for a Protestant.[1] At the outset he was presented with a plea for the preferment of twenty-eight of the most forward Protestant divines[2] which based itself on their utter rejection of 'Antichriste and al his Romishe rags'.[3] In the early fifteen-sixties he took a 'special care' of Jewel's defence of his *Apologie* for the Anglican settlement against Harding.[4] What is more, he lent his name to a succession of Calvinist tracts, whose authors acknowledged his favour and generosity and even brandished his device of the bear and ragged staff on the title page.[5] Thomas Lever testified in 1565 that 'heretofore I and mani others have bi your meanes had quietnes, libertie and comfort to preach the Gospel of Christ'.[6] When the Church divided on the issue of the vestments, the puritans addressed themselves to Leicester and based their hopes mainly on him,[7] not apparently in vain.[8] While Archbishop Parker was

was in favour of a league with Spain and the restoration of Catholicism. In 1571, a common enmity towards Cecil drew Leicester into alliance with Norfolk and the dissident Catholic earls, but this was as short-lived as the circumstances which dictated it. (Read, *Cecil*, pp. 431–68.)

[1] Except in the pages of *Leycesters Commonwealth*, where it is stated that 'for his gaine' Leicester was for some years the 'secret friend' of the papists against the Protestants, until persuaded by Lord North to 'step over' to the puritans. (*Copie of a leter*, p. 15.)

[2] All but seven on the list had been exiles, nine of them at Geneva. In order, those named are: Miles Coverdale, William Turner, Richard Alvey, John Foxe, (John, Ralph or Thomas) Lever, Thomas Sampson, William Whittingham, Laurence Humphrey, Anthony Gilby, Thomas Cole, Adam Halliday, Robert Crowley, Mr. Buskit, Percival Wiburn, Thomas Horton, John Philpot, Walter Austin, William Cole, (James or Leonard) Pilkington, Edmund Allen, Thomas Hancock, Richard Harvel, Richard Tremayne, Mr. Courthop, Mr. Stanton (John Staunton?), John Gough, Arthur Saule and Mr. Reth.

[3] Magdalene College, Pepys Library, MS. 'Papers of State', ii. 701.

[4] Jewel to Leicester, 30 Jan. 1565, printed John Whitgift, *Works* (Parker Soc., 1853), iii. 624.

[5] In 1561 Jean Veron (later a preacher to the army at Newhaven) dedicated to Dudley *A Moste Necessary Treatise of Free Wil*, addressing him as 'the Mecenas and patron of all godlye learninge and true religion'; in 1562 the translator of *The Lawes and Statutes of Geneva* (probably Robert Fills) dedicated his work to Dudley, testifying to his 'zeal . . . to the advancement of God's glorye in this realme, and the singuler gentilnes and favour that you usually shewe to the furtherers thereof.' In 1564, Leicester received the translation of Peter Martyr Vermigli's commentary on Judges; in 1565 *The Firste Parte of the Christian Instruction*, a Swiss catechism of Calvinist inspiration; and in 1566 an anti-Roman treatise by John Bartlett. The last two books carried Leicester's device. (Rosenberg, pp. 202–12.)

[6] John Strype, *The Life and Acts of Matthew Parker* (Oxford, 1821), iii. 138.

[7] James Pilkington, the bishop of Durham, Whittingham, the dean and Thomas Lever, the Master of Sherborne Hospital, Durham, all defended the nonconformist position in letters to Leicester. (Pilkington, *Works*, pp. 658–62; Strype, *Parker*, iii. 76–84, 138–41.) Whittingham's letter was still in circulation among the puritans nearly ten years later. (See p.89below.) Parker warned Cecil of a rumour current among the puritans that Leicester would persuade the queen to withdraw the demand for conformity 'and this thinge is nowe done in his absence'. (*Parker Correspondence*, pp. 237–8.)

[8] In a second letter, Bp. Pilkington reminded Leicester that 'you did put yourself betwixt and helped to stay the displeasure conceived and intended'. (Hist. MSS. Comm., *Pepys MSS.*, pp. 42–3.)

striving to reduce Thomas Sampson and Laurence Humphrey to conformity, Leicester was putting both of them up to preach at Paul's Cross.[1] Wood later acknowledged that 'in the begining of Mr Sampson's and Mr Goodman's first truble' Leicester was 'theire chiefest and in manner their only patrone'.[2] In 1571 Leicester undertook 'earnest travell' with Archbishop Parker on behalf of the Genevan outcast Christopher Goodman and incurred the queen's displeasure as a result.[3] Yet in the following year, he persuaded Bishop Downham of Chester to install Goodman as archdeacon of Richmond and promised to shield the bishop from the queen's anger.[4]

Nevertheless, it was only after the readjustments in the pattern of domestic and external politics which took place between 1569 and 1572[5] that Leicester's public image became thoroughly infused with progressive Protestantism. The eclipse of the conservative opposition to Cecil and changes in England's relations with France and Spain both seem to have influenced him in this direction. The turning-point probably came with the abortive Anjou marriage project of 1571. Leicester seems at first to have favoured a marriage between Elizabeth and Anjou, but later to have attempted to frustrate it by exploiting the difficulty of religion.[6] Whether he thought in sincerity that the proposed marriage endangered the Protestant establishment or only that it threatened his own influence with the queen, he praised Elizabeth's determination not to allow Anjou the practice of his religion and acted as 'the chief prompter of her conscience in the matter'.[7] In the following year he adopted the same attitude towards the proposal that Elizabeth should marry Catherine de Médici's younger son, the Duc d'Alençon. On 7 July 1572 he reported to Robert Beale, Walsingham's secretary in Paris, that Alençon meant to stick to his religion and concluded with palpable complacency:

And so wyll the matter breake of I suppose. And so must we pray to the Almighty to protect and defend us, who only hath hetherto so done and without whose only hand we are lyke to fall, having as yt were all the great princes of the world uppon us and at this day no aliaunce at all with anyone. But better ys yt to trust in God than in man and yf we do lose our frendes and neyghbours for his cause with a synceare hart, then ys no doubt but he wyll as he ys able myghtyly defend us against all his enymyes.[8]

Walsingham could now assume that Leicester shared his own theological conception of what English foreign policy should be. In commenting on both French and Dutch affairs at about this time, he advocated his policies to Burghley in terms of political expediency, but to Leicester 'in respect of the spiritual fruits that thereby may ensue'.[9] Henceforth Leicester was always one with the closely-interrelated group of zealous Protestants in the Court and the council

[1] Dixon, vi. 59; Strype, *Parker*, ii. 164.
[2] See p. 101 below.
[3] Goodman to Leicester, 28 July 1571, B.M., Add. MS. 32091, fos. 246–7.
[4] Downham to Leicester, 31 Mar. 1572, *ibid.*, fos. 268–9.
[5] Accounts in Conyers Read, *Mr. Secretary Walsingham and the Policy of Queen Elizabeth* (Oxford, 1925), i. 59–262; *Cecil*, pp. 431–68; *Burghley*, pp. 17-108.
[6] Read, *Walsingham*, i. 110–46.
[7] *Ibid.*, i. 125.
[8] Leicester to Beale, 7 July 1572, B.M., MS. Eg. 1693, fo. 9.
[9] Read, *Walsingham*, ii. 142–5; *Burghley*, p. 75.

who equated the safety of the realm with the cause of the Gospel and favoured preventive measures against a supposed international Catholic conspiracy.[1] If Walsingham was its intellectual inspiration, Leicester was the greatest courtier of the group, so that in *Leycesters Commonwealth* the whole faction could be represented as 'the Erle of Leycester and his friendes in England'.[2] 'When the Earl of Leicester lived' remembered a puritan writer at the end of the reign, 'it went for currant that all Papists were traitors in action or affection'.[3]

Within England, Leicester's great influence continued to be exerted in the interests of the Reformed sector of the Church. He protected the prophesyings, subsidized preachers, and when in the country appeared at the preaching exercises, publicly lending his credit to the godly cause.[4] When the queen and Parker attempted to enforce the uniform use of wafer bread in the communion service,[5] provoking religious disorders in some counties, Leicester represented the grievances of the radical Protestants to the queen and obtained the rescinding of the order.[6] Leicester was probably more responsible than any of his colleagues for the favour which the privy council almost habitually showed to puritan preachers in the fifteen-seventies and early fifteen-eighties.

Such actions won Leicester the firm friendship of the radical Protestant gentry and corporations, especially in the Midlands and East Anglia. Even in North Wales he was told that the expense of planting preachers would be more than repaid by the credit which would redound to his name.[7] King's Lynn and Yarmouth both elected him as their high steward after the execution of the duke of Norfolk in 1572.[8] In both towns puritan factions were in the ascendant at the time and religion may well have guided their choice.[9] Maldon, another

---

[1] Conyers Read, 'Walsingham and Burghley in Queen Elizabeth's privy council', *Eng. Hist. Rev.*, xxviii (1913), 34–58. The group included Leicester's brother Warwick, his brother-in-law Huntingdon, his father-in-law Sir Francis Knollys and Warwick's father-in-law, Bedford.

[2] Part of the title of *A copie of a leter*.

[3] Thomas Digges, *Humble Motives for Association to Maintain Religion Established* (1601), p. 25. Miss Rosenberg has demonstrated Leicester's importance as a patron of anti-Catholic literature. In 1572 Leicester received the dedication of the semi-official translation of Bullinger's *Confutation of the Popes Bull . . . against Elizabeth*. The bear and ragged staff was reproduced on the title-page. (Rosenberg, pp. 212–18.)

[4] In 1584 a Shrewsbury preacher called Leicester a 'provident peregrine', feeding on the Word of God in his travels. (Rosenberg, p. 226.)

[5] Strype, *Parker*, ii. 32–5. This was an attempt to resolve in the conservative interest an anomalous situation. The 1559 Prayer Book prescribed the use of common table bread, while the Injunctions of the same year ordered the use of wafers resembling in form those 'heretofore named singing cakes'. (Anthony Sparrow, *A Collection of Articles, Injunctions, Canons* (1661), p. 79.)

[6] Cambridge Univ. Library, MS. Ee. 11. 34, fo. 145; *Seconde Parte of a Register*, i. 187.

[7] William Herle to Leicester, 14 Aug. 1579, De L'Isle and Dudley papers (Baskerville transcripts), i. 170.

[8] J. E. Neale, *The Elizabethan House of Commons* (1948), pp. 179, 209. Besides the fees—at Lynn £10—the positions carried parliamentary patronage and other means of influence.

[9] The town preacher of Yarmouth later congratulated the bailiffs on their choice of so godly a high steward. (Bartimaeus Andrewes, *A Very Short Catechisme* 1586), epistle.) At Lynn, the puritan recorder Robert Bell chose Leicester in

borough with strong puritan elements, appointed Leicester as its recorder.[1] In county politics, Leicester supported the puritan justices of Norfolk and Suffolk in a factional dispute with Bishop Freke of Norwich and his friends in 1578[2] and later extricated three of the Suffolk justices from the disgrace of suspension from the commission of the peace into which their puritanism had brought them.[3]

To turn to the Midlands: in 1567 Leicester procured the letters patent of incorporation which constituted a group of Protestant magnates[4] governors of certain funds for the support of preachers in Warwickshire.[5] In 1572 he twice wrote to Bishop Scambler of Peterborough on behalf of the puritan gentlemen of Northamptonshire to defend the Northampton prophesying and its founder and moderator, the radical town preacher Percival Wiburn, urging Scambler to establish similar conferences elsewhere. When the bishop assured him that there were more orderly exercises in other parts of his diocese and that Wiburn was a troublesome nonconformist, Leicester retorted with a favourite puritan argument: contention over such matters inevitably followed where preaching 'sharplie and preciselie sought the reformation of the lycentious sort'.[6] Four years later he simulated righteous anger when Scambler deprived another radical Northampton moderator, Arthur Wake, of his mastership of St. John's Hospital. At the time Wake was in Jersey where he and Wiburn were helping to draft the book of discipline for the presbyterian church of the Channel Islands.[7] When in the same summer the queen heard of the disorders at Southam, Leicester had no choice but to sacrifice the exercise and its clerical leaders, but he made efforts to rescue the justices who had maintained it

preference to Burghley. Soon after his election, the town was divided between the puritans and their opponents at the same time as all Norfolk was agitated by the communion bread controversy in which Leicester was known to have taken the puritan side. (King's Lynn Borough Records, Corporation Book 1569–91, fos. 55–6, 61v. (I owe this reference to Miss N. M. Fuidge); *Seconde Parte of a Register*, i. 98–9.)

[1] Collins, i. 45.

[2] This dispute (which concerned the attempts of the bishop's faction to unseat Dr. Becon, the chancellor of the diocese) is copiously documented in P.R.O., S.P. 15/25, 12/126, 127, and discussed in A. H. Smith, 'The Elizabethan Gentry of Norfolk: Office-Holding and Faction' (unpublished London Ph.D. thesis, 1959), pp. 176–84. The evidence for Leicester's interest in the case is in a letter from the puritan justices, now among Nathaniel Bacon's papers, Folger Shakespeare Library, Washington, D.C. (Photostat (lacking reference) supplied by Dr. Smith.)

[3] *Rushbrook Parish Registers 1567 to 1850 with Jermyn and Davers Annals* (Suffolk Green Books, vi, 1906), p. 214.

[4] Huntingdon, Warwick, Sir Ambrose Cave, Sir Nicholas Throckmorton, Sir Thomas Lucy, Sir Richard Knightley, Clement Throgmorton.

[5] *Cal. S.P. Dom., 1547–80*, p. 304.

[6] Leicester to Scambler, 28 Jan. 1572, Magdalene College, Pepys Library, MS. 'Papers of State', ii. 647–8; Scambler to Leicester, 5 Feb. 1572, De L'Isle and Dudley papers (Baskerville transcripts), ii. 160; Leicester to Scambler, 19 Feb. 1572, MS. 'Papers of State', ii. 389–90. The orders of the Northampton prophesying are in P.R.O., S.P. 12/78/38; printed, R.M. Serjeantson, *A History of the Church of All Saints, Northampton* (Northampton, 1901), pp. 104–8.

[7] Scott Pearson (who wrongly identifies the recipient of the letter as the bishop of Lincoln), *Thomas Cartwright*, pp. 161–3.

'Aske them, I meane the gentlemen . . . who helpt to deliver them hence and
to qualify her Majestie's displeasure towards them.'[1] Perhaps for this reason
no permanent harm was done to Leicester's credit with the puritan gentry of
the Midlands. In 1581, after he had attended sermons in the course of a journey
through these shires, Sir Richard Knightley of Fawsley, one of the governors
of the Warwickshire preachers' revenues, assured him:

You have therby gotten yow such frends as wolde be readie to venture their
lyves with your Lordship in a good cause, even suche as wold not do yt so muche
in respecte of your hye callinge, as for that they espie in your Lordship a zeale and
care for the helpinge and relevinge of the poore Churche which hath so manye and
myghtie enimyes that fewe such as your Lordship ys are frends to yt.[2]

In the following year, Leicester urged on Walsingham the necessity of a
thorough purge of the commissions of the peace and of a greater reliance to be
placed upon 'honest and relygyous gentlemen'.[3] In making his recommendation for a gentleman to be appointed as keeper of the recusants in Banbury
Castle, he told Burghley: 'I hear of one Cope greatly commended.'[4] Anthony
Cope of Hanwell, who would present the presbyterian bill and book in the
1586/7 parliament, lived twelve miles from Southam and was almost certainly
among the gentlemen who had supported the exercise there. So notorious was
Leicester's familiarity with these circles that the author of *Leycesters Commonwealth* could plausibly represent the preaching communions held in gentlemen's
houses in the Midlands[5] as secret meetings of Leicester's faction.[6]

The common link between Leicester's political views and his factional backing
in the country was demonstrated in 1585 when many of his puritan friends
joined his expedition to the Netherlands. 'The Lord's cause', Sir Robert
Jermyn of Suffolk called it on the eve of his departure,[7] while the preacher
Giles Wigginton in his sermons in London at the same time used to pray for
'all hir Majesty's faithfull councellors and namely my Lord the Earle of
Leicester in his expedition and warfare for the church and the gospell etc.'[8]

It would be profitless to ask whether the puritan gentry adhered to Leicester

[1] See p. 96 below.
[2] Knightley to Leicester, 17 Oct. 1581, P.R.O., S.P. 12/150/42.
[3] Leicester to Walsingham, 9 Sept. 1582, P.R.O., S.P. 12/155/42.
[4] Leicester to Burghley, 20 July 1580, P.R.O., S.P. 12/140/23.
[5] See evidence for such practices at George Carleton's house at Overston,
Northants., and Peter Wentworth's at Lillingston Lovell, Oxon. (*Acts of the
Privy Council*, xi. 132–3, 218–19.)
[6] *Copie of a leter*, pp. 119–20. It was a major thesis of *Leycesters Commonwealth*
(pp. 61–4) that Protestant gentlemen and officials throughout England were linked
with Leicester in a treasonable plot to divert the succession from the legitimate
Stuart line. For this to be plausible, the writer must have depended on the
common knowledge that all these men were Leicester's clients.
[7] Jermyn to William Davison, 25 Aug. 1585, Bodleian Library, MS. Tanner
78, fo. 73. Cf. the East Anglian puritan preacher Oliver Pig, addressing 'a christian
knight imployte in the service of her Majestie in the lowe countries': 'The cause
which you have in hande I nothing dout is the Lord's, as well in respect of releeving
his present pore distrest churches, as in preventing the ruine of owers here now
in some sort florishing.' (Letter prefacing MS. copy of *Meditations concerning
praiers* (pr. 1589), Cambridge Univ. Library, MS. Dd. 11. 76, fos. 21, 24r.)
[8] *Seconde Parte of a Register*, ii. 247.

in the first place because of his godly reputation, or whether Leicester borrowed his religious and political views from the gentlemen of his following. All that can be safely said is that Leicester's staunchest adherents in some of the counties where his influence was paramount were radical puritans. The alliance between them was one of mutual profit, promoting the local credit and authority of the puritan justices while adding to the dignity and influence of the courtier. Quasi-feudal connexions of this kind ran persistently through the social and political fabric of Elizabethan England,[1] but Leicester's faction approximated more closely than most to the modern conception of a party, based on a politico-religious principle. Great harm could be done to all the interests involved in such a connexion by the spread of the general suspicion that Leicester was 'a slyder or a faller from the Gosple', as was tacitly understood by both sides in this correspondence.

Many of the preachers and gentlemen whom Leicester befriended were presbyterians, who hoped to replace episcopacy with an egalitarian ministry, congregational discipline and government by consistory, *classis* and synod:[2] a reorganization of the English Church more drastic than the Tudor Reformation itself. How far did Leicester share these ambitions, perhaps with a less than spiritual interest in the dissolution of the temporalities of bishoprics and cathedral churches? Leicester was at pains to convince Wood that he was far from favouring any such drastic alteration of the Elizabethan Settlement. 'For my owne parte, I am so resolved to the defence of that is already established as I mean not to be a maintaynor or allower of any that wold troble or disturbe the quiett proceeding thereof.' While manifestly not true of his actions hitherto, this statement means that although Leicester had shielded individual presbyterians out of consideration for their worth as preachers, he had no intention of being known as a patron of the presbyterian cause.

In July 1572 Leicester had argued from the same moderate position against Robert Beale, then Walsingham's secretary in Paris. Beale had sent an attack on the English bishops which may have been inspired by the recently published *Admonition to the Parliament* and Leicester's reply can be read as a statement of his attitude to that diatribe against the government of the Church. Unlike Beale he held both sides to blame for the faults of the Church,

for as some of the higher sort hath bin over hard perchaunes to some of ther inferior brethren, so ar they of the inferior sort that shew more wylfulnes in some cases then reason or charyty wyll well allowe. For undowbtedly I found no more hate or dyspleasure almost betweene papyst and protestant then ys now in many places betweene many of our owne religione. . . . For my owne parte, none hath travelled more from the first than my self hath done to have the sincere concyences of faythfull preachers and mynisters to be preserved nether have I left all meanes undone that might make reconcylement betwene them and others, and thereby have sondry tymes had conferences betwene them, I meane have hard them of both sydes together in conferences and dysputaciones. I have hard what can be sayd by both and nearly I cannott excuse those I wold faine shuld be faultles. And

[1] J. E. Neale, 'The Elizabethan Political Scene', *Essays in Elizabethan History* (1958), pp. 59–84.

[2] Wiburn and Wake helped to erect the presbyterian church of the Channel Islands. (Scott Pearson, *Thomas Cartwright*, pp. 161–3.) Sir Richard Knightley sheltered the Marprelate press at Fawsley in 1588. (W. Pierce, *An Historical Introduction to the Marprelate Tracts* (1908), pp. 156–8.)

as our bysshopes ar in many thinges to be reproved, so assuredly, in ther dealings with such menn as dyffer from them, I doe not perceave that they doe yt with such extremyty as desarves so great myslyke as ys layd to them. For I must needes say that by many they be over much urged to do as they have done, or without dowbt we shuld have no certen relygyon in this realme shortly. . . . And I could never yet hear any reasone that could make me thinke otherwyse of these common quarreles in our Church but that they wear for matters simply indyfferent and nothing concerns doctryne, and therefore ought they to be concluded in our obedyence to the Magistrate. And I doe pray God dayly to send that spiritt amonge our preachers that may unyte them in doctryne and leve this discension and controversye for tryfles.[1]

Leicester's exercise of his ecclesiastical patronage and influence seems to have been generally consistent with these views. So were some of his attempts to arbitrate in religious controversy. In 1573 he made apparently sincere efforts to obtain the opinions of the leading German and Swiss reformers on the issues of the vestments controversy.[2] In December 1584 he convened and helped to preside over the conference at Lambeth between representatives of the bishops and of the puritans.[3] By the evidence of his letter to Beale, this was not the first time that he had listened to disputation between the two sides.

For all these professions, there was a time, for perhaps twelve months after the publication of the *Admonition*, when not only Leicester but many other courtiers may have concluded that the days of diocesan episcopacy were numbered; when the privy council held aloof from Archbishop Parker,[4] some of its members actively undermined the bishops' attempts to defend themselves against the fashionable presbyterian agitation and Parker feared that Leicester 'purposed to undo him' with the help of 'certain precisians'.[5] The authors of the *Admonition* themselves petitioned Leicester for relief from imprisonment in the Fleet, and he was presumably among the 'sundry noblemen' who secured their transfer to more comfortable lodgings with the archdeacon of London.[6]

But by her proclamations against the puritans of June and October 1573,[7] the queen made plain her determination to defend the established order and displayed the sensitivity to encroachments upon her ecclesiastical prerogatives which she had already shown in the parliaments of 1571 and 1572.[8] Whatever his personal sympathies, Leicester was forced to recognize that the puritan

---

[1] Leicester to Beale, 7 July 1572, B.M., MS. Eg. 1693, fos. 9–10. This was written in no spirit of formal propriety, for although Leicester told Beale that he would welcome further private discussion of the matter, he warned him to avoid mention of it in his despatches, which he was accustomed to show to the queen 'and the last I durst not, for this respect.'

[2] Sir John Wolley (on Leicester's behalf) to John Sturmius, 24 July 1573. (*Zurich Letters*, 2nd ser. (Parker Soc., 1845), pp. 220–1.)

[3] Account of the conference by Walter Travers in *Seconde Parte of a Register*, i. 275–83; mentioned by George Paule, *Life of Whitgift* (1612), p. 30.

[4] Collinson, 'Classical Movement', pp. 144–51.

[5] *Parker Correspondence*, p. 472.

[6] *Seconde Parte of a Register*, i. 91; *Puritan Manifestoes*, ed. W. H. Frere and C. E. Douglas (Church Hist. Soc., 1954), p. 153; *Acts of the Privy Council*, viii. 90, 93.

[7] *Tudor and Stuart Proclamations, 1485–1714*, ed. Robert Steele (Oxford, 1910), i. 74, nos. 687, 689.

[8] Neale, *Elizabeth I and her Parliaments, 1559–1581*, pp. 191–217, 291–304.

hotheads could provoke a reaction in which the Reformed religion itself might be overthrown; besides endangering his own credit, which rested ultimately on Elizabeth's favour. In 1571 Christopher Goodman had told Leicester that he was sorry that 'for my sake your Lordship shoulde growe in suspicione to be a mayntenor of such as go abowt the undermininge of the estate'.[1] Warwick told the puritans that his brother's actions on their behalf 'had not bene done without some danger of displeasure to himself and with more difficulty then is fitt shold be knowen'.[2] Leicester himself warned Wood that if the puritans continued to disregard the law 'such inconveniences must follow to the Church as all true gospellers in deed shalbe sory for'. The 'over busy dealing of some' at Southam had done 'so much hurt in striving to make better perforce that which is by permission good enough already, as we shall nether have it in Southam nor any other where els, and doe what we can all, and those all yow thinke more zealous then I. And this have I feared long agoe wold prove the fruict of our discention for trifles first and since for other matters.'[3] Walsingham gave the same advice to William Davison and his presbyterian friends among the English Merchant Adventurers in Antwerp: 'If yow knew with what difficulty we retain that we have, and that the seeking of more might hazard . . . that which we already have, you would then, Mr Davison, deal warily in this time when policy carrieth more sway then zeal.'[4] Here is the explanation of many of the apparent vacillations in Leicester's religious policy exploited in *Leycesters Commonwealth*. The puritan preachers could be encouraged only within prescribed limits, beyond which there was danger of arousing the queen's displeasure and playing into the hands of the many enemies of the Reformed faction in Court and country. When the queen was informed of the irregularities at Southam, Leicester was forced himself to complain of the conduct of the preachers. And when a sermon was preached in Oxford in 1578 which condemned the suppression of the prophesyings, Leicester expressed his extreme displeasure and made no attempt to rescue the preacher from imprisonment by the high commissioners.[5]

Apart from the dangers it entailed, it is doubtful if presbyterianism can have corresponded with Leicester's interests. It certainly failed to engage his sympathy. His letter to Wood betrays the profoundest distaste for the carping zeal and uncharitable divisiveness of the extreme puritan spirit: 'he that wold be counted most a sainct I pray God be found a plain trew Christian.' Leicester supported the religious radicals principally because puritan preachers and magistrates were a sure safeguard against the danger of Catholic subversion; his church policy was the complement of the Protestant state policy which he derived from and shared with Walsingham. For this reason, principally, the puritan ministers were to be protected if possible from the penalties of any minor breach of the ecclesiastical laws. But those puritans who concentrated their attack on the English bishops rather than on the bishop of Rome were in a different category. By provoking what Thomas Norton called 'civil warres of the Church of God'[6] they aggravated the divisions of the Church, offended

---

[1] Goodman to Leicester, 28 July 1571, B.M., Add. MS. 32091, fos. 246–7.
[2] See p. 93 below.
[3] See p. 97 below.   [4] Read, *Walsingham*, ii. 265.
[5] Thomas Randolph to Leicester, 28 Aug. 1578, B.M., MS. Cott. Tit. B. vii, fo. 18v.
[6] *Seconde Parte of a Register*, i. 190–1.

the queen and brought the whole Reformed cause into disrepute. Leicester had
no sympathy for the divisive tendencies of puritanism.[1] Although he accepted
dedications of books from John Field in 1579 and 1581[2] and used his influence
to procure him an Oxford preaching licence,[3] this was significantly at a time
when the presbyterian leader was directing most of his energies into anti-
Catholic controversy.[4] When the bishops went to extreme lengths to impose
uniformity and silenced the preachers, Leicester laid the blame on the bishops;[5]
but when the preachers stood too nicely on points of controversy, or wantonly
attacked the government of the Church, he blamed them. The peace of the
Church was to be defended within the existing frame of government by tolerance
on the part of the bishops and by forbearance from the side of the preachers.
Leicester wanted the Protestant latitudinarianism of Grindal rather than the
severe discipline of Whitgift or, at the other extreme, the drastic revisions
demanded by the presbyterians.

It may be argued that Leicester had a financial motive for encouraging the
presbyterian movement. The opponents of the puritans commonly insinuated
that their great patrons in the Court befriended them only with the intention of
using them to despoil the Church. John Whitgift hinted at this as early as
1574,[6] and it became one of the stock arguments of his protégé and chaplain
Richard Bancroft. In his Paul's Cross sermon of 1589 Bancroft boldly declared:
'I am fully of this opinion, that the hope which manie men have conceived of
this spoile of bishops livings, of the subversion of Cathedrall churches, and of a
havocke to be made of all the church revenues, is the chefest and most principall
cause of the greatest schismes that we have at this day in our Church.'[7] The
argument was crudely distorted by seventeenth-century controversialists[8] but
has received a sophisticated restatement from a modern scholar.[9] After his

[1] Here I am in substantial agreement with Miss Rosenberg's opinion (pp.
274–7) that Leicester was primarily interested in the puritans as anti-Roman
protagonists; that it was 'the national consciousness of the puritan writers, rather
than their separatist tendencies' which he found useful.

[2] Philippe de Mornay du Plessis, tr. Field, *Treatise of the Church*; *A Caveat
for Parsons*.

[3] *Register of the University of Oxford*, ed. C. W. Boase and A. Clarke (Oxford,
1884–9), II. i. 149. See also Field's letter of thanks to Leicester (printed R. F.
Brinkley, *Nathan Field, the Actor-Playwright* (New Haven, 1928), pp. 148–9) and
the petitions sent to Leicester by Field's auditors at Aldermary after his suspension
in 1585. (*Seconde Parte of a Register*, i. 135 (misdated).)

[4] Rosenberg, pp. 243–56.

[5] At the Lambeth conference of Dec. 1584, Leicester said 'it was a pitifull
thing that so many of the best mynisters and painfull in their preching, stood to be
deprived for these things'. (*Seconde Parte of a Register*, i. 282.)

[6] See his sermon preached before the queen in that year (John Strype, *Life
and Acts of John Whitgift* (Oxford, 1822), i. 126) and his *Defense of the aunswere*
(*Works*, i. 11, ii. 389).

[7] *A Sermon preached at Paules Crosse* (1589), pp. 23-4. Cf. parallel statements
in a tract written perhaps seven years earlier (*Tracts ascribed to Richard Bancroft*,
ed. Albert Peel (Cambridge, 1952), pp. 59–60) and in *A Survay of the Pretended
Holy Discipline* (1593), pp. 244–6.

[8] Notably by Peter Heylyn.

[9] Christopher Hill, *Economic Problems of the Church from Archbishop Whitgift
to the Long Parliament* (Oxford, 1956), esp. pp. 14–47.

death, Leicester in particular was stigmatized as the type of the courtier who had championed the puritans for base designs of his own[1]—a charge already made in his lifetime by *Leycesters Commonwealth*.[2]

It is one thing to accuse Leicester of robbing the Church, but quite another to argue that he hoped for the dissolution of the temporalities of bishoprics and cathedral churches as the by-product of a presbyterian revolution. The first charge is certainly true, but there is little to be said for the second. If John Penry later dangled the material advantages of the destruction of episcopacy before the earl of Essex,[3] there is no evidence that Leicester devoted any serious attention to such a possibility. He perhaps hardly needed Bancroft's disingenuous warning[4] that once the presbyterians were in power, far from allowing their erstwhile patrons to plunder the Church, they were likely to insist on the restitution of church property already alienated to secular uses.[5]

Leicester's material interests lay in the preservation rather than the overthrow of the Elizabethan ecclesiastical establishment. It was to well-worn channels in the existing machinery of church government and patronage that he looked for financial relief. The period of the Reformation witnessed a continuous 'unofficial dissolution'[6] of the temporalities of the Church under the pressure of the Court which was profoundly secular and owed little directly to the presbyterian rejection of episcopacy.[7] The most common form which this process of secularization took was the securing by laymen of long leases of church land (normally for ninety-nine years) which were highly favourable to the farmer in an age of rising prices and the rapid depreciation of all fixed payments.[8] By an act of Elizabeth's first parliament, archbishops and bishops

---

[1] See Thomas Nashe, *Pierce Pennilesse His Supplication to the Divell* in *Works*, ed. R. B. McKerrow and F. P. Wilson (Oxford, 1958), i. 221–6, which represents Leicester as a bear scheming to fatten himself on ecclesiastical honey; Harington, pp. 62, 113–15, 171–2, 203; Walton (p. 39) accused Leicester of using the puritans 'by their means to bring such an *odium* upon the *Bishops*, as to procure an Alienation of their lands, and a large proportion of them for himself: which avaritious desire had so blinded his reason, that his ambitions and greedy hopes had almost put him into a present possession of *Lambeth-House*'.

[2] *Copie of a leter*, pp. 15, 68–9.

[3] *The Notebook of John Penry*, ed. Albert Peel (Camden Soc., 3rd ser., lxvii, 1944), pp. 90–2.

[4] *Sermon preached at Paules Crosse*, pp. 27–8; cf. *Tracts ascribed to Bancroft*, pp. 59–60.

[5] The same point is made in a possibly apocryphal anecdote which descended from Walter Travers through Archbishop Usher to the Maldon antiquary, William Plume: it was said that Leicester and his friends had agreed with Cartwright on the confiscation of the bishops' lands, until Cartwright told them that this would be sacrilege, whereupon they remembered that the bishops were their friends and gave them hospitality and broke off their negotiations with the presbyterians. (*Essex Rev.*, xiv. 161–2.)

[6] P. M. Hembry, 'The Bishops of Bath and Wells, 1535–1647: a social and economic study' (unpublished London Ph.D. thesis, 1956), p. ii.

[7] Hill, pp. 14 *seq.* Dr. Hembry has explored in detail the spoliation of church property in the diocese of Bath and Wells. See also Lawrence Stone, 'The anatomy of the Elizabethan aristocracy', *Econ. Hist. Rev.*, xviii (1948), 29–31.

[8] Hembry, *passim*. Many cases are referred to in F. O. White, *Lives of the Elizabethan Bishops of the Anglican Church* (1898). In 1581 Walsingham proposed

were forbidden to make leases of longer than three lives or thirty years or at less than the normal rent, except to the queen,[1] and in 1571 this prohibition was extended to the lands of deans and chapters and colleges.[2] But the effect of these statutes was no more than to provide for the centralization of these transactions through the Court, where those with the greatest influence found the richest pickings.[3] It was therefore through his influence with the queen that Leicester could best hope to acquire the profits of church lands. In 1587 he petitioned Elizabeth for a grant in fee-simple of lands to the annual value of £1,000 from four vacant dioceses, suggesting that the queen could compensate the bishoprics with impropriations to the same value,[4] as she was authorized to do by a statute of 1559.[5] There is some evidence that Leicester on occasions put direct pressure on the bishops to grant him leases or loans or that he took them as his reward for service.[6] There is therefore some foundation for the story later retailed by Archbishop Samuel Harsnet that Leicester and his faction had been in league to force the bishops and deans to part with their lands by ninety-nine year leases.[7] Among other sources of income which Leicester exploited were the fees of offices attached to bishoprics and cathedral churches which bishops and deans were glad to grant to a great courtier in return for his patronage. Leicester was steward to the archbishop of Canterbury (at a fee of £10), the bishop of Ely and the bishop of Bristol (at a fee of £4), reversionary steward to the bishop of London, high steward and Master of Game to the archbishop of York, Master of Game to the bishop of Coventry and Lichfield, steward to the dean and chapter of Norwich and to the dean and chapter of Durham.[8] The evidence suggests that these were the rewards which Leicester took after successfully preferring his candidate to high ecclesiastical office.[9] They were not, perhaps, the only rewards.[10]

to cover the cost of intervention in the Netherlands by converting a substantial proportion of the bishops' temporalities into fee-farms. (Read, *Walsingham*, ii. 94.)

[1] 1 Eliz., c. 19, cap. iv.   [2] 13 Eliz., c. 10, cap. ii.
[3] Hill, pp. 14–15.   [4] Strype, *Annals*, III. i. 689–90.
[5] 1 Eliz., c. 19, cap. i.

[6] Harington's report (p. 62) that the Master of the Horse (Leicester) 'swept some provender out of the manger of Winchester' may refer to the rent-charge of £100 given to Leicester by Horne. (See p. 63, n. 6 above.) Leicester is probably the 'great Lord in the Court' whom Harington reports (pp. 171–2) as forcing Abp. Young of York to lend him £1,000. He further charges Leicester (pp. 113–15) with joining with another courtier to force Bp. Godwin of Bath and Wells to make a 99-year lease of the rich manor of Banwell. In 1577 Leicester took advantage of the preferment of Bp. Barnes to Durham and the disgrace of the previous bishop (Pilkington) to obtain from the queen a lease of the coal-mines of Gateshead for his servant, Thomas Sutton. (Trevor-Roper, *ubi supra*, 54–5.)

[7] *Essex Rev.*, xiv. 161–2. Cf. Walsingham's project of 1581, p. xxxiii, n. 8 above.

[8] Collins, i. 45 ; Strype, *Annals*, III. i. 682 ; see references on p. xxi, n. 3 and p. xxii, notes 3, 6, 13.

[9] Leicester was appointed to the high stewardship of Norwich Cathedral two months after he had preferred George Gardiner to the deanery. (See p. 64, n. 13 above.)

[10] One may cite the case of a law-suit between the dean and chapter of Chester and the gentlemen who held disputed leases of the greater part of the lands of Chester Cathedral. The dean had initiated this suit for the recovery of the lands

In that puritans of all shades of opinion favoured some reduction in the status and power of the bishops, they assisted in Leicester's exploitation of the weakness of the Church; while those bishops who set themselves most resolutely against the puritans—notably Whitgift—were at the same time the outspoken defenders of the Church against the rapacious laity. In this sense Leicester's encouragement of puritanism was connected with his financial interests. But he was unlikely to serve the interests of the presbyterians by promoting the wholesale dismantling of an institution in which he had an almost proprietary interest.

This interest was much more than financial. Many of the bishops had been, or still were, Leicester's servants, and he treated them as such, delivering orders on the conduct of their dioceses which betray a low opinion of the men if not of their office. After a visit—or rather a visitation—to Northampton in 1578, he wrote to Bishop Scambler of Peterborough:

Remember, my Lord, how before you were bishopp you woulde finde faulte with negligence of bishopps, how much yow cryed out to have preachers and good ministers to be increased and carefully placed. And soe did you all almost that be now bishops. But let me now looke into your deedes, and behold in every diocese the want of preachers, nay the great discouragement that preachers finde at your handes . . . And you are noe more a private man; you have a great charge and therefore it behoveth you to have a great and marvellous diligence; not to live at home and teach or to looke only to your particular family . . . But soe it is for the moste parte amongst you all at this day throughout England, the more is the pitty, and to remedy this ye lack neyther power nor authority. Yow have both dignityes in name and power by jurisdiction. But my Lord, I neede not tell you the fault, you knowe it well enough. The care of this worlde truly hath choked you all yea allmost all . . . But look to it, my Lord, or else it will cost you more deare then all your goods will redeem againe.[1]

Bishop Overton of Coventry and Lichfield was of the stuff of which Leicester's bishops were made. As treasurer of Chichester he had written to his master:

Consyder with yourself I besech you what I am and what I have been towardes your Lordship. I am your chapleyn of olde; I have ben alwaies servisable at your commandement; I have been plyable to your letters and suytes; I have ben and am in case both able and ready to do you honor if you will use me.[2]

The presbyterians might address pragmatic appeals to the nobility and gentry, but they could not adopt this tone; nor could their doctrine of the Church be easily reconciled with the superiority which Leicester and others of the governing class instinctively assumed when dealing with the clergy. As high Calvinists

on Leicester's advice. Yet Leicester accepted from the fee-farmers a bribe of six years' rent of the lands in question in return for his good offices in having the case transferred from the exchequer to the privy council, where he saw that judgment was given in the fee-farmers' favour. (R. V. H. Burne, *Chester Cathedral from its Founding by Henry VIII to the Accession of Queen Victoria* (1958), pp. 72–5, 83–4.)

[1] Leicester to Scambler, 27 Sept. 1578, B.M., MS. Harl. 677, fos. 37–8. (On the basis of faulty copies this letter is sometimes mistakenly attributed to Sir Nicholas Bacon.) Cf. Leicester's peremptory command to Scambler to reinstate Arthur Wake as Master of St. John's Hospital, Northampton, 'as you intende to have me favorable in anye your requests hereafter, and as you will gyve me cause to contynue your frende and thinke well of you'. (P.R.O., S.P. 12/24/52 (2).)

[2] Overton to Leicester, 22 May 1571, De L'Isle and Dudley papers (Baskerville transcripts), i. 237.

they were as inflexibly opposed as Rome itself to the subordination of the Church
to magistrates and proclaimed their intention of restoring the integrity of
Christ's Kingdom.[1] Within a presbyterian commonwealth Leicester himself
would have been made subject to the Church's discipline, a point which he would
not have missed in reading Thomas Wood's letters. By contrast, the reforms in
diocesan organization commonly envisaged by more moderate puritans who
stopped short of presbyterianism, to which the exercises of prophesying rightly
belong, were certain to augment the authority in religious matters of the aristocracy and gentry.[2] Some of these projected reforms would have reduced the
wealth and social status of the bishops[3] and all of them proposed to dilute
episcopal jurisdiction either by multiplying the number of dioceses or by
delegating some of the bishops' powers to coadjutors or rural deans and to rural
synods.[4] Proposals which had much in common with such a programme were
put forward by the house of commons in 1581, energetically pursued by Sir
Francis Walsingham and Robert Beale, and seriously entertained by others in
the privy council.[5] The intention of these schemes was to restore the pastoral,
preaching character of the episcopal office, but the effect in Elizabethan society
would have been a further reduction in the authority of the bishops without the
substitution of any alternative form of church discipline which could have
stood on its own feet, and so to increase the Church's dependence upon the
secular authorities. Indeed such projects often gave the justice of the peace a

[1] The classical statements of English presbyterian theory are in Thomas
Cartwright's controversial writings against Whitgift (reprinted in a conflated text
in Whitgift's *Works* and abbreviated by D. J. McGinn in *The Admonition Controversy* (New Brunswick, 1949)) and in Walter Travers, *Ecclesiasticae Disciplinae et
Anglicanae Ecclesiae . . . Explicatio* (Heidelberg, 1574). English presbyterian doctrine on the relations of Church and Commonwealth is the subject of a monograph
by A. F. Scott Pearson: *Church and State: Political Aspects of Sixteenth-Century
Puritanism* (Cambridge, 1928).

[2] See an account of non-presbyterian ideas of reform in church government
and of the relation of the prophesyings to these projects in my 'Classical Movement', Ch. 3, ii, pp. 214–97.

[3] See, for example, William Turner, *The Huntyng of the Romishe Vuolfe* (Zurich,
1554), sig. Fii. Cf. an Elizabethan programme, surviving among Robert Beale's
papers, by which the dioceses were to be multiplied and the revenues of the old
sees divided between the new bishops and 'other good things'. The new bishops
were to receive an annual stipend of 200 marks besides a house and the profits of
visitation and justice. Cathedral and collegiate churches were to be dissolved and
their revenues diverted to the support of the ministry, education, the relief of the
poor and the repair of highways; bells and the lead from roofs were to be melted
down for munitions. (B.M., Add. MS. 48066 (Yelverton 72), fos. 2–14.) These
proposals were more drastic than many, but they represent the ideas of many
Reformers who wanted to retain the principle of subordination in the ministry
while removing the abuses of large dioceses and lordly bishops. They should be
compared with Northumberland's plan for the bishopric of Durham. (Trevor-
Roper, *ubi supra*, 50.)

[4] John Knox, *Works*, v. 518–19; John Aylmer, *An Harborowe for Faithfull and
Trewe Subjects* (Strasbourg, 1559), sig. O4; William Stoughton, *An Assertion for
True and Christian Church Policie* (Middelburg, 1604), pp. 13–14; John Rylands
Library, English MS. 374, fo. 28v; Hist. MSS. Comm., *Hatfield MSS.*, ii. 195–8;
P.R.O., S.P. 12/282/71.

[5] Collinson, 'Classical Movement', pp. 279–85.

watching brief over the conduct of church government and emphasized the shire rather than the diocese as the working unit of ecclesiastical organization. In one such proposal, the commissions of justices were to appoint six learned preachers from each county who were to assist the bishop in visiting, excommunicating and ordaining.[1] In another project of reform proposed by the chancellor of Norwich Cathedral, Thomas Becon, such justices as were zealous in religion were to help and fortify the bishops' coadjutors and to be 'present at their solemn assemblies or preachings'.[2] These proposals were sent either to Leicester or to the whole privy council by Becon's supporters among the puritan justices of Norfolk and Suffolk as an indication of 'his desire of good proceedings'.[3] Bishop Overton, who was Leicester's creature, later attempted a modest experiment on the same lines in his diocese of Coventry and Lichfield.[4] The prophesyings were essentially a first step in the partial delegation of the bishop's pastoral functions to permanent moderators of local synods who were rural deans or bishops' coadjutors in all but name.[5] The warm support which the country gentry and Leicester himself gave to these exercises is a sign that proposals for the moderate reform of the diocesan organization of the Church were much to the taste of the Elizabethan governing class. There is no evidence that the doctrinaire attack by the presbyterians on the principle of imparity in the ministry made the same appeal.

The conclusion drawn from this argument is that both discretion and self-interest disposed Leicester to favour the moderate puritans but deterred him from consciously or willingly patronizing the presbyterian movement. His religious outlook was substantially as he defined it to Wood, although we may put our own interpretation on some of his declared motives.

There is some evidence to suggest that Leicester was drawn closer to the more extreme wing of the puritan movement in the last four or five years of his life and as his influence in the Church and over its bishops waned. This decline had its beginnings in the suppression of the prophesyings and Archbishop Grindal's sequestration. There is a clue to the politics which may have been concealed behind these events in a statement appended to a near-contemporary copy of Grindal's famous letter to the queen that Elizabeth had been 'moved by Hatton and some other' to put down the exercises.[6] There seems little doubt that Sir Christopher Hatton had estimated the personal advantages of making the queen's views on church policy his own, perhaps in conscious rivalry to Leicester.[7] John Aylmer became bishop of London in 1577 by Hatton's means[8] and received instructions from the queen through Hatton

[1] P.R.O., S.P. 12/282/71.

[2] Hist. MSS. Comm., *Hatfield MSS.*, ii. 195–8.

[3] *Ibid.*, p. 198.

[4] W. P. M. Kennedy, *Elizabethan Episcopal Administration* (Alcuin Club Collections, 1924), iii. 161–72; *Seconde Parte of a Register*, i. 260–7; B.M., MS. Eg. 1693, fo. 118.

[5] Collinson, 'Classical Movement', pp. 235–40.

[6] Hist. MSS. Comm., *Hastings MSS.*, i. 433.

[7] Thomas Digges wrote at the end of the reign: '[Leicester] was no sooner dead, but Sir Christopher Hatton . . . bearing sway, Puritans were trounced and traduced as troublers of the state.' (*Humble Motives*, pp. 24–5.)

[8] Aylmer to Hatton, 8 June 1578, 20 Mar. 1582, Harris Nicolas, *Memoirs of Sir Christopher Hatton* (1847), pp. 59, 240.

'to correct offenders on both sides which swerve from the right path of obedience . . . both the Papist and the Puritan'.[1] Later, as his secretary has recorded, John Whitgift 'lincked himself in a firme league of friendship' with Hatton,[2] who proved to be his only constant supporter in the struggle with the puritan ministers over subscription in 1584.[3] Richard Bancroft was chaplain to Whitgift and Hatton in turn, and Hatton made use of his expert knowledge of the doctrines and behaviour of the puritans.[4] It is not too much to say that both the lord chancellor and the future archbishop used the exposure of presbyterianism to further their own careers.[5]

Apparently it was not at first clear to Leicester that Whitgift's rise to power would lead to a more severe repression of the puritans than had yet been seen and the curtailing of his own influence in the Church. Whitgift's secretary and biographer noted Leicester as one of his master's especial friends before his elevation to Canterbury.[6] According to Robert Beale, both Leicester and his brother had satisfied themselves when Whitgift was bishop of Worcester that he was disposed to encourage a preaching ministry and to deal leniently with nonconformists.[7] But once at Lambeth Whitgift's strenuous efforts to stamp out nonconformity and to restore the dignity and independence of the clergy rapidly won Leicester's hostility. Paule tells us that when he and other privy councillors 'saw that they might not sway (as formerlie in the restraint of Archbishop Grindal) and prefer whom they listed unto ecclesiastical promotions: they with some other linked themselves against the Archbishop'.[8] In December 1584 Leicester attempted to arbitrate between the bishops and the puritan ministers by calling a two-day conference at Lambeth between representatives of the two sides.[9] Paule is not to be believed when he says that this experience satisfied Leicester of the justness of the archbishop's proceedings.[10] Three months later Leicester delivered a vigorous attack on Whitgift in the house of lords.[11] Later in the same year Whitgift snubbed him by refusing his request to grant Thomas Cartwright a preaching licence on his return to England from the Netherlands.[12] Leicester's ecclesiastical influence suffered its most severe set-back when, in his absence in the Netherlands, not only Whitgift but his supporters Lord Buckhurst and Lord Cobham, all enemies of Leicester, were admitted to the privy council, apparently by Burghley's means.[13] Thereafter,

[1] Aylmer to Hatton, 28 May 1578, Nicolas, p. 56.
[2] Paule, p. 36.
[3] Whitgift to Hatton, 9 May, 17 July 1584, Nicolas, pp. 371-2, 379-80. See my 'Classical Movement', pp. 389-478.
[4] Bancroft helped to draft the parliamentary speech which Hatton delivered against the presbyterians after Anthony Cope had presented the presbyterian bill and book ir. Feb. 1587. (Collinson, 'Classical Movement', p. 575 n. 1.)
[5] *Ibid.*, pp. 1040-7.
[6] Paule, p. 21.
[7] Beale to Whitgift, (early summer) 1584, B.M., Add. MS. 48039 (Yelverton 44), fos. 1r, 2r.
[8] Paule, p. 31.
[9] *Seconde Parte of a Register*, i. 275-83.
[10] Paule, pp. 30-1.
[11] J. E. Neale, *Elizabeth I and her Parliaments, 1584-1601* (1956), p. 81.
[12] Scott Pearson, *Thomas Cartwright*, p. 231.
[13] Paule, p. 36; Thomas Morgan to Mary queen of Scots, 31 Mar. 1586, Hist. MSS. Comm., *Hatfield MSS.*, iii. 136-7.

Paule tells us, Whitgift's 'courses . . . were not so much crossed nor impeached as heretofore; but by reason of his daily attendance and accesse he thus oftentimes gave impediment to the Earles designments in Clergie causes'.[1] In 1585 Whitgift secured Thomas Bickley's preferment to the bishopric of Chichester in spite of the fact that as archdeacon of Stafford he had won Leicester's enmity by suspending one of his chaplains for nonconformity.[2] In 1587 Leicester failed to secure the translation of Bishop Piers from Salisbury to Durham.[3] Walton preserves the tradition of a quarrel between Leicester and Whitgift in the queen's presence after the archbishop 'by his interest with her Majesty' had 'put a stop to the Earl's sacreligious designs'. After both had left the room, Whitgift 'made a sudden and seasonable return' and successfully pleaded the integrity of the Church and its wealth.[4] Whether or not such a scene took place, the story accurately points the direction in which the Church was now moving. Crown and bishops were discovering their mutual dependence and were drawing together in a protective alliance against the puritans and the courtiers who had attempted to direct the affairs of the Church to their own advantage.[5]

These developments may well have thrust Leicester into a somewhat closer alliance with the puritans who were resisting Whitgift. He was probably impelled in the same direction by the increasing Catholic danger and by his involvement in the war in the Netherlands, which the puritans regarded as a crusade for the Gospel. There is some indication of this in Leicester's choice of chaplains and servants in his later years. Whereas in the fifteen-seventies he had employed men of moderate puritan churchmanship, he now seemed to favour presbyterians. After trying in vain to obtain a preaching licence for Thomas Cartwright, he made him Master of his hospital at Warwick.[6] He took to the Netherlands as his chaplains John Knewstub[7] and Humfrey Fen,[8] befriended Dudley Fenner[9] and employed as a secretary John Hart, an Oxford puritan.[10] All these men were deeply implicated in the presbyterian classical movement and Fen and Hart applied to John Field and the *classis* in London for approval of their appointment under Leicester.[11]

Nevertheless, it remains doubtful whether Leicester ever concerned himself with the activities of the organized presbyterian movement or would have sympathized with them if he had. Leicester was first and last a courtier and it

[1] Paule, p. 37.

[2] Strype, *Whitgift*, i. 464–5.

[3] Strype, *Annals*, III. i. 682–4.

[4] Walton, pp. 46 *seq.*

[5] Hill, pp. 31–5.

[6] Scott Pearson, *Thomas Cartwright*, pp. 290–304.

[7] Alexander Southaicke to Walsingham, 27 Oct. 1585, P.R.O., S.P. 12/183/52; *Leycesters Correspondence*, ed. James Bruce (Camden Soc., xxvii, 1844), p. 238 n.; Hist. MSS. Comm., *Ancaster MSS.*, p. 25.

[8] B.M., Add. MS. 48014 (Yelverton 14), fo. 161. In July 1585 Leicester asked Whitgift to relieve Fen of a suspension from preaching. (B.M., Add. MS. 22473, fo. 246.)

[9] Rosenberg, p. 242. Fenner was preacher to the Merchant Adventurers at Middelburg in the years in which Leicester was in the Netherlands.

[10] Bancroft, *Survay of the Pretended Holy Discipline*, p. 368.

[11] *Ibid.*, pp. 304, 368; Richard Bancroft, *Daungerous Positions and Proceedings* (1593), pp. 122–3.

was in the Court that he pursued his ambitions, rather than in the plots of a minority of puritan extremists. In the last months of his life he was pressing a suit with the queen for a grant of episcopal lands for the repair of his 'decayed estate'.[1]

[1] Walsingham to Leicester, 5 Mar., 8 June 1588, B.M., MS. Cott. Tit. B. vii, fos. 32, 34.

LETTERS OF THOMAS WOOD,
PURITAN, 1566–1577[1]

[*fo. 1r*]

The copie of my father Captaine Thomas Wood his lettres to certaine noble personages and other his good freinds out of the copies under his owne hand; which, being in loose papers, I have here exemplified for myne owne encouragement and good of mine; that both I and they may tread in his religious steps, being a strong engagment to godlines, having so worthy a pattern before us, as it wilbe a foule blott and a double staine to degenerate from the good courses of a parent so religious.

Wood to Sir William Cecil, 29 March 1566.

[*fo. 13r*]

To the Lord Treasurer [*sic*] SIR WILLIAM CECILL.

Though our neglect or rather contempt (Right Honorable) of the plentifull preaching of [*fo. 13v*] God's word, especially here in London, hath justly deserved that the same should utterly be taken from us; yet such cannot be excused in his presence as have bene instruments to provoke the Queen's Majestie by hir bishops to put from their livings and ministery (and so from the feeding of their flocke) 36 godly men at one instant, amongst which were divers that traveyled in preaching of the word with more zeall and dilligence then many others of greater callyng, by meane whereof all exercises almost of interpretacion of the scriptures used every morning and evening in sundry churches within this city are utterly overthrowne; and in some places nether preacher nor curett left to say the common service; besides the utter overthrow of a most frutfull and comfortable exercise named prophesying used once a week at St. Peter's, where 2 or 3 hundred were assembled before th'accustomed houre on Thursday last and, seeing themselves disapointed, departed, not without abundance of teares, to the great discomfort of all godly hartes. These three dayes past, the accustomed exercise at St. Tantlyns[2] hath bene manteyned at five of the clocke in the morning by such godly young men as having no spirituall [*fo. 14r*] lyvings were not called before the Commissioners,[3] but how long it will continewe the Lord knoweth, for all those that ordinarily furnish the same are amongst the rest discharged. The pitifull complaint of all the godly here, which many utter dayly with teares and greif of hart, with the wonderfull rejoysing also of the Papistes, enemyes to God and the Prince, move me not only to signify this much unto yow, but also to let yow understand that in common opinion and brute of all sortes of men (so farr as I heare) yow are taken and named to be one of the cheife instruments and procurers of this present calamity, whether worthely or unworthely God and your owne conscience best knoweth. But howsoever it be, I am as it were forced, both in conscience and respect of sundry benefites received

---

[1] In transcribing the letters I have preserved the original spelling, but have modernized punctuation and capitalisation and have extended abbreviations and suspensions. The letters are printed in chronological order.

[2] St. Antholin's.

[3] But these too were silenced by 12 Apr. (*Parker Correspondence*, pp. 277–9.)

at your handes, to advertise yow hereof. Which I protest before the lyving God I have done without advice or consent of any, trusting that yow will accept it in no worse parte then I have ment it and also that yow wilbe a meane to the uttermost of your power to salve in time this so greivous a soare. And thus I most humbly take my leave, [*fo.* 14*v*] wishing unto yow the increase of honor and true felicity. At London this 29 of March, 1566.

Sir William Cecil to Wood, 31 March 1566.

The Lord Treasurer [*sic*] his answere.

Mr Wood, I hartely thanke yow for your frendly admonition of me in such thinges as yow heare me by many touched and condemned, as though I were the cheif instrument and procuror of a calamity which you doe describe to be in that cittie by inhibition of the ministery, preaching and of the interpretation of the Scriptures, which yow call prophecying. And though in slaundering me herein some may use more liberty then truthe and more mallice then charity, yet finding my conscience free not only from the occasion of that which yow mention but from any allowance or intention to have ether ministery of the word or of sacraments empayred, I doe rest the more quiett, not dowting but in this, as in many other God hath, so now he will give me some portion of patience that I may effectually say '*Deo subiecta est anima mea, quoniam ab ipso patientia mea.*'[1] If I shold looke for that which I have through God's goodnes merited of the faithfull in promoting the edification of this His Church [*fo.* 15*r*] and compare it with these popular noyses rising of mallicious plantings, I should then have a disquiet mind. But some contentation it is to modest men, that meaning well receave evill report, to heare the saying of our Lord: '*Vae cum benedixerint vobis homines etc.*'[2] God of his mercy inspire us all with his spirit of myldnes and symplicity and increase his Church with ministers hable to performe that which the Apostle earnestly warneth: '*Fratres magis satagite ut per bona opera certam vocationem vestram faciatis.*'[3] But I hold best with yow to end any longer writing, seing my intention was but to thank yow and to assure yow my conscience is free from any fault in this matter. At Grenwich, the last of March 1566.

Your assured good frend,

W. CECILL.

Wood to Francis Cave, Esq., LL.D., of Bagrave, Leicestershire, undated.

[*fo.* 19*v*]
To MR. DR CAVE.

Sir, I have bene earnestly requested by yor cousin Dilkes to speake or write to yow in a matter wherein I was lothe to deale. And yet if I had utterly refused he had ere this communicated the whole with Mr Hastings[4] and requested his

[1] Psalm lxii. 5.
[2] Luke vi. 26.
[3] 2 Peter i. 10.
[4] Francis Hastings, brother of the earl of Huntingdon and the leading personality in Leics. during his brother's prolonged absences in the North. (Cross, 'The Career of Huntingdon', p. 251.)

lettres unto yow, for the staye whereof I thought good to lett yow knowe bothe what I have heard and thinke in that behalf. Your cosin Dilkes, understanding that yow are purposed shortly to send your sonne Mr Thomas into Cornewall to make sale of all his brother-in-lawe's woodes, not only to the great hinderance of his said brother, but also of those whom God hath appointed to succeed him, thinketh it a very hard and extreme dealing, consydering the great and lardge sommes of money by yow receaved by the space of thirty yeares or more, by what title yow best knowe, and if it be noe better then it is reported I wishe yow shold in tyme consider of it, lest it be a burden to your conscience hereafter. For if it be not good and just before God it is not the lawe of the realme that will dischardge yow in his presence. And surely I take this to be a certeyn and infal[*fo. 20r*]lable rule bothe in religion and common reason, that a man can never dispose justly and lawfully of that which he commeth unjustly by (unles it be in restoring it to the right ownor). But your predicessor (as it is said) did subtelly and wickedly defete his simple brother and his children of all that his inheritance, and therefore could not justly nor lawfully dispose thereof as he did. For it is a maxime (as I have heard) in yor law:[1] '*Quod ab initio non valet, tractu temporis convalescere not potest.*' And yet by that title, which yow knowe and have confest to others (as it is sayd) to be noght, yow have during your wife's life kept the most parte of the whole benefitt to your self, and also have procured a further estate in parte of it during your owne life, besides other devises that were drawne (though not performed) to the furder damage of the partie. Yf these thinges be true, whether yow have delt herein with that good simple man as yow wold have bene delt with if yow had bene in his case (which is the surest rule to judge all our doings by) I leave it to the consideracion of your owne conscience. For this yow knowe is the expresse commandement of Christ, that we do to others as we wold be done unto, *Luk* 6; which precept hath moved me to be thus plaine with yow, lest, as yow have heard and seen God's sharpe [*fo. 20v*] and speedy judgments executed upon your predecessor and his seed, he be also offended with yow for communicating with so wicked a facte. Yow knowe Christ's wordes, 'what availeth a man to wynn all the world and lose his owne soule'; then the which nothing ought to be so deare unto us. God graunt yow may consider of it accordingly and direct yow to doe that which may continue his manifolde mercies bestowed upon yow and yours. Thus trusting both yow and Mr Thomas will take in good parte this which of good will and care of your well doing I have writt, I commit yow and all yours to the grace of God. From Leicester etc.

Wood to Thomas Cave of Bagrave, Esq., undated.

The answere to Mr Thomas Caves lettre.

Yf that yow tolde me at your being here had bene of effect I had bene satisfied indeed; but when upon better consideracion I finde the contrary, I thought good to let yow understand that I was not so simple but that I was able to discerne betwixt a shadowe and a substance, which was the cheif cause of my writing to yow then. Where yow say I put all the fault in Dilkes, if you remember well I only chardged him with one point of the lettre, which yow with sharp wordes denyed, and yet he hath your owne [*fo. 21r*] hand (as he saith) to showe

---

[1]Cave was a Doctor of Civil Laws.

against yow. At our departing, I desired yow to showe your father that if I had
failed in the pointes of my lettre, it was through ill informacion, not naming
any man. For of this matter I heard something before Dilkes knewe of it and
also before yow were borne. Though indeed I have heard of him more then I
understood before in some respects, as partly in my first lettre is touched, which
he is ready to justefie. To conclude: I am sorie that my good and godly meaning
towards your father is no better accepted. And for my lettre to yow, I trust my
motion therein was neither ungodly nor unreasonable, if thinges may be weyed
with indifferency. If any thing in my lettres can justly be reproved I will
willingly acknowledg my ignorance; if not, I hope they wilbe better thought of
hereafter or at the least that your father will not be offended with me (as yow
write he is) whom I will see (God willing) so soone as I may, and wold now have
write to him, but that I knowe yow will make him privie to this as yow have done
to the rest. And thus I comitt yow etc.

Wood to Thomas Cave, 9 March 1573.

To SIR THOMAS CAVE KNIGHT [sic].

Because I purpose (God willing) with my wife to ride to morow towards
London for the better recovery of my health, being thereunto advised by a godly
phisition, [fo. 21v] I thought good of good will (how ever yow take it) to let yow
knowe what I have seene since I last spake with yow. First, I will tell yow that
which will seem strange unto yow, as it did to me, and yet trewe. There was
never a letter that yow wrote to your father or Mr Wilde that concerned Mr
Randoll, but if they once came to his handes and that he colde by any means
gett opportunity, he copied them out of his owne hand playnly and distinctly,
besides divers other indentures and articles writ by others, the knowldege [sic]
whereof I have not sought, but they have bene brought unto me. And to let
passe other of your lettres, I will only note this: that in one of them yow advised
your father for his better assurance to offer unto Randoll vl. a yeare annuitie,
to th'end that he should not only confirme his estate, but also Mr Wilde's; and
that yow thought it might be very easily compassed. What this dealing ment I
leave it rather to your conscience and hart, fearing God (which is advertised
dayly by his ministers as well in this as in other cases) then entre my self into
judgement of it. God give us grace to see and follow the right in all matters,
as well to the proffet of our neighbours as our owne. But to let this passe: it
appeareth also [fo. 22r] by the deede yow devised (which with great vehemencie
of wordes yow denied unto me and yet it is to be shewed of your owne hand)
that if your father's conscience had not bene the better, Randall had bene a pore
Randall at this day. Yea I doe verely beleve if it had not bene more by others
persuasions then of your father's owne inclination, he wold never have sought
that at that simple mans handes which he now cleymeth, such I knowe to be his
good and godly nature, whereof I wish yow the like portion. I have not writ
any thing to him of this matter now, for that yow requested and I promised the
contrary. But if yow continue in your extremities, I will from hensforth be free
from this promise, and will bothe write and speak as occasion shalbe offered and
as to the dutie of a faithfull frend appertayneth. And for my part (God willing)
I will performe that which yow in words protested touching your frendship
towards me: namly to beare my good will to your father and all his during my

life. Which thing I never performed better then in this case, how ever yow take it. And so fare yow hartely well, being sory that yow departed hense in such collor, where no such cause was given, as I will alwayes be ready to avouch without any feare to incurr the danger of an action of the case. At Leicester this present Munday, 9 March 1572[3].

Yours in Christ,
T. Wood.

Wood to Richard Beaumont, Esq., of Whitley, Yorkshire, 12 December 1573.

[fo. 18r]
To Mr Beaumont.

Mr Beaumont, since I heard of the death of of [sic] my cosyn Thomas Wood, I heard also that he hath made yow overseer of his last will, as his sister in lawe had done of hers before. Yf it be so, I praye God yow may better dischardge this then yow have done the other, or els yow will have an heavy accompt to make to the just revenger of all injuries, especially when they are committed against the widoes and fatherles. Adam's excuse will not then serve, who when God charged him with the breach of his Commandement answered: 'The woman thou gavest me did deceive me.' It may be that as wicked Jezabell could not be satisfied till for the pleasure of her husband she had gotten pore Naboth's vineyeard, even so it is not unlike but that your wyfe could not be at rest nor would not suffer yow to be in quiett till for the preferment of hir brother (as she thought) she had caused yow to take from those fatherles and motherles children their vineyeard, the Thornes. God grant hir, if this were hir fault, a better end then Jezebell had. But beholde the just judgment and plague of God: how that, very shortly after, your brother was not onely [fo. 18v] forced to leave the farme, but also to flye his contry to the great shame of yow all. And yet, not satisfied with this injurie nor warned by this punishment, when as that pore simple man had sold certaine cattle for iiiil. xvis. iiiid. a practise was devised, no doubt by one of your parasites, that the monye should be brought to yow to keepe, which, when yow of policie (as it seemeth) had refused, your wife required to have the custodye of it, as olde Eastwood confeste unto me in your house; and shortly after, she delivered it to her brother, so as when the pore man should have had his monye, he was borne in hand that he had lent it to Netleton and so lacketh so much of his portion to this day. Was it likely that he wold sell his cattle and lend the mony to him that had bene one of the cheif instruments of his undoing? But he was indeed so ill handled amongst yow that he was almost berefte his wittes, which appeared plainly in that the said Eastwood tolde me and others in your house that he solde Netleton so much stuffe for xxs. as was worth five poundes, and in th'end (as I heard) was paide with an olde frese cote. Was this, Mr Beaumont, ether the parte of a good overseer, or of a good Justice, not only to take from the pore orphanes a good [fo. 19r] lease, wherein was nere xxv yeares to come (as he that made it will justefie) being reserved in the sale, as appeareth by the indentures of covenants, which I sawe at my being there under your hand and seall, but also to suffer your wife and brother so wickedly to deceyve so simple a man? Thinke yow that God will not revenge these so manifest injuries without repentance and spedy restitution? Deceyve not your

self for God will not be mocktt. I will speake nothing of the xxl. yow held in your
hands seven yeares, which no doubt yow wold still have kept from them (with
as good conscience as the rest) if with much a doe I had not gotten a bill of your
hand for it. I have not rehearsed these thinges of any malice or ill will, for God
is my witnes I have alwayes wisht yow well; but only (if yow have any remorse
of conscience) to move yow in time to prevent God's wrathe, which hangeth over
your head till these injuries be redressed. And surely, if this my frendly admonition take no effect, and that God spare me life and health that I may be able to
travaill, I will ere it be a yeare to an end make the best in Yorksheir knowe as
much and more then I have here written, which I wold be sorie to be driven
unto for your owne credite sake. And so fare yow well. From Groby beside
Leicester, this xiith of December 1573.

By him that wisheth yow well in the Lord,

THO: WOOD.

Wood to William Whittingham, Dean of Durham, 15 February 1574.

[*fo. 15v*]
To MR WHITTINGHAM, Deane of Durham.

Salutem in Domino. Albeit yow liked not, Mr Whittingham, to satisfie my
desire in touching my man, yet I thought having so convenient a messenger
yow would have vouchedsafe to have answered my lettre. As for the partie by
whom yow promest to write, I have not heard any thing of him. But I thinke
my former plainnes hath offended yow, and thereby the old proverb verifyde,
Veritas etc. Surely if I had writt otherwise I shold have dissembled, and therefore I thought best, as I have since our first acquaintance (for God's good giftes
in yow) loved yow interely, so to deale with yow bothe frendly and plainly. For
if ever I did or thought yow harme, it was in procuring the lettre whereof this
inclosed maketh mention; which I doe the rather send unto yow for that I
have heard to my greif the good Earll of Warwick once or twise complaine of
your ingratitude, who as yow best knowe hath well deserved at your handes.
But to let this passe: I will once againe make a new sute unto yow in the behalfe
of our persequuted brethren, desiring yow as yow tender God's glorie and their
comforte not to denie it me. It is to sende unto me Mr. Calvin's lettre of his
judgment touching the booke of service, which both men and women[1] are
urged by subscription to approve, as that there is [*fo. 16r*] nothing in it evill or
repugnant to the word of God. Se what it is to yelde never so litle, specially in
matters of religion, against the which yow have often godly inveyed bothe
publiquely and privatly. As for th'apparell, there is now skarce any inforcement
at all unles it be for the surples. But whosoever denieth to subscribe to the boke,
to prison he goeth, whether he be minister or other; of which number our

---

[1]In London both lay men and women known to be puritans were called to
subscribe. (*Seconde Parte of a Register*, i. 93.) The preacher Edward Dering
wrote to his brother on 24 Dec. 1573 of his wife, Anne Locke: 'My wyfe hathe bin
(I thanke God) in no troble, neither was any towardes her that I knowe of. Yf any
fall, God hathe made her riche in grace and knowledge to gyve accompt of her
doynge.' (Kent County Record Office, Maidstone, MS. Dering CI/1, fo. 6r.)

brother Mr Fuller is one.[1] And as yow were the first that made me and many others mislike with the said boke, so are the corruptions thereof best knowne unto yow; being as touching th'order therof (as yow have affirmed) papisticall, and many thinges in it superstitious, yea and something that is therin allowed mere wicked, so as upon the notes yow drewe out of it Mr Calvin termed them in his said lettre *faeces papisticae*.[2] That therfore not only they which suffer for that truthe may, as they have heard of it, so to their more full contentacion see it indeed, as also to stopp the mouthes of the adversaries and to perswade some that yet are ignorant of the corruptions therof; for these causes (I say) in their behalf I desire it; or at the least a coppie of it of your owne hand, for that his is hard to read, as yow knowe. And I doe protest unto yow before the Lord that none (no, not my brother Williams[3]) shall knowe but that I found it amongst my papers, as [*fo. 16v*] yow are not ignorant that bothe that and the rest were in my custody till my departure from Geneva. There is a lettre of yours in many men's handes writt to the Earll of Leicester,[4] wherein after divers and many learned argumentes and authorities you conclude thus: that whosoever shall weare any of the popish garments either for holines or pollicie, *Anti-Christi mancipium est*. And as that lettre (as also your former doctrine) hath bene a comfort and confirmacion to many, so hath your doings to the contrary bene no small offence to the Church of God; and what the danger thereof is, yow knowe better than I. Yet many do hope that seeing thinges growe dayly from worse to worse, and that for the maintenance of the thinges above mentioned the pore famished shepe of Christ are daylie spoiled of their godly and learned shephardes by xii at a clap in some one dyocesse;[5] they hope, I say, that God will not only give yow hartie repentance for your backsliding, but also restore yow to your former zeale and boldnes to acknowledg all that truthe which heretofore yow have taught to others, which I pray God I may live to see and that speedely. You know th'old proverb: '*Mora trahit periculum*'.

[1] William Fuller, sometime of Princess Elizabeth's household at Hatfield and an elder of the exile congregation at Geneva. (Garrett, pp. 158–9.) There are references to Fuller's imprisonment in the Counter and his removal to house-arrest in Mar. 1574 in letters of Thomas Wilcox to Anthony Gilby. (Cambridge Univ. Library, MS. Mm. 1. 43, pp. 439, 441.) Cf. Fuller's own 'book to the Queen', 1586. (*Seconde Parte of a Register*, ii. 49–64.) Wilcox speaks of 'divers óthers . . . prisoners' and names William White, a vociferous layman with separatist leanings, and Robert Johnson, preacher of St. Clement's without Temple Bar.

[2] The original passage to which Wood refers runs as follows: 'Nunc quum eversis illis principiis [the form of religion established in England under Edward VI], alibi instituenda vobis sit Ecclesia, et liberum sit formam, quae ad usum et aedificationem Ecclesiae maxime apta videbitur, de integro componere: quid sibi velint nescio, quos faecis Papisticae reliquiae tantopere delectant.' (Printed by Laing in Knox, *Works*, iv. 51–3, from the text in Calvin's *Epistolae et Responsae* (Amsterdam, 1667), p. 98. Cf. Whittingham's translation in *Brieff Discours off the Troubles Begonne at Franckford*, pp. xxxiiii–xxxvii.)

[3] William Williams, Wood's brother-in-law and with him an elder at Geneva.

[4] Whittingham to Leicester, 28 Oct. 1564. Strype, *Parker*, iii. 76–84.

[5] This seems to be an exaggeration, unless the county of Northants. (diocese of Peterborough) is meant. Elsewhere outside London, the 'inquisition' disturbed few puritans. (Collinson, 'Classical Movement', pp. 169–72.)

There are three lately dead by the bishops' imprisonement,[1] whereof Evans a godly brother was [*fo.* 17r] one.[2] See what mischeif the maintenance of their lordly pompe and desire to make their sonnes gentlemen hath brought them unto.[3] And will yow for any wordly respects joyne handes with such bloudy persequters? God forbid, and be it farr from yow (as it is from a remnant of your old acquaintance, which God be praised have not yelded, but stood faithfully for the defence of his cause) as to the sincerity and simplicity of his word appertayneth. There were lately burnt in the Stationers' Hall at London so many of Mr. Beza's Confessions in English as could be found amongst the said stationers. The cause is imputed to the translation, but as I heare credibly Fitz, the doer thereof, is well able to avouche that it is faithfully translated according to the French.[4] The Warden of that compeny in his protestacion then affirmed that the writinges of Mr. Beza and his Master was almost in as great credit with many as the Bible.[5] And there is a brute in London that our Geneva Bibles shalbe called in;[6] if that be true, other thinges will follow ere it be long. God's will be done with mercie, to whose providence I committ yow and yours. From Groby, this 15 of February 1573[4].

Yours in the Lord,

THO: WOOD.

[1]Wilcox, who wrote to Gilby two weeks earlier (Cambridge Univ. Library, MS. Mm. 1. 43, p. 439) reports the same: 'Three of them that they have imprisoned' were 'dead allreadie'. These did not include Robert Johnson, preacher of St. Clement's, who died in the Westminster Gatehouse in Apr. (*A Parte of a Register* (Middelburg or Edinburgh ? 1593), pp. 94–118.)

[2]Possibly Lewis Evans, a Roman Catholic controversialist converted to Protestantism in the fifteen-sixties and the author of a number of anti-Catholic pamphlets in circulation among the puritans. (*D.N.B.*, *s.v.* Evans; *Short Title Catalogue* nos. 10588–10593; Cambridge Univ. Library, MS. Mm. 1. 43, p. 439.)

[3]See p. 19, n. 5 below for some discussion of the argument in puritan controversy which attributed the schism in the Church to the worldly ambition of the higher clergy.

[4]Theodore Beza's *A Briefe and Piththie* [sic] *Summe of the Christian Faith made in the Forme of a Confession* was translated by Robert Fills and printed in 1563, 1566[?], 1572 and 1585. (*Short Title Catalogue* nos. 2007–12.) That Wood renders his name 'Fitz' is sufficient indication of the fancifulness of Garrett's suggestion (pp. 152–3) that Fills may have been the father of John Field. No copies survive of the edition which Wood says was burned at Stationers' Hall in Feb. 1574. The fault of the translation, the reason given for burning the tracts, may have involved some alteration in the section on the ministry of the Church, which as translated in the earlier editions (fo. 108v) contains an acknowledgment of the legitimacy of episcopacy. Fills in a dedicatory epistle addressed to Huntingdon claimed (sig. Avii): 'I have added nothyng of myne owne, but symple, and playnelye, according to my small understandyng, I have kept the wordes and meanyng of the authoritie, as neare as our English wyl suffer mee, rather shewing mee selfe homelye and playne, then by over much fynenesse to dissent from the mynde of hym, who in the feare of God and for his Bretherns sake set it foorth.'

[5]This was a common saying at the time. (See, for example, *Seconde Parte of a Register*, i. 97.)

[6]Until 1576 the Geneva Bible was not printed in England, although there had been three successive Geneva editions of 1560, 1562 and 1570. The *Brieff Discours off the Troubles Begonne at Franckford* in its concluding pages (pp. cxcii–cxciiii) gave prominence to an appeal for the reprinting and more general dispersal of the Geneva Bible.

Postscript. Yf without all fayned excuses yow will satisfye the godly request of your brethren by sending the said lettre, this bearer Mr Parker of Leicester [*fo. 17v*] will savely bring it to me, who hath requested me to crave your helpe for his furtherance and expedition in a sute he hath there, as the justnes of his cause shall require.

The coppie of my Lord of Leicester lettres before in this former lettre mentioned.[1]

My good brother, I have now at the last gotten Captaine Reads bill dispatched, and the same being delivered to his man under the Seall, I thought good like as to let yow understand of that, so of your request for Mr Whittingham for the Deanery of Durham, whereunto the Queen's Majestie hath also condiscended, which she wold not I assure yow do nether at myne or Mr Secretaries sute, but upon your[2] last lettres written in his behalfe hir Highnes hath graunted it unto him. He is therefore next unto hir Majestie to thanke yow for it. And thus with my most harty commendacions I bid yow as my self farewell. At the Court the 14[3] of July 1563.

Your loving brother,
R. D.

The postscript of his owne hand.

I pray yow in your next lettres give her Majestie thankes for the favour she hath shewed Mr Whittingham for your sake.

And looke well to your health my deare brother.

Wood to the Earl of Warwick, 4 August 1576.

[*fo. 1r*]
This letter was sent unto that right noble Lord Ambrose, Earle of Warwick.[4]

The mighty comfort of the Holy Ghost for salutacions.

Many verie ill and dishonorable brutes (Right Honourable and my singular good Lord) are spred abrode of my Lord your brother, which I doe ofte heare to my great greif; specially now of late touching the overthrowe of a most godly exercise at Southam in Warwicksheir cheifly maintayned by Mr. Oxenbridge,[5] a zealous and godly learned man, which is commonly reported to be his Lordship's only deed. As this is a matter that toucheth the glory of God (which all men ought to promote) so is the taking away thereof no small greif and discouragement to all good men, who by this feare also the taking awaye of the rest. I have therefore thought it my duty [*fo. 1v*] (considering how much I am bound to his Honour and your Lordship) to advertise him thereof, that wayeing with himself what an ungodly fact he hath comitted (if this be true) he

---

[1] This letter occurs also in the 'Life of Mr William Whittingham', pp. 13–14. The text printed here bears the correct date and appears to be the better copy.

[2] The other copy has 'the'.

[3] The other text has '24th'. But see Warwick to Dudley, 24 July, P.R.O., S.P. 70/61/967.

[4] This heading appears as a marginal note in the MS.

[5] See a biographical note on Oxenbridge, p. 59 , n. 5 above.

may be moved to repentance and to labour most earnestly for the speedy restoring of the said exercise, the taking awaye whereof (I feare) hath taken from him the harts of all godly men, that knowe what singular benefitt doth daylie growe by such most godly exercises, the like whereof were never erected in England before. I have sent your Lordship his lettre unsealed, to thintent yow may peruse it and so cause it to be sealed and delivered to his Lordship's owne hands. It is plaine, and peradventure may be thought to plaine; but if the rest touching his ungodly life (as the common report goeth) be as true as that before mencioned, God's judgments in the opinion of all godly men without speedy repentance is not far of, and therefore had need to be plainly dealt withall, that in time they may be prevented if God so will; to whose great mercies I commit your good Lordship with my good Lady and all yours, beseeching him to increase his zeall and love to his truthe in yow bothe, that yow be not drawne backe by the wickednes of these dangerous times, wherein vertue and vertuous men are least regarded. Grooby, 4 August 1576.

Wood to the Earl of Leicester, 4 August 1576.

[*fo. 1v*]
The copy of the inclosed lettre to the Earll of Lecester, Lord Robert Dudlye.

Your Lordship's great good will alwayes shewed me (Right Honourable and my singular good Lord) doth force me to utter that by my pen, which more willingly I would have declared [*fo. 2r*] to your Honour by mouth, if long sicknes and want of strength to traveill did not lett me. It is commonly reported amonge the godly (which I doe ofte heare with great greif of hart) that your Lordship hath bene the cheife instrument, or rather the only, of the overthrowe of a most godly exercise at Southam, to the great hinderance of God's glory and the greif of all good men that hath heard it or heard of yt, which maketh them afraide lest the rest of such most profitable exercises bothe for the preachers and people (the like were never erected in England before) shall likewise be overthrowne; which God forbyd. Ah, my Lord, I have knowen yow and so yow have bene taken to be an earnest favorer and as it were a patrone of theise zealous and godly preachers who have bene the setters forth and maintainners of these worthy exercises; they are the same men now they were then, and only seek God's glory as zelously as ever they did. And can yow then become enemye to them now and not show yourself enemye to him whose faithfull messengers they be, and whose glory they only seek to advance? It is not possible? Loke therefore, my good Lord, against whom yow bende yourself; surely against him that hath said: 'He that persecuteth yow, persecuteth me'; who no doubte is toe strong for yow, as experience by many yet fresh in memory ought to teach yow. There is an other that was thought at the first to have bene a dealer with your Lordship in this case, but it is now plainly affirmed that he hath cleared himself and laid the whole burden one your shoulders. Yf this be true, and that yow doe not spedilye by true repentance cast of this burthen, yt will surely overthrowe yow. For there is no counsell against God, who, thoughe [*fo. 2v*] he suffer long where no repentance is, he payeth home in the end. There be other verie common brutes verie dishonorable and ungodly, but I will not committ them to writing. If God give life that I may once againe speak with your Honour, I will declare them particularly, which I thought to have done the last yeare at

Killingworth[1] if oportunity had served; trusting that as I have of zeall and love I beare to your Lordship's well doeing (God is my witnes) now in parte uttered them, so my hope is that yow will take well that which in conscience I could no longer kepe from yow, most humbly beseeching God to give your Honour is [sic] Holy Spirit right to reforme all that is amisse, to make yow a zealous gospeller indeed, which cannot be unles yow showe your self a harty lover bothe of the true preachers and professors thereof; and finally to grant yow his true feare and love to thend that yow may receave the the Crowne of Glory only prepared for suche; to whose mercifull protection I humbly committ your good Lordship. Grooby, 4 August 1576.

The Earl of Warwick to Wood, 16 August 1576.

The Erle of Warwick's answer to the former lettre, copied from his owne hand writing.

I have receaved your lettre wherein it sheweth yow are greatly greived with slaunderous reports the which are come to yow of my brother. If they were as true as they be reported, there is none hath so much cause to be greived there-withall as my self, but [fo. 3r] since there is no man knoweth his doings better then I my self, I must therefore declare my knowledg without any brotherly affection, but even as the truth shall lead me. First, where as he is charged to be the only overthrower of the godly exercise used at Southam, I can assure yow there is nothinge more untrue. For that if he had beene so disposed, he might have done that long before this time as well as now, but that he hath alwayes had a spetiall care in maintaining of it, so far forthe as it might tende to the edefying of the Church of God, But when ther began some abuses amongst them to be reformed, I thinck then not only he but my self also with divers others did seke by all the good means we coulde to have them brought in that order indeed as that they might continew in their well doing and not to be cut of; so that if by any other means this be done without the knowledg of my brother, God defend that he should beare the blame of other mens' doings. I cannot a litle marvell that ether yow or any other will so lightly condem him upon every slight reporte, who hath done so great good amongst yow as he hath done. It is well knowne if he had not byn, a greate sorte the which hath their mouthes opened at this day had not byn suffered nether to preach nor yet to teach, and peradventure it had not bene done without some danger of displeasure to himself and with more difficulty then is fitt shold be knowen. Therefore I thinck it to be very hard dealing towards him who hath deserved [fo. 3v] so well at their hands as he hath done, to be so hardly rewarded. But the best is that God the which hath made him an instrument for his Church heretofore will continue or rather increase his zeall in him to the end, whatsoever it shall please his enemyes ether to thincke or say. And where as yow wrote to me that some other whome was more suspected in the matter then my brother hath not only cleared himself therein but also hath layde it to my brother's chardge as the only author thereof, I doe not a litle marveill that men the which seem to be so great professors of the gosple hath so litle charity in them as that they will rather lay the faulte in him who hath alwayes bene their greatest stay and ayde then on some souch on that nether hath nor yet will ever doe them that good that he hath

[1] Kenilworth.

done. Assuredly Thomas you did well in writing that they came to yow as reportes and that yow hoped they were not true, yet I must advise yow as a freind somewhat to qualify your affection from hence forth and not to write after so vehement a manner as that a man may rather judge yow beleive it then otherwise. And but that my brother doth knowe the great good will yow beare him indeed, els it had bene inoughe to have caused him to have conceived some evill opinion of yow for your over hasty judgment. Also I perceive by yow that this reporte of him yow feare will make a great sorte of godly men withdraw their [*fo. 4r*] good wills from him. As it is not the parts of godly men to be caryed away with every flying tale, even so, if there be no more holde in their frendship, then so they are as good lost as founde. Yet I doubt not thorough God his helpe his behaviour hath bene and shalbe such as that he will deserve to keep as good or better frends then they, since I dare boldely answere on his behaulf all that he hath done for them hath bene only for conscience sake and for no popularity sake. The last matter yow write to me of I cannot answer yow any way therein, for that it is such as that yow will nether committ to letter nether to message, but as God shall make yow able yow will declare it to him your self; the which is so honest and freindly dealing as that I cannot but in my brother's behalfe greatly to thanke yow whatsoever the matter be. But in the end I hope yow shall finde th'one as true as the other, although I must needs confesse we be all flesh and blood and fraill of nature, therefore to be reformed. Well, at what time it shall please God yow be able to deale with my brother about these matters, I will then give yow to understand of one that carieth the countenance of a very precyse fellowe and a preacher of no small reputacion, who hath used my brother so vyllenously as never vyle person did use any noble man. I can terme him no otherwise, considering he was most bound to my brother of any creature in the world, so [*fo. 4v*] that I doubt not but God of his justice will make him an example to all false hypocrites. As yow confesse yow are greatly bound to my brother, even so my good Thomas play the parte of a faithfull frend as in answering such evill reportes as may come to your hearing. In so doing it wilbe an occasion for him to thinke his benefits bestowed not upon an ungratefull man. And so I end, praying God to make yow so strong and that yow may be the sooner able to styr abrode to the end yow may be fully resolved of all your doubts. My harty commendacions to yow and from my wyfe not forgotten.

From the Courte, the 16 of August 1576,

Your very assured freind,

A. WARWYKE.

The Earl of Leicester to Wood, 19 August 1576.

[*fo. 23r*]
The Earll of Leceister lettre copied from his owne hand writing.

I perceave you have mett with some good frendes of myne (Thomas Wood) whose reportes I thinke be also as easily beleeved of some as lightly reported of others. And such good hap have I often had and even at their handes of whom I have best [*sic*, least?] deserved to have such dealings used towards me. But first for the matter of Sowtham. If it had bene true yow shold as well have suspended the opinion first of my doing as so hastely to judge of it; as though it had not bene possible aswell for a minister to have disordered himself as to deserve reformacion. As for me to be thought an enemye so sone to God's Church, I dare thus farr vaunt of my self, and the rather being a just and good cause I may well doe it: that there is no man I knowe in this realme of one calling or other that hath shewed a better minde to the furthering of true religion then I have done, even from the first day of her Majestie's reigne to this. And when tymes of some troble hath bene amonge the preachers and ministers of the Church for matters of ceremonies and such like, knowing many of them to be hardly handled for so small causes, who did move for them, bothe [*fo. 23v*] at the bishops' handes and at the Prince's ? Or who in England had more blame of both for the successe that followed thereby then my selfe ? I wold fayne knowe at the most divilyshe enemie's hand that I have what one act have I done to hinder or dimynish the Church of God synce the begining of this time to this day ? I defye their worst. For my conscience doth witnes the contrary. And for proofe of it, looke of all the bishops that can be supposed that I have commended to that dignity since my creditt any way served, and looke whether they were not men as well thought of as any amonge the clergye before. Looke of all the deanes that in that time also have bene commended by me. Looke into the University of Oxford lykewise, whereof I am Chancelor, and see what heads of houses be there now in comparison of those I found. And doe but indifferently examine howe the ministery is advanced there, even where were not long agoe not only many ill heads, but as many th'worst and untoward schollers for religion. Beside this, who in England hath had or hath more learned chapleyns belonging to him then I, or hath preferred more to the furtherance of the Church of learned preachers ? Or what bysshop (since I must now speake for my self) in England, besyde the number of preachers that I countence of myne owne, doth give so lardge [*fo. 24r*] stypendes out of his purse to them as I doe ? And where have I refused any one preacher or good minister to doe for him the best I could at all times, when they have need of me either to speake or write for them ? I thinke no man will thinke I did it for fear; I trust there lives not that ever can say I did it for gayne, except to give them of mine withall to. Then if it was nether for feare nor gayne, it is like it was for good will, and that was not for any other cause but for their profession sake. And even so may I conclude for the hole. If from the begining I have (as all the world knoweth) bin a furtheror to the advancement of our religion as far as any man hath bene of any calling, if I have alwaies sought to prefer the meetest men and best preachers in God's Church as may appeare by the persons yet living, though some dead, that I have and doe maintaine as many preachers as the best bishopp in England doth, and reformed the universities as is manifest, there is no cause for any man to doubt or report of me as yow say, nor for yow or any good man to beleive lightly of such a man as hath performed this that I write, which I hope no man can reprove. But I have manifest wrong to be thus charged to be a slyder or a faller from the Gosple or I cannot tell what. No (Thomas Wood) I am no hypocrite nor Pharisy; my doings are plaine, and cheifly in the causes of religion. I take Almighty God to my record, I never [*fo. 24v*] altered my mind or thought from my youth touching my religion, and yow knowe I was ever from my cradle brought up in it; and I thank God I never rejoysed in no wordly thing so much as in this good establishment of it which we ought to be thankfull for, and to use the good ministers thereof better then when I have bene oftentimes amonge yow. But the cause is His, who knoweth best the wrong they have done me now and before this; and their malitious dealing shall no way hurt me, I trust. God amend them. I will not justefy my self for being a sinner and flesh and blood as others be. And beside, I stand on the topp of the hill, where I knowe the smallest slipp semeth a fall. But I will not excuse my self; I may fall many wayes and have more witnesses thereof then many others who perhapps be no saintes nether, yet their faults lesse noted though somewayes greater then myne. But let not them triumph in that theirs is more covered or that they are not so greatly touched. For my faults, I must fly to the mercifull God, who I knowe can and will forgive myne, though they were greater then any earthly man is able to chardge me with, as sone as they that thinke they are most cleane in his sight. And for my faults, I say, they lye before him who I have no doubt but will cancell them [fo. 25r] as I have byn and shalbe most hartely sorrey for them. But for th'other false and evell reportes that yow write to me of touching Southam: I doe assure yow they are most false and untrue, and lye most shameleslye of me. Albeit there be and have bene some places of exercises used that I doe mislike, and some over curious ministers also that give cause of the breach of the unity of our Church; and I doe and must condemne them in my opinion as great offenders, and so doth the most of the godly of our Church, and since I feare that their unthankfulnes and yll dealing wilbe one day the cause of God's just scourge to the whole religion. And I wold not have yow so lightly thinke of me, Thomas Wood, though [sic, through?] dwelling in Court I may be easely abused and caryed away for lack of zeall. No, I trust God will not so abridge his grace from me. Nether, I humbly thanke him, do I finde that decay of spirit in me, howsoever yow deall with me abrode, which I must say playnly is both unthankfully and uncharitably done. For there is none of yow all that seem to beleve this tale of me but I thinke hath found good at my handes even for religion sake many times or this, and had found, I am sure, lack enough otherwise but for me. But I thanke God for whose sake [fo. 25v] it was done, He is able to double and treble any others' unthankfull requitalls with greater comfort and contentacion a thousand fold. Yow write others have discharged themselves and leye this matter uppon me. I scarse beleeve that, but if they did so, is that well receaved of the good and godly, or well judged? I assure yow, being in my dyett,[1] the Queen her self first of any told me of that matter, and had been most greevously informed both against preachers and gentlemen. And aske them, I meane the gentlemen (the others I saw not) who helpt to deliver them hence and to qualify her Majestie's displeasure towards them.[2] I have much combred my self with this my owne justification in a matter which I thought wold have bene needles to yow or a great number of others of whom I have better deserved then to beleeve so lightly of one that hath given to yow all both generall and particular (though I say it) better cause. But we be all men I se, and he that wold be counted most a sainct I pray God be found a plain trew Christian. For I never saw or knew in my life more envye styring and lesse charity used, every man glad to hear the worst, to thinke the worst, and to beleeve the worst of his neighboure, which be very uncomfortable fruits of our profession. But God amend all and make [fo. 26r] us not so self lovers or

---

[1] The meaning is probably of an appointed day of formal attendance at Court.

[2] Grindal to Burghley, 10 June 1576: 'I heare that the sayd parties [the puritan moderators, Eusebius Paget and John Oxenbridge] are supported by some of cowntenance in those contrees, beynge off the laitie: and then your Lordships off the Councell had nede in myne opinion to take some paynes with them.' (B.M., MS. Lansd. 24, no. 4, fo. 7.)

weenors of our selves that we thinke none good but our selves. I have often found lest good in deed in such in the end. And for the matter of Southam once againe, I knowe no such thing of it one way or other as to praise it or mislyke it, only I hope the best of it, whatsoever hath bene said. But I wold have yow and all men thinke this of me (Thomas Wood) that I am not, I thanke God, fantastically perswaded in religion, but being resolved to my comfort of all the substance thereof, doe finde it soundly and godly set forth in this Universall Church of England, by the good consent of many ancyent learned and godly men and marters of our owne tyme, which doctrine and religion I wish to be obeyed dewly as it ought of all subjects in this land, and that men seek not so farr to perswade the mislyking thereof for some particular respects that they doe more hurt to the generall then ever it may lye in them to repay agayne. For my owne parte, I am so resolved to the defence of that is already established as I mean not to be a maintaynor or allower of any that wold troble or disturbe the quiett proceeding thereof; nether wishe them, who so ever they be, for any small pretence to have such coul[*fo. 26v*]lerable tolleracions as in times past for other causes then of no moment. Nether doe yow thinke or any other that ought to wish the prosperity of this religion but if these divisions or discentions shold continue awhile as it hath done of late yeares but such inconveniences must follow to the Church as all true gospellers in deed shalbe sory for. Therefore for my religion I tell yow how it is. And for any dealing against Southam exercise yow heare, untrue it is also. And generally for the exercises which I have knowne and heard of in many places, there was never thing used in the Church that I have thought and do thinke more profitable both for people and ministers; or that I have more spoken for or more laboured in defence of even from the begining, spetially where it is used with quietnes to the conservacion and unity of the doctrine established already and to the encrease of the learned ministery. Now, judge yow whether it is like I wold be against so good a thing in Southam in my countrie or no. But to be plaine with yow, I knowe not what is the cause. I feare the over busy dealing of some hath done so much hurt in striving to make better perforce that which is by permission good enough already as we shall nether have it in Southam nor any other where els, and doe what we can all, and those all yow thinke more zea[*fo. 27r*]llous then I. And this have I feared long agoe wold prove the fruict of our discention for trifles first and since for other matters. There be other matters yow say also yow have heard of me. When yow let me knowe them, whatsoever they be, I must thanke yow for it, being one of the frendly parts yow can dischardg to your frend, and will more thanke yow for these offices then to be easily perswaded to beleeve the worst of your frend by others' reportes. I have many ill wyllers, and I am none of those that seek hypocritically to make my self popular. I use no indirect instruments nor dealings (I thanke God) and thereby lye the more open to all mens' judgments. And he had need be a perfect sainct that shold escape in any place slaunderous tongues. I see more private persons then I cannot eschew it, no not the preciest that I knowe. But if I wold give myne eares open of them, I shold heare more then truth I am sure of them, and so many times I take it when I have heard it. I trust my place, all things considered, shold crave some indifferency also, spetially at their handes of whom I have deserved best of and who for many respects ought rather to be means to preserve my credite then to hinder it. But I have troubled my self to much and yow both (Thomas) for this matter though I [*fo. 27v*] thanke yow for your good will, hoping I have alway given yow none other cause but to continue it. And so wishing your perfect health, and to answere for me as yow knowe yet (and not as others shall say) till yow have other cause, I bid yow fare well this xix of August 1576.

Your old acquaintance,
R. LEYCESTER.

Wood to Warwick, 20 August 1576.

[*fo. 11r*]

To the EARLL OF WARWICK.

My hope is (Right Honourable) that my last lettres to yow and my good Lord your brother are safely come to your handes and that yow bothe will well accept my bolde enterprise, for that I thought my self bound in conscience to utter that which very ofte to my great greif I have heard concerning my Lord your brother, for whose preservation in the feare of God I doe dayly pray, as I am most bound. God make your Lordship with my Lord your brother zealous mayntainers of his glory and of the true professors thereof, I meane specially of those faithfull ministers whom none can justly reprove either in doctrine or life, and yet of the wicked worldlings and vaine courtiers falsly termed Puritanes,[1] parte whereof have had their mouthes stopped of late by our byshopes for (saving your Honour) a filthy popish ragg,[2] to the great discouragement of the godly and rejoysing of the enemies. As for the Pluritanes[3] which make no conscience to take 2 or 3 benefices, and yet not discharging one well, your Lordship shall not need to speak for them; they with the help of their patrons will shift for themselves well enoughe, though their pore sellie sheep perish for it, as they doe in great nomber thoroughout England for want of faithfull teachers. And yet our bishops make no conscience to stopp their [*fo. 11v*] mouthes for triffles, that have bene and would be most diligent in this behalfe. God for his great mercies amend those that be the occasion thereof. And if your Lordship have any of the said double and treble beneficed men to your chaplens[4] (which are worse then cormorants[5]) for God's sake rid your handes of them, least yow be partaker of their sinnes. One shephard is litle enough for one flock. And so I humbly take my leave, beseeching God to increase his graces in yow and my good Lady. 20 August 1576.

Wood to Warwick, 7 September 1576.

[*fo. 4v*]

An answere to the former lettre.

My singular good Lord: I have received of late two lettres, one from your Lordship and an other from my Lord your brother, bothe tending to one effect,

---

[1] 'Puritan' as a nickname for the most extreme Protestants was about ten years old by this time, but the godly themselves still refused to acknowledge a label which to them implied the pure 'perfecti' of a dualist heresy. (Collinson, 'Classical Movement', App. I, 'The Name of Puritan'.)

[2] The surplice.

[3] I.e. pluralists. I have not come across this pun anywhere else in Elizabethan writing.

[4] By the statute of 21 Hen. VIII, c. 13, earls were entitled to retain five chaplains each, who could purchase licence or dispensation to keep two benefices with cure of souls. (Richard Burn, *Ecclesiastical Law* (1797), iii. 100.)

[5] In this sense an insatiably greedy or rapacious person.

and therefore I thought it best to answere both in one, which I have done at large in this inclosed, which I have not sealed, to th'intent your Lordship may first peruse it and after cause it to be delivered. I prayse God that my Lord is cleare in that matter of Southam which I feared as I must neds confesse had bene toe trew, as many godly men did, a good parte whereof I have [*fo. 5r*] and shall, I trust, ere it be long satisfy in that behalf, for they are so far from being my Lord your brother's enemies that I am fully perswaded they wish him well in their harts, as to their profession appertayneth. Yet this I add more then is in my Lord's lettre, that besides his cheif accuser (of whom I thincke no good man hath any good opinion) I doubt lest some of my Lord's owne chaplaines and servants have by unjust reportes done great harme in that matter. For as I have credibly heard, there was a brute given out that Mr Gryffen, Master of my Lord's Hospitall,[1] wold come and confute the exercise. And he came thether in deed to one of the last assemblies, placing himself beyond a piller with pen and inke. And at th'end of the exercise, one of the moderators, seeing he did not offer to speake, requested him to say his opinion, which he refused. Then he desired him agayne if he had heard any thing to be misliked to confute it, if not, in few wordes to confirme it, but it would not be. Which thing (considering the former bruite) bred a suspition in many that he came not thether ether to teach or learne.[2] The same day, also, a man of my Lord's met with a gentleman of his acquaintance going to the exercise and askte him whether he loved to be out of troble. Th'other an[*fo. 5v*]swered that willingly he wolde not enter into it. 'Then', said he, 'kepe yow from th'exercise this day, for I and others have commission to take the names of all such as shall be there.' To the which he answered that if that was the matter, he perceaved he shold have compeny and therefore ment to take such parte as they did. Judge yow now, my Lord, what men might deeme hereof. But to let this passe: I beseech yow, my Lord, to put to both hart and hand with my Lord your brother, that the exercise, which of all other without comparison was esteemed the best in this realme, may speedily be set up againe. So shall yow doe bothe to God and your country one of the best services that ever yow did. Touching the disorder mentioned in your lettre that began amongst the ministers, surely I can heare of none, no not the least from the first day to the last, as more playnly yow shall see in my Lord your brother's lettre. Where your Lordship saith that divers of the ministers' mouthes had bene stopt long agoe if my Lord your brother had not bene; I pray God both your Lord and he may be means to keep them open still. When they are stopt, perseqution is like to followe which some looked for

---

[1] Ralph Griffin was the first Master of Leicester's Hospital in Warwick. Leicester was licensed to found this hospital by an act of the 1571 parliament. He endowed it with lands worth £200 a year and obtained possession of the 14th-cent. premises of the dissolved guilds of Holy Trinity and St. George after promising the corporation that he would make provision for a new burgess hall, school and schoolhouse. Griffin was preferred to the deanery of Lincoln in Dec. 1584 at Leicester's 'earnest sute'. Thomas Cartwright was appointed in his place on 21 Nov. 1585. (Collins, i. 45–6; Scott Pearson, *Thomas Cartwright*, pp. 290–3.)

[2] This story contains unique evidence of the conduct of an exercise of prophesying. It was evidently the custom for the moderator, after the 'table' of preachers had finished speaking to the text, to call upon any other learned man who might be present in the auditory to confirm or confute the doctrine.

long agoe and wilbe as ready to suffer for the truth as our young Popes wilbe to
persecute, who charge those good men to be troublers of the peace of the Church,
where indeed it is the byshopes their [*fo. 6r*] accusers whom the Prince of this
world hath bewitched with such welth and pufte up with such pride as they will
not be content to submitt themselves to God's word in all points, but will have
it to give place to their traditions or rather to Antichrist's, as more largly is
touched in the other letter. And if God begin once with his dearest children,
as he did in Queen Marie's time, let not the rest thincke to escape skotfree. But
your Lordship will thinck I am to vehement. Thinke also my Lord I besech
yow that it is God's cause, wherein we must ether be hott or colde, for there is
no meane. Go forward then, my Lord, with my Lord your brother, to seeke
his glory zealouslye; wherein yow may not looke to please both him and the
world, for yow knowe they be contrary. It is sufficient if He allowe of it, though
all the world condemne it. I am sory to heare that my Lord your brother hath
bene so ill dealt with by a preacher, but I hope he is a Pluritan and none of
those that in this time is charged with precisenes as the best men be, yet your
Lordship knoweth that amonge twelve there was a divell. Thus I have trobled
your Lordship longer then I ment, beseeching God to direct yow with my good
Lady in his true feare, and increase his graces in yow bothe to th'end. 7 September 1576.

Wood to Leicester [7 September 1576].

The answer to the Earll of Lecester's lettre.

I have receaved (Right Honourable and my singular good Lord) your lettre
of the 19 of this last moneth, whereby I perceave to my great comforte that yow
are cleare as touching the overthrowe of the exercise of Southam, the contrary
whereof I ofte heard by sundry both wise and godly which I am fully perswaded
wishe well unto your Lordship and that unfaynedlie, as to their profession
appertayneth. And that made me to affirme it more boldly in my lettre to my
Lord your brother then was meett, which fault I trust your Lordship will
pardon. And yet, if I shold write unto yow the words and protestacions that
your Lordship's accuser made, yow would thincke a wiser man then I might
be abused, as divers other were which upon such reportes thought it had bene
your Lordship's fact indeed. But I hope eare it be long to pūt some of them out
of that errour. God amend them that have bene the cause thereof, and graunt
that that exercise may be speedily set up againe, the rather by your good means.
Wherein I beleve your Lordship shall doe one of the best servises, both to God
and your country, that ever yow did, for it was undoubtedly without exception
counted the best exercise in this realme, both for the number of the learned that
repaired thether, as also of gentlemen and others moe then the church could well
holde. [*fo. 7r*] And for the ministers generally, I cannot learne of any disorder
that hath bene amongest them from the first day to the last, not the least that
could be. For they kept precisely the same orders (as they affirme) which they
receaved from the High Commissioners, as divers Justices of Peace can witnes
(for there were commonly 3 or 4 at every exercise) who according to their duties
would have found fault if any had bene. And this not withstanding, two of the
cheif preachers were sent for up, and being there nether cold they knowe their
accusers, nor, as they say, had not one word said to them touching the said

exercise, but being examined of 3 or 4 points by the Archbishope touching the booke of service and surples, were dismissed. Surely, my Lord, this was hard dealing, whosoever was the cause thereof, and a great discouraging to those godly men who are much commended for God's great giftes bestowed upon them. For your Lordship's well deserving towards the learned ministers, specially those that of long time have bene troubled about the unprofitable ceremonies (for the other cold shifte well enough for themselves) I can be a witnes when I was an humble suiter unto your Lordship in the begining of Mr Sampson's and Mr Goodman's first truble, that yow were theire cheifest and in manner their only patrone, as in my former lettres is mentioned, and that I never knewe no man better bent to the setting forth of God's glory and helpe [fo. 7v] of such as were the unfayned professors thereof then yow shewed your self at many times when it pleased your Lordship to talke with me. This both I have and will confesse (God willing) so long as I live, as the truth is, and as I am in conscience bound, if I had never receaved benefitt at your Lordship's handes. As for the byshops whom your Lordship hath commended, I knowe not. But there was one Younge, preferred in the beginning to be one of the cheifest,[1] and of many thought to be your Lordship's doing, who was no divine but a simple civilian,[2] and never preached at Yorke but one sermon (as the reporte was) which he conde so ill by harte that he was forst to cut it of in the midest. I wrote to your Lordship at the same time (if yow remember) Mr Calvin's opinion out of his Institucions touching such bastard byshops.[3] Touching the use of them, I will shew your Lordship a godly gentillman's opinion, and now of very good calling,[4] which he was wonte ofte merely [merrily] to utter, thus: 'Let the godliest man, and best learned within this realme be chosen, and put once a rochet on his backe, and it bringeth with it such an infection as that will marr him for ever.' I would experience had not taught this thing to be as true as it was merily spoken. Theise are they that burthen others to be disturbers of the peace of our Church, where in[fo. 8r]deed they have bene and are the doers of it. For if they had at the begining sought a full reformation according to God's word, and an utter abolishing of all Papists' dreges, theise controversies had never come into question. But every one sought how to catche a welthy and rich bishopricke, some paying well for it, xxxxl. pention to some one man during his life, as I have credibly heard. And thus neglecting God's glory, they sought their owne, and therefore God never blest their doings to this day, nor never will so long as they continue in this pompe and great wealth.[5] Looke

---

[1] Thomas Young, archbishop of York 1560–1571. See p. 63 above.

[2] Young proceeded B.C.L. in 1538 and disputed for his D.C.L. in 1564. (*D.N.B., s.v.* Young.)

[3] The reference is to Bk. iv, cap. 5, of Calvin's *Institution of Christian Religion*, 'That the olde forme of governement is utterly overthrowne by the tyranny of the Papacie'; in the 1562 edition of Thomas Norton's translation, fos. 26–32 of the fourth book.

[4] Possibly Sir Francis Knollys. The reported saying is similar to the sentiments of several of his letters.

[5] Wood here represents an important element in puritan thought, or rather emotion. The Genevan party were excluded from the best preferments in the early Elizabethan church and many lived in poverty and comparative obscurity. The result was that they made a virtue of necessity, while many of their brethren of Frankfort or Strasbourg who obtained rich preferments seem to have hankered

upon Winchester, what large sommes of mony he hath given with his daughters, and how he hath matcht them.[1] Looke upon the rest, and for the most parte your Lordship shall finde no better frutes, but every one seeking to set themselves up a name. Thus with their covetous example, they have done farr more harme then they have done good by their preaching. But in this point, I have holden your Lordship to long, and peradventure touched the quick to neare if the bishops might be my judge. But now I will tell yow of a good byshope indeed. There is not far from Asheby a pore town called Mesham; the most parte there are colliers.[2] They have had one Peter Eglesall, a grave and godly man to their minister [fo. 8v] not much above a yeare and halfe,[3] who with his continuall diligence in this time hath brought to passe that there is not one in his parish of lawfull years but they are able by harte to make a good and godly confession of their faith, which they use to doe before the receipte of the Communion, besides the paines he hath taken with catechising of their children. This man being of late cited before Bishop Bentame for the surples as he had bene ofte before, two aunciient old men above threescore yeares a pece wold needs goe with him, who coming to the Bishop fell downe upon their knees and besought him for the passion of Christ not to take from them their minister, confessing that at his coming to them they were ignorant and obstinate papists, and had bene cast away for ever if God had not sent them that man by whose painefull travell they had attayned to a comfortable feeling of their salvation in Christ. Wherewith the Bishop, being as it were astonied, turned his backe and slypt awaye, and so, God be praysed, they injoye their minister still to their great comfort.[4] And this man hath not of his parish (as I thinke) above xxl. a

regretfully for the simplicity of the exile. Thus in early puritanism there was an element reminiscent of medieval heresy which found wealth in a churchman irreconcilable with godliness. (Collinson, 'Classical Movement', pp. 19–31.)

[1] I have been unable to discover whether this assertion has any foundation. Bishop Horne died in debt to the queen and White states that he left his five daughters 'quite unprovided for'. (*Lives of the Elizabethan Bishops*, p. 157.) The meaning of this statement is not clear, since all five daughters (Anne Dayrel, Mary Hales, Margery Hales, Rebecca Hayman and Elizabeth Dering) were married at the time of his death and Elizabeth Dering predeceased him. (*D.N.B.*, *s.v.* Horne.) It may well be, as Wood reports, that Horne had strained the resources of his bishopric in order to settle substantial marriage-portions on his daughters; it would be a misfortune to any diocese to be served for twenty years by a bishop with a family of five daughters.

[2] Measham is $3\frac{1}{2}$ miles S.W. of Ashby-de-la-Zouch, on the Leics.–Derbs. border. At the time of Wood's letter the parish was a donative curacy in the gift of the earl of Huntingdon. (J. C. Cox, *Notes on the Churches of Derbyshire* (Derby, 1875–9), iii. 447.)

[3] Peter Eckershall occurs on a clergy-list for 1593 as curate of Burton-on-Trent; he is described as 'scholaris ruralis et predicator publicus'. He was ordained by Bishop Bentham of Coventry and Lichfield. (W. N. Landor, *Staffordshire Incumbents and Parochial Records, 1530–1680* (Collections for a History of Staffs., 1916), pp. 42–3.) In 1596 he was active in a puritan exercise held every Monday in Burton and a supporter of John Darrell, the puritan exorcist. (Samuel Harsnet, *A Discovery of the Fraudulent Practises of J. Darrel* (1599), pp. 270–1; John Darrel, *A Detection of that Sinful Shamful Lying and Ridiculous Discours of Samuel Harsnet* (1600), pp. 182–3.)

[4] Thomas Bentham, bishop of Coventry and Lichfield from 1560 to 1579, had spent part of the Marian exile at Geneva and had assisted with his Hebraic learning

yeare, besides a litle farme of his owne not far of.[1] I doe feare, my Lord, [*fo. 9r*] that all they bishops, deans and chaplens in England are not able in these 19 yeares by past to shew forth the like fruites. This is one of those men, my Lord, that is counted precise and curious. The Lord increase the number of them to a thousand thousand, for such they be indeed that have bene both the beginners and cheif maintayners of all the godly exercises. And if the Gosple has had any increase in England these yeares before named, it hath bene cheifly by their preaching and godly example of life. For the deanes, I never heard but that your Lordship hath bene toe good to them in preferring some to 2 deanries a peece, and others to moe livings then they were able to discharge or can keep with good consciences. And till this be amended, let it never be said our ministerie is reformed. For the universities, there is a brute of late that the cheif and towardest young men and such as wold have proved the fittest for the ministery are either gone or will goe, for that the surples and such like trifles are of late so urged as they must either receave them or loose their standing, which, if it be true, is lamentable, as was the driving away of some of the best and zealous preachers in Cambridge not long agoe. Concerning the bishops' chaplens, I thinke there is scarse [*fo. 9v*] one mayntained of the bishops' charges but they have one or 2 benefices abrode, and so live of the sweat of other mens' browes, which perish for want of that spirituall foode they ought to have at their handes. And shall not they that be preferrers and mayntayners of such (far worse then cormorants) be partakers of their sinnes? No doubt of it. A byshope by St. Paul's canon ought to rule his owne house well, and in it is not so much as the name of a chaplaine. Your Lordship with many moe are (no doubt) gyltie in this most dangerous offence. For God's sake therefore rid your handes of such unnessesarie chaplins, of whom assuredly the blood of all such as perish thorough their default shalbe required. One man can but supply but one place at once, and therefore litle enough for one flocke, which no one man is able to discharge to the full. Yf your Lordship will have a learned man or 2 to confer withall and so instruct your family, let them be maintayned of your owne purse, and suffer not the pore to to be spoyled, nor your chaplines to keep moe lyvings then one under pretence of your servant. Every one hath to many synnes of their owne, though they beare not the burden of others. For our religion by law established, as all good men praise God [*fo. 10r*] for it, so doe many of good and sound judgment affirme that there be great wants in it; and that of such importance as nether ours nor any other church can be counted reformed without it, I mean Discipline, which that godly learned Beza affirmeth to be one parte of the word of God and the ordinance of Christ, without the which it is not possible but the whole building shall fall downe.[2] Yf this be true, as it is most true indeed, how

in the translation of the Geneva Bible. He was on excellent terms with Anthony Gilby, the preacher of Ashby-de-la-Zouch, in 1565. Hence, no doubt, his embarrassment on this occasion. (Garrett, pp. 86–7; Bentham to Gilby, 12 Nov. 1565, Cambridge Univ. Library, MS. Mm. 1. 43, p. 434.)

[1] Wood is here making use of a technique of propaganda which developed in the successive editions of Foxe's *Actes and Monuments* and was adopted by John Field and his presbyterian friends in the MS. collections of *A Parte of a Register* and 'The Seconde Parte of a Register' and especially in the 'Survey of the Ministry' which the latter includes: the 'registering' of specific case-histories which tended to demonstrate the righteousness of the puritan cause.

[2] For Beza's teaching applied to the English situation, see his letter to Bullinger

can it be avouched that our Reformacion is good enough, seeing that the want of this Discipline cannot be as is said but the overthrow of the whole building? And shall not then such godly ministers whose harts the Lord hath touched with an unfayned zeall of his glory crie out still for the obtayning of it, and abolishing of that popish discipline yet retayned for the gaine of a fewe, which doe far more harm then good, as many good men thinke? Strive, saith Salomon, for the truthe to the death. And no doubt there be no small nomber that by all good means will prosecute this so good a cause, as also the reformacion of divers other things, so long as God giveth them liberty and life; who give to your Honor and all other that feare him zeall and courage boldly to joyne with them in this behalfe to the [*fo.* 10*v*] perfitt building up of Sion. And if in this attempt yow be ill spoken of or frowned upon, remember it is the Lord's worke yow have in hand, who both is able and will maintaine his owne cause, though all the world shold bend it self against it. And forget not that it is the portion of all God's faithfull servants to heare evill for well doing, which ought to be a sufficient comforte to yow against all enemies. The Lord direct yow by his Holy Spiritt to do that in all your enterprises which may please him, for that is praise worthy indeed. Yf that do come to passe which your Lordship and many others feare, that is, not only the taking away of the exercises, but of the rest toe, it is, my Lord, for that men wilbe wiser then God and will not submitt themselves to his word in all pointes, but willingly, or rather stubbernly, refuse and reject Christ's ordinance, being, as is sayd before, a parte of God's word, without the which Religion never flourished in any city or country; and therefore they do great injury to God that shall put fault in those his most faithfull servants, which only labour to obtayne that which wold be the preservacion of all, namely that nothing be wanting in our religion which God's word requireth, nor any thing allowed which that word doth not warrant. And this, my Lord, is the marke they shote at.

Wood to Leicester and Warwick, undated [1577].

[*fo.* 11*v*]

To the EARLLS OF LECESTER AND WARWICK.

It is now come to passe (Right Honourable and my singuler good Lordes) to the great greif of all that truly fear God, which your Honors feared long agoe, namely not only the overthrowe of Southam exercise but of all the rest, which is not only a great rejoysing to all God's enemies but such a service to Sathan as unles the whole religion shold be overthrowen a greater could not be done. For surely, if they had continued they wold in short time have overthrown a great part of his kingdome, being one of the greatest blessings that ever came to

of 3 Sept. 1566. (*Zurich Letters*, 2nd ser. (Parker Soc., 1845), pp. 127–36.) The addition of 'discipline' to Calvin's two 'marks' of the Church—preaching of the Word and administration of the sacraments—was in itself no novelty. What was new in Beza's doctrine was the narrow definition of 'discipline' as the presbyterian system of government. (G. Donaldson, 'The Relations between the English and Scottish Presbyterian Movements to 1604', unpublished London Ph.D. thesis, 1938), pp. 17, 106–8.) In the period 1566–9 the London puritans frequently quoted a statement of Beza in his Exhortation to the Prince of Condé that 'when discipline lacketh, there is a licentious life and a schoole of wickednes.' (*Seconde Parte of a Register*, i. 56, 64, 98.)

England. And therefore a [*fo. 12r*] heavy account have they to make that have bene his instruments in that behalfe, of what calling so ever they be. But it is to be feared that this is but the begining of greater plagues, whereof the stopping of the course of Christ's Gosple is a most fearfull signe. Surely the terrible example first of Callice, and now at Andwarpe,[1] ought to move England not only to speedy repentance, but also to bring forth better fruites. The like sinnes no doubt that raigned there do raigne in England both in Court and Cuntry, and therefore the like judgemente is to be feared, for God is not partiall; he hateth sinn in all countries alike. In the last dayes of King Edward, the godly preachers cried out against the wickednes of those times and told playnly of the plagues that shortly after came to passe (as some good men doe in these dayes) but no amendement followed. That godly father Latimer was said to dote, and Hoper, Bradford and Knox were counted (as our best men be now) toe precise and curious. And yet that worthy bishop Mr Ridley writt to Mr Grindall, now of Canterbury, in a lettre a litle before his marterdome (which is in print) these wordes: 'We pastors, many of us, were to colde, and bare toe much (alas) with the wicked world; our magistrates did abuse to their owne gaine both God's Gosple and the ministers of the same; the people in many places were wayward and unkinde, and thus of everie side and everie [*fo. 12v*] sorte we have provoked God's angre and wrath to fall upon us.'[2] Mark theise wordes, my Lords, and consider whether these times are not far more dangerous. In this point I am sure it is much worse: for then the faithfull ministers might freely tell both Prince and people their faultes, but such as wold doe the like indeed either have their mouthes stopped or cannot be suffered to come in place where it ought cheifly to be done. And therefore such as for the most parte will speake *placentia* must supply that place, then the which there cannot be a more fearfull signe, the fruites whereof are too apparent. For as it is commonly said, the nommber of Papists and Atheists are marvelously increased and such as be zealous for God's glory, whether they be preachers or professors, are least regarded; so as it may be truly said that for the state of religion, it was better in King Edward's time then now; for then they went forward as knowledg increased (though slowly) but now having greater light we go most shamfully backwarde. Of the rest, I will make no comparison, but leave them to your Honors' consideracion; as also whether after such great mercies receaved at God's handes, not only in delivering England from bondage, but in restoring to it his glorious Gosple, our state is not far more dangerous [*fo. 13r*] then theirs was in the raigne of that most godly young King. What followed then we knowe. And what is like to come to passe now, all godly men tremble to thinke of it, and feare least for our toe shamefull abusing of God's Gosple and contemning Christ's ordinance (*Discipline* I meane) we shall drincke the dregs of that cup which our neighbours have tasted of already. Looke to it therefore (my Lordes) in time. Better late then toe late. There is no doubt but if your Lordships with the rest of your calling wold doe that for the which the Lord God hath placed yow in theise high roomes, which is above all to seeke the advancement of his glorie, the promoting of his Gosple, and the welth of your Prince and Country, and to the

---

[1] Antwerp was sacked by mutinous Spanish troops in Nov. 1576.

[2] See 'An Answer of Bishop Ridley to Master Grindal's Letter sent from Frankfurt' in John Foxe, *Actes and Monuments*, ed. Josiah Pratt, vii. 434–6. Wood quotes correctly from Day's 1570 edition (ii. 1902) except for the omission of 'worldly' before 'gaine'.

uttermost of your powers to suffer nothing to be done (for the will and pleasure of any) against the same, there is no doubt (I say) but God wold yet, upon repentance, shew mercy to England and repent him of the evill spoken against it, as he did to *Nineve*, when Jonas by his commandement preached the destruction thereof within 40 dayes.

APPENDIX

This letter survives among Thomas Baker's transcripts of Anthony Gilby's correspondence. It is included here because of the strong resemblance it bears to the other letters printed in this volume. As in the Gorhambury letters, Wood is here edifying the reformist cause by castigating the defection of a lost leader. As far as I know, this is the only Wood letter of this type to survive outside Ambrose Wood's commonplace book, and Ambrose might well have included it if he had possessed a copy.

The Robert Beaumont referred to in this letter became Master of Trinity College, Cambridge, in 1561. He had at one time been a member of the exile congregation at Geneva. In 1565 he was vice-chancellor, and as such was burdened with the distasteful task of imposing Parker's 'Advertisements' on the university. In enforcing the surplice he followed the explicit instructions of the archbishop and of Cecil as chancellor. But Wood was only one of many who 'at tables and other common places' accused him of turning back 'to the toyes of popery and pudles of superstition.' Beaumont's reply to these charges was also transcribed by Baker (Cambridge Univ. Library, MS. Mm. 1. 43 (Baker 32), pp. 427–30) and includes a reasoned consideration of the problem of the surplice both for the private conscience and for the person set in public authority. As for the report of riding with a foot-cloth, he told Gilby: 'I mervayle one of Mr Wodds yeares wolde so lightly eyther credite or write of so unlyke a matter. I ryde styll as homely as ye do, or at least as homely as ye have sene me ryde in Leicestershire in all points.' Both Wood's letter and Beaumont's rejoinder have been given prominence in H. C. Porter's recent study of *Reformation and Reaction in Tudor Cambridge* (pp. 115–18). Unfortunately Dr. Porter identifies Wood with a young graduate who entered Trinity as a sizar in 1561. He therefore misses the point of the correspondence, as he does when he suggests that Beaumont showed condescension in defending himself at such length to the mere vicar (in fact the preacher) of Ashby-de-la-Zouch. Wood, Beaumont and Gilby were all, apparently, Leicestershire men and—what is more—all three were veterans of the Geneva congregation. Of the three, 'Father' Gilby had incomparably the greatest reputation. It is this which gives Wood's letter its sting, especially when he reports to Gilby that Beaumont covers his horse with a stately foot-cloth. The returned exiles felt themselves to be deserted by any of their number who accepted high office for what were often assumed to be 'worldly considerations'. (Cf. John Foxe's letter to Laurence Humphrey when the latter accepted the Presidency of Magdalen, J. F. Mozley, *John Foxe and His Book* (Oxford, 1940), p. 66.) Gilby could probably have been a bishop had he so chosen.

Thomas Wood to Anthony Gilby, 4 October 1565 (Cambridge University Library, MS. Mm. 1. 43 (Baker 32), pp. 430–1.[1])

Salutations in the Lorde to you and all yours. Sinse the delivery of my lettre to our good Erle,[2] I have hearde that my countryman Mr Beaumont hath bene very

[1] There is another transcript of this letter in a Baker MS. in B.M., MS. Lansd. 841, fo. 52.

[2] Presumably the earl of Huntingdon. The letter was probably a protest against the enforcement of vestiarian conformity.

ernest at Cambridge about capp matters, upon a lettre written to him from Mr Secretary, to the great greif and mislykinge of the godlye, which hath bene stomaked even of the poore lytle boyes, insomuch as they sought to utter their good devotion towards him in this sorte following.

Upon a certen daye, Mr Beaumont rode with his footeclothe[1] to the churche (a maner not used in our tyme as you knowe). While he was at his sermon, certen of the boyes clipt of all the heere of his horse tayle and toppe, and made him a crown like a popishe prest. Wherupon proclamation was made that whosoever wuld bring forth the doer of this heynous fact shall have a certen summe of money. But all were dom, and none wold utter any thing. [p. 431] In the meane tyme he made many protestations of his good will and meaninge towards all, and that it was agaynst his conscience to hurte any, save for his dutie towards the Magistrate. The Sonday following, all the fellowes and scollers use to fetch the Master to the churche, going before him two after two. The said boyes to make my countryman amends cutt all the heere of his horse taken before in short peces and strewde it in the waye as he went (insted of a carpet) from his chambre to the churche. What hath followed therof I have not heard. But if they had served all our bishops (or their horses) in like sorte, they shuld never be accused for me.[2] This storye is so pretty and pleasant that I could not but make ye partaker therof etc.

With most hartie commendations to you and your good bedfellowe, whom my wyfe salutes. She and Mrs Wythers[3] have sent her 2 lytle tokens by this bearer. Mr Bodley[4] and Mr Keth[5] and all the rest be in helthe and pray for you. At London, scribled as you see this 4th of October 1565.

Yours assuredly in the Lorde,

THOMAS WOOD.

[1] A large richly-ornamented cloth laid over the back of a horse and reaching the ground on either side; a mark of state.

[2] 1565 is an early date for such a markedly anti-episcopal sentiment.

[3] The wife of either Francis, Henry, Stephen or William Withers: all four were at Geneva. (Garrett, pp. 340–2.)

[4] John Bodley, the printer of the Geneva Bible and father of Sir Thomas Bodley.

[5] William Kethe, a member of the Geneva congregation, versifier of many metrical psalms and with Wood and Whittingham at Newhaven. (Garrett, pp. 204–5, and see p. 51 above.)

Note (1983): After the original publication of *Letters of Thomas Wood* Dr. Claire Cross supplied me with further biographical information from the Hastings collection in the Huntington Library, California, which establishes that whereas Wood was described in 1568 as 'Thomas Wood of Tottenham' in 1570 he was known as 'Thomas Wood, late of Leicester Esq.' and is referred to after his death as 'Thomas Wood, late of Groby'. His widow was still alive in 1598 and is described as 'Agnes Wood of Sunnynge Hill, Berkshire'. (Huntington Library, H. A. Accounts & Inventories, Boxes 2-5.) Dr. Simon Adams has corrected me on two points. Wood did not leave Geneva in May 1560 (p. 47), for he wrote a letter from Portsmouth on 9 March 1560, the contents of which suggest that he had been back in England for some time. The letter from the earl of Leicester to Robert Beale quoted on pp. 61-2 should be dated 7 July 1571, not 1572. Its contents refer not to *An admonition to the Parliament*, which was published in the summer of 1572, but to moves made against nonconformity by the bishops in the previous year. Dr. Adams is preparing a study of Wood which will shed further light on his career.

Archbishop Grindal's Birthplace

One of the oldest houses in the Cumbrian village of St Bees, traditionally known as Cross Hill and now no. 19 Finkle Street. When my biography of Grindal was published in 1979, an old controversy about the birthplace, whether in St Bees 'town' or in an outlying hamlet, was still unresolved. Now the detective work of Cumbrian antiquarians has established that this was the house in which a future archbishop of Canterbury grew up and which passed, by virtue of his neice's marriage, into the possession of the Dacre family. Work undertaken by the present owners, Mr and Mrs Noel Carr, has uncovered ancient wall decorations featuring griffins, the supporters of the Dacre arms. The photograph is reproduced by courtesy of Mr Clifford Turner and much of the research was undertaken by John and Mary Todd of St Bees.

4

IF CONSTANTINE, THEN ALSO THEODOSIUS
ST. AMBROSE AND THE INTEGRITY OF THE
ELIZABETHAN *ECCLESIA ANGLICANA*

The proud boast of Bishop John Jewel in *Apologia Ecclesiae Anglicanae* that 'we lean unto knowledge, they unto ignorance' brought a swift retort from his catholic opponent: 'Ye lean to the favour of secular princes.' To which Jewel replied: 'We flatter our princes, M. Harding, as Nathan flattered King David; as John Baptist flattered Herod; as St Ambrose flattered Theodosius; and as salt flattereth the green sore.'[1] How much credibility was there in this resounding riposte when it was made in 1567, and how much would survive three more decades of Tudor royal supremacy? Not many Nathans in bishops' clothing were prepared to confront monarchy itself with a bold 'Thou art the man', and it was scarcely in the Tudor character to confess with King David: 'I have sinned against the Lord.' Nor were the sins of Henry VIII's children of the kind to provide many occasions to play Nathan or John the Baptist. But the integrity of the Church and its faith are always in need of defence, even against misguided Christian princes. Or, to put the case less prejudicially, the possibility of a difference of opinion between Christian princes and Christian bishops can never be excluded. For all such occasions the appropriate model was the third of Jewel's *exempla*, that notable father of the Church, St Ambrose. In the words of Jewel: 'We say to the prince as St Ambrose sometime said to the emperor Valentinian: "*Noli te gravare, imperator, ut putes te in ea quae divina sunt imperiale aliquod jus habere*: Trouble not yourself, my lord, to think that you have any princely power over those things that pertain to God."'[2]

* I acknowledge the advice and comments of Dr William M. Lamont of the University of Sussex. Dr Lamont has been this way before me in his article 'The Rise and Fall of Bishop Bilson', *Journal of British Studies*, v (1965–6), 22–32.
[1] *The Works of John Jewel*, ed. J. Ayre, iv (Parker Society, Cambridge 1850), 898.
[2] Ibid.

Our late colleague Professor Greenslade, whose absence we must regret on this occasion, once remarked that 'a treatise on church and state from the pen of Ambrose would be an exciting thing to read', noting that in place of it we have to rest content with the remarks occasioned by political circumstances.[3] For the purpose which we share with the Tudor controversialists those circumstances are reducible to three dramatic encounters with an imperial authority which was no longer wholly alien but which required instruction by the representative of the Church on the limit and mode of its operation in areas where there were overriding religious and moral considerations: *causae Dei*. These episodes prompted the seminal *topoi* which were never long absent from the perennial dialectic of Church and State. Almost the whole matter of Ambrose in this connexion may be distilled in three affirmations, characteristic of the gift for clear-cut and 'passionate overstatement'[4] possessed by this Roman aristocrat and rhetorician: in God's cause bishops are to be judges of emperors and not emperors of bishops; palaces belong to the emperor, churches to the bishop; the emperor is within the Church, not over the Church. '*Quid enim honorificentius, quam ut imperator Ecclesiae filius esse dicatur?*'[5]

The first of the three episodes was the Battle of the Basilicas of 385–6, provoked when the Arian sympathies of the lady Justina, exercised in the name of her son, the young Valentinian II, threatened Ambrose and the whole 'orthodox' community of Milan with the expropriation first of the suburban *Basilica Portiana* and then of the more prestigious and centrally located *Basilica Nova*. With the facts and the problems of chronology and topography surrounding their interpretation we are not concerned. It is sufficient for our purpose that there was a crisis of naked force when Ambrose shared the state of siege in one of the contested basilicas; and another crisis of legal process, when he was summoned to meet his opponent in the Consistory, where the matter was to be arbitrated by a secular tribunal. In the sermon 'Contra Auxentium', preached in the besieged basilica, Ambrose insisted that God's church was not his to surrender.[6] In describing these events to his sister, Ambrose glossed Matthew xxii. 21, appropriating the text to his own office and converting it into an original dictum: '*Scriptum est: Quae Dei Deo, quae caesaris caesari. Ad imperatorem palatiae pertinent, ad sacerdotem ecclesiae.*'[7] The refusal of Ambrose to submit his cause to secular arbitration was conveyed to Valentinian in *Epistola XXI*, which included these rhetorical questions: '*Quando audisti, clementissime imperator, in causa fidei laicos de episcopo*

---

[3] *Early Latin Theology*, ed. S. L. Greenslade (Library of Christian Classics, v. London 1956), 178.

[4] Hans von Campenhausen, *The Fathers of the Latin Church*, tr. Manfred Hoffmann, London 1964, 90.

[5] *Oratio Contra Auxentium de Basilicis Tradendis*, P.L., xvi. 1018.

[6] Ibid., cols. 1007–18.

[7] *Epistola XX*, ibid., col. 999.

judicasse? . . . Si docendus est episcopus a laico, quid sequetur? Laicus ergo disputet, et episcopus audiat: At certe si vel scripturarum seriem divinarum vel vetera tempora retractemus, quis est qui abnuat in causa fidei, in causa inquam fidei, episcopus solere de imperatoribus Christianis, non imperatores de episcopis judicare?'[8]

By 388 Ambrose was consolidating a new relationship with the emperor Theodosius who had mastered the West and was often resident at Milan. Among other disturbances in and around the town of Callinicum on the distant Euphrates, the Christians had burned down the synagogue at the instigation of their bishop. When Theodosius ordered restitution to be made Ambrose protested, first in writing (*Epistola XL*), and then in a sermon preached in the imperial presence. Only when Theodosius solemnly promised to rescind his order did Ambrose consent to continue with the celebration of the eucharist. The merits of the case are of no more concern to us than they were to the sixteenth century. (Ambrose described the synagogue as '*perfidiae locus, impietatis domus, amentiae receptaculum*'.) What matters for the present purpose is that in *Epistola XL* Ambrose asserted that in *causa Dei* it was the part of a bishop to speak his mind freely and of an emperor to listen: '*Sed neque imperiale est libertatem dicendi negare, neque sacerdotale quod sentiat non dicere. Nihil enim in vobis imperatoribus tam populare et tam amabile est, quam libertatem etiam in iis diligere qui obsequio militiae vobis subditi sunt. Siquidem hoc interest inter bonos et malos principes, quod boni libertatem amant, servitutem improbi. Nihil etiam in sacerdote tam periculum apud Deum, tam turpe apud homines, quam quod sentiat, non libere denuntiare . . . Malo igitur imperator bonorum mihi esse tecum quam malorum consortium, et ideo clementiae tuae displicere debet sacrerdotis silentium, libertas placere. Nam silentii mei periculo involveris, libertatis bono juvaris . . . In causa vero Dei quem audies, si sacerdotem non audias, cujus majore peccatur periculo? Quis tibi verum audebit dicere, si sacerdos non audeat?*'[9]

Two years later Ambrose dared for a second time to play Nathan to Theodosius's David, after an imperial order had contributed to a hideous massacre of the inhabitants of Thessalonika. Unlike modern scholars the sixteenth century had no reason to doubt the accounts in Sozomen and Theodoret of a dramatic confrontation between Ambrose and Theodosius in which either the very doors of the basilica were barred to the emperor or he was put to the ban before the altar. What is more certain is that in *Epistola LI*, written with his own hand for the sight of the emperor alone,[10] Ambrose successfully induced a mood of chastened repentance, which Theodosius publicly exhibited by the performance of penance before regaining access to the altar.

The utility of these precedents for the bishops and fathers of the sixteenth-century *Ecclesia Anglicana* may not be immediately apparent. We tend to assume that even if some Tudor churchmen had it in them to be

---

[8] Ibid., cols. 1005–6.
[9] Ibid., cols. 1101–6.
[10] 'Postremo scribo manu mea, quod solus legas.' Ibid., col. 1163.

lions, preferment made them lions under the throne. Those who retained the character of lions, or escaped preferment, have been reclassified as puritans, not churchmen at all, or scarcely churchmen. In the most notorious of all sermons preached before Elizabeth I, Edward Dering assumed the person of Nathan to the queen's David and led her on a tour of the 'intolerable evils' allowed by her government. 'And yet you, in the meanwhile that all these whoredoms are committed, you at whose hands God will require it, you sit still and are careless. Let men do as they list. It toucheth not belike your commonwealth, and therefore you are so well contented to let all alone. The Lord increase the gifts of his Holy Spirit in you, that from faith to faith you may grow continually, till that you be zealous as good king David to work his will.'[11] But Dering was a puritan, which serves as the explanation for his conduct. And he did not preach before the queen a second time. When John Whitgift preached before the court at Greenwich four years later he denounced the 'sinister affection' of flattery. 'Well saith Ambrose: "... We must take heed that we give no ear to flatterers."'[12] But how successful was Whitgift himself in warding off the disease of flattery in his own splendid career, then scarcely begun? Sir John Harington's epitaph for Bishop Richard Fletcher might seem to serve for the Elizabethan episcopate as a whole, more especially in Whitgift's time: 'He knew what would please the queen, and would adventure on that though that offended others.'[13]

It was not Theodosius but Constantine who is supposed to have supplied all that was needed from antiquity to bolster a polity which attributed so much to the benevolent initiative of the godly prince. We speak, of course, of an almost mythical Constantine, not of the Constantine whose far from self-evident *locus standi* in ecclesiastical affairs our chairman Professor Ullmann has recently investigated in this JOURNAL.[14] In the *Apologia* Jewel cited the relevant places from Theodoret to prove that Constantine had established an enduring tradition of imperial supremacy in the affairs of the Church: 'Continually, for the space of five hundred years, the emperor alone appointed the ecclesiastical assemblies, and called the councils of the bishops together.'[15] While in the newly written Ecclesiastical History of John Foxe the Elizabethan reader learned how 'gentle Constantine' in the manner of a new Moses led the Church of God out of the Red Sea of persecution.

---

[11] *A sermon preached before the Queenes Maiestie the 25 day of Februarie ... 1569(70)* was published at least a dozen times between 1570 and 1603. It has been reprinted in *Elizabethan Puritanism*, ed. Leonard J. Trinterud (A Library of Protestant Thought, New York 1971), where the quotation appears at p. 159. See Patrick Collinson, *A Mirror of Elizabethan Puritanism: The Life and Letters of 'Godly Master Dering'* (Friends of Dr. Williams's Library Seventeenth Lecture (1963), 1964).

[12] *The Works of John Whitgift*, ed. J. Ayre, iii (Parker Society, Cambridge 1853), 578.

[13] John Harington, *A Briefe view of the state of the Church of England* (1608), 1653, 30.

[14] 'The Constitutional Significance of Constantine the Great's Settlement', xxvii (1976), 1–16.

[15] *Works of Jewel* (above n. 1), iii. Cambridge 1848, 98.

'Such was the goodness of this emperor Constantine, or rather such was the providence of Almighty God toward his church in stirring him up, that all his care and study of mind was set upon nothing else, but only how to benefit and enlarge the commodities of the same ... No less beneficial was his godly care also in quieting the inward dissensions and disturbance within the church, among the christian bishops themselves.' The intended comparison was sufficiently plain with 'the flourishing and long-wished for reign' of 'our dread and sovereign mistress and governess queen Elizabeth', 'such a chosen instrument of his clemency, so virtuously natured, so godly disposed', in her very person the 'amends and recompense, now to be made to England, for the cruel days that were before.'[16]

So sharply was the focus set on the 'godly zeal and princely care' of this 'singular spectacle for all christian princes to behold and imitate' that the place of the godly bishop in this happy dispensation was often blurred. It has been baldly stated that 'the Elizabethan bishops were all Erastians, from the point of view that they rested the government of the Church on the civil ruler.'[17] Foxe composed prefaces to Jesus Christ, to the queen, to the learned reader, 'to the true and faithful congregation of Christ's Universal Church', and even to 'the persecutors of God's truth, commonly called papists'. But there was no dedication to the bishops and fathers of *Ecclesia Anglicana*. Nor was room found in *Acts and Monuments* for the bishop of Milan, except to inform the reader that it was Ambrose, in his funeral oration for Theodosius, who started the unfortunate rumour that Constantine's mother was not a British princess but the daughter of an innkeeper.[18]

Certain ideological difficulties, even contradictions, make Foxe's neglect of Ambrose understandable. The occasions were few when Elizabethan controversialists would wish to explore the possibility of the royal power being abused to bring injury to the Church. The most apparent rock of offence was the fact of the excommunication of Theodosius, the first step on the road to Canossa and a precedent for papalist, not imperialist publicists. As Bishop Thomas Bilson observed, it was 'the onely example in all antiquitie which fully proveth that a bishoppe did prohibit a prince to enter the church and to bee partaker of the Lordes table: which wee neither deny nor dispraise, considering the cause and the manner of the fact.'[19] Alexander Nowell professed to find no embarrassment in the precedent, claiming that 'we profess', with Calvin, that the prince ought to be obedient to the minister in executing his office according to God's word, 'yea though it be against the prince

---

[16] *The Acts and Monuments of John Foxe*, ed. S. R. Cattley, i. London 1848, 292–303, viii. London 1839, 600–1.

[17] F. J. Shirley, *Richard Hooker and Contemporary Political Ideas*, London 1949, 108.

[18] *Acts and Monuments*, i. 293.

[19] Thomas Bilson, *The true difference betweene christian subiection and unchristian rebellion*, 1585, 372.

himself, according as Theodosius the emperor was in this case obedient to
St Ambrose.'[20] But Richard Hooker, who later discussed such precedents
at length, regarded it as an extraordinary case, involving extraordinary
people, 'strange and admirable patterns', which had no bearing on the
exercise of ordinary ecclesiastical jurisdiction, from which Hooker was
sure that kings were exempt.[21]

An added difficulty was the dualism of Church and State very nearly
implied by the rhetoric of the Battle of the Basilicas, but a hair's breadth
from the question of Donatus 'What has the emperor to do with the
Church?' Thomas Cartwright could cheerfully render the dictum 'that
palaces belong unto the emperors, but the churches unto the ministers',
for it was entirely consistent with the high presbyterian doctrine of the
two kingdoms.[22] His opponent John Whitgift could only employ
Ambrose sophistically, as providing a precedent for the pronunciation of
excommunication by a single individual.[23] To be sure, the dualism of
Contra Auxentium enabled both Thomas Becon and John Jewel to recruit
Ambrose in support of civil obedience and the payment of taxes ('Si
tributum petit imperator, non negamus') but that was hardly the point.[24] Only
in the Marian persecution was it possible for English protestants to follow
the natural thrust of Ambrose's rhetoric, as when John Philpot told his
judges: 'St Ambrose saith, that the things of God are not subject to the
power and authority of princes.'[25] The Marian Martyrs were indeed to
prove invaluable when catholic apologists accused their opponents of
'leaning to the favour of secular princes'. 'If we make princes to be judges
of faith,' Bishop Bilson asked 'Philander the Jesuit', 'why were so many of
us consumed not long since in England with fire and faggot, for disliking
that which the prince and the pope affirmed to be faith?'[26]

Yet it was difficult to disguise the fact that with the peace of the Church
restored princes were in some sense judges of faith, and impossible to
escape the truth that they were makers and unmakers of bishops. A queen
who had begun her reign with the deprivation of an entire episcopal
bench could not very plausibly be asked: 'Quando audisti . . . in causa fidei
laicos de episcopo judicasse?' The days of jure divino episcopacy in England

[20] Alexander Nowell, A reproufe of a booke entituled A proufe of certayne articles by T. Dorman,
1566, fol. 51.

[21] The Works of . . . Mr. Richard Hooker, ed. John Keble, Oxford 1874, iii. 444–55.

[22] The rest of the second replie of Thomas Cartvuright (sic), (Heidelberg) 1577, 156. See A. F.
Scott Pearson, Church and State: political aspects of sixteenth century Puritanism, Cambridge
1928.

[23] Works of Whitgift (above n. 12), iii. 242–6.

[24] The Early Works of Thomas Becon, ed. J. Ayre (Parker Society, Cambridge 1843), 221;
Works of Jewel (above n. 1), iv. 835.

[25] The Examinations and Writings of John Philpot, ed. R. Eden (Parker Society, Cambridge
1842), 11.

[26] Bilson (above n. 19), 173.

were not yet, not even as a theoretical proposition.[27] Archbishop Parker
could tell Burghley: 'I refer the standing or falling altogether to your own
considerations, whether her Majesty and you will have any archbishops or
bishops, or how you will have them ordered.'[28] And when Archbishop
Grindal wrote his otherwise defiant letter to the queen, far from uttering
threats of excommunication he told her: 'If it be your Majesty's pleasure,
for this or any other cause, to remove me out of this place, I will with all
humility yield thereunto, and render again to your Majesty that I received
of the same.'[29]

Moreover the fact that the Tudor Polity was not neatly divided as
between Church and State could cut both ways. It was not merely in their
'Erastian' pusillanimity that the Elizabethan bishops inhabited a church
remote from the basilicas of Ambrosian Milan. Some of their bolder
utterances were in matters of state, *causae Dei* for the sixteenth century but
scarcely for the fourth. We recall the remarkable political sermon
preached at the opening of the 1563 Parliament by Alexander Nowell, the
dean of St Paul's, with its insistent demand that the queen should marry
and the posing of an unanswerable question: 'For if your parents had
been of your mind, where had you been then?'[30] And, from the other end
of the reign, the occasion when Archbishop Hutton devoted an entire
sermon to the succession, with a finger pointed unmistakably towards
Scotland. 'I no sooner remember this famous and worthy prelate,' wrote
Sir John Harington, 'but me thinks I see him in the chappell at White-
hall, Queen Elizabeth at the window in the closett, all the lords of the
Parliament spirituall and temporal about them, and then after his three
courtsies that I heare him out the pulpit thundring this text: "The
kingdomes of the earth are mine, and I doe give them to whom I will, and
I have given them to Nebuchodonozor and his sonne, and his sonnes
sonne."' Elizabeth might have interrupted to reverse Ambrose's question
and ask when it was ever heard that bishops were judges of the succession.
Instead she calmly thanked Hutton for his very learned sermon 'as if she
had but waked out of some sleepe', and only later sent two councillors
'with a very sharp message'.[31]

[27] Norman Sykes, *Old Priest and New Presbyter*, Cambridge 1956; William M. Lamont,
Godly Rule: Politics and Religion 1603–60, London 1969; W. D. J. Cargill Thompson,
'Anthony Marten and the Elizabethan Debate on Episcopacy', in *Essays in Modern English
Church History in Memory of Norman Sykes*, ed. G. V. Bennett & J. D. Walsh, London 1966,
44–75; W. D. J. Cargill Thompson, 'Sir Francis Knollys' Campaign Against the *Jure Divino*
Theory of Episcopacy', in *The Dissenting Tradition: Essays for Leland H. Carlson*, ed. C. Robert
Cole & Michael E. Moody, Athens Ohio 1975, 39–77.

[28] *Correspondence of Matthew Parker*, ed. J. Bruce (Parker Society, Cambridge 1853), 454.

[29] *The Remains of Edmund Grindal*, ed. W. Nicholson (Parker Society, Cambridge 1843),
387.

[30] An evidently secondhand and abbreviated version of this famous sermon, preserved
in a seventeenth-century hand in Gonville and Caius MS. 64 was printed as an Appendix
to *A Catechism . . . by Alexander Nowell*, ed. G. E. Corrie (Parker Society, Cambridge 1853),
221–9. See J. E. Neale, *Elizabeth I and her Parliaments 1559–1581*, London 1953, 92–5.

[31] Harington (above n. 13), 216–22.

Ambrose was more than likely to be projected into the argument by opponents of the Elizabethan Church, obliging its defenders to handle this hot potato as best they could. When Harding quoted *Epistola XXI* to Jewel, '*Quando audisti . . .*', Jewel replied that the letter must be read in context. Valentinian was 'a rash young man', not yet baptised, an Arian heretic and a tyrant.[32] The implication was that Ambrose would not have objected to the arbitration of a truly Christian emperor. When Cartwright quoted the same text to Whitgift Whitgift referred him to the bishop of Salisbury's answer to Harding, leaving Cartwright to protest with some reason that tender years and other impediments had nothing to do with the case. An emperor was an emperor.[33] Cartwright did not remind his opponent of Edward VI. Whitgift would not have wished to repudiate the English Josiah and for the purpose of Cartwright's argument he was an embarrassment. Later Hooker in his comments on the Battle of the Basilicas placed the stress where Jewel had placed it. Unlike Jewel he expressed positive approval of the resistance of 'the holy bishop', but added: 'A cause why many times emperors did more by their absolute authority than could very well stand with reason, was the over great importunity of heretics, who being enemies to peace and quietness cannot otherwise than by violent means be supported.'[34] How different from ecclesiastical life under 'virtuous' Constantine!

But a more ingenious and fruitful way to handle Ambrose was not to explain him away by an appeal to special circumstances but to transfer attention to Theodosius as a model of how a prince should behave when instructed and admonished by the minister of God. Bishop Pilkington pointed in this direction when he said of the excommunication of Theodosius that he was unsure whom to praise the more: he who durst do it or the other that would humbly obey it.[35] That was neat, but not original. As Hooker later remarked: 'The very histories, which have recorded them, propose them for strange and admirable patterns; the bishops, of boldness; the emperors, of meekness and humility. They wonder at the one, for adventuring to do it unto emperors; at the other, for taking it in so good part at the hands of bishops.'[36] Bishop Bilson developed the argument by observing, as modern scholarship for more disinterested reasons has done, the lack of any evidence that Theodosius was forcibly coerced by Ambrose. We know only that the words of the bishop struck the emperor to the heart and that he repented, not that Ambrose commanded him to put off his robes and leave his seat in the sacristy. 'The Jesuites helpe the storie with their admixtions.' 'You care not, to fit your purpose, though you make S. Ambrose a sturdie rebell.'[37]

[32] *Works of Jewel* (above n. 1), iv. 1027–9.
[33] *Works of Whitgift* (above n. 12), iii. 308–9; Cartwright (above n. 22), 161.
[34] *Works of Hooker* (above n. 21), iii. 442–3.
[35] *The Works of James Pilkington*, ed. J. Scholefield (Parker Society, Cambridge 1842), 381, 491.
[36] *Works of Hooker*, iii. 453.
[37] Bilson (above n. 19), 172–6, 372–3.

Bishop William Barlow would later teach that bishops and priests used the power of the keys for winning the souls of kings, 'not for disturbing their states; for preaching to them, not factiously against them.'[38] The protestant account of the episode was as Archbishop Sandys expressed it, that Ambrose 'brought the emperor Theodosius himself to unfeigned humility and hearty repentance.'[39] The master card was to represent such sublime condescension as no derogation from the imperial dignity but the noblest of all kingly attributes. It was sufficient to quote what Ambrose had himself written in *Epistola XL*: 'Sed neque imperiale est libertatem dicendi denegare ... Nihil enim in vobis imperatoribus tam populare et tam amabile est, quam libertatem etiam in iis diligere qui obsequio militiae vobis subditi sunt.'

Once this had been grasped attention could shift back to Ambrose, who had also said in *Epistola XL* 'neque sacerdotale quod sentiat non dicere.' The emperor would suffer from his silence and benefit from his outspokenness. Peter Wentworth in the House of Commons handled a secular version of the same *topos*. 'The liberty of free speech' was justified by 'the commodities that grow to the prince and the whole state' by the use of it.[40] For that matter Elizabeth's ministers, frustrated men grappling daily with the problem of counsel, knew that it was implicit in their oaths as privy councillors that they must preserve the safety of the queen and commonwealth by their frankness: and none franker than Sir Francis Knollys, whom James Cargill Thompson illuminated for us.[41]

Thus armed, William Fulke could deal confidently with *Epistola XXI*. 'And who saith the contrary, but that in causes of faith the emperor is ordinarily to be instructed of the bishops and not the bishops of the emperor?' Princes were to follow the direction of God's word, 'the knowledge whereof, especially in difficult matters, he is to receive of the ministers of the Church; as of the lawyer the knowledge of law, although he be bound to see justice executed.'[42] Bilson developed the same point. It was 'evident that princes must be directed unto truth the same way that al other christians are, to wit, by perswasion and not by coaction.' Princes were not to teach bishops, 'much lesse to professe themselves judges of trueth.' One might as well look to princes to prescribe medicines. So what Ambrose wrote was 'stout but lawfull; constant but christian'. 'He refused to put his consent to the princes will: but he resisted not the princes power.'[43]

[38] Quoted, Lamont (above n. 27), 40.

[39] *The Sermons of Edwin Sandys*, ed. J. Ayre (Parker Society, Cambridge 1841), 72.

[40] Wentworth's speech in the House of Commons, 8 Feb. 1576, printed in Trinterud (above n. 11), 166–90. See J. E. Neale, 'Peter Wentworth', *English Historical Review*, xxxix (1924); and *Elizabeth I and her Parliaments 1559–1581*, esp. 318–32.

[41] 'Sir Francis Knollys' Campaign' (above n. 27).

[42] *Fulke's Answers to Stapleton, Martiall, and Sanders*, ed. R. Gibbings (Parker Society, Cambridge 1848), 267.

[43] Bilson (above n. 19), 124, 173, 174, 176.

Both Jewel and Hooker glossed the royal supremacy not as the intelligence by which matters were determined but as the authority by virtue of which they were to be effected, the distinction later developed by Bishop George Carleton between execution, belonging to the king, and interpretation, the property of the priest.[44] 'We flatter not our prince with any new-imagined extraordinary power', wrote Jewel, explaining else-where in the *Defence* that 'that unused and strange style' of Supreme Head had been abandoned. As the Church's nurse and lawmaker the prince was 'to hear and take up cases and questions of the faith, *if he be able*[45]; or otherwise to commit them over by his authority unto the learned.'[46] Hooker wrote that 'in principal matters belonging to christian religion' it would be 'very scandalous and offensive' if kings or laws should dispose of the law of God 'without any respect had to that which of old hath been reverently thought of throughout the world.' Consequently Hooker experienced no difficulty with the dictum of Ambrose that the emperor was *'intra ecclesiam, non supra ecclesiam.'* 'For the received laws and liberties of the Church the king hath supreme authority and power, but against them, none.' And who was to define such matters? 'The most natural and religious course in making of laws is, that the matter of them be taken from the judgment of the wisest in those things which they are to concern. In matters of God, to set down a form of public prayer, a solemn confession of the articles of the christian faith, rites and ceremonies meet for the exercise of religion; it were unnatural not to think the pastors and bishops of our souls a great deal more fit, than men of secular trades and callings.'[47] This doctrine was not theoretically in conflict with Elizabeth's own understanding of how the royal supremacy should operate. When subjected to lay, parliamentary pressure to alter the ecclesiastical settlement, she was especially remindful that such matters belonged properly to churchmen, saving her own prerogative. Only in the reverse situation, when her policy was opposed by ecclesiastics, would the naked 'Erastianism' which was implicit in the Elizabethan polity reveal itself fully.

Historians have yet to explore the practical possibilities contained within these not unfamiliar expositions of the constitution of the Elizabethan Church, preferring to work with the doubtless realistic but perhaps over-realistic assumption that the queen was mistress of her Church and the bishops mere instruments of her will. Certainly Elizabeth was not one to forget that the bishops were her creation and her servants. And as with any other servant or subject the penalty of independence

---

[44] Lamont (above n. 27), 36–8.
[45] My italics.
[46] *Works of Jewel* (above n. 1), iii. 167, iv. 974.
[47] *Works of Hooker* (above n. 21), iii. 358, 410. See W. D. J. Cargill Thompson, 'The Philosopher of the "Politic Society": Richard Hooker as a Political Thinker', in *Studies in Richard Hooker: Essays Preliminary to an Edition of his Works*, ed. W. Speed Hill, Cleveland & London 1972, 3–76.

could be temporary or permanent rustication from her favour. But the ineluctable fact remains that there was no easy or summary procedure for the dismissal of a bishop and that no bishop appointed by Elizabeth was ever deprived.[48] Modern studies have made much of the role in the Elizabethan Church of the governing class ('lay intervention'), but the study of bishops remains anchored to biography and episcopal administration, a system which in practice belonged to professional administrators and judges and functioned with only occasional intervention by the bishops themselves. This is not the place to develop these potentially expansive themes, but only to note that the loss of the records of Convocation and the relative obscurity of most of the proceedings in the House of Lords are accidents which have led to the unconscious neglect of the synodical and political activity of the Elizabethan episcopate, while the personal and pastoral influence which some bishops may have exerted in more informal ways, at Court and elsewhere, by its very nature was rarely a matter for record.

On this occasion we are concerned only with the power of utterance, which for protestants was in a sense the only power belonging to the ministry: and not properly its own power but the power inherent in the word of God. 'And touching the . . . safest way for princes to be guided unto the truth,' wrote Bilson, as to a Jesuit opponent, 'though we differ about the meanes, yow reserving it as a speciall privilege to the pope, we referring it as a common duetie to the preacher: yet this is evident, that princes must be directed unto truth . . .' 'To conclude, pastors may teach, exhort and reprove, not force command or revenge: only princes be governors.'[49]

An investigation of those occasions when senior ecclesiastics besought Queen Elizabeth, in the bowels of Christ, to think it possible that she might be mistaken would lead most naturally to the subject of court preaching. How often has it been said that Elizabeth 'tuned the pulpits'? The evidence for such tuning is quite slender, if we look beyond some London pulpits and except certain moments of political emergency. It is not so often remarked that the queen was herself the hearer of hundreds of sermons, seated behind the window of her closet, which when the Court was at Richmond was *vis-a-vis* the pulpit, as we say, eyeball to eyeball.[50] We do not know that the preachers on such occasions were restrained by any influence other than their own sense of decorum and self-preservation.

---

[48] The case of Bishop Marmaduke Middleton of St Davids is obscure, but it is not clear that he suffered deprivation. (R. E. Head, *The Royal Supremacy and the Trials of Bishops 1558–1725*, London 1962, 23–7.)

[49] Bilson (above n. 19), 124, 127.

[50] Harington (above n. 13), 187–8. The context is a description of a sermon by Bishop Anthony Rudd of St Davids: 'The bishop discovering all was not well, for the pulpit stands there *vis a vis* to the closet . . .'

Lenten sermons would offer the best scope for such an enquiry, since not only was this the principal season for court preaching but in Lent there was a kind of role reversal, a religious anti-carnival. Even Queen Elizabeth might have experienced a sense of disappointment if her Lenten preachers had failed, albeit within conventional limits, to cut into the proud flesh of the auditory, her own included. Dering's controlled outburst, which exceeded those limits, was on the occasion of a Lenten sermon, and it was a Lenten sermon in which Whitgift attacked the 'sinister affection' of flattery. On other occasions the preacher, like Agag, may have come unto the queen more delicately (1 Samuel xv. 32, which the Geneva Bible rendered 'pleasantly'). But it should not be forgotten that when Alexander Nowell was accused of flattering the queen in his sermons he replied that 'he had no other way to instruct the queen what she should be, but by commending her.'[51] There was no older trick in the persuasive rhetorician's repertoire, and court preachers were no more likely to neglect it than authors in framing their dedicatory epistles.

In what remains of this article I propose to look not at sermons, some of which may have been uttered in the spirit of *Epistola XL*, but at two written orations in which Ambrose was extensively cited in defence of the temerity of the author in addressing the queen with reproof and admonition. Unlike some of the more outspoken of court sermons, which were political in substance, these addresses concerned what any protestant would regard as quintessential *causae Dei*: the priority of the preaching ministry and the enormity of image worship.

We turn first to the more celebrated of the two addresses; Archbishop Grindal's 'Book to the Queen' of 8 December 1576. Some of the circumstances surrounding this celebrated document are well known and others I have discussed elsewhere.[52] After Elizabeth had been incensed by reports of 'disorders' involving preachers in the midlands, and the preaching conferences known as prophesyings, Grindal was twice interviewed on the matter at Court. On the second of these occasions his attempt to justify the practice of prophesying with scholarship and the declared support of eight of his suffragans was brushed aside. Faced with a peremptory demand not only to 'utterly suppress' prophesying but to 'abridge' the number of preachers, Grindal returned to Lambeth to compose a letter of great length[53] in which he expressed astonishment

[51] Ralph Churton, *The Life of Alexander Nowell*, Oxford 1809, 92.

[52] 'The Downfall of Archbishop Grindal and its Place in Elizabethan Political and Ecclesiastical History', in *The English Commonwealth 1547–1640*, ed. Peter Clark, Alan G. R. Smith & Nicholas Tyacke, Leicester 1979, 39–57; and my forthcoming study of Grindal, *Archbishop Grindal and the Struggle for a Reformed Church. See below*, 371-98.

[53] Among the many MS. copies of this document two are of especial interest, since they seem to be copies prepared for two privy councillors, Lord Burghley and Sir Walter Mildmay: BL, MS. Lansdowne 23, no. 12, fols. 24–9^r, and Northamptonshire Record Office, F.(M).P.54. The Lansdowne copy is printed in Grindal's *Remains* (above n. 29), 376–90.

that the queen should favour a reduction of preaching and attempted with an array of pragmatic arguments and scriptural and patristic 'proofs' to convince her of the utility of prophesying. The climax was reached in an unqualified refusal to lend either conscience or hand to the promulgation of the queen's order. 'I am forced, with all humility, and yet plainly, to profess that I cannot with safe conscience, and without the offence of the majesty of God, give my assent to the suppressing of the said exercises; much less can I send out any injunction for the utter and universal suppression of the same.' There followed an offer to vacate his office, fitting perfectly Bishop Bilson's model of an answer 'stout but lawfull; constant but christian', refusing to consent to the prince's will but resisting not the prince's power. The subsequent play of political forces determined that Grindal should not be deprived, which legally and constitutionally might have proved a dubious and perilous undertaking. But he was suspended from many of his functions and remained in some degree of sequestration until his death in July 1583.

It underlines a point already made that on the evidence of this letter Grindal is as often as not labelled a 'puritan'. But when W. H. Frere called it 'a particular piece of characteristically puritan crankiness'[54] he mistook the rhetorical currency in which Grindal dealt and chose to overlook its source. For when Grindal wrote: 'Bear with me, I beseech you, Madam, if I choose rather to offend your earthly majesty than the heavenly majesty of God' this was an echo not of Calvin or Knox but of Ambrose in the *Oratio contra Auxentium*: 'Quia plus Dominum mundi quam saeculi hujus imperatorem timerem.'[55] It was in the peroration required by rhetorical convention that Grindal leaned most heavily on Ambrose. These final periods were built, perhaps gratuitously and no doubt unwisely, around two 'short petitions' which generalised from the matters at issue to provide a sketch of the proper relationship which in Grindal's view should obtain between the queen and her Church, a view somewhat remote from reality but not from what Hooker would later write in the 8th Book of the *Laws of Ecclesiastical Polity*. The first petition was to the effect that the queen should follow the example of all godly emperors and princes in referring 'all these ecclesiastical matters which touch religion or the doctrine and discipline of the Church' to the bishops and divines of her realm. The second was that 'when you deal in matters of faith and religion, or matters that touch the Church of Christ, . . . you would not use to pronounce so resolutely and peremptorily, *quasi ex auctoritate*, as ye may do in civil and extern matters . . . In God's matters all princes ought to bow their sceptres to the Son of God, and to ask counsel at his mouth, what they ought to do.' These positions were supported from two Ambrosian epistles, *Epistola XL*, to Theodosius, and *Epistola XXI*, to Valentinian: '*Si de causis pecuniariis*

[54] W. H. Frere, *The English Church in the Reigns of Elizabeth and James I*, London 1904, 192.
[55] P.L., xvi. 1007.

comites tuos consulis, quanto magis in causa religionis sacerdotes Domini aequum est consulas?' *'Si docendus est episcopus a laico, quid sequetur?'* And it was Theodoret's account of the words purportedly spoken by Ambrose after the massacre of Thessalonika[56] which furnished Grindal with what may have proved the most offensive passage in the entire letter: 'Look not only (as was said to Theodosius) upon the purple and princely array, wherewith ye are apparelled; but consider withal, what is that that is covered therewith. Is it not flesh and blood? Is it not dust and ashes? Is it not a corruptible body, which must return to the earth again (God knoweth how soon)?'[57] There is a certain irony in the adverse reaction of Bishop Frere, of all people, to these fragments of the fourth century assembled for the instruction of the sixteenth.

The argument is not that Grindal was somehow 'influenced' by Ambrose in the formation of views on Church and State which were to be found in the writings of such contemporary theologians as, for example, his old mentor Martin Bucer:[58] only that he chose to compose his discourse out of a mosaic of quotations of or relating to Ambrose. It was only when I saw Grindal's own copy of the Erasmian edition of the *Opera* of Ambrose in the Basle edition of 1538[59] that I appreciated that the 'Book to the Queen' was in form an oration in the manner of Ambrose, making of prophesying an issue in relations between the basilica and the palace equivalent to the Battle of the Basilicas itself. Even for Grindal to claim to have written *'manu mea, quod sola legas'*[60] was to borrow from *Epistola LI* of Ambrose.

Grindal only rarely annotated his books. But his pen was never still as he read the Ambrosian epistles. His distinctive hand first appears in the margin of Erasmus's dedication of the edition to John à Lasco where Grindal took note of the fact that Theodosius had been praised for suffering himself to be subdued by Ambrose: *'Theodosio laudi fuit, quod se a Ambrosio vinci passus est.'*[61] From *Epistola XL* he noted: *'Sacerdotium est, libere denuntiare quod sentiunt'* and *'Speculatores non Adulatores'*[62] The

---

[56] *A History of the Church . . . by Theodoret and Evandrius* (Bohn's Ecclesiastical Library, London 1854), 219–23.

[57] The brackets have been restored from the MS. They appear to strengthen the force of Grindal's aside.

[58] See my article 'The Reformer and the Archbishop: Martin Bucer and an English Bucerian', *Journal of Religious History*, vi (1971), 305–30. *See above*, 19-44.

[59] *Omnia quotquot extant divi Ambrosii Episcopi Mediolanensis opera cum per des. Erasmum Roterodamum tum per alios eruditos viros*, 5 tom. in 2 vols., Basle 1538. I am greatly indebted to Miss Helen Powell, Assistant Librarian of the Queen's College, Oxford, for assistance in locating Grindal's copy of this work, bequeathed to the college among a large collection of books by his will of 1583.

[60] Yet no copy in Grindal's hand or bearing his signature survives, whereas, as noted above, copies seem to have been prepared almost at once for the benefit of members of the Privy Council.

[61] *Ambrosii opera*, tom. 1, Sig. AA 5[r].

[62] Ibid., tom. 3, 129.

critical passage *'in causa vero Dei quem audies si sacerdotem non audies'* was prominently underscored and given an identifying mark in the margin, while the point of the passage *'si de causis pecuniariis comites tuos consulis . . .'* was extracted as *'causa religionis episcopi consulendi'*.[63] When he reached *Epistola XX* to Valentinian Grindal noted *'sacerdotes de sacerdotibus iudicare'*; and from the *Oratio contra Auxentium 'imperatoribus deferrendum, non cedendum'*, and also three pregnant words *'imperator filius Ecclesiae'*.[64] In his study of *Epistola XX* Grindal took no special notice of the seminal dictum *'ad imperatorem palatia pertinent, ad sacerdotem ecclesiae'*. Was this a significant omission? But he underlined the immediately preceding sentences and wrote in the margin *'imperator Deo subditus'*.[65]

This was not the first time that Elizabeth had been treated to a dose of Ambrosian rhetoric. In the winter of 1559–60 it was intended that she should receive an address of much the same length as the 'book' of 1576, and bearing a close family resemblance to it. This initiative was taken in the midst of the first and perhaps most serious ecclesiastical crisis of the new Elizabethan dispensation.[66] In the autumn of 1559 the newly appointed but still unconsecrated bishops were deeply troubled by the presence of a little silver cross, together with candles, on the communion table in the queen's chapel. The symbolism of these small objects was in itself a cause of offence to protestant churchmen frequenting the Court. But a greater cause of concern was their significance as a portent of a general reaction in ecclesiastical policy which threatened to restore to parish churches the crucifixes and rood statuary so recently dismantled in the course of the Royal Visitation of the Church.[67] It appears that the cross had been removed from the royal chapel only at the time of the visitation, when the queen was herself absent on progress, and that it had been promptly restored on her return. The holocaust of imagery in the summer of 1559 had exceeded her expectations and the letter of the Royal Injunctions and she did not intend to let the matter rest. Since the removal of rood lofts had been a contentious and costly undertaking in thousands of parish churches nothing could be more calculated to discredit the leaders of the newly reformed Church than a decision to reverse the process yet again. This daunting prospect coincided with another cause of grave discouragement to the new bishops: the implementation of the Act of Exchange of 1559, which threatened to make a drastic alteration in episcopal finance

[63] Ibid., tom. 3, 130, 134.

[64] Ibid., tom. 3, 145, 147, 154.

[65] Ibid., tom. 3, 156.

[66] The fullest account is in William P. Haugaard, *Elizabeth and the English Reformation: the Struggle for a Stable Settlement of Religion*, Cambridge 1968, 185–200.

[67] So much is implied by the Spanish ambassador (*Calendar of State Papers, Spanish*, i. 105) and Bishop Sandys (letter to Peter Martyr, 1 April 1560, *The Zurich Letters*, ed. H. Robinson (Parker Society, Cambridge, 1842), 72–5).

without a corresponding reappraisal of episcopal duties.[68] The affair of
the silver cross or 'offendicle' came to a head in February 1560 with the
staging of a disputation between two pairs of bishops before a tribunal
appointed by the Privy Council: Parker and Cox on one side, Jewel and
Grindal on the other. The arrangements in a formal disputation are not
necessarily indicative of the private convictions of the participants. If Cox,
as seems likely, was one of those required to defend the use of images, he
had also drafted a letter to the queen offering reasons why 'I dare not
minister in your grac[es] chappell the lights and crosse remayning.'[69] But
the Zürich correspondence points to some real difference of opinion
between those, like Jewel and Sandys, for whom the cross was not
negotiable and who were ready to resign or face dismissal rather than
submit to its use, and others, perhaps including Parker and Cox, for
whom the matters at issue were of the nature of *adiaphora* and within the
prince's discretion.[70]

These were the circumstances which seem to have prompted the
preparation of an elaborate address to the queen, of which a copy
survives among Parker's MSS. in Corpus Christi College Cambridge.[71]
The document is of a composite nature. First there is a letter to the queen,
which speaks of renewing 'our former sute' and of having 'at sundrie
tymes made petition to yor Majestie, concerning the matter of images',
but without hitherto exhibiting 'any reasons for the removing of the
same.' 'We have at this tyme put in wryting and do most humblie exhibite
to your gracious consideration those authorities of the Scriptures, reasons
and pithie persuasions, whiche as they have moved all suche our brethren
as now beare the office of bisshops, to thinke and affirme images not
expedient for the Churche of Christ, so they will not suffer us withowt the
great offending of God, and grevouse wounding of our owne consciences
(which God deliver us from) to consent to the erecting or reteaning of the
same in the place of worshipping. And we trust and most earnestlie aske it
of God that they may also persuade your Majestie by your regall authoritie
and in the zeal of God utterly to remove this offensive evill owt of the
Churche of England, to Godds great glorie and our great comforth.' The
letter is undated and unsigned and it is not known whether it was in fact
presented to the queen. In ascribing it to 'Archbishop Parker and others'
the editors of *Correspondence of Matthew Parker* followed the ancient lead of
Burnet and Strype, although, as more recent authors have pointed out,

---

[68] Felicity Heal, 'The Bishops and the Act of Exchange of 1559', *Historical Journal*, xvii
(1974), 227–46.

[69] Haugaard, op. cit., 194.

[70] Ibid., 189–96.

[71] Corpus Christi College Cambridge MS. 105, art. 11, pp. 201–15ʳ. I am grateful to the
Master and Fellows for permission to consult and cite this document. It bears no
endorsement or other identifying marks. There is no significant palaeographical evidence,
the document being written in a standard mid-sixteenth century secretary hand. It was
printed in *Correspondence of Matthew Parker* (above n. 28), 79–95.

there is no justification for connecting the document with the arch-bishop.[72] Indeed, the reference to 'suche our brethern as now beare the office of bisshop' may indicate that the authors were not bishops at all but some of the returned exiles who stood outside the ranks of the episcopate in making and would form the nucleus of the nonconformist group which was to emerge by the mid-sixties.[73] Yet Dr Haugaard is probably right to see in the letter the hands of those bishops who took a hard line against the 'offendicle': 'men of the party of Jewel, Grindal and Sandys'.[74]

The treatise which follows, 'Reasons Against Images in Churches', is divided into two sections: first a catena of biblical texts, from Exodus xx to 1 John, followed by reasoned argument; then a collection of 'Proofs out of the Fathers, Councils and Histories', which ends with the bleak verdict that in spite of the heavy weight of iconoclastic tradition, nothing had overcome the images for as long as they were permitted by authority to stand. 'For thies blinde bookes and domme scholemasters (whiche they call laye mens bokes) have more prevailed by their carved and paynted preching of idolatrie than all other written bokes and preachinges in teaching the truth and the horror of that vice.' The final peroration finds us on familiar ground. The writers humbly beseech the queen 'not to strean us any further', but to consider that God's word threatens judgment to pastors and ministers who consent to what they are persuaded in conscience to be idolatrous. 'We pray your Majestie also not to be offended with this our plannesse and libertie, which all good and christiane princes have ever taken in good parte at the handes of godlie bishops. Saynt Ambrose writing to Theodosius the emperor useth thies wordes', and then follow the very passages from *Epistola XL* which Grindal was to use in 1576 and which will now hardly bear, or need repetition. Moreover the writers continue with a plea that 'in thies and such like controversies of religion' the queen would 'referr the discussement and deciding of them to a synode of your bisshops and other godlie learned men, according to the example of Constantinus Magnus and other christiane emperors; that the reasons of both partes being examined by them, the judgement may be given uprightlie in all dowbtfull matters.' We may note in passing that the question at issue was not referred to a specially convened synod: there can have been no question of that. Instead, as we have seen, the bishops were required to debate before a lay tribunal, so illustrating the discrepancy between the Ambrosian and Elizabethan polities. For it was in protest against a demand to submit his

---

[72] Gilbert Burnet attributes the document to 'the reformed bishops and divines': *The History of the Reformation of the Church of England*, Oxford 1829, II. i. 794–6, ii. 487–90. John Strype attributed this 'humble free letter' to 'the Archbishop and Bishops'; *Life of Parker*, Oxford 1821, i. 191–3, *Annals of the Reformation*, Oxford 1824, I. i. 330–2. See the modern views of V. J. K. Brook, *A Life of Archbishop Parker*, Oxford 1962, 78 and Haugaard, op. cit., 190.

[73] Patrick Collinson, *The Elizabethan Puritan Movement*, London 1967, 45–55, 71–83.

[74] Haugaard, op. cit., 192.

cause to secular arbitration that Ambrose had written *Epistola XL*. Finally the memorialists pointed out that the establishing of images by royal authority 'shall not onlie utterlie discredite our ministeries, as builders of the thinges which we have destroyed, but also blemishe the fame of your most godlie brother, and suche notable fathers as have given their liefes for the testimonie of Goddes truthe, who by publik lawe removed all images.'

Comparison with Grindal's peroration of 1576 may lead to the plausible conclusion that Grindal was the author of both documents. Unfortunately there are complications which will not allow the matter to be so tidily settled. For if John Foxe is to be believed, the treatise 'Reasons Against Images in Churches' was written by Nicholas Ridley in the reign of Edward VI. If this is true then only the letter to the queen which prefaced it was an original composition of 1559–60. In the Appendix of hitherto unpublished documents added to the 1583 edition of *Acts and Monuments* Foxe included the treatise in its entirety, heading it with this description: 'A Treatise of M. Nich. Ridley, in the name, as it seemeth, of the whole Clargie, to King Edward the vj concernyng Images not to be set up, nor worshipped in Churches'.[75] This differs from the copy in the Corpus Christi MS. in one word only: where the MS. speaks of 'the fame of your most godlie brother' Foxe's text has 'the fame of your most godly father'. Among the editors of the Parker Society the right hand did not know what the left was doing. In 1843 Henry Christmas reprinted the Treatise Against Images from Foxe in *The Works of Nicholas Ridley*.[76] In 1853 John Bruce and T. T. Perowne included the Corpus Christi document in *Correspondence of Matthew Parker*.[77]

An Edwardian treatise against image worship, penned by Ridley in the name of a party among the clergy, is not an impossibility. The matter of images was a storm-centre of controversy in the early months of 1547, which witnessed episodes of apparently spontaneous iconoclasm of the kind which marked a certain stage in the progress of the protestant movement in other parts of Europe. On Ash Wednesday 1547 Ridley (still 'Master Nicholas Ridley') preached against images at Court, and the details of his sermon are known from Bishop Stephen Gardiner's reply to it.[78] But within the next twelve months the removal of all images became official policy, while at no point had the Edwardian government expressed public support for a reaction in their favour of a kind which

[75] Pp. 2126–31; in the Cattley edition (above n. 16), viii. 701–7.

[76] *The Works of Nicholas Ridley*, ed. H. Christmas (Parker Society, Cambridge 1843), 81–96.

[77] Among modern authors only Ridley's descendant and biographer Jasper Ridley has noticed that the two documents are identical, although even he appears to have known the Elizabethan version only from the account in Jeremy Collier, *An Ecclesiastical History of Great Britain*, London 1852, vi. 300–2. (*Nicholas Ridley: A Biography*, London 1957, 119n.)

[78] *Acts and Monuments* (above n. 16), vi. 58–63.

would have provoked a measured démarche on the part of the protestant clergy. More seems to be required than the alteration of 'brother' to 'father' to turn what looks very like an Elizabethan document into something Edwardian. What would it have meant, in 1547, to speak, as the Treatise does, of 'the restitution' of images?[79] Moreover it must be doubted whether Ridley would have thought it appropriate to write in 1547 of 'suche notable fathers as have given their liefes for the testimonie of Goddes truthe, who by publik lawe removed all images.' It seems more likely that Ridley himself was among the 'notable fathers' intended by the reference.

Nor was Foxe without motives for falsifying the evidence. No 'precisian' but a convinced iconoclast, it would have suited his purpose to suggest that an uncompromising denunciation of images, not as *adiaphora* but as utterly inadmissible, was made in the time of Edward VI by such a notable father and martyr as Ridley, 'in the name, as it seemeth, of the whole clergy'. By the same token he would have no wish to make public a serious disagreement between the Elizabethan bishops and the queen with whose godly purposes he could find no fault. Moreover Foxe had not concealed where his sympathies were to be found in the Edwardian controversy over vestments between Ridley and Bishop John Hooper. This was how he introduced his account of this affair: 'For notwithstanding that godly reformation of religion then begun in the Church of England, besides other ceremonies more ambitious than profitable, or tending to edification, they used to wear such garments and apparel as the popish bishops were wont to do.' What followed was hostile to 'the bishops' but refrained from naming Ridley since he had later become reconciled to Hooper and had shared his martyrdom.[80] So Foxe gave prominence to the letter of reconciliation which Hooper received from his old opponent in which he was addressed as 'dear brother' and assured that the two were in complete agreement on 'the grounds and substantial points of our religion'.[81] And in his account of Ridley's degradation Foxe took evident pleasure in the moment when the bishop rejected the surplice as foolish and abominable apparel, 'yea, too fond for a vice in a play'.[82] Finally, in printing a letter from Ridley in prison to Grindal in exile Foxe omitted a passage which was critical of John Knox's 'puritan'

[79] The only recorded incident of 1547 which would fit the circumstances implied in the Treatise was the Privy Council order of 10 February requiring the churchwardens of the London parish of St Martin's, Ironmonger Lane, to restore the crucifix and images which they had removed on their own authority. (*Acts of the Privy Council*, ed. J. R. Dasent, n.s. ii. 25–7.) A year later Archbishop Cranmer's mandate on the subject spoke of images having been restored in some places 'and almoste in every place ys contentyon for images', but this was not a reference to officially inspired action. (Edward Cardwell, *Documentary Annals*, Oxford 1844, i. 47–9.)

[80] *Acts and Monuments*, vi. 640–2.

[81] Ibid., vi. 642–3.

[82] Ibid., vii. 543–4.

role in the Frankfurt troubles.[83] It is no longer in doubt that Foxe was prepared to tamper with the evidence in order to disguise cracks in the edifice of protestant unity. Yet to attribute to Ridley something written four years after his death in wholly different circumstances approaches the sloppily dishonest scholarship of which Foxe was accused by his Victorian critics. It remains a teasing problem.

We are left with two or perhaps three possibilities. The first, the least likely, is that Ridley indeed wrote the Treatise Against Images in 1547. It would follow that he was responsible for the Ambrosian note sounded in the peroration and for giving currency to the important *topos* that 'plainness and liberty' had always been taken in good part by Christian princes at the hands of Christian bishops. And that would tend to locate the source of Grindal's interest in Ambrose and even of his 'puritan crankiness' in one of the most impeccable of all the founding fathers of the reformed English Church. This is an attractive thesis, since Ridley and Grindal were the closest of friends and associates, first in Cambridge and then in London, where Grindal formed part of Ridley's 'general staff' in the chapter of St Paul's and became his designated successor. According to William Turner, Grindal was Ridley's *'fidus Achates'*, and there is only room for one Achates in a man's life.[84] But on balance it appears more likely that the Treatise was composed in 1559–60 and that Grindal was its author. The third possibility is that Grindal or some other correspondent of Foxe supplied him with the Treatise in its Elizabethan form but with the information that it had been prepared from notes left behind by Ridley. But in this case we should expect to find some resemblance between the Treatise and Ridley's Ash Wednesday sermon on the same subject, which was a more restrained statement and, so far as appears from Gardiner's response, lacking in the specific citations which we find in the Treatise. Here we must leave this triangular enigma, noting the curious circumstance that Ridley made Foxe a deacon and Grindal made him a priest.

Only after this argument had been constructed and these paragraphs written was it discovered that another copy of the letter of protest to the queen about images is preserved among the Laud–Selden–Fairhurst MSS. recently restored to Lambeth Palace Library in MS. 2002:[85] the letter only and not the treatise 'Reasons Against Images in Churches'. The fact that this copy exists apart from the treatise makes it more likely that the Treatise Against Images had another origin and was pressed into service

[83] Ibid., vii. 434–6. Miles Coverdale omitted the same passage in his edition of the letter in *Certain most godly fruitful and comfortable letters*, 1564, 51–6. The missing passage was printed in part in William Covell, *A briefe answer unto certain reasons by way of an apologie . . . by M. Iohn Burges*, 1606, p. 69 and in full in the Supplement to *The Works of Ridley* (above n. 76), 533–4 (but without disclosing its relationship to the remainder of the letter printed elsewhere in the same volume, 388–95.) The letter is found in its original integrity in Emmanuel College Cambridge, MS. 260, fol. 114.*

[84] *Works of Ridley*, 493.

[85] Lambeth Palace Library, MS. 2002, no. 5, fol. 29.

on this occasion. But this copy of the letter is dated, 5 February 1559(/60), and the date appears to be written in the hand of Edmund Grindal. Lambeth Palace Library MS. 2002 (a miscellany of papers connected with four archbishops of Canterbury) contains another paper which in its very form suggests a kinship with the two other documents on which this article has focused, and which both appear to have emanated from Grindal. This is 'Certeyne reasones to be offred to the quenes majesties consideracion why it is not convenient that the communion shulde be mynystered at an altare'.[86] Although Strype printed this document from another copy in the Petyt MSS.[87] it has not attracted as much attention as it may deserve. In this paper, as with the other documents under consideration, 'proofs' from the Bible and the Fathers are followed by pragmatic and circumstantial arguments, in this case nine in number. If altars are retained the 'adversaries' will note the inconsistency with Edwardian policy. Honest preachers who have denounced altars in their sermons will be discredited. Mass priests, on the contrary, will be encouraged, while the offence to the godly would threaten schism. To reinstate altars would be incompatible with the Prayer Book, already enacted. It would also be inconsistent with practice under Edward VI. With the single and eccentric exception of the Saxon churches the protestant world had removed altars and had abolished related ceremonies. So to maintain altars would be to go against 'the greatest learned men of the worlde' and against Cranmer, Ridley and other English martyrs. 'And last of all, it maie please your Majestie to tender the consent of suche preachers and learned men as nowe do remayne alyve, and do earnestle and of conscience and not for lyvinges sake desyre a godly reformacion, who if they were required to utter their mind or thought it necessarie to make petition to your grace would with one mynde and one mouthe (as maie be reasonably gathered) be most humble suters to your Majestie that theie might not be inforced to retourne unto suche ordinaunces and devises of man not commaunded in Goddes worde. Beinge also once abrogated and knowen by experience to be thinges hurtfull, and onely servinge either to nourishe the superstitious opinion of the propiciatorie masse in the myndes of simple, or elles to minister an occasion of offence and division amongst the godly mynded.' This trenchant address may account for the injunction appended to the Royal Injunctions of 1559 which, while not requiring the removal of altars, recognised the *fait accompli* 'in many and sundry parts of the realm' and provided an orderly procedure for the removal and for the erection of holy tables.[88] In the Lambeth Palace Library copy the address is endorsed in Grindal's hand: 'Reasons why the communion should not be

[86] Ibid., no. 18, fols. 107–10.

[87] Strype, *Annals*, I. i. 237–41, from Inner Temple Library, MS. Petyt 538. 38, no. 9, fols. 29–31.

[88] Henry Gee, *The Elizabethan Clergy and the Settlement of Religion 1558–1564*, Oxford 1898, 63–4.

ministred at an alter². It appears that the story of the construction of the Elizabethan Settlement, somewhat against the desires of the queen, has not yet been told in full.

Whatever the origins and provenance of the Treatise Against Images it ought not to be our conclusion that only Edmund Grindal was concerned about the threat to the integrity of *Ecclesia Anglicana* occasionally represented by Elizabeth's government, or that he alone was capable of calling upon the fourth century to redress the balance of the sixteenth. In 1561 there was another crisis of protestant conscience when the queen revealed to a scandalised Archbishop Parker the depth of her old-fashioned prejudice against a married clergy. 'I was in an horror to hear such words to come from her mild nature and christianly learned conscience, as she spake concerning God's holy ordinance and institution of matrimony.' The queen had gone so far as to express 'a repentance' that the bishops had been appointed to office and Parker for his part, not for the last time, professed to rue the day that he had consented to become her archbishop, 'to whom resorteth daily and hourly such complaints as I send you herewith', apparently from fellow bishops and churchmen. Elizabeth had already issued a new injunction against the residence of women in colleges and cathedral closes and she threatened others, which would doubtless have rescinded the measure of toleration for clergy wives allowed in the Royal Injunctions of 1559. We do not know that Parker was so incautious as to express his feelings on this subject, or indeed on any other subject, to the queen in person, as Grindal would do in parallel circumstances in 1576. That was a measure of the difference between the two primates. But he reminded Cecil that princes were supposed to cherish the ecclesiastical state as 'conservators of religion', and he hoped that the clergy would not be forced to 'show disobedience' in the spirit of Acts v. 29. *Oportet Deo obedire magis quam hominibus.* This was not the text most frequently on Parker's lips. (He once had occasion to tell a suffragan: 'It is pity we should shew any vanity in our obedience.'[89]) But showing that ancient precedents were not far from his mind he hoped that the queen would 'use Theodosius' days of deliberation in sentence-giving, in matters of such importance', and ended with citations in favour of clerical marriage from Jerome, Augustine and Chrysostom.[90]

The storm over the married clergy blew itself out and revived only intermittently, at the expense of individuals like Bishop Richard Fletcher, whose second marriage in 1595 cost him the royal favour. But the affair of the little silver cross had a famous sequel. In 1560 Bishop Sandys had rejoiced that God had 'delivered the church of England from stumbling-blocks of this kind.'[91] But he appears to have meant that there was no

[89] *Correspondence of Parker* (above n. 28), 458.

[90] Ibid., 156–60, and also 146, 148, 151–2.

[91] *Zurich Letters* (above n. 67), 72–5. For the subsequent clarification of arrangements in parish churches, see *Orders taken the x. day of October in the thirde yere of the raigne of . . .*

longer a threat to the work of the Royal Visitation of 1559, not that the queen had allowed the bishops to have their way with the furnishing of her chapel. The cross remained. On Ash Wednesday 1565 the preacher at Court was the dean of St Paul's, Alexander Nowell. We know that Nowell believed that the prince should be obedient to the minister in carrying out his office in accordance with the word of God.[92] From the Spanish ambassador's account of this Ash Wednesday sermon and the preacher's own report[93] it appears that this was a rare occasion when he put his convictions to the test. The opportunity occurred in the course of an intentional digression from the text in order to attack a book recently published in Antwerp, John Martiall's *Treatyse of the crosse*, which James Calfhill was about to answer in print.[94] Martiall had dedicated this latest salvo in the battle of the books to the queen, who was 'so well affectioned to the cross' that she kept it reverently in her chapel.[95] Consequently Nowell's reply was likely to scratch an old sore, and this indeed may have been its purpose. So Elizabeth must have assumed when she intervened with 'Do not talk about that'; and, when the preacher, not having heard, forged on: 'Leave that; it has nothing to do with your subject and the matter is now threadbare.' The words have been filtered through Spanish and back into English and they do not ring entirely true. But their effect registered high on the Richter scale for it was felt as far away as Rome, where Cardinal Charles Borromeo was encouraged by the intelligence that the queen had 'censured the preacher that preached against images and the saints.'[96] Thomas Harding later congratulated Elizabeth for her 'princely word commanding a preacher that opened his lewd mouth against the reverent use of the cross in your private chapel to retire from that ungodly digression unto his text.'[97]

It is possible that, as catholics hoped, the royal outburst was premeditated and intended to signal a reactionary turn in ecclesiastical policy but it is unlikely. As Elizabeth indicated, the subject of images was now somewhat *passé*. The dean of St Paul's was a preacher whom she heard

[92] See above, pp. 113–14.
[93] *Calendar of State Papers, Spanish*, i. 405: Nowell to Cecil, 8 March 1564(/5); Strype, *Parker* (above n. 72), iii. 94.
[94] James Calfhill, *An Answer to John Martiall's Treatise of the Cross*, ed. R. Gibbings (Parker Society, Cambridge 1846).
[95] *A treatyse of the crosse*, Antwerp 1564, Sig. A 2^v; quoted by J. E. Booty in the Introduction to his edition of *An Apology of the Church of England by John Jewel* (Folger Documents of Tudor and Stuart Civilization, Ithaca 1963), x.
[96] *Calendar of State Papers, Rome*, i. 171.
[97] Quoted by Booty, loc. cit., x.

Elizabeth quene of Englande, 1561; and 'The Interpretations of the Bishops' in W. H. Frere, *Visitation Articles and Injunctions of the Period of the Reformation*, iii (Alcuin Club Collections xvi. 1910), 59–73. See also W. P. M. Kennedy, *The Interpretations of the Bishops*, London 1908, and Haugaard (above n. 66), 197–200.

frequently,[98] on this and other subjects an old sparring partner. At a service in St Paul's on 1 January 1562 he had arranged that the queen should find on her cushion what he hoped would prove an acceptable New Year's gift: a Prayer Book richly illustrated with German pictures 'representing the stories and passions of the saints and martyrs'. But the little plot badly misfired when Elizabeth rounded on Nowell to ask whether he was unaware of her aversion to idolatry and had forgotten her proclamation against images and pictures in churches.[99] This must surely have been said with tongue in cheek.

But the queen's anger on Ash Wednesday 1565 was not feigned and may have had some permanent effect on the style and content of court preaching. Parker wrote to Cecil on the following day: 'For pure pity I took home to dinner with me M. dean of Paul's yesterday; he was utterly dismayed.'[100] A year later he had difficulty in filling the list of preachers for another Lent since there was a general fear of 'the like sequel of reproof.' 'I would wish the dean of Paul's to be one: whom, if the Queen's Majesty shall not like after her accustomed manner to favour and to give him hearing, he shall be hardly entreated to occupy the place.'[101] Whether or not, as Ambrose had suggested, it was offensive above all else in God's sight for a bishop to remain silent there were some eloquent episcopal silences in the years that followed Nowell's discomfiture, until pent-up frustration found at least one voice in December 1576. And the consequences of Archbishop Grindal's fatal utterance were such that it was not until the next reign that bishops felt free to justify openly the liberty of prophesying which was their proper heritage within *Ecclesia Anglicana*.[102]

With the accession of James I, whose very table was said to be 'as Constantine's Court, *ecclesiae instar*, a little universitie compassed with learned men',[103] the example of Ambrose could be commended with less inhibition. In his *Iurisdiction, royall, episcopall, papall* Bishop George Carleton roundly asserted that 'for the preservation of true doctrine in the Church, the bishops are the great watchmen. Herein they are authorised by God. If princes withstand them in these things, they have warrant not to obey princes, because with these things Christ hath put them in trust.' There followed an almost ecstatic exposition of the role of Ambrose in the Battle of the Basilicas. 'This example of Ambrose his courage is worthily commended by all posterity, wherein this worthy man seemeth to direct a true rule of obedience ... There appeared in him courage, godlinesse, and exact obedience, all truly tempered. He denieth

---

[98] In 1562 Nowell preached before the queen in St Paul's on 1 January and no less than four times at Court in the ensuing Lent. (Churton (above n. 51), 70–4.)

[99] Strype, *Annals*, I. i. 408–10.

[100] *Correspondence of Parker* (above n. 28), 235.

[101] Parker to Cecil, 29 Jan. 1565(/6), ibid., 254–5.

[102] Lamont (above n. 27), 36–41.

[103] William Barlow, *An answer to a catholike Englishman*, 1609, 105.

the emperour to be a sufficient judge in a cause of faith and religion. *In causa fidei, in causa inquam fidei*. For this hee repeateth precisely, desirous to be rightly understood: he would rather die then admit such an example as to betray the trueth, and that commission and charge wherein God had set him. And yet if the emperour would by force doe any thing, he denieth that there is any power in him, or in the Church, to resist by force and armes, but by prayers and teares. Thus resolute is this godly man in the cause of faith against the emperour . . .'[104]

This is a special occasion which invites an occasional tailpiece. Some readers of this article may recall, with the author, that it was Clifford Dugmore who first made them consider the relevance of Ambrose for the sixteenth century, when he discussed the Ambrosian and Augustinian strains in eucharistic theology in *The Mass and the English Reformers* (1958). It was also Clifford Dugmore who first suggested that I should make a study of Archbishop Edmund Grindal. This article has been born of a marriage between the two hares which he started. It is fitting at this time of celebration that we should also remember our loss in James Cargill Thompson, until his untimely death our Assistant Editor and the originator of the plan to present Clifford Dugmore with a special number of the JOURNAL, as a *Festschrift*. The name of Cargill Thompson will always be associated with the study of theories of political obligation in the age of the Reformation, to which this essay has appended a modest footnote. Moreover it was James, not long before his death, who suggested to me that in spite of a report to the contrary[105] the books bequeathed by Archbishop Grindal to the Queen's College Oxford might still be in place on the shelves of the college library. Happily he proved to be right and enquiries soon revealed the annotations in Grindal's hand on the pages of Ambrose which suggested the composition of this piece.

[104] George Carleton, *Iurisdiction, regall, episcopall, papall*, 1610, 44–5.
[105] Sears Jayne, *Library Catalogues of the English Renaissance*, Berkeley & Los Angeles 1956, 20, 125.

Sir Nicholas Bacon, Lord Keeper of the Great Seal.
The portrait bears Bacon's motto *'Mediocria firma'*.
(*National Portrait Gallery*)

5

SIR NICHOLAS BACON
AND THE ELIZABETHAN *VIA MEDIA*

I

There exists in the British Museum a copy of the prayer book of 1559 bearing the signature of Sir Nicholas Bacon.[1] It would be reasonable to infer that the book was once the lord keeper's property, but a pleasing fancy to pretend that he autographed it for a friend and well-wisher. He was not the author of this all but final recension of the Anglican liturgy but he was one of its principal sponsors. For in the words of Ralph Churton, 'the business of that important parliament...in which the acts of uniformity and supremacy for the settlement of religion were passed was principally managed by the Lord Keeper Bacon'.[2] It was Bacon who presided, not only in the House of Lords but over the theological disputation in Westminster Hall which was staged as a public signal that the English Church was to be once more reformed according to the protestant model. In a speech at the conclusion of the 1559 parliament he defended the newly made settlement against opponents and detractors, and in so doing scratched in the sand, as it were, the line of the Anglican *via media*: 'Amongst thease I meane to comprehende aswell those that be to swifte as those that be to slowe, those I say that goe before the lawe or beyond the lawe as those that will not followe.'[3]

There was no original content in these sentiments. The lord keeper was merely working his own rhetorical variation on a theme first heard a quarter of a century earlier, when the English government advised the court of Saxony that their king would 'neither go in any part beyond the said truth, ne for any respect tarry or stay on this side the truth, but would proceed in the right straight mean way'; and when the publicist Thomas Starkey spoke of setting forth 'the indyfferent mean betwyx the old and blynd superstycyon and thys

* Based on a lecture given for Corpus Christi College in the Mill Lane Lecture Rooms, Cambridge on 31 October 1979 as part of the quatercentenary celebrations of Sir Nicholas Bacon (1510–1579).

[1] Press-mark c.25.m.7.

[2] Ralph Churton, *The life of Alexander Nowell* (Oxford, 1809), pp. 39–40.

[3] British Library, MS Harley 5176, fo. 113ᵛ. I am grateful to the History of Parliament Trust and specifically to the general editor of the History of Parliament, Mr P. W. Hasler, for enabling me to employ transcripts of Sir Nicholas Bacon's parliamentary speeches made by Sir John Neale. Some of these transcripts I checked against the originals when I was employed as Professor Neale's research assistant in 1955–6.

lygt and arrogant opynyon lately entryng here among us'.[4] In 1547 the duke
of Somerset instructed Bishop Stephen Gardiner that the magistrate's duty lay
'in a mean' between those who were so ticklish and tender-stomached that they
could not abide the reform of abuses and the rash who 'headlong will set upon
every thing'.[5] Presently Archbishop Cranmer set the Church squarely between
those who were 'addicted to their old customs' and those who were 'so
new-fangled that they would innovate all thing'.[6] These words, applying to
'ceremonies, why some be abolished and some retained', continued to preface
the prayer book in the Elizabethan version. Other embroideries of this
standard text were still to come. In 1633 George Herbert admired the 'British
Church' for

> A fine aspect in fit array,
> Neither too mean, nor yet too gay.[7]

In 1660 Archbishop Bramhall commended the religion of the Anglican Church
as 'neither garish...nor yet sluttish.'[8]

Recent attempts to reconstruct the inner, parliamentary history of the
Elizabethan settlement, together with generally changing perspectives, have
detracted from R. W. Dixon's majestic sense of 'great religious enactments
...vast and permanent',[9] and they have overtaken the sense of 'golden
mediocrity' as the native genius of the Church of England, predetermining the
shape of the settlement. Sir John Neale conceded that on looking back
everything seemed 'natural and inevitable' – 'the *via media* of tradition'. But
he came to the conclusion that the compromise symbolised by the Acts of
Supremacy and of Uniformity was not deliberate, still less of a philosophical
character, but accidental and political. It was not a path deliberately chosen
between two religious extremes but the arbitrary outcome of a parliamentary
struggle between Queen Elizabeth's addiction to old customs and the new-
fangledness of the House of Commons.[10] In a recent Cambridge thesis Dr
Norman Jones has challenged this version of events but without rehabilitating
the notion that the settlement was inspired by the *via media* as a positive value.
His case rests on a skilful re-reading of the same slender political documentation
which was available to Neale and to earlier historians.[11] Yet the settlement,

[4] W. Gordon Zeeveld, *Foundations of Tudor policy* (Cambridge, Mass., 1948), pp. 119–22, 128–56,
163. Cf. Bernard J. Verkamp, *The indifferent mean: adiaphorism in the English Reformation to 1554*,
Studies in the Reformation, 1 (Athens, Ohio, 1977).

[5] John Foxe, *Acts and monuments*, ed. S. R. Cattley, VI (London, 1838), 30.

[6] *The two liturgies of Edward VI*, ed. J. Ketley, Parker Society (Cambridge, 1844), p. 197.

[7] *The works of George Herbert*, ed. F. E. Hutchinson (Oxford, 1941), p. 109.

[8] James Brogden, *Illustrations of the liturgy and ritual of the United Church of England and Ireland:
being sermons and discourses selected from the works of eminent divines who lived during the seventeenth century*
(London, 1842), III, 473.

[9] R. W. Dixon, *History of the Church of England from the abolition of the Roman jurisdiction*, v (Oxford,
1902), 57.

[10] J. E. Neale, 'The Elizabethan Acts of Supremacy and Uniformity', *English Historical Review*,
LXV (1950), 304–32; J. E. Neale, *Elizabeth I and her parliaments 1559–1581* (London, 1953), pp. 51–84.

[11] Norman L. Jones, 'Faith by statute: the politics of religion in the parliament of 1559',
unpublished Cambridge Ph.D. thesis (1978). See also Dr Jones's article, 'Profiting from religious
reform: the land rush of 1559', *Historical Journal*, XXII (1979), 279–94.

however arrived at, was an act of policy in the eyes of the world, and the moderation which it brought to the religious divisions of the time and of which Bacon spoke in his closing speech was of the essence of policy as the Tudor humanists and 'adiaphorists' understood it.[12]

Bacon's own preference for 'policy' in this Aristotelian sense was not something to which he was converted by his experience of the 1559 parliament: for him at least this was no U-turn. In his speech at the opening of the parliament the Aristotelian mean was already invoked. Members of parliament were instructed that the mark they were to shoot at was 'concorde and unitie', eschewing 'all contentions, contumacious or opprobious words, as heretike, schismatike, papist and such like names.' Their aim should avoid on the one hand 'any kinde of idolatrye or superstition', and 'soe on the other side' licentiousness, irreverence and 'any spice of irreligion'.[13] Indeed, Bacon's moderation had been in evidence even earlier, in the approaches which he began to make to his fellow East Anglian and old Corpus contemporary Matthew Parker. It was a mere three weeks after Mary's death, in early December 1558, that Parker was asked to make urgent contact either with Bacon himself or with 'my brother-in-law Sir William Cecil' 'touching such matters as he and I did talke of concerning you'. And it was to Bacon that Parker eventually came, overcoming illness and profound misgiving, to hear his 'signification' of 'a certaine office ye named to me.'[14] Archbishop Parker was the very soul of 'golden mediocrity', a principle held in contempt by some of his contemporaries as 'leaden mediocrity'.[15] 'I think', the archbishop wrote in 1563, 'divers of my brethren will rather note me, if they were asked, too sharp and too earnest in moderation, which towards them I have used, and will still do, till mediocrity shall be received amongst us'.[16] The taste for mediocrity is sometimes said to be 'innate in the English temper'.[17] How far it extended in the early Elizabethan ecclesiastical and governing class we cannot say. In Neale's judgement the active running in 1559 was made by the two extremes. Yet it is clear that the principal devotees of the middle way were that trinity of glittering prizemen from Henrician Cambridge and the pillars of the Elizabethan church and state, Archbishop Parker, Mr Secretary Cecil and Lord Keeper Bacon. Indeed for Bacon a total philosophy was subsumed in the motto inscribed above his front door at Gorhambury and on his portrait: *Mediocria firma* – Moderate Things Endure, or, Safety in Moderation. One may speak properly and not in any spirit of denigration of the mediocrity of Sir Nicholas Bacon.

[12] Zeeveld, *Foundations of Tudor policy.*   [13] British Library, MS Harley 5176, fo. 106.
[14] Correspondence between Bacon, Cecil and Parker, December 1558–September 1559, *Correspondence of Matthew Parker*, ed. J. Bruce & T. T. Perowne, Parker Society (Cambridge, 1853), pp. 49–63, 67–71, 76.
[15] John Jewel to Peter Martyr, n.d., *The Zurich letters*, ed. H. Robinson, Parker Society (Cambridge, 1842), p. 23.   [16] *Correspondence of Matthew Parker*, p. 173.
[17] P. E. More, 'The spirit of Anglicanism', in *Anglicanism: the thought and practice of the Church of England, illustrated from the religious literature of the seventeenth century*, ed. P. E. More & F. L. Cross (London, 1935), p. xxii.

II

In so far as mediocrity is acquired rather than innate it is certain that Bacon came by it in the course of his exposure to the rhetorical tradition, at Cambridge and Gray's Inn. It was rhetoric, laced and braced with dialectic which provided the intellectual formation for his legendary eloquence as judge and counsellor of state.[18] That Bacon was, in Sir Robert Naunton's phrase, 'an arch-piece of Wit and Wisdom'[19] needs no emphasis. Anyone attempting a study of the lord keeper's career is of necessity driven back on surviving examples of his oratory by the relative dearth of political papers, whereas collections of his speeches have been preserved in quantity and are now accessible to scholars not only in London but in Washington, Chicago and San Marino. Nor is it necessary to make heavy weather of Bacon's evident familiarity with the standard rhetorical handbooks and models, including the relevant texts of Cicero, the *Ad Herennium*, and Quintilian's *De Institutione Oratoria*; nor of his thorough acquaintance with the contemporary pedagogical culture reflected in Thomas Wilson's textbook, the *Art of rhetorique*.

But it is necessary to clear up a misunderstanding and to insist on the particular importance for Bacon's formation of both the prose style and philosophical content of the works of Seneca. An anti-Ciceronian preference for Seneca is conventionally dated from the last years of Elizabeth, in the time of Francis rather than Nicholas Bacon. Moreover on the dubious evidence of editions printed in England and listed in the *Short-title catalogue* it has been argued that Seneca was not well-known to the mid-Tudor generation.[20] It is true that there was a world of difference between Bacon's spare and plain prose and the form of Senecan discourse which Bishop Earle in 1628 characterized as 'Lipsius his hopping style'. Earle attributed such affectations to 'a self-conceyted man' and this Bacon was not.[21] Nevertheless there is no doubt that Bacon cultivated the 'pointed', silver, Senecan amble, with its terse and strikingly antithetical figures of speech. For example, in his 1563 speech conveying the views of the Lords on the question of the hour, the queen's marriage, he begged Elizabeth to dispose herself to marry 'where you will, with whom you will, and as shortly as you will'.[22] On another occasion he spoke of 'the wante of the number of ministers that ought to be, and be not, and the insufficiencye of those that be'.[23] In a Star Chamber speech delivered to Archbishop Grindal in his disgrace, Bacon expressed the fear that 'religion, which of his own nature should be uniform, would against his nature have

---

[18] R. J. Schoek, 'Rhetoric and law in sixteenth-century England', *Studies in Philology*, I (1957), 110-27.

[19] Sir Robert Naunton, *Fragmenta regalia*, English Reprints ed. E. Arber (London, 1870), p. 38.

[20] Earl Miner, 'Patterns of Stoicism in thought and prose styles, 1530-1700', *P.M.L.A.*, LXXXV (1970), 1023-40. But see George Williamson, *The Senecan amble: a study in prose from Bacon to Collie* (Chicago, 1951).

[21] John Earle, *The autograph manuscript of microcosmographie*, Scolar Press Facsimile (Leeds, 1966 p. 47. Cf. Williamson, *The Senecan amble*, p. 121.

[22] British Library, MS Harley 5176, fo. 93ᵛ.   [23] Ibid. fo. 89ᵛ.

proved milliform, yes, in continuance nulliform...'.[24] All these are examples of 'silver', Senecan discourse.

There was more involved in such verbal constructions than taste or aesthetic preference. Bacon was as conscious as his contemporaries in late Renaissance Europe that the vivid and tough-minded oratory of the early Roman Empire was more fitting than republican amplitude, not only for advocacy and jurisprudence but also for the counselling of princes. Seneca and Quintilian were the aptest models, and for churchmen, St Ambrose.[25] For the purpose of style Bacon found his rhetorical *via media* somewhere between Cicero and Seneca in Quintilian. For Quintilian shared Seneca's moral values but in prose style veered away from his artificial figures and far-fetched conceits towards a preference for Cicero as the only 'perfect orator'.[26] George Puttenham recorded a vignette of Bacon at his book: 'I have come to the lord keeper Sir Nicholas Bacon and found him sitting in his gallery alone with the works of Quintilian before him.'[27]

But style was subordinate to content and moral purpose. What Bacon chiefly absorbed from both Quintilian and Seneca was their common Stoicism, a personal commitment, deeply felt, to Quintilian's proposition that 'no man can be an orator unless he is a good man'.[28] For the purpose of taking hold of the Stoic virtues and commending their practice to others a sententious rhetoric was the perfect vehicle, conveying by its very form the moral discipline it preached.[29] Puttenham taught that *sententiae* were to be employed 'in waightie causes and for great purposes', when 'wise perswaders use grave and weighty speeches, specially in matter of advise or counsel'.[30] How Bacon would have delighted to instruct modern politicians or even perpitatetic academics with the pungent dictum: 'Nusquam est, qui ubique est.' He aspired above all to the Stoic ideal characterized by Erasmus as the *quadratus homo*, the foursquare man who is indifferent to worldly success and serene in the face of all adversity.[31] This man was Seneca. In a poem addressed to his wife Bacon spoke of 'your Tullye and my Senecke'. 'Mediocria Firma' comes from a chorus in Seneca's tragedy *Oedipus*.[32]

---

[24] *The remains of Edmund Grindal*, ed. W. Nicholson, Parker Society (Cambridge, 1843), p. 471.

[25] See my article 'If Constantine, then also Theodosius: St Ambrose and the integrity of the Elizabethan *Ecclesia Anglicana*', *Journal of Ecclesiastical History*, xxx (1979), 205–29. *Above*, 109 f.

[26] Quintilian, x. i. 125–31, xii. i. 19. On Quintilian's criticism of Seneca, see George Kennedy, *Quintilian* (New York, 1969), pp. 112–13.

[27] George Puttenham, *The art of English poesie* (1589), ed. G. D. Willcox and Alice Walker (Cambridge, 1936), pp. 139–40. L. A. Sonnino remarks in *A handbook to sixteenth-century rhetoric* (1968) that 'the influence particularly noticeable in this period is that of Quintilian' (p. 2). Dr Lisa Jardine has observed the value of the *Institutio Oratoria* for a training in the art of 'arguing on one's feet' as a lawyer and politician. ('Humanism and dialectic in sixteenth-century Cambridge: a preliminary investigation', in *Classical influences on European culture A.D. 1500–1700: proceedings of an international conference held at King's College Cambridge, April 1974*, ed. R. R. Bolgar (Cambridge, 1976), p. 145.)   [28] Quintilian, xii. i. 3.

[29] Moses Hadas, *The Stoic philosophy of Seneca* (New York, 1958), esp. pp. 17–19.

[30] Quoted, Elizabeth McCutcheon in her edition of *Sir Nicholas Bacon's Great House Sententiae* (see n. 33 below), p. 24.   [31] Ibid. p. 58.

[32] Robert Tittler, *Nicholas Bacon: the making of a Tudor statesman* (London, 1976), p. 57.

Bacon's Stoicism has two enduring monuments: the *sententiae* painted and perhaps incised on the walls of the long gallery in his house at Gorhambury. A still more public affirmation of his mediocrity no longer exists: Gorhambury itself, which Queen Elizabeth called a 'little house' and which Horace Walpole later praised for its air of 'sober simplicity'. In Fuller's *Worthies* we read of Bacon: 'He was not for invidious structures...but delighted in *domo domino pari*.'[33] Fortunately the Gorhambury *sententiae* outlived the house they adorned. Written on vellum, in richly decorated but stately Roman inscriptional capitals, they were sent to Jane, Lady Lumley as an accession to what has been called 'the largest private library of the Elizabethan period'. From there they passed to the Royal Library.[34]

In a scholarly and sensitive edition of the *sententiae* Elizabeth McCutcheon has helped us to see that in place, on the walls of the lord keeper's gallery, these texts formed 'a memory-theatre of a verbal sort', conveying thought made concrete and fixing it in the mind's eye. The spare sententious instinct was implicit in the process of selection itself: from thousands of possible adages fewer than sixty to express Bacon's profoundest convictions, forty-three from Seneca or a Senecan source (mostly from the *Epistulae morales*), fifteen from Cicero. As Bacon remarked in one of his speeches, 'in very deede, few wordes be best remembered'.[35] An Aristotelian maxim travels from the walls of Gorhambury to underline a point in Chancery: OMNE IVS AEQUABILE, ALITER IVS NON EST. The themes of the *sententiae* include moderation, the treachery of ambition, friendship, fortune, the greatest good. AD VIVENDUM MULTIS: AD BEATE VIVENDUM, PAVCIS OPUS EST – One needs many things to live, few to live happily.

The same philosophy pervades 'The recreations of my age',[36] poems which distil the experience of early married life with Bacon's second wife, Ann Cooke, an experience which in itself was Stoic in character, since the Stoics advocated mutuality and parity in marital relations:

> I must nedes saye and with good harte
> You have well played a good wyves parte.[37]

The occasion was the enforced semi-retirement of the Marian interlude, and of a spell of convalescence after a 'sickness both greate and longe'. The train of thought is hostile to ambition, covetousness, lust:

[33] Quoted, McCutcheon, *Bacon's Great House Sententiae*, p. 13. There is a University of Chicago doctoral dissertation by Ernest R. Sandeen, 'The building activities of Sir Nicholas Bacon' (1959).

[34] British Library, MS Royal 17 A XXIII. Edited with English translation and introduction by Elizabeth McCutcheon, *Sir Nicholas Bacon's Great House Sententiae*, English Literary Renaissance Supplements, III (Amherst, 1977).

[35] British Library, MS Harley 398, fo. 7^r.

[36] Privately printed 1903, issued (Oxford, 1919) as *The recreations of his age*, from a MS in the possession of the Rev. M. H. Marsden of Moreton, co. Dorset.

[37] 'It is really the Stoa that first recognized the full equality of husband and wife' (Ludwig Edelstein, *The meaning of Stoicism* (Cambridge Mass., 1966), p. 73).

> Nothing in earth so good I fynde
> As in a mann a contented mynde.

'In commendacion of the mean estate' Bacon wrote:

> The surest state and best degree
> Is to possess mediocritye.

And 'at the desire' of his wife Bacon 'turned' an ode of Horace on the same theme:

> The golden meane whosoe loves well
> Shall fare and free therby eschue
> The lothesome howse with filthe and smelle
> And envious spight the which is due
> To suche as in the Palace dwell...
> A mynde well taught standes suer and faste,
> When fortune frownes hopeinge of better.

The Anglican *via media* converted into a spiritual and ecclesiastical norm what was in origin a precept of classical ethics, related primarily to a man's expectations and conduct, the secret of happiness.[38] When Bacon commended the middle way to parliament he was not an ecclesiastical statesman charting a course between Rome and Geneva but a philosopher who believed that one should neither have too much religion (superstition) nor yet too little (irreverence) but just the right amount. Yet the strength of the Aristotelian mean lies in its ambiguity. Courage is a mean between rashness and cowardice. However, one cannot be over-courageous. To be truly religious is a mean. But no one can be too religious. In the 1563 parliament Bacon rebuked those who in religion were 'colde, luke-warme, doubtfull and doubledealinge.'[39] The Senecan *quadratus homo* was no Laodicean.

III

The modern age is suspicious of rhetoric. Was the rhetorical and sententious Bacon the real Bacon? Miss McCutcheon has called his theatre of *sententiae* 'a psychological survival kit', enabling a man in high office to survive the treacheries of a slippery world.[40] Was it also a mask, concealing Bacon's true nature even from himself? We are told that the late President Lyndon B. Johnson affected a sonorous and even sanctimonious style of public speaking because of the need to restrain his natural lack of inhibition and preference for salty speech well peppered with 'cuss words'. Bacon's public voice was the voice of Jacob. Were the hands the hands of Esau, hairy hands sprung of a long line of grasping East Anglian sheep farmers, projecting incongruously from the folds of a Roman toga?

Bacon's wit and wisdom had its familiar side. He was the source of once

---

[38] F. E. More in *Anglicanism*, p. xxiii.
[39] British Library, MS Harley 5176, fo. 89.
[40] McCutcheon, *Bacon's Great House Sententiae*, p. 32.

famous jests and apophthegms,[41] some of them very indicative of his true character. Confronted with a certain nimble-witted barrister who was a compulsive interruptor, Bacon said: 'There is a great difference betwixt you and me: a pain to me to speak, and a pain to you to hold your peace.'[42] This was the plain Bacon we see in the portrait, not so much warts and all as all warts. Bacon often said that he loved 'plain dealing', and, we may add, plain speaking too. We catch his everyday voice in a business letter to one of his sons: 'Yt is much a worse pennyworth then Rokewoodes bargayne which was yll enowghe. To be short, except Mr Bozome will yeld in this matter of iiij acres in Gunthorp...I meane not to conclude with hym.'[43] In a celebrated letter to Cecil Bacon said that to care for the lands of young persons in wardship and to neglect their minds was 'plainly to set the cart before the horse'.[44] Such homely proverbs were deliberately but sparingly used in formal oratory, with a nice sense of decorum. Even on parliamentary occasions the lord keeper could speak with an almost brutal frankness on a matter which aroused his deep prejudices, and perhaps there would have been many more such speeches if he had not been restrained by his occupation of the Woolsack. He could tell the Lords: 'That there be in England to many Frenchmen and that it were much better yf there were none at all I cannot perceive that anie man denieth.' The question was 'how to be ridd of that noysome multitude, howe to have fewe French men or none at all. The way is offred by this bill....'[45]

Sometimes even Bacon's close friends and colleagues felt the rough edge of his tongue. In July 1563, at an anxious moment in his career, facing disgrace and perhaps worse for tampering with the succession question,[46] Bacon handled Cecil very unkindly for using what he considered to be too much of his own discretion in the drafting of a privy council letter. Cecil protested to his brother-in-law that he was 'no clerk to write your resolutions...There be clerks for that purpose.' 'I know not', Cecil's letter began,

upon what just ground your Lordship should use me thus strangely as you many times do in open speech and not in private...For though I lack the wit, the great wealth, the credit that you easilier get then I can, I will never, howsoever you use to nip me with speeches, that you *love plain dealing*, which words I often mark, lack any portion of truth, plainness or honesty that you have.[47]

It appears that this letter was drafted but never sent. And it was to Lady Bacon, not her husband, that Matthew Parker poured out his heart in similar

[41] Some were collected by his son Francis: see *Apophthegmes: the works of Francis Bacon*, ed. J. Spedding, R. L. Ellis and D. D. Heath, vII (London, 1861).

[42] Ibid. 171.

[43] Sir Nicholas Bacon to Nicholas Bacon, 23 Aug. 1573; E. R. Sandeen, 'Correspondence of Nicholas Bacon, Lord Keeper', University of Chicago A.M. dissertation (1955), p. 149.

[44] Quoted, J. Hurstfield, *The Queen's wards: wardship and marriage under Elizabeth I* (London, 1958), p. 26.

[45] British Library, MS Add. 33271, fo. 15ᵛ.

[46] Mortimer Levine, *The early Elizabethan succession question, 1558–1568* (Stanford, 1966), pp. 74–85.

[47] Conyers Read, *Mr Secretary Cecil and Queen Elizabeth* (London, 1955), pp. 281–3.

circumstances.[48] There was a matter at issue between the archbishop and the lord keeper and Parker had written a letter which produced the worst of results. Bacon sent him 'a hard answer in word', employing for this purpose a servant whom Parker would have wished to have no knowledge of the matter. He told Ann Bacon that even the queen was careful to chide him only in private, giving him good looks in public so that his authority should be countenanced before the people. One observes in both these letters a rhetorical word-play with Bacon's reputation for 'plainness', reminiscent of Martin Luther's play with the theme of moderation in a letter to Erasmus: 'I say this, excellent Erasmus, as an evidence of my *candid moderation*.'[49] So Parker wrote to Ann Bacon: 'Madam, be not offended with my plainness, as though I would make comparison with him. I know his office, I know his gifts of God, and his place, and yet may Matthew Parker write privately to Nicholas Bacon in matter of good friendship without offence.' Shades of Churchill and the generals! But unlike Winston, Bacon was perhaps unaware of his capacity to inflict deep wounds. Parker was fond of saying 'homines sumus',[50] and within the conventions of decorum such 'plain dealing' was not in conflict with the lofty and disinterested style adopted by Bacon on more formal occasions. Indeed it could be said to have arisen from the same unemotional, Stoic personality and to have had its roots in a philosophy of life.

In the remainder of this essay I propose to examine two aspects of Bacon's career which may or may not provide more substantial evidence of a contradiction between the mediocrity to which he gave rhetorical expression and his actual designs and dealings. The first of these spheres will be his estate management. Did his care of what Elizabethans called 'commodity' exceed the measure placed on covetousness in his poems and *sententiae*? Was he in truth a mean and greedy man, consequently a hypocrite to boot? According to the moralist, the voice of this generation said: 'It is mine own: who shall warn me to do with mine as myself listeth.'[51] The second area of enquiry will concern Bacon's views and policies in the matter of religion, and on those critical considerations where religion and politics intersected. Was he or did he become more radical than the parliamentary speeches commending the *via media* would suggest? Was he even a puritan?

There is a further possibility: that Bacon the courtier was more devious than Bacon the plain-dealer and readier to climb high than Bacon the Stoic was willing to admit, even to himself. Sir Robert Naunton in *Fragmenta regalia* had cryptic things to say about Bacon as 'abundantly factious, which took much with the Queen when it was suited with the season'.[52] And Cecil, comparing his estate with that of his brother-in-law, wrote: 'In pains I exceed, in rewards

[48] Archbishop Parker to Lady Bacon, 6 Feb. 1568; *Correspondence of Matthew Parker*, pp. 309–16.

[49] Preserved Smith, *The life and letters of Martin Luther* (London, 1911), p. 206.

[50] This perhaps prompted Professor Gordon Rupp to entitle his 1975 quatercentenary lecture on Parker 'Matthew Parker, a Man', and to give to the volume of 'historical pieces' in which it appears the general title *Just men* (London, 1977).

[51] *The select works of Robert Crowley*, ed. J. M. Cowper, Early English Test Society, xv (London, 1872), 156.   [52] Naunton, *Fragmenta regalia*, p. 38.

and worldly commodities I would I might come near you', adding, 'and yet
your wealth I wish were doubled.'[53] But in a rare begging letter to the earl
of Leicester Bacon wrote that he did

> of purpose determine with myself to forbear eighteen years to crave by word any manner
> of suit touching my self, thinking it better by deeds and good service to crave then by
> worde or other meanes, a course that in my opinion ought to be followed by all good
> servants.[54]

This resembles something said by Bacon's equally Stoical contemporary,
Archbishop Grindal: 'Those men that sue for bishoprics do in that declare
themselves unmeet for the room.'[55] Such pronouncements were not inconsistent
with what Anthony Esler has called the 'paradoxical attitude' of Bacon's
generation to ambition, an ambivalence perhaps instilled by the awesome rise
and fall of their predecessors in power and aspiration, Wolsey and Cromwell,
Somerset and Northumberland.[56] They may have been ambitious. They were
mortally afraid to appear ambitious. But the almost total loss of Bacon's courtly
and political correspondence makes this a no go area for the historian.

IV

On Bacon's care of his East Anglian estates we are in a better position to judge.
Deeds, accounts and acquittances survive in plenty, together with some scores
of letters to his sons, Nicholas at Redgrave in Suffolk, Nathaniel at Stiffkey
in Norfolk. Although this correspondence is dispersed in a dozen collections,
including the Folger Shakespeare Library and the University of Chicago
Library, the work of Professor Alan Simpson of Chicago and his pupils, and
more recently of Dr Hassell Smith of the University of East Anglia has made
it generally accessible.[57] A prayer survives in which the lord keeper thanks his
maker that he is so placed 'as neyther for wante or penurye I mighte be moved
to growche or repyne, nor yet for excesse and wealthe or vayne glorye and
carefull cumber that growed therby be withdrawne from walkeinge thy
wayes'.[58] The middle way between wealth and poverty! But if Bacon's aim
was to avoid riches he fell lamentably short of his target. Professor Simpson
has shown that as attorney of the Court of Augmentations and later of the Court
of Wards Bacon purchased land at an annual outlay of about £600; as lord
keeper his annual investment rose to about £1,380. The sum total of his
acquisitions was in the region of £35,000 to £40,000.[59]

[53] Conyers Read, *Mr Secretary Cecil*, p. 283.

[54] Nicholas Bacon to the earl of Leicester, n.d.; British Library, MS. Harley 1877, fo. 27.

[55] Patrick Collinson, *Archbishop Grindal 1519–1583: the struggle for a reformed Church* (London, 1979), p. 295.

[56] Anthony Esler, *The aspiring mind of the Elizabethan younger generation* (Durham N.C., 1966), pp. 4–10.

[57] Alan Simpson, *The wealth of the gentry 1540–1660: East Anglian studies* (Cambridge, 1961); E. R. Sandeen, 'Correspondence of Nicholas Bacon'; A. H. Smith, *County and Court: government and politics in Norfolk, 1558–1603* (Oxford, 1974); ed. A. H. Smith, *The papers of Nathaniel Bacon of Stiffkey*, I (1556–1577), Norfolk Record Society CLVI (Norwich, 1978 & 1979).

[58] *The recreations of his age*, p. 38.   [59] Simpson, *Wealth of the gentry*, pp. 45–52.

But Simpson's account of how this substantial estate was acquired and administered tends to acquit Bacon of any charge of rapacity or of unfeeling 'economic individualism'. 'The predominant impression is conservatism', remarks Simpson, and 'immemorial shrewdness'.[60] Bacon was no speculator and no opportunist. Having bought at twenty years' purchase he proceeded to rent at the assessed annual value. Nor was he one to neglect the obligations of a good countryman for the sake of private advantage. In the course of a prolonged negotiation to marry his daughter to one of his wards he wrote: 'Surely yt is not for lyvelod or welth that I have ben contented to com to this matche...But yt was neighborowod and bycause I hadd brought hym up amongest myn own children as one of my own sonnes.' Nevertheless, Bacon had been careful to protect himself against financial loss if the enterprise should fail, as fail it did.[61]

Bacon's success seems to have been achieved by the same time-honoured methods which had raised other Bacons from obscurity and which had given him his own start in life, the qualities typical of the 'individualism' which Dr Alan Macfarlane believes had deep taproots in the English soil,[62] but not necessarily anti-social or un-neighbourly. Simpson notes the absence in Bacon's dealings of anything which could be described as 'rationalisation'.[63] The lesson to be drawn is that in accounting for the rise of Nicholas Bacon we have no need of the Weberian hypothesis of the manic drive of the 'inner-worldly ascetic', induced by the protestant ethic: only what has been called 'constant attention to detail'.[64] There is scarcely one of Bacon's letters which fails to confirm his eye for detail. In April 1573, when there were doubtless other matters on his mind, we find the lord keeper writing thus to his son Nathaniel about the construction of a little quay in the tidal creek at Stiffkey:

I have thowght since Mountfordes goyng from me that yf the turfe which maye be cutt of the upper sword of the grownd where the trench shall go be layed in forme of a little walle on the sides of the trench I thinke therby the earthe that is cast out of the trenche beyond that walle shalbe kept from falling in agayne when Spring tides come.[65]

A few months later, with his attention on a small piece of woodland in Suffolk, Bacon wanted to know 'what men will take for the hedging, dikinge and quycke settyng of a rodde'.[66] In the following year it was a matter of concern 'how my howse of Redgrave eyther is alredie, or hereafter maye be provided of conyes',[67] and how best to supply fencing for the yard of his school at Botesdale, which the schoolmaster had planted with crab apple trees.[68] Both Nicholas and Nathaniel were bombarded with demands for detailed

[60] Ibid. p. 78.
[61] Sandeen, 'Correspondence of Nicholas Bacon', pp. 17-77.
[62] Alan Macfarlane, *The origins of English individualism: the family, property and social transition* (Oxford, 1978).
[63] Simpson, *Wealth of the gentry*, p. 78.
[64] *Sir Nicholas Bacon: an address given by Dr J. P. T. Bury in St Bene't's Church at the Commemoration of Benefactors* [of Corpus Christi College] *on 5th December 1975.*
[65] *The papers of Nathaniel Bacon*, 1, 69.
[66] Sandeen, 'Correspondence of Nicholas Bacon', p. 157.
[67] Ibid. p. 162.   [68] Ibid. p. 164.

information and action, which in the case of Nicholas was rarely forthcoming. After the acquisition of the Stiffkey property the more diligent Nathaniel spent long days 'treading out' its fields. His father wanted to know how many lambs 600 ewes were likely to bear, taking one year with another; how many fleeces would make a stone of wool; how much the local farmers would pay for the privilege of fold-coursing these 600 ewes on their land.[69] As Simpson observes, sheep-farming was in the blood. 'He must have learned all this in his cradle.'[70] To a not very businesslike son-in-law, Henry Woodhouse, Bacon explained his plain and simple way with money matters: 'Call to remembraunce and put in wrightinge all maner of sommes of money that you owe to any person.' 'This beyong done, you are also to cause to be set downe in wrightinge in another note all the debtes that be owyng unto you and the tyme of those paymentes, and all the goodes which you have that you may convenyently make money of.'[71] This was more practical advice than that given by a certain sententious character in Shakespeare: 'Neither a borrower nor a lender be.' But neither here nor in any other record of his financial affairs is there inconsistency with Bacon the public and rhetorical figure, or with Bacon the Stoical and foursquare man.

V

We come finally to a problem less easily disposed of. Did Bacon in his patronage of religious men and religious causes betray the ecclesiastical *via media* which he preached in 1559? In crude modern parlance, was his true ideological position to the left of centre, or did it tend in that direction between 1559 and his death twenty years later? Bacon's most recent biographer, Professor Robert Tittler, suggests that it did.[72] He speaks of Bacon's 'reputation for radical Protestantism', and of his 'support of radical protestants'. He makes much of the puritan divines who enjoyed Bacon's patronage and the shelter of his roof and of the puritan magistrates in East Anglia whom the lord keeper advanced in the local politics of the region. Tittler's private Bacon is a puritan in contention with Bacon the public man and politique.

This is the moment to admit what is self-evident. When Bacon spoke in parliament he was either representing the views of the queen or speaking in circumstances which were prejudicial to the free expression of his own opinions. Of his speech at the end of the 1559 parliament Neale wrote: 'Here spoke the statesman, not the *dévot*. And it was for the Queen that he spoke; perhaps on her brief.'[73] Nevertheless the words were his own and so personal that the medium was more than half the message. On other occasions there is good reason to suspect that Bacon's high office obliged him to defend policies which were in conflict with his private convictions. At the time of Archbishop Grindal's disgrace and sequestration, Bacon prepared a speech for delivery in

---

[69] *The papers of Nathaniel Bacon*, I, 46.   [70] Simpson, *Wealth of the gentry*, pp. 64, 79.
[71] *The papers of Nathaniel Bacon*, I, 143–4. .
[72] *Nicholas Bacon: The Making of a Tudor statesman*, esp. pp. 61–2, 92, 158–63, 168–71.
[73] Neale, *Elizabeth I and her parliaments*, p. 81.

the Star Chamber in the presence of the judges on an occasion which the queen may have intended to conclude with the archbishop's summary deprivation. The speech consisted of trenchant reproof for Grindal's rank disobedience, 'wherein it must be concluded that you have very greatly offended her Majesty'. Yet from other sources it appears likely that Bacon participated in the dismay with which many in the governing class observed the queen's treatment of her primate. The Star Chamber hearing was preceded by a privy council meeting held in the lord keeper's house at Charing Cross in which a strategy was devised for frustrating the course of action which the queen had dictated. Whether as part of this strategy or as the consequence of genuine illness, Grindal failed to keep his appointment in the Star Chamber so that the crisis was averted. Sir Thomas Wilson later reported to Burghley that his mistress 'disliketh our darings for dealing with the archbishop so at large', and it is likely that the lord keeper was included in her displeasure.[74]

But on the evidence available we should resist the temptation to call Bacon a puritan and we should be careful not to read too much into those episodes and circumstances which sometimes linked him with the puritan clergy and their cause. Indeed it may not be entirely improper to wonder whether a man born within months of the death of Henry VII and who never ceased to punctuate his discourse with the oath 'Mary' or 'Marry' was ever a protestant in any profound sense. His pronouncements on matters of divinity (some poems, a prayer and the preamble to his will)[75] are marked by genuine devotion, but it is protestant devotion only in the sense that it lacks distinctively catholic features. There is no deep impression made by the great protestant doctrines, still less by Calvinism. In their absence Bacon's piety can be best characterized as 'mere Christian'. Bacon's brother-in-law Cecil was seventy-five years of age before a theological dispute in Cambridge obliged him to discover what Calvinism was about. He was apparently astonished to discover that theologians whom he had trusted with his patronage for many years should believe that God might be so cruel as to will the wickedness and consequent destruction of a portion of mankind.[76] It is possible that Bacon lived and died without acquiring a lively interest in such matters.

But what he shared with Cecil was a lifelong addiction to that suspicious jealousy of the higher clergy which was almost instinctive for this generation. In a speech to the 1563 parliament Bacon asked that the clergy be treated with more respect. The laity were to yield 'that estimacion, countenance and creditte to the ministers of this doctrine which of right they oughte to have...For howe can any thinge be well sett forthe and governed by them that wante creditte?' But this was at once followed by a characteristic exclamation: 'Marye, for my parte let the tyme of theire offices last as their doeinges doe deserve.'[77] This sector of Bacon's mental world is illuminated by a day in 1573 when a number

[74] Collinson, *Archbishop Grindal*, pp. 259–63.

[75] *Historical Manuscripts Commission 11th Report*, appendix IV (Marquis of Townshend MSS), 4–7.

[76] Humphrey Tyndall to Lord Burghley, 19 Dec. 1595; Trinity College Cambridge MS B/14/9, fos. 127–8. I owe this reference to the kindness of Dr Peter Lake.

[77] British Library, MS Harley 5176, fo. 89.

of notorious puritan agitators (including one of Bacon's own chaplains) were interviewed in a leisurely way before the privy council, with Bacon in the chair. Archbishop Parker and Bishop Sandys of London were in attendance but without any clear role and they were not invited to speak. When Parker at last protested he was told that their lordships were bound to hear what the puritans had to say. 'We may not deal with them as in popish time.' Nevertheless, Bacon seems to have ensured that the afternoon ended satisfactorily for the bishops, who gained a proclamation against religious extremists.[78]

It would be a mistake to overlook Bacon's serious interest in the reformation of ecclesiastical discipline. In 1563 he delivered himself of a major parliamentary speech on church government which broke important new ground and was characteristically practical in its approach.[79] It contained a rare stricture on the moral licence enjoyed by 'men of wealth and power' who 'in their contryes' lived as dissolute and licentious lives as they chose. There was also a striking comment on the laxity of popular religious practice which deserves to be better known to ecclesiastical historians of the catastrophist school.[80] 'Howe commeth it to passe that the common people in the countrye universallie come so seldome to common prayer and devine service, and when they doe come be there manye tymes so vainely occupied...? In 1559 an Act of Uniformity had been passed, 'but hitherto noe man, no, noe man or verye fewe hath seene it executed'. Bacon's cure for such a radical disease was the same medicine he so regularly prescribed in the secular sphere: due execution of the existing laws. 'Lawes for the furtheraunce of this discipline unexecuted be as roddes for correcion without handes.' One specific remedy indicated was the division of dioceses into rural deaneries 'as I knowe commonly they be', and the committing of the deanieries to men well chosen 'as I thinke commonly they be not'. There should be 'certain ordinarye courtes' at prescript times 'with a severe controllment of thease inferiore ministers by the bisshoppe or his chauncellor, not byenuallie or tryennuallie but every yeare twice or thrice'. Bacon's interest in a revivified ruridecanal structure may seem to associate him with advanced schemes for ecclesiastical reorganization and reform.[81] Yet his remarks have a vagueness not entirely consistent with such an interpretation. The speech contains no recognition of the ordinary routine of bishops' consistory courts and no mention of the archdeacons and their 'bawdy courts', the principal instrument of ecclesiastical discipline at a grassroots level. Was this disingenuousness or lofty ignorance? Bacon was content that the bishops, at the time of his speech assembled in the Convocation of 1563, 'should take the chiefe

[78] Inner Temple Library, MS Petyt 538/47, fo. 479.

[79] British Library, MS Harley 5176, fos. 89–92. Simonds D'Ewes, *The journals of all the parliaments* (1682), misplaces this speech in the 1572 parliament (pp. 192–5). This has perhaps encouraged some historians to connect its burden with the radical puritan agitation which came to the surface in the parliaments of the early 1570s, and in the pamphlet of 1572, *An admonition to the parliament*.

[80] Christopher Haigh, 'Puritan evangelism in the reign of Elizabeth I', *English Historical Review*, XCII (1977), 30–58.

[81] Patrick Collinson, 'Episcopacy and reform in England in the later sixteenth century', *Studies in Church History*, III, ed. G. J. Cuming (Leiden, 1966), 91–125. *See below*, pp. 155–89.

care to conferre and consulte of thease matters'. Nevertheless, his speech was inspired by lay suspicion of the motives and quality of ecclesiastical administration. But none of this made Bacon a puritan.

It was far otherwise with Bacon's sons by his first marriage, Nicholas, Nathaniel and Edward, and with his second wife, Ann Cooke. The three sons all settled into the pattern of godly, severe magistracy which by the later years of Elizabeth's reign was increasingly dominant in East Anglia, and they worked hand in glove with the godly preaching ministry.[82] Nathaniel in particular was an outstanding example of this type, while Edward's settled years in the country outside Ipswich were preceded by exotic theological experience abroad, where he had consorted with Beza, Danaeus and other famous divines.[83] Reading Nathaniel's correspondence and comparing it with the letters of his fellow Norfolk puritan John Stubbs[84] it seems likely that both Edward and Nathaniel contracted their lifelong protestant enthusiasm at Gray's Inn, in a shared atmosphere of youthful religious seriousness reminiscent of the christian union in a modern university.[85] In the 1570s Edward's letters from London to his brother in the country were filled with reports of sermons and of the religious sensations of the moment: the madness of the fanatic Peter Birchet, the silencing of the preacher Edward Dering, the sermons for and against the presbyterian discipline at Paul's Cross.[86] Another of Nathaniel's correspondents wrote of 'that chearfull remembraunce one of another wherein we may delite'.[87] This is the same epistolary style which we find in John Stubbs: 'The Lord knit us faster and faster in our faith and love and hope of our everlasting life, when we shall be forever one with our head, Jesus Christ.'[88] This was not the rhetoric which Sir Nicholas had learned at the Inns of Court in the 1530s.

Bacon's second wife, Lady Ann, was probably the reason for much of the hospitality and patronage which her husband extended to puritan divines, both in a private capacity and as lord keeper, an office which dispensed much of the ecclesiastical patronage of the Crown.[89] Perhaps her equally pious sister Mildred had no less of an interest in Cecil's capacity to do the godly cause some good. One of Bacon's more radical chaplains was Percival Wiburn. (It was Wiburn who defined the puritans as 'the hotter sort of Protestants'[90] and few

[82] Patrick Collinson, 'Magistracy and ministry: A Suffolk miniature', in *Reformation conformity and dissent: essays in honour of Geoffrey Nuttall*, ed. R. Buick Knox (London, 1977), pp. 70–91; Kenneth W. Shipps, 'Lay patronage of East Anglian Puritan clerics in pre-revolutionary England', unpublished Yale Ph.D. dissertation (1971). *See below*, pp. 445-66.

[83] Tittler, *Nicholas Bacon*, pp. 61–2, 154.

[84] Printed in *John Stubbs's Gaping Gulf with letters and other relevant documents*, ed. Lloyd E. Berry, Folger documents of Tudor & Stuart civilization (Charlottesville, 1968).

[85] Wilfrid R. Prest, *The Inns of Court under Elizabeth I and the early Stuarts 1590–1640* (London, 1972), esp. chapter 9, 'Preachers, puritans and the religion of lawyers', pp. 187–219.

[86] *The papers of Nathaniel Bacon*, 1, 90–1, 95–7, 122–3, 161, 174, 281–2.   [87] Ibid. 73–4.

[88] John Stubbs to William Davison, 30 April 1578, in *John Stubbs's Gaping Gulf*, pp. 106–7.

[89] Rosemary O'Day, 'The ecclesiastical patronage of the Lord Keeper, 1558–1642', *Transactions of the Royal Historical Society*, 5th ser., XXIII (1973), 89–109.

[90] Quoted, Patrick Collinson, *The Elizabethan puritan movement* (London, 1967), p. 27.

were hotter than Wiburn himself.) On no less than sixteen occasions in as many years Wiburn successfully petitioned the lord keeper to bestow a Crown living on one of his friends.[91] After his own deprivation this radical presbyterian veteran would finish up as Lady Bacon's pensionary at Gorhambury, long after Sir Nicholas was dead and gone.[92]

The learning and virtues of the wife of Bacon's second age and of her scarcely less remarkable sisters were legendary in their own time and have remained so for posterity. Macaulay disparaged these bluestockings, suggesting that it was not so extraordinary that they were well read in Latin and Greek since in mid-Tudor England there was nothing else to read. A woman was either 'uneducated or classically educated'.[93] Macaulay chose to forget that Ann Cooke was equally fluent in Italian and French. In any case, to remain uneducated would have been the reasonable expectation of the Cooke sisters if they had not chosen their father so well. Of their mother the best that could be said was that her beauty never interfered with her husband's studies: 'Tibi fuerat quamvis pulcherrima conjux, diminuit studium non tamen....'[94]

Questions hang over Sir Anthony Cooke and his daughters. What was Cooke's role in the 1559 parliament? Leader of the protestant opposition, according to Neale, almost overlooking the circumstance that he was father-in-law to the two principal columns of the state, Cecil and Bacon.[95] Why at this time did Bishop John Jewel reveal his dislike of Cooke and what did he mean when he told his friends at Zürich that Cooke was obstinately defending some scheme of his own 'and is mightily angry with us all'?[96] And why, nevertheless, did Ann Cooke do Jewel the friendly office of translating his *Apologia Ecclesiae Anglicanae*? Why did she also translate the sermons of Bernardino Ochino as he began to wander far from protestant orthodoxy?[97] Why did her father, who had been tipped for the very office to which Bacon was advanced, live out the remainder of his days in provincial obscurity? And why was the last will and testament of this religious zealot so lacking in tokens of faith, hope and tangible charity?[98] We know only enough about the Cookes to suspect that the stereotype of 'radical puritan' will not fit.

However, in the case of Ann it is clear that there was a radical progression from the 'mediocrity' which she initially shared with her husband to the bigoted puritan partisanship for which she was notorious in her widowhood. In the 1550s her conscience allowed her to serve Mary the Catholic as a gentlewoman of the bedchamber. In the 1580s she was reluctant to come to the Court of protestant Elizabeth except to plead for her puritan friends.[99] The

[91] O'Day, 'Ecclesiastical patronage', pp. 101–2.

[92] Lambeth Palace Library, MSS 648, no. 103, 649, no. 79, 650, no. 69.

[93] T. B. Macaulay, *Critical and historical essays*, ed. A. J. Grieve (London, n.d.), II, 300.

[94] John Strype, *Annals of the Reformation* (Oxford, 1824), II, ii, 605.

[95] Neale, *Elizabeth I and her parliaments*, pp. 57, 59.

[96] John Jewel to Peter Martyr, 28 April 1559; *Zurich letters*, p. 21.

[97] Philip McNair, 'Ochino's apology: three gods or three wives?', *History*, LX (1975), 353–73.

[98] M. K. McIntosh, 'Sir Anthony Cooke: Tudor humanist, educator and religious reformer', *Proceedings of the American Philosophical Society*, CXIX (1975), 233–50.

[99] Collinson, *Elizabethan puritan movement*, p. 257.

subscription imposed by Archbishop Whitgift on the puritan ministers in 1584 was perhaps a watershed. In that year she told Burghley that she had little personal contact with the ministers but that she had heard their sermons for the past seven or eight years, and as 'one that hath found mercy' had profited more by 'such sincere and sound opening of the Scriptures' than from hearing 'odd sermons' at Paul's Cross for twenty years.[100] Ten years on, as the formidable and cranky dame of Gorhambury, she was never without the company of the most intransigent of the puritan clergy. What Anthony Bacon called her 'soveraigne desire to over-rule [her] sons in all things', regardless of the circumstances, has its memorial in numerous letters preserved among the Bacon papers at Lambeth. [101] Anthony's papist friend Sir Anthony Standon admired his patience with such a termagent. 'And although I well know my lady your mother to be one of the sufficientest without comparison of that sex, yet, at the end of the career, *il y a toujours de la femme*.'[102] Another correspondent reported that the only people with whom Lady Bacon remained on civil terms were her clerical protegees.[103] As Bishop Goodman remembered, 'she was but little better than frantic in her age.'[104] It was a great age. Forty years of widowhood had followed twenty-five years of marriage. But was the root of Ann Bacon's dottiness intellectual frustration? Did the marriage that had begun with Stoic parity ('your Tullye and my Senecke') go awry? On one occasion when someone tried to discuss Nathaniel's business with his father he made little progress, 'beinge both chidden and oft interrupted by my ladie'.[105]

Those who made the transition from humane learning and its Stoic values to puritanism experienced an intensification of the same austere virtues and sought more convincing answers to the same inner questions. Lady Bacon who wrote of her 'inward feeling knowledge of God his holy will'[106] was one of many whose life described this pilgrimage. But Sir Nicholas remained on the far side of Jordan, convinced that as faction was the root of all civil disorders, 'so certainlye there is no faction so violent and daungerouse as the faction of religion'.[107] He was of a different generation after all, fully eighteen years older than his second wife.

Yet we cannot conclude that Bacon remained a man of the *via media* to the end without acknowledging that the median position in religion and politics was moving to the left before the end came for Bacon in 1579. There was no such thing as a fixed mean. Henry VIII's 'right straight mean way' was not the

---

[100] Lady Ann Bacon to Lord Burghley, 26 Feb. 1584(/5); British Library, MS Lansdowne 43, no. 48, fos. 119–20. This copy is holograph. There is a further copy in MS Lansdowne 115, no. 55, fo. 125.

[101] Anthony Bacon to Lady Ann Bacon, 12 July 1594; British Library, MS Add. 4112, fo. 49ʳ. See the *Index to the papers of Anthony Bacon (1558–1601) in Lambeth Palace Library (MSS. 647–662)* (1974).

[102] Thomas Birch, *Memoirs of the reign of Queen Elizabeth* (London, 1754), 1, 67–8.

[103] Edward Spencer to Anthony Bacon, 16 Aug. 1594; Lambeth Palace Library, MS 650, nos. 169–70.

[104] *D.N.B.*, art. Lady Ann Bacon.   [105] *The papers of Nathaniel Bacon*, 1, 89–90.

[106] British Library, MS Lansdowne 43, no. 48, fo. 120.

[107] British Library, MS Harley 398, fos. 8ᵛ–9ʳ.

same path which his daughter trod. Dr Peter Lake has demonstrated that by the 1580s the true gravitational centre of the English Church was defined by the Calvinist theologians who presided over so many Cambridge colleges, of whom the *primus inter pares* was Whitaker of St John's.[108] Moreover as Bacon's career matured what Sir John Neale called 'the *via media* in politics'[109] became progressively harder to preserve against the pressure of the contrary extremes. In the 1560s the healing of confessional divisions was still an inspiring and even plausible dream. But towards 1580 the search for the middle ground was almost abandoned in an atmosphere of religious partisanship and of ideological commitment. As a privy councillor and the author of measured memoranda on the major questions of the day, Bacon was a consistent politique, his caution and moderation tempered only by suspicion of the French and dislike of Mary Queen of Scots. In 1559 he opposed military intervention in Scotland, basing his objections on 'just and indifferent consideration of the equallitie and inequallitie of this matter, I meane of the power of Englande and of Fraunce'.[110] Four years later, at the time of the Newhaven expedition, he supported war, 'if sufficient provisions of money might be made', but on wholly secular grounds and without reference to the cause of French protestantism.[111] Bacon was never enthusiastic about war. 'What is peace?' he asked the 1571 parliament. 'Is it not the richest and most wished for ornament that pertaines to any publique weale? Is not peace the marke and ende that all good governmentes direct their actions unto?...By this we generally and ioyfully possesse all, and without this generally and ioyfully possesse nothinge.'[112]

But in the last year of his life the increasingly menacing international scene with its cockpit in the Netherlands persuaded Bacon that peace was unlikely to be obtained. He began to draw closer to those more militant elements in the Council which favoured a forceful foreign policy directed against what Bacon now called 'the twoe mighty and potent princes' who were the queen's 'inward enymyes'. Soon he was writing of his 'great grief' that Elizabeth had not given more timely assistance to the prince of Orange. 'Surely Madam the feare of this growethe so great in me that I could not be quiet in my selfe without remembering the same unto your Majestie according to my bounden dutye.'[113] But it was still a politique and a moderate who advised Walsingham that although the hope of peace appeared to be taken away the fortunes of war were such that it was hard to judge where victory would fall. The best to be hoped for was stalemate, to be obtained by dividing and confusing the

[108] Peter Lake, 'Laurence Chaderton and the Cambridge moderate puritan tradition, 1570–1604', unpublished Cambridge Ph.D. thesis (1978).

[109] 'The Via Media in politics: an historical parallel', in *Essays in Elizabethan history* (London, 1958). For the cultural implications, see J. A. van Dorsten, *The radical arts: first decade of an Elizabethan renaissance* (Leiden & Oxford, 1970).

[110] British Library, MS Harley 398, fos. 12ᵛ–15ᵛ.

[111] Ibid. fos. 44ᵛ–5.

[112] British Library, MS Cotton Titus F. i, fos. 123–6.

[113] Tittler, *Nicholas Bacon*, pp. 173–86. Three letters from Bacon to the queen on matters of foreign policy discharged his responsibility as a councillor in this respect in the last months of his life. Copies in British Library, MS Harley 168, nos. 6, 23, 24, fos. 52–3, 91–2, 97.

queen's enemies. It was an outlook singularly free of the ideological simplicities which moved Walsingham himself: a mind with shades of mediocre grey, not composed of black and white.[114] Bacon died in this uncertain and troubled state, facing the choice between evils rather than hoping for any good, doubtless aware that the *via media* was unlikely to rest where he had drawn it.

VI

In a book called *The aspiring mind of the Elizabethan younger generation* Anthony Esler asks: 'How could Anthony and Francis Bacon take seriously their father's motto *Mediocria Firma* when old Sir Nicholas had begun life as a sheep-reeve's son and died Sir Nicholas Bacon, K.G., P.C., Lord Keeper of the Great Seal?'[115] This is a crude question, improperly put. Yet it is true that Sir Nicholas Bacon and his sons by his two marriages confront us with what Esler calls a 'generational mechanism', and with three generations rather than two. The first is represented by the lord keeper himself, pre-protestant and Stoical in his formation; the second by his East Anglian progeny, prototypes of the godly country magistrate and saved from impossible ambitions by the mundane necessities of provincial life, treading out the fields and punishing bastard-bearers; the third by the aspiring but aberrant and ultimately burnt-out case, Anthony, in full revolt against 'the abnormal prudence and conservatism of his elders'.

But the youngest son, who somehow escaped youth, will not fit this attractive model. The lord chancellor was as sententious as the lord keeper, if ten times more inventive and, according to Macaulay, a hundred times more ambitious and servile. In his *Advertisement touching the controversies of the Church of England* Francis Bacon addressed some of the attributes of his father's mind to those religious problems of later Elizabethan England which threatened to wreck not only the *via media* but the Church itself. This too was a layman's mind, plain, possessed of moderation, and uncontentious. Let a sentence from this remarkable *eirenicon* bring us to an end: 'If we did but know the virtue of silence and slowness to speak commended by St James our controversies of themselves would close up and grow together.'[116] Sir Nicholas would have said Amen to that.

[114] Bacon to Walsingham, 24 July 1578; ibid. no. 25, fo. 94.
[115] Esler, *The aspiring mind*, pp. 69–70.
[116] *The letters and life of Francis Bacon*, ed. J. Spedding (London, 1861), I, 75.

THE
SEES OF ENGLAND
AND WALES
AS RE~ARRANGED
IN 1541
AND
1555

THE HEAVY LINE SHOWS THE BOUNDARIES OF THE NEW SEES FOUNDED
BY HENRY VIII IN 1541 AND RECOGNISED BY POPE PAUL IV IN 1555

THE STIPPLE MARKS THE AREA OF THE SEE OF WESTMINSTER, i.e., MIDDLESEX, FOUNDED
BY HENRY VIII IN 1541 AND SUPPRESSED BY EDWARD VI IN 1550

Diocesan Map of England and Wales in the Later Sixteenth Century. This map appeared originally in Philip Hughes, *The Reformation in England*, Vol. II (*Religio Depopulata*), p. 7. (*By courtesy of Search Press Ltd.*)

6

EPISCOPACY AND REFORM
IN ENGLAND IN THE LATER SIXTEENTH CENTURY

On the second day of the Hampton Court Conference of January 1604, King James I rebuked Dr John Reynolds of Oxford in words which are almost painfully familiar. A Scottish presbytery, pronounced the royal theologian, 'as well agreeth with a monarchy as God and the Devil,' and there followed what a Scot later remembered as 'that unkoth motto,'[1] 'no bishop, no king.' The king's *bon mot* so perfectly epitomises an important principle of Stuart policy that it may seem an act of pedantry to ask whether in fact the proposals which provoked it included the extirpation of bishops. But Dr Barlow, author of the *Summe and substance of the conference*, seems to have appreciated that Reynolds had spoken of no such thing. The king was 'somewhat stirred,' he explains, 'thinking that they aymed at a Scotish presbytery.' Knowing James's erudition in the whole range of questions under review at Hampton Court, we may suspect that this was rather how he chose to understand the Puritans, to create an opportunity to denounce the presbyterian discipline. Reynolds had spoken of a 'presbytery,' to be sure, but the context of his remarks was one which many modern Anglicans would find unexceptional, and which the king should not have mistaken or wholly rejected, since it resembled his own view of the proper conduct of spiritual government, expressed in some of the calmer and more constructive exchanges of the same conference, and even partly embodied in the Canons

---

[1] The phrase occurs in a fragment of correspondence, discovered by Mr Alistair C. Duke, and deposited in London University Library, MS 610. Professor Gordon Donaldson has suggested that it should be placed in the 1630s.

of 1604.[1] The essence of Reynolds's proposal was that the bishop should be responsibly related to his presbytery. As one account puts it: 'For the last point, of jurisdiction, their desire was that the bishops should not execute it alone by themselves, but jointly with the presbitery of their brethren, the pastors and ministers of the Churche.'[2] This was evidently a plea for a measure of what the twentieth century has learned to call 'constitutional episcopacy.'

Behind the puritan spokesmen at Hampton Court hovered, not a Scottish elder, but that insubstantial figure, conjured out of the past by Christian humanism, the ideal bishop, an image which continued to haunt the English Church from the earliest years of the Reformation to the days of the Long Parliament, for almost as long after Hampton Court as before it. 'Nowe whiche is the true image and forme of a bysshop,' explains a tract of the 1530s, 'the Apostle Paul doth descrybe in the thyrde chapytre of the fyrst epystle to Tymothe.'[3] 'Let us not destroy bishops,' said Lord George Digby in the Root and Branch debate more than a century later, 'but make them such as they were in primitive times.' 'Certainly, sir,' echoed another speaker, 'this superintendency of eminent men, bishops over divers churches, is the most ancient, primitive, spreading, lasting government of the Church.'[4] The theme of this paper is provided by the attempts of English reformers and would-be reformers, more especially in the reign of Elizabeth I, to give this phantom substance, and to make effective and salutary use of the 'superintendency of eminent men.'

It should be made clear at the outset that this is not intended as another contribution to the extensive literature devoted to

---

[1] E. Cardwell, *A History of Conferences ... Connected with the Revision of the Book of Common Prayer*, Oxford 1841, 202-3, 172, 215; R. G. Usher, *The Reconstruction of the English Church*, New York 1910, II, 351-2; Canons XXXV, CXXII.

[2] British Museum, MS Additional 38492, f. 81^r; printed by Usher from another copy, op. cit., II, 335-8.

[3] *The descrypcyon of the images of a verye chrysten bysshop and of a counterfayte bysshop*, 1536? (*S.T.C.* 16963), Sig. Cvi^v.

[4] W. A. Shaw, *A History of the English Church during the Civil Wars and under the Commonwealth, 1640-60*, 1900, I, 32, 30.

the doctrine of the ministry in the post-Reformation Church of England. Rather it has been born out of a conviction that almost too much has already been said about that side of the question. In this century, opposed doctrines of ministerial order have formed the crux of the great debate about the Church's essence which has accompanied the movement towards reunion. For the Church of England, at once claiming 'the historic episcopate' and commending it as an essential bond of peace to those Christian bodies which lack bishops, the sixteenth century is a court of appeal. It has also been made a battle-ground, since Anglicans are unable to agree on the value which their Church has itself attached to this possession in the past. Consequently, the post-Reformation Church has been asked and asked again the great question of our own day: can the Church exist without episcopacy? The interrogation may serve a legitimate polemical purpose, but only at the cost of some historical distortion, for the question was not considered in the same terms or from the same motives by the Elizabethan fathers of the Church of England. The conclusion of Dr A. J. Mason's study, *The Church of England and Episcopacy* (1914)[1]—announced almost on the first page—was that 'among the catholic principles which have been dear to the church of England, none has been dearer to her than the principle of episcopacy.'[2] But the apologists of the Elizabethan Church could not have regarded episcopacy as a catholic principle, properly so-called, or as an essential attribute of the Church of God. Neither the medieval background to their thought, nor the political conditions obtaining under the royal supremacy, still less the principles of the Reformation which they had embraced, allowed such a notion to obtrude. In common with the whole protestant world in the mid-sixteenth century, the English reformers of the first and second generations were inclined to regard the division between bishops and

---

[1] This was a scholarly polemic, commissioned by Archbishop Davidson in his search for a solution to the Kikuyu crisis of 1913-14. Similarly, the symposia *Episcopacy Ancient and Modern* (1930) and *The Apostolic Ministry* (1946) contemplated, the one obliquely, the other less so, the problems arising in South India and elsewhere.

[2] p. 23.

inferior clergy as a distinction of rank rather than of order, an indifferent, political matter rather than a point of doctrine.[1] Statements can be found in the formularies and the writings of Elizabethan divines which indicate a sense of the normality of an episcopally ordained and governed ministry, and by the last decade of the century a whole treatise, Bishop Bilson's *Perpetual government of Christes Churche* (1593), which argues for its divine necessity. But Bilson belonged to the coming age, as did the later books of Hooker's *Laws of ecclesiastical polity*, and to make too much of these swallows is to impress on the age of the Reformation a cast of mind which was alien to it. If the Elizabethans took a pride in the regularity of the episcopal succession, as preserved in England, anything resembling the doctrine of apostolic succession held by Roman Catholics or modern Anglo-Catholics would have been regarded as rank error. These are flat, unsubstantiated assertions, but this is not the place to develop arguments which have been effectively stated by others.[2] My concern is rather to divert at least some attention from questions of doctrine to what was, for the reformers, a matter of prior concern: the proper employment of bishops in the renovation of Christian society.

It has to be admitted that to turn from the study of episcopacy as a 'principle' to questions of its expediency and of its organic properties is to be no less a child of one's own time than Mason was of his. Since Archbishop Fisher's Cambridge sermon of 1946, the Church of England has had much to say about the benefits conferred with the historic episcopate, and has been asked in its turn to explore the relation of episcopacy to the

[1] John Jewel, *Works*, ed. J. Ayre, Parker Socy., I, 1845, 340, 379, III, 1848, 439; James Pilkington, *Works*, ed. J. Scholefield, Parker Socy., 1842, 493-4.

[2] Norman F. Sykes, *Old Priest and New Presbyter*, 1956, 1-57; Gordon Donaldson, *The Scottish Reformation*, 1960, 102-29, and in his unpublished London Ph. D. thesis, 'The Relations Between the English and Scottish Presbyterian Movements to 1604,' 1-96. The extent to which this paper follows Professor Donaldson's lead will be apparent. His work casts almost as much light on the English sixteenth-century polity as it does on Scotland. For a different view of the problem, see H. F. Woodhouse, *The Doctrine of the Church in Anglican Theology, 1547-1603*, 1954, 78-123.

other ministries contained in the total life of the Church. Consequently, those who took part in the Anglican-Presbyterian Joint Conferences which reported in 1957 found that 'the question of Episcopacy did not prove (as it had sometimes done in the past) an obstacle to discussion, but rather a means of its movement along fresh lines'; while the Anglican delegates were at pains 'to emphasize that the Bishop's office is rightly exercised only within the context of the corporate life of the whole Church.'[1] The 1963 Anglican-Methodist Report spoke with the same voice in its insistence that 'each should bring all its riches to the other.'[2] Whatever the theological merits of these insights, which lie beyond my present concern, they bring us into more appreciative contact with the view taken of the episcopal office in the sixteenth century. For if the reformers had little use for episcopacy as a mark of catholicity, they were keenly interested in the proper relation of the bishop to the Church's other members, magistrates, ministers and people, and in restoring what they conceived to be its proper functions to a much-abused office. The succession in which they were conscious of standing was one of doctrine and faithful service rather than of sees and titles. 'God's grace is promised to a good mind, and to one that feareth God,' wrote Jewel, 'not unto sees and successions.'[3] The true bishop proved his right to the title by doing the work of a bishop, just as the false bishop was disqualified by its neglect. 'Is he an officer,' asked Bishop Pilkington, 'that does not his office? Nay, surely, but only in name . . .'[4]

The dualistic theme of the true and the false bishop was an indispensable polemical weapon in the justification of the protestant schism, as was the whole apocalyptic scheme of church history to which it belonged, and which the reformers borrowed from the sects and visionaries of the later Middle

[1] *Relations between Anglican and Presbyterian Churches: A Joint Report*, 1957, 11-12.
[2] *Conversations between the Church of England and the Methodist Church: A Report to the Archbishops of Canterbury and York and the Conference of the Methodist Church*, 1963, 24.
[3] Jewel, *Works*, III, 103.
[4] Pilkington, *Works*, 604.

Ages. It dominates almost everything written about church polity from the protestant side until a point well beyond the middle of the century. One thinks, for example, of Calvin's preoccupation in the *Institutes* with the faults of 'bastard bishops.' And in England of Latimer's preaching: in the Apostles' time, Latimer's hearers were told, 'they preached and lorded not. And now they lorde and preache not.'[1] In this country the tradition can be traced back at least as far as Tyndale's *The practyse of prelates* (1530), and to an anonymous tract published about 1536 by the notable protestant publicist, William Marshal: *The descrypcyon of the images of a verye chrysten bysshop and of a counterfayte bysshop*.[2] Of these antithetical figures, we learn that 'even as it is impossyble in descrybynge the good bysshoppe to saye any thynge of hym but that whiche is good, honeste, vertuous and godly, oneles he shuld deadlye belye hym: even so contrarywyse, in descrybynge the evyll bysshoppe, it is as impossyble to saye any thynge of hym that good, honest or vertuous is . . .' God neither acknowledges nor elects the false bishops, 'this dysgysed and paynted deceytefull people, . . . for as moche as they doo neyther teache, neyther yet do execute any poynte belongynge to the offyce of a bysshop.'[3] The same theme was later elaborated in the voluminous historical writings of Bale and Foxe,[4] and it was the whole burden of Jewel's defence of the course taken by his Church, where the charge of 'variety' from the apostolic pattern was firmly unloaded onto those who occupied Peter's chair, only to depart from his example.

To dwell upon the abuse of the episcopal order in the Roman Church was to imply some positive estimation of the office, rightly used. The novelty of the neo-Calvinist teaching which

[1] *Sermons*, ed. G. E. Corrie, Parker Socy., 1844, 66.
[2] In the *Short-Title Catalogue* and elsewhere this tract has been attributed to Luther, on grounds that for me remain obscure. Efforts by the British Museum staff to relate it to any of the reformer's known works have not been fruitful. At one point the writer compares the performance of popish will-works to a man who 'wolde go about to stoppe the ryver of Thaymes of his course with a banke made of straw.' (Sig. hvi[r].)
[3] Sigs. av[v], bvi[v].
[4] William Haller, *Foxe's Book of Martyrs and the Elect Nation*, 1963.

emanated from Geneva in the time of Theodore Beza lay in the assault on the office itself, and on the principle of imparity, as inherently Antichristian. This was consistent with a dogmatic treatment of matters of polity which was foreign to earlier protestant teaching, and which cannot be attributed to Calvin.[1] Presbyterianism was a militant and persuasive force in England from about 1570 until about 1590, and thereafter its theoretical appeal remained strong, but there is no need to suppose that these doctrines represented the only alternative to uncritical acceptance of the *status quo* of the Anglican settlement. If it were so, episcopacy and reform might have seemed wholly incompatible concepts in the last thirty years of the sixteenth century. But it hardly needs to be said that not all Puritans were Presbyterians. Among those who remained convinced that the English Church stood in need of further reformation, there were many, in all probability a majority, who found nothing offensive in the subordination of one minister to the permanent oversight of another, and whose attitude to questions of church order continued in the original protestant tradition.[2]

As for the writers who answered the first Presbyterians, it is notorious, and has been since John Keble's day,[3] that through thirty years of controversy, they were not for the most part to be drawn into a counter-assertion of the *jus divinum* of bishops. Naturally, when Cartwright was the opponent, the defence of the established polity was more positive than when Jewel wrote

[1] Donaldson, *Scottish Reformation*, 183-202; Basil Hall, 'Calvin against the Calvinists', *Proceedings of the Huguenot Socy. of London*, XX, 1962, 284-301. The origins and progress of Presbyterianism in England are reviewed in my unpublished London Ph. D. thesis, 'The Puritan Classical Movement in the Reign of Elizabeth I,' 1957, and in my forthcoming book, 'The Elizabethan Puritan Movement.'

[2] When Bishop Cooper of Lincoln explained that the Ordinal and the 36th Article of Religion 'alloweth not three distinct orders in the mynistery' but a distinction 'in government politicall,' three hundred Leicestershire ministers, virtually the entire clergy of a county subject to the pervasive puritan influence of the Hastings family, professed their willingness to subscribe to both. (John Rylands Library, Rylands English MS 874, f. 39r).

[3] See his disappointed comment on the Elizabethan estimation of the episcopal succession, in the introduction to the Oxford edn. of Hooker's *Works*, 1888, I, lix.

against Harding. The office of a bishop was said to be traditional, ancient, even apostolic. But it was none the less represented as an office and a dignity, rather than a distinct order of the ministry, just as the ministry itself was thought to be a divine calling, rather than a divine gift, sacramentally imparted.[1] Moreover these Anglicans were at one with Dr Erastus of Heidelberg: 'Ubicunque igitur magistratus est pius et Christianus, ibi nullo est opus, qui alio nomine ac titulo vel gubernet vel puniat: quasi nihil a profano magistratu pius differet.'[2] To suggest that the bishop received his jurisdictional powers from any other source was to ask for trouble, as Bancroft discovered when his Paul's Cross sermon of 1589 implied that it might be heresy to deny the superiority of bishops.[3] Until the end of the reign, the case for episcopal government was rested on its antiquity and the sense that it was answerable to the state of an established Church under a Christian prince.[4]

There was wide agreement in the mid-sixteenth century, not merely among Protestants, but on both sides of the great divide, on the qualities required of a true Christian bishop, and on the proper functions of his office. Reformers in both camps were seeking to escape from the same abuses: the dissociation of benefices from pastoral duties through the pluralism and absenteeism of episcopal magnates; the excessive concern with rule and jurisdiction to the neglect of instruction. And the consequences of these conditions: the vicarious care of souls by officials, largely through judicial processes; and the lordly bear-

---

[1] Sykes, op. cit., 17-29.

[2] *Explicatio gravissimæ questionis*, London 1589 (*S.T.C.* 10511), Thesis LXXIIII, 61.

[3] The controversy, stirred up by Sir Francis Knollys, is documented in P.R.O., S.P. 12/223/23; B.M., MS Lansdowne 61, ff. 78-80, 151-2; ibid., MS Additional 48064, ff. 94-5, 226-38; *H.M.C. Report, Hatfield MSS*, III, 412-13.

[4] See, for example, the last will and testament of Archbishop Sandys: 'The state of a small private church, and the form of a learned christian kingdom, neither would long like nor can at all brook one and the same ecclesiastical government.' (*Sermons*, ed. J. Ayre, Parker Socy., 1842, 448). Cf. John Whitgift, *Works*, ed. J .Ayre, Parker Socy., II, 1852, 265, III, 1853, 166, 175-8, 535-6.

ing of bishops on their infrequent appearances in their dioceses. To be a false bishop was

> to beare in theyr handes a shepehoke of sylver bounde about with a towell, to weare a mytre with hornes, to go after the maner of pageaunts, in processyons, ... to leade aboute with a certayne pompe goodlye palfrayes, and that a great many of them, after the maner of one tryumphynge, to be proude with all maner pompe and gorgyousnes after the courte facyon, to keepe offycyalls, that is to say, certayne robbers and pyllers of provynces, and tormentours of pore men, to kyll soules by tyranny and excomicacyons [*sic*].

So runs the vivid propaganda of *The images of a verye chrysten bysshop and of a counterfayte bysshop*.[1] Protestant and catholic reformers alike were indebted to the Christian humanists for their conception of the Church's mission as primarily educational and exemplary, rather than regal and jurisdictional; and for their ideal image of the bishop, recovered from the Pastoral Epistles and the Fathers. For the English reformers, no longer troubled by the vested interests of the friars, the bishop was above all things a preacher. 'For surely,' we read in *The institution of a Christian man* of 1537, 'the office of preaching is the chief and most principal office, whereunto priests or bishops be called by the authority of the gospel.'[2] Secondarily, the bishop's charge was discipline and oversight, but these he was to exercise as a true father in God, not like a lord or a secular judge. Lord Burghley spoke for his generation when he complained that 'such as shold be feders of the flocke only fede themselves, and turne teaching into commaunding.'[3] 'We require our bishops to be pastors, labourers and watchmen,' Jewel told Josiah Simler in 1559. 'Those oily, shaven, portly hypocrites' had been sent packing to Rome, and their successors were to enjoy a diminished and 'reasonable' substance, so that, 'being relieved from that royal pomp and courtly bustle, they may with

---

[1] Sigs. di^v-ii.
[2] C. Lloyd, *Formularies of Faith*, Oxford 1825, 109-10.
[3] Burghley to Sandys, 22 August 1573; B.M., MS Lansdowne 17, f. 101.

greater ease and diligence employ their leisure in attending to the flock of Christ.'[1]

Much of this was echoed, where it was not anticipated, in the thought of the southern European Erasmians who inaugurated the Catholic Reformation. The debates at Trent in 1546 on the proclamation of the faith and on episcopal residence were inspired by the same vision of the urgent, preaching bishop, the stock figure of the exemplary biographies and 'mirrors' of the Catholic Reform movement. Preaching was here officially described as the bishop's chief duty (*munus praecipuum*).[2] In England, these aspirations are preserved like a fly in amber in that curiously unreal document, the decrees of the National Council convened by Cardinal Pole in 1555. Here there is the same insistence on the faithful performance of the pastoral office, 'which chiefly consists in the preaching of the divine word,' and on the personal duty of bishops to preach, which no-one can discharge for them. Discipline is to be exercised 'like a father and with all the affection of charity.' The lives of the higher clergy should be an example, and ostentation and superfluity of all kinds are explicitly condemned.[3]

For some of the English reformers, the name of 'superintendent' perfectly described the episcopal office as they understood it. Since episcopacy was not a separate order of the ministry, the humdrum Latin conveyed the bishop's function without the accretions with which the name of bishop was contaminated.[4] So when the papists slighted the Elizabethan bishops as mere superintendents, Jewel gladly owned the title: 'Your own Thomas of Aquine saith,' he reminded Harding: 'Episcopi dicuntur

[1] Jewel to Simler, 2 Nov. 1559; *Zurich Letters*, ed. H. Robinson, Parker Socy., 1842, 50-1.

[2] Hubert Jedin, *A History of the Council of Trent*, tr. Graf, II, 1961, 99-124.

[3] Wilkins, *Concilia*, 1837, IV, 121-6. The decrees are available, if not easily accessible, in translation; *The Reform of England by the Decrees of Cardinal Pole*, tr. Henry Raikes, Chester 1839. Cf. W. Schenk, *Reginald Pole*, 1950, 142-4.

[4] Bishop John Ponet of Winchester made a positive suggestion that the title should be altered: John Strype, *Ecclesiastical Memorials*, Oxford 1822, II. ii, 141.

ex eo, quod superintendunt.'[1] Archbishop Cranmer was not one
to substitute indifferent Latin for good Greek, but the most
notable exposition of reformed superintendency occurs in the
abortive programme of canon law revision for which he was
primarily responsible, the *Reformatio Legum Ecclesiasticarum*.
Although the bishop is here described as exercising authority
over the 'inferiores ordines cleri', his own office is no 'ordo,'
but a 'gradus ac dignitas in Ecclesia'; and he is said to hold the
first place 'inter ceteros Ecclesiæ ministros.' If a code of church
law can be said to have such a thing, the bishop is the hero of
those sections of the *Reformatio Legum* devoted to the pastoral
office. Here there is the same emphasis as in Pole's decrees of
two or three years later on preaching, lively pastoral care, and
exemplary life.[2]

These were the ideals of the returned exiles who stepped into
the shoes of Pole's bishops in the first two years of Elizabeth's
reign, as we know from those transparent documents, the
Zurich Letters, their correspondence with their erstwhile hosts.
The task facing them was formidable: to repair what one authority has called the 'inherited spiritual and moral exhaustion'[3] of
the time, which was nowhere more pronounced than among
the clergy themselves. The prospects in a Church not profoundly shaken by reformation were sufficiently daunting to
deter a number of those who were considered for bishoprics
from undertaking the burden.[4] But it was characteristic of this
generation of humanists to take more account of character than

[1] Jewel, *Works*, IV, 906.

[2] *The Reformation of the Ecclesiastical Laws*, ed. E. Cardwell, 1850, 103-4.

[3] W. M. Kennedy, *Elizabethan Episcopal Administration*, I, Alcuin Club
Collections XXVI, 1924, lxxxix.

[4] An undated list of 'bishops elect' (May 1559?) shows that Thomas
Sampson was first choice for the bishoprics of Hereford and Norwich in
turn; that Miles Coverdale was expected to return to Exeter; and that
Alexander Nowell was considered for Coventry and Lichfield. (P.R.O.,
S.P. 12/11/12). Sampson wrote to Peter Martyr on 6 Jan. 1560: 'Let others
be bishops; as to myself, I will either undertake the office of a preacher, or
none at all . . .' (*Zurich Letters*, 63). Rumours that David Whitehead had
first refusal of the archbishopric of Canterbury were not entirely discounted
by A. F. Pollard in the *D.N.B.*, and he certainly rejected the mastership of
the Savoy. (P.R.O., S.P. 12/19/48).

of institutions, and those who cast off the *nolo episcopari* greatly overestimated the power of good intentions. In its organization, the Church of England in the reign of Elizabeth was far from being one of 'the best reformed churches,' a fact which no amount of respect for the positive virtues of the Anglican settlement can alter. The first Elizabethan bishops took on an administrative structure typical of the later Middle Ages which stood on altered foundations but was otherwise remarkably undisturbed by recent events; and they were obliged to administer a canon law modified piecemeal in those undefined sectors where it infringed on the common law, but otherwise unreformed. The procedure in courts and visitations still implied a view of pastoral care which was primarily jurisdictional; and it was inevitable that the bishop should continue to be represented in most of these processes by officials who were now more often than not laymen, whose working knowledge of the canons was married to a training in civil law. Excommunication as most commonly invoked had no moral or censorious quality, but served as the mere 'pain of contumacy.' As the reign progressed, there was a tendency for this apparatus to be strengthened, for in the hands of energetic administrators the church courts shared in the growth and elaboration of the institutions of government which accompanied internal security and rising prosperity. This was reconstruction, to be sure, but its ethos was not that of Protestantism. The bleak view of the Puritan was that 'discipline' had not been established in England.[1] Moreover, if the wealth of the bishoprics was now reduced, as Jewel had boasted, it was not so far diminished as to confine the bishops to the modest living envisaged by the early reformers. With the same large establishments and a measure of the old estate to maintain, and now with wives to keep and clothe and children to advance, the new bishops were open to the very same charges of worldliness and fiscality which they had levelled against their predecessors, especially in a period of inflation which threatened ruin to anyone who failed to make

[1] Thomas Lever to Bullinger, 10 July 1560; *Zurich Letters*, 84.

the best use of his office and possessions. The grant of long and ultimately unprofitable leases against substantial entry-fines, the sale of reversions to office, the wastage of timber: these were the most familiar of the shabby devices by which the bishops of the *Zurich Letters* clung to solvency.[1]

Foremost among the institutional obstacles to the establishment of a genuinely reformed order was the size of the English diocese. The point had been made at Trent that the notion of the bishop as the official teacher of his diocese made sense in the numerous small sees of Italy, where every little city had its bishop.[2] It was not immediately obvious how it could be applied to the great territorial dioceses of northern Europe. The diocese of Lincoln, to give the extreme English example, extended at this time from the Humber to the Chilterns, and embraced nine counties in whole or part. The newly-created Henrician bishop-rics somewhat eased the burden without substantially altering the scale of English diocesan administration. William Harrison, boasting in his *Description of England* that the bishops were no longer 'idle in their callings,' thought that there were very few who would not be found preaching at some place within their jurisdiction, every Sunday or oftener.[3] This may not have been all wishful thinking, for the Elizabethan bishops are not to be too lightly underestimated. But the most exemplary of episcopal preachers must have been a stranger to most of his hearers. The regular observance of triennial visitations may have been restored by the Elizabethan bishops, but to the reformed eye this was no substitute for constant pastoral vigilance, and it was not easy to dissociate these proceedings from the more occasional triumphal progresses of the past. In 1576 the ministers of Ashby-

---

[1] Christopher Hill, *Economic Problems of the Church from Whitgift to the Long Parliament*, 1956, 3-49. These general problems are exemplified from the history of a single diocese in the unpublished London Ph.D. thesis of Mrs P. M. Hembry, 'The Bishops of Bath and Wells, 1535-1647: a social and economic study,' 1956. Cf. much illustrative material in Sir John Harington, *A briefe viewe of the state of the Church of England* (1608), 1653; and F. O. White, *Lives of the Elizabethan Bishops*, 1898.

[2] Jedin, op. cit., II, 103-4.

[3] ed. F. J. Furnivall, 1877, 16.

de-la-Zouch complained to Bishop Cooper of Lincoln, as to any pre-Reformation prelate, that 'you yourselves that be great bishops would not joigne with Christ's poore mynisters, either for your great affaires which you commonly alleadge, or for your great travaile or great chardges, that cannot come without some great troupe of horses,' and they begged him to 'come amongest us sometymes in Christian humilitie, layeng asyde all popishe lordlynes, and so exercise your good guiftes amongest us your bretheren that we of your great light may receave some light.'[1] 'I see such worldlines in many that were otherwise affected before they came to cathedrall chairs,' was Burghley's complaint, 'that I feare the places alter the men.'[2] It could hardly have been otherwise.

The drastic prescription of the Presbyterians offered one kind of cure for these diseases. Theirs was a doctrine supposedly based on the unchanging requirements of God's word, but it is not hard to see that the practical deficiencies of the Elizabethan Church lent it much of its force and appeal, just as in Scotland the chaos of ecclesiastical finance gave Andrew Melville his opportunity.[3] But Presbyterianism was strong medicine, impossible to contemplate apart from a general institutional and social revolution from which all but the strongest stomachs shrank. Bishops in one form or another belonged to the hierarchical arrangement of Tudor society, and it was more natural to think of them as instruments of reform than as an insuperable obstacle. As I have argued elsewhere,[4] it was only in the conditions of conflict created by nonconformity on the one hand, and the quest for an unvarying uniformity on the other, that bishops appeared even to the more radical of the Puritans intolerable. The ideal system of many progressive minds continued to include bishops, and even to make them the very linchpins of

---

[1] B.M., MS Additional 27632, ff. 47r, 48r.

[2] Burghley to Archbishop Whitgift, 17 Sept. 1584; B.M.,MS Additional 22473, f. 12.

[3] Donaldson, *Scottish Reformation*, 194-9.

[4] 'John Field and Elizabethan Puritanism,' *Elizabethan Government and Society*, ed. Bindoff, Hurstfield and Williams, 1961, 127-62. *Below*, 335-70.

the reformed order, but bishops who were almost of another species from the lords spiritual of the past.

Even before 1559, the sobering experiences of the Marian reaction had persuaded some protestant publicists of the need for reconstruction of the units of pastoral oversight, if bishops were ever to be made credible instruments of reform in England. For those who saw the bishop's office as simple superintendency, it was but a short step to the radical opinion that only the superintendent of a small and manageable area could be a true bishop. On this at least John Knox and his English opponent John Aylmer were agreed. 'Let no man be chardged in preaching of Christ Jesus, above that which one man may do', wrote Knox from Geneva in 1558,

I mean that your bishoprikes be so devided, that of every one as they be nowe (for the most part) be made ten: and so in every citie and great towne there may be placed a godly learned man, with so many joyned with him, for preaching and instruction, as shalbe thoght sufficient for the bondes committed to their charge.[1]

Aylmer, writing a few months later against Knox's *First blast of the trumpet*, looked for the day when 'every parishe church may have his preacher, every city his superintendent, to live honestly and not pompously.'[2] (Thirty years later these words provided Martin Marprelate with a stick to beat an older and more conservative Bishop Aylmer of London). William Turner, the radical dean of Wells and the father of English natural history, indulged in similar thoughts while on his botanical wanderings around Europe in the same years. For the avoiding of confusion and the maintenance of good order, he believed that in every little shire there should be at least four bishops. 'I meane no mittred nor lordlye, no racchetted bishoppes,' but such as should be chosen annually by the rest of the clergy.[3]

Turner was no more than groping for the as yet unformulated presbyterian polity, and it might be thought that such a primitive

[1] *A brief exhortation to England*, in *Works*, ed. D. Laing, V, 1864, 518-19.
[2] *An harborowe for faithfull and trewe subjectes*, Strasbourg 1559 (*S.T.C.* 1005), Sig. 04ᵛ.
[3] *The huntyng of the Romyshe Vuolfe*, Zurich 1554 (*S.T.C.* 24356), Sig. Fiᵛ.

scheme would have been superseded by the graduated system
of representative synods devised within Calvinism, which contrived to satisfy the need for order without raising one man
permanently above another. Yet long after the presbyterian
polity had been elaborated in theory, and practised in other
Reformed churches, the case was still made in England for the
multiplication rather than the abolition of bishops. For example,
an Elizabethan 'plot for reformation,' evidently a parliamentary
device, complains that the bishops have 'wonderfullie neglected'
their duty, seldom preaching or visiting, but admits that if they
had studied never so hard they could not have done it, 'by
reason the same dioceses be so wyde and large.' It insists that
no bishopric should be so extensive that the farthest minister
could not resort to the bishop or he to him, once a week or
oftener, to read or hear a lesson of divinity; and proposes that
the existing dioceses should be divided among 150 new sees.[1]
In 1604, a puritan civil lawyer, practised in ecclesiastical administration, declared in *An assertion for true and christian church-
policie* that he was 'so farre from mislikyng of the state, order or
government of divine bishops' that, where one bishop served
five shires, as in the diocese of Lincoln where his experience lay,
he would rather 'that every one of these shyres had fyfteene
bishopps, to teach and to governe the same.'[2]

But more may well mean worse, and it is not clear that the
cause of reform would have been well served by a process of
ecclesiastical balkanization. In the early years of the reign it
would not have been easy to find 150 episcopal men of sound
religion and requisite talent. And there was little to be said for
restricting the exceptional gifts of a Grindal or a Jewel to the
limits of a market town and a few villages. Moreover there was
no overlooking the position which the bishops still retained in
the commonwealth, and their effective function as commission-

[1] B.M., MS Additional 48066, ff. 2-15.
[2] William Stoughton, *An assertion for true and Christian Church-policie*,
Middelburg 1604 (*S.T.C.* 23318), epistle, 13-14. For Stoughton, see my
Letters of Thomas Wood, Puritan, 1566-1577, *BIHR* Special Supplement no.
5, 1960, x.

ers for the royal government of the Church, a rôle which must have been altered out of recognition if their numbers had been multiplied by ten. Such a drastic reorganization as this would have entailed almost as much constitutional disturbance as a presbyterian revolution, and under Elizabeth it could never have been practical politics. A more constructive line of thought is represented by a succession of proposals to preserve the existing diocesan boundaries, while providing the bishops with co-adjutors to represent them in subdivisions of their jurisdictions. These lesser superintendents or *chorepiscopi*, if we may so call them, were to be joined with the bishop as a synod; and they were themselves to preside over local assemblies of their fellow-clergy. For a strong motive in all these projects was to restore to episcopal government the synodal context which was suggested in such patristic sources as Ignatius, Tertullian, and Cyprian. As the Strasbourg reformer, Martin Bucer, had insisted in his *De regno Christi*, composed in Edwardine England, the bishop could not properly fulfil his office 'sine reliquorum presbyterorum consilio.'[1] If there was no inherent difference of order between the bishop and the inferior clergy; if the bishop was himself primarily a teacher and the inferior ministers themselves pastors of souls; and if jurisdiction was by delegation from the Christian magistrate: then there were no necessary grounds on which pastoral discipline need be reserved exclusively to the bishops. The parish clergy should be recognised as pastors within their own congregations; while at the diocesan level, the bishop should be assisted by other pastors according to their capacities, rather than by officials who were pastorally irresponsible.

There is some evidence that in the reign of Edward VI, John Hooper attempted to base his administration of the diocese of Gloucester on some such principles. He appointed quarterly meetings of the clergy in each deanery, 'synods, councils and assemblies,' to be presided over by himself or his deputies, and he wrote of 'such as I have made superintendents in Gloucester-

---

[1] Bucer, *De Regno Christi*, II, xii; ed. Wendel, *Opera Latina*, XV, 1955, 118.

shire.'[1] Later, when Hooper and John Rogers were awaiting martyrdom under Mary, they took steps to warn their brethren, 'as well in exile as others,' that only by the use of such lesser superintendents could the failings of the Edwardine Church be avoided in the future. For every ten churches, they advised the appointment of 'one good and learned superintendent,' to be subject to annual episcopal visitation and to 'oversee the profiting of the parishes' and the readers who were to serve them. This advice was in print, for everyone to read, in the pages of Foxe's *Acts and Monuments*.[2]

To have planted such auxiliary superintendents in the Church of England would not have been a rank innovation, as those with some knowledge of ancient practice were able to show. These 'devices' amounted, in effect, to a proposal to revive the use of rural deans and rural chapters.[3] The rural deanery was still a working unit of ecclesiastical administration in the sixteenth century—often co-extensive with the hundred—and the dean of Christianity himself was not quite an extinct species. But where the office survived, its attributes seem to have been largely formal, whether granted for life by patent [4] or supplied from the beneficed clergy by annual nomination.[5] If rural deans were

[1] Hooper, *Later Writings*, ed. C. Nevinson, Parker Socy., 1852, 132, xix.

[2] ed. Cattley, VI, 610.

[3] Robert Beale, the learned clerk of the Privy Council, even contrived to relate the clandestine *classes* and synods of the Presbyterians to these ancient institutions: 'And further, if men will without partiallitie looke into the first foundacions in the auncient cannons for the *Ruralle Deanyries*, what were they but Classes? and the bishopes visitacions but colloquies and conferences? to see howe the churches had profitted and the people bin taught? . . . Wherefore, although the tearmes be somewhat straunge, yet the matter is good and auncient. . .' (B.M., MS Additional 48046, f. 135ᵛ.)

[4] The rural deanery was a life tenure in the diocese of Norwich, where their continuance was 'perpetual, and their admission more solemn than elsewhere,' and by collation; and in the diocese of Chester, where deaneries were sometimes granted *en bloc* by patent, to be held with the office of commissary. (William Dansey, *Horæ Decanicæ Rurales*, 1835, I, 146-7, 133-4; II, 379-84; A. Hamilton Thompson, *Diocesan Organization in the Middle Ages: Archdeacons and Rural Deans*, Raleigh Lecture 1943, 39-41.)

[5] In the time of Bishop Cox (1559-81), as earlier in the sixteenth century, rural deans were nominated in the diocese of Ely as part of the business of the annual synods, held at or near Whitsun. (Cambridge University Library, Ely Diocesan Records, B2/1, 7).

still saddled with some administrative chores,[1] their function as arch-priests had long since been usurped by the archdeacon, along with the power to assemble the clergy of the deanery in monthly assemblies and quarterly solemn chapters.[2] It was not common at this time to see a remedy for the excessive centralisation of spiritual government in the person of the archdeacon, in spite of his traditional function of *oculus episcopi*, or in the bishop's commissary. Few callings were more unpopular, and the familiar abuses of the archdeacons' and commissaries' courts were an embarrassment even to Archbishop Whitgift.[3] But rural deans were another matter. The office was uncontaminated by recent history, and had an aura of primitive purity. The seminal mind of Martin Bucer was perhaps the first to advocate, in effect, their resuscitation when, in *De regno Christi*, he made explicit recommendations for the employment of *chorepiscopi* (whom he mistakenly identified with rural deans) and for the holding of regular synods, to be attended 'non civitatum modo episcopi, sed etiam chorepiscopi, aliique presbyteri et diaconi.'[4] It may have been under the influence of his presence and teaching in England that detailed provision was made for the office in the *Reformatio Legum*, which restored to the rural dean his important responsibilities as *testis synodalis*.[5]

At least one early Elizabethan bishop, Thomas Bentham of Coventry and Lichfield, made some attempt to put this projected reform into practice. Among his highly original injunctions of 1563 was an order that the parish officers should report moral offences to their 'dean . . . every quarter once when he shall sit

---

[1] In Bury St Edmunds on 3 Febr. 1596, one George Atherston of Bury, rural dean, affirmed on oath before a notary that a certain induction had taken place on 2 June 1582. (Seckford Library, Woodbridge, MS V. B. Redstone 3.1, p. 24). There is no clergyman of Atherston's names in any clergy-list for the diocese of Norwich.

[2] Dansey, op. cit., II, 101-8, 120-7; A. Hamilton Thompson, op. cit., 34-44, and *The English Clergy and their Organization in the Later Middle Ages*, 1947, 63-70; Edmund Gibson, *Codex Juris Ecclesiastici Anglicani*, Oxford 1761, II, 973; Richard Burn, *Ecclesiastical Law*, 1797, II, 123.

[3] John Strype, *Life of Whitgift*, Oxford 1822, III, 445-52.

[4] *Opera Latina*, XV, 129.

[5] *The Reformation of the Ecclesiastical Laws*, 100-1.

at any church within the deanery, calling you before him for the same purpose.'[1] Archbishop Parker's constitutions and canons of 1571 defined the procedure for the appointment of deans, by which the archdeacon was to nominate suitable candidates to the bishop at the end of his annual visitation.[2] At the opening of Parliament in May of the following year, the lord keeper, Sir Nicholas Bacon, dwelt upon the scandalous lack of effective church discipline, and indicated the remedy in 'the dividing every one of the dioceses according to their greatness into deaneries, as I know commonly they be; and the committing of the deaneries to men well chosen, as I think commonly they be not . . .' He suggested that the rural deans might henceforth keep 'certain ordinary courts at their prescript times for the well executing of those laws of discipline,' and should themselves be closely observed by the bishop or his chancellor. This was a 'plot', he thought, 'which in this Parliament may very well be brought to pass.'[3] But no legislation followed. A year earlier a renewed attempt to obtain statutory recognition of the *Reformatio Legum*, promoted by John Foxe, who prepared the first printed text, and by the great 'parliament man' and Cranmer's son-in-law, Thomas Norton, who commended it to the House of Commons, came to nothing.[4] Even the canons enacted in the Convocation of the same year failed to secure royal approbation. The queen's jealous conservatism towards the conduct of church affairs was doubtless responsible, directly or indirectly, for each of these checks, and for the institutional immobility of the

[1] P.R.O., S.P. 12/36/41; printed, R. W. Dixon, *History of the Church of England*, VI, 1902, 80 (77n.).

[2] *Synodalia*, ed. E. Cardwell, 1842, I, 117. Burn remarks (op. cit., II, 125) that this was 'rather a permission, than a positive command, for the continuance of that office.'

[3] Simonds D'Ewes, *The Journals of all the Parliaments during the Reign of Queen Elizabeth*, 1682, 193. Cf. the interest taken in the ancient practice of rural deans by William Harrison: 'Unto these deanerie churches also the cleargie in old time of the same deanrie wer appointed to repaire at sundrie seasons, there to receive wholesome ordinances, and to consult upon the necessarie affaires of the whole jurisdiction, if necessitie so required: and some image hereof is yet to be seene in the north partes.' (*Description of England*, 15-16.)

[4] J. E. Neale, *Elizabeth I and her Parliaments, 1559-1581*, 1953, 194-7.

Church of England throughout a period which might otherwise have been filled with improvisation. Well over a century later, Francis Atterbury indulged in no more than a pipe-dream when he declared in a famous archidiaconal charge that 'if ever a re-establishment of church-discipline in its vigour be sincerely intended, one, and a chief, method of promoting it must be by a restoration of *rural deans* and *chapters*, to the full extent of their ancient powers.'[1] It was left to a busier age of improvement —the nineteenth century—to breathe some new life into these old bones, but by then the effect could hardly be to re-establish church discipline 'in its vigour.'

But if rural deans and chapters were not effectively revived in Elizabethan England under those names, the practice of associating the clergy in local assemblies and entrusting the better equipped with a pastoral responsibility for their weaker brethren was widely, if informally, established. Over much of the country in the later sixteenth and early seventeenth centuries, ministers met regularly to engage in mutual edification and discipline in meetings known at first as 'exercises of prophesying,' and latterly simply as 'exercises.'[2] This was an institution known in one form or another in many of the Reformed churches, and deriving its authority from a text in 1 Corinthians xiv: 'Let the prophets speak two or three, and let the other judge . . . For ye may all prophesy one by one, that all may learn and all may be comfort-ed.' One Leicestershire minister writing to another called these exercises 'the universities of the pore ministries,'[3] which in-dicates their prime function. The clergy were brought together regularly, usually once a month or every two or three weeks, to the local market town, or the principal church of their deanery, to take part in a kind of preaching conference. Under the pres-idency of a moderator, three or four exegetical sermons would be preached in turn on the same text by the learned of the com-

[1] Dansey, op. cit., II, 187.
[2] A full account of the prophesyings will be found in my doctoral thesis, op. cit. ,173-214; and in my forthcoming 'Elizabethan Puritan Movement.'
[3] John Ireton to Anthony Gilby, May 1578; Cambridge University Library, MS Mm. 1.43, p. 452.

pany, the purpose being, as one order of proceedings puts it, 'to rippe up the texte, to shewe the sense of the Holie Ghoste, and brieflie, pithylie and plainly to observe such thinges as hereafter maie well be applied in preaching, concerninge either doctrine or maners.'[1] By this means the unlearned were initiated in the word of God and trained to become preachers themselves, and agreement in doctrine was promoted among all the ministers associated in the exercise. This last purpose was served by the process of formal censure to which all speakers were subjected, the moderator acting as the mouthpiece of the assembly. This censure might extend to the lives and conduct of the ministers, serving the general interests of discipline. This part of the proceedings was conducted in private, but when the prophesying itself took place before a lay audience, it supplied the want of preaching and provided an impressive public vindication of the Reformed faith in what might still be a largely hostile environment.[2] The day would end with a dinner for the clergy at a local inn, an opportunity for informal discussion of matters of common interest.

[1] The order for the prophesying at Bedford, Lambeth Palace Library, MS 2007, ff. 106-7; similar to the Hertfordshire order, ibid., ff. 108-9, printed, S. E. Lehmberg, 'Archbishop Grindal and the Prophesyings,' *Historical Magazine of the Protestant Episcopal Church*, XXXIV, 1965, 93-7; and from another copy by Strype, *Annals*, Oxford 1824, II. i, 473-7; and to the 'Rules and orders agreed unto by the mynysters in Buckinghamshyre tochynge the exercyse of theym selves together in the interpretation of the scriptures,' Cambridge University Library, MS Ff. 5.14, no. 8, f. 85; these all sanctioned by Bishop Cooper of Lincoln. Cf. the commission for the holding of an exercise granted to the preachers of Bury St Edmunds by Bishop Parkhurst, Cambridge University Library, MS Ee.11.34, f. 106; the 'order of Northampton,' P.R.O., S.P. 12/78/38, often printed; and the Norwich order of 1575, 'sede vacante,' Dr Williams's Library, MS Morrice B I, pp. 268-70, printed, J. Browne, *History of Congregationalism in Norfolk and Suffolk*, 1877, 18-20. Apart from these documents, most of what is known of the history and conduct of the prophesyings is contained in a collection of reports from fifteen bishops, and three archdeacons of the diocese of London, Lambeth Palace Library, MS 2003; printed, Lehmberg, loc. cit., 87-145.

[2] When the prophesyings were put down in 1577, Thomas Wood described this as 'not only a great reioysing to all God's enemies, but such a service to Sathan as unles the whole religion shold be overthrowen a greater could not be done.' (*Letters of Thomas Wood*, 22.)

These meetings have left only occasional traces in the formal ecclesiastical records,[1] which may account for the scant attention which they have received from historians. The impression usually given is of an enthusiastic and probably dangerous practice which came briefly into prominence in the time of Archbishop Grindal. But although they flourished in the early 1570s, the prophesyings dated in some places, for example, Coventry, much of Essex, and Norwich, from the earliest years of Elizabeth's reign.[2] As such they were officially suppressed in the southern province by the queen in person, in 1577,[3] but meetings of ministers for 'exercise' continued in many districts, with a single sermon taking the place of public 'prophesying.' The most significant part of the proceedings, the private conference of the ministers themselves, was a regular feature of clerical life in numerous market towns, before and after the turn of the century.[4] Exercises of this kind were begun throughout the great diocese of Chester in 1583 and continued for about ten years, and in some places for much longer.[5] On the other side of the Pennines they began in the early seventeenth century and continued without interruption until the advent of Archbishop Neile in 1632. Dr Marchant believes that in Nottinghamshire they lasted without a break from 1570 until about the same time.[6]

[1] There are some references in the register of Bishop Cooper of Lincoln. (*Lincoln Episcopal Records in the Time of Thomas Cooper*, ed. C. W. Foster, Lincoln Record Socy., II, 1912, 114.)

[2] For Coventry and Essex, evidence in Lambeth Palace Library, MS 2003, ff. 5, 12-13; for Norwich, evidence in a letter in P.R.O., S.P. 15/12/27.

[3] Much of the documentation for this episode, and for the subsequent troubles of Archbishop Grindal, is in *The Remains of Archbishop Grindal*, ed. W. Nicholson, Parker Socy., 1843, 372-403. The queen's letter to Whitgift, as bishop of Worcester, ordering the suppression of the exercises, is in Lambeth Palace Library, MS 2003, ff. 40-1, printed, Lehmberg, loc. cit., 142-3.

[4] The evidence is gathered in my doctoral thesis, op. cit., 261-79.

[5] Francis Peck, *Desiderata Curiosa*, 1732, I. iii, 29; iv, 33; Gonville and Caius College, Cambridge, MS 197/103, pp. 175-84; *H.M.C., 14th Report, Appendix IV, Kenyon MSS.*, 15.

[6] R. A. Marchant, *The Puritans and the Church Courts in the Diocese of York, 1560-1642*, 1960, 29-39, 115, 134-5, 169; J. A. Newton, 'Puritanism in the Diocese of York, Excluding Nottinghamshire, 1604-1640,' unpublished London Ph.D. thesis, 1956, 218-38.

In the diocese of Lincoln, the exercises had a troubled but continuous history from the 1570s at least until 1614.[1] There was a similar picture in the diocese of Norwich.[2]

If these institutions had been no more than an emergency In the diocese of Lincoln, the exercises had a troubled but conmeans of meeting a famine of sermons and of preachers they would merit little more than the passing mention which they have usually received. But at a time when the Church itself was thought to be primarily an instrument of edification, meetings devoted to the instruction of both ministers and people, and which provided means of self-discipline for the clergy, necessarily assumed a place of some importance in the organic life of the Church, even to the extent of modifying its polity. In other Reformed churches where the ministers successfully asserted their claim to a voice in church discipline, the organs of their government invariably grew out of similar meetings which were at first restricted to biblical conference; and in Scotland, when the General Assembly came to set up presbyteries, it ruled that, wherever an exercise already existed, it was to be 'judged a presbytery.'[3] It would seem, therefore, that the English prophesying had at least a potentially administrative function.

Where these potentialities have been appreciated, it has usually been with the assumption that the prophesyings were simply presbyteries in embryo, and that their tendency was entirely subversive. Admittedly, the Elizabethan Presbyterians in their

[1] The exercises in the diocese of Lincoln are described in the report of a visitation made to Bishop Neile in 1614. (Original in Muniment Room of the dean and chapter of Lincoln Cathedral, MS 4/3/43; Ralph Thoresby's transcript in John Strype's papers, Cambridge University Library, MS Baumgartner 8, double ff. 199-202; whence copied by William Cole, B.M., MS Additional 5853, ff. 166v-8). Dr Mark C. Curtis has recently referred to this document in his article 'The Alienated Intellectuals of Early Stuart England,' *Past and Present*, XXIII, 1962, reprinted, *Crisis in Europe, 1560-1660*, ed. T. Aston, 1965, 310. But *pace* Dr Curtis, the seventy 'lecturers' who maintained these exercises were mostly beneficed clergy, and not 'lecturers' in the professional sense.

[2] *The Registrum Vagum of Anthony Harison*, I, Norfolk Record Socy. XXII, 1963, 96-103.

[3] Janet G. Macgregor, *The Scottish Presbyterian Polity*, 1926, 53, 115-16; B. J. Kidd, *Documents Illustrative of the Continental Reformation*, 1911, 592; Donaldson, *Scottish Reformation*, 204-8.

early manifestoes and parliamentary projects anticipated the same kind of progression from exercise to *classis* which served to set up the presbyterian polity in Scotland.[1] It is also true that some conferences of Elizabethan preachers developed into secret *classes*, which applied presbyterian principles to the management of their own affairs, and that for a time, in the 1580s, some of these groups were involved in a bold and co-ordinated design to take over the central direction of the Church from within.[2] But the prophesyings were neither inevitably presbyterian in their tendency, nor at all incompatible with the episcopal principle of imparity. One might apply to the original form of these meetings a later comment on the presbytery mentioned by St Ignatius: 'Here was a fellowship, yet such a fellowship as destroyed not presidency.'[3]

If the preachers themselves often took the initiative in setting up the exercises, they were seldom reluctant to seek episcopal confirmation of their orders of meeting, while several of the bishops were willing to meet them half-way in issuing these orders as their own. 'Thes orders of exercise, offred to me by the learned of the clergie of Hertfordshire, I think good and godly,' wrote Bishop Cooper on an order which seems to have served as a model for other areas in the diocese of Lincoln.[4] Cooper reserved strictly to himself both the enrolment of the ministers attached to each exercise, and the appointment of the moderators. He could later assure his archbishop: 'Trulie, my lord, there is no one thinge in the charge of my diocese wherunto I have had a more carefull eye than to the moderate using of those conferences.' His contemporaries in the sees of Chichester and Exeter went one better, and could claim to have played the part of moderator in person.[5] When the queen threatened the future

---

[1] *Puritan Manifestoes*, ed. W. H. Frere and C. E. Douglas, repr. 1954, 107-8; *The Seconde Parte of a Register*, ed. A. Peel, 1915, II, 217.

[2] See my thesis, op. cit., and my forthcoming 'Elizabethan Puritan Movement.'

[3] *A collection of speeches made by Sir Edward Dering . . . in matter of religion*, 1642, 72.

[4] Lambeth Palace Library, MS 2007, f. 109.

[5] Ibid., MS 2003, ff. 29-30, 4, 8.

existence of the prophesyings in 1576, and Archbishop Grindal canvassed his suffragans for their views, no less than ten were in favour of the exercises continuing, subject to careful regulation, and only four of those who replied were wholly unsympathetic.[1]

The hall-mark of a presbyterian assembly is that the office of moderator should circulate, so compromising in no way the equal status of the members. But where a bishop sanctioned an order of prophesying, he appointed two or three permanent moderators who exercised his own delegated powers in convening the other clergy. These were not voluntary gatherings,[2] and there is evidence that Bishop Cooper constrained attendance through his consistory court.[3] The moderators were already, in effect, superintendents or deans of the other inferior clergy, their responsibilities extending in practice beyond the simple regulation of proceedings. Offenders could be bound by the consistory court to do penance in the exercise, presumably under the eye of the moderator.[4] And the unlearned clergy were examined on the same occasions in the written tasks laid upon them by royal and episcopal injunctions.[5] In Suffolk, the powers conferred by Bishop Parkhurst on the three moderators at Bury St Edmunds were wide and imprecise. They were to take 'chardge and order' of the exercise to the extent that they could by their order and direction assemble 'the hole clergie ther aboutes' to meet at such times and places as they or any one of them should think convenient. They were to report disobedient persons to the bishop's commissary, and anything lawful which they thought fit to order and decree 'for the better execution of the premysses,' the bishop undertook to 'ratify, continue and allow.'[6]

[1] Lambeth Palace Library, MS 2003, passim.

[2] Unlike the Norwich prophesying of 1575 (Browne, op. cit., 18-20) and the Dedham conference of 1582-9, led by 'exiles' from Norwich, (the minutes and other papers printed, *The Presbyterian Movement in the Reign of Queen Elizabeth*, ed. R. G. Usher, Camden Socy, 3rd ser. VIII, 1905), which were voluntary, and where the office of moderator circulated.

[3] *Lincoln Episcopal Records*, 114.

[4] Ibid.

[5] Lambeth Palace Library, MS 2003.

[6] Cambridge University Library, MS Ee. 11.34, f. 106.

It was in this same diocese of Norwich in 1578 that the chancellor, Thomas Becon, who was both a forward-looking reformer and an antiquarian, suggested how the administration of the diocese might be transformed by the revival of the office of rural dean within the modern innovation of prophesying. The medieval rural dean had been a potent figure in this diocese,[1] and Becon was impressed with what he deduced of his activities from certain thirteenth-century records. Such men should now be appointed as superintendents in each deanery, to summon the ministers and churchwardens of every parish to a monthly prophesying or, failing that, to a sermon. They were to exercise discipline on these occasions, dealing summarily with minor offences, and certifying others to the bishop. They were also to have charge of probate, a cunning device to secure the attendance of those who would not come of mere devotion. And they were to make regular reports on the recusants in their divisions. A regular opportunity to confer with the bishop or chancellor would be provided by appointing the superintendents to preach the Sunday sermons in the Green Yard at Norwich. Collectively, they were to be associated with the bishop and the chancellor in their synods, 'sitting openly as their assistance,' so that offenders would be 'rebuked or suspended before all the clergy of the diocese and the whole congregation there assembled.' They were to be further employed as examiners of candidates for the ministry and for admission to benefices. By such means, the bishop would be enabled to be 'pastor of his whole diocese,' with 'a special knowledge of every particular man of his diocese as near as possibly he may,' while the abused jurisdiction of commissaries, which Becon took to be the chief cause of the unpopularity of ecclesiastical government, would be superseded.[2] Other projects, bearing a general generic resemblance, survive in a number of parliamentary papers and other addresses, most of them dating from the encouraging years of Grindal's

[1] Collated to a life-tenure of the office by patent, and empowered to impose acts of penance. (Dansey, op. cit., I, 146-7; J. F. Williams, 'Ecclesiastical Discipline at South Creake in 1317,' *Norfolk Archaeology*, XXIII, 1929, 305-7).

[2] *H.M.C. Report, Hatfield MSS.*, II, 195-8; Strype, *Annals*, II. ii, 695-701.

archiepiscopate.[1] It was a scheme with the same pedigree which James I chose to misinterpret at Hampton Court. Dr Reynolds's desire was

> that, according to certain provincial constitutions, they of the clergy might have meetings once every three weekes. First, in rural deaneries, and therein to have prophecying ... Secondly, that such things as could not be resolved upon there, might be referred to the archdeacon's visitation, and so Thirdly, from thence to the episcopal synode, where the bishop with his presbytery should determine all such points as before could not be decided.[2]

If these not unreasonable demands had been even partially satisfied at any time between 1559 and 1640, it must have taken much of the wind out of the sails of the rigid presbyterian demand for parity.

From a pragmatic point of view, the merit of proposals of this kind was that they answered, as Presbyterianism surely did not, to the actual conditions and real needs of the Elizabethan Church. Applied to the whole of a ministry in which only a minority was capable of imparting instruction, and where livings were so unequally endowed, the dogma of the parity of all

---

[1] Of particular importance is a schedule of articles of 1581, which distil the reforms pursued by the Puritans in the House of Commons with some consistency between 1576 and 1584, and which were referred by Sir Walter Mildmay and Sir Francis Walsingham to the queen, and by the queen to the attention of the bishops. (Neale, op. cit., 349-53, 398-406; copy of the articles bearing the bishops', and mostly Whitgift's, comments, Inner Temple Library, MS Petyt 538/54, ff. 247-62; printed by Strype, *Whitgift*, III, 47-63, from B.M., MS Lansdowne 30, ff. 203-10.) There is also a project drafted for the eye of Parliament which, like the 1581 articles, provides the bishop with six learned preachers, appointed by the justices of the peace, 'his six annexed,' to assist him in most of his functions, including ordination. (P.R.O., S.P. 12/282/71.) Cf. Thomas Norton's 'Devices,' 'A note of such thinges as are mete to be considered of, for the stay of the present corruption in religion,' drawn up in 1581, apparently at the instigation of Walsingham and perhaps other councillors. (B.M., MS Additional 48023, ff. 41v-58v.) Cf. also Thomas Lever's 'notes for some reformation of the ministry and ministers' (Inner Temple Library, MS Petyt 538/38, ff. 71-4) which may have prompted a modest experiment on similar lines undertaken by Bishop Overton of Coventry and Lichfield in 1584. (Kennedy, *Elizabethan Episcopal Administration*, III, 161-74; *Seconde Parte of a Register*, I, 260-7.)

[2] Cardwell, *Conferences*, 201-2.

presbyters was, as Sir Edward Dering was to remark in the Long Parliament, 'a fancy, a dream, a meer *non entity*.'[1] Certainly it was only entertained by the Presbyterians themselves in the context of a fundamental financial and administrative reorganization. Failing any such upheaval, its necessary corollary was the drastic doctrine that non-preaching ministers were no ministers at all, and along that road lay separatism, a path which few took willingly or lightly. If the integrity of a comprehensive, established Church was to be maintained, with institutional continuity, it was necessary to recognise that, while the calling of all ministers might in the strictest theory be equal, some were more equal than others. In practice, there were not a few famous preachers and pastors in the Elizabethan Church whose reputations and powers of leadership gave them a kind of natural episcopal status. This was the position of 'Father' Anthony Gilby at Ashby-de-la-Zouch, a kind of bishop in Leicestershire, where his patron, the earl of Huntingdon, was uncrowned king. John Aylmer as archdeacon of Leicester could speak of 'Ashby, where Gilby is bishop,' and Leicester, 'where Johnson is superintendent.'[2] In Norwich, two preachers—John More of St Andrew's and Thomas Roberts, for two years archdeacon of Norwich—stood out, and are described by one of their admiring contemporaries as 'presidents, or leaders of an armie.'[3] A primary fact of Tudor social geography can help us to understand this situation. The market town was the centre of a still partly self-sufficient world, and it was natural that both the town and its leading preacher, often not an incumbent but enjoying a singular status as a lecturer or town preacher, should exert an equal influence over the clerical life round about them. Aylmer had in mind Tudor England and no imaginary Utopia when he wrote in 1559 that every city should have its own honest and moderate superintendent.

Quite apart from the prophesyings, and short of a revision

---

[1] *Speeches*, 139.

[2] B.M., MS Additional 29546, ff. 56^v-7^v.

[3] Erasmus, tr. William Burton, *Seven dialogues both pithie and profitable*, 1606 (*S.T.C.* 10457), Sig. A2^v.

of the diocesan system, there were already many ways in which the Church exploited the superior gifts of its more able inferior clergy. The leading preachers of a county, or of an archdeaconry, could be employed to assess the other ministers for a clerical subsidy, or to collect contributions under a charitable brief, or to represent the bishop or archdeacon at assizes and sessions.[1] Above all, the Church depended upon this class of clergy to preach the quarter sermons in the parishes where the incumbent was not a licensed preacher, and to supervise in those same parishes the extramural studies of the non-graduate clergy. In the years after the queen's suppression of the prophesyings, some individual bishops, and eventually Archbishop Whitgift and Convocation, laid the imposition and examination of these tasks on 'one or two of the best learned and most discreet preachers' in each deanery.[2] In the diocese of London, the effect of these orders was to divide the clergy into three ranks: 'commissioners of the exercise,' with power to assemble their charges, other graduate clergy, and the unlearned.[3] In such ways as these the English diocese already bore some marks of what in the language of the time would be called a mixed polity, monarchy tempered with aristocracy.

If these developments were in keeping with the actual state of the Elizabethan Church, it is certain that they were equally in harmony with the aspirations and prejudices of those who had the running of the Elizabethan commonwealth. The religious Elizabethan gentleman or borough magistrate looked to the clergy to promote godliness by the preaching of the word and

[1] These examples drawn from *Victoria County History of Derbyshire*, II, 21-2; *Records of the Old Archdeaconry of St Alban's*, ed. H. R. Wilton Hall, St Alban's & Herts. Architectural and Archaeological Socy., 1908, 46-7; Herts. Record Office, Records of the Archdeaconry of St Albans, Act Book, 1582-6, ASA 7/11, f. 18ᵛ.

[2] The development of 'exercises' in the sense of tasks for the unlearned clergy is reconstructed in my thesis, op. cit., 244-60. For Whitgift's orders of 1585 'for the increase of learning in the unlearned sort of ministers,' see *Records of the Old Archdeaconry of St Alban's*, 45, 49-50; for the similar orders promulgated from Convocation in 1586/7, Lambeth Palace Library, Whitgift's Register, I, f. 131ʳ, whence printed, Strype, *Whitgift*, III, 194-6.

[3] Guildhall Library, MS 9537/6 (Liber visitationis, 1586), ff. 173-83.

wholesome moral discipline; and above all to cultivate obedience to the laws of God and of the realm, and an attitude of
deference to the local representatives of authority. The proper
relationship of preachers and governors is indicated in a contemporary account of their cooperation in Norwich: 'The
magistrates and ministers imbracing and seconding one another,
and the common people affording due reverence, and obedience,
to them both.'[1] 'Ministry' and 'magistracy' were but separate
arms of the same Christian government, and conflict between
them was abhorrent. This tended to mean that the clergy should
never withstand the Council or the local justices, and that a
bishop must never set himself against the gentry, as Archbishop
Whitgift was accused of doing in Kent.[2] The function of the
clergy was to underpin, not undermine, the authority of the
prince and her agents, as well as the social order. Bishops, in a
phrase of Sir Francis Knollys, were themselves 'under-governors
to her Majestie.'[3] Excessive wealth and display in the higher
clergy suggested a pretension to some other authority, inherent
in themselves, or in the pope. But if the governing class ab-
horred prelacy, it is probable that all but a minority would have
regarded the neo-clerical claims of Presbyterianism with equal
distaste. Like Lord Digby in the Long Parliament, they had no
wish to see 'a pope in each parish,' and they would surely have
agreed with Sir Edward Dering's complaint, uttered in that same
assembly, that parity of degrees in church government was 'as
absonous to reason, as parity in a state or family.'[4] 'I am none of
them that would have archbisshoppes or bisshoppes pulled
downe, or the forme of the Churche altred,' wrote a learned
Elizabethan official, Robert Beale, clerk of the Council, 'for I
am not so foolishe, but see that the estate [5] cannot beare it
without some harme . . .' But was there, he asked, a church
'under the cope of Heaven' which tolerated two such absurdities

---

[1] Erasmus, tr. Burton, *Seven dialogues*, Sig. A2.
[2] Dr Williams's Library, MS Morrice L, no. V, pp. 8-11.
[3] Knollys to Burghley, 4 Aug. 1589; B.M., MS Lansdowne 61, f. 151^v.
[4] Shaw, op. cit., I, 32; Dering, *Speeches*, 139.
[5] 'of the Churche' erased.

as the maintenance of a dumb ministry, and the whole exercise of discipline and excommunication by a single individual?[1]

The church of the prophesyings, on the other hand, was to the taste of the protestant gentry. The exercises themselves seemed to contain the best hope for a disciplined and useful clergy, and so eventually for the general amelioration of society. It is not surprising to learn that the local justices were often assiduous attenders. At Southam in Warwickshire there were usually three or four on every occasion, while at Shrewsbury the entire Council in the Marches would grace the proceedings if their meeting in the town coincided with an exercise. At St Albans, the 'masters of the towne and the gentlemen of the cowntrey' took it in turns to supply the preachers with free wine, and saw to it that they were charged a fair price for their dinners and that their horses were fed for nothing. 'This is a sygne that oure doinges is well lyke of,' wrote the archdeacon and principal moderator.[2] If these assemblies had been enabled to assume an administrative function, there is no doubt that the gentlemen in attendance would have underwritten the discipline of the moderator-superintendents. Becon, the chancellor of Norwich, expressly provided for their presence at all the 'solemn assemblies' to be held by his superintendents, and it is significant that a faction of Norfolk justices, all godly protestants, forwarded his scheme to the Privy Council as proof of his 'desire of good proceedings.'[3] Behind these proposals one senses the notion that the shire rather than the diocese should be the working unit of church government; that the pattern of ecclesiastical discipline should be accomodated to that of civil administration. One's mind reaches forward to the proposition put to the House of Commons by Sir Edward Dering in June 1641: allowing that the existing dioceses were 'too vast,' the circuits of church government should be reduced to 'the common boundaries and limits of our severall shires.'[4]

[1] B.M., MS Additional 48039, ff. 49ᵛ, 67ᵛ.
[2] *Letters of Thomas Wood*, 18; Lambeth Palace Library, MS 2003, ff. 5, 17.
[3] *H.M.C. Report, Hatfield MSS.*, II, 196, 198. For the politics underlying this project, see my thesis, op. cit., 882-5.
[4] *Speeches*, 69-70.

No form of church polity can be considered apart from the structures of the secular society in which it is set, or from its values. If the Elizabethan and Jacobean bishops were virtually commissioners for the Crown, or at least, as James I insisted at Hampton Court, complementary to monarchy, then these reduced bishops and their auxiliaries would probably have exposed a Church already deeply penetrated by lay patronage to the greatly augmented influence of the nobility and gentry. Such devices as we have discussed for the reform—or emasculation— of episcopacy often proposed a more or less drastic paring of bishops' temporalities, or even their replacement by stipends, with the diversion of the revenues so released to education, poor relief, military expenditure, and 'other good things.'[1] There were plenty of Elizabethans who would have agreed with Nathaniel Fiennes in 1641 that if the bishoprics were felled, or at least topped, 'a great deal of good timber might be cut out of them for the use of the Church and of the kingdom. . .'[2] Not the least of the attractions of all such schemes of disendowment was the promise they contained of 'abating the pride of the clergy,' and admittedly the effect of any of the proposals which have been discussed in these pages must have been to reduce in some degree the social status of the bishops, and with it their largely illusory independence. Yet a partnership of ministry and magistracy, such as William Burton claimed to have witnessed in Elizabethan Norwich,[3] was a real alternative to clericalism on the one hand and naked Erastianism on the other. It was, after all, the authentic, primitive, Calvinist ideal.

The policies and actions of Archbishops Whitgift and Bancroft, as later those of Laud and his bishops, seem to have been based on the assumption that there could be no such inter-

---

[1] For example, Turner, *The huntying of the Romyshe Vuolfe*, Sig. Fii. The anonymous 'plot for reformation' referred to above contains elaborate plans for the redeployment of the bishops' revenues. (B.M., MS Additional 48066, ff. 14-15r.) For a very early calculation of the same kind, see *Henry Brinklow's Complaynt of Roderyck Mors*, Early English Text Socy., extra ser. XXII, 1874, 50-3.

[2] Shaw, op. cit., I, 36.

[3] Erasmus, tr. Burton, *Seven dialogues*, Sig. A2.

dependence, and that the Church must defend itself against lay interference by the reinforcement of its ancient claims of spiritual government. Queen Elizabeth's suspension of Archbishop Grindal and her appointment of Whitgift as successor mark a watershed of major consequence. Insofar as the life of the Church and its government was controlled from the centre, and in particular from Lambeth, the episcopal office became more and not less monarchical; the prospect of reform in its vexatious and exorbitant apparatus of government receded; and with the growth of government by High Commission, the organization of the Church became more rather than less centripetal, a far cry from Martin Bucer's ideals. The Crown, waking up belatedly to its interests in the maintenance of episcopal government in its traditional forms, and in resisting the attack on episcopal wealth and dignity, actively promoted these developments.[1] The axiom 'no bishop, no king' exposed interdependence of another kind, so that the Puritans were uncertain whether to accuse the Laudians of promoting popery or tyranny. For as long as the exercise of the royal prerogative, in the ecclesiastical sphere as in others, was not effectively challenged, the notions and projects which have concerned us here were remote from practical politics. A decentralised Church which sought its mind in conferences and synods, albeit under episcopal presidency, was scarcely compatible with the claims and pretensions of Elizabethan and early Stuart government. Yet those pretensions were themselves intolerable to English seventeenth-century society. It is not the historian's place to condemn the ends pursued by Whitgift or Laud, but he may feel bound to declare them unattainable. In the creative resentment which found a voice in the Long Parliament, the vision of a moderate, reformed, and, in the language of the 1640s, 'reduced' episcopal government, consistent with current social and political values, again sprang to the fore. That it was a vision too moderate to hold its own in what had become a revolutionary situation is quite another story.

[1] Hill, op. cit., 3-13. These concluding remarks owe much to Mr Christopher Hill's fertile suggestions.

The best-known of the new devices for the moderation of episcopacy was Archbishop Ussher's *Reduction of episcopacy unto the form of synodical government*. One thinks besides of Bishop Williams's formula, of some of the parliamentary speeches of Sir Edward Dering, and of the Scottish devices associated with the names of Robert Leighton and the 'Aberdeen Doctors,' Forbes, Lindsay, and Ross. All these proposals had this much in common: they were conceived as means to reconcile two already sharply defined positions, episcopalian and presbyterian, and they suffered the common fate of most such mediating formulæ at a time of intense ecclesiastical and political strife. The virtue of the much more obscure projects discussed in this paper is that they partly antedated the entrenchment of the parties, and are to be considered on their merits as relatively disinterested attempts to restore to episcopal government what were thought to be its primitive qualities. They do not deserve to be totally forgotten.

John Whitgift, Archbishop of Canterbury (1583-1604)
(*National Portrait Gallery*)

7

THE AUTHORSHIP OF *A BRIEFF DISCOURS OFF THE TROUBLES BEGONNE AT FRANCKFORD*

The *Brieff discours off the troubles begonne at Franckford*,[1] an anonymous tract commonly ascribed to William Whittingham, dean of Durham, and printed in Heidelberg in 1574 and 1575, enjoys a unique reputation among the polemical writings of the Elizabethan puritans for its well-documented if partisan account of the controversies of the Marian exiles in their German and Swiss congregations. The importance of the *Brieff discours* as a source for the history of the Exile has hitherto tended to divert attention from the circumstances of its origin in the Elizabethan puritan controversy.[2] This note is intended to introduce new evidence on the activities of a group of puritan propagandists responsible for organising the publication of this and other tracts in the early years of the Elizabethan Presbyterian Movement; to call in question the traditional attribution of the *Brieff discours* to Whittingham; and to suggest that the author may have been a relatively obscure exile, Thomas Wood.

The historical account of the Frankfort troubles[3] which constitutes the bulk of the *Brieff discours* is constructed largely from original documents. These fall into two sections: letters, forms of church order and (apparently) minutes of meetings and conversations relating to the history of the Frankfort church from its foundation through its earlier troubles to the secession of many of its original members in the autumn of 1555; and, derived by the compiler from an independent and unnamed source, a narrative history of the renewed troubles of the residual Frankfort congregation in 1557: *The historie of that sturre and strife which was in in* [sic] *the Englishe church at Franckford from the 13 daie off Jan. Ar o Domini*

---

[1] *A brieff discours off the troubles begonne at Franckford in Germany anno domini 1554 abowte the booke off off* [sic] *common prayer and ceremonies and continued by the Englishe men theyre to the ende off Q. Maries raigne.* Printed by Schirat of Heidelberg in two editions, 1574 and 1575 (see below, 209). The tract has been reprinted three times: in *The Phoenix* (ii. 1708), 44–204; in quasi-facsimile (preserving the original pagination) by John Petheram in 1846 with a critical introduction largely contributed by Thomas McCrie; and by Edward Arber in 1908 as the first volume of 'A Christian Library'. The best modern text is Petheram's. Arber's suffers from his editorial idiosyncracies and is sometimes inaccurate. All references here are to the edition of 1575.

[2] Noted by A. F. Scott Pearson, *Thomas Cartwright and Elizabethan Puritanism, 1553–1603*, Cambridge 1925, 145.

[3] For modern accounts of the Exile, see M. M. Knappen, *Tudor Puritanism: a Chapter in the History of Idealism*, Chicago 1939, and Christina H. Garrett, *The Marian Exiles: a Study in the Origins of Elizabethan Puritanism*, Cambridge 1938.

1557 forwarde. This *Historie*, with its own appendix of documents, forms by far the longest section of the tract.[1] The first section tells the story of that celebrated quarrel between the factions of Knox and Cox over the liturgical forms to be employed in the exiled congregation which anticipated the puritan controversy in the Elizabethan Church. The second records a later controversy in which a minority of conservatives in the congregation resisted the adoption by the majority of a Reformed 'New Discipline' which would have more than satisfied the aspirations of the seceded Knoxians.[2] These records are connected by a narrative and are set within a preface and concluding section which relate the history of this 'old grudge'[3] to the troubles of the Elizabethan puritans at the time of publication. The design is to construct from original records of the Exile an historical justification of the puritan cause as it stood in the winter of 1573/4 when conformity and subscription to the Elizabethan Settlement were being required of all puritans under severe penalties. In conclusion, two further and more recent documents are published: a letter from the General Assembly of the Church of Scotland dated 28 December 1566[4] and a letter from Theodore Beza and his fellow Genevan ministers of 24 October 1567,[5] both addressed to the ministry of the Church of England, the former carrying a searching criticism of the deficiencies in Reformed discipline of the Elizabethan Church, and both defending the stand taken against the vestments by the original Elizabethan nonconformists.

The *Brieff discours* is, therefore, a compilation in which the editor has reduced his narrative to a minimum and has relied extensively on original documents, including, for more than half of the whole tract, a narrative of distinct authorship, *The historie of that sturre and strife*. Continuity of style and intention allows us to assume—what cannot always be assumed in deciding questions of the authorship of anonymous puritan tracts[6]— that the compiler of the whole publication and the writer of the topical preface and conclusion was also the author of the history of the Frankfort troubles up to the secession of 1555. It is, therefore, most plausible to suppose that the tract was compiled shortly before its publication, although the documents of which it largely consists date from the Exile itself. The compiler was probably an original member of the Frankfort congregation and a radical of the faction led by Whittingham and Knox who left for Geneva in October of that year. He owes *The Historie of that*

---

[1] *Brieff discours*, lxii–clxxxi.
[2] Besides giving the church an advanced congregational polity, the New Discipline directed that in the use of the 1552 Prayer Book 'certaine rites and ceremonies' were to be left out 'as we at this present doo'. (*Brieff discours*, cxvii.)
[3] *Brieff discours*, cxciiii.   [4] Ibid., ccxii–ccxv.   [5] Ibid., cxcix–ccxi.
[6] See below, 203, for examples of the pirating of MSS. by the Elizabethan puritans. Tracts printed by these means had often been written some years before their publication and were furbished with a topical introduction by an anonymous editor (see, for example, the anonymously printed *Dialogue concerning the strife of our Churche*, 1584). It is important for the arguments to be developed here to establish that the *Brief discours* was not a composite production in this sense.

sturre and strife of 1557, as he acknowledges, to 'the handes off such as are bothe lerned and off credit, but yet, I muste needes say, by those that were parties in this broyle'.[1] To account for the presence in the tract of *The Historie of that sturre and strife* may be to cast light on the circumstances in which the documentary materials edited in the *Brieff discours* were first assembled. Hitherto, students seem to have assumed that the anonymous author of this *Historie* was a willing and active participant in the project of the *Brieff discours*[2] and have attempted to identify him with a member of the Knox-Whittingham faction who remained in Frankfort after the exodus of most of his party: David Whitehead or Thomas Cole.[3] Yet the assumption that whoever transmitted the MS. of the *Historie* to the compiler of the *Brieff discours* must have sympathised with the puritan cause and approved of the publication of a tendentious history of the Exile is not justified: the methods employed by the Elizabethan puritans to obtain material for publication were often far from direct.[4] In fact, although the author of the *Historie* was an apologist for the radical faction of the 'New Discipline' in the Frankfort troubles of 1557, there is nothing in the *Brieff discours* to suggest that he consciously collaborated with any member of the Genevan party either during or after the Exile. Although the development of Frankfort in the later stages of the Exile was towards a simpler liturgy and a congregational polity,[5] the compiler of the *Brieff discours* makes it clear that he has printed the *Historie* less as an indication that Frankfort and Geneva had come close to agreement on questions that had earlier divided them than as proof that the secession of Knox and his followers had not brought peace but a sword to the Frankfort church. 'From whiche tyme forward the troubles and contentions were so sore amonge them, that who so shall well waie it with due consideration, I ween, he shall think it to be the juste judgement of our righteous God that fell upon them, for supplantinge a churche there before them in great quietnes and off muche sinceritie.'[6] The margins of this part of the *Brieff discours* are scattered with the editor's hostile and satirical annotations.[7] On internal evidence alone there can be no doubt that the

[1] *Brieff discours*, clxxxi.

[2] Miss Garrett, for example, is concerned to identify the exile 'who continued Whittingham's narrative after the latter's departure'. (op. cit., 122.)

[3] McCrie suggested Whitehead in his introduction to the 1846 edition; Miss Garrett (op. cit., 122) preferred Cole.

[4] See the evidence on this point gathered on p. 203 below.

[5] For most of our knowledge of these developments and for the Frankfort New Discipline itself we are entirely indebted to the *Historie of that sturre and strife*.

[6] *Brieff discours*, lxii.

[7] Where the New Discipline remarks that the pastor, Robert Horne, later bishop of Winchester, may 'wilfully and suddenly leave his flocke' (cxxxviii), the margin notes with glee: 'Yea; but though he did so then he will not doo so nowe I warrant yow.' There is a reference to 'the simple sutteltie of H[orne's] factious head' (xc). Where Horne hesitated to subscribe a certain article: 'Yff maister Horne tooke such deliberation before he would subscribe to that article: what meanethe this that poore ignorant men and wemen must thus subscribe upon the sudden or ells to newgate' (xcv). The detachment of the Editor is best shown by a marginal note on p. cxii: 'This article I find rased in the copie, what they ment by it, I know not.'

Historie was composed before the end of the Exile and probably very soon
after the events which it describes; and that it was written for the eyes of
exiles in other congregations and in defence of the Frankfort New Discipline and its protagonists.[1] The Frankfort exiles were in poor circumstances by the summer of 1557,[2] but such was the scandal which attached
to their troubled church, that no supply was forthcoming from wealthier
Englishmen in other places.[3] Attached to the *Historie* is a copy of a letter
dated 25 July 1557, which was apparently sent to all the churches by one
of their number Edmund Sutton. This appeals for relief and essays a
defence of the church and an explanation of its troubles.[4] Whether or not
Sutton's letter was accompanied by the *Historie*, it is likely that this longer
document (which, like Sutton's letter, ends with an appeal to the reader's
charity) was written and dispersed with the same motive and at the same
time. Presumably it was received in Geneva and filed among the records
of that congregation. Here it took its place beside papers belonging
properly to the Genevan congregation and the records of the original
Frankfort church,[5] which we must presume to have been carried to
Geneva by the secessionists of 1555. It was from this collection of documents that the *Brieff discours* seems to have been compiled. Some, at least,
of these materials were still in the possession of the author and compiler
in 1574.[6]

From this analysis of the contents of the *Brieff discours* it is possible to
make some definite assertions about the identity of the author. Although
his knowledge of the foundations and early history of the Frankfort
congregation could have been derived at second-hand, he was most
probably an early if not an original member of the Frankfort church;[7]
he sided consistently with the party of radical reform; involved himself
closely in the disputes about church order and worship; had access to if
not custody of the archives of the congregation; and left with most of

---

[1] The text of the *Historie* ends with this appeal: 'In the meane time nothinge dis-
trustinge the lordes mercie (how soever the deceites off men would let it) hopinge that
neither livinge nor foode shall ever want to oure poore congregation, [through him]
who also feedeth the ravens, and that he will allwaies be present by his spirit to us and
to oure whole churche continually whiche thinge that it maie please him to bringe to
passe, we beseche the good reader (who soever thow art) praie unto god, togither with
us, and fare well!' (*Brieff discours*, cv.)

[2] In April 1557 the ministers were in debt to their landladies for four months' rent.
(Ibid., ciiii.)

[3] Ibid., cv, clxxv.   [4] Ibid., clxxiii–clxxxi.

[5] On the evidence of a letter from Thomas Wood to William Whittingham (printed
below) it appears that a letter of John Calvin written to the Frankfort congregation in
holograph in January 1555 was in the possession of the Genevan congregation as late
as 1559.

[6] The documents described as 'yet to be seen' are an undated letter from Whittingham to a friend in England, recounting events in the Frankfort church; an undated
letter of Thomas Cole sending on news of fresh quarrels in Frankfort to a former member
of the congregation who had seceded to Geneva; and a letter of Richard Chambers
dated from Strasbourg, 20 June 1557, to a number of Frankfort exiles. (*Brieff discours*,
xlvii, lix, clxxxi–clxxxii.)

[7] In any case he speaks of 'keepinge of theis thinges almoste by the space off theis
twentie yeares in secret.' (Ibid., cxcviii.)

his faction for Geneva in the autumn of 1555. In Geneva he was close to the conduct of affairs in Knox's congregation and had access to its correspondence. On his return to England he remained a supporter of a further Reformation and in 1574 was a fervent puritan and one of an inner group of propagandists intent on frustrating the demand of the authorities for conformity and subscription.

Hitherto there has seemed to be an overwhelming case for identifying this figure with William Whittingham. Whittingham was the leader of the original party of exiles which arrived at Frankfort on 27 June 1554 and which founded the English congregation a few days later. Of this small company, he was the only member who achieved any prominence either before or after the exile and who has hitherto been more than a mere name to history. Even the basic biographical data on his companions—William Williams, Edmund Sutton, Thomas Wood—have been uncertain[1] and nothing has been known of their literary capabilities. Whittingham was the leader of the radical faction in the congregation in its struggle with the conservatives, and on most occasions its spokesman. In many of the negotiations recorded in the *Brieff discours* he was the central figure. It was he who led the secession to Geneva. As early as 1603, Whittingham's authorship was assumed by George Johnson, the separatist and author of *A Discourse of Some Troubles in the Banished English Church at Amsterdam*,[2] a tract modelled closely on the *Brieff discours*.[3] This attribution is carefully noted by an early seventeenth-century reader in the margin of a copy of the 1575 edition preserved in the British Museum.[4] The tract was also attributed to Miles Coverdale at about this time.[5] The modern tradition of Whittingham's authorship rests on the critical introduction contributed to Petheram's edition of 1846 by Thomas McCrie. McCrie argued Whittingham's authorship from internal evidence, and placed especial emphasis on the evidence of style. Some of his arguments carry weight,[6] but others apply equally well to other

---

[1] Garrett, op. cit., 335–6, 300–1, 343.

[2] *S.T.C.*, no. 14664. I am grateful to the Librarian of Sion College for granting facilities to inspect the only copy of this tract listed in the *Short Title Catalogue* (Sion College, press-mark Arc in Lib. A/69/.3/355).

[3] Johnson was not a contemporary of Whittingham, but was born about the time of Whittingham's death. Against his attribution of the *Brieff discours* to Whittingham it should be said that the author of an anonymous life of Whittingham, written (but not printed) in the same year as Johnson's tract, who was a personal acquaintance of Whittingham, does not ascribe the *Brieff discours* to him, although he refers to it as 'a large Discourse, in an ancient book'. (*A Brief Discourse of the Troubles at Frankfort*, ed. E. Arber, 1908, 3).

[4] *Brieff discours*, 1575 edn., B.M. Press-mark 697. g.20, xlix.

[5] A copy of the 1575 edition of the tract in the B.M. (press-mark 697.b.26) bears 'By M.C.' on the title-page and 'M. Coverdale' as a signature to the Preface, entered in a near-contemporary hand in imitation of the letter-press.

[6] For example, the argument that private interviews in which Whittingham took part are fully reported and Whittingham's speeches given *verbatim*. Yet McCrie is not justified in saying that 'none could have reported, or would have thought of reporting' these transactions except Whittingham himself, since he could have communicated notes to another exile at the time.

candidates for the authorship[1] and some do not bear close investigation.[2] Certainly they were not conclusive, as several writers have pointed out,[3] but they have been accepted, among others by A. F. Pollard,[4] W. D. Maxwell,[5] Miss Garrett,[6] and M. M. Knappen,[7] while in the *Short Title Catalogue* the tract has been ascribed to Whittingham without query.[8] Edward Arber, in editing the *Brieff discours* in 1908, assumed the traditional ascription without further discussion and prefaced the text with a reprint of an anonymous early seventeenth-century life of Whittingham.[9]

On the internal evidence of the *Brieff discours* and from what we know from other sources of the history of the Exile, the case for ascribing the tract to Whittingham is quite plausible. It is not so much the material in the tract as the circumstances of its publication in 1574 which make his authorship unlikely if not incredible. Scott Pearson, the biographer of Thomas Cartwright, was the first to point out that the *Brieff discours* cannot be considered in isolation but must be connected with the other puritan tracts which appeared from the same press at about the same time.[10] These were the *Ecclesiasticae disciplinae et Anglicanae ecclesiae . . . explicatio*, a presbyterian manifesto attributed to Walter Travers, Thomas Cartwright's translation of the *Explicatio* under the title of *A Full and plaine declaration of ecclesiastical discipline*[11] and Cartwright's own *Second Replie*[12] to John Whitgift in the Admonition controversy. It has recently been established[13] that all these tracts were printed at Heidelberg by Michael Schirat, presumably under the general supervision of Thomas Cartwright, who had escaped from England to the Palatinate in December 1573.[14] Schirat had evidently taken over from the secret presses in England on which the first and second *Admonitions* and their ancillary pamphlets and Cartwright's first *Reply* had been printed.[15] By the end of 1573 a more

---

[1] McCrie's most plausible arguments concerned Whittingham's whereabouts and the events of which we know him to have had personal experience. Yet all arguments based on Whittingham's movements, both during and after the exile, apply equally to Thomas Wood.

[2] It is not true, for example, that Whittingham is usually styled plain Whittingham while the other figures in the story are 'Maister Knox, Maister Goodman, etc.'

[3] Notably by Froude (*Edinburgh Review*, lxxxv. 424), R. W. Dixon (*History of the Church of England*, iv. 689n) and P. Hume Brown (*John Knox*, i. 67 n. 1).

[4] *D.N.B.*, art. Whittingham.

[5] *John Knox's Genevan Service Book, 1550*, Edinburgh 1931, 10n.

[6] Op. cit., 1 n. 1.   [7] Op. cit., 119n.

[8] Entry nos. 25442 and 25443.

[9] *The Life and Death of Master William Whittingham, Dean of Durham, who departed this life, Anno Domino 1579, June 10*. Previously edited by M. A. E. Green as *The Life of Mr William Whittingham, from a MS. in Anthony Wood's Collection* in Camden Miscellany, vi (1870).

[10] Op. cit., 135–48.   [11] *S.T.C.*, no. 24184.   [12] *S.T.C.*, no. 4714.

[13] A. F. Johnson, 'Books Printed at Heidelberg for Thomas Cartwright', *Library*, 5th ser., ii (1948), 284–6.   [14] Scott Pearson, op. cit., 130–5.

[15] For information on the secret presses which produced presbyterian propaganda between June 1572 and June 1573, see Scott Pearson, op. cit., 81–7, 109–14; *Puritan Manifestoes*, ed. W. H. Frere and C. E. Douglas, Church Historical Society, reprinted 1954, xvii–xxv; *The Seconde Parte of a Register: being a Calendar of Manuscripts under that title intended for publication by the Puritans about 1593, and now in Dr. Williams's Library, London*, ed. Albert Peel, Cambridge 1915, i. 108–14.

intensive repression of the puritans had made the printing of puritan tracts for the time impracticable in England. Thus the *Brieff discours* appeared from a press which at the time of its publication was the principal organ of expression for the radical, presbyterian wing of the Puritan Movement and, apparently, as part of a co-ordinated literary apology for the cause.

Cartwright's *Second Replie* continued the debate on the principles of church order provoked by Whitgift's *Answer* to the attack of the *Admonition* on the constitution of the Elizabethan Church. The *Explicatio* and its English translation gave the first definitive exposition of English Presbyterianism.[1] The function of the *Brieff discours* was less theoretical: it was to demonstrate that the dispute between the puritans and the bishops was not, as some spokesmen for the bishops had alleged, of recent and superficial origin and that the principles on which the puritans stood were not the invention of an insignificant and youthful *coterie*. Doctor Young,[2] in a Paul's Cross sermon, had insinuated that the strife in the Church sprang from the frustrated ambitions of 'certaine speciall persons' who had been disappointed in their hopes of a bishopric;[3] others had blamed the influence of foreign churches, both overseas and refugee in England.[4] Archdeacon Mullins (in the days of the Exile a member of the Frankfort congregation), indeed, traced the controversy to a 'hot Contention" at Frankfort in queen Mary's time, but implied that the puritans had been the trouble-makers.[5] To all these damaging insinuations, the *Brieff discours* was designed as a retort. 'By this discours . . . yt maie be seene, bothe when, where, how and by whom, this controversie firste began, who continued it, who was on the suffring side and who readieste to forget and forgive, that godly peace and concord might be had.'[6] In this appeal to history, the *Brieff discours* employs a controversial technique taken straight from the pages of Foxe's *Actes and Monumentes*,[7] a mode of

---

[1] *An Admonition to the Parliament* and *A Second Admonition to the Parliament* are reprinted in *Puritan Manifestoes*, cited above (first published in 1907). Whitgift's *Answer*, Cartwright's *Reply*, Whitgift's *Defence of the Answer* and Cartwright's *Second Replie* and *The Rest of the Second Replie* are reprinted in a conflated text in *The Works of John Whitgift*, ed. John Ayre, Parker Socy, 3 vols., Cambridge 1851–3. An abbreviated conflated text of the whole controversy is printed in D. J. McGinn, *The Admonition Controversy*, Rutgers Studies in English v., New Brunswick 1949. The *Explicatio* and the *Full and plaine declaration* have not been reprinted.

[2] Later bishop of Rochester.   [3] *Brieff discours*, ii.

[4] Ibid.   [5] Ibid., iii.   [6] Ibid., cxcvii.

[7] For John Foxe and the appeal to history, see William Haller, 'John Foxe and the Puritan Revolution', *The Seventeenth Century: studies in the History of Thought and Literature from Bacon to Pope*, ed. R. F. Jones, Stanford, California 1951, 209–24. The *Brieff discours* acknowledged its indebtedness to Foxe and to earlier writers in the same tradition; the Preface claims that the tract follows 'the steppes off such, whome god off his goodnes hath raised up at all tymes and amonge all nations, to commit thinges to memorye, whiche hath passed in commonweales, who have with great freedom and libertie byn suffred to make manifest to the whole worlde the ill dealinges even off Popes, Cardinalls, Emperours, Kinges and Princes, where as (in this discours) the highest that I touche (and that with great grieff of hart) are (to my knowledge) but certeine Bishopps, and therefore I hope the more to be borne withall.' Specific reference is made in the margin to 'Platina, Paulus Jovius, Sledein, Fox with many other'. (*Brieff discours*, iii.)

apologetic which the Elizabethan puritans were to make very much their own. The author of the *Brieff discours* assured the reader that his story would be 'from time to time continued, till it be brought even to this present tyme',[1] a promise which the puritans fulfilled in their organised 'registering' of documents illustrating the righteousness of their cause and in their collection for publication in *A Parte of a Register* and the projected 'Seconde Parte of a Register'.[2]

The need to establish a respectable pedigree for Puritanism was especially acute in the winter of 1573–4. In the previous summer the cause of radical Puritanism had seemed to be running high. Since the publication of the *Admonition to the Parliament* by two young London preachers, John Field and Thomas Wilcox, a year before, Presbyterianism had gained in popularity, especially in London, while the bishops had suffered a series of moral defeats in their attempts—often desultory—to restore conformity.[3] A royal proclamation prohibiting possession and dissemination of the inflammatory presbyterian tracts,[4] wrung from a reluctant Privy Council by archbishop Parker in July,[5] had served only to demonstrate the popularity of the *Admonition* and its authors.[6] All this was changed in October 1573 when, in a further proclamation, the queen trounced her bishops and magistrates alike for their failure to deal effectively with the puritan threat to the Church and demanded the strictest enforcement of the Act of Uniformity with imprisonment for those who spoke against the Prayer Book.[7] By order of the Privy Council, special commissions were set up in every diocese and exempt jurisdiction to conduct a general enquiry into the extent of puritan disobedience and to demand subscription from the clergy to articles defining the law of the Church on the questions in controversy.[8] Moreover, the Assize Judges, by an order delivered by Burghley in the Star Chamber, were made instruments of the 'Iniquisition', a commission which those on the South-Eastern Circuit, at least, carried out with thoroughness.[9] In London, where ecclesiastical discipline was comparatively effective, and where the puritans were well-known to the courts, the 'Iniquisition' was conducted with conspicuous success. Subscription was pressed on both ministers and

---

[1] *Brieff discours*, cxciiii.   [2] See below, 203-4.

[3] See Scott Pearson, op. cit., 58–109; *Puritan Manifestoes*, xvii–xxv; my own unpublished Ph.D. thesis, 'The Puritan Classical Movement in the Reign of Elizabeth I', London 1957, 138–45.

[4] *Tudor and Stuart Proclamations, 1485–1714*, ed. Robert Steele, Oxford 1910, i. no. 687, 74.

[5] See a memorandum by Parker, Inner Temple Library, MS. Petyt 538/47 f. 479 r and v; printed in part, J. Strype, *The Life and Acts of Matthew Parker*, ed. Oxford 1821, ii. 239–41.

[6] See Bishop Sandys to Burghley, 2 July 1573, printed *Puritan Manifestoes*, 154–5.

[7] *Tudor and Stuart Proclamations*, i. no. 689, 74.

[8] *Acts of the Privy Council*, N.S., ed. J. R. Dasent, viii. 1894, 140, 171; *A Seconde Parte of a Register*, op. cit., i. 93–7.

[9] See the printed charge delivered at Chelmsford, 15 December 1573, Inner Temple Library, MS. Petyt 538/47 f. 510; and the record of the indictment at the Middlesex Assize of Robert Johnson, preacher of St. Clement's without Temple Bar (*Seconde Parte of a Register*, op. cit., i. 124).

laymen known to be puritans, some were imprisoned and others wavered in their puritan profession.[1] These were the events which formed the immediate background to the *Brieff discours* and to which the preface and conclusion of the tract make specific reference.[2]

A source of weakness in this crisis, of which the presbyterians themselves were painfully aware, was that their movement had failed to win the approval of older and more moderate puritans, the radicals of the Exile and of the Convocation of 1562 and the Vestments Controversy of 1564–5.[3] Few of these revered veterans had lent any support to the new and more drastic programme of reforms proposed in the *Admonition* and some, among them Laurence Humphrey,[4] John Foxe[5] and Thomas Norton 'the Parliament man',[6] had not hesitated to condemn it. Many other famous reformers, among them Thomas Sampson,[7] Robert Crowley[8] and William Fulke,[9] were either dropping out of active participation in the movement or were declining to endorse presbyterian extremism. It has hitherto escaped notice that by 1574 Whittingham, the supposed author of the *Brieff discours*, was among these 'lost leaders'. In 1563 he had been presented to the deanery of Durham—a rich preferment— through the combined influence of the Earl of Warwick and his brother Lord Robert Dudley (later Earl of Leicester),[10] procured by an old friend in exile and Warwick's retainer, Thomas Wood.[11] He had introduced a Reformed order into Durham cathedral, apparently supplanting its liturgical worship with preaching and exercises of prayer and fasting.[12] On the promulgation of the Advertisements, he had taken a firm stand against conformity and had written to the Earl of Leicester, his patron, a letter of protest[13] which had circulated widely among the puri-

---

[1] *Seconde Parte of a Register*, op. cit., i. 92–7. See the private letters of puritans reporting on these events: the letter of Thomas Wood to William Whittingham, printed below; two letters of the puritan preacher Thomas Wilcox to Anthony Gilby, preacher of Ashby-de-la-Zouche in Leicestershire, 21 December 1573 and 2 February 1573[/4], Cambridge Univ. Lib. MS. Mm.I.43 (Baker 32), 441–2, 439; Edward Dering, the famous preacher to his brother, Richard Dering, 24 December 1573, Dering, *Certaine godly and comfortable letters*, in *Works* (ed. 1597), Sig. A 4.

[2] For a fuller account of these events, see my thesis (cited above), 160–72.

[3] I have discussed this question at some length in my thesis, 111–22.

[4] See his letters to Anthony Gilby, 17 January 1572[/3], Cambridge Univ. Lib., MS. Mm. I. 43, 431–2; and to Burghley, 6 February 1576[/7], B.M. Lansd. MS. 24 no. 25 f. 52.

[5] J. F. Mozley, *John Foxe and His Book*, 1940, 111–2; Thomas Nashe, *Works*, ed. R. B. McKerrow, i (1904), 85.

[6] Norton to John Whitgift, 20 October 1572, Inner Temple Library MS. Petyt 538/38 f. 65 r and v.

[7] *Zurich Letters*, ed. Hastings Robinson, Parker Socy., Cambridge 1842, 292; Sampson to Gilby, 8 March 1584[/5], Cambridge Univ. Lib. MS. Mm. I. 43, 433.

[8] Albert Peel, *Robert Crowley*, Manchester 1937, 22. John Field to Gilby, 28 February 1580[/1], Cambridge Univ. Lib. MS. Mm. I. 43, 446.

[9] [William Fulke], *The Examination of M. Doctor Whytgiftes Censures*, 1573, Sig. Ai.

[10] *The Life of Mr William Whittingham*, ed. M. A. E. Green, *Camden Miscellany*, vi (1870), 13–14.

[11] See below, 219.　　[12] *The Life of Mr William Whittingham*, op. cit., 23 n. 1.

[13] Whittingham to Leicester, 28 October 1564, printed Strype, *Parker*, iii. App. xxvii, 76–84.

tans.[1] Yet in March 1567 he had conformed in the wearing of the vestments,[2] an act which seems to have severed his connexion with those of his old friends who persisted in their nonconformity and who, after 1572, became associated with the presbyterian attack on the established order of the Elizabethan Church.[3] A letter written to Whittingham by Thomas Wood in February 1574 (printed here for the first time)[4] contains evidence of the bitter resentment with which his defection was still regarded in these extreme circles in the very year of the publication of the *Brieff discours*. Wood wrote, evidently not for the first time—an earlier letter written with some 'plainnes' remained unanswered—begging Whittingham to come to the assistance of his old friends in their trial. Wood reminds Whittingham that it was he who first convinced him 'and many others' of the errors of the Prayer Book. His letter to Leicester of 1565 was still 'in many men's hands' and was a source of comfort to many. But his conduct since had caused 'no small offence to the Church of God'. The hope of a remnant of his old acquaintance who still stood firmly in the cause was that God would use the growing persecution of his brethren, not only to 'give yow hartie repentance for your backsliding' but to 'restore yow to your former zeale and boldnes to acknowledg all that truthe which heretofore yow have taught to others, which I pray God I may live to see, and that speedely'. Wood remarks bitterly that the only harm he ever did Whittingham was in procuring the letter from his patron which had brought him to Durham.[5]

The particular request which Wood makes of Whittingham is highly significant: it is to make and send a transcript of a celebrated letter of John Calvin of 25 January 1555, then in Whittingham's possession, in which the Reformer, who had been sent an account of the 1552 Prayer Book by the radical party at Frankfort, described the contents as 'Popish dregs'. It was hoped to circulate this letter to confirm the wavering and 'to stoppe the mouthes of the adversaries'. Whittingham seems to have relented sufficiently to send Wood a translated transcript of the letter, for it was printed by the puritans within the year; not, indeed, as a separate document, but as an important part of the *Brieff discours*.[6] Here it is duly acknowledged as having been 'faithfully translated owte off Latten by Maister Whittingham'. Significantly enough, this is the only section of the *Brieff discours* to which Whittingham's name is specifically attached. Yet it is unlikely that Whittingham sought to associate himself any closer

---

[1] See the evidence of the letter from Thomas Wood to Whittingham, printed below.
[2] *Life of Mr William Whittingham*, op. cit., 22, n. 3.
[3] See Wood's letter referred to in the next note and printed below.
[4] Thomas Wood to William Whittingham, 15 February 1573[/4], MS. Gorhambury VIII/B/143, ff. 15v–17r. My thanks are due to the Earl of Verulam for permission to print this letter and to the staff of the Hertfordshire Record Office, Hertford (where the MS. is deposited) for enabling me to transcribe it.
[5] See below, 209.
[6] *Brieff discours*, xxxiiii–xxxvi. The Latin original of Calvin's letter, preserved in Geneva, is printed in *The Works of John Knox*, ed. David Laing, iv. Edinburgh 1855, 51–3.

with the puritan party in 1574 and it is now hardly possible to believe that the *Brieff discours*, which seems to have been assembled in its entirety at about this time, was of his authorship. In the circumstances he could hardly have written this sharp condemnation of the time-serving conformist which the *Brieff discours* carries in its concluding pages:

'I wil not saie that (in the meane time) such as are turn-coates and can chaunge with al seasons, subscribinge to what so ever, and can cap it can cope it an curry for advantage, that such, I saie, how ignorant, how vicious, and ungodly so ever they be, live at their ease in all pleasure and in some place are thought to be moste meete men for the ministerie. But this I maie be bolde to affirme, that (although in very dede I neither do nor dare condemne certeine godly persons, who off infirmitie, but yet with most sorowfull and heavy hartes (as hathe well appeared by their most lamentable protestations with plentie off teares to their congregations) have yelded to more then expedient it were they shulde (prayinge the lorde to let them se it in time) yet, it maie not onely be saide, but proved too I truste, that neither is subscribinge alwaies a sure note off good subject nor yet the refusall dew proffes off a rebell.'[1]

If Whittingham was not behind the *Brieff discours*, who was? The answer seems to be that the idea of a polemical history of the Exile originated with a group rather than with any single individual and that it was this group which procured the writing, printing and dispersal of the tract. That the *Brieff discours* and other important puritan manifestoes were printed at Heidelberg in itself argues the existence of an organisation in England which maintained links with Thomas Cartwright, perhaps despatched the MSS. to him and certainly received and dispersed the printed tracts.[2] A correspondence survives between such a group and Cartwright from 1576 and 1577, in which the puritans in England debate with their leader (by this time in Basel) an important case of conscience which concerned the response of the puritan minister to the demands of authority.[3] Moreover, the letter of Thomas Wood to Whittingham, printed below, contains clear evidence of the corporate conscience and activity of 'the brethren' and of their plan to strengthen the cause by distributing copies of Calvin's letter of January 1555. Since the *Brieff discours* incorporates this letter, we seem to have here the original idea from which the tract as it was eventually projected sprang. There can be little doubt that those responsible for the *Brieff discours* were a group of London puritans, for the few topical allusions in the preface and conclusion refer only to London events: to Paul's Cross sermons and to the

---

[1] *Brieff discours*, cxcv.

[2] John Strowd, the printer-preacher who had printed Cartwright's *Reply* in June 1573, had a copy of the *Explicatio* as early as November 1574 and in that month passed it on to an acquaintance. (*Seconde Parte of a Register*, op. cit., i. 109.)

[3] *A Parte of a Register*, Middelburg or Edinburgh? 1593, 401–8; *Seconde Parte of a Register*, op. cit., i. 136–43.

imprisonment of staunch puritans refusing subscription.[1] From June 1572, when the *Admonition to the Parliament* had appeared, the vocal leadership of the movement for further reformation had been captured by a group of extremists in London who were later to be the nucleus of an organised English Presbyterian Movement.[2] We know from the deposition of a London incumbent, Thomas Edmunds, given in the Star Chamber in 1591,[3] that there was in London at this time, and had been from about 1571, an association of radical puritan ministers organised as a presbyterian *classis* and holding frequent meetings. Edmunds himself was a member and, in the autumn of 1573, was imprisoned for refusing subscription,[4] although in later years he abandoned his Puritanism and turned queen's evidence against the association to which he had belonged. The leaders of this group were two young preachers, John Field and Thomas Wilcox, the authors of the *Admonition*. Its remaining members were unbeneficed and somewhat obscure preachers. This association maintained an unbroken existence throughout the 'seventies and 'eighties, and it subsequently received into membership such important presbyterian leaders as Walter Travers, William Chark and Stephen Egerton.[5] These ministers, with their collaborators and supporters among the laity,[6] constituted a small but active association of radical puritans which formed a focal point for the developing presbyterian organisation in the counties, especially between 1583 and 1590.[7] It was this group, with some representation from the country, which in 1576 and 1577 was in correspondence with Thomas Cartwright at Basel. Undoubtedly it was the same group which in its early days had organised the publication of the *Admonition* and its ancillary pamphlets, and it is almost certain that the *Brieff discours* originated in the same circle.

The leader of this London association and the principal corresponding secretary and organiser of the English Presbyterian Movement was John Field, to whom we owe the more pungent and spiteful pages of the *Admonition*.[8] Field was one of the most brilliant organisers and publicists of his age.[9] His authorship, with Thomas Wilcox, of the *Admonition* needs no mention, but his other activities in the publication of puritan propaganda, both before and after June 1572, deserve to be better known.

---

[1] *Brieff discours*, ii–iii, and cxciiii–cxcv.

[2] See Chapter ii of my thesis (cited above), passim.

[3] P.R.O., Star Chamber 5 A 49/34. For a detailed analysis of the case in which this deposition was made, see my thesis Chapter xi. ii.

[4] See references to his imprisonment in letters of Thomas Wilcox to Anthony Gilby, 21 December 1573 and 2 February 1573[/4], Cambridge Univ. Lib. MS. Mm. I. 43, 442, 439.   [5] Edmunds's deposition.

[6] For a discussion of the identity of these active lay puritans, see my thesis (cited above), 105–12.   [7] See my thesis, Chapters iv, v, vi, xi, passim.

[8] Field acknowledged to archbishop Parker's chaplain that the 'bitterness of the stile' was his and expressed his conviction that it was 'no tyme to blench, nor to sewe cushens under mens elbowes, or to flatter them in their synnes'. (*Seconde Parte of a Register*, op. cit., i. 89.)

[9] For his leading part in the organisation of the Puritan Classical Movement, see my thesis, especially Chapters iv–vi.

Field was not always the author of these tracts himself: much of his material was acquired through the organisation which he controlled and was printed for the sake of 'the common cause', as often as not without the knowledge of those who had supplied the MSS. In November 1571 he informed Anthony Gilby, the Earl of Huntingdon's preacher at Ashby-de-la-Zouche, that a pamphlet of his had come into his possession 'and had there not bin wyser men then I, it had bin or this tyme published, together with that of Mr Samsones. Howbeit upon the advise of the Brethren it is stayed'.[1] Two months later he told Gilby that a short epistle of his authorship—probably that which later prefaced Gilby's *Pleasaunt dialogue betweene a souldior of Barwicke and an English chaplaine*[2]— had been translated. 'I hope you will not be angrie with Mr Wodde for sendinge it unto me, sith it is yet at your Commaundment.'[3] Of William Fulke's presbyterian handbook, the *True and Short Declaration*, probably written in 1572 but not printed until 1584, Matthew Sutcliffe reported: 'When John Field contrary to his mind did publish the pamphlet called *the learned discourse*, hee was offended with him and if he had lived would have confuted the same himselfe.'[4] In 1580 Field secured for translation and publication Theodore Beza's *De Triplicatu Episcopatu*, a forthright denunciation of diocesan episcopacy which in origin was a private letter sent to some of the Reformed Scottish nobility.[5] Three years later, in collaboration with the puritan printer, Robert Waldegrave, he brought out a posthumous work of John Knox, *A notable and Comfortable exposition ... upon the Fourth of Matthew*. The MS. of this tract had been obtained from a Mrs. Anne Prouze, wife of William Prouze, three times Mayor of Exeter, who was none other than Anne Vaughan, sometime wife of Henry Lock and the confidante of Knox, and subsequently the wife and widow of the famous puritan divine, Edward Dering.[6] Field printed the Knox MS. without the knowledge or permission of its owner, and in a preface apologised to Mrs. Prouze, pleaded the necessity of allowing the whole Church to share such a possession and appealed to her to release any other Knox MSS. which might still be in her possession.[7] Field was the originator of the plan for using the developed organisation of puritan conferences with which he corresponded in the 'eighties to 'register' and send to London records of the troubles of the puritans[8]: these were the

---

[1] Field to Gilby, 22 November 1571, Cambridge Univ. Lib. MS. Mm. I. 43, 447.

[2] Edn. 1581, *S.T.C.*, no. 11888.

[3] Field to Gilby, 10 January 1571[/2], Cambridge Univ. Lib. MS. Mm. I. 43, 447.

[4] Quoted, Scott Pearson, op. cit., 273.

[5] Printed as *The iudgement of a most reverend and learned man from beyond the seas concerning a threefold order of bishops*; *S.T.C.*, no. 2021.

[6] Edward Dering to Anne Lock, n.d., Kent County Record Office, Maidstone, MS. Dering CI/2 ff. 28v–29r; Hazel Mathews, 'Personnel of the Parliament of 1584–5', unpublished London M.A. thesis 1948, biog. Prouze. For evidence of Anne Prouze's own literary activities, see Doris Mary Stenton, *The English Woman in History*, 1957, 136.

[7] Field's Epistle Dedicatorie to 'The Vertuous and my very godly friend, Mrs Anne Prouze of Exeter', *A Notable and Comfortable exposition of M. Iohn Knoxe upon the Fourth of Mathew*, Knox, *Works*, ed. David Laing, Edinburgh 1855, iv. 91–4.

[8] See a directive, probably emanating from a General Assembly held in London at

collections which survive as the printed *Parte of a Register*[1] and the MS.
'Seconde Parte of a Register'[2] and which supplied some of the materials
for the Marprelate Tracts.[3] These records—indispensable for the study of
Elizabethan dissent—we owe to the organising genius of John .Field.
Do we also owe to his initiative our principal source for the history of the
Exile? The intention behind the *Brieff discours* and the 'Register' is the
same, and, moreover, the *Brieff discours* was introduced as the first instal-
ment of a continuous history of the godly cause.[4]

Field may have organised the printing and distribution and even the
writing of the *Brieff discours*, but he belonged to the generation after the
Exile and cannot himself have written the tract, unless we are to conclude
that the whole account is secondary, which seems unlikely.[5] Pending
more conclusive evidence than has yet come to light, the problem of
authorship must remain unsolved, but on the evidence available there is
only one candidate who fulfils all the requirements as we have defined
them in this discussion: Thomas Wood, a founder-member of the Frankfort congregation, later an elder of Knox's church at Geneva and
Whittingham's correspondent of 1574. Wood was a Leicestershire man,[6]
sometime a student, though not perhaps a graduate of Cambridge,[7] and
on the eve of the Exile a resident and perhaps a merchant of London.[8]
He may or may not have been the Thomas Wood described as a mercer
and servant of Henry Lock in Privy Council proceedings of November

the time of the 1586/7 Parliament, instructing the country conferences that the oppression of the bishops and their courts and officers both towards clergy and people 'but
especially towardes the mynisters' are to be 'registered and gathered'. (*The Presbyterian
Movement in the Reign of Queen Elizabeth as illustrated by the Minute Book of the Dedham
Classis, 1582–1589*, ed. R. G. Usher, Camden Socy., 3rd, ser., viii., 1905, 93.) See also a
note accompanying the account of his troubles by Ezechias Morley, an East Anglian
preacher: 'If yt will then any thinge help the common cause I pray yow then use your
discretion.' (Dr. Williams' Library, MS. Morrice B.II. f. 91v.) For evidence that these
documents were received by Field in London, see his attestation of a copy of the record
of a Sussex minister's suspension: '*Concordat cum originali ut ipsemet* [the minister] *testor.*
Joh. Fielde.' (*Seconde Parte of a Register*, op. cit., i. 221.) In a MS. catalogue of these
collections, dating perhaps from 1588, the items concerning Field and Thomas Wilcox
are referred to in the first person—'our offer to the Lords of the Councell'—'our wives'
supplication'. (B.M. Harl. MS. 360 ff. 87, 86, 85.)

    [1] *A parte of a register, contayninge sundrie memorable matters, written by divers godly and
learned in our time, which stande for and desire the reformation of our Church, in discipline and
ceremonies, according to the pure worde of God, and the Lawe of our Lande*, Middelburg or
Edinburgh ? 1593.
    [2] 'The Seconde Parte of a Register' and 'Old Loose Papers', Dr. Williams' Library
MS. Morrice A and MS. Morrice B; calendared in 1915 by Dr. Albert Peel as *The
Seconde Parte of a Register* and referred to above.
    [3] *Seconde Parte of a Register*, op. cit., i. 16–17.   [4] *Brieff discours*, cxciiii.
    [5] Some of the marginal comments, however (see above, 206 n. 7) are very reminiscent
of his style and could conceivably have been added by him to the MS.
    [6] He referred to Robert Beaumont, Master of Trinity, who certainly came from
Leicestershire, as 'my country man'. (Wood to Anthony Gilby, 4 October 1565, B.M.
Lansd. MS. 841 f. 52.)
    [7] In the letter to Gilby referred to above, he speaks of Beaumont's behaviour in
Cambridge—'a maner not used in our tyme you knowe'. There is no record of Wood in
Venn's *Alumni Cantabrigienses*.
    [8] Garrett, op. cit., 343.

1553.[1] He was a pioneer of the Exile and arrived at Frankfort in June 1554, one of the small company led by Whittingham.[2] Although the circumstances in which this group came together are unknown, it is clear that Whittingham and Wood were already close friends. Wood himself testified in 1574 that it was Whittingham who had first made him a puritan.[3] Thereafter they seem to have remained inseparable companions throughout the Exile. Wood was a consistent supporter of Whittingham in the Frankfort troubles and seceded with him to Geneva, where he became an elder of the congregation in 1557. Like Whittingham, he remained in Geneva long after Elizabeth's accession and was still there in September 1559.[4] Any arguments for Whittingham's authorship of the *Brieff discours* which rely on his movements during the Exile must, therefore, apply with equal force to Wood. The numerous transactions in which Whittingham played a central, and sometimes a solitary rôle,[5] and of which the author of the *Brieff discours* seems to have inner knowledge, would naturally have been communicated by Whittingham to Wood, if only in the course of ordinary conversation. Yet Wood may have recorded them in an official capacity, for there is evidence that he was both clerk and archivist of the Geneva congregation and he had perhaps undertaken the same duties at Frankfort. In September 1559 Knox wrote to his friend Mrs. Lock, then one of the surviving members of the Geneva church, informing her that he had written to Wood of a certain matter at large, 'asking him to communicate the same with you and with other brethrein at Geneva'.[6] In his letter to Whittingham of February 1574, Wood speaks of his possession of Calvin's 1555 letter 'and the rest' before his departure from Geneva. There is more than a suggestion here that the Frankfort and Geneva documents may still have been in his possession in 1574, for he points out to Whittingham that if Calvin's letter be published, those in a position to know, such as his son-in-law and sometime co-elder at Geneva, William Williams,[7] will assume that it came from his own papers. There is, therefore, a strong case for believing that these papers were the same as those printed in the *Brieff discours*, some of which the reader was informed might still be consulted in the originals in 1574.

On Wood's return from exile, he became a retainer of Ambrose Dudley, Earl of Warwick,[8] and by January 1563 was serving as secretary

---

[1] Ibid. Miss Garrett thought this a fair presumption, but Thomas Wood is a not uncommon combination of names and our Thomas Wood had a cousin of these names. (Wood to Mr. Beaumont, 12 December 1573, MS. Gorhambury VIII/B/143, f. 18r.)

[2] *Brieff discours*, v.   [3] In the letter printed below.

[4] Garrett, op. cit., 343.

[5] For example, his negotiations with the Frankfort magistrates.

[6] Knox to Mrs. Lock, 2 September 1559, *The Works of John Knox*, op. cit., vi. 78.

[7] Williams is described as Wood's son-in-law in his will of 1577. (Principal Probate Registry, Somerset House, P.C.C. wills, 16 Daughtry.)

[8] There are frequent references in Wood's correspondence to his 'good Lord' the Earl of Warwick. He named his son Ambrose after his master, and in his will of 1577 bequeathed to him a memento which Warwick had given to him.

to his master in the army at Le Havre,[1] where Whittingham was preacher. Possibly it was Wood who obtained this appointment for his friend: certainly he later claimed that he had procured Warwick's letter from Le Havre to the Court which secured Whittingham the deanery of Durham from a reluctant queen.[2] After the return of the French expedition, Wood seems to have lived at first in London.[3] By 1571 he had returned to his native Leicestershire and had purchased the lease of a manor-house and demesne at Groby,[4] in the country of the puritan Hastings family and not far from his old Geneva pastor, Anthony Gilby, preacher at Ashby-de-la-Zouch. He was now a man of moderate substance, for not long after the purchase of Groby he bought other lands from Richard Martin, the puritan goldsmith, and he lent £800 to the Earl of Huntingdon at about the same time.[5] He died in 1577, appointing Francis Hastings and Anthony Gilby as his overseers.[6]

Wood remained throughout his life a passionately outspoken puritan. An important collection of his correspondence has recently come to light[7] —piously copied by his son Ambrose Wood, a member of Francis Bacon's

[1] Letters from Wood to Cecil, Lord Robert Dudley and the Privy Council, and documents bearing his signature or referring to him are calendared in *Calendar of State Papers, Foreign 1562*, nos. 1012, 1060, 1127, 1214; *Calendar of State Papers, Foreign, 1563*, nos. 53, 307–9, 550, 552(3), 584(1), 605, 710(2), 835, 948, 968; a letter sent from Portsmouth to Lord Robert Dudley, reporting on Warwick's health on his return, occurs in the domestic series, *Cal. State Papers Dom. 1547–1580*, 229.

[2] See the reference in the letter printed below to 'procuring the letter whereof this inclosed maketh mention'. Attached to the letter is a copy of Lord Robert Dudley's letter to his brother (already known to us from the *Life of Mr. William Whittingham*, op. cit., 13–14) in which he reports the signing of Whittingham's patent for Durham and acknowledges Warwick's letter written in support of Whittingham which alone persuaded the queen to agree to his appointment. Whittingham was a comparative late-comer to Le Havre. The original preachers in the English army had been Broadbridge and Viron and on their departure Warwick had expressed a preference for Christopher Goodman or Percival Wiburn. (*Life of Mr. William Whittingham*, 12.)

[3] His correspondence includes letters written from London on 4 October 1565 and 29 March 1566. (B.M. Lansd. MS. 841 f. 52; MS. Gorhambury VIII/B/143 ff. 13r–14v.)

[4] The details of this purchase are in Wood's will, P.C.C. 16 Daughtry. The manor of Groby was leased from Lord Grey and the lease was purchased from a Mr. Henry Sekeford. Wood had evidently settled in Leicestershire as early as January 1572, when John Field refers to his presence there. (Field to Gilby, 10 January 1571[/2], Cambridge Univ. Lib. MS. Mm. I. 43, 447.) It is worth noting that by settling at Groby, Wood escaped virtually all ordinary ecclesiastical discipline. Groby was a peculiar of the Court of Arches, visited only by a commissary appointed by the Lord of the Manor. (John Nichols, *The History and Antiquities of the County of Leicester*, i (1815), 624, iv (1811), 632.) In 1575 the Commissary was William Stoughton, a puritan civilian who as M.P. for Grampound introduced the puritan petitions from Leicestershire into the 1584 Parliament and later wrote *An assertion for true christian church-policie* (*S.T.C.*, no. 23318, Middelburg 1604) to prove that a presbyterian Church polity was not inconsistent with English law or custom. (Nichols, op. cit., iv. 632; Simonds D'Ewes, *The Journal of all the Parliaments during the Reign of Queen Elizabeth*, 1682, 349.)

[5] Wood's will of 1577, P.C.C. 16 Daughtry.   [6] Ibid.

[7] MS. Gorhambury VIII/B/143, at present deposited in the Hertfordshire Record Office at Hertford, is a note-book in which Wood's son Ambrose has copied letters illustrative of the puritan cause from the Elizabethan and early Jacobean periods. These include a collection of his father's letters 'to certaine noble personages and other his good freinds out of the copies under his owne hand: which, being in loose papers, I have here exemplified . . .'

household, and so preserved at Gorhambury—which shows him to have
been a prolific letter-writer in the godly cause. Besides private letters of
godly rebuke to erring Leicestershire neighbours, this collection includes
a number of letters of a more public nature. From these and from references in Gilby's correspondence it is clear that Wood was a most active
member of the small and militant group led by John Field which controlled the organised Puritan Movement from the centre. In the Vestments Controversy of 1564–5, he appealed to the Earl of Huntingdon,[1]
petitioned the Earl of Leicester for Thomas Sampson and Christopher
Goodman[2] and wrote to Cecil on 29 March 1566, the day after thirty-five
London ministers had been suspended for their refusal to conform,
charging the Secretary with responsibility for this severe application of
the *Advertisements*.[3] In 1565 he had spread damaging reports in puritan
circles about the behaviour of Robert Beaumont, Vice-Chancellor of
Cambridge, who, although an old Geneva man, had assisted in the
application of the *Advertisements* in the University.[4] In 1573–4 he wrote
two letters to Whittingham in an effort to restore him to active membership of the puritan movement.[5] In 1576 and 1577 he wrote a series of
letters to the Earls of Warwick and Leicester which charge Leicester
with conspiring the suppression of the puritan exercises of prophesying
and with certain unspecified moral lapses and call on both brothers to
lend all their weight to the cause of reformation.[6] In all these letters,
Wood seems to be speaking for others besides himself and makes constant
references to what is 'commonly reported among the godly'. It is clear
from Warwick's and Leicester's replies (which are preserved in the same
collection)[7] that they regarded Wood as something more than a troublesome retainer and were well aware that he was capable of damaging or
salvaging their credits in circles to which they attached importance.[8] It
is arguable that, as Wood had had charge of the correspondence at
Geneva and as he had been a secretary at Le Havre, so he was now an
accredited corresponding secretary of the organised Puritan Movement.

[1] Or so one would deduce from a reference in a letter to Gilby to 'the delivery of
my letter to our good Erle'. (B.M. Lansd. MS. 841 f. 52.)

[2] Reference in a letter from Wood to Leicester [20 August 1576], MS. Gorhambury
VIII/B/143 f. 7r.

[3] Wood to Cecil, 29 March 1566, Cecil to Wood, 31 March 1566; MS. Gorhambury
VIII/B/143 ff. 13r–15r.

[4] Wood to Gilby, 4 October 1565, B.M. Lansd. MS. 841 f. 52, (another copy)
Cambridge Univ. Lib. MS. Mm. I. 43, 430; Beaumont to Gilby, 25 January 1565[/6],
ibid., 427–30.

[5] See the letter printed below.

[6] Wood to Warwick, 4 August 1576, MS. Gorhambury VIII/B/143 f. 1; to Leicester,
4 August 1576, ibid., ff. 1v–2v.; to Warwick, 20 August 1576, ibid., f. 6 r and v; to
Leicester, [20 August 1576], ibid., ff. 6v–10v; to Warwick, 7 September 1576, ibid.,
ff. 4v–6r; to Warwick and Leicester [1577], ibid., ff. 2v–13r.

[7] Warwick to Wood, 16 August 1576, MS. Gorhambury VIII/B/143, ff. 2v–4v;
Leicester to Wood, 19 August 1576, ibid., ff. 23r–27v.

[8] This correspondence is particularly valuable for the light it sheds on Leicester's
religious position and his attitude to the controversy between the bishops and the
puritans. I hope to publish it elsewhere.

He and Field were both retainers of the Earl of Warwick[1] and there is evidence that they knew each other and collaborated in securing propagandist material for the puritan press. In 1571, Wood apparently borrowed a MS. tract from Anthony Gilby and promptly sent it to London without Gilby's knowledge, where Field took steps to have it translated from the Latin and published.[2] If Wood was not the author of the *Brieff discours*, then he was evidently being employed as an intermediary in the same way when he asked Whittingham in 1574 for Calvin's letter. Although Wood was no longer resident in London at the time when the *Brieff discours* was written, he seems to have been in constant touch with the brethren in London and he probably visited London frequently.[3] His letter to Whittingham proves that he was thoroughly acquainted with the events in London which stimulated the writing of the *Brieff discours*.

On comparing the style of the *Brieff discours* with that of Wood's letters and allowing for the difference of *genre*, there is no doubt that both could have come from the same hand, although neither style is sufficiently distinctive to allow an identification of Wood as the author on these grounds alone. Both tract and letters are written in the forthright but ponderously parenthetical prose common to so many puritan writers.[4] Two points are worthy of mention. A slight archaism—the word 'bruit'—which Wood employs frequently in his letters occurs twice in the *Brieff discours*.[5] And there is a remarkable similarity in the balance of the phrases which both Wood and the author of the tract employ to describe the application of the 1573 'Inquisition' against the London puritans. Wood writes to Whittingham:

'But whosoever denieth to subscribe to the boke, to prison he goeth, whether he be minister or other, . . .'

The author of the *Brieff discours* remarks:

'But also yff he come once in presence off the Bishopps, and subscribe not to what so ever they will, then (yf he have livinge) to be deprived, or whither he have livinge or not, be he lerned or unlerned, be he man or woman, halt or blinde, to prison he muste, withowte all redemption.'[6]

---

[1] Field's auditory at the London Church of Aldermary, in a petition to Leicester of 1585, referred to Field having been 'towards your Honorable brother these twenty yeares'. (*Seconde Parte of a Register*, op. cit., i. 135). For my reasons for re-dating this document see my thesis (cited above) 372 n. 2.

[2] Field to Gilby, 10 January 1571[/2], Cambridge Univ. Lib. MS. Mm. I. 43. 447.

[3] See Wood to Sir Thomas Cave, 9 March 1572[/3]; 'I purpose (God willing) with my wife to ride tomorrow towards London for the better recovery of my health, being thereunto advised by a godly phisition.' (MS. Gorhambury VIII/B/143, f. 21r.)

[4] Thomas McCrie, in his introduction to Petherham's edition of 1846, went too far when he wrote (ix) that the style is 'clearly identical with the writings of Whittingham'. The characteristics he specifies are common to much puritan writing of the time.

[5] *Brieff discours*, clxxxiii: 'The brute thereoff was the cause that moo Englishe people in short time resorted thither.' Cf. lxii.   [6] Ibid., cxciiii–cxcv.

If it cannot as yet be proved that Wood wrote the *Brieff discours*, there is no single count on which it can be shown that he did not. On the contrary, everything that we know of him favours his authorship. On the evidence available this seems to be true of no other exile.

APPENDIX

Letter of Thomas Wood to William Whittingham, dean of Durham, 15 February 1573[4].[1]

Salute in Domino. Albeit yow like not, Mr. Whittingham, to satisfie my desire in touching my man, yet I thought having so convenient a messenger, yow would have vouchedsafe to have answered my letter. As for the partie by whom yow promest to write, I have not heard any thing of him. But I thinke my former plainnes hath offended yow, and thereby the old proverb verifyde, *Veritas* etc. Surely if I had writt otherwise, I shold have dissembled, and therefore I thought best, as I have since our first acquaintance (for God's good gifts in yow) loved yow interely, so to deale with you both friendly and plainly. For if ever I did or thought yow harme, it was in procuring the letter whereof this inclosed maketh mention, which I doe the rather send unto yow, for that I have heard to my greif the good Earll of Warwick once or twise complaine of your ingratitude, who as yow best knowe hath well deserved at your hands. But to let this passe, I will once againe make a new sute unto yow in the behalfe of our persequuted brethren, desiring yow as yow tender God's glorie and their comforte not to denie it me. It is to sende unto me Mr Calvin's letter of his judgment touching the booke of service, which both men and women are urged by subscription to approve, as that there is nothing in it evill, or repugnant to the Word of God. Se what it is to yelde never so litle, specially in matters of religion, against the which yow have often godly inveyed bothe publiquely and privately. As for th'apparell, there is now skarce any inforcement at all, unles it be for the surples. But whosoever denieth to subscribe to the boke, to prison he goeth, whether he be minister or other, of which number our brother Mr Fuller[2] is one. And as yow were the first that made me and many others mislike with the said boke, so are the corruptions thereof best knowne unto yow; being as touching th'order thereof (as yow have affirmed) papisticall, and many things in it superstitious, yea and something that is there alowed mere wicked, so as upon the notes yow drewe out of it, Mr Calvin termed them in his said letter *faeces papisticae*. That therefore not only they which suffer for that truthe may as they have heard of it, so to their more full contentation see it indeed, as also to stopp the mouthes of the adversaries, and to perswade some that yet are ignorant of the corruptions thereof; for these causes (I say) in their

---

[1] In this transcription I have preserved the original spelling, but have modernised the capitalisation and punctuation and have extended some abbreviations.

[2] William Fuller, sometime of princess Elizabeth's household at Hatfield and an elder of Knox's congregation at Geneva. (Garrett, op. cit., 158–9.) In 1586 he presented the queen with a book in which he recalled her to repentance and recounted his own experiences during and after the Exile (*Seconde Parte of a Register*, op. cit., ii. 49–64). There are references to Fuller's imprisonment in the Counter and his removal to house-arrest in March 1574 in letters of Thomas Wilcox to Gilby (Cambridge Univ. Lib. MS. Mm. I. 43, 441–411). Wilcox speaks of 'divers others . . . prisoners' and names William White, a prominent puritan layman and Robert Johnson, preacher of St. Clement's without Temple Bar (ibid.).

behalf I desire it; or at least a coppie of it of your owne hand, for that his is hard to read, as yow knowe. And I doe protest unto yow before the Lord, that none, (no, not my brother Williams[1]) shall know but that I found it amongst my papers, as yow are not ignorant that bothe that and the rest were in my custody till my departure from Geneva. There is a letter of yours in many men's hands, writt to the Earll of Leicester,[2] wherein, after divers and many learned arguments and authorities, yow counclude thus: That whosoever shall weare any of the popish garments either for holines or pollicie, *Antichristi mancipius est*. And as that letter (as also your former doctrine) have bene a comfort and confirmation to many, so hath your doings to the contrary bene no small offence to the Church of God, and what danger thereof is, yow knowe better then I. Yet many doe hope that seinge things growe dayly from worse to worse, and that for the maintenaunce of the things above mentioned, the poore famished shepe of Christ are daylie spoiled of their godly and learned shephards by xii at a clap in some one dyocesse,[3] they hope, I say, that God will not only give yow hartie repentance for your backsliding, but also restore yow to your former zeale and boldness to acknowledg all that truthe which heretofore yow have taught to others, which I pray God I may live to see, and that speedely. Yow knowe th'old proverb *Nova trahit periculum*. There are three lately dead by the bishops' imprisonment,[4] whereof Evans, a godly brother was one.[5] See what mischeif the maintenaunce of their lordly pompe and desire to make their sonnes gentlemen hath brought them unto. And will yow for any worldly respects ioyne hands with such bloudy persequters? God forbid, and be it farr from yow, (as it is from a remnant of your old acquaintance, which, God be praised, have not yelded but stood faithfully for the defence of his cause), as to the sincerity and simplicity of his word appertayneth. There were lately burned in the Stationers Hall at London so many of Mr Beza's Confessions in English[6] as could be found amongst the said Stationers. The cause is imputed to the translation, but as I heare credibly, Fitz,[7] the doer thereof,

[1] William Williams, sometime an elder of the Genevan congregation and Wood's son-in-law.

[2] Whittingham to Leicester, 28 October 1564, printed in Strype, *Life of Parker*, iii. App. xxvii, 76–84.

[3] This seems to have been an exaggeration, except perhaps in the case of Northamptonshire. For evidence that the 'Inquisition' was conducted with leniency elsewhere, see my thesis (cited above) 169–72.

[4] Thomas Wilcox, who wrote to Gilby a fortnight before this, reports the same: 'three of them that they have imprisoned' were 'dead allreadie' (Wilcox to Gilby, 2 February 1573[/4], Cambridge Univ. Lib. MS. Mm. I. 43, 439). These three did not include Robert Johnson, preacher of St. Clement's without Temple Bar who died in the Westminster Gatehouse in April (*A Parte of a Register*, op. cit., 94–118).

[5] Was this Lewis Evans, a Catholic controversialist converted to Protestantism in the 'sixties and author of a number of anti-Catholic pamphlets? (*D.N.B.*, art. Evans; *S.T.C.*, nos. 10588–10593.) Cf. Wilcox to Gilby, 2 February 1573[/4] 'You shall receave by the bearer hereof . . . Beza his Epistles, and Lewis Evans his pamphlet.' (Cambridge Univ. Lib. MS. Mm. I. 43, 439.)

[6] Theodore Beza, *A briefe and piththie* [sic] *summe of the Christian Faith made in the forme of a confession*, transl. R[obert] F[ills], edns. 1562, [1566?], 1572, 1585.

[7] I.e. Robert Fills, the translator. Fills, who was a member of Knox's Genevan congregation, also translated *The Lawes and Statutes of Geneva*, published in 1562 and dedicated to Lord Robert Dudley (*S.T.C.*, no. 11725). (Garrett, op. cit. 152–3.) That Wood renders his name 'Fitz' is sufficient indication of the fancifulness of Miss Garrett's suggestion that, since he was registered in Geneva as 'Fielde' he may have been the father of John Field.

is well able to avouche that it is faithfully translated, according to the French. The Warden of that Company in his protestation then affirmed that the writing of Mr Beza and his Master was almost in as great credit with many as the Bible. And there is a brute in London that our Genevan Bibles shalbe called in[1]; If that be true, other things will followe ere it be long. God's will be done with mercie, to whose providence I committ yow and yours. From Groby, this 15 of February, 1573.

Yours in the Lord

Thomas Woode

Yf without all fayned excuses yow will satisfye the godly request of your brethren by sending the said letter, this bearer Mr Parker of Leicester will savely bring it to me, who hath requested me to crave your helpe for his furtheraunce and expedition in a sute he hath there, as the justnes of his cause shall require.

[1] Until 1576 there was no edition of the Geneva Bible printed in England, although there had been three successive Genevan editions, of 1560, 1562 and 1570. The *Brieff discours* in its concluding pages (cxcii–cxciiii) gives prominence to an appeal for the reprinting and more general dispersal of the Geneva Bible.

SERMONS

OF JOHN CAL-
VIN, VPON THE SONGE
that Ezechias made af-
ter he had bene sicke, and
afflicted by the hand of
God,
conteyned in the 38. *Chapi-*
ter of Esay.

¶ Translated out of Frenche
into Englishe.
1560.

☞ Newly set fourth and allowed, accordyng to
the order appointed in the Quenes Maiesties Iniunctions.

℄ Imprinted at London, ouer Aldersgate,
by John Day.
And are there to be solde at his shoppe
vnder the Gate.

¶ *Cum Gratia & priuilegio*
Regiæ maiestatis.

Anne Locke's translation of Calvin's *Sermons* on Isaiah xxxviii. A copy in the British Library bears an inscription in the hand of Mrs Locke's husband: 'Liber Henrici Lock ex dono Annae, uxoris suae, 1559'. (*By courtesy of the trustees of the British Library.*)

8

CALVINISM WITH AN ANGLICAN FACE
THE STRANGER CHURCHES IN EARLY
ELIZABETHAN LONDON AND THEIR
SUPERINTENDENT

SOMETIMES a useful point is scored by reminding students whose Latin is rusty that John Jewel's *Apologia Ecclesiae Anglicanae* is not an apology *for* the Church of England, still less for a newly invented religion called Anglicanism, but an apology *of* the Church of England, in defence of a religion deemed to be universal, catholic and of a primitive character. But one is in danger of being caught out by the alert and troublesome pupil who may know that the English version of the *Apologia* was entitled *An apologie or aunswer in defence of the Church of England*. There is ambiguity in the very construction of Jewel's title, as there will prove to be in any attempt to reconcile the various senses in which the post-reformation English church was and was not considered to be a distinct and self-sufficient entity.[1]

Scholars currently absorbed in the study of Tudor apocalyptic writings (a considerable literary edifice, all erected on the proposition that the pope is antichrist) are telling us that Haller's theme of 'the elect nation' has been overdone. 'God is English' was not after all, a phrase on the lips of the divines. The church transcended nationality.[2] As for Jewel himself, there are striking indications in his controversial writings of the lack of any sense either of a separate Anglican identity or of a specifically English protestant cause. And few of these disclosures are more likely to embarrass any modern Anglican who reads Jewel than something which the bishop of Salisbury said about Michael Servetus 'and such other the like'. Thomas Harding had been unkind

---

[1] Denys Hay, 'The Church of England in the Later Middle Ages', *History*, 53 (1968) pp 35–50.

[2] Katherine Firth, 'The Apocalyptic Tradition in Early Protestant Historiography in England and Scotland', unpubl Oxford DPhil thesis 1971; V. N. Olsen, *John Foxe and the Elizabethan Church* (Berkeley 1973); Paul Christianson, *Reformers and Babylon: English Apocalyptic Visions from the Reformation to the Eve of the Civil War* (Toronto 1978); Richard Bauckham, *Tudor Apocalypse, Courtenay Library of Reformation Classics* 8 (np 1978).

enough to suggest that this hunted and ultimately extinguished heretic
and others as bad might be some of Jewel's spiritual kindred. But Jewel
corrected him. 'We detected their heresies . . . We arraigned them.
We condemned them. We put them to the execution of the laws. It
seemeth very much to call them our brothers, because we burnt them.'[3]
When Servetus died in October 1553 Jewel was no nearer to Geneva
than Oxford. But later he was content to be reckoned among the
whole community of the reformed who had consented unto his
death. The theme in this essay is one of international protestant
solidarity, and in a context not remote from heresy-hunting and the
burning of Servetus. The ashes of Servetus were again and again to be
whipped up and blown into the faces of the characters in our story.

Most of these characters were 'strangers', members of the immigrant community in early Elizabethan London. Rather more than
half of some four thousand foreigners made up the membership of the
Dutch and French churches, with smaller groups constituting an
Italian congregation and a Spanish-speaking group which only
sporadically achieved the viable independence of a separate church.[4]
A substantial minority adhered to the English parish churches or were
'of no church'. In each of these categories of strangers there were
intellectuals and political and ecclesiastical activists who tend to
throw into the shade of C. S. Lewis's 'drab age' all but a few of their
English opposite numbers. 'Only they, occasionally, relieve the general
barrenness of the sixties'.[5]

Many of these strangers were still identified with events across the
Channel and the North Sea where the progressive consolidation of
French and Dutch protestantism within the structures of Calvinism
coincided and interacted with convulsive political and popular movements. The decade which for Anglican historians was a time of
consolidation for the Elizabethan settlement witnessed elsewhere in
protestant Europe, from Poland westwards, the joining of a struggle
between the disciplined, jealously orthodox faith and ecclesiastical
polity demanded by such stern times and alternative, relatively liberal
visions of what it might mean to be a Christian man. Some of the
resistance to hardening Calvinism expressed the mild eclecticism or
'syncretism' of those who were indebted to Melanchthon or Bucer

---

3 *The Works of John Jewel*, ed J. Ayre, 3, PS (1848) p 188.
4 R. F. G. and E. F. Kirk, *Return of Aliens in London*, H[uguenot] S[ociety of] L[ondon],
q[uarto] s[eries] 12 (1900) pp 1–154.
5 [J. A.] van Dorsten, [*The Radical Arts: First Decade of an Elizabethan Renaissance*]
(Leiden 1970) p 15.

for some of their theology and were reluctant to grant Geneva total spiritual hegemony. Others displayed the pertinacity of the true heresiarch and 'fanatic'. Others still the heresy of the free spirit (a good name if it had not been otherwise appropriated) to which the Spaniard Antonio del Corro subscribed when he wrote: 'What is hee of any iudgment at all who wyll not feare to forsake the tyrannie of the papistes to enter into an other, almost of lyke condition?'[6] This was the crisis of reformed protestantism, theological and structural. But it was also a series of personal crises: on the one hand, men of individuality and, perhaps, some innate instability of temperament, for whom the reformation had been an adventure; on the other, men of discretion, self-possessed and capable of providing the coherence and stability required for effective institutionalisation. In this critical engagment between the orthodox and those whom we are almost forced, with Calvin, to call 'libertines' London as a sanctuary and source of support had a signal importance and provided the stage for a succession of rounds in what was really a single contest to determine the future of protestantism itself.

When the mannered Anglican historian R. W. Dixon dismissed such 'intestine commotions' as meriting 'in some interval of languor' the interest of the reader he not only chose to ignore their importance but wrongly assumed that the protestant strangers inhabited a ghetto.[7] There were to be sure linguistic and cultural differences, even barriers. Nevertheless the true situation was not one of mutual isolation. Some of those Englishmen who shared Jewel's sense of identity with a supra-national protestantism, themselves no doubt a tiny national minority, were deeply involved in the concerns of the stranger churches and had no sense that the Church of England was in a detached or special position in relation to their often turbulent affairs. Whether attention was directed to Strasbourg or Emden or Geneva, or to the Dutch-speaking church in the Austin Friars in London, intercourse was indifferently on the basis of 'our churches', 'your churches', or so it appears from much surviving correspondence.

Elsewhere I have written of the attraction of the stranger churches as models for the English puritans in their aspirations for a further

---

6 Antonio del Corro, *An epistle or godlie admonition of a learned minister of the gospel . . . sent to the pastoures of the Flemish church in Antwerp (who name themselves of the Confession of Auspurge)* (1569) fols 25ᵛ–6ʳ.

7 *History of the Church of England from the Abolition of the Roman Jurisdiction*, 3 (London 1885) p 236.

reformation.[8] The not wholly appropriate paradigm was one of fellow-travelling. On this occasion, in a different perspective, we are concerned with more formal contacts between the stranger churches and the Church of England. These contacts invariably involved Edmund Grindal, bishop of London from 1559 to 1570, and as bishop also superintendent of the stranger churches. But besides Grindal other English churchmen were from time to time active in attempts to stabilise the stranger churches. They included another bishop, James Pilkington of Durham, some of the London parish clergy, and members of Grindal's own staff, such as his chancellor Thomas Huycke, who as an old Genevan exile must have taken more than a merely professional interest in these matters. The effect of English intervention in general, and of Grindal's continual participation in particular, was to underpin Calvinist orthodoxy and to promote the pastoral and political arrangements associated with Geneva, in a word, 'the discipline'. Fortunately burning was no longer in question, except for two Dutch anabaptists who perished in Smithfield in 1575. But by the end of the first Elizabethan decade the bishop of London could have paraphrased his brother of Salisbury by saying of the Dutchman van Haemstede and the Italian Acontius: 'We excommunicated them.'

But there was a consistent, qualitative difference between what might be called the minimising policies of Grindal in his tactful handling of individual cases and the maximisation of theological, political and personal disagreement by the ministers and elders of the stranger churches, together with those exercising leadership on a wider scale, especially in the French-speaking reformed churches. This was partly a difference of temperament. Taking them as representative figures, Edmund Grindal and Theodore Beza, born in the same year and known to each other in Strasbourg[9] were so different in character as to seem to belong to different generations: the one open in his dealings and always hoping for the best, the other less generous and tending to fear the worst. But also implicit was the divergent experience of the English church from that of other reformed churches. The Church of England was settled, the essentials of worship, polity and doctrine placed beyond legitimate dispute. Or so the situation could be represented. The role of the ecclesiastical authorities was

---

8 Patrick Collinson, 'The Elizabethan Puritans and the Foreign Reformed Churches in London', P[roceedings of the] HSL 20 (1964) pp 528–55. *See below*, pp. 245–72.

9 Grindal wrote to Calvin on 10 February 1561: 'Salutes, quaeso, meo nomine D. Theod. Bezam (cum quo aliquam familiaritatem Argentinae contraxi), caeterosque tuos collegas . . .', Calvin, *Opera*, 18, no 3337, cols 358–9.

already a conserving role. Subscriptions and formal concurrence were sufficient tests of conformity, and conformity was tantamount to orthodoxy. The case was different among the French and Dutch. Their churches were not devoid of political support but by comparison with the Church of England were suffering 'under the cross'. Confessions of faith and forms of discipline were not the basis of a unity and a peace already enjoyed but the instruments by which such unity was to be won, nominally through the processes of consensus, actually by the suppression of opposition, which as often as not involved the coercion of majorities by an élite, 'the best'. These insecure conditions induced an extreme sensitivity towards any sign of deviation, intellectual, political or moral, an atmosphere of heresy-hunting. To be sure these differences were far from absolute. The continental churches already exhibited some of the features of institutionalisation. The English church was not without a sense of being threatened, although internal cohesion was protected by referring the threat to the alien 'antichristian' enemy. Nor could protestant Englishmen indulge in complacency about the state of a church which still possessed little more than its foundations in a wilderness of ignorance and pastoral neglect. Nevertheless, one can detect in Grindal's relatively relaxed approach to the problem of orthodoxy the authentic trace of Anglican rather than Calvinist churchmanship. Shall we call it Calvinism with an Anglican face?

Turning from generalities to specific cases we shall have space for only three of several *causes célèbres* of the sixties;[10] the affair of Nicolas des Gallars and his opponents in the French church, a story with touches of black comedy; the truly tragic tale of Adriaan van Haemstede and his 'subtle patron' Jacobus Acontius; and the picaresque adventures of the two Spaniards, Casiodoro de Reina and Antonio del Corro. The account which follows has few claims to originality. Each of these episodes has its modern historians, and the Spaniards have been particularly well served by the studies in English of McFadden, Hauben and Kinder.[11] But not since baron de Schickler wrote in

10 This article omits consideration of the case of the perfectionist 'fanatic' Justus Velsius and of a more recalcitrant crisis in the Dutch congregation at Austin Friars which centered on the minister Godfried van Winghen and his controversial views on baptism and on iconoclasm and other manifestations of active resistance in the Netherlands.

11 W. McFadden, 'The Life and Works of Antonio del Corro, 1527–1591', Queen's University of Belfast PhD thesis 1953; [Paul J.] Hauben, [*Three Spanish Heretics and the Reformation*], *Études de philologie et d'histoire* 3 (Geneva 1967); [A. Gordon] Kinder, [*Casiodoro de Reina: Spanish Reformer of the Sixteenth Century*] (London 1975).

the last century[12] has any scholar looked at these episodes as part of a coherent plot, still less with the intention of interpreting the policy of the English ecclesiastical authorities, as a means of characterising Anglican churchmanship in the first years of the Elizabethan settlement.

Des Gallars provides a convenient starting point, for he obliges us to deal with the constitution of the London stranger churches and the connection between their domestic government and ministry and the bishop-superintendent. When the churches were first constituted, in Edward's reign, they comprised an autonomous corporation, a *corpus corporatum et politicum*', with the right to elect officers, determine forms of worship and exercise pastoral discipline.[13] 'We are altogether exempted . . . from the jurisdiction of the bishops', exulted one of the original leaders.[14] Admittedly the charter spoke of a superintendent, a quasi-episcopal office which symbolised the ultimate authority of the English crown. But the first superintendent was himself a stranger, the Polish nobleman and prelate turned reformer, John à Lasco. Under his regime the churches enjoyed a form of guided democracy and proved an awkward thorn in the side of bishop Ridley. Later, in commenting on the troubles of the English strangers at Frankfurt, Ridley insisted that in such circumstances, and in respect of *adiaphora*, the godly man should 'forbear the custom of his own country' and conform to local practice. 'And surely, if I might have done so much with our magistrates, I would have required Mr Alasco to have done no less when he was with us.'[15]

When the stranger churches came together again under Elizabeth the privy council insisted on a modification of the Edwardian arrangements which made the bishop of the diocese superintendent *ex officio*, and further required that no religious forms be used 'contrary to our law'.[16] The queen perhaps expected that the bishop-superintendent would use his office to comprehend the strangers in orderly conformity to the Church of England, the policy of Laud seventy-five

---

[12] [Baron F. de] Schickler, [*Les églises du refuge en Angleterre*], 3 vols (Paris 1892).

[13] *Ibid* 1, pp 24–31. See also [J.] Lindeboom, [*Austin Friars: History of the Dutch Reformed Church in London 1550–1950*] (The Hague 1950); and Basil Hall, *John à Lasco 1499–1560: A Pole in Reformation England*, Friends of Dr Williams's Library 25th Lecture (London 1971) pp 31–4.

[14] Martin Micronius to Henry Bullinger, 28 August 1550; *Original Letters Relative to the English Reformation*, ed H. Robinson, 2, PS (1847) p 568.

[15] *The Works of Nicholas Ridley*, ed H. Christmas, PS (1843) pp 534–5.

[16] Schickler, 1, pp 84–6; Lindeboom, pp 30 *et seq*.

years later. The strangers themselves were moving in their thinking beyond à Lasco's primitive polity towards the more sophisticated presbyterian institutions of developed Calvinism, and alongside these the superintendent would seem an anachronistic and irksome survival: still more the person of the bishop with whom the churches would have to deal directly when, in due course, the office of superintendent was allowed to lapse. Yet paradoxically relations between the strangers and the bishop were at first more harmonious and productive under the new régime than they had been in the Edwardian days of fuller independence. This owed something to the fact that Grindal, as superintendent, had less cause than Ridley to feel threatened by the existence of separate churches within his diocese, but more to Grindal's benevolent attitude towards foreign protestants, a 'religious' rather than 'liberal' attitude,[17] and his determination to exercise his office within the economy of the stranger churches and not as an alien intruder in their affairs. Ordinarily he intervened only at the invitation of the church officers, and with an heroic and self-effacing patience which was the mark of the man and a rarity in his age. When some rebels against the discipline of their own congregation sought refuge in the more permissive atmosphere of the parish churches Grindal ordered that they should be refused communion: *acte de levesque remarquable*, as the clerk of the French church called it in his minutes.[18] Baron de Schickler regarded Grindal's appointment as *singulièrement heureux. Comme superintendant, il cherchait à exercer plutôt la protection que la surveillance et le controle.*[19]

At first there was some resentment that the new superintendent was not the Flemish man of affairs Jan Utenhove. Utenhove was the companion of à Lasco in his last days and returned to London with the charter and, as it were, à Lasco's mantle to negotiate with the government for the renewal of the strangers' privileges.[20] But hostility to the bishop was not sustained, partly because Utenhove did nothing to fuel it, partly because of the excellent relations which Grindal

---

[17] Grindal told Cecil on 8 September 1562 that London was 'marvellously abused by straungers'. Of large numbers who had recently arrived few were good protestants. He proposed that there should be a census of church members 'for the better separatynge off the gode from the badde.' He held no brief for such as were 'not trewly religiouse'. (PRO, SP 12/24/24.)

[18] *Actes du consistoire* [*de l'Eglise française de Threadneedle Street, Londres*], I (1560–1565), ed Elsie Johnston, *HSL*, qs 38 (1937) p 97.

[19] Schickler, I, pp 85–6.

[20] F. Pijper, *Jan Utenhove: zijn Leven en zijn Werken* (Leiden 1883).

maintained with the Dutch elders, not only in church affairs but in a grand design to link England economically and politically with the port of Emden, the mother church of Dutch protestants.[21] When Calvin heard of the campaign to displace Grindal he condemned it as shortsighted, telling the French that in the bishop they had a faithful and sincere protector of their librety.[22] Later it was only as they faced the possibility that Grindal, *bonus hic episcopus*,[23] might be taken from them that the churches worried about the constitutional position and about their future.

The mutual confidence between Calvin and Grindal assisted negotiations between London and Geneva for the supply of a minister of some eminence to assume pastoral direction of the French congregation. The French community which had regrouped in London in 1559 was not without resources of its own for supplying the ministerial office. These included Ebrard Erail, an Antwerp preacher favoured by those whose consciences had allowed them to hear mass in Mary's reign. There was a certain Jean Janvier, best described as a failed divinity student. But above all there was Pierre Alexandre, recently arrived from Strasbourg, an agent in dealings with the government to recover the use of St Anthony, Threadneedle Street. Alexandre was an erudite man,[24] like the Englishman John Bale an ex-Carmelite, sometime chaplain to Mary of Austria, sometime professor at Heidelberg and the holder of a prebend at Canterbury who had delivered learned

21 Grindal to Cecil, 4 August 1562, PRO, SP 12/24/3; Utenhove to Cecil, 20 December 1563, PRO, SP 70/66/1319; Grindal to Utenhove, 10 February 1564, [*Ecclesiae Londino-Batavae Archivum*, ed J. H.] Hessels, 2 (Cambridge 1889) pp 210–13; Utenhove to Cecil, 11, 18, 21 March 1564, BL, MS Lansdowne 7, nos 64–5, 68, fols 149–51, 157; George Needham to Cecil, 13 April 1564, PRO, SP 12/34/38, 41. Compare G. D. Ramsay, *The City of London in International Politics at the Accession of Elizabeth Tudor* (Manchester 1975) pp 229–43.

22 Calvin to des Gallars, [June 1560]; Calvin, *Opera*, 18, no 3216, cols 116–17. The editors mistakenly concluded from this letter that it was des Gallars whom some favoured as superintendent. The true position is stated in the letter from des Gallars to Calvin, 2 August 1560; *ibid*, no 3233, cols 161–6. In later years what Calvin had said was hardly questioned, particularly among the French. In 1565 Grindel was told: 'Nous confessons plainement que ne pouvons avoir ung refuge plus asseure que vostre bien veuillance et authorite, a fin que les molestes et fascheries que nos font telles gens soient reprimees.' Grindal's response to this testimonial, presented on 10 December, was to invite the French consistory to celebrate one of the twelve days of Christmas with him. (*Actes du consistoire* pp 124–5.)

23 *Kerkeraads-Protocollen* [*der Nederduitsche Vluchtelingen-Kerk te Londen 1560–1563*, ed A. A. van Schelven], Werken uitgegeven door het Historisch genootschap, series 3, 43 (Amsterdam 1921) pp 134–5.

24 *Actes du consistoire* pp xv–xvi; Schickler, 1, pp 92–3, 97–8.

courses of lectures in the cathedral in Edward's reign.[25] The annals of the Huguenots would later record that *des siens* (and he was a man who flourished on partisanship) Alexandre was known as *la merveille d'Arras*.[26] But a party in the congregation, in Schickler's estimation *les plus serieux*,[27] had set their sights higher. They were ambitious that 'a Viret, a Theodore de Beze, a Macar or a Pierre de Collonges' might be sent to them from Geneva.[28] They had named the ranking Geneva pastors and what they wanted was the sure hand of Calvin himself on the helm. In the event they were given Nicolas des Gallars, sieur de Saules, a pastor with the aristocratic background which French protestantism found so invaluable,[29] and a trusted lieutenant who had served as moderator in Geneva in Calvin's absence and had recently acted as his envoy to the first national synod of the French reformed church in Paris. In Edward's reign he had been Calvin's nuncio to London.[30]

The fact that Calvin was willing to spare a man of this calibre, *non sine acerbo dolore*,[31] may connect with the sense of unease which Grindal had conveyed about the state of the English church. The winter of 1559–60 was a time when the presence of a silver cross in the queen's chapel was thought to portend a reaction against the thorough purge of parish churches in the royal visitation of the preceding summer, and these fears were linked with a disturbing threat to episcopal revenues as the crown helped itself to bishops' lands under the terms of the 1559 act of exchange.[32] Calvin wrote: *Ecclesias totius regni nondum ita compositas esse ut optarent boni omnes, et principio*

---

25 Treatises on predestination and on matrimony, Corpus Christi College Cambridge MSS 115, 126; treatises on ecclesiastical discipline and excommunication and on purgatory, BL, MS Add 48040, no 3.

26 Schickler, 3, p 173.

27 *Ibid*, 1, p 90.

28 *Ibid*, 1, p 91.

29 R. M. Kingdon, *Geneva and the Coming of the Wars of Religion in France, 1555–1563*, *Travaux d'humanisme et renaissance* 22 (Geneva 1956); H. G. Koenigsberger, 'The Organisation of Revolutionary Parties in France and the Nrtherlands During the Sixteenth Century', *JMH* 27 (1955) pp 335–51.

30 Geneva pastors to ministers and elders of Flemish church in London, 4 May 1560, Hessels, 2, pp 132–3; Calvin to Grindal, 15 May 1560, Calvin, *Opera*, 18, no 3199, cols 87–8. For des Gallars, see Eugène and Émile Haag, *La France Protestante*, ed Henri Bordier, 5 (2 rev ed Paris 1886) cols 298–305.

31 Calvin to Grindal, 15 May 1560; Calvin, *Opera*, 18, no 3199, cols 87–8.

32 William P. Haugaard, *Elizabeth and the English Reformation* (Cambridge 1968) pp 185–200; Felicity Heal, 'The Bishops and the Act of Exchange of 1559', *HJ* 17 (1974) pp 227–46.

speravarant, vehementer dolet.[33] The mere presence of des Gallars would strengthen the still wavering cause of reform in England. Later it was arranged that he should preach twice a week in Latin, for the edification of learned men outside his own nation.[34] Grindal was to assure Calvin that apart from settling the French church which was in total confusion at the time of his arrival des Gallars had been of the greatest assistance to himself 'and to our own churches', while the French pastor for his part wrote the most glowing of testimonials for Grindal: *Nisi certe talis vir his ecclesiis praeesset, nullo modo subsistere possemus.*[35]

By the time this was written the alliance of Grindal and des Gallars had been severely tested. Des Gallars was in London to rescue what Calvin called 'the yet tender and unsettled church'[36] from unsound leadership. Nevertheless a majority of church members seems to have been unhappy about his appointment. Since des Gallars made no secret of his dislike of majorities it was perhaps more disturbing that some of 'the best', including two physicians and other professional and affluent men, opposed his ministry in favour of the prior claims of Pierre Alexandre.[37] On a small scale these factions resemble the forces marshalled behind Jean Morély, sieur de Villiers, in the struggle which was about to develop in France itself between protagonists of 'the discipline' and those who favoured a more decentralised church government, lay and popular in character.[38]

Grindal was bound to intervene in the disputes which were now to threaten the very existence of the church in Threadneedle Street, but he was compromised by the personal circumstance that as a stranger himself he had enjoyed the hospitality of Pierre Alexandre in Strasbourg.[39] When des Gallars waited on him with Calvin's letters of commendation Grindal exhorted the elders to be both submissive and friendly and reminded the whole church of its duty towards a duly appointed pastor. But he then said something more about the need to treat as a colleague Alexandre, who was acceptable 'to the people' and had begun to gather the church before the arrival of the

---

33 Calvin to Grindal, 15 May 1560; Calvin, *Opera*, 18, no 3199, cols 87–8. See also Grindal to Calvin, 10 February 1561; *ibid* no 3337, cols 357–9.
34 *Actes du consistoire* p 42.
35 Des Gallars to Calvin, 14 February 1561; Calvin, *Opera*, 18, no 3341, cols 366–8.
36 Translation by G. C. Gorham of Calvin's letter to Grindal of 15 May 1560, *Gleanings of a Few Scattered Ears During the Reformation in England* (London 1857) pp 415–17.
37 Schickler, I, pp 93, 96n.
38 [R. M.] Kingdon, *Geneva and [the Consolidation of] the French Protestant Movement 1564–1572* (Madison 1967).
39 Schickler, I, pp 96, 132.

pastor. He also mentioned that Alexandre's English benefices would enable him to serve the congregation without charge.[40] This was the first of many fruitless attempts by Grindal to hold the ring between the two French fighting cocks and the opposed factions in the church. Those hostile to des Gallars now contested the validity of his election and demanded a popular vote. This Grindal refused, insisting that a pastor could not be chosen twice, that des Gallars had been duly called by leading elements in the congregation, and that to reject him would be an insult, not least to Calvin. Nevertheless the installation of the pastor was delayed for a week, while Ebrard suggested that under the terms of the charter it was necessary to secure royal confirmation of the appointment, which Elizabeth might refuse, since des Gallars had been sent from Geneva 'by those who have greatly offended her.' Grindal dismissed this objection, insisting that his office placed him between the strangers and the government and that he would assume responsibility for the church's action.[41] On 24 June 1560 he came to Threadneedle Street to instal des Gallars as pastor. Happier with the German language than with French[42] he spoke through an interpreter and exhorted the church to follow the teaching of its minister and to submit to ecclesiastical discipline. At this point des Gallars intervened to ask the bishop to allow any objections to be voiced. There was silence, but since Grindal's interpreter was none other than Pierre Alexandre this was perhaps the silence of resentful and stifled opposition rather than of satisfaction. Des Gallars revealed his insensitivity to these undercurrents when he announced to Geneva that this was the end of the matter.[43]

It was only the beginning. Grindal had ordered new elections, presumably with the intention of removing from the consistory elements hostile to des Gallars. The elections seem to have been carefully managed, with the help of the Dutch elder, Utenhove, the leading English merchant adventurer Thomas Heton, not long returned from Strasbourg, and two other Englishmen 'newly come from Geneva'. The deacons, who were members of Ebrard's faction, were defeated and Ebrard now retired to France, where he was to meet a violent

---

[40] *Ibid* pp. 93–4; *Actes du consistoire* p xvi.
[41] Schickler, 1, pp 94–5.
[42] Grindal's proficiency in German is well documented. On one occasion he wrote to Cecil to say that so far as he could understand the language in which they were written the proposals of a group of French protestants in Southampton appeared reasonable. (PRO, SP 12/43/29.)
[43] Schickler, 1, pp 95–6; *Actes du consistoire* p 4.

end in the first of the religious wars.[44] The remodelling of the church
on Genevan lines was completed when des Gallars published first
in French and later in Latin a new *Forme de police ecclésiastique*. This
book of discipline, heavily impressed with Calvin's hand, continued
to provide for popular election to the church offices but looked towards further constitutional modifications of an aristocratic and clerical
character which would be made in the time of des Gallars's successor,
Jean Cousin.[45] It was of a piece with this political tendency that des
Gallars now replaced congregational prophesying with a sermon.[46]

But Alexandre was still a force to be reckoned with, still proud to
recall that he was preaching in the congregation *iusques a le venue de
celuy qui estoit envoyé de Geneve*.[47] Grindal had persuaded des Gallars
to admit his rival as an honorary colleague, to preach on Sunday
afternoons and alternate Thursdays, but without the title of minister.
Both parties found the terms of this compromise unacceptable.
Towards the end of the year des Gallars was tempted to throw in the
sponge and required Calvin's steadying voice: *Iam electus es pastor:
cuius esset, levitatis mox te revocare?*[48] In December violent words were
uttered in the consistory[49] and it was perhaps at this juncture that
Alexandre addressed Grindal in a formal *Apologia* to which des
Gallars responded.[50] On the last day of the year Grindal effected a
formal reconciliation over dinner.[51] But Alexandre soon disregarded
the arrangements made for alternating the ministry and open hostili-
ties resumed.[52] When in July 1561 the annual elections failed to go his
way Alexandre alleged electoral impropriety from the pulpit and

44 *Ibid* p 4; Schickler, 1, pp 98–100. Heton, one of the 'sustainers' of the Marian exile, is
mentioned in several of the *Zurich Letters*, [ed H. Robinson], PS (1845). For his participation with Grindal and Utenhove in the Emden scheme, see Grindal to Utenhove,
10 February 1563, Hessels, 2, pp 210–13. See also C. H. Garrett, *The Marian Exiles*
(Cambridge 1938) pp 18n, 27, 48, 182–3.
45 Schickler, 1, pp 103–15. An apparently unique copy of the printed Latin text, *Forma
polititae ecclesiasticae*, which includes a dedication to Grindal, is bound up with BL,
MS 48096. It was originally in the possession of the puritan activist John Field.
46 *Actes du consistoire* pp 11–12.
47 *Ibid* p 5.
48 Calvin to des Gallars, 5 October, November 1560; Calvin, *Opera*, 18, nos 3257, 3276,
cols 211–15, 242–3.
49 *Actes du consistoire* pp xxiii, 20.
50 Corpus Christi College Cambridge MS 340 (no 19, pp 425–34) (i) 'Apologia Petri
Alexandri adversus animadversiones domini Galasii ad reverendum patrem et dominum episcopum Londinensem'; (ii) 'In scripto domini Petri inquit haec sunt ani-
madvertanda'; (iii) 'Responsio Petri Alexandri ad animadversionem domini Galasii'.
51 *Actes du consistoire* p 21.
52 *Ibid* pp 22, 42.

absented himself from the communion with his faction. Grindal was warned of the impending ruin of the church and was persuaded to suspend Alexandre from preaching while the matter was investigated.[53] Early in August everyone went to Fulham: des Gallars, Alexandre, the elders and the leaders of the Dutch church. The meeting lasted from ten in the morning until six in the evening, while all the bitterness of the past twelve months was raked over. Des Gallars offered a presumably tactical resignation and obtained a vigorous endorsement from Grindal. At last Alexandre was persuaded to withdraw his charges and all parties agreed to forgive and forget.[54] Reconciliation was probably sealed on this as on another occasion by the bishop joining the hands of those present and by a general drinking of healths.[55]

Not long after this des Gallars left London to take part in the colloquy of Poissy, from which he sent reports to Grindal and through the English ambassador, Throckmorton, to Cecil.[56] Since Alexandre served as *locum tenens* in his absence it was scarcely surprising that when he turned his back on attractive offers to remain in France and returned to his bed of nails in London des Gallars found the congregation once again in disarray, his party among the elders faltering and the *Forme de police* under fire. In regaining control he received less support from the superintendent than he may have expected. When Alexandre refused to submit his cause to the arbitration of the consistory and was again suspended he found that Grindal gave him a sympathetic hearing and even asked des Gallars to nominate him as his successor. When des Gallars indignantly refused Grindal proposed to make the nomination himself.[57] Des Gallars was reduced to asking the meeting of the two churches, the *coetus*, how the French church might be rid of Pierre Alexandre.[58] Alexandre supplied the answer himself. Finding that des Gallars had control of the consistory he reverted to underhand tactics and accused the deacons of embezzlement. When the deacons were exonerated in a formal enquiry des Gallars chose to strike, and faced the church with a demand to choose between himself and

---

53 *Ibid* p 48; *Kerkeraads-Protocollen* pp 234–5.
54 *Actes du consistoire* p 50.
55 *Ibid* p 87.
56 *Ibid* p 51; Schickler, 1, pp 127–31. Des Gallars to Throckmorton in *CalSPF, 1561–2,* nos 458, 485, 492, 507, 511, 569, 583, 611, 636. Des Gallars to Grindal, 29 October 1561, PRO, SP 70/31/486.
57 *Actes du consistoire* p xxv; Schickler, 1, pp 131–2; *Kerkeraads-Protocollen* pp 280–1.
58 *Ibid* pp 285–6.

Alexandre. His rival accepted defeat and left for France, where he died a few months later.[59] This was the end of organised resistance to 'the discipline'. But as if to make the point that he had fought not for his private interest but for the public cause des Gallars himself resigned in the spring of 1563, after his wife and several children had succumbed to the plague. As he proceeded to the next and most distinguished chapter of his career at Orléans[60] the London church, now according to Grindal *placatam ac bene institutam*, passed into the care of Jean Cousin of Caen, a sound appointment which must have been welcomed in Geneva, where indeed it may have been made.[61]

From our point of view the most intriguing part of this drama was Grindal's conduct in the last act. Why did he give Alexandre encouragement when des Gallars was poised for the kill? There was perhaps sufficient motive in the old debt incurred in Strasbourg. But it may be that Grindal was also moved by some distaste for the uncompromising and uncharitable way in which des Gallars had handled his opponent. He endorsed the *res* of the Genevan policy but perhaps found the *modus* hard to stomach. This is speculation. We can only note that our information is dependent upon the correspondence of des Gallars with Calvin,[62] and that we have only his rival's word for it that Alexandre was so deficient in character as to be disqualified from the pastoral office to which, in the view of his supporters, he had the prior claim.

Even des Gallars conceded that Alexandre was orthodox in doctrine, hostile to sectaries and opposed to sin.[63] His faults were wounded pride and an uncontrollable temper. The fracas in Threadneedle Street

59 Schickler, 1, p 133.

60 *Ibid* pp 133–6; *Actes du consistoire* p xxv; Grindal to Calvin, 19 June 1563, Calvin, *Opera*, 20, no 3696, cols 43–5, English translation in *Zurich Letters*, 2, pp 96–7; testimonials for des Gallars from the French and Dutch churches, 14, 25 May 1563, Hessels, 3 (1897) pp 29–31.

61 Cousin was doubtless more welcome to lovers of 'discipline' than Adrian Saravia whose appointment was earlier mooted—Des Gallars to Calvin, 31 December 1561; Calvin, *Opera*, 20, no 3680, cols 226–7. Saravia would later dissent from Calvinist dogmatics and was already suspected of holding the Lutheran doctrine of ubiquity, *Kerkeraads-Protocollen* p 266.

62 Letters from des Gallars to Calvin of 1 July, 2 August, 2, 13 September, 14 October 1560, 25 January, 14 February, 14 April, 7 June, 6 October, 31 December 1561, 16 March 1562; Calvin, *Opera*, 18, nos 3226, 3233, 3241, 3244, 3261, 3327, 3341, 3373, 3412, cols 142–5, 161–6, 174–5, 180–2, 219–21, 340–2, 366–8, 423–5, 504–6; 19, nos 3551, 3680, 3744, cols 18–19, 226–7, 338–43.

63 Des Gallars to Calvin, 13 September 1560: 'Unum me solatur, quod Alexander purae est doctrinae, sectariis infestissimus, vitiaque acriter insectatur.', Calvin, *Opera*, 18, no 3244, cols 180–2.

had important implications but its substance was a clash of personalities. The van Haemstede affair which concurrently convulsed the Dutch church at Austin Friars was of an altogether more serious nature, concerning as it did not only profound differences in doctrine but a difference in the evaluation of doctrines, and hence the very coherence of the reformed churches and their faith.

Adriaan Cornelis van Haemstede shared at least one quality with Pierre Alexandre: a constitutional reluctance to submit to church discipline. As a cultivated preacher in Antwerp with access to the homes of the well-to-do he refused to maintain the low and defensive profile which for some years had protected the protestant community in that great city from harrassment, and which was a policy enforced by the church leadership. His preference for preaching and debating in public was thought to have contributed to the revived persecution of the later 1550s. By March 1559, when he published the first martyrology in the Dutch language, *De geschiedenisse ende den doodt der vremer martelaren*, van Haemstede was himself on the run with a price on his head and could be said to have created some of his own copy.[64] Having extricated himself from the dangers of Antwep he made his way through Emden to London in the early summer of 1559, before the return to Utenhove and the arrival of Peter Deleen, the future minister of the Dutch congregation. Although without accreditation he began preaching, perhaps supporting himself as a bookseller.[65]

In London van Haemstede attracted a following among the same sort of erudite and affluent people with whom he had mingled in Antwerp, and who were to cultivate a lifestyle in Elizabethan London at a certain distance from the worthies of the church at Austin Friars. They included the merchant-scholar van Meteren and relations of the great Ortelius. Presently there moved into this circle the Italian Jacobus Acontius (Aconcio), one of the more notable of protestant 'libertines' and a mathematician and logician of the first rank, author of a *De methodo* from which a route is traced to Descartes.[66] Acontius's acquaintance with the Strasbourg group of English exiles and his reputation as an engineer had brought him to London, where he enjoyed the patronage of the queen and of her favourite, Lord Robert Dudley.

[64] J.-F. Gilmont, 'La génèse du martyrologe d'Adrien van Haemstede (1559)', *RHE*, 63 (1968) pp 379–414. See also the study by A. J. Jeslmas, *Adriaan van Haemstede en zijn Martelaarsboek* (The Hague 1970).

[65] See the heading on p 23 of *Kerkeraads-Protocollen*: 'De Adriano bibliopola'.

[66] W. K. Jordan, *The Development of Religious Toleration in England*, 1 (London 1932) pp 303–64; van Dorsten pp 16–18.

Ideologically he belonged to the loose association of liberally minded Italian heretics whom Calvin called 'academic sceptics', for whom the execution of Servetus had provided a cause.[67] He was now at work on the book called *Stratagematum Satanae* which would be published in Basle in 1565 with a dedication to queen Elizabeth. Besides enunciating a reductionist theology of truths deemed to be beyond dispute and advocating a policy of practical religious toleration this book included an original and psychologically powerful analysis of the motive springs of intolerance. These were the 'stratagems of Satan'.[68]

Des Gallars was to inform Calvin that Acontius was van Haemstede's *patronus subtilior et acutior*.[69] That may well have been a plausible inference about the intellectual relationship of these two dissimilar individuals. It is possible that van Haemstede in the secrecy of his own conscience had wandered far from orthodox protestantism. If, as one scholar has considered possible, he was an adherent of the Family of Love we should almost expect to know nothing about this since to conceal the nature of one's true beliefs was for Familists a way of life.[70] But it is more likely that van Haemstede, while more of a Melanchthonian than a Calvinist, was not unorthodox,[71] and that he merely shared with his fellow martyrologist, the Englishman John Foxe, a profound dislike of violence used in the cause of religion. He included no anabaptist martyrs in his *Geschiedenisse* but in London he befriended a group of anabaptists and undertook to help them at a time when they were threatened with deportation by a royal proclamation.[72] It was his opinion, which acquired a certain formality in the

---

[67] Philip McNair, 'Ochino's Apology: Three Gods or Three Wives?', *History*, 60 (1975) pp 353–73. McNair remarks that the Italian exiles mixed with the 'severe and doctrinaire divines' of northern Europe like oil with water. 'Wherever there was trouble, there was an Italian behind it.'

[68] There is a modern edition, *Jacobi Acontii Satanae Stratagematum libri octo*, ed Walther Koehler (Tübingen 1927); and an English translation of books 1–4 with an introduction by C. D. O'Malley, Sturo branch, California state library, *Occasional Papers*, English series 5, pt 1 (San Francisco 1940). See Erich Hassinger, *Studien zu Jacobus Acontius*, *Abh zur Mittleren und Neueren Geschichte* 76 (Berlin 1934).

[69] Des Gallars to Calvin, 25 January 1561; Calvin, *Opera*, 18, no 3327, cols 340–2.

[70] Van Dorsten pp 27–33; B. Rekers, *Benito Arias Montano* (1972) pp 70–104.

[71] Lindeboom p 41.

[72] *Tudor Royal Proclamations*, ed P. L. Hughes and J. F. Larkin, 2 (New Haven 1969) no 470, pp 148–9. Was a formal petition presented? The archives of the Dutch church contain a letter from Grindal to Utenhove and Deleen, dated 4 September 1560, referring to a supplication submitted by certain anonymous persons, 'apparently anabaptists'. Grindal reports the opinion that the author was 'Adrianus'. But Hessels knew of evidence which identified this man as a certain Adrianus Gorinus, Hessels, 2, pp 139–41.

proceedings of the next two years, that 'among the anabaptists as well as among the papists and other pestiferous sects weak members of Christ are found.'[73]

Dutch protestants were divided in their attitude towards the anabaptists and sometimes individuals were torn in their own minds. So much would emerge from the confused reaction which would greet the betrayal of the Dutch anabaptist congregation in London in 1575.[74] But if Mennonites sometimes looked like simple god-fearing folk, it was hard to deny that the opinion commonly held among them, that Christ's flesh was not derived from the Virgin but was a 'celestial' flesh, was a dangerous heresy. Without doubt it was liable to endanger those who meddled with it. One version of this near-Gnostic doctrine was associated with Servetus, while another had persuaded the protestant government of Edward VI to burn the English woman Joan Bocher.[75] We do not know that van Haemstede himself held the doctrine of the heavenly flesh. Indeed he said that he did not hold it. But he would not allow 'weak members of Christ' to be constrained in such a matter against their consciences. This was where the 'patronage' of Acontius became significant. Van Haemstede adopted the formal, adiaphoristic position that the Christological question was 'circumstantial', not 'fundamental', and that implies a capacity to extract the philosophical essence from a practical situation which is unlikely to have been entirely his own.[76]

In early July 1560 a series of unhappy meetings began in the Dutch consistory. Van Haemstede was required to confess his fault in describing the anabaptists as brethren and weak members of Christ, and in bringing his church into danger with the civil authorities. Far from submitting he soon walked angrily out of the consistory, compounding his offence with contempt for church discipline.[77] Like other heresiarchs he would now deploy against the consistory a polemic which identified the elders with 'the rulers of the Jews' and his own cause with that of the rejected Christ.[78] When he was suspended from

[73] *Kerkeraads-Protocollen* pp 6–10, 445–7.

[74] Hessels, 2, pp 522–3, 552–8.

[75] G. H. Williams, *The Radical Reformation* (London 1962) pp 325–37.

[76] Acontius wrote to Grindal in 1564: 'Ac quoniam quod fuit in Hadriani condemnatione praecipuum, et quo propemodum solo nomine videtur haereticus fuisse habitus, id in usu vocabuli circunstantiae erat positum: arbitror ego super hoc puncto potissimum a me satisfactionem requiri', Hessels, 2, p 227.

[77] *Kerkeraads-Protocollen* pp 11, 445–7.

[78] *Ibid* p 455.

preaching this will have strengthened his sense of embittered *anomie*.[79] The consistory now devoted itself to almost daily discussion of the scandal of van Haemstede. By the end of August the French were also involved and des Gallars began to report the case to Geneva.[80] In early September there was a critical debate before the *coetus* of the two churches when Acontius supported van Haemstede in the contention that the doctrine of the celestial flesh was circumstantial.[81] Up to this point the Dutch had shown their usual reluctance to involve the bishop-superintendent,[82] but when van Haemstede refused to recognise any other jurisdiction they no longer had any choice. All parties now appeared before Grindal, his chancellor, and the archdeacon of London, John Mullins. Before this tribunal van Haemstede professed himself willing to subscribe to orthodox articles concerning the incarnation and to renounce any doctrine incompatible with the Belgic confession of faith.[83]

It illustrates the argument developed earlier that whereas Grindal would have been happy to let the matter rest with van Haemstede's formal subscription Utenhove and Deleen now assembled a dossier of evidence from his writings and public utterances, *loca pugnantia* which were inconsistent with what he had subscribed.[84] At another hearing attended by all parties Grindal was confronted with this evidence and pressed to issue a punitive sentence against van Haemstede.[85] Instead he set in motion a protracted judicial process. Questions were referred to van Haemstede through the chancellor and further testimony was delated against him. Meanwhile Grindal was lobbied by van Haemstede's eloquent friends, including van Meteren and Acontius, who shared van Meteren's house.[86] And Acontius had des Gallars engaged in an exchange of polemics in which the subject at issue transcended most theological controversies of the sixteenth century, concerning as it did the fundamental essence of Christianity. This exchange has recently been given the felicitous title of *Un combat aux frontiéres de*

---

[79] *Ibid* pp 27–8.
[80] There are entries relating to the affair of van Haemestede throughout the main series of *Kerkeraads-Protocollen* for this period (pp 6–353). These are followed by a special register (pp 445–66): 'De Moeilijkheden met Adriaen van Haemstede'. Des Gallars to Calvin, 2 September 1560; Calvin, *Opera*, 18, no 3241, cols 174–5.
[81] *Kerkeraads-Protocollen* p 459.
[82] *Ibid* pp 455, 458–61, 135.
[83] *Ibid* pp 43–4, 462.
[84] *Ibid* pp 44–6, 463.
[85] *Ibid* pp 48–9, 464–5.
[86] *Ibid* pp 50–4, 465, 59–60.

l'orthodoxie.[87] Acontius also found time to visit Grindal with a major manifesto.[88] In mid-October the various documents were undergoing scrutiny by Grindal's staff while the church officers pressed the bishop for a definitive and summary sentence and the Haemstedians played for time with demands for a full and unprejudiced debate.[89] Eventually Utenhove overcame Grindal's obvious reluctance to see the issue forced to a punitive conclusion. On 17 November 1560 the bishop appeared in person at Austin Friars before the combined congregations and after Deleen had pronounced the sentence of excommunication against van Haemstede in Dutch confirmed it in English and addressed the company from the pulpit.[90] Van Haemstede thus became, on the face of it, the noblest kind of martyr: victim not of his own belief but of defending, if not to the death to the loss of security and livelihood, the right to believe of others.

If van Haemstede had chosen to stand his ground the case might have rivalled any other theological *cause célèbre* of the century. A disputation was planned, to be conducted in Latin so that its character might be international. At first it was thought that Grindal would preside, but then there was talk of a tribunal composed of bishop Pilkington of Durham, the dean of St Paul's and the Scottish reformer, John Willock. Deleen and Utenhove were busy despatching copies of the documents overseas and corresponding with the major centres of Dutch and French protestantism.[91] But van Haemstede, who had no ambition to be a second Servetus, tried to confine debate to the Dutch congregation, where he still enjoyed a measure of support. And then, in the midst of this frenetic activity, he slipped away from London to face an uncertain welcome at Emden. On the way his ship almost sank, he was robbed of all his possessions, including his library, and his wife gave birth to triplets.[92] One of the two surviving

87 Corpus Christi College Cambridge MS 113 no 37 pp 281–6 contains an autograph letter from Acontius to des Gallars, for which the date of 4 September 1560 is inferred. It bears marginal annotations in the hand of des Gallars. The letter is printed and discussed in [Philippe] Denis, ['Un combat aux frontières de l'orthodoxie: la controverse entre Acontius et des Gallars sur la question du fondement et des circonstances de l'église'], *BHR*, 38 (1976) pp 55–72.

88 *Kerkeraads-Protocollen* p 68. This manifesto has not survived. But its argument is rehearsed in a letter from Acontius to Grindal of 1564: Hessels, 2, pp 224–34.

89 *Kerkeraads-Protocollen* pp 59, 64, 65, 68, 70.

90 *Ibid* pp 72–3; *Actes du consistoire* p 14. The sentence is printed by Hessels from the archives of the Dutch church, Hessels, 2, pp 142–3.

91 *Kerkeraads-Protocollen* pp 76–9, 89, 90, 103–4; *Actes du consistoire* pp 17–18.

92 Adriaan van Haemstede to Mayken, wife of Jacob Cool, 10 February 1561; Hessels, 2, pp 144–6.

infants was christened Charitas. Was that to give away a secret about the *Domus Charitatis*, the Family of Love?[93]

Van Haemstede's supporters rallied to his defence. Even Utenhove's half-brother wrote from Antwerp to deplore what had happened.[94] Grindal now had to deal with the Haemstedians, including van Haemstede's sister Katrijn who arrived in London to swell the clamour of *feminae inquietae*.[95] On pain of themselves suffering excommunication these people, *circiter viginta*, were required to acknowledge the error of representing the incarnation as less than fundamental and their own fault in impugning the justice of the sentence imposed on their hero.[96] It was in the context of this major struggle between 'the discipline' and dissidence that des Gallars published the Latin edition of his *Forme de police ecclésiastique*.[97] Some submitted but most stood their ground.[98] By May 1561 there was nothing for it but to excommunicate ten of van Haemstede's supporters, including his sister and van Meteren.[99] An obviously reluctant Grindal confirmed the sentence and took steps to prevent the excommunicates from taking up a new home in the parish churches.[100] One of the dissidents boasted in a pub of having said to the bishop's face: 'My lorde, so you hadde the popes power, you wolde be more cruel then the pope him self.'[101] Grindal now revealed characteristic reservations about the rigour of the discipline which he himself had administered. Some of the Haemstedians made a qualified submission in which while remaining critical of the manner in which the affair had been handled they agreed to refrain from further criticism and to ask forgiveness for any offence given from their side. Grindal hoped that the Dutch elders would meet this offer half way: *forte enim aut nimio rigore aut animi altertatione verbis ac moribus usi sumus ex quibus offensionem dedimus*.[102] And he was ready to discuss the terms on which van Haemstede's own ban

93 Van Dorsten p 33.
94 Carolus Utenhove to [John Utenhove], 16 May 1561; Hessels, 2, pp 162–4.
95 *Kerkeraads-Protocollen* p 111.
96 *Ibid* pp 117, 163, 166, 175. See the document in Hessels, 2, pp 149–50 beginning 'Conditiones duae offerendae quibusdam in Ecclesia Germanica, qui hactenus visi sunt adhaerere Hadriano'.
97 *Actes du consistoire* p 39.
98 Statement by 'denuntiati fratres', 2 May 1561, Hessels, 2, pp 150–1.
99 *Kerkeraads-Protocollen* pp 185–8, 201, 209.
100 *Ibid* p 209.
101 *Ibid* pp 293–4.
102 *Ibid* p 226; a statement, apparently from Grindal, to the elders of the Dutch church, 1 July 1561, Hessels, 2, pp 152–3.

might be lifted. But Grindal must have known that any display of weakness on his part must strengthen the ambition, never far below the surface of the Dutch consistory, to escape from his tutelage and regain the full autonomy enjoyed in Edwardian days.

Any chance of compromise was destroyed by the instinct of van Haemstede and his 'patron' for direct and provocative action. It was Acontius who persuaded van Haemstede to return to London.[103] In July 1562 the clerk of the Dutch congregation had a sufficiently dramatic entry to make in his register: *Adrianus Hamstedius compt opentlick in de kercke, hoort die predicatie*.[104] Shades of Michael Servetus who had placed himself in the arena, nine years before in Geneva! A warrant was immediately issued for his arrest,[105] while Utenhove began all over again the tireless amassing of evidence to persuade the bishop to act decisively.[106] On 4 August Grindal confronted van Haemstede with a humiliating form of recantation which bore the names of four English 'doctors' besides his own: Miles Coverdale, David Whitehead, Robert Crowley and John Philpot.[107] Three of these would soon be revealed as recalcitrant nonconformists, while the fourth, David Whitehead, had already distanced himself from leadership in the Elizabethan church. When van Haemstede refused to subscribe Grindal came to Austin Friars again and ratified a second sentence of excommunication. And this time van Haemstede was deported to Emden, where not long afterwards he died. He was thirty-seven. This second excommunication provoked another protest from Utenhove's half-brother. *Sed de hoc baste, ut loquuntur Itali*.[108]

The rationale of the Calvinist discipline required that it should be watertight. Excommunication should be equivalent to severance from the body of Christ and the erring brother to whom this last extremity of the pastoral ministry had been extended should be to the faithful as a heathen man and a publican. As we have seen, Grindal was willing to fence the tables of his own London churches against those who had been barred from the communion of Austin Friars or Threadneedle Street. But the Haemstedians and other recalcitrants had another refuge, a bolt hole which the strict Calvinists were unable

---

103 Van Haemstede to Acontius, 14 June 1561; *ibid* pp 165–8.
104 *Kerkeraads-Protocollen* p 331.
105 *Ibid* p 332.
106 *Ibid* p 334.
107 Dated 31 July 1562, Hessels, 2, pp 201–4; also printed, with translation, in [*The Remains of Archbishop*] *Grindal*, [ed W. Nicholson], PS (1843) pp 441–5.
108 Carolus Utenhove to Joannes Utenhove, 4 September 1562; Hessels, 2, pp 205–7.

entirely to stop. This was the Italian church in London, containing a
nucleus of strangers of Italian origin but also diverse elements which
were not of Italian extraction at all.[109] When the London Italian
church finds its historian, or the editor of its minutes, we may understand the modality of these anomalies, and how they may have been
handled in the *coetus* which linked the stranger churches in a loose
association.[110] What is apparent is that the hard-liners, Utenhove, des
Gallars and, presently, des Gallars's successor Jean Cousin, regarded
the Italian church with justified suspicion. From no later than January
1561 it was a field which Acontius cultivated.[111]

Somewhat earlier the only intermittently viable church of the
Spanish strangers had similarly earned the hostile attention of the
guardians of Calvinist orthodoxy. Acontius was to be found there as
well, bearing the office of elder.[112] To the story of two of the Spaniards, Casiodoro de Reina and Antonio del Corro we finally turn, in
search both of the clearest demonstration of the clash of free thought
and discipline, and of the temperamental and intellectual differences
dividing Grindal from the leaders of French-speaking Calvinism.

Two interpretations of this story are possible. Either Casiodoro and
Corro were wrongly accused of gross heresy, not to speak of moral
delinquency, when they were guilty only of intellectual integrity,
proudly defended: victims of what Hauben has called 'heretical
packaging'.[113] Or the instinct of the Calvinist witch-hunters was
sound. A Spanish protestant in the age of Philip II was the ultimate
outsider, the freest of free spirits. Necessity forced these spiritual
vagabonds to find sanctuary and employment in Calvinist communities. But their Calvinism was a cloak, worn lightly, for convenience.

Casiodoro de Reina and Antonio del Corro (who assumed the
French name of 'Bellerive') were two of a group of Spanish evan-
gelicals whose spiritual progress had begun as young monks with
'Erasmian' and cryptically protestant leanings in the monastery of

[109] A list in BL, MS Lansdowne 10 no 61 fol 177 of 'those which are of the Italian church
being born in Flanders and other places under the dominion of the king of Spain'
lists fifty-seven names, of which only twelve are self-evidently Italian.

[110] BL, MS Add 48096 contains the minutes of the Italian church. The earliest surviving
'Livre de *Coetus*' runs from 1575 to 1598, library of the French protestant church,
Soho Square.

[111] Des Gallars to Calvin, 25 January 1561; Calvin, *Opera*, 18, no 3327, cols 340-2.

[112] Denis p 63.

[113] Hauben p xii.

San Isidro del Campo, outside Seville.[114] With a younger associate, Cypriano de Valera, who was also resident in London in the sixties but as an orthodox Calvinist kept out of the limelight, they were dedicated to the project of a Spanish bible. Building on foundations laid by earlier translations of the new testament Casiodoro was to achieve the first complete translation of the scriptures into Castilian, the so-called Bear bible printed at Basle in 1569. This was the basis of all Spanish protestant bibles printed from that time to this, and it required only superficial revision by de Valera in the definitive edition of 1602.[115]

In 1557 Casiodoro fled from Spain with other members of a nascent protestant church and after brief sojourns in Geneva and Frankfurt came to London in 1559, perhaps in company with returning English exiles. He attached himself to the French church but then began negotiations with Grindal and Cecil for recognition and accommodation for a separate Spanish congregation. According to the ambassador, de la Quadra, who was careful to keep the Spanish heretics under surveillance, the little church first gathered in the bishop of London's house, with preaching three times a week.[116] Later the Spaniards were granted the use of the church of St Mary Axe after Casiodoro had insisted on the need to make their meetings public and above suspicion. As pastor of this little body Casiodoro composed a confession of faith[117] which was markedly expressive of what the age knew as 'syncretism', a mediating position between Calvinism and Lutheranism, and of 'adiaphorism', the distinction between essentials and nonessentials. There were other traces of unsoundness, easily detected by sensitive noses, and rumours of Casiodoro's contact with the Genevan antitrinitarians. When he appeared before the French consistory to defend himself and other Spaniards against imputations of Servetianism he was asked questions about van Haemstede and Acontius. Evidently the French and Dutch already expected the Spanish congregation to become a cave of Adullam for dissidents.[118]

---

114 The fundamental account of this circle and of the divergent careers of its members is in the work of [Edward] Boehmer, [*Bibliotheca Wiffeniana. Spanish Reformers of Two Centuries from 1520*], 'According to the late Benjamin B. Wiffen's plan and with the use of his materials', 2, 3 (Strasbourg/London 1883, 1904). The account which follows is drawn from Boehmer, making use of Hauben and Kinder.

115 E. M. Wilson in *CHB*, 2 (1963) pp 127–8.

116 *CalSP, Spanish, 1558–1567*, no 170, p 247.

117 Grindal's copy, endorsed (possibly in 1578) 'De causa Cassiodori Hispani, Confessio Hispanica', in Lambeth Palace Library, MS 2002, fols 31ᵛ–48ᵛ.

118 *Actes du consistoire* pp xx, 13.

A gap in the minutes has obscured what subsequently happened in Casiodoro's negotiations with the French consistory, but it is unlikely that these ended to the satisfaction of both parties. And then, in 1563, all hopes and fears for the little Spanish church were extinguished when Casiodoro suddenly disappeared from London and after a period of hiding in Antwerp made himself a new home in Frankfurt.

A thorough investigation of the circumstances of his flight, such as Kinder has undertaken, carries us down into an obscure underworld inhabited by Spanish agents and their even more shadowy accomplices. The ostensible cause was a charge of homosexuality, *peccatum sodomiticum* as Grindal put it explicitly in an account sent to Cecil some years later.[119] This was not a total fabrication, yet it is likely that the commission of enquiry appointed by Grindal to enquire into these allegations, consisting of Cousin, Utenhove and two London ministers, Robert Crowley and James Yonge, and which was interrupted by Casiodoro's flight, would have found that no criminal offence had been committed.[120] Casiodoro had fled in the mistaken belief that sodomy was a capital offence in England, which in 1563 it was not, and perhaps out of fear of abduction by Spanish agents.[121]

The Calvinist jungle telegraph now hummed with rumours. Casiodoro was said to have kissed a book by Servetus and to have declared that only Servetus understood the mystery of the Trinity. Des Gallars wrote from Orléans to tell Utenhove how much the news about de Reina had upset him. *Avertat Dominus tantas pestes a grege suo.*[122] Theodore Beza was not one to be carried away with rumours and in 1565 he was prepared to recommend Casiodoro to the French church at Strasbourg, where Calvin himself had once ministered. But an interview with the Heidelberg theologian Olevian aroused new fears about his doctrinal purity and moral reputation, and renewed the utterly damaging charge of Servetianism.[123] From a position of

---

119 BL, MS Lansdowne 11, no 67, fol 150; printed Boehmer, 3, pp 89–91.
120 The depositions of Casiodoro's accuser Balthasar Sanchez and his own protestation survive in the archives of the French church in Frankfurt, Boehmer, 3, p 30 n; 2, pp 220–1. A deposition from the London enquiry of 1564 is in Hessels, 3, pp 35–6. See Kinder esp p 27.
121 *Ibid* pp 29–31, and appendix.
122 Des Gallars to Utenhove, 25 March (1564); Hessels, 2, pp 236–7.
123 The charge may have had its origin in Casiodoro's dependence upon Servetus, or on a rabbinical source which he shared with Servetus, for certain marginal notes on the old testament. Casiodorus himself suggested as much in writing to Theodore Beza, 1 March 1566, *Correspondance de Théodore de Bèze*, 7 (1566), ed H. Maylou and others, *Travaux d'humanisme et renaissance*, 136 (Geneva 1973) no 453, pp 48–9.

cautious neutrality Beza was later persuaded to set his face against Casiodoro. It was true, he recalled, that he had never heard the Spaniard expressly dissociate himself from Servetus. (He had been heard to say that when living in Geneva he could never pass the site of Servetus's execution without tears.)[124] Ultimately Beza's verdict was: *Dieu vieille le laver si a tort on lui a mis ceste tache, sinon, le plonger du tout et noyer en son ordure affin qu'il n'en infecte des aultres plus avant.*[125]

Grindal's part in this affair was honourable and consistent. He thought well of Casiodoro and perhaps recognised some theological affinity, derived from a common veneration of Martin Bucer. In the midst of the débacle Grindal was instrumental in preserving the manuscripts of the Spanish bible and this was not forgotten when the completed work was published. A copy of the Bear bible was among the books which were bequeathed to the Queen's College, Oxford, at the time of the archbishop's death, with a graceful inscription by Casiodoro recalling Grindal's action in rescuing his manuscripts *ex hostium manibus*.[126] Many years later, when Casiodoro needed a complete clearance of his name in order to qualify for a post at Antwerp, he returned to London and the commission of enquiry which his flight had interrupted was reconvened, under Grindal as archbishop of Canterbury. It found in his favour on all points. But the London French remained hostile, declining to comment on the archbishop's sentence or to issue a testimonial in de Reina's favour, or even to admit him to its fellowship.[127] Beza, after all, had pronounced the sentence that mattered, in *Epistola LIX*, by then in print and in international circulation.

The affair of Casiodoro de Reina was only the overture to a more prolonged and serious heresy hunt in which the quarry was Antonio del Corro, *dit Bellerive*. Corro came to England in 1567 on a visit which lasted a lifetime, but only after many years did he cease to be a highly controversial figure. The fact that in the end he found a home for himself and his eclectic theology in the Church of England has a certain symbolic value for the argument of this essay.

[124] Kinder p 19.
[125] Beza to Corro in *Epistola LIX* of *Epistolarum [theologicarum Theodorii Bezae Vezelii liber unus, secundo editio]* (Geneva 1575) pp 248–61. See also Beza to Jean Cousin, 14 February 1571; Hessels, 2, pp 370–6.
[126] Boehmer, 2, p 172. I am grateful to the assistant librarian of the Queen's College for helping me to trace Grindal's copy of the Bear bible.
[127] Schickler, 1, pp 231–5.

On Christmas Eve 1563 Corro wrote to his 'dear friend' Casiodoro
de Reina in London. The letter concerned their joint plans for printing
a Spanish bible, but it also initiated, or perhaps continued, a theolo-
logical discussion, with what Corro's accusers later considered to be
affirmations but Corro insisted were innocent questions, and which
we may call leading questions.[128] Corro seemed to regard fundamental
articles of faith as legitimate matters for argument and expressed a
desire to read writers whom no good Calvinist could wish to consult,
such as the spiritualist Schwenkfeld. And he asked Casiodoro what he
thought of the enthusiast Justus Velsius, who had recently suffered
deportation from London, and of Acontius. Beza knew the answer
to that question. Velsius was insane and Acontius 'full of paradoxes'.[129]
Corro's letter was included in a packet directed to a member of the
French congregation and endorsed (but it was not the letter to Casiodoro which was so endorsed) 'for matters of great importance touching
the church of God'. Casiodoro's whereabouts by this time were unknown (he was in hiding in Antwerp) and the French consistory
waited three months, then opened the letter, found that it contained
nothing of a public nature, advised Corro that his friend was un-
available, and filed the letter away. It was one of at least twenty-one
which Corro wrote to Casiodoro at this time without receiving a
reply.[130] It remained an embarrassment to his detractors that the root
of the matter lay in a private letter which had been tampered with,
albeit in good faith: 'providentially' as was said, to put a bold face on
a dubious procedure.[131] We may compare the 'extraordinary miracle'
and 'singular providence of God' which enabled des Gallars to discover a collection of letters in Orléans and with them to discredit
Jean Morély, the leader of an alternative French Calvinism.[132] Corro
would later complain that his letters had been intercepted over a
period of four years.

By the time that he arrived in London with the intention of preaching in Spanish and perhaps of regrouping the Spanish congregation
Corro was an object of suspicion, the good standing in which he had
left the Lausanne academy and Beza's company in 1559 already
damaged beyond repair. The portmanteau charge of Servetianism

[128] Schickler (1, p 169 n 1) prints the relevant sections of the fateful letter, with bibliographical details of the extant copies. The text is also printed in Boehmer, 3, pp 79–81.
[129] In *Epistola LIX*; *Epistolae* p 253.
[130] Hessels, 3, p 32.
[131] Boehmer, 3, p 40.
[132] Kingdon, *Geneva and the French Protestant Movement*, pp 86–8.

had been mentioned in correspondence between France and Geneva and he had acquired the reputation of an 'ambitious' man, which may mean only that he conducted himself like a Spaniard, as one report suggests. Driven from pillar to post by the violent disturbances of the French religious wars he came to Antwerp in 1566 with excellent recommendations from the church of Montargis and Châtillon, south of Paris, and from Renée de France, dowager duchess of Ferrara.[133] At Antwerp he tried to establish himself as minister of the Walloon church, but succeeded in causing multiple offence with 'a godly admonition', a notable but in the circumstances provocative essay in eirenics addressed to the local Lutheran community. Calvinists of all people were unlikely to derive much comfort from an apologia which in the course of its criticism of those who would make of the confession of Augsburg 'a fifth gospel or new symbol of the Creed' denigrated all 'confessions, catechisms, commentaries and traditions' and those who would make 'gods or idols of our doctors'.[134]

When Corro recommended himself to the French church in London all this and much more was remembered. Even the testimonial from Montargis and Châtillon, like some modern university placement file, was rendered suspect 'by the excessive eulogy it contains.' Corro could only be admitted to fellowship if he would subscribe to true doctrine and publicly admit that his letters to Casiodoro were *imprudenter scriptae*. This he declined to do, choosing instead to 'run to the bishop', as his enemies contemptuously put it. Grindal conferrred with the Spaniard in the presence of his advisers and issued a formal certificate of soundness in doctrine.[135] It was the van Haemstede case all over again. Grindal was satisfied when Corro renounced the heresies alluded to in his letters, failing, or refusing, to tune his ear to theological undertones. He would continue to praise Corro's 'good learning' long after he had been repelled by his conduct, which is to say that Grindal did not have the mind to translate faults of character into a suspicion of intellectual deviance. He granted Corro a small pension and did what the French church had been careful not to do: handed him a copy of the notorious letter which he had written three years before.[136]

133 Boehmer, 3, pp 14–17.
134 A version of this *Epistle or godlie admonition* was published in London in 1569. See above n 6.
135 *Grindal* pp 313–14. The French version is printed by Schickler from a copy in Geneva, Schickler, 3, pp 73–4.
136 Boehmer, 3, pp 30–6.

Armed with the bishop's testimonial, Corro successfully applied for membership of the Italian congregation, where he began to preach to the Spanish-speaking members. He had no ambition, he said, to become a minister in the more prestigious French church, which brought from Jean Cousin the comment 'sour grapes'.[137] But now what Corro called 'an atrocious war against me by tongue and pen' intensified, orchestrated by Cousin. There was slanderous talk in Lombard Street and at public eating places, which Grindal advised the victim to ignore. But Corro could not disregard a stream of letters from the French consistory to Paris, to des Gallars at Orléans, and to other churches, giving wide publicity to the affair and adding to his incriminations. This bore fruit in a sentence of the French national synod which barred him from exercising his ministry anywhere until he had cleared his name.[138] As with Casiodoro, it appears that Cousin's fear was that Corro's ministry in the Italian church would provide a haven and a rallying point for 'libertines' who had abandoned their own churches.

Corro gave as good as he got. He circulated copies of Grindal's testimonial with an added endorsement which implied quite improperly that the bishop had condemned the 'malice' of his opponents. He prepared an *Apology*, no longer extant, which upset Grindal with its 'sharp invectives' and untruths. He supplied the bishop with details of an elaborate conspiracy with its roots in Paris and the machinations of a certain Balthasar Sanchez, the same man who had denounced Casiodoro.[139] He wrote besides to archbishop Parker and secretary Cecil and sent his *Apology* with many other papers to Beza.[140] His invective is very quotable. Cousin and his henchmen were said to be more cruel and tyrannical than the Spanish inquisition, worse than Turks or pagans. With clear reference to Acontius's notorious book the disintegration of the Spanish group within the Italian church was said to be 'a stratagem of Satan'. And he had this to say at his trial before the ecclesiastical commissioners: *Apparet vos Anglos non solum civile, sed et ecclesiasticum bellum gerere contra Hispanos, civile capiendo ipsorum naves ac pecunias, ecclesiasticum in persona mea.*[141] It was in the midst of this trial, in December 1568, that Alva's pay-ships

---

[137] *Ibid* p 32. What Cousin actually said was: 'The fox did not wish what he could not reach.'
[138] *Ibid* pp 32–9, 89–91. Grindal to Cousin, 18 July 1567; Hessels, 2, pp 271–3.
[139] Boehmer, 3, pp 36–9, 89–91.
[140] *Ibid* p 39; Hauben pp 36–40.
[141] Boehmer, 3, pp 41, 91.

were impounded and their cargo of bullion diverted to the queen's coffers. If this was a little too apt it was ingenious to send the French text of his Antwerp *Admonition* to archbishop Parker with the suggestion that his daughters might care to use it in their French lessons.[142]

It was this provocative conduct rather than any suspicion of actual heresy which turned Grindal against Corro. He may also have been stung by a frank 'remonstrance' from the French consistory. Why have a magistrate and why have a superintendent if such a man could conspire against the church and claim the bishop as his supporter?[143] The French church prepared a dossier under four heads, dealing with Corro's ambition, his calumnies, his lies and his jests, the man being *versé en l'art de moquerie*: all to the effect that here was *un troubleur des églises reformées*, but not impugning his doctrine.[144] In response Grindal took the unusual course of referring the case to a joint commission composed of staff members of the ecclesiastical commission and no less than six French pastors. After a protracted hearing he pronounced sentence in March 1569. On account of his evil speaking, slander and unshakeable obstinacy, Corro was suspended from preaching, teaching and all other ecclesiastical functions.[145] Beza, by no means happy about an affair of which the details were intercepted letters 'and other crudities' was content that judgment should rest with the bishop.[146] But the sentence was confirmed, in effect, in a devastating letter which Beza wrote to Corro in response to his *Apology*, which would later gain notoriety in a watered-down version as his *Epistola LIX*.[147]

Once again Grindal appeared in the role of Pontius Pilate, sadly confirming the sentence of the Sanhedrin when his instinct was probably to scourge Corro and let him go. But unlike the verdict of the Roman governor, his sentences were acts of conscience and pastorally motivated. No sooner had he pronounced against Corro than he was labouring for his restitution. That was the purpose of ecclesiastical discipline which was in no ultimate sense punitive. But he was also under some pressure from Cecil and perhaps other courtiers

---

142 Corro to Parker, 16 January 1569; *Correspondence of Matthew Parker*, ed T. T. Perowne, PS (1853) pp 339–40.

143 'Une remonstrance a Mr Levesque touchant le libelle d'Anth. Corran.' (so endorsed by Cousin); Hessels, 3, pp 81–2.

144 Articles of the French church against Corro, 28 November 1568; Hessels, 3, pp 62–72.

145 Sentence printed from a Genevan source by Schickler, 3, pp 84–5.

146 Beza to Cousin, 11 March 1569, *Epistola LVII*, in Hessels, 2, pp 308–10; Schickler, 1, p 172, n 2.

147 *Epistolae* pp 248–61.

who may have heard only Córro's side of the story.[148] In August 1569 Corro undertook to admit the fault of his slanderous speeches and to live peaceably hereafter. It was not until November that Grindal forwarded this partial retraction, apparently because a suspicion of plague in the French pastor's house had interrupted communications. But he now begged Cousin to meet Corro half-way. *Nihil mihi gratius efficere potestis.* Corro had already sustained eight months of suspension, and for a matter of conduct rather than of doctrine. But the consistory was not impressed. Corro must explicitly retract the scandalous imprudence of his 1563 letter to Casiodoro, and of his Antwerp *Admonition.* In other words, he must thoroughly purge himself theologically. This Corro could not or would not do, not ever.[149]

Grindal's refusal to admit that the root of the matter was theological may appear in the retrospect of centuries to have been a very Anglican attitude. It was an attitude all the more remarkable in that Grindal well knew of a new provocation on Corro's part: the publication at Norwich of a controversial theological statement in the form of a broadside, *Table d'oeuvre de Dieu.*[150] The eloquent silence of this publication on the subject of the Trinity and its casually incidental mention of predestination were suggestive, a new *Apology* which followed indicative of Corro's digression from Calvinist dogmatics.[151] Again it is revealing of Grindal's attention to niceties, and perhaps of an essentially untheological mind, that he considered this latest scandal to be a domestic matter between Corro and the Italian congregation of which he was a member. Grindal expressed no view of his own on Corro's doctrine but merely noted that the *Tableau* had been printed without ecclesiastical approval, an offence against discipline, and that the Italian church disapproved of its doctrine.[152] Early in 1570 the Italian consistory excommuni-

---

[148] Grindal to Cecil, 20 September 1569; *Grindal* pp 309–12.

[149] Grindal to Cousin, 7 November 1569, Hessels, 2, pp 328–9; Cousin to Grindal, 12 November 1569, *ibid* p 331; consistory to Grindal, 22 November 1569, *ibid*, 3, pp. 95–8. Hauben (p 49) finds it 'mysterious' that Grindal sat on Corro's 'semi-apology' for two months. But it is likely that Grindal and his staff complied with the plague orders made in the city in 1563, Corporation of London Record Office, JOR 18, fols 123ᵛ, 136, 139, 154, 184, 189ᵛ–90.

[150] One copy of the printed text extant in Cambridge University Library. Printed from a MS copy by Hessels, 3, pp 75–80.

[151] Boehmer, 3, pp 47–8; Hauben p 49.

[152] *Grindal* pp 309–12.

cated Corro.[153]   The long arm of Cousin, Beza's arm, had reached even into that pleasingly varied assembly.

Corro had now burned his boats with the stranger churches and was looking for a future in the Church of England. Copies of the Latin version of the *Tableau* were sent as new year's gifts to the queen and various notables. As Grindal prepared to leave London for York episcopal hearings continued, and Cousin and successive national assemblies of the French church maintained unrelenting pressure.[154] In 1573 Corro made a new and more comprehensive submission, but it is likely that by this date his motive was to impress the Anglican authorities. In consequence Grindal's successor as superintendent, bishop Sandys, did nothing to impede his appointment to a lectureship at the Temple, which seems to have been favoured and perhaps actively promoted by his principal patron, the earl of Leicester, and other magnates.[155] Later the further help of Leicester established Corro in Oxford as a theological teacher, albeit deprived by the successful resistance of Oxford Calvinists of the doctorate which Leicester as chancellor had sought to secure for him, and which was conferred with alacrity on one of his principal French-speaking opponents.[156] In international Calvinist circles it became a commonplace that Corro was tolerated 'by the silence of the bishops'. Eventually the dominant note in his theology became the repudiation of Calvinist predestinarian doctrine, so that he appears to posterity as a proto-Arminian, together with Peter Baro, another foreigner who held a divinity chair at Cambridge, a pioneer of the intellectual reaction against John Calvin.[157] When Richard Hooker's views first became known, in the same Temple church where Corro had lectured, comparisons were at once made with the Spaniard.[158] International Calvinism had known what it was about.

153 Details in the MS minutes of the consistory of the Italian church, which record a bitter dispute between Corro and his Calvinist compatriot Cypriano de Valera, BL, MS Add 48096, no 2, fols 21–31ᵛ.
154 Boehmer, 3, pp 49–62, 114–19; Hauben pp 50–6.
155 R. M. Fisher, 'The Origins of Divinity Lectureships at the Inns of Court, 1569–1585', *JEH*, 29 (1978) pp 150–1. See Corro's letter to the earl of Huntingdon, 18 January 1571, and critical notes on the letter, Hessels, 3, pp 129–36.
156 Pierre Loiseleur, seigneur de Villiers, present in London from 1572 and a successor to Cousin, who died in 1574. Details in Boehmer, 3, pp 63–72, Hauben pp 59–62.
157 Corro's intellectual progress and its significance for English Arminianism are discussed in McFadden and in the unpublished Oxford DPhil thesis by N. R. N. Tyacke, 'Arminianism in England in Religion and Politics from 1604 to 1648' (1969) pp 83–8.
158 Boehmer, 3, p 74.

This has not been an essay about Anglicanism, for the distinctive and coherent body of divinity implied by that title had no apparent existence in the days of the Elizabethan Calvinist *consensus*. But one of its themes has been Anglican attitudes, which in the days of Grindal, bishop and superintendent, were anomalous and conflicting attitudes. It was the acute mind of Jacobus Acontius which pointed out the anomalies to Grindal and which may perform the same service for us. In a manifesto intended to assist an attempt to regain membership of the French church[159] the 'academic sceptic' reminded the bishop that whereas he, Acontius, had attributed salvation to those who denied but a single article of the faith there were precedents for declining to unchurch those who were ignorant of the faith in its entirety. Zwingli, for example, had been willing to offer as it were retro-spective baptism to noble pagans such as Socrates. If this was a shrewd thrust, the letter ended with a truly Parthian shot. It was remarkable, Acontius suggested, that as a stranger he was denied membership of the stranger church while the English parish churches were not only willing to admit him but were required by law without any effective test of belief to compel the adherence not only of himself but of countless others whose grasp of gospel truth was at best uncertified.[160]

Acontius may have found it stranger still that these inconsistent policies, one of extreme narrowness, the other of excessive latitude, were both administered in the name of the same individual: Edmund Grindal, bishop and superintendent. What he could not have forseen (and within two years he was dead, not long after the publication of *Stratagematum Satanae*) was that the tolerant latitudinarianism and advanced adiaphorism of which he was a lonely advocate would have its most secure future within the Church of England.

---

[159] Acontius to Grindal, 1564, Hessels, 2, pp 224–34. The letter has been printed more recently in Koehler's edition of *Stratagematum Satanae*, pp 235–42. For the circum-stances see *Actes du consistoire* pp xxiv, 108–9, 115.

[160] 'Sed illud satis mirari non possum. Cum peregrinis Ecclesiis peregrinus communicare non permittor. Anglicae non permittunt solum; sed etiam, nisi sponte accessero, invitant, et cogunt, neque id faciunt solum cum mei similibus: sed cum plurimis a sincero Evangelii doctrina dissidentibus non uno in puncto, sed propemodum in omnibus.'

9

THE ELIZABETHAN PURITANS AND
THE FOREIGN REFORMED CHURCHES IN LONDON

On 13 October 1584 an unusually large funeral procession made its way through the London streets. At its head, carrying the bier and competing for the honour ' thicklie, comelie and curteouslie ', walked more than twenty pastors of the Reformed faith : twelve of them Scotsmen, eight of them English and three French. The corpse was that of a Scottish minister, by name James Lawson, who with his brethren had taken refuge in England from a régime in Scotland unfavourable to their presbyterian cause.[1] The procession was on its way to the new Bedlam churchyard outside parochial limits where it was feasible to use a Reformed order of burial service taken from the Geneva book.[2] Behind the bier walked, we are told, ' gentlemen, honest burgess[es], famous and godlie matrons ', . ' manie godlie brethren, ministers and citicens ' to the number of above five hundred persons, ' an unaccustomed frequencie, yea even with the chefest men in the citie '. Like funerals in Reformed communities in France, this was an occasion for a show of strength ; and it was a demonstration by people to whom a common faith meant more almost than blood. The native-born Englishmen among the mourners would have been marked out by the onlookers as ' gospellers ', ' curious and precise persons ', ' puritans '. And

---

[1] An account of Lawson's death and funeral was sent north to Scotland by one of the Scots ministers who was in London at the time ; (British Museum, MS. Additional 4736, f. 166ᵛ ; printed, imperfectly, *Miscellany of the Wodrow Society*, ed. David Laing, I, [Edinburgh, 1844], pp. 451–2, (Wodrow Society)).

[2] Richard Bancroft cited the practice at ' the newe Churchyard in London ' as proof that the puritans had put their Book of Discipline into practice with respect to burials ; (*Daungerous positions and proceedings*, (1593), p. 104). On 12 May 1590 the High Commission made an order regulating the use of Bedlam Churchyard which had been employed by the puritans for the burial of the dead outside the orders of the Church ; (Somerset House, Consistory Court of London records, Liber Vicarii Generalis, Stanhope, I, 1583–90–5, f. 343ᵛ ; I am indebted for this reference to Dr. H. G. Owen of Reading University).

with them walked the three ministers of the church of the French strangers with ' manie Frenchmen '.

In this paper I propose to look at the foreign Reformed communities in Elizabethan London—and especially the French congregation—in the setting suggested by this vivid snapshot. As Calvinists, the strangers must have enjoyed some fellowship with their English co-religionists, even if these contacts were restricted by barriers of language, English insular prejudice and the inward-looking tendencies of the refugee group.   As members of organised Calvinist churches which were largely self-governing and free to elect their own officers and to exercise Reformed, congregational discipline, the foreign Protestants must have exercised a fascinating influence over their English brethren who longed for these rights but could not as yet enjoy them.   It should be made clear at the outset that these native London Calvinists, whose dealings with the strangers we shall be exploring, were not much more numerous than the immigrants themselves ; we are talking, of course, about the hard core of English Calvinism, the convinced, the instructed and the zealous.   Most of these English Reformed saw no necessity to make a formal separation from the established parish churches, but their rule of life, corporate as well as personal, owed little to Anglican formularies and regulations, and their idiosyncratic behaviour, which often involved them in breaches of the ecclesiastical laws, won them a name : ' puritans '.   What they lacked in numbers they made up for in both individual zeal and the disciplined strength of their brotherhood, led by preachers who were for the most part salaried lecturers rather than beneficed parsons and whose connection with the established Church was rather tenuous. Within ten years of Elizabeth's accession, secretly and in defiance of the law, they were using among themselves orders of Reformed worship and discipline akin to those used publicly and with permission by the stranger churches.

I cannot offer the results of any very prolonged research, or mature reflection, on the influence that these two Reformed groups—foreign and native—exercised over each other.   All that I can hope to do is to show that a relationship existed and deserves more attention than it has yet received.   As I see it, we are in possession of two considerable bodies of information, but almost nobody has acquainted himself with both or has used the one to deepen our understanding of the other. The history of the stranger churches has been pursued along many lines of enquiry, but often authorities in this field have ignored the fact that these congregations existed in a Protestant English environment. While our knowledge of the advanced wing of the English Reformation has been enormously extended in recent years, it has hardly ever been thought relevant to mention in accounts of the puritan movement that living models of a Reformed Church flourished by permission no farther afield than, for example, at Canterbury, Norwich, Southampton, Sandwich and London itself. Yet in 1568, after the renewal of civil war in France, there were no less than nineteen émigré ministers gathered in London from that country alone ; and in 1572, after St. Bartholomew's night, more than sixty French pastors took refuge in England.[1] Admittedly, from the viewpoint of the foreign congregations, the English puritan movement represented only one and no doubt the least important of the dimensions in which they moved, but it is the most neglected by their annalists. Lindeboom, in his history of the Dutch congregation at Austin Friars,[2] shows the church in its dealings with other refugee congregations in London, with Dutch communities elsewhere in England and with the mother Church in the Netherlands ; but he has nothing to say about its relations with English Protestantism, apart that is from the ecclesiastical authorities, who are represented far from sympathetically. This criticism does not apply to Baron Schickler's superb history of the Huguenot churches ;[3] but we now know much more about the English puritans than was known in Schickler's day.

The particular problem which interests me as a student of English nonconformity is this. In the reign of Edward VI, when the Polish reformer John à Lasco organised the twin refugee congregations and obtained the original royal charter, it was recognised and is familiar to modern historians that these moves were meant to be as significant for the English Church as they

[1] Le Baron F. de Schickler, *Les Églises du Refuge en Angleterre*, (Paris, 1892), I, pp. 148-9, 198-200.
[2] J. Lindeboom, *Austin Friars : History of the Dutch Reformed Church in London, 1550-1950* : English tr. D. De Iongh, (The Hague, 1950).
[3] Schickler, *Les Églises du Refuge*, 3 vols., (Paris, 1892).

were for the strangers.[1]   John Hooper, the chief hope of the
more radical English Protestants who hoped to establish a
Church on the pattern of Zwingli's Zürich, probably employed
the considerable influence which he possessed in high places to
secure à Lasco's charter.   He was certainly an intimate of
à Lasco, whose admiration for Zürich was equal to his own, and
of the leader of the Dutch community, Martin Micronius, who
told Bullinger that Hooper would prove ' the future Zwingli of
England '.   Bishop Nicholas Ridley's hostile reaction to the
privileges granted to the strangers to form a distinct religious
corporation outside his jurisdiction is evidence from another
quarter that à Lasco's church was intended to serve as a model,
closer at hand than Zürich, of ' a Church rightly reformed '.[2]
To take a leap of eighty years : it is equally well known that
Archbishop Laud objected to the continued separate existence
of the foreign Reformed congregations because of the distracting
example they provided for the English puritans.[3]

Since these circumstances from the reigns of Edward VI and
Charles I are relatively familiar, it is odd that so little attention
has been paid to the influence of the stranger churches on the
English Church in the time of Elizabeth I, when they played
the part of a Trojan horse, bringing Reformed worship and discipline fully armed into the midst of the Anglican camp.   These
were the years when the English puritans were most concerned
with urging a further reformation of their Church in worship and
discipline ;   when the example of the ' best reformed churches '
overseas was most admired, and when English puritanism was
anything but an insular phenomenon.   The puritan manifesto,
An Admonition to the Parliament, asked rhetorically in 1572 :
' Is a reformation good for France ? and can it be evyl for England ?   Is discipline meete for Scotland ? and is it unprofitable

---

[1] In 1555 à Lasco wrote in the epistle which dedicated to King Sigismund
of Poland his *De ordinatione ecclesiarum peregrinarum in Anglia :* ' Nous pensions, en effet, qu'encouragés par cet exemple les Églises Anglaises elle-mêmes
seraient unanimes dans tout le royaume à revenir au culte apostolique dans
toute sa pureté.'   (Quoted, *Actes du Consistoire de l'Église Française de Threadneedle Street, Londres,* I, 1560-65, ed. Elsie Johnston, (1937), p. xiii n.,[Huguenot
Society, Q.S. XXXVIII].)

[2] W. Morris West, ' John Hooper and the Origins of Puritanism ', *Baptist
Quarterly,* XVI (1955-6), 24, 29-30.

[3] Schickler, *Les Églises du Refuge,* II, pp. 3-63 ; Lindeboom, *Austin Friars,*
pp. 136-48.

for this Realme ?   Surely God hath set these examples before
your eyes to encourage you to go foreward to a thorow and a
speedy reformation.' [1]   A Scottish presbyterian who received in
consecutive days letters from one of the authors of the *Admonition*
in London and from the French Protestants of La Rochelle was
moved to tell his English correspondent, John Field : ' It is no
small comfort brother, . . . to brethren of one natione to
understand the state of the brethren in other nationes. . . .' [2]
But there were godly examples nearer at hand, in London itself,
as some contemporary puritan documents remind us.   One
writer acknowledges as ' members and parts ' of the Church
universal ' the Church of Christ in Geneva, in Fraunce, in Germany, in Scotland, etc. : allso in London the Italian Church, the
Dutch and the French '.[3]

The French congregation in London derived a particular
lustre in the early years of Elizabeth's reign from the quality of
its senior pastor, Nicholas des Gallars, sieur de Saules, who
arrived in London in June 1560.[4]   Des Gallars had not yet
arrived at the full stature which he would achieve in the French
Reformed Church after his appearance at the Colloquy of Poissy
in 1562, when he would serve as chaplain to the Queen of
Navarre,[5] but he was already one of the most trusted of Calvin's
lieutenants, to be ranked with Beza and Viret.   He was responsible for the Latin translations of several of Calvin's Biblical
commentaries and controversial writings and had defended his
master against Cochlaeus ; he was also the learned editor of an
annotated edition of Irenaeus and was at work on an edition of
Cyprian at the time of his death.   Calvin entrusted to des Gallars
some missions of the first importance : in 1551 he had come to
England with Calvin's letters to the King and the Duke of

[1] *Puritan Manifestoes*, ed. W. H. Frere and C. E. Douglas, 2nd edn., (1954),
p. 19, (Church Historical Society Series, LXXII).
[2] Quoted, R. M. Gillon, *John Davidson of Prestonpans*, (1936), pp. 262–3.
[3] *The Seconde Parte of a Register : Being a Calendar of Manuscripts under
that title intended for publication by the Puritans about 1593, and now in Dr.
Williams's Library, London*, ed. Albert Peel, (Cambridge, 1915), I, p. 106 n. 2.
[4] For des Gallars, see Eugène and Émile Haag, *La France Protestante*,
2nd edn. revised Henri Bordier, V, (Paris, 1886), cols. 298–305 ; R. M. Kingdon,
Geneva and the Coming of the Wars of Religion in France, 1555–1563, (Geneva,
1956), pp. 6–7, 11, 17, 19, 34, 46, 61, 82, (Travaux d'Humanisme et Renaissance, XXII).
[5] Schickler writes : ' Depuis le colloque de Poissy, sa situation n'avait cessé
de grandir.' (*Les Églises du Refuge*, I, p. 135.)

Somerset—that is to commend the Genevan example to the English government—and had taken the opportunity to present Edward VI with Calvin's commentary on Isaiah which he himself had translated into Latin.[1] In 1559 he had conveyed Calvin's directions to the first national synod of the French Reformed Church in Paris which had adopted a Confession of Faith and a Discipline which were virtually dictated from Geneva.[2] And now in London he was responsible for a recension of à Lasco's *Forma ac ratio* for the government of the stranger churches which retained some of the distinctive features of that interesting early experiment in Reformed church order, but otherwise remodelled it extensively on lines suggested by the *Ordonnances ecclésiastiques* of Geneva.[3] (Members of the Huguenot Society may be interested to hear that what may well prove to be a unique copy of the printed, Latin edition of des Gallars's *Forme de police ecclesiastique*, the *Forma politiae ecclesiasticae*, with its dedication to Bishop Grindal as superintendent of the foreign churches, has recently been acquired by the British Museum among the Yelverton collection of MSS., where it is bound with the MS. minutes of the Italian congregation from 1570 to 1590.)[4]

Invaluable though des Gallars's presence was for the well-being of the French congregation—Grindal told Calvin that on his arrival he had found it ' in a most disturbed condition ', but that he passed it on to his successor ' in a state of quietness and good order ' [5]—one may doubt whether such a valuable man was spared from Geneva and France merely to salvage the affairs of the refugee congregation in London. Dr. Robert M. Kingdon and Dr. H. G. Koenigsberger have both recently drawn attention to the importance of the political rôle played in the affairs of French and Dutch Calvinism by aristocratic pastors, Beza and des Gallars in France, Philippe Marnix van Sint Aldegonde in the Netherlands, men well-fitted by their social standing to act as intermediaries between the clerical leadership of the Reform

---

[1] John Strype, *Memorials of Thomas Cranmer*, (Oxford, 1840), I, p. 592.
[2] Kingdon, *Geneva and the Coming of the Wars of Religion*, p. 46.
[3] *Form de police ecclesiastique institutee a Londres en l'Eglise des Francois*, (1561). Schickler writes : ' Les principaux passages de la Discipline sont empruntés textuellement à Calvin:' (*Les Églises du Refuge*, I, p. 103.)
[4] MS. Additional 48096, (Yelverton 150).
[5] *The Zürich Letters*, 2nd series, ed. Hastings Robinson, (Cambridge, 1845), p. 96, (Parker Society).

and its princely patrons, Condé, Coligny, Orange.[1] It is more than possible that des Gallars was sent to London to develop fruitful contacts with the great patrons of English Calvinism such as Francis Russel, Earl of Bedford, and to guide the development of Elizabeth's newly-settled Church in lines acceptable to Geneva and profitable for the hard-pressed churches in France and the Low Countries. In asking Geneva for a pastor, the French in London had written : ' Quel honneur, en effet, non pas seulement pour les Églises étrangères, mais aussi pour celles d'Angleterre, si un Viret, un Théodore de Bèze, un Nicolas des Gallars, un Macar, un Colonges, s'unissait à nous ! ' [2] And when Calvin somewhat reluctantly released des Gallars from Geneva there is little doubt that he had the needs of the English Church in the forefront of his mind. ' Je deplore vivement ', he told Grindal, ' que les Églises de tout le royaume ne soient pas organisées comme tous les gens de bien le désireraient et l'avaient espéré à l'origine.' [3] This is not to say that Calvin utterly condemned the episcopal polity or even the conservative liturgy of the Church of England as Beza would condemn them within a few years, although he disapproved of the Erastianism which lay behind the shadow of episcopal forms in Elizabethan church government. He was on the best possible terms with some of the new English bishops, especially with Grindal, and Grindal himself had pressed for des Gallars's appointment, adding his personal plea to that of the French congregation.[4] Calvin, in common with the more Protestant of the English bishops and many of the most prominent lay patrons of the English Reform, had good cause for uncertainty about the course in which the English Church was pointed in these early years of the reign, and des Gallars may have been sent to strengthen the hands of those who were determined to emphasise the complete agreement of the Church of England with the continental Reformed

[1] Kingdon, *Geneva and the Coming of the Wars of Religion*, p. 6 ; H. G. Koenigsberger, ' The Organisation of Revolutionary Parties in France and the Netherlands during the Sixteenth Century ', *Journal of Modern History*, XXVII (1955), 335-51.

[2] Schickler, *Les Églises du Refuge*, III, p. 45.

[3] *Ibid.*, III, pp. 47-48.

[4] *Ibid.*, III, pp. 46-47.   Grindal wrote on 18 March 1560 : ' Je recommande à vos prières et à celles de tous les autres frères l'état de nos Églises, non encore suffisamment constituées selon notre gré.'

churches. When des Gallars left London for the last time in
1563, Grindal told Calvin that his advice and prudence had been
' of great use both to myself and our churches '.[1] It will demonstrate the omissions to which I wish to draw attention in this
paper to say that I do not know of a single modern account of
Elizabethan history which so much as mentions des Gallars's
presence in London at this time.

Des Gallars's successors included other illustrious pastors
who were hardened by years of service in exposed and dangerous
places in France. Des Gallars's successor and the pastor until
his death in 1574 was Jean Cousin, who came to London from
Caen. In 1574 the ministers were Pierre Loiseleur, seigneur
de Villiers, a contributor to the work on the Geneva New Testament,[2] and Robert le Maçon, sieur de la Fontaine—maintaining,
one notices, the tradition of employing aristocratic pastors in the
strategic London church. De la Fontaine had been des Gallars's
colleague at Orléans, an important church which was deci-
mated by the siege and massacre of 1568. Villiers had built up
the church in Rouen, where he seems to have entertained the
English presbyterian leader, Thomas Cartwright, in the spring
of 1572.[3] After Villiers had left London for Antwerp, in the
late 'seventies, there is ample evidence in the English diplomatic
correspondence of the close understanding which existed between
him and highly-placed English Calvinists, a relationship which
possibly dated from friendships formed in Geneva and Rouen in
the 'fifties. ' I pray you commend me to Monsieur de Vylliers ',
wrote Henry Killigrew, Burghley's brother-in-law, to William
Davison, English ambassador in the Netherlands, in August
1577, and asked him to assure Villiers that the troubles of Archbishop Grindal, sequestered by the Queen for his too earnest

---

[1] *Zürich Letters*, 2nd series, p. 96.

[2] He is usually stated to have been pastor from 1574 to 1575, but the
Comptes des Diacres for 1572-3 (f. 17) show him to have been in England as
early as December 1572, which suggests that he left Rouen for this country
soon after the August disturbances. (Library of the French Protestant Church,
Soho Square.) I am most grateful to the pastor of the French Church, M.
Dubois, for his courtesy in allowing me to consult this and other MSS. at Soho
Square, and to the Honorary Librarian, Miss Turner, for giving up her time
in order to introduce me to these remarkable archives. All subsequent references will be to ' Soho Square '.

[3] A. F. Scott Pearson, *Thomas Cartwright and Elizabethan Puritanism,
1535-1603*, (Cambridge, 1925), pp. 54-56.

defence of preaching and prophesying, did not extend to restraint of his personal liberty.[1] ' My harty commendations to Monsieur de Villiers ', Killigrew wrote in the following year, and five months later, ' I desire to know how Monsieur de Vylliers and his famely doe '.[2] When Walter Travers went over to Antwerp to take charge of the congregation of English merchants in that city, Villiers took part in his presbyterian ordination and acted as a constant friend and adviser to Travers and Cartwright in their ministry in the Netherlands.[3] Another English puritan who received presbyterian orders from Villiers among other Antwerp ministers was the Essex preacher, Robert Wright.[4]

One reason why some annalists of the refugee churches have underestimated the relevance of their subject for the history of the English Reformation may be their misunderstanding of what was implied in the episcopal government of the stranger churches under Elizabeth I. After 1560 the foreign churches no longer comprised an autonomous ' corpus corporatum et politicum ' and they were obliged to accept a superintendent who was not a minister elected from their own membership but the bishop of London.[5] Admittedly the government of ' monsieur l'evesque ' impeded the full participation of Dutchmen and Frenchmen in the life of the developing presbyterian churches of their own nations.[6] But it did not prevent the churches from exercising congregational government in consistory, from electing their own officers in the first instance, or from framing their own orders

---

[1] Public Record Office, S.P. 83/2/43.

[2] Public Record Office, S.P. 15/25/98, 117.

[3] Scott Pearson, *Thomas Cartwright*, pp. 56, 182–4, 193 ; S. J. Knox, *Walter Travers: Paragon of Elizabethan Puritanism*, (1962), p. 44.

[4] *Actes du Consistoire*, Hug. Soc., Q.S. XXXVIII, p. xiv.

[5] *Actes du Consistoire*, Hug. Soc., Q.S. XXXVIII, p. xiv.

[6] In June 1572 the consistory of the Dutch church in London informed its sister churches on the Continent which were urging it to accept the decrees of the first national synod of the Dutch Reformed Church held at Emden and to signify its assent to Geneva : ' Minime nobis permittendum fore, ut classicos in hoc Regno conventus habeamus, multominus, ut vel ad exteras Synodos transeamus, vel ut illorum decretis subscribamus.' (J. H. Hessels, *Ecclesiae Londino-Batavae Archivum*, II, (Cambridge, 1889), no. 117, pp. 410–11.) See also the letter from the consistory of the Dutch church to the *classis* of Walcheren, September 1574 ; (*ibid.*, no. 135, pp. 504–7). On the other hand, on 19 May 1581, the first *colloque* of the French churches in England agreed to send a minister and an elder to a synod of the Dutch Church to be held at Middelburg, ' pour témoignage de l'union que les Eglises de la langue françoise réfugiées en Angleterre veulent avoir avec les Freres qui seront assemblez au dit Synode '. *Les Actes des Colloques*, Hug. Soc., Q.S. II, p. 1.

for sermons and discipline. And to suppose that in the first ten years of the reign the powers of the superintendent implied more than a minimal limitation of the autonomy of the congregations is to misjudge totally the first bishop and superintendent under the new régime, Edmund Grindal. Grindal was thoroughly at home in international Reformed circles, anything but an insular Anglican. He had spent more than five years in continental exile, when he learned German and established the friendly contacts with many of the leaders of the continental Reformation which he was careful not to neglect as bishop of London. He was the acknowledged leader of a group of émigré bishops who were dissatisfied with the ambivalence and half-measures of the Elizabethan church settlement, and who handled the puritan clergy who refused to be bound by the rubrics of the Prayer Book with tact and sympathy. Although his duty to authority sometimes obscured this, there is no doubt that Grindal believed that ' the best reformed churches ' represented the ideal towards which the English Church should strive. While he could regard with equanimity a foreign church in London which followed its own Reformed orders, and as superintendent step gladly into a rôle far removed from that of an Anglican prelate, he advised the preacher to an English congregation which found itself in an analogous situation overseas—in Antwerp —not to use the Prayer Book ceremonies but to be guided by the usages of the churches round about him.[1] When des Gallars first paid his respects to Grindal on his arrival from Geneva, he requested that all disputes in his congregation might be determined by the bishop's authority, ' by which means our people would be more effectually kept to their duty '. But Grindal, who told the elders that ' they had obtained more than they had dared to hope for ' in des Gallars, assured him that he resigned all his authority to him, ' but that he would willingly attend if he could be of any use '.[2] Later Grindal would refer to des Gallars's successor, Jean Cousin, as ' my very dear brother in the Lord '.[3]

Grindal's conception of government and discipline was nothing

[1] Grindal to William Cole, 17 May 1564 ; Corpus Christi College, Oxford, MS. 297, f. 18.
[2] *Zürich Letters*, 2nd series, pp. 49-50.
[3] *Ibid.*, p. 170.

if not Reformed.   Consistently, throughout his career, he chose
to exercise his authority over Protestant brethren fraternally
rather than judicially.   His method of dealing with the recurrent
fractious disputes over doctrine, discipline or precedence in the
stranger churches was the method that he always preferred :
bringing the parties together and composing them.   And he did
all and more than might have been expected to prevent the disintegration of the congregations through the assimilation of their
members into their Anglican parishes.   When Gabriel Goodman,
the dean of Westminster, ordered two members of the French
congregation to worship in their parish church, Grindal upheld
the rights of the French church, but told the elders that ' nevertheless it were good to speak to the Dean of Westminster and
to tell him we had spoken to the Bishop '.[1]   After a renewed
appeal from the French congregation in January 1565, Grindal
ordered all the clergy of his diocese not to admit foreigners to
the communion in their parishes unless they brought the written
consent of their own ministers.   Someone has noted in the margin
of the Acts of the Consistory which record this gracious gesture :
' Acte de levesque remarquable '.[2]   In short, it is far truer to
say that Grindal was playing the part of a Reformed superior
pastor, representative of the civil power, than that the foreign
churches were subjected to episcopal government.   As Schickler
says, Grindal exercised ' plutôt la protection que la surveillance
et le contrôle.'   ' Vous avez en lui ', Calvin told des Gallars, ' un
fidèle et sincère protecteur de votre liberté.' [3]   Grindal was succeeded as bishop of London and superintendent of the stranger
churches in London by Edwin Sandys, who came from the same
Cumberland parish as Grindal and was his friend from boyhood.
Sandys lacked Grindal's warmth and charity, but he was a bishop
of the same churchmanship.   In 1574 he protested to the Privy
Council against a decision to prohibit the stranger churches to
admit any new members.[4]   It was only in 1577, when Sandys
gave way to John Aylmer—no friend to puritans—that the
strangers had cause to fear a new and chillier wind.   Not that
any nervousness is necessarily to be read into the decision of the

[1] *Actes du Consistoire*, Hug. Soc., Q.S. XXXVIII, pp. xxvi, 108.
[2] *Ibid.*, pp. xxvi–xxvii, 97.
[3] Schickler, *Les Églises du Refuge*, I, pp. 85–86.
[4] Hessels, *Ecclesiae Londino-Batavae Archivum*, II, no. 133, pp. 499–501.

coetus to salute ' Monsieur l'Evesque nouvellement élue pour luy recommander nos Eglises '.[1]

The mild government of Grindal was proof that the powers of a superintendent, representing the supreme authority of the Queen, were not necessarily incompatible with the liberty of a congregation to choose in the first instance its own officers and to exercise discipline through its own consistory. In their subordination to the Crown through the bishop, the foreign churches enjoyed a status not unlike that of the English parishes, particularly since virtually all English Protestants would at this time have understood episcopacy as nothing more than superintendency. ' *Quoad ministerium* ', it was believed, bishops were the equals of other ministers. It was only their powers of jurisdiction and government that marked them out from other pastors, and these they received from the Queen. So the parish churches of London and the foreign congregations alike had their superintendent in Grindal. But whereas the stranger churches had autonomous powers of discipline, there was no discipline in the parishes, only the bishop's and archdeacon's courts, regarded by the puritans as a relic of popery ; and the parishioners (in most cases) had no voice in the choice of their pastors. Moreover the foreign churches were free to adopt orders of sermons and other services which were ' most pure ', whereas Englishmen were bound to the use of a Prayer Book culled from the old popish service books.

This is to explain the position as the puritans themselves understood it. One London incumbent who was suspended from his ministry in 1565 for refusing to wear the prescribed vestments wrote at the end of his life : ' Yt semethe ryghtfull that subiects naturall receve soe much favoure as the churches of natyonall straungers have here with us. But we can not once be harde soe to obtayne. Thys with them : they an eldershippe ; we none. They frely electe the doctor and pastor ; we maye not. They their deacons and churche servauntes with dyscyplyn ; and wee notte.'[2] The same observer's view of the puritan

---

[1] Soho Square, MS. Livre de *Coetus* de l'année 1575 à 1598, p. 6. The MS. volume of Actes du Consistoire, 1578–88 leaves one in no doubt that Aylmer took less interest in the affairs of the French congregation than either of his two predecessors.

[2] Thomas Earl's notebook, Cambridge University Library, MS.Mm.1.29,f.2.

agitation in London during his life-time was that ' the stryffe
of this desyryd Refformatyon hath contynued from the tyme of
Mr. John Hooper byshope and mertir, . . . ffrom the yere
1548 [sic] unto this daye.   And yt was grauntyd to the Belgique
Neytherlanders churche, also graunted unto the Freanche
churche, the Italian churche and the Spanyshe churche, . . .
whiche natyons neyver dyd receive our Booke of Common Prayers
by Acte of Parlament to use in their temples and congregatyons
unto this daye, from 1546 [sic] unto 1600, . . . and so was
raysed a grett hart boournyng with wyse men.' [1]

In 1573 many were attributing the troubles in the Church to
the influence of the ' strange Churches, as well beyond the seas
as here among us remaining ', thereby, as the puritans thought,
' to provoke the displeasures of the Magistrates against them '.[2]
Seventeen years later, the radical puritan John Udall, giving an
account of his religion to Sir Walter Raleigh, would state that
he believed in congregational discipline by ' ministers assisted
with elders ', such as he had observed to be used in the best
reformed churches in Europe ' and even by these exiles which her
Majestie to her great honour hathe hetherto protected.' [3]   The
Genevan liturgy used by the stranger churches was an equal
incitement for the English puritans.   An anonymous set of
' Articles of the Discipline of the Church ' recommends the use of
'the liturgie used by our country men persecuted in Queen Maries
tyme, and now used in Fraunce, Scotland, Flanders, and others
for the profession of the gospell within this Citye and by other
abroade at Geneva and els where '.[4]

I believe that the contribution of the foreign congregations
to the developing puritan movement becomes particularly
significant if the activities of the puritans in London are given
their due centrality, especially in the period from 1566 to 1572.
In these six years, the puritan protest grew from a relatively
trivial objection to vestments and certain ceremonies retained
in Anglican worship to a more fundamental rejection of the

---

[1] Cambridge University Library, MS. Mm. 1.29, f. 1.
[2] *A Brief Discourse of the Troubles begun at Frankfort*, ed. Edward Arber,
(1908), pp. 21–22, (A Christian Library, I).
[3] A paper headed by Robert Beale, ' Articles sent by Mr. Udall to Sir Walter
Rawley ', British Museum, MS. Additional 48064, (Yelverton 70), f. 130 v.
[4] *Seconde Parte of a Register*, ed. Peel, I, p. 165.

Prayer book *in toto*—a protest against the whole ethos of Prayer Book worship—and of the unreformed, episcopal government of the Church. Hitherto accounts of the puritan movement have suggested that these new and more radical developments had their origin in Cambridge, where Thomas Cartwright as Lady Margaret professor of divinity enunciated the essential dogmas of presbyterianism in his lectures on the Acts of the Apostles delivered in the spring of 1570. But both my own researches and those of Dr. H. G. Owen of Reading University [1] have drawn attention to a particular puritan group in London as the crucible, so to speak, in which this new and disturbing revolt was first incandescent. Those who have posited a purely academic origin for English presbyterianism have been inclined to suggest that the cardinal doctrines of the system—a parity of pastors and churches, the congregational eldership, regional synods—were novelties in 1570 which were derived from one place only— Geneva. Yet these principles of Reformed church order were commonplaces well before 1570 and would have been known from the organization of the refugee churches in London, to name no more remote influence. The presbyterian agitation in England between 1570 and 1574 reflected an urge which was widely felt in the Reformed churches—even if it was stimulated from Geneva —to draw together in classical and synodical assemblies and through these to strive for uniformity of faith, worship and order. In April 1572, for example, Petrus Dathenus (Pieter van Bergen), writing on behalf of the Palatinate *classis*, reminded his fellow-countrymen in London of the decisions taken at the first national synod of the Dutch churches held at Emden in the previous autumn, and called upon them to notify their assent to the French Church, ' de qua nos nihil dubitare Domino Bezae et Sijnodo Gallicanarum Ecclesiarum proximo mense Maijo habendae, ante hoc tempus non nihil scripsimus '—the eighth national synod of the French Reformed Church which met at Nîmes in May 1572.[2]

---

[1] P. Collinson, ' The Puritan Classical Movement in the Reign of Elizabeth I ', unpublished London Ph.D. thesis, (1957), especially pp. 33–172 ; G. H. Owen, ' The London Parish Clergy in the Reign of Elizabeth I ', unpublished London Ph.D. thesis, (1957), especially pp. 515–40.

[2] Hessels, *Ecclesiae Londino-Batavae Archivum*, II, nos. 110, 111, pp. 391–396.

There was nothing new, in the early 1570's, in synodical organisation as such.   What was novel and distinctive in the presbyterian assertion was the claim that the particular form of church order and discipline to be found in the Calvinist churches was alone apostolic and necessary for all times and places.   It was Theodore Beza, Calvin's successor, who made this point more emphatically than any, and Beza's narrow and dogmatic conception of discipline was being quoted by the London puritans a year or two before Cartwright's famous Cambridge lectures.[1] The letters from Beza and other members of the Honourable Company of Pastors at Geneva to the English puritans [2] were received and passed on by the French congregation in London, ' a thing they do very frequently ' according to the puritan emissary Percival Wiburn, who visited Geneva and Zürich in 1567.[3]   No doubt when the English communicated with French-speaking Reformed churches across the Channel they also employed the same intermediary, as for example when ' nos Freres les Ministres Anglois ' wrote on a certain matter to the Nîmes synod of the French Reformed Church in 1572.[4]

The London puritans were served and led partly by seasoned veterans from the congregation of Marian exiles in Geneva, partly by younger men, fresh from the universities.   The movement was running to extremes in sharp reaction to the episcopal repression of nonconformist clergy which had driven it for the most part outside the parish churches and into the more or less sectarian congregations grouped around preachers who were in a state of virtual separation from the established Church.[5]   An important centre of their activities was the parish of Holy Trinity, Minories, where the parishioners exercised the right of choosing their own curates and preachers.[6]   It was in this

[1] Seconde Parte of a Register, ed. Peel, I, pp. 56, 64.
[2] See an example printed in Epistolarum Theologicarum Theodori Bezae Vezelii, I, (Geneva, 1575), no. XII, pp. 94–103.
[3] The Zürich Letters, ed. Hastings Robinson, (Cambridge, 1842), p. 190, (Parker Society).
[4] Jean Aymon, Tous les Synodes Nationaux des Eglises Reformées de France, (The Hague, 1710), I, ii, p. 122.
[5] Much material on the history of these groups is gathered in Albert Peel, The First Congregational Churches, (Cambridge, 1920) and in Champlin Burrage, The Early English Dissenters in the Light of Recent Research, 1550–1641, 2 vols., (Cambridge, 1912).
[6] E. M. Tomlinson, A History of the Minories, London, (1907), passim ; Owen, ' London Parish Clergy ', pp. 517–24.

parish, says John Stow, that they were first known as puritans.[1]
Some of these people were on the verge of an open separation.
But an able and militant young Oxford graduate, John Field,
was seeking to impress on the whole puritan movement, in
London and beyond, his Calvinist ideal of a national Reformation to be upheld by public authority.[2] To this end he and
another young preacher, Thomas Wilcox, composed in the
summer of 1572 the trenchant *Admonition to the Parliament*
which called upon Parliament to apply stringent Calvinist
remedies for the deep blemishes which still, in their opinion,
marred the face of the English Church almost beyond recognition
as a true Church of God.[3] Amongst Field's admired models
was des Gallars's form of discipline for the French congregation
in London. The copy of the *Forma politiae ecclesiasticae* which
is now to be found bound up in a volume of the Yelverton MSS.
in the British Museum [4] (which may be unique) bears John Field's
signature on the title-page and the information that he paid
fourpence for it. To find what use he may have made of his
purchase, we must look at certain proceedings in Parliament
in May 1572.

The *Admonition* embodied a declaration of open war against
the bishops and a peremptory demand that Parliament should
make a clean sweep of the existing constitution of the Church.
Not only much of the English puritan leadership—men like
Laurence Humphrey and Thomas Norton—but Beza himself
deplored this rash and headstrong course. In a letter to Jean
Cousin, minister of the French church, of 3 August 1572, Beza
asked to be sent a copy of the offensive tract and for instructions
to prevent him being ' meslés en telles procedeures bien indiscrettes
autant que i'en puis preveoir '.[5] The *Admonition* was published,
I believe, only after a last attempt had failed to provide the
puritans with a wide toleration within an episcopal polity.
This attempt embodied a proposal of great interest for our present

[1] *Three Fifteenth Century Chronicles*, ed. James Gairdner, (1880), p. 143,
(Camden Society, New Series, XXVIII).
[2] See my ' John Field and Elizabethan Puritanism ' in *Elizabethan Government and Society : Essays Presented to Sir John Neale*, ed. S. T. Bindoff,
J. Hurstfield and C. H. Williams, (1961), pp. 127–62.   *Below*, pp. 335-70.
[3] Reprinted in *Puritan Manifestoes, op. cit.*, pp. 5–55.
[4] MS. Additional 48096, (Yelverton 150).
[5] Hessels, *Ecclesiae Londino-Batavae Archivum*, II, no. 121, pp. 426-7.

theme. In May 1572 an unofficial ' Bill concerning Rites and Ceremonies ' was introduced into the House of Commons, which proposed that the penalties under the Act of Uniformity for violating and infringing the Prayer Book should remain in force only against the popishly inclined, and that the bishops should be empowered to license their clergy to omit parts of the Prayer Book in order to increase the time available for preaching or ' to use any other godlie exercise '.[1] What concerns us is the specific proposal which follows that the bishops should be enabled to consent to the use of ' such forme of prayer and mynistracion of the woorde and sacraments, and other godlie exercises of religion as the righte godlie reformed Churches now do use in the ffrenche and Douche congregation, within the City of London or elswheare in the Quenes maiesties dominions and is extant in printe '. The Speaker, Robert Bell, understood by the bill that the bishops were to be free to license their clergy to use rites and ceremonies differing from those provided in the Prayer Book ' so as the same alteracions dyd nott differ from the order now allowed and sett forth in the french and dutch churches '.[2] In debate, one member emphasised that this order of service was available in print ' and therefore wilful ignorance not to knowe it ',[3] an interesting comment on the model which des Gallars had provided.

The 1572 bill is presumptive evidence that English puritan congregations were already utilising the material provided in the printed orders of the foreign congregations. One ' godly exercise ' which they had certainly adopted, perhaps from this source, if not from à Lasco's original scheme, was the institution of ' prophesying ', in the sense of a weekly congregational conference on doctrine, which was practised in one London parish before 1566.[4]

[1] J. E. Neale, *Elizabeth I and her Parliaments, 1559–1581*, (1953), pp. 297–304. A conflated text of the earlier and later forms of the bill is printed in *Puritan Manifestoes*, pp. 149–51.

[2] Bell to Burghley, 20 May 1572 ; printed, *Puritan Manifestoes*, p. 152.

[3] The sentiment was Robert Snagge's and it was recorded by Thomas Cromwell, the parliamentary diarist, on 19 May. I am grateful to Sir John Neale for permission to consult his transcript of the diary from Trinity College, Dublin, MS. N.2/12.

[4] See my *Letters of Thomas Wood, Puritan, 1566–1577*, (1960), pp. xi–xii (Bulletin of the Institute of Historical Research, Special Supplement, no. 5). *See above*, 53-4.

The Minories was not so far from Austin Friars and Threadneedle Street and there were not so many Calvinists—of whatever
nation—in Elizabethan London that the English Reformed
were likely to be content merely to admire or even to imitate
the orders of the foreign congregations from afar. There is
evidence that some English puritans were rather actively involved in the affairs of the stranger churches, and that they
received some positive encouragement from that quarter.
With Grindal's approval, des Gallars preached in Latin twice
a week, on Mondays and Wednesdays at eight in the morning,[1]
and these sermons must have attracted a learned English audience, especially of London clergy. Moreover there always seem
to have been some Englishmen ready to receive the communion
in the French church, and one or two perhaps did so with
regularity. On 6 April 1561 the communicants included ' maistre
foulan gentilhomme englois et sa femme ' (probably William
Fuller, a member of Knox's congregation in Geneva in Mary's
reign, and later to be in repeated trouble for his puritan activities),
William Whittingham, the translator of the Geneva Bible and
future dean of Durham who must quite recently have returned from
Geneva (his wife, one recalls, was French-speaking), ' et plusieurs
aultres englois '.[2] On 3 May 1565 there is a record of a remarkable episode which it would not be hard to discredit on less
reliable evidence than the consistory minutes of the French
congregation itself. The clerk notes that on that day there was
no sermon since the church had been lent, at the request of Sir
Henry Sidney, for the baptism of his sister's child by an English
minister called Gough, ' ung de ceulx quy ne veult point porter
le bonet Cornu ny le surplys '.[3] This was John Gough, rector
of St. Peter Cornhill (the probable location of the congregational exercise of prophesying) and lecturer of St. Antholin's,
with Robert Crowley and John Philpot one of the ringleaders
of the puritan anti-vestments agitation in London a year later.[4]
The Queen was to be a sponsor at this baptism, and when she
heard that Gough was employed to officiate she sent another
minister ' avec le surplys et avec le bonet cornu lequel administry

[1] *Actes du Consistoire*, Hug. Soc., Q.S. XXXVIII, pp. xvii, 42.
[2] *Ibid.*, pp. xxvii, 38.   [3] *Ibid.*, pp. xxvii, 109.
[4] *Three Fifteenth Century Chronicles*, ed. Gairdner, pp. 135–40.

le baptesme avec une casuble sans faire sermon '.   The Earl of
Warwick was present and the Countess of Rutland represented the
Queen.   On 2 December 1565 the congregation was joined for
the communion by the puritan courtier and diplomatist Henry
Killigrew, whom we have already met as a friend of Pierre
Loiseleur de Villiers, and by his wife.[1]   Catherine Killigrew
was one of the four learned daughters of Sir Anthony Cooke of
Gidea Hall, the sister-in-law of Burghley and Sir Nicholas Bacon.
She was an intimate friend of the famous puritan preacher
Edward Dering.[2]   When she died in 1583, Calvinist divines of
three nations contributed elegiac verses to her tomb ;   the
Englishman William Chark, the Scot Andrew Melville and
Robert le Maçon de la Fontaine, pastor of the French church.[3]
In 1568 the French congregation had an even more distinguished
guest.   In that year the French ambassador reported that the
Queen's favourite, the earl of Leicester, now setting himself
up as the peculiar patron of the best Protestant preachers, had
publicly associated himself with the Reformed religion by
taking the communion at the strangers' church, ' ce que aucun
de ce conseil ny mesme seigneur notable d'Angleterre n'a jamais
faict . . .' [4]

When des Gallars first took up his ministry, Grindal asked
him to use a reasonable discretion in admitting Englishmen to
communion :   he should not encourage English schismatics who
were forsaking their own parishes, but he need not repel those
who merely wished to give expression to the unity in faith
which the two churches enjoyed.   From the French side it
was agreed that none should be offended if the English came
to communicate with them, ' a cause qui sont unis de foy avec
nous '.[5]   But with the development of schism in the English
Church, the superintendent, and for that matter the Privy
Council, could no longer afford to be so liberal.   In August

[1] *Actes du Consistoire*, Hug. Soc., Q.S. XXXVIII, p. 124.

[2] Edward Dering, *Certaine godly and comfortable letters*, in *Works*, (1597),
Sigs. C3–7.

[3] John Stow, *A Survey of the Cities of London and Westminster*, (edn. 1720),
Bk. iii, pp. 7–8.

[4] Bochetel de la Forest to King Charles IX, 25 March 1568 ; Public Record
Office, Baschet Transcripts, 31/3/26, f. 207.   I am indebted for this reference
to Professor Wallace T. MacCaffery.

[5] *Actes du Consistoire*, Hug. Soc., Q.S. XXXVIII, pp. 25, 28.

1573, at the height of the presbyterian agitation against the ministry, government and liturgy of the Elizabethan Church, Bishop Sandys complained that Edward Dering, the most prominent nonconformist in London, had conferred with the French ministers and had their consent before delivering to the Council a statement of his position with respect to the questions in controversy. Sandys asked Burghley and Leicester for a sharp letter as from the Queen or the Council to require the French neither to meddle in matters of this state, nor to admit any of the Queen's subjects to their communion.[1] On 22 October the Council (at last persuaded by an uncompromising royal proclamation[2] to take the nonconformist threat seriously) addressed a sharp letter to the Dutch church (and no doubt to the French as well) which reported the Queen's fear that ' tumultuous spirits ' among the English puritans would lead them into a misuse of their privileges. They were told that ' if there be any that, out of a wanton conceitedness, leave and come from the use and custom of their native country, and will joyne themselves with you, such wee think ought not to be received by you, that so they may not occasion discord and contention '.[3] The Dutch ministers and elders replied obediently enough that they would not take amongst them ' any English, who from such principles seek to separate themselves from their own country customs ' ; adding the incidental information that ' in our congregation are not above four English, whereof two since their comming hither from their exile, have continued amongst us. The third is one that married a Dutch woman. The fourth came in their company, and continueth for the improoving in the language.' They had communicated the wishes of the Council to the congregation.[4] Yet eight years later, in 1581, Convocation received a petition from a group of London clergy complaining of the behaviour of ' manie citizens ' who deserted

---

[1] British Museum, MS. Lansdowne 17, no. 43, ff. 96–97.

[2] See my ' John Field and Elizabethan Puritanism ', *Elizabethan Government and Society*, pp. 138–9.

[3] The original letter will be found in Hessels, *Ecclesiae Londino-Batavae Archivum*, II, no. 127, pp. 456–9. I have used Strype's translation of a copy of the document which was supplied to him by a contemporary member of the Dutch church ; (*Annals of the Reformation*, (Oxford, 1824), II, ii, pp. 517–519). Strype, however, misdates the letter to April 1573.

[4] Hessels, *op. cit.*, II, no. 130, pp. 482–5 ; Strype's rendering, *op. cit.*, II, ii, pp. 519–21.

their parishes to join with the Dutch and French congregations. The blame was laid on English preachers in Flanders and Germany—Thomas Cartwright and Walter Travers would be meant—whose lectures and other ministrations sent London merchants home again ' contemptuous and rebelling against our state ecclesiasticall '.[1]

The scope of this paper must be restricted to the earlier Elizabethan years, but looking forward briefly to the third decade of the reign, one is bound to notice how closely developments within the English puritan movement kept pace with what was happening in the foreign congregations in England. Of course we should not be surprised that the Reformed churches throughout western Europe were taking similar steps at the same time, but it is not a point which very often emerges from histories of the Elizabethan Church, largely because the post-Tractarian Anglican assumptions of so many of our church historians have not disposed them to relate the unauthorised activities of the English puritan nonconformists to the more public events in other Reformed churches in the same years. I myself spent some considerable time on a study of the conference movement among the English puritans[2] without, I think, being distinctly aware that at precisely the same time the French and Dutch communities in this country were developing a regular pattern of colloquies representing their own widely scattered congregations. Conferences of English preachers developed rather spontaneously out of the local associations of ministers for the exercise of prophesying which many bishops had encouraged before the Queen ordered their suppression in 1577, and these were assuming a more formal character from about 1582. Between 1584 and 1586 the presbyterian leaders of the movement, John Field especially, were attempting to build these bodies into a coherent, national synodical structure of the presbyterian type.[3] In effect, though these conferences were of ministers only and lacked representative elders, these were the *classes* distinctive of presbyterian church order, concealed

---

[1] Bodleian Library, MS. Wood F 30-2, p. 87; quoted, Owen, ' London Parish Clergy ', p. 551, to whom I am indebted for the reference.

[2] See my unpublished Ph.D. thesis, cited above.

[3] See my ' John Field and Elizabethan Puritanism ', *Elizabethan Government and Society*, pp. 147-60. *See below*, pp. 355-68.

under an innocuous name. Similarly, the French refugee
churches in England disguised their *classes* under the name of
'colloques'. The first of their colloquies, representing the
congregations of London, Norwich, Rye, Winchelsea and
Southampton, met in London in May 1581, and annual meetings
were held from then until 1590 with the exception of 1585.[1] In
1587 it was agreed at the sixth colloquy, held at Rye—the decision
was abortive—to hold all subsequent colloquies in London, at
the time of the St. Bartholomew's fair in late August.[2] The
English presbyterians held an annual national synod in London
at this same convenient season, when a large gathering of clergymen would not attract any unfavourable notice.[3] The Dutch
colloquies began rather earlier, in 1575, when seven congregations were represented in London.[4] Between 1586 and 1589
the English presbyterians were busy hammering out their own
Book of Discipline, which was under discussion in their *classes*
and synods up to the time when the presbyterian movement
was broken up by vigorous episcopal and governmental intervention.[5] The French churches, in their colloquies, were concerned at precisely the same time with the adaptation of des
Gallars's *Forme de police* for the needs of all the French congregations in England.[6] Fasts of the Reformed type (which involved
a day or more of preaching as well as abstinence) became more
and more frequent in the hard-pressed puritan congregations
in the 1580's,[7] and in the French churches, which had their own
troubles, they were no less popular. The minutes of the *coetus*
of the stranger churches of London contain numerous references
at this time to co-ordinated fasting. On 9 January 1588, for
example, a fast was agreed upon because of ' les afflictions des
Eglises, tant en France que au pais bas, ensemble l'estat de ce
Royaume '.[8] In August 1586 one of the motives for holding
a fast in English puritan circles in Suffolk was said to be ' the

---

[1] *Les Actes des Colloques*, Hug. Soc., Q.S. II, pp. 1–20.
[2] *Ibid.*, p. 12.
[3] See my ' Puritan Classical Movement ', pp. 484–596.
[4] Lindeboom, *Austin Friars*, pp. 111–13.
[5] My ' John Field and Elizabethan Puritanism ', *Elizabethan Government
and Society*, pp. 156–8. *See below,* pp. 364-6.
[6] *Les Actes des Colloques*, Hug. Soc., Q.S. II, pp. 3, 5, 10, 14.
[7] My ' Puritan Classical Movement ', pp. 323–46.
[8] Soho Square, MS. Livre de *Coetus*, 1575–98, p. 32.

state of the ffrenche churche ',[1] no doubt meaning the French church in London which was in sore financial straits at the time.

Some Englishmen seem to have been even more deeply involved in the affairs of the immigrant congregations than we have yet implied.   On the occasion of the election of the elders in the newly-reorganised French church on 7 July 1560, Thomas Heton, an English merchant newly arrived from Strasbourg, and two other English brethren fresh from Geneva were employed to sit at a table and count the votes.[2]   Heton was a cousin of the reformer Thomas Lever and a close friend of Grindal. He spent the whole of Mary's reign in Strasbourg and seems to have impoverished himself with the help that he gave to other exiles and later to the scheme in which he cooperated with Grindal and Utenhovius, minister of the Dutch church in London, to develop Emden as a Protestant port to rival Antwerp.[3]   In 1561, when new elders were elected in the French church, des Gallars and Utenhovius were assisted by ' mr yong . . . ministre englois '.[4]   It appears that it was not impossible for the Queen's subjects to become members of the foreign congregations and even to bear office.   In October 1564 the French church admitted to membership a servant of Sir Nicholas Throckmorton, the diplomatist, one John Roger, described as an Englishman, born near Winchester.[5]   Of course, it is more than likely that Roger had been domiciled in France and had entered Throckmorton's service there.   More intriguing is the association with the French church of John Bodley, the father of the founder of the Bodleian Library.   Bodley was another merchant whose purse-strings were loosened by the needs of his Calvinist co-religionists and he had helped to arrange the printing of the Geneva Bible during Mary's reign.   He had served with Miles Coverdale as an elder in John Knox's Geneva congregation,[6] and it is perhaps not altogether surprising to find him occupying the same office

[1] *The Presbyterian Movement in the Reign of Queen Elizabeth as Illustrated by the Minute Book of the Dedham Classis, 1582–1589*, ed. R. G. Usher, (1905), p. 58, (Camden Society, 3rd Series, VIII).

[2] *Actes du Consistoire*, Hug. Soc., Q.S. XXXVIII, p. 4.

[3] C. H. Garrett, *The Marian Exiles*, (Cambridge, 1938), pp. 182–3.

[4] *Actes du Consistoire*, Hug. Soc., Q.S. XXXVIII, p. 48.

[5] *Ibid.*, pp. 83, 86.

[6] Garrett, *Marian Exiles*, pp. 92–4.

in the community of French religious refugees in London twenty years later. On the revised form of discipline of the French church of August 1579, Bodley's signature appears first among those of the ' anciens ', immediately after that of Robert le Maçon, the pastor.[1] No less than three Englishmen, no doubt merchants with continental connections, served as elders in the comparatively weak and struggling Italian congregation. Their names were William Winthrop, Michael Blount and Bartholomew Warner, and their election is recorded on 16 September 1570 in the Acts of the Italian consistory recently acquired by the British Museum in the Yelverton collection of MSS.[2] I am particularly interested in the activities of William Winthrop. In April 1564, when the remnants of the Spanish Protestant congregation were received into the French church, Winthrop was sent for because it was known that he had helped the Spaniards by soliciting money for the poor of their congregation from ' les bons marchans englois '. He was asked if in future he would channel this assistance through the French church, but replied that men were cold in this cause and that he dared not ask more of them but that he would do his best.[3] He was as good as his word, for eight years later, in 1572, when the earliest surviving accounts of the deacons are available for inspection, we find recorded the receipt of £2 for the poor ' per les mains de M. Wyntroppe, venant de Maister Turneur, gentilhomme '.[4] Winthrop was present three years later with the martyrologist, John Foxe, the preacher, John Field, and other puritans when two Dutch Anabaptists were burned in Smithfield.[5] This was not ' to consent unto their deaths ' as might be supposed. Foxe had added his plea for mercy to those of the *coetus* of the foreign churches and of the Dutch consistory.[6] Winthrop's presence at

[1] Schickler reproduces a facsimile of this document as the frontispiece of the first volume of his *Églises du Refuge*. He gives no reference for it and I have been unable to consult the original MS.

[2] British Museum, MS. Additional 48096, (Yelverton 150), f. 17. Further references to the participation of these English elders occur on ff. 18ᵛ, 19, 32ᵛ.

[3] *Actes du Consistoire*, Hug. Soc., Q.S. XXXVIII, pp. xx, 57.

[4] Soho Square, MS. Comptes des Diacres, 1572–3, f. 1ᵛ.

[5] *Seconde Parte of a Register*, ed. Peel, I, 105.

[6] A full account of the efforts of the Dutch church in London on behalf of the Anabaptists was supplied to Hendrik van den Corput on 19 July 1581 ; (Hessels, *Ecclesiae Londino-Batavae Archivum*, II, no. 191, pp. 700–8). The MS. Livre de *Coetus*, 1575–98 at Soho Square records the decision of the Franco-Flemish community to petition the Council and to speak to the bishop of

the execution is merely a further indication of his close concern for the interests of the foreign Protestants.

This leads me to the last aspect of the relations between the refugee congregations and the English puritans with which I can deal on this occasion, and it is the pleasantest to record. There is no doubt that the puritans were foremost among those charitably minded Englishmen who collected and gave money for the support of the poor among the strangers. ' To the aflicted churches, either of the straungeres or of our owne, tenne pounds ' runs the will of Robert Smith, servant to the Northamptonshire puritan gentleman, George Carleton,[1] which his master helped him to compose in 1573.[2] The subject of the international organisation of relief for needy Protestant communities and the financing on an international scale of Protestant enterprise, educational and military as well as merely charitable, is an enormous and largely neglected field, and it would be foolhardy for me to embark upon even a corner of it in the closing paragraphs of an already prolix essay. All that I can hope to do on this occasion is to indicate the flow of funds which more than anything else served to bind the godly English puritans to their French and Dutch co-religionists. If one examines the lists of receipts in the earliest extant account-book of the French deacons which runs from November 1572 to December 1573, and if one has some knowledge of the leading personnel, lay and clerical, of Elizabethan puritanism, familiar names will at once leap out from the page and others will painfully follow, so soon as they can be disentangled from the curious orthography of the far from bilingual French scribe. Robert Johnson, Sir Nicholas Bacon's puritan chaplain (' ministre de melord kuipre '), gives a mark;[3] Monsieur Lever brings £13 6s. 8d. from the mayor and aldermen of Leicester, a town where the godly earl

London to moderate the sentence passed on the Anabaptists, emphasising ' la simplicité de ces gens ' (p. 3). For Foxe's efforts on their behalf, see *Acts and Monuments*, ed. Josiah Pratt, introduction by John Stoughton, (n.d.), I, pp. 51–52.

[1] For Carleton, see Neale, *Elizabeth I and her Parliaments, 1559–1581*, pp. 183, 209–11.

[2] Principal Probate Registry, Somerset House, Wills Proved in the Prerogative Court of Canterbury, 23 Martyn. I owe this reference to the kindness of Miss Katharine Longley, late of the Surrey County Record Office.

[3] Soho Square, MS. Comptes des Diacres, 1572–3, f. 1.

of Huntingdon, the leading magnate of the shire, saw to it
that there was ample puritan preaching ;[1] and Huntingdon's
brother, Sir Francis Hastings, one of the most zealous of Elizabethan puritan gentlemen, brings £10 4s. ' venant des gentils
hommes de conté de Lecestre '.[2] Villiers brings ten shillings
from Thomas Cartwright.[3] William Whittingham, now dean
of Durham and no longer the radical that he once was, is nevertheless not forgetful of his old Calvinist friends and sends £10
by William Williams, who had been a fellow-member of the
English congregation in Geneva in Mary's days ;[4] Whittingham
had sent forty shillings in March 1563.[5] On another occasion
Williams, who was brother-in-law to another Genevan veteran
of whom I have written elsewhere, Thomas Wood, himself gives
£1.[6] A total of £22 is received from ' Monsieur le compte de
Bedfort ' ;[7] £21 3s. 4d. ' des fidelles de la conté de Bucking-
ham ' ;[8] and £10 from ' la conptes de Suceques ', the foundress
of Sidney Sussex College, Cambridge.[9] A group of young men
from Grays Inn, including Nicholas Fuller, later a celebrated
puritan opponent of the ecclesiastical courts, sends £24.[10]
Edmund Chapman, the town preacher of Bedford and later
lecturer of Dedham in Essex and leader of the puritan *classis*
in that part of the country, brings £6 13s. 4d. from various
benefactors in Bedfordshire.[11] John Bodley brings the same
sum from Alderman Richard Martin, Master of the Mint and
host to Cartwright in his house in Cheapside at this time.[12]

The puritans' own papers shed some light on the way that
these funds were solicited and collected. In the 1580's the
French community suffered extreme hardship and made direct
approaches to the conferences of puritan ministers in several
counties. A letter survives from the ministers Jean Castel

---

[1] Soho Square, MS. Comptes des Diacres, 1572–3, f. 17.
[2] *Ibid.*, f. 30.
[3] *Ibid.*, f. 17. If ' monsieur quartier, englois ' was meant for Cartwright,
which I think is probable. Cartwright had been Villiers's guest in Rouen a
few months earlier ; (see p. 535 n. 3 above).
[4] Soho Square, MS. Comptes des Diacres, 1572–3, f. 41v.
[5] *Actes du Consistoire*, Hug. Soc., Q.S. XXXVIII, p. 99.
[6] Soho Square, MS. Comptes des Diacres, 1572–3, f. 62v. See my *Letters
of Thomas Wood, Puritan, 1566–1577*.
[7] Soho Square, MS. Comptes des Diacres, 1572–3, ff. 72v, 145.
[8] *Ibid.*, f. 17v.   [9] *Ibid.*, f. 41v.   [10] *Ibid.*, f. 17v.
[11] *Ibid.*, f. 41v.   [12] *Ibid.*, f. 145.

and Robert le Maçon ' to our lovinge brethren Mr. Pigge,
Mr. Dyke, and the rest of our brethern of Buckingshier and
Bedfordshire ' [1] which outlines the history of the church and
its present difficulties and asks for relief.[2]   It was perhaps a
copy of the same letter which was produced in the conference
of puritan ministers meeting in the neighbourhood of Dedham
on the Suffolk–Essex border, of which the minutes are still
extant.   On 27 June 1586 ' Mr. D. Chapman shewed a letter
that came from the ffrench churche requiring aide and relieff,
to which every one professed themselves willing to helpe toward
it so much as they could '.[3]   Two months later it was agreed
not to make a public collection ' bicause the people were not so
much charged, but to deale privately with the best affected '.[4]
This seems to confirm that the needs of the Protestant immigrants were recognised to be the responsibility of the preachers
and other initiated puritans rather than of the population at
large.   The almost conspiratorial way in which the puritans
organised their charity attracted the suspicious attention of
Richard Bancroft, later archbishop of Canterbury and at this
time the enemy of the puritans and the exposer of their clandestine ways.   They used, he reported, ' to make collection of
money for their brethren that travell for them beyond the Seas,
and the monye gathered is commonlye delivered to one Field
a Preacher in the Citie, and one Culverwell in Tamyse streete '.[5]
John Field, the Admonitionist, we already known.   Richard
Culverwell, a member of the Mercers' Company and uncle of a
celebrated Essex preacher, Ezechiel Culverwell, later bequeathed
to his daughter Judith ' the chaine of golde which the quene of
Navar gave me, willing her safely to kepe and preserve the
same, and after her deathe to leave it to some childe of her

[1] Oliver Pig was beneficed first in Colchester and then in Rougham, Suffolk,
and later (with an interval in the Home Counties) he appeared at Dorchester,
Dorset.   William Dyke was an unbeneficed preacher successively at Yarmouth,
Rochford and Coggeshall and in the parish of St. Michael's, St. Albans.   In
1587 Dyke and Pig represented Hertfordshire in a national puritan synod held
in Cambridge.   (British Museum, MS. Harley 7029, p. 128.)   Nothing is known
to connect either of these preachers with Buckinghamshire or Bedfordshire,
but in 1586–7 they seem to have been the leading presbyterians in the Home
Counties.
[2] Seconde Parte of a Register, ed. Peel, I, p. 156.
[3] Presbyterian Movement, ed. Usher, p. 57.   [4] Ibid., p. 58.
[5] Tracts Ascribed to Richard Bancroft, ed. Albert Peel, (Cambridge, 1953),
p. 12.

bodye lawfullye begotten as a remembraunce of the honorable
zeale of that good quene, whiche franckly gave that chaine to
me, and manye other her jewells of greate value to others for
the furtheraunce and defence of the Ghospell and suche as
sincerely professed the same '.   John Bodley, whom we have
already found serving as an elder of the French congregation,
was appointed an overseer of Culverwell's will.[1]

If the Protestant strangers found themselves quite literally
in the debt of their English friends, as the queen of Navarre's
pawned jewels remind us, this paper may have shown that in
the less tangible sphere of church polity and worship, the English
Reformed were indebted to the immigrant communities settled
among them.   It was this obligation which the puritans of
the Long Parliament would acknowledge in 1641 when, after
the long ordeal of Archbishop Laud's onslaught on their privileges, the Dutch of Austin Friars and the French of Threadneedle
Street would obtain a new guarantee of security from the Act
of Parliament ' for settlinge the free exercise of Religion and
Discipline for the reformed Forreine Churches in this Kingdom
accordinge to the Order of their Churches beyond the seas '.[2]

---

[1] Principal Probate Registry, Somerset House, Wills Proved in the Prerogative Court of Canterbury, 9 Windsor.   Culverwell's will was drawn up on
1 December 1584.
[2] Lindeboom, *Austin Friars*, p. 147.

10

THE ROLE OF WOMEN IN THE ENGLISH REFORMATION ILLUSTRATED BY THE LIFE AND FRIENDSHIPS OF ANNE LOCKE

THE notable part played by women in the Reformation has rarely been given its due recognition in English historical studies. In recent years Professor Wallace Notestein has written with characteristic authority and grace on 'The English Woman, 1580-1650,'[1] but one does not learn from this essay that the English women of this age had any religious propensities at all. And leaving aside the more prominent figures such as Queen Catherine Parr, Lady Jane Grey, and Catherine Brandon, duchess of Suffolk, women make but few appearances in most accounts of the English Reformation. This is no doubt only one symptom of the tendency of so many of our histories to dwell upon the officially inspired aspects of the Reformation to the neglect of the spontaneous and the local; to be concerned with the making of settlements and their enforcement rather than with the means by which Protestantism actually spread in families, towns, and other communities. And of course there are special factors which obscure the female contribution to history, the legal disabilities of the sex, which so often hide the married woman and allow us to catch glimpses only of the widow, a 'person' in law. Yet in France, where by the nature of the case a more sensitive historical criticism has had to be directed towards what Americans might call the grass-roots of Protestantism, the supreme importance of women in its propagation has not been missed. Professor Romier, for example, has written: 'Plus on étudie les commencements de la Réforme dans les provinces, plus l'action

---

[1] In *Studies in Social History: A Tribute to G. M. Trevelyan*, ed. J. H. Plumb, 1955, 69-107.

féminine y apparaît considérable... C'était le plus souvent par les femmes, mères ou épouses, que la Réforme gagnait les familles de l'aristocratie et du peuple...' And he notes 'un zèle enflammé et une inflexible ténacité' in 'les huguenotes.' [1] In England, studies devoted to Elizabethan Roman Catholicism, an analogous movement of unauthorised religious idealism, have for long recognised that the staunchest and most zealous recusants were often women.

But the same observation was often made of the more fervent Protestants by their contemporaries. When vestiarian conformity was first enforced on the London clergy in 1566 it provoked more than one female riot, and Bishop Grindal was 'howtyd at' in one church with cries of 'ware horns,' 'especially the wymen.' [2] And at the end of the reign the diarist Manningham described the principal puritan auditory of St Anne's, Blackfriars, as 'a great congregacion, specially of women,' wealthy and fashionably dressed women according to another, hostile observer.[3] Richard Hooker notes that 'most labour hath been bestowed' among the Puritans 'to win and retain towards this cause them whose judgments are commonly weakest by reason of their sex,' and this, he believes, because women are naturally 'propense and inclinable to holiness.' Moreover, they are character-ised by 'the eagerness of their affection, that maketh them, which way soever they take, diligent in drawing their husbands, children, ser-vants, friends and allies the same way.' The Puritans knew how to exploit both good and bad feminine qualities. Their 'natural inclina-tion unto pity' makes women more bountiful towards needy preachers than their husbands. And even their tendency to gossip may be put to good use, for women are marked by the 'singular delight which they take in giving very large and particular intelligence, how all near about them stand affected as concerning the same cause.' [4]

These judicious remarks may serve instead of any general dis-cussion of why women have sometimes been inclined to an intensity of religious enthusiasm not so often found in their husbands, a problem which lies beyond my present scope and my competence.

[1] Lucien Romier, *Le Royaume de Catherine de Médicis: La France à la Veille des Guerres de Religion*, Paris 1922, II, 234-40.

[2] *The Remains of Archbishop Grindal*, ed. William Nicholson, Parker Society 1843, 288-9; *Three Fifteenth-Century Chronicles*, ed. J. Gairdner, Camden Society n.s., XXVIII (1880), 140.

[3] *The Diary of John Manningham, 1602-3*, ed. John Bruce, Camden Society, XCIX (1868), 101, 74-5.

[4] *Works*, ed. J. Keble, revised R. W. Church and F. Paget, 1888, I, 152-3.

But we may note in passing two factors which may help to account for the strong force of attraction which undoubtedly drew together English protestant divines and women of the higher ranks of society, the one theological and pastoral, the other social. These women belonged to a Church which had only recently abandoned the regular practice of spiritual direction, while laying great emphasis on the doctrine of election, which most of these ladies seem to have found perplexing. From the 'godly and comfortable letters' which the preachers addressed to them it is apparent that women sought assurance on this matter especially, and that they leant on the preachers as a Catholic would lean on his confessor. Thomas Cartwright writes to one of his female correspondents in the 'fearefull temppest' of her perplexities.[1] Most of such letters can be reduced to one simple exhortation: 'Most hartilie I beseech you, good madam, goe on forward and faint not in the course of godlines.' [2] The preacher Thomas Wilcox corresponded in this vein in the 1570s with the countess of Bedford, the countess of Sussex (foundress of Sidney Sussex College), Lady Anne Bacon, Lady Walsingham, Lady Mary Grey, and other ladies.[3] Secondly we must remember that some of these gentlewomen and merchants' wives had received a liberal education and that many enjoyed a degree of personal liberty which were shining achievements of the society to which they belonged. The erudition of a number of choice girls of the generation of Lady Jane Grey perhaps needs no emphasis, but one is inclined to forget how liberal the treatment of women in general could seem to the eye of a foreign observer. The Dutchman Van Meteren noted that when not engaged in managing their households, English middle-class women spent their time 'in walking and riding, in playing at cards or otherwise, in visiting their friends and keeping company, conversing with their equals (whom they term *gosseps*) and their neighbours, and making merry with them at child-births, christenings,

---

[1] Two letters from Cartwright to 'Mrs D.B.', Corpus Christi College, Oxford, MS 294, ff. 163-83; printed in part, *Cartwrightiana*, ed. Albert Peel, Elizabethan Nonconformist Texts, I (1951), 105-8.

[2] Edward Dering to Lady Elizabeth Golding, n.d., printed in *Certaine godly and comfortable letters*, in Dering's *Workes*, 1597, Sigs. C7-8; Lady Golding is identified from a copy of the letter in Dering's hand in the Kent Archives Office, Maidstone, MS Dering U 350, C1/1, f. 3. I am indebted to the County Archivist of Kent, Dr Felix Hull, for permission to make several citations from the Dering Papers in his care.

[3] Various dedicatory epistles in Wilcox's published works; notes by Roger Morrice on a folio volume of Wilcox's letters in MS no longer extant, Dr Williams's Library, MS Morrice 'A Chronological Account of Eminent Persons,' II, 617 (2), (4).

churchings . . . and funerals; and all this with the permission and knowledge of their husbands, as such is the custom.' [1] The example of modern Islamic societies leads one to expect the enthusiastic, even violent adoption of political causes by a partially emancipated womanhood. Translated into sixteenth-century categories, we are perhaps witnessing something of the same sort in the vigorous religious partisanship of the women of that time. And in a society of arranged marriages, in which the wives nevertheless had leisure to cultivate religious neuroses and sufficient freedom to move outside the household, it is not to be wondered at if an intimate friendship with some physician of the soul was not seldom the result. A theme which creeps into some of these letters is this: 'Hath your husband beene unkind to you? Beare it and you shal winne him at the last; if not, thank God that you can continue loving and obedient even unto an unkind husband.' [2]

One could speak of many godly matrons in Tudor England, but at this point I propose to leave generalities and to concentrate our attention on one, best known to posterity as Anne Locke, although she won a mention from Lady Stenton under the name of Anne Prowse. [3] In all, this lady had four names, her own and those of her three husbands, and she might as well have borne a fifth, that of John Knox, for no one was ever closer to the Scottish reformer. In all these roles, and under all her names, the career of Mrs Locke has something of interest in it, and I propose to attempt what has not, I think, been done before, and draw her life together as a whole.

Anne Locke was the elder daughter of Stephen Vaughan, an entrepreneur and diplomatist of the reign of Henry VIII, whose diverse interests have been the subject of a recent monograph by Professor W. C. Richardson. [4] Vaughan was the son of a London mercer and himself an active Merchant Adventurer. Common business interests seem to have drawn him into contact with Thomas Cromwell and a career in government service. From 1538 he was governor of the Merchant Adventurers' factory at Antwerp besides

---

[1] W. B. Rye, *England as Seen by Foreigners in the Days of Elizabeth and James the First*, 1865, 72.

[2] Edward Dering to Mrs Honeywood, 19 April n.y., Dering, op. cit. Sigs. C 2ᵛ-3; Mrs Honeywood identified from MS Dering U 350, C1/1, f. 5.

[3] D. M. Stenton, *The English Woman in History*, 1957, 136.

[4] *Stephen Vaughan, Financial Agent of Henry VIII. A Study of Financial Relations with the Low Countries*, Louisiana State University Studies, Social Science Series, III, Baton Rouge 1953.

acting, in effect, as the permanent financial agent for the English government from that time until 1546.[1] As for his religion, with one foot in Cromwell's entourage and another in the Antwerp trade, it is not surprising that Vaughan was moving in these years into a definitely protestant position, part of that largely unrecorded but highly significant process of conversion which was going forward steadily in the thirties and forties. In 1530 Vaughan had been sent to Flanders to persuade William Tyndale to return to England and bend his pen to the king's policies. Although, as he wrote in his own defence, 'neither Lutheran nor yet Tyndalin,' Vaughan's despatches show an utterly untheological mind predisposed to heresy, and one understands why he was regarded with enduring suspicion by Sir Thomas More. For his own faith, he wrote, 'I have the holy scripture, given to me by Christ's church, and that is a learning sufficient for me, infallible and taught by Christ.' When Tyndale was arrested in 1535, Vaughan urged Cromwell to intervene to save his life.[2] By 1546 there is very little doubt of what his religious profession had become. His first wife and the mother of his three children, a woman of some culture, 'witty and housewifely,' had died in the previous year, and he now sought 'a sad, trusty and womanly matron' to succeed her. He chose Margery Brinklow, the widow of the London mercer who had written that bitter and excessive diatribe, *The Complaynt of Roderyck Mors*. She brought him only a small estate, but Vaughan was content to quote Scripture: 'Riches is the gift of God, but an honest woman that feareth God is above all riches.' So the probability is that Anne Vaughan, now perhaps in her early teens, spent some of these most formative years in the care of a stepmother of uncompromising protestant profession.[3]

Stephen Vaughan died in the winter of 1549-50, a substantial parishioner of St Mary Bow, Cheapside, leaving a twelve-year-old son, Stephen, and two daughters, Anne and Jane, who were older but still minors and unmarried.[4] Some time in the next six years Anne was married to Henry Locke (or Lok), a mercer with interests in Antwerp and her father's neighbour in Cheapside. Locke came of a

[1] Ibid. 1-20; *D.N.B.* art. Vaughan.
[2] Richardson, op. cit. 25-34; J. F. Mozley, *William Tyndale*, 1937, 207-10.
[3] Richardson, op. cit. 21-2; *Henry Brinklow's Complaynt of Roderyck Mors*, ed. J. M. Cowper, Early English Text Society, Extra Series XXII, 1874; *D.N.B.* art. Brinklow.
[4] Richardson, op. cit. 79, 23; *Abstracts of Inquisitions Post Mortem Relating to the City of London*, I, ed. George S. Fry, Index Library, 1896, 85-7; Principal Probate Registry, Somerset House, P.C.C. wills, 5 Coode.

long line of mercers. His great-grandfather, John Locke, was sheriff of London in 1460; his father, Sir William Locke, who died in 1550, was a friend of Henry VIII and as sheriff helped to conduct Somerset to the Tower in October 1549. Another of Sir William's thirteen sons was Michael Lok, the famous traveller, a friend of Sir Martin Frobisher and an early adventurer in the Cathay and Levant Companies.[1] Michael Lok's second wife was the widow of Caesar Adelmare and thus the mother of that highly successful Elizabethan official who took the name of Julius Caesar, so that Anne Locke was Caesar's aunt by marriage.[2] The Lockes seem to have been Protestants from the generation of Sir William, and their numerous connections, many within the closed circle of their business associates, suggest that a study of early Protestantism in the Mercers' Company would prove rewarding. For example, Thomas Wood, the friend and companion of William Whittingham, later an elder at Geneva and an active member of the organised Puritan Movement in Elizabethan England, seems to have been a mercer and a factor to Henry Locke before his departure for Frankfurt in 1554.[3] However, Henry Locke himself would appear to have been a somewhat formal Protestant, cast in another mould from that of his wife. The Lockes were also a cultivated family, and more than one of them had some literary pretensions. Michael Lok translatéd part of Peter Martyr's *Historie of the West Indies*.[4] Henry Locke, Anne's husband, could write Latin in an elegant Italian hand,[5] and their son, Henry Locke, was an indifferent religious poet, author of a pedestrian versification of Ecclesiastes, 'paraphristically dilated in English poesie'[6] and of two hundred religious sonnets, published in 1593 as *Sundry Christian Passions*, besides some scores of secular sonnets addressed to many late Elizabethan notables, with which he attempted to advance an equally unfruitful career as a courtier.[7] His cousin, Michael

[1] *D.N.B.* arts. Sir William Locke, Henry Locke (the younger), Michael Lok.

[2] In 1590, when Anne Locke was married to Richard Prowse of Exeter and Caesar Master of Requests, Prowse tried to exploit the relationship to assist a Chancery suit concerning a £20 annuity which his wife claimed against 'Mr Locke, her adversarie'; B.M. MS Lansdowne 163, f. 379.

[3] See my *Letters of Thomas Wood, Puritan, 1566-1577*, Bulletin of the Institute of Historical Research, Special Supplement no. 5, November 1960, iv. *See above*, 45-108.

[4] *De Novo Orbe, or the Historie of the West Indies*, 1612.

[5] An example of his calligraphy is noted on p. 266 below.

[6] *Ecclesiastes, otherwise called The Preacher*, 1597.

[7] Printed in *Miscellanies of the Fuller Worthies' Library, Poems by Henry Lok, Gentleman, (1593-1597)*, ed. A. B. Grosart, 1871.

Cosworth, son of one of Sir William Locke's daughters married to yet another London mercer, contributed commendatory verses to Henry Locke's *Ecclesiastes* and himself turned the Psalms into English metre in a version which was widely circulated in MS.[1] As we shall see, Anne Locke was not out of place in this family of pious poetasters.

John Knox first met Anne Locke in the winter of 1552-3, when he wrote to his future mother-in-law, Mrs Elizabeth Bowes, from London and described himself sitting with 'thrie honest pure[2] wemen,' sharing their infirmities and their tears.[3] One of these may well have been Anne Locke, another the wife of a merchant called Hickman, and in the later months of 1553 Knox was living with the Lockes and the Hickmans before his departure for the Continent.[4] Most of Knox's biographers have had their say about his friendship with Mrs Locke,[5] but none has handled it with more perception and tact than Robert Louis Stevenson in a little-known essay, 'John Knox and his Relations to Women.'[6] Stevenson felt with some justification that Anne Locke was the woman that Knox loved best. She was pious and learned, and yet lacked the morbid scrupulosity which made Elizabeth Bowes a spiritual hypochondriac. Certainly, as Professor Croft Dickinson has remarked, Knox's letters to Mrs Locke reveal aspects of his character of which we should have remained in ignorance if they had never met.[7] There are thirteen letters in the series, extending from 1556 until 1562, and besides containing an eloquent memorial of Knox the man, the later letters carry valuable reports of events in Scotland after his return in 1559.

The first letters were written by Knox in Geneva to Mrs Locke in London, and with the scarcely concealed motive of inciting her to leave her husband and family and to join God's saints in exile. In November 1556 he wrote: 'Ye wryt that your desyre is ernist to sie me. Deir Sister, yf I suld expres the thrist and langoure whilk I haif

[1] *D.N.B.* art. Cosworth.

[2] I.e. poor.

[3] *Works of John Knox*, ed. David Laing, III (1854), 379-80.

[4] Thomas McCrie, *Life of John Knox*, 3rd ed., Edinburgh 1814, I, 114.

[5] Perhaps the most discreet comment is that of Dr McCrie who represents Knox's letter inviting her to Geneva as having been written to 'Mr Locke.'

[6] Originally published in *Macmillans Magazine*, Sept. and Oct. 1875; reprinted in *Familiar Studies of Men and Books*, Tusitala ed. of the *Works*, XXVII, s.d., 202-44.

[7] *John Knox's History of the Reformation in Scotland*, ed. William Croft Dickinson, I, lxxxiii-lxxxv.

had for your presence, I suld appeir to pass measure.' [1] In his next
letter, written on 9 December, he attempted to draw her to Geneva
with that classic phrase which has lost some of its original freshness
for university teachers and examiners. In spite of her husband's
opposition and 'so gud occasioun as God hath now offrit yow to
remane whair ye ar,' Knox longed that it would please God 'to gyd
and conduct your self to this place, whair I nether feir nor eschame
to say is the maist perfyt schoole of Chryst that ever was in the erth
since the dayis of the Apostillis.' [2] Five months later, on 8 May,
Mrs Locke arrived in Geneva with two infants, Harrie and Anne,
and a maid, but without her husband. Little Harrie was, of course,
the future poet; Anne was buried within four days of their arrival.[3]
Mrs Locke's desertion of her husband for the cause of religion was
not without parallel. Romier tells of a citizen of Nîmes whose wife
had decamped to Geneva taking the portable assets of the household
with her, and who complained to Calvin that plenty of other women
would like to do the same, on the pretext that their protestant faith
received no encouragement from their husbands.[4] Anne Locke must
have been an asset to the congregation of English exiles gathered in
Geneva. Part of her time was spent in translating Calvin's sermons
on the song of Hezekiah from Isaiah xxxviii, the first of her literary
ventures to be published. This she dedicated to that intrepid
adventurer and fellow-exile Catherine Bertie, dowager duchess of
Suffolk. Discoursing elegantly on the diseases of the soul and their
cure, a characteristic feminine theme, she wrote pleasantly: 'This
receipte God the heavenly Physitian hath taught, his most excellent
Apothecarie Master John Calvine hath compounded, and I, your
grace's most bounden and humble, have put into an Englishe box and
do present unto you.' The sermons are followed by *A meditation of
a penitent sinner*, a metrical paraphrase of the fifty-first Psalm, perhaps Knox's work, which 'was delivered me by my frend with whom
I knew I might be so bolde to use and publishe it as pleased me.' [5]
A copy of this little volume in the British Museum[6] bears on the

[1] Laing, ed. cit. IV (1864), 237-9.

[2] Ibid. 239-41.

[3] Charles Martin, *Les Protestants Anglais Réfugiés à Genève au Temps de Calvin,
1555-1560*, Geneva 1915, 64, 333, 338.

[4] Romier, op. cit. II, 236.

[5] *Sermons of John Calvin upon the songe that Ezechias made after he had bene sicke
and afflicted by the hand of God, conteyned in the 38 chapiter of Esay*, London 1560, Sig.
A 3.; *A meditation*, sig. Ai.   [6] Press-mark 696.a.40.

fly-leaf what is surely one of the most curious and touching comments on a sixteenth-century marriage partnership: 'Liber Henrici Lock ex dono Annae, uxoris suae, 1559.'

Knox left Geneva for the last time in January 1559 and within a month Mrs Locke was asking why he had not written and if he had already forgotten her. In April he wrote from Dieppe:

Of nature I am churlish, and in conditions different from many: Yet one thing I ashame not to affirme, that familiaritie once throughlie contracted was never yet brocken on my default... However it be, as tuiching remembrance of yow, it cannot be, I say, the corporall absence of one year or two that can quenche in my hart that familiar acquaintance in Christ Jesus, which half a yeare did engender, and almost two yeares did nourish and confirme.[1]

This letter contained strangely ambiguous advice for a Geneva congregation uncertain whether or not to entrust itself to the inadequately reformed Church of Elizabeth. As Knox put it later: 'That we ought not to justifie with our presence such a mingle mangle as now is commaunded in your kirks,' but that those who stayed away 'onlie for negligence' were to be condemned. Mrs Locke herself had told Knox her own reasons for not 'assisting to their assemblie,' which Knox implied were rather superficial—objections to the surplice and 'external monuments of idolatrie.' But his rule for these problems of conscience was the same puritan maxim which she had so often heard from his mouth: 'That in the Lord's actioun nothing ought to be used that the Lord Jesus hath not sanctified, nather by precept nor by practise.' [2] The next letter, of 3 May, came from Edinburgh, and the next, of 23 June, from St Andrews, and there were five more in the course of eight months, packed with reports of the rapidly developing Scottish scene.[3] Knox relied on Mrs Locke to pass on this news to other members of the Geneva congregation, and to convey messages to Christopher Goodman, Miles Coverdale, John Bodley, and others. It may or may not be significant that among the many personal messages which Knox channelled through Mrs Locke during the next three years—including more than one compliment to Michael Lok and his wife, whom Knox had never met—there is hardly a word for her husband.

Anne Locke was in Frankfurt in late March and was back in her

[1] Laing, ed. cit. VI (1864), 11-15.
[2] Ibid. 83-5.
[3] Ibid. 21-7, 30, 83-5, 100-1, 103-4, 107-9.

husband's house in Cheapside by mid-June 1559, when Knox wrote:

Communicate the contents heirof . . . with all faithfull, but especiallie with the afflicted of that little flock now dispersed, and destitute of these [*sic*] pleasaunt pastures in which they sometime fed abundantlie. If anie remaine at Geneva, lett ather this same, or the double of it be sent unto them, and likewise unto me deir brother, Mr Goodman. . .

In November he had further instructions: to send Calvin's latest works, including the last, definitive edition of the *Institutes*; and to influence the English faithful to send money for the support of the protestant army in Scotland—otherwise 'if we perishe in this our interprise, the limits of Londoun will be straiter than they are now within few yeeres.' 'I cannot weill write to anie other, because the actioun may seeme to appertaine to my countrie onlie.' In February 1560 he wrote:

I know not what of our brethren of Geneva be with you; but to such as be there, I beseeche you to say that I think that I myself doe now find the truthe of that which oft I have said in their audience, to witt, that after our departure frome Geneva sould our dolour beginne.

In October 1561 he sent her an early copy of the Scottish Confession of Faith, in quires, unbound;[1] in May 1562, the last letter that we have.[2]

With the end of this correspondence, we lose sight of Mrs Locke for more than ten years. During this period we can assume that she held a commanding and respected position among the London 'godly,' who began to earn the label of 'puritan' in the troubles about church ceremonies and discipline which began in 1566. In 1571 her husband died after a lingering illness. His will[3] bequeathed all his worldly goods to his wife and appointed her sole executrix. A woman of Anne Locke's qualities and substance was not allowed to remain a widow for long, and perhaps we should not be surprised that she now married, not another mercer, but the godliest and most promising young preacher of the day, Edward Dering, a successor, surely, to Knox rather than to Henry Locke. One of Dering's letters of proposal survives[4]—no doubt the decisive one—and this is surely the

---

[1] Ibid. 129-31.

[2] Ibid. 140-1.

[3] Principal Probate Registry, Somerset House, P.C.C. wills, 39 Honey; made 28 January 1570/1 when he was 'sicke and weake in bodie,' proved 31 October 1571.

[4] Kent Archives Office, Maidstone, MS Dering U 350, C1/2, ff. 28ᵛ-29ʳ. The Dering Papers include two collections of Dering's letters (U 350, C1/1, 2), most of which

earliest extant document of this kind to have been penned by a clergyman of the Church of England. In it Dering mingles an obsessive puritan conscientiousness with more normal instincts and calculations in a way that I find utterly disarming, and Mrs Locke must have found it equally pleasing:

Thoughe I atempte nothyng but that which ys verye laufull and becomethe any Christian in plac and condition agreeable to every mane's estate, yet our nature is so full of nedeles shamfastnes that bothe nowe it makythe me almoste afearde to write unto you, and sync my last letters it hathe made me carefull to shunne your good companye.

He depended upon a trustworthy intermediary, 'Mysterys Martin,' to assure her of the state of his feelings. This Mrs Martin was probably the wife of Richard Martin, goldsmith and Master of the Mint, a notable Puritan who entertained Cartwright on the eve of his exile in 1573. In the same year Mrs Martin was reported by Bishop Grindal to have been the stationer in her house in Cheapside for the first impression of Cartwright's *Replie* to John Whitgift's *Answer to the Admonition*.[1] And in 1584 she would help to nurse one of the Scottish presbyterian ministers in exile in England through his last illness, lavishing on him expensive medicines, 'so careful was she of his health and restoring.'[2] 'Yf God shall worke all that I desyre,' Dering went on, with rather more piety than tact,

it is nether the first nor the gretest benefit that I have receevid. Yf he shall worke otherwise, I trust his grac shall gide me that I shall accompte best of myne owne will when it is framed unto his. In this mynde, good Mysterys Locke, I write unto you as as [*sic*] before, sekinge you alone, whome the grace of God in myne opinion hathe made a good possescion, and my minde is so setled (and yet in the fear of God) that nether as I am I wolde remove it unto any, nether yet yf I were as highe as in the world I colde rise, I wold change it from you; and you shall do as the Lorde shall move you. Yf your affection shalbe enclyned as I doo wyshe it to be bent, God's name be praised. Yf you shall better like other where, I pray God blesse you. I wyll endure my losse under thys hope: when we shall have better eies that shalbe able to se God, our faythe shall lead us bothe into a happye societie. . . . But for the worlde, I am at a pointe, and whensoever I shall thinke of you, I wyll think of you with the Lorde, where your body shalbe better. . . For the worldlye estate in which I

occur among the *Godly and comfortable letters* (earliest extant edition in Dering's *Workes*, 1597). The letter to Mrs Locke (which is undated) does not appear in the published collection.

[1] Grindal, *Remains*, ed. cit. 347–8.
[2] B.M. MS Additional 4736, f. 166ᵛ.

hope to lyve, I will signyfie somwhat that you shall not thynk that I
meane thoroughe me to make your estate or your childrene's the worse,

and he ends with an allusion to expectations from an elderly uncle.
If Mrs Locke found this fervent preacher, perhaps ten years her
junior, irresistible, so did a number of other ladies with whom she
must always have had to share him: Lady Mary Mildmay, Lady
Golding of East Peckham, Kent, Mrs Mary Honeywood, whose
notorious spiritual hypochondria and enormous progeny and lon-
gevity won her a place in Fuller's *Worthies*,[1] a Mrs Barrett of Bray,
and above all Mrs Catherine Killigrew, one of the four learned
daughters of Sir Anthony Cooke of Gidea Hall, who was Burghley's
sister-in-law and Francis Bacon's aunt. Dering was often detained
in the Killigrew household at Hendon.[2] But Anne seems to have
enjoyed her sisterly relationship with these other women who had
their own claims on her husband's spiritual comforts. 'Mrs. H. and
my wife wish to see you,' Dering wrote to Catherine Killigrew on
one occasion.[3]

The first year of the Derings' married life can have brought them
little peace. Dering was lecturing on the Epistle to the Hebrews at
St Paul's, and was thought by some to be the most notable preacher
of his day.[4] But this was 1573, the year after *An Admonition to the
Parliament* had declared open war on the bishops from positions
which Dering was helping to defend. In May Archbishop Parker and
Bishop Sandys of London persuaded the Council to examine him in
the Star Chamber and to sound him out on a set of twenty articles
based on the arguments of Thomas Cartwright's *Replie* to John
Whitgift's *Answer to the Admonition*.[5] To Parker's exasperation, the
Council did nothing effectual to stop Dering's lectures, but in
December he was silenced at the Queen's personal command, in
spite of Mrs Killigrew's efforts on his behalf.[6] In the same month the
Puritans generally, and especially in London, were subjected to a

[1] Thomas Fuller, *The History of the Worthies of England*, 1662, II, 85-6.
[2] Dering's correspondents appear as initials only in most of the *Godly and comfortable
letters*, but are identified from the copies in MSS Dering U 350, C1/1, 2 in the Kent
Archives Office.
[3] Dering, op. cit. Sig. C 5. The printed text has 'Maister H.'; the correct reading is
supplied from the Dering Papers.
[4] *Correspondence of Matthew Parker*, ed. John Bruce, Parker Society, 1853, 410.
[5] Inner Temple Library, MS Petyt 538/47, ff. 479-80.
[6] *Parker Correspondence*, ed. cit. 434; *Acts of the Privy Council*, ed. J. R. Dasent,
VIII (1894), 133; Dering, op. cit. Sigs. A 4-5. For fuller details of Dering's affairs in 1573

vigorous campaign of repression announced in a royal proclamation.[1] Not only ministers but laymen and women, 'such as they call Puritans,' were committed to prison in numbers on their refusal to subscribe.[2] Dering told his brother on Christmas Eve: 'My wife hath beene I thanke God in no trouble, neyther was any toward her that I know of; if any fall, God hath made her rich in grace and knowledge to give account of her doing.'[3] But troubles of another kind were not far away. Dering was a consumptive and by the summer of 1575 he was spitting blood; he died a year later, on 26 June 1576, aged thirty-six.[4]

Anne Locke's third and last marriage took her out of London and down to Devon. She married, some time before 1583, Richard Prowse, an Exeter draper and a substantial figure in West Country affairs. Prowse was successively bailiff, sheriff, and alderman of Exeter, and mayor three times. He sat in Parliament in 1584 and showed a keen interest in anything which had to do with cloth. His son by his first marriage, John Prowse, was to be a very prominent Exeter M.P. Prowse was a godly gentleman, allied with other firm Devon Protestants, Carews and Periams.[5] I have not followed Anne Locke down into the West Country and I have little to add on this last, more placid period of her life. But in 1583 an old friend from Geneva days, Christopher Goodman, appeared in Exeter and preached a controversial sermon in the cathedral,[6] and I can think of nothing that would have drawn him so far from his usual haunts but Anne Locke. In any event there are two episodes left to describe which suggest that all the godly exhortation which Anne Locke had received was not in vain, and that the wife of the mayor of Exeter remained steadfast to the end.

see my Friends of Dr Williams's Library Annual Lecture (1963), *A Mirror of Elizabethan Puritanism; the Life and Letters of 'Godly Master Dering.'*

[1] *Tudor and Stuart Proclamations, 1485–1714*, ed. Robert Steele, 1910, I, no. 689; Dasent, ed. cit. VIII, 140, 171.

[2] *Letters of Thomas Wood*, ed. cit. 6–8; Cambridge University Library, MS Mm.1.43, 441.   [3] Dering, opt. Sig. A 4.

[4] Ibid. Sigs. C 3–7; A. F. Scott Pearson, *Thomas Cartwright and Elizabethan Puritanism, 1535–1603*, 1925, 117.

[5] J. C. Roberts, 'The Parliamentary Representation of Devon and Dorset, 1559–1601,' unpublished London M.A. thesis, 1958, unpaginated biographies; Hazel Matthews, 'Personnel of the Parliament of 1584–1585,' unpublished London M.A. thesis, 1948, 183–4; Principal Probate Registry, Somerset House, P.C.C. wills, 83 Huddlestone, will of Richard Prowse, made 20 May 1607, proved 10 November 1607.

[6] Albert Peel, 'A Sermon of Christopher Goodman's in 1583,' *Journal of the Presbyterian Historical Society of England*, IX (1949), 90.

In January 1583 that restless opportunist John Field, commissar and propagandist of the organised Puritan Movement, published part of a minor work on the Temptations of Christ which Knox had sent to Mrs Locke in 1556.[1] The MS had been in Field's possession for some time, but it was still unquestionably Mrs Locke's property and probably a treasured keepsake. No one was ever more eager than Field to record, gather, and publish anything which could conceivably help the cause of 'further Reformation,' and, as was his way, he published Knox's MS without asking leave, arguing that it was the common possession of the Church. In compensation he dedicated the volume to Mrs Prowse—seizing the opportunity to urge her to send any other Knoxiana which she might still possess:

And if by yourselfe, or others, you can procure any other his writinges or letters, here at home or abroad, in Scotland or in England, be a meane that we may receive them. It was great pittie that any the least of his writings should be lost. . . . And his Letters, being had together, would together set out an whole Historie of the Churches where he lyved.[2]

This may explain how the Knox-Locke correspondence was preserved and found its way into Calderwood's *History*, which is the earliest text that can be traced.[3] At least one of these letters was already known to Field (that which had accompanied the *Exposition on the Temptations*),[4] and perhaps Mrs Prowse now parted with the rest. They would then have passed into the possession of the Scottish presbyterian ministers, Andrew Melville and others, who were exiles in England in 1584-5. Some of these ministers held regular meetings that winter with Field in London and they were entertained by Anthony Martin and his sister-in-law, Mrs Martin, an old intimate of Anne Locke.[5] Field went on to tell Mrs Prowse that he kept by him 'many of the writings, labors and letters of that worthy and godly man's, your late and deare husband, Mr Edward Dering (whom I name even for honor's sake) and gather them in dayly as I can get them, of his and my good friendes.' This tends to confirm what is clear from one or two of Dering's individual printed sermons: that Field was the editor of Dering's collected *Workes* as we have them

[1] Reprinted in Knox's *Works*, ed. cit. IV, 85-114.
[2] Ibid. IV, 92.
[3] Ibid. VI, 7.
[4] Ibid. IV, 92.
[5] *A Seconde Parte of a Register*, ed. Albert Peel, 1915, I, 284; B.M. MS Additional 4736, f. 166ᵛ.

in the 1597 edition.[1] Although, as Field acknowledged, Mrs Prowse was 'no young scholler in [God's] school,' he ended with the exhortations which ladies like this, with their fearful trials and tearful temptations, expected to hear from a preacher of the Gospel. 'Remember the hope of your calling . . . strive on forwarde with good courage.' [2]

The last word comes in 1590 when Anne Locke for the second time brought a work of her own to the press:

Everie one in his calling is bound to doo somewhat to the furtherance of the holie building, but because great things by reason of my sex I may not doo, and that which I may I ought to doo, I have according to my duetie brought my poore basket of stones to the strengthning of the walles of that Jerusalem whereof (by grace) wee are all both citizens and members.

Her basket contained a translation from the French of Jean Taffin, *Of the markes of the children of God, and of their comfort in afflictions*, solace originally intended for the oppressed Protestants of the Netherlands, but which Mrs Prowse believed would soon be needed in England. This was a time when Archbishop Whitgift and the High Commission were delivering a crippling blow to the Puritan Movement, if not to puritan religion, and in the epistle which presents her little book to another elderly lady of proven godliness, Ann, countess of Warwick, there is an old person's perspective: the good days—'*Halcyon* daies' she calls them—of Gospel liberty under Elizabeth are already passing, and nothing but trial lies ahead.[3] I know of no earlier trace in literature of the retrospective legend of the Elizabethan golden age which was to be so emotive in seventeenth-century religion and politics, and perhaps for this reason the volume was reprinted in 1608 and 1634. Thus Anne Locke's life spans the whole story of the Reformation in England, from Tyndale in the Netherlands and the *Complaynt of Roderyck Mors* to the post-Reformation atmosphere of the Stuart conflicts, which is dimly foreseen in this touching last testament.

[1] See my essay, 'John Field and Elizabethan Puritanism,' *Elizabethan Government and Society: Essays Presented to Sir John Neale*, ed. S. T. Bindoff, J. Hurstfield and C. H. Williams, 1961, 144-5. *See below, 352-3.*
[2] Laing, ed. cit. IV, 92-3.
[3] *Of the markes*, Sigs. A 2-5^v.

EDOVARDVS DERINGVS.

Sedulus inculcans diuini semina Verbi
Expers DERINGVS ambitionis erat

This engraving, probably the work of C. van de Passe senior, was included by
Henry Holland in his *Herwologia Anglica* (1620). The portrait from which it was
engraved was 'from Mr John Harison's' according to a cryptic MS. note in a copy
of the *Herwologia* in the British Museum (C.38.h.2). Reproduction by courtesy of
the Trustees of the British Museum.

11

A MIRROR OF ELIZABETHAN PURITANISM
THE LIFE AND LETTERS
OF 'GODLY MASTER DERING'

WHEN I was invited to have a share in this distinguished series I was told that the intention was to devote these lectures over the next few years to the more or less coherent if not consecutive theme of post-Reformation English Church History, and I was asked to deal in some way with the puritanism of the Elizabethan period. My first thought was to attempt a summing-up of some impressions of the character and ideals of the Elizabethan puritan movement, but on futher consideration it seemed that the particular might prove more illuminating than the general, and certainly more manageable in the space of one lecture. So I have chosen 'godly Master Dering' as a mirror in which to catch I hope some authentic reflections of the spirit and the aspirations of the godly Elizabethan preachers who first established the English puritan tradition. To those who know this ground the choice may seem a strange one. Edward Dering's active and public career was only seven or eight years in duration and included little of the eventful history of the puritans and their opponents in the Elizabethan Church. Certainly his premature death in 1576 will make it impossible in a lecture devoted to Dering to touch on some of the more celebrated and important episodes in that history. Nevertheless, I hope that you will agree with me that Dering is worth an hour. For the late Professor A. F. Scott Pearson, Thomas Cartwright was 'the representative puritan'.[1] More recently Dr. S. J. Knox has called Cartwright's close collaborator Walter Travers 'the paragon of Elizabethan Puritanism'.[2] And I myself have made some large claims on behalf of yet another preacher and puritan leader of that generation, John Field.[3] Without wishing to prolong an obviously artificial discussion, I believe that Dering was in some ways more representative than any of these three of the kind of person and of

[1] *Thomas Cartwright and Elizabethan Puritanism, 1535-1603*, Cambridge 1925.
[2] *Walter Travers: Paragon of Elizabethan Puritanism*, 1962.
[3] 'John Field and Elizabethan Puritanism', *Elizabethan Government and Society: Essays Presented to Sir John Neale*, ed. S. T. Bindoff, J. Hurstfield and C. H. Williams, 1961, pp. 127-62. *See below*, pp. 335-70.

the philosophy that we should have in mind when we speak of puritans and puritanism in the Elizabethan context. I would go further and call him the archetype of the puritan divine, whose life and works were a model for the many who would come after him in the seventeenth century. Certainly Dering provides an incomparable illustration of some of the more positive qualities of the puritan spirit which have too often been obscured, not only by those totally out of sympathy with the puritan tradition, but also by its heirs and well-wishers who, as nineteenth-century liberals, have viewed puritanism primarily as a movement of nonconformity and dissent, which are, after all, negative concepts, however notable their place in the history of religious liberty. What I propose to do is to approach Dering and Dering's religion with no preconceptions and with a mind as free as it is possible to be from the limitations imposed by denominational or theological labels. I hope that this will not prove an altogether unrewarding exercise.

Edward Dering belonged to that diminished company of Eliza-bethan clergy who partially redeemed a devalued profession by belonging to respectable gentry stock. The Derings who settled in the hamlet of Surrenden near Ashford in the Weald of Kent in the fifteenth century and hyphenated the name with their own as Surrenden-Dering were one of the most ancient of all Kentish families. Sir Edward Dering, the great seventeenth-century parlia-mentarian and lay scholar, was to make the celebrated discovery of an original copy of Magna Charta in Dover Castle and to add it to his collection at Surrenden-Dering, but his own family was much older than Magna Charta, older even than the Conquest. This Sir Edward, the first baronet, was named for our Edward Dering who was the first of the family to bear that name. Edward Dering the divine was the brother of Sir Edward's grandfather, and he was born in about the year 1540, the third son of John Dering Esquire of Surrenden-Dering.[1]

---

1 *Visitation of Kent, 1619-21*, ed. R. Hovenden, Harl. Socy. Pubns. xlii. 1898, p. 140; *Proceedings Principally in the County of Kent in Connection with the Parliament Called in 1640*, ed. L. B. Larking, Camden Socy. 1862, intro. by J. Bruce. There is much information on the Derings scattered throughout Dr. A. M. Everitt's unpublished London Ph.D. thesis, 'Kent and its Gentry, 1640-60: A Political Study', 1957. I am grateful to Dr. Everitt for his permission to refer to this valuable dis-sertation. See also C. E. Wright, 'Sir Edward Dering: A Seventeenth-Century Antiquary and his "Saxon" Charters', in *The Early Culture of North-West Europe: H. M. Chadwick Memorial Studies*, 1950, pp. 371-93.

Edward Dering was marked with the strong local patriotism of a county which was a world in itself, and where, we are told, when people spoke about the West they often meant the West of Kent.[1] As a preacher in London, he was like any other Kentish exile, longing to escape to his native county, which was by no means the annexe to the metropolis which it has sometimes been represented. 'I am holden heere,' he wrote to a Kentish correspondent on one occasion, 'that I could never yet have opportunitie to ryde farre, or to see my native country and nighest friends.'[2] Loyalty to family was another powerful instinct in this county where Sir Robert Filmer was to write his *Patriarcha*.[3] We have some of Dering's letters to his eldest brother, Richard Dering, in which deference to the head of the family is combined with godly exhortation to embrace the Protestant gospel as unreservedly as his youngest brother had done:

You are my eldest brother, and you know not how glad I would be to see you goe before me in religion. God hath given you neyther a light hed nor little understanding; if you would apply your selfe unto knoledge you should then reape the fruite of your labor in more gladnes of hart then yet you can imagine. Begin once but a litle, and tast how sweete the Lord is, and you shall feele the riches of his glory and say: Happy be the time that ever I knew it. Let not, good brother, let not the world deceive you. It is faithlesse and deceitfull; when you shall love it best, it will soonest deceive you.[4]

---

1 Everitt, loc. cit., p. 5.

2 Dering to Lady Elizabeth Golding, n.d., *Certaine godly and comfortable letters,* 1597, Sig. C7. Dering's letters of spiritual counsel are a principal source for this lecture. The fullest collection survives in two volumes of copies, some of them in Dering's own hand, in the Dering papers now deposited in the Kent Archives Office, Maidstone; (MSS. Dering U 350, C1/1 & 2.) I am indebted to the County Archivist of Kent, Dr. Felix Hull, for permission to quote from these MSS. Most, but not all of the letters were included in the printed collection, *Certaine godly and comfortable letters, full of Christian consolation,* first printed by Richard Schilders in Middelburg in 1590 (one copy in Cambr. Univ. Libr., press-mark Syn. 8. 59. 42) and subsequently as part of Dering's collected *Workes,* separately printed and not continuously paginated but bound together in the editions of 1597 and 1614. A few of the printed letters do not occur in the Dering Papers. I shall quote Dering's letters, where possible, from the 1597 printed edition, cited as *GCL;* and those which occur only at Maidstone as Dering MSS. C1/1 and C1/2. In many cases personal names which appear only as initials in the printed text have been supplied from the copies in the Dering papers.

3 See Mr. Peter Laslett's introduction to *Patriarcha* in the Blackwell Political Texts edn., Oxford 1949.

4 *GCL,* Sig. A3. The correct date for this letter is no doubt 19 Dec. 1570, as in the Dering Papers, not 19 Nov. as in *GCL.*

To another brother, John Dering, he wrote of his concern for his maternal uncle, Thomas Brent of Charing, and for his aunt, Jane Brent:

And I beseech God blesse my good uncle Brente, and make him now to know which in his tender yeares he could not see, for the world was then darke, and we were blind in it. But since we have beene lightened with the Gospell of the Lord Jesus, and so much the more earnestly now we must pray that it may be unto us the Gospel of health, and we may increase in the knowledge of the mistery of it. And the Lord open his gracious countenance revealed in it unto my aunt, that she may also make a blessed change, to leave vaine imaginations of her owne mind, which are full of ignorance, and learne the Scripture, which can make knowne unto her the living God.[1]

Uncle Brent was a person of some importance for the Derings, for he was childless and they were his co-heirs.[2]

These pious sentiments will have served to introduce the obsessive theme of Dering's life, which must necessarily dominate any account of the man: the intense evangelical experience by a first-generation Protestant of justification and union with Christ through the renunciation of 'will-works' and of the world and the exercise of a lively faith; and the consuming desire to convey this experience to others. It will serve too as a reminder that much of what we call puritanism at this time was nothing but authentic Protestantism, and that the reign of Elizabeth was not conspicuously a post-Reformation age, as some Anglican interpretations of history would have us believe, but the age of the English Reformation *par excellence,* when Protestantism was for the first time taking a strong hold on families of the country gentry and on the urban middle classes. Both these brothers whom Edward Dering exhorted in the 'seventies were among the Kentish gentlemen who rode up to Lambeth in 1584 to confront Archbishop Whitgift with the cause of their suspended ministers.[3]

I propose to say little more about Dering's divinity than this, if only because it lies outside my competence as a mere historian, except to notice these few things. That it was of no particular pro-

---

[1] *GCL*, Sig. A6.
[2] *The Visitations of Kent, 1530-1 and 1574*, ed. W. Bruce Bannerman, Harl. Socy. Pubns. lxxiv, 1923, pp. 3, 15; *Visitation of Kent, 1619-21, op. cit.*, pp. 140, 211-12.
[3] B.M., MS. Lansdowne 43, fol. 7; Dr. Williams's Library, MS. Morrice L V 7.

fundity, and that Dering was not in any systematic sense a theologian. (In this sense there *was* no puritan theology before Dudley Fenner in the eighties and William Perkins in the nineties.) And although Dering seems to have enjoyed the reputation with some of being 'the greatest learned man in England',[1] this presumably referred to his prowess as a Greek scholar. As a preacher, Dering deliberately set aside all humane knowledge and cited nothing but Biblical texts. 'If I speak out of the Fathers of the Church, and knowe it to bee the woord of God,' he wrote in his Lectures on the Epistle to the Hebrews, 'why doo I attribute it to man rather than to God, whose truth it is? or if I speake of the Fathers and knowe it not to be the word of God, bee it never so true in the Doctor's mouth, in mine it is sinne, because I speake not as I am taught of God.' He condemned 'bretheren who knowe not their calling, but fill the pulpit with Doctors and Counsells and manie vanities' and who 'use the pulpit like a philosopher's chaire.'[2] Dering's conception of God's transcendence and of the work of Christ, however, were expressed with a rich and even mystical imagination. 'If all the world were a flowing water,' he could write, 'and every yeare one drop should be diminished, the sea shold be all made dry and the bottomes of the deepe should appeare before He shall cease to live whom God hath raysed from the dead.'[3] There is in all his teaching a strongly ascetical emphasis, and he has as much or more to say about relinquishing the world and its vanities than the worthlessness of meritorious religious works, perhaps because he addressed himself for much of the time to nominal Protestants of the wealthier classes whose spiritual enemy was the materialism of the age. But the consequence is that he often seems to be upholding a simple philosophy of renunciation and an ideal of spirituality which are 'merely Christian' and transcend the controversies of the sixteenth century. 'Increase still in fayth, in love, in hope,' he wrote characteristically to one correspondent, 'till with a wise hart you have such a feeling of the glory of God and of eternall life that you have made your account up with the worlde and are at a poynt with all that is under the sunne.'[4] It is remarkable that apart from

[1] *The Correspondence of Matthew Parker*, ed. J. Bruce, Parker Socy., Cambridge 1853, p. 410.
[2] *XXVII lectures or readinges upon part of the Epistle written to the Hebrues*, in *Workes*, 1597, Sigs. A5v, T5v.
[3] Dering to Mrs. Mary Honywood, n.d., *GCL*, Sig. B3.
[4] Dering to Lady Golding, n.d., Ibid., Sig. C7v.

occasional unexceptional references to 'the elect' he has nothing whatever to say in his writings and letters about the doctrines of prevenient grace and election. For these reasons it seems to me that Dering shares the strongly ethical emphasis of some of the Edwardine preachers and by comparison with many of his contemporaries appears to have been very little indebted to continental Reformed theology.

Where Dering became infected with something more than the formal Protestantism of the rest of his family is not known, but it is a safe guess that it was at Cambridge, where he entered Christ's College, probably early in Mary's reign. There is a typically partisan recollection of life in Marian Cambridge in the earliest of his published works: 'Such priestes as I have knowne some in Cambridge that when they have played all night at dice, in the morning being called away to Masse have sworne a great othe that they would make hast and come againe.'[1]

Dering was never the kind of gentleman scholar who would later come to the university for a superficial polishing. 'I have been a scholar almost this twentye yeares', he wrote when he was perhaps twenty-eight years of age.[2] He commenced Bachelor of Arts in 1560, the first in the somewhat shrunken *ordo* of that year. He was at once elected a fellow of Christ's and retained his fellowship until 1570. During these years he was recognized to be one of the foremost Greek scholars of the university. He was ordained deacon in 1561 by the bishop of Ely; (there seems to be no record of his ordination to the priesthood). He commenced Master of Arts in 1563.[3]

Christ's College at this time was a seed-bed of puritan religion, a society with a character of its own which was not exactly matched by any other college in either university, and which it owed to a remarkable succession of tutors.[4] While St. John's was thrown into a turmoil in the sixties by the determination of the authorities to impose the surplice and the square cap and by the truculent nonconformity of a faction of the fellows, and while the heads of

[1] *A sparing restraint of many lavishe untruthes which M. Doctor Harding doth chalenge in the first article of my lorde of Sarisburies replie,* 1568, pt. ii, p.4.

[2] Ibid., pt. i, p. 52.

[3] J. A. Venn, *Alumni Cantabrigienses,* I. ii. Cambridge 1922, 36.

[4] H. C. Porter, *Reformation and Reaction in Tudor Cambridge,* Cambridge 1958, pp. 236-8.

Christ Church and Magdalen at Oxford, Thomas Sampson and Laurence Humphrey, postured as national leaders in the same anti-vestiarian cause, a quieter and yet more potent movement was at work in Christ's. Here there grew a puritan tradition moderate in its reaction to those questions of ceremonies and church order which are usually represented as the main ground of the puritan protest, but passionately indignant against the practical inadequacies of the Elizabethan Church and above all against its pastoral deficiencies. It was a tradition established and begun, in all probability, by Dering himself. It was continued by Laurence Chaderton who became a fellow in 1568 and who soon gave up ordinary tutorial responsibilities in order to devote himself wholly to his plans for harnessing the university more effectively to the supply of preaching ministers for the Church at large,[1] a conception which found some fulfilment in the foundation by Sir Walter Mildmay—another old Christ's man—of Emmanuel College, of which Chaderton became the first master. He was succeeded in Christ's by that prince of puritan divines, William Perkins, who in his turn bred up some of the giants of the seventeenth century, Samuel Ward, Paul Baynes, William Ames. For these puritans of the Christ's succession, matters of ceremonial and church government were never more than side issues. In 1573, when he was in the thick of the puritan controversy in London, Dering stated quite explicitly that 'whyle any lawe did binde me to weare cappe and surplesse, I did weare both', and he claimed never to have persuaded anyone else to refuse them; and, in spite of serious doubts about the Anglican forms of service, he had never preached against the Prayer Book.[2] Three years earlier, Cambridge had been torn in two by Thomas Cartwright's presbyterian teaching, delivered in the context of a course of lectures on the Acts of the Apostles, which asserted the necessity of conforming in all points to the primitive, Apostolic Church; and by John Whitgift's successful bid to impose a narrowly oligarchical form of government on the university in order to curb the puritanism of the younger regent masters. Dering at this time told Cecil: 'I have never

---

[1] John Ireton to Anthony Gilby, 8 May 1578, Cambridge Univ. Libr., MS. Mm.1.43 (Baker 32), pp. 437-8; *The Seconde Parte of a Register: Being a Calendar of Manuscripts under that title intended for publication by the Puritans about 1593, and now in Dr. Williams's Library, London,* Cambridge 1915, i. 133-4.

[2] 'An aunswere unto 4 articles by Maister Edwarde Dering', *A Parte of a Register,* Edinburgh or Middelburg? 1593, p. 84.

broken the peace of the Churche, nether for cappe nor surplesse, for archbyshop nor byshop.' And although the occasion of this letter was to make a plea on Cartwright's behalf and against Whitgift's new university statutes, he implied a difference between his own position and that of Cartwright which is of the first importance for a true evaluation of Elizabethan puritanism. Cecil was urged to exhort Cartwright 'to use Christian libertie, and to beare with the time', that is, not to stand so stiffly on secondary and indifferent matters. Yet he was asked not to punish Cartwright 'becawse he is afrayd of the shadow of sinne. We have a common sayinge: "He that hath byn strooken with the swoorde is afrayde of the scabberde." I would yow had seene the horror of sinne; I am sure yow woold also be afrayde of the shadow.'[1]

What Dering's puritanism amounted to was a limitless concern with the substance of sin and with its remedy, the practical, dominant note of the English Reformation from the Edwardine preachers through to the fruitful, plain preaching of the seventeenth century. It was inspired by a vivid sense of divine retribution, 'the everlasting curse of God', from which 'none are discharged saving those that take hold upon Christ and his merits with a true fayth'; and the conviction that the preaching of the word was the ordinary and indeed the only means of faith. 'Without this preaching of the word, wee can never have fayth.'[2] For those who really believed this, all other abuses in the Church of England were as nothing compared with the cardinal scandal of the insufficient, nonpreaching ministry. That this was an insight especially of the puritan tutors of Christ's is suggested by a comparison of Dering's pronouncements on these questions with those of his contemporary, John More, whose fellowship dated from 1568.[3] More went from the university to Norwich where he became preacher at St. Andrew's, city lecturer, and a kind

---

1 Dering to Cecil, 18 Nov. 1570, B.M., MS. Lansdowne 12, fols. 190-1ᵛ.

2 Dering and John More, *A briefe and necessarie catechisme or instruction, very needfull to be knowne of all householders*, here quoted from Dering's *Workes*, Sigs. B1, 5.

3 That this was an emphasis especially of the Christ's puritans is further suggested by what we know of an objectionable sermon preached in Great St. Mary's in October 1573 by John Millen, another fellow of the college. He was said to have taught 'that ignoraunt ministers were no ministers, bycause they were not chosen by God' and that 'the common sorte of the cleargie which (although they had lerninge) were eyther negligent in teachinge or preachinge, or dissolute in ther lyf wer no preachers nor mynisters before God.' (B.M., MS. Lansdowne 17, fols. 176-7.)

of apostle to the whole of Norfolk, with a more than episcopal reputation throughout the shire. We are told that he preached 'many hundred sermons, or rather certaine thousandes' in Norfolk in the space of twenty years, preaching every day of the week and three or four times on Sundays.[1] Of all these sermons only three have survived, but they are on a typical theme, *declaring first how we may be saved in the day of judgement and so come to life everlasting: secondly, how we ought to live according to God's will during our life.* 'Alas, what shall we say to the state of this people here in this land,' More exclaims in one of these sermons, delivered before an audience of Norfolk justices gathered for the quarter sessions,

skarsly the twentie parish hath a preacher, and can they be saved then? Shal we make God a lyer? He saith, whosoever doth not beleeve is damned; and none can beleeve without a preacher. If then we will have the people of the Lord to be saved, let them have preachers.

'But alas,' he goes on,

I can not preach to the whole land, but for the discharge of my conscience I desire you, good brethren, so many of you as have any voyces in place and parliament where these things may be reformed, consecrate your tongues to the Lord in the behalfe of your poore brethren, that ignorant and blind guides ... be remooved, and true preachers placed in their roomes.

In the meantime he urges the gentlemen of Norfolk to resort to a policy of self-help: 'Wherefore (good brethren) if ye will be saved, get you preachers into your parishes, ... bestow your labour, cost and travell to get them. Ride for them, runne for them, stretch your purses to maintain them. We shall begin to be riche in the Lord Jesus.'[2]

While they were both still at Cambridge, Dering and More collaborated in the composition of *A brief and necessary catechism* to be used by householders for the catechising of their families. Such was their obsession with the pulpit that Dering and More could not regard a household catechism as anything more than the emergency provision of basic instruction for a situation in which

1 John More, *Three godly and fruitful sermons,* Cambridge 1594; epistle by the Suffolk preacher Nicholas Bownd who married More's widow and later occupied his pulpit of St. Andrew's, Norwich.
2 Ibid., pp. 66-9.

scarcely one parish in twenty enjoyed a preaching ministry.[1] But
none of the unofficial catechisms which did so much to shape the
English religious consciousness in the sixteenth and seventeenth
centuries can have had a greater or more extended influence than
this *Short catechism for householders*. In Norfolk where it seems to
have been widely used it was known as 'Mr. More's Catechism'[2]
and justly so, for his was the principal hand in it. But elsewhere it
was attached to Dering's more famous name and Dering initialled
the preface. More's part in it has since been altogether forgotten.[3]
Eighteen editions survive from the years 1572 to 1631, nine of them
from after 1603,[4] and with such a small book which was used up
so rapidly, these must represent only a fraction of the total number
of impressions. In his preface, Dering echoes the complaints which
we have already heard from More: 'Scarce one of a great many can
give an account of their fayth . . . A very small number have tasted of
the beginnings of the Gospell of Christ.' What do we mean when we
pray daily 'Let thy kingdom come' 'if we speak not like the
parrets?' No nation ever had such ignorant ministers. 'Wee may
heerein compare with the man of sinne him selfe.'[5] Against this
state of affairs Dering holds up, not a certain dogmatic view of
how the ministry should be ordained and regulated, but an idealized
image of the true minister of Christ in the form of a kind of
scriptural collage:

The true minister is the eye of the body, the workman of the harvest,
the messenger that calleth unto the marriage, the prophet that telleth the
will of the Lord, the wise-man that teacheth to discerne betweene good
and evill, the scribe that doeth expound the Law, the servant that
occupieth his maister's talents unto gaine, the witnesse that beareth testimony of Christ to all people, the dispensers of the misteries of God, the

[1] Dering's Epistle 'to the Christian Reader', *A briefe and necessarie catechisme*,
Sigs. A1v-3.

[2] Folger Shakespeare Libr., Washington D.C., MS. Bacon I. T. 10 (a reference to
More's catechising which I owe to Dr. A. H. Smith of Homerton Training College);
R. G. Usher, *The Reconstruction of the English Church*, New York 1910, i. 263.

[3] The editions of the catechism of 1603, 1614, 1617 and 1625 have on the title-
page the words 'first made by Maister Moore'. The British Museum and Folger
Shakespeare Library catalogues correct this statement and mistakenly attribute the
catechism to Dering alone.

[4] This figure has been arrived at by comparing the entries in Pollard and Redgrave's
Short-Title Catalogue with the catalogue cards of the Folger Shakespeare Library.

[5] *A briefe and necessarie catechisme*, Sigs. A2-3.

steward that giveth meate in due time unto the residue of the housholde, the sacrifice of the Gospell of God, to make the oblation of his flocke acceptable, the minister by whom the people doe beleeve . . .

Such a minister was to be found in 'scarce one parish of an hundred'.[1]

'The minister by whom the people doe beleeve'! Few English Protestants have held such a 'high' doctrine of the ministry as Edward Dering. If the minister was not a priestly mediator between man and God, he was nevertheless the only reconciler of God to man. 'Yf yow doe not beleeve me,' he told Cecil, 'yow doe me wronge. I am a minister of Christe and I have sworne to speake the truthe.'[2] On another occasion he told the same correspondent that the minister was 'but the mouthe of God, in whose person Christ Him selfe is ether refused or receavyd, before whome to exalt a man is to sett up the clay above the potter . . .'[3] Dering was the only early Protestant writer that I know of to insist in controversy with Catholics that the mere fact of preaching itself—distinct from the sincerity of the doctrine preached—was an essential mark of the Church. The very name 'Ecclesia', he wrote, signified 'a companye caulyd together by the voice of a precher . . . Therfore the Roman Churche in which many ceremonies and longe servis occupiethe all the time, preachinge for the most parte altogether pretermittid, it cannot be the Churche of Christ.' Every Biblical phrase descriptive of the Church of God was turned to this account: 'Children of the kingdom, that ys, who have repentyd of the preachinge of the Gospell which is the Kingdome of Heaven, Matthew 3. 2; the flocke of Christ, that is, the shepe which have herde his voice calinge them, John 10. 16; the heires of grace, that is, of reconsilyation preachid in the Gospell which ys the word of grac, Acts 14. 3; they are called holy, that ys, sanctified thorow the worde preachid, John 17. 17.'[4] This seems to have been written in part refutation of the papist Nicholas Sanders's *De visibile monarchia ecclesiae,* and it failed to please Archbishop Parker who had commissioned the work, and who wrote that it contained 'too much childishness'.[5] By

1 Ibid., Sig. A3.

2 Dering to Cecil, 18 Nov. 1570, B.M., MS. Lansdowne 12, fol. 190.

3 Dering to Burghley, 3 Nov. 1573, ibid., MS. Lansdowne 17, fol. 198.

4 'Of the viseble Churche, how it may be knowne', Kent Archives Office Maidstone, MS. Dering U 350, C1/2.

5 Parker to Burghley, 22 Nov. 1572, *Parker Correspondence*, pp. 409-10.

Dering's argument, of course, not merely the Church of Rome, but most of the parishes of England stood condemned.

Dering's sense of his own office as the very mouth of God and the unchallenged rule of his conscience within his own personality have left some remarkable memorials in his letters. In the late sixties he and another fellow of Christ's, Edward Hansbie, were made chaplains to England's only living duke, Thomas Howard, duke of Norfolk. (John Foxe the martyrologist was another fervent Protestant to be entertained in this household, and yet Norfolk is still more often than not called a Catholic!) In September 1569, when Norfolk was becoming hopelessly entangled in a web of intrigues against the Cecilian regime, Dering and Hansbie prepared a collection of prayers for the use of his household, which they presented to the duke, accompanied by an elegant Latin epistle.[1] This seems to represent faithfully enough the formal character of the spiritual offices which they performed for their great patron, for when a year later Norfolk's foolish entanglements brought him to the Tower and a death-sentence for high treason, Dering decided that he had served his master ill. In a remarkable letter he invited the duke to join him in repentance for both their failings. 'Now therfore my Lord, let us take counsell together, and as a wise maister, learne of a faythful servaunt what is best to be done.' After much exhortation of Norfolk he turns to himself:

And now my Lorde I beseech you, pray for mee, and humbly uppon my knees I aske you harty forgivenes wherin I have not done as it becam me touching you. You knowe howe in my time I have perswaded you from your wicked servaunts, from your popish friends and from your adulterous woman. But (alas) my Lord, your high calling hath bridled my wordes. I could not speake as I should, my wordes were too soft to heale so olde a disease. Why should I have tarried in your Lordship's house except these things had bin amended? This bearing with your evill was the greatest evill I coulde have done you. And I beseech you, forgive me, and God for his mercies sake shall make me strong that hereafter I shall not feare to reprove the sinner, and God shall forgive you your dulnes of spirit that could not be moved with a little counsell.[2]

[1] B.M., MS. Lansdowne 388, no. 14, fols. 320-42.
[2] Dering to Norfolk, dated in MS. marginal note '1572' in B.M. copy of 1614 edition of *Works*, GCL, Sigs. D3-E2v.

As early as March 1570, Dering had asked Cecil to allow Norfolk access to the sermons which he preached as chaplain in the Tower. 'Your longe experience and greate wisdome can not choose but see that yf all strange fancies weare out of mie Lord of Norfolke's hed, his unfeyned godlines weare a great preparation to the best waye.'[1] Apparently Norfolk gave his chaplain some indication of a repentant spirit before the end, for on the very eve of the day on which the clamour of the House of Commons at last secured the execution which the queen had so long deferred, Dering wrote again, now not so much to his master as to his 'Christian brother, from whome Christ hath taken away the pride of honor which was a fadinge flower, and given insteed of it the hoape of his electe which never shalbe confounded . . .'[2]

There is no reason to suppose that Dering ever again had cause to reproach himself for over-soft words. This, for example, is how he wrote to the Kentish magnate Henry Neville, Lord Abergavenny:

Thoughe I knowe that our Saviour Christ hath geven us a straight chardge not to cast precious stones before swine, nor to geve that which is holye to doges, yet I see so manye examples of his unspekable mercies that I know not anye swyne so walowinge in the myre, nor any dog so retourninge to his vomet, of whome I have not some hope that he may be a pure and a clene creature in Israell. This makythe me bolde with a good conscience to write unto your honor . . .

Later in the letter comes this peroration:

Loke from your verye childhod and examyne your times. Alas, it grevethe me on your behalfe. The comlynes of a manly countenaunce you have changed into brutishe affections; the strenght [sic] of nature you have geven to harlotes; the use of your tongue to ungodly talke; your desire to unclennes; your sences to wickidnes, your riches unto riot, your honor to shame, and what sholde I saye, your dayes unto vanities and life unto deathe. It is trewe, it is trewe, God grante you to beleve it. The wayes of your walkinge, they have byn suche that you above other seeme a lothesome example, in whome you may behold an evell man, an enemie to the crosse of Christ, whose belly is his God, whose ende is distruction, and whose glorie is torne into endles shame. I love you in the Lorde and therfore I speake so playne . . .

1 Dering to Cecil, March 1569(/70), B.M., MS. Lansdowne 12, fol. 98.
2 Dering to Norfolk, 1 June 1572, B.M., MS. Add. 33271, fols. 40ᵛ-41ʳ.

It is only fair to add that the letter contains much besides of the positive side of the evangelical doctrine: 'The Lorde ys ryche in mercye and abounding in compassion, able to forgeve us more then we cann trespass.'[1]

In 1569 Dering was to all appearances poised for high preferment. He was one of the outstanding Greek scholars of his generation ('the greatest learned man (so thought) in England', as Archbishop Parker wrote caustically[2]) and up to this point he had not put a foot wrong in the pursuit of a career. He was chosen to make a Greek oration on the occasion of the queen's visit to the university in 1564. In 1567 he was Lady Margaret preacher. In the following year he commenced Bachelor of Divinity[3] and he was expected to proceed to the doctorate in the course of time.[4] At some point in his career he had lived in Archbishop Parker's household, perhaps as a chaplain,[5] and what could have been more fitting than for the archbishop to have promoted a scion of one of his own Kentish families? In 1568 Parker collated Dering to the rectory of Pluckley, the parish which contained the family seat of Surrenden-Dering.[6] He was nonresident and employed a curate; there is a conflict of evidence as to whether the curate was or was not a preacher.[7] In the same year Dering entered the lists against the English papists of Douai and defended Bishop Jewel against Stephen Harding in a book which contained this assertion, remarkable in the light of Dering's future development: 'Our service is good and godly, everie title (i.e. tittle) grounded on holie scriptures . . . '[8] (Dering was later asked to subscribe to this very expression, quoted from his own book, when he was examined before the Council in May 1573.[9]) He

---

1 Dering to Lord Abergavenny, n.d., MS. Dering C1/2.

2 *Parker Correspondence*, p. 410.

3 Venn, *op. cit.*, I.ii. 36.

4 Dering reported in November 1573 that Dr. William Chaderton had said to him in December 1572 that 'he was sure the universitie wold willingly geve me againe my grace to commence this next yere.' (B.M., MS. Lansdowne 17, fol. 203ᵛ.)

5 Dering to Parker, 1 June 1572, B.M., MS. Stowe 743, no. 1, fol. 2.

6 *Registrum Matthei Parker*, ed. E. M. Thompson, ii. Canterbury & York Socy., xxvi. Oxford 1928, 835.

7 Canterbury Diocesan Archives, 1569 Clerical Survey, fol. 6ᵛ. I am indebted for this information to Mr. John Daeley of St. John's College, University of Manitoba, Canada.

8 *A sparing restraint, op. cit.*, pt. i, p. 5.

9 Inner Temple Libr., MS. Petyt 538/47, fol. 480. I am indebted to the Treasurer and Masters of the Bench of the Inner Temple for permission to refer to the Petyt MSS.

was chaplain to England's premier nobleman and held in addition a chaplaincy in the Tower.[1] 'I am knowne now bothe in Cambridge and London, and to some also in the Courte'[2] he told Cecil in a letter which shows that he was far from indifferent to his own reputation and prospects.

And then came some kind of watershed, a crisis of conscience, possibly connected with Cartwright's radical lectures of the spring of 1570, but more probably with the marked deterioration in his health which set in at this time.[3] By March 1570 he had resigned Pluckley.[4] And then he proceeded to burn his boats in turn with Cecil (the chancellor of his university), Archbishop Parker (his patron in the Church) and with the queen herself. On each of these three—the principal personages in the kingdom—Dering unloaded the blame for the debased state of the ministry and other evils. It was here, in this indignant, even arrogant confrontation with authority that the passionate practical concerns of a Protestant like Dering became those of a puritan, in revolt against the existing order in the Church. Parker was blamed for the lax administration of his province and for the religious condition of Kent in which only two in six hundred parishes, in Dering's opinion, had adequate instruction. But he was equally reproved because 'in all your speeches which you comenly use both private and publick you thunder oute frequent oathes', and because his sons wore gaudy garments and his retainers 'monstrous great breches'. In this astonishing attack there was at least some show of deference. If Parker's own conscience did not convict him of these faults 'by your authority revoke me from error; for I doe willingly both reverence your great wisdome . . . and exceedingly honor your gravity and great yeeres.' In this letter Dering expresses disappointment that Parker had not thought of him for the profitable cure of Bocking in the archbishop's peculiar in Essex, lately vacated by the death of James Calfhill. 'If my necessarie wants were supplyed, I wold not desire greate things . . .; if that had byn bestowed upon me, it should not have bene unwillinglie accepted . . .' But he insists that

1 See The *Sermon preached at the Tower of London by Mr. Edward Dering the 11 of December 1569* and reprinted as one of *Two godly sermons*.

2 Dering to Cecil, 18 Nov. 1570, B.M., MS. Lansdowne 12, fol. 191.

3 On 5 Sept. 1570 he reminded Parker that his constitution would not allow him to live 'sparingly and hardlie'. (B.M., MS. Stowe 743, fol. 10.)

4 *Registrum Matthei Parker*, ii. 861.

he mentions the matter, not because he would seek anything for himself, but so that it should not be thought that he is unwilling to shoulder the painful burdens which he would lay on others.[1] Dering's assault on Burghley was for maladministration of the university, specifically for sending down the new statutes which Whitgift had devised. For Dering these were merely a cover for the sins of those (himself amongst them until a few months before!) who lived in the university on the proceeds of parochial benefices. 'While they are clothed in scarlet ther flockes perishe for cold; and while they fare deliciouslie ther people are faint with a moste miserable hunger.' Again and again Cecil was told that if he had had any personal experience of the Gospel of Christ he would not have lent himself to such calculated wickedness.[2] Not surprisingly, both Parker and Cecil took this ill. The archbishop could never bring himself to say a good word for Dering again. As for Cecil, a letter of similar tone on a later occasion would elicit the kind of pained and self-righteous reaction which was characteristic of the sixteenth century and of Cecil especially.[3] What foolish and yet what superb contempt for everything that was expedient and tactically wise!

But it was in a sermon preached before the queen in her chapel on 25 February 1570 that Dering had passed the point of no return. Such an occasion could have been the making of an ecclesiastical career. When Whitgift had been chosen to preach before Elizabeth in 1567 he had at once been made a royal chaplain and proceeded in the same year to the masterships in quick succession of Pembroke and Trinity. Dering chose to use the opportunity to appoint himself as Nathan the Prophet to the queen's David. He took his text from Psalm 78: 'Hee chose David his servant also and took him from the sheepefoldes . . . to feed his people in Jacob and his inheritance in Israell.' This was boldly applied to God's dealings with the queen and to her duty towards the Church. Elizabeth was reminded that she had not chosen God but that God had chosen her

[1] Dering to Parker, 5 Sept. 1570, B.M., MS. Stowe 743, no. 1, fols. 1-2. The original letter in Latin is followed immediately in the MS. by an English translation in a near-contemporary hand which I have used for these quotations.

[2] Dering to Cecil, 18 Nov. 1570, B.M., MS. Lansdowne 12, fol. 190-91v.

[3] Dering to Burghley, 24 March 1572, P.R.O., S.P. 12/85/75; Burghley's reply in John Strype, *Annals of the Reformation*, Oxford 1824, II.ii. 483-6; for an account of this correspondence, see Conyers Read, *Lord Burghley and Queen Elizabeth*, 1960, pp. 113-15.

as His instrument, and it was strongly implied that He could unmake her again if she fell into unthankfulness or neglect of her duty.

I neede not seeke farre for offences whereat God's people are grieved, even round about this chappell I see a great many, and God in his good time shall roote them out. If you have sayde sometime of your selfe, *tanquam ovis,* as a sheepe appoynted to be slayne, take heede you heare not now of the prophet, *tanquam indomita luvenca,* as an untamed and unruly heifer.

Later in the sermon Dering took the queen on a conducted tour of her Church.

I would first leade you to your benifices, and behold, some are defiled with impropriations, some with sequestrations, some loaden with pensions, some robbed of their commodities. And yet behold more abhominations then these. Look after this upon your patrons, and loe, some are selling their benefices, some farming them, some keepe them for their children, some give them to boyes, some to servingmen, a very few seeke after learned pastors. And yet you shall see more abhominations then these. Looke upon your ministery, and there are some of one occupation, some of another: some shake bucklers, some ruffians, some hawkers and hunters, some dicers and carders, some blind guides and can not see, some dumb dogs and will not barke. And yet a thousand more iniquities have now covered the priesthood. And yet you in the meane while that all these whordoms are commited, you at whose hands God will require it, you sit still and are carelesse, let men doe as they list. It toucheth not belike your comon wealth, and therfore you are so well contented to let all alone.[1]

Elizabeth never heard another sermon like this one, and she never forgot the preacher. 'It is now a great many yeeres as I account them,' Dering later told the queen, 'and they have passed exceeding slowlie, . . . since first I heard howe muche your Highnesse misliked of mee.'[2] Nor did the puritans forget this remarkable performance: no Elizabethan sermon was more often reprinted.[3]

[1] *A sermon preached before the Queenes Maiestie* in *Workes,* pp. 8, 27.
[2] 'Mr. Dering's own preface to her Majestie' set before the above sermon in the *Workes* (Sigs. *1-3) but probably written as a preface to the Lectures on Hebrews.
[3] See the list of editions in Appendix 1 below. The sermon seems to have been printed by the puritan propagandist John Field. Two of the earliest extant editions (1570? and 1575?) carry an epistle signed 'I.F.' which was reprinted as a preface to the *Two godly sermons* in the collected *Workes.* Dr Williams's Library possesses a copy of the 1575 (?) edition, S.T.C. no. 6701, press-mark 564.B.28. This is a great rarity.

Dering's eldest brother was appalled at his rashness, especially in forfeiting Cecil's good will which might have done the family so much good. 'For Maister Secretarye, whether he be angry or no I know not,' Dering told him, 'if he be, God is witnes between him and me, how little I have deserved it. True it is hee seemed not very well pleased . . .' As for his own worldly prospects: 'I had lever be your brother not worth a groate but having a good conscience to pray for you then have (as I might) great living and encomber my conscience with muche sinne.' 'And perswade your selfe of this,' he concluded, 'that a lively zeale and holy knowledge in you and in my sister shal make me gladder then any bishoprick in England.'[1]

By now Dering had resigned his fellowship and was living in London, possibly in Norfolk's household, and although his friendship with Parker was at an end, his relations with Bishop Sandys of London were as yet undamaged. 'My Lord of London is a good man,' he told his brother, 'I am often with him. I have seene in him so good tokens of a good spirit that I reverence him in my heart, and will serve him in Christ all wayes that I may.'[2] In 1572 Sandys appointed him to be reader of the divinity lecture in St. Paul's Cathedral, and he began a course of lectures on the Epistle to the Hebrews which enjoyed a tremendous vogue and established him— if he was not already so established—as the great preacher of his day, the Elizabethan Spurgeon. The confident hold which Dering had of his weekly auditory is suggested in the dedication of the twenty-fourth lecture, preached on 6 December 1572, which was printed and presented 'for a New Yeares gift to the godly in London and elsewhere.'[3]

Such a prominent figure could not escape involvement in the hurricane of religious controversy which struck London in 1572 and raged for the next two years. In June 1572 two young and disgruntled London preachers, John Field and Thomas Wilcox, suspended from preaching for nonconformity and stung into desperation by the failure of the Parliament of that summer to obtain

1 Dering to Richard Dering, 19 Dec. 1570, *GCL*, Sigs. A3-4.

2 Ibid., Sig. A 3ᵛ.

3 *A lecture or exposition upon a parte of the v. chapter of the Epistle to the Hebrues*, 1573. The dedicatory epistle addressed 'to his very loving friend Mayster M.F.' was reprinted in *GCL*, Sigs. A1-2ᵛ. Here the letter was dated 6 Dec. 1572 rather than 1573 as the earliest editions. 1572 is no doubt correct.

relief for ministers in their condition, published their composite tract called *An admonition to the Parliament,* a virulent attack on the shortcomings of Elizabethan Anglicanism which offered to display 'a true platforme of a Church reformed' so that its readers might 'beholde the great unlikenes betwixt it and this our English Church.'[1] The *Admonition* lifted—or lowered—the quarrel in the Elizabethan Church to a new level of seriousness and vituperance. It represented the issues at stake as no longer a matter of the 'shells and chippings of popery' but the cause of 'the awful ministry of the word and the right government of the Church'. It demanded not reform but a revolution in which the bishops together with all other relics of the pre-Reformation Church would be swept away, and it did so with a violence of expression not hitherto publicly used between English Protestants. The bishops were described as 'drawne out of the pope's shop' and their government as 'Antichristian and devilishe and contrarye to the scriptures'.[2] Although Field and Wilcox were sent to Newgate, they continued to preside triumphantly over an enthusiastic and growing following. When Whitgift elected to answer the *Admonition* and Cartwright to defend it this was assured to be no nine day's wonder.[3] And in London and in governing circles, even to the Council board itself, the mood of the hour was in favour of an assault on popery and prelacy in this year of the St. Bartholomew massacres in France. 1573 was a year of bishop-baiting, when Archbishop Parker wrote: 'The comfort that these puritans have, and their continuance, is marvellous, . . . and but that we have our whole trust in God, in her Majesty, and in two or three of her council, I see it will be no dwelling for us in England.'[4] And Bishop Sandys who three years before had been moved to accept the bishopric of London by an assurance of 'the ful consent and calling of the people of London'[5] was now attacked in offensive libels printed and cast in the streets.[6] He now wrote:

1 *Puritan Manifestoes,* ed. W. H. Frere & C. E. Douglas, repr. 1954, p. 8.

2 Ibid., p. 30. For the circumstances of the publication of the *Admonition* see my 'John Field and Elizabethan Puritanism', loc. cit., pp. 129-41. *See below,* 337-49.

3 The whole controversy is printed in Whitgift's *Works,* Parker Socy., 3 vols., Cambridge 1851-3; and in summary form in D. J. McGinn, *The Admonition Controversy,* Rutgers Studies in English, v. New Brunswick 1949.

4 *Parker Correspondence,* pp. 418-19.

5 Sandys to Cecil, 26 April 1570, B.M., MS. Landowne 12, fol. 179.

6 *A parte of a register,* pp. 371-81. The dating of this document (1567) is a mistake, it clearly relates to the troubles of this summer.

'Our estimation is litle, our autoritie is lesse, so that we are become contemptible in the eies of the basiste sorte of people.'[1]

Dering would never himself have written the *Admonition*—this was to mistake the shadow of sin for the substance—and he could make a clear distinction between 'suche as wold be rashe' and 'suche as have preached faythfully.'[2] In his St. Paul's lectures he protested 'that I have neither part nor fellowship in this division, but in love and unitie I beare him witnesse who speaketh truth, and beare with his errour who is deceived, acknowledging my selfe more unworthie than either of both.'[3] For this reason he was regarded uneasily as a doubtful ally by the most extreme of the London puritans.[4] Yet he had been associated with the Admonitionists when in 1571 they and other leading puritan divines had offered Bishop Sandys their terms—inadmissible terms—for respecting the peace of the Church.[5] He visited them now in Newgate.[6] Moreover he was an old friend and defender of Cartwright. On 24 March 1572 he had written to Cecil—whom we must now call Lord Burghley—asking him to facilitate Cartwright's return to England from Geneva and to support his candidature for the chair of Hebrew at Cambridge.[7] It is not surprising that he was now an object of suspicion. In late April 1573 Burghley asked Sandys in the presence chamber at Court what he thought of Dering's lecturing and the bishop replied that he misliked it 'for it tended not to edifyinge'. Burghley went on to ask Sandys whether Dering approved of Cartwright's *Replie* to Whitgift's *Answer to the admonition* which had appeared from a secret press in the country a few days before and was causing a sensation. Sandys confirmed that Dering and two other preachers whom he named 'were favorers of it'.[8] The likelihood is that the queen, who had not forgotten Dering, had instructed Burghley to take these soundings. Moreover Gabriel Goodman, the dean of Westminster, probably acting on Burghley's be-

---

1 Sandys to Burghley, 5 Aug. 1573, B.M., MS. Lansdowne 17, fol. 96.
2 Dering to Richard Dering, n.d., Dering MS. C1/1, fol. 3v.
3 *Lectures on Hebrues*, in *Workes*, Sig. X8.
4 See William White's letter to Dering, *Seconde Parte of a Register* i. 101-2.
5 Ibid., i. 82.
6 Inner Temple Libr., MS. Petyt 538/47, fol. 481.
7 P.R.O., S.P. 12/85/75.
8 Sandys to Burghley, 28 Aug. 1573, B.M., MS. Lansdowne 17, fol. 100v. MS. Lansdowne 17 is the principal source for this part of our story and it will be cited on the next few pages as L17.

half, had already obtained from Parker a list of 'whoe were noted the most precisians', that is, those who had visited Field and Wilcox in prison, which included Dering's name; and with it an abstract of the principal matters in Cartwright's book.[1] This information clearly formed the basis of Burghley's enquiries. And so on Friday 29 May,[2] in spite of his studious avoidance of any controversial matter in his St. Paul's lectures, Dering was called before the Council in the Star Chamber, together with the other ministers named by Sandys. Field and Wilcox were examined on the same afternoon.

A strange kind of comedy was enacted on this occasion. Parker and Sandys were in attendance, and according to Burghley the hearing was held at their request and they were expected to prefer charges against Dering. But neither of the bishops said anything all afternoon, appearing, as Burghley thought, not to wish to be his accusers in that place. Sandys was later 'bytterly rebuked' by the queen (his own words) for his silence, but both he and Parker explained that they had been called for unprepared, on the morning of the hearing, and that they did not know that Dering would be present or for what cause they had been summoned. Parker's version of the story was that he had not been invited to speak and that when at the end of the afternoon he at last protested that something must be done if the queen's expectations and those of the city of London were to be satisfied he was told that the time was spent and 'we see what they aunswere, we maye not deale with them as in popishe tyme.' At last it was agreed to require the ministers, 'specially Mr. Deering', to declare their opinions of certain positions extracted from Cartwright's book and in the meanwhile to suspend Dering from his lectures and the others from their preaching.[3]

The truth was that Dering was so well-connected that nobody wanted to bear the odious responsibility of suspending him. The courtier Henry Killigrew and his wife were close personal friends and Mrs. Killigrew was sister-in-law to Burghley and Sir Nicholas Bacon who took the most active part in examining Dering in the

---

[1] Inner Temple Libr., MS. Petyt 538/47, fol. 470.

[2] I conclude that this was the day of the Council hearing from these circumstances: Sandys referred to it in a letter of 3 June; Sir Thomas Smith sent the articles to Dering to subscribe on Sunday 7 June; and Parker refers to the proceedings as having taken place on a Friday. (L17, fol. 67, MS. Petyt 538/47, fols. 467, 470.)

[3] Parker's memorandum of the afternoon's business in MS. Petyt 538/47, fols. 470, 479-80; see also Burghley to Sandys, 22 Aug., Sandys to Burghley, 28 Aug. 1573, L17, fols. 101, 100v.

Star Chamber. The earl of Leicester regarded him with favour.[1] We must remember, too, that Dering's own social status gave him a measure of immunity. When Sir Thomas Smith wrote to him with the articles of which he was to subscribe his opinion, he addressed him as 'the right worshipfule and my lovinge frend Mr. Edwarde Deringe' and he seems to have regarded the procedure as a mere formality. 'The said articles I send you here enclosed, to the which the soner you shall aunswer, the soner I trust you shall returne to the good which you weare noone [i.e. known] to doe.'[2] There can have been few stranger affairs in the whole history of ecclesiastical discipline. Five days after the Council hearing, Sandys wrote to Burghley to say that he thought that Dering had shown great simplicity in offering to declare his mind on Cartwright's opinions, and that he should be released from the necessity of subscribing and restored to his lecture. The sore demanded a soft plaster rather than a sharp corrosive and if Dering were 'somewhat spared and yet wel scholed' others 'beinge manifest offenders' could be 'dealt withall according to their deserts.'[3] Burghley 'misliked and sharply impugned' him for this letter.[4] Yet on 28 June the Council, meeting in Burghley's absence, wrote to Dering, lifting his suspension, regardless of the answers which he now made to their articles and without reference to Parker and Sandys.[5] Dering called on his bishop with the news and told him that 'he never thought that he should be longe kepte from it [his lecturing], for the whole Counsell favored hym, except the Lord Treasurer [Burghley]'; and, reported Sandys, it was generally spread about in London that the queen and the Council favoured Dering and 'that yt was only the malitiouse proud bishops that sought his troble.'[6] It was the bishops' turn to be angry, and Parker, Sandys and Cox of Ely all com-

---

[1] For Dering's friendship with the Killigrews see p. 29 below. On 28 Sept. he told to Burghley: 'Of this yf your Honor will vouchsafe to send me woord by Mr. Killigrewe, what I shall doe or wher I shall attende, it is all I can crave at your handes . . .' (L17, fol. 195.) In December 1573 Dering was anxious that his position should be made clear to the earl of Leicester 'whose good opinion it would greeve me to loose.' (*A parte of a register*, p. 85.)

[2] Smith to Dering, 7 June 1573, Inner Temple Libr., MS. Petyt 538/47, fol. 467.

[3] Sandys to Burghley, 3 June 1573, L17, fol. 67.

[4] Sandys to Burghley, 28 Aug. 1573, L17, fol. 100ᵛ.

[5] *Acts of the Privy Council*, ed. J. R. Dasent, viii. 1894, 120; *Parker Correspondence*, pp. 434-5.

[6] L17, fol. 100.

plained.[1] At the end of July the Council again attempted to silence Dering, but their order seems to have taken no effect.[2]

And so it went on for months. When Sandys renewed his complaints in early August, Burghley showed his letter to the queen, who commanded him to charge the bishop not merely to silence Dering but to remove him from his lectureship. But when Burghley heard that Sandys had no specific charges to make against Dering he wrote that he could not 'in conscience procede to hasten her Majestie's commaundement, untill I may heare more from your Lordship wherin he hath offended worthy to be removed'. Yet a lectureship was no freehold! By this time Burghley had fallen out with Sandys because of a report that the bishop should have informed Dering before witnesses that he was being deprived solely on Burghley's warrant. A heated correspondence went on between the two men, each striving to establish that it was not he who had wanted Dering silenced. Soon the Lord Treasurer was revealing his secret sympathy for men of Dering's stamp, or rather his deep suspicion of the ways of clerical government, telling Sandys that bishops 'shoulde rather be feders then punishers' and complaining that 'such as shold be feders of the flocke only fede them selves and turne teaching into commaunding'.[3] Later in the year the same kind of comedy was repeated. On the Friday before Christmas, as Dering was about to deliver his lecture, Dr. Wilson, the Secretary, forbade him to preach 'in her Majestie's name', so, as he wrote, 'I stand now forbidden, not by the bishops but by our princesse, whom I beseech God make a happy governour in his Church and many yeares [sic] to give peace unto His people'; 'whereupon', as he wrote in a later letter, 'I long absteined'. But when his great friend Mrs. Killigrew blamed Wilson for bringing Dering such a message 'he denied that ever he spake yt, or had any suche message'. He was commanded, he said, only to tell the bishop to suspend Dering, but although Dering had been with the bishop many times, nothing had been said on his part. And so Dering again resumed his lectures, whereupon the queen was angrier than ever. 'Now the question may be,' Dering told his brother, 'whether her Majestie wyll better

---

1 *Parker Correspondence*, pp. 434-5; Cox to Burghley, 5 Aug. 1573, L17, fol. 94.

2 *Acts of the Privy Council*, viii. *133*.

3 Sandys to Burghley, 5 Aug., Burghley to Sandys 22 Aug., Sandys to Burghley, 28 Aug., Sandys to Burghley 9 Sept., 19 Sept., L17, fols. 96, 101, 100, 104, 106.

beleve the bishop of London and the Master of the Requestes or elles your brother.'[1]

Dering's final case was that he was 'forbidden to preach any more openly' in the queen's dominions.[2] He consoled himself with preparing his lectures for the press and prefacing them with an epistle addressed to Elizabeth herself, which was not, however, printed in his lifetime. Here there is the same kind of struggle to find a safe course for conscience between God's demands and the anger of the prince which we find in the letters and speeches of the great Elizabethan parliament men, Peter Wentworth and Thomas Norton.[3] 'In the disfavour of the prince wee must feele a greate overthrow of the happinesse of our life.' But what if the cause be just? By ceasing to preach he would acknowledge his fault and 'should I not be injurious to the graces of God? Should I not pul downe whatsoever I have built? Should I not betray the truth of God to the slaunderous tongues of many envious men?'[4] In private Dering spoke of the queen's displeasure rather more frankly: 'She hath spoken angrie wordes, but I trust they are but wordes and theire substance but wynd.'[5] With so many eager to insulate the puritans from the queen's displeasure, such affairs rarely had a tidy conclusion. When Parker went to the Court more than a year later, in March 1575, he was told once again that 'her Majesty disliked Deering's reading'.[6]

As for Dering, it must be admitted that his behaviour throughout these troubles was by any standards insufferable, if we are to believe the complaints of Bishop Sandys who began with a high opinion of him. In one of his interviews with the bishop he told him that he thought he would respect his order not to preach 'lest some disordered fellow byd youe come of your horse when as youe shal ryde down Cheape syde'. Sandys told him that these threats would not terrify him and that he would 'forth with ride downe Cheape syde to try what his disordered schollers wold do, and so I

---

1 Dering to Richard Dering, 24 Dec. 1573, same to same, n.d., *GCL*, Sigs. A4-5, Dering MS. C1/1, fol. 4.

2 *A sermon preached before the Queenes Maiestie*, in *Workes*, Sig. *.

3 J. E. Neale, 'Peter Wentworth', *English Historical Review*, xxxix. 1924, 36-54, 175-205. The letters of Norton that I have in mind are in B.M., MS. Add. 48023 (Yelverton 26), fols. 32-3ᵛ, 42-3ᵛ.

4 *A sermon preached before the Queenes Maiestie*, in *Workes*, Sig. *v.

5 Dering to Richard Dering, n.d., MS. Dering C1/1, fol. 3ᵛ.

6 *Parker Correspondence*, p. 476.

did'.[1] Behaviour on both sides was nearly hysterical in that summer of 1573.

And what, we may well ask after all this, was Dering's position with regard to bishops and to the new presbyterian doctrines which were so much in the air? and to the questions of authority in Church and State which were at the root of the crisis of 1573? The materials for an answer exist in Dering's attempts to defend himself at this time, and it is worth stating, for Dering's ideas on church polity were, I believe, those of a great number of Elizabethan puritan ministers. In the most fundamental and important respect Dering was a presbyterian. This is to say that his high conception of the ministry of the word had as its corollary a doctrine of the two kingdoms: of the Church as a sphere removed from the competence of the magistrate, in which the word of God, declared from the pulpit by the preacher, was alone sovereign. 'The prince alone is the person in the world to whome God hathe committed the seate of justice, and they onlie to execute the duetie of it to whome it is committed, at whose handes God will require it . . . The minister is apointed for another defence wher horsemen and chariottes will doe no good. They may hindre the minister and make him forgett his duetie, they cannot profitt him in his office and function. He must frame the hart, uppon which yow cannot sett a crowne; and edefie the soule, which fleashe and bloud cannot hurt.'[2] That this doctrine undermined the ecclesiastical supremacy of the queen and the Tudor conception of Church and State as contained within a single indissoluble Commonwealth needs no emphasis. Yet it was characteristic of Dering that he chose to turn the implications of his teaching, not so much against the kind of church government represented by the Elizabethan bishops or against the royal supremacy, but against the confusion of the spiritual and temporal spheres by the pope and those popish bishops who claimed temporal sovereignty and a title of lordship. 'The lordship or civile goverment of a byshop', he told Burghley, 'is utterlie unlawfull in the Churche of God.' The lordship of a bishop had 'byn ever a plague-sore in the state of a kingdome, and is at this day a swellinge wound, full of corruption in the bodie of a commonwealthe'. The word of God knew Christ's ministers as 'felow elders, felow healpers, felow woorkmen, . . . in which names

1 Sandys to Burghley, 28 Aug. 1573, L17, fol. 100.
2 Dering to Burghley, 3 Nov. 1573, L17, fol. 198ᵛ.

they are forbidden lordship over ther brethren.'[1] This emphasis is
sufficient to account for the popularity of Dering and his friends
with the governing class and for Burghley's reluctance to see him
silenced. For on the surface Dering's teaching was calculated to
appeal to the laity: its neo-clerical tendencies were obscured behind
a highly popular attack on the pride of prelates. Dering knew this
well enough and was quick to inform the Council of a preacher at
Paul's Cross who had much to say about the authority of bishops
'and what a thinge it were to have them honorable' and told his
auditory: 'I would five or six of the Counsell weare Aarons. I would
the lord keeper weare a bishop.' 'It greveth me', wrote Dering, 'to
see one pretend the persone of Christ and to speake woordes of so
great vanitie.'[2] 'Humbly I obaye you as godly magistrates,' he told
the Council in June 1573, 'hartely reverence you as thos under whose
govermente God hath sent us libertie, and trulie love you as thos
that ar partakers of the same grace of Christe. . . This callinge is
precious in the daies of the Gospell.'[3]

In his teaching on the ministry Dering had more in common with
the first generation of Protestant reformers than with the new and
more narrowly dogmatic Calvinists who were coming to the fore in
the 1570's. Which is to say that he was more concerned with condemning the popish abuses of church offices than with dogmatically
defining the offices themselves. This practical concern with the sins
of prelacy rather than with the unlawfulness of episcopacy would
always be characteristic of the main stream of the English Protestant
tradition. True, Dering was reluctant to subscribe to the article of
the consecration of archbishops and bishops and wrote 'let him
allowe of it that hath profit by it; and hee that liketh not of it, let
him have no bishopricke'.[4] And at a supper-table in December 1572
when he met one of the clerical hacks employed on Archbishop
Parker's Lives of the Archbishops of Canterbury, the *De antiquitate
Ecclesiae Britannicae*, he told him 'that he should do well to be
somewhat long in this bishopes lyf, for peradventure he should be
the last that should sitt in that plase', but that was said 'merrily', to
amuse a sick man in whose chamber the supper-party took place

---

1 Ibid., fols. 197-9.
2 L17, fol. 204.
3 Inner Temple Libr., MS. Petyt 538/47, fol. 467ᵛ.
4 *A parte of a register*, p. 82.

(Mr. Lonison of the Mint) and it was in any case the expectation of the hour.[1] It is by no means certain that Dering was interested in abolishing altogether the superintendency of bishops or that he would place emphasis on a complete pastoral parity like a doctrinaire presbyterian. When challenged on this point he replied, as even the bishops of the time would have done, 'that all ministers are equalie called to the preaching of the worde and ministration of the sacraments'. But as touching government, while he would not allow any Christian minister dominion, 'nor give to one of them authoritie above the other', some ministers—by implication the bishops—were worthy 'of double honour . . . of singular love . . . of great reverence . . . yea of all humble duetie.'[2] What, Dering asked finally in pursuit of this question, was to be said about the fathers and martyrs of the English Church, Cranmer, Latimer, Ridley and Hooper, 'all byshopes and lordes'? and what about the present bishops of the Church? Of Cranmer and his fellow-martyrs, Dering wrote: 'The Lord had not yet revealed it unto them, but leaft them in that infirmitie, as he leaft manie of his saintes before them . . . Notwithstandinge, we reverence ther memorie and love ther ashes . . .' Of the Elizabethan bishops he had this to say: 'We knowe ther doinges and our hope is of them as of the members of the Churche. We love them as brethren and honor them as elders. And the Lorde grawnt that we may have no cawse to call back this praise and dare not geve it them. But this I must needes say and freelie confesse, yf I weare in one of ther places I am afraide I showld not have byn so sone perswaded.'[3]

At the end of 1573 Dering had less than three years more to live. The sickness which, as he told the duke of Norfolk in 1572, had 'taken nowe long hold upon me'[4] was pulmonary tuberculosis, and his health now suffered a rapid deterioration. These last years were spent free from public controversy, which, indeed, subsided throughout the Church in the course of 1574, and they found Dering once

---

[1] L17, fol. 204. The episode had been reported as though Dering should have made a solemn prophecy of the end of bishops in England, putting off his cap and lifting up to his eyes and saying: 'Masters, hearken, I will prophecy, after Matthew Parker I trust there shall be no more Archbishops of Canterbury', to which Thomas Cartwright is supposed to have added: 'Accipio omen.' (H.M.C. Report, Hatfield MSS., ii. 64; Petyt MS. 538/38, fol. 68+.)
[2] A parte of a register, p. 76.
[3] L17, fol. 200v.
[4] GCL, Sig. D3.

again immersed in the private cultivation of godliness which was his proper and natural sphere. In December 1573 a Twysden cousin tried to procure a Kentish parsonage for him which he was not disposed to refuse, but there is no evidence that he received the presentation, perhaps because he was not prepared to sue for it.[1] He probably never exercised a public ministry again. Most of the 'godly and comfortable letters' which were collected after his death survive from this time, and they show that Dering was first and always 'a physician of the soul', a practical divine whose letters were full of little but encouragement to forsake the world and to go forward in the pursuit of godliness. It has sometimes been implied that the puritans discovered this practical divinity only in the early seventeenth century, when their attempts to reform the externals of worship and church government were finally defeated, but I have no doubt that 'mere religion' had always been the first concern of the majority of the godly preachers of the Elizabethan Church.

Most of Dering's spiritual patients were women, and this too was no uncommon situation. Thomas Wilcox corresponded with the countess of Bedford, Lady Ann Bacon, Lady Walsingham, Lady Mary Grey, Lady Fielding, Lady Rogers and the countess of Sussex, and most of his letters contained 'little but godly, plain and necessary exhortations and directions for the exercise of godlynesse.'[2] Dering counted among his intimates Mrs. Catherine Killigrew, Lady Mary Mildmay and Lady Elizabeth Golding. I am sorry to have reached almost the end of this paper without having drawn attention to Dering's relations with these and other ladies, because this is certainly one of the most interesting and even important aspects of his career. As was so often the case with Catholic recusants, Protestant wives were frequently more deeply committed to the cause of religion than their husbands. It was noted by contemporary observers, Richard Hooker amongst them, that the largest and most enthusiastic following of the puritan preachers were often women, London merchants' wives, 'famous and godly matrons' and gentlewomen. And in French Reformation studies the fervent Protestantism of the womenfolk has been recognized as a factor of primary

---

1 Dering to Richard Dering, 24 Dec. 1573, *GCL*, Sig. A5.
2 See the dedicatory epistles to Wilcox's various *Works* in the collected edition edited by his son-in-law John Burgess in 1624; and Roger Morrice's account of Wilcox's spiritual letters, now lost, Dr. Williams's Library, MS. Morrice 'A Chronological Account of Eminent Persons', ii. pp. 617 (2) & (4).

importance in the propagation of the Reform. These women were often afflicted with doubts and fears about their salvation and in the worst cases with a kind of spiritual hypochondria. But herein lay the bond which tied them to the preachers. They needed their comfort and casuistry and their very physical presence as much as any seventeenth-century French Catholic of a similar station in life needed the services of her Jesuit or Jansenist director.[1]

In 1572 Dering married Anne Locke, a gifted and pious city widow who in her youth had been so drawn to the Scottish reformer John Knox that she left her husband in London and took her babies to join him in Geneva.[2] Dering must have seemed to her to be Knox reborn. We have his letter of proposal, surely the earliest surviving document of this kind to have been penned by a clergyman of the Church of England. 'I write unto you as before,' he wrote, 'sekinge you alone, whome the grac of God in myne opinion hathe made a good possescion.' If God should work all that he desired, 'it is nether the first nor the gretest benefitt that I have receavid, yf he shall worke otherwise, I trust his grac shall gide me that I shall accompte best of myne owne will when it is framed unto his.'[3]

But Dering's marriage in no way released him from his obligations to other importunate ladies. Those with the strongest claims upon him seem to have been first and foremost Catherine Killigrew, one of Sir Anthony Cooke's four learned and famous daughters, sister-in-law to Burghley and Sir Nicholas Bacon and wife of that versatile government servant, Henry Killigrew; Lady Elizabeth Golding of East Peckham and Mrs. Mary Honywood of Charing, both Kentish ladies; and a Mrs. Barret of Bray, near Windsor. Hardly a letter to any of these women begins without apologies and explanations for his failure to be with them in the flesh. 'I am sorie that hetherto I coulde not come unto you, and I would be sorry if you shold thinke that I had lever bee anywhere then in your house', he wrote to Mrs. Barret.[4] 'It greeveth me, good Mistris Killigrew, that you should be so long at Hendon as now you have beene, and all this while I could finde no leysure to come unto you.'[5] And then he

---

1 See my communication, 'The Rôle of Women in the English Reformation, Illustrated by the Life and Friendships of Anne Locke', to appear in *Studies in Ecclesiastical History*, ii. *See above*, 273-87.
2 Ibid.
3 Dering to Mrs. Locke, n.d., MS. Dering C1/2.
4 *GCL*, Sig. B7.
5 Ibid., Sig. C3.

would invariably proceed with the kind of evangelical exhortation which he would otherwise have delivered verbally. 'Let us not then, good Mistrisse Killigrew, bee hencefoorth sorrowfull[1] or faynt-harted. Paule and Peter and all the Apostles and Prophets have spoken glorious thinges unto us and we will beleeve them.'[2] Dering's letters to Mrs. Honywood contain interesting confirmation of a tradition preserved by Thomas Fuller in his *Worthies of England*. As the story went, this remarkable lady, who lived to be 93 and could count 367 children and children's children at the time of her death, was notoriously oppressed by a troubled conscience and the certainty that she could not be saved. On one occasion she told John Foxe the martyrologist (another famous physician of the soul) that she was 'as surely damn'd as this glasse is broken', violently throwing it to the ground. 'Here happened a wonder, the glasse rebounded again and was taken up whole and entire.'[3] Dering's letters to Mrs. Honywood are entirely occupied with the comforting of what he calls her 'heavie estate' and with assuring her that her afflictions were a singular token of God's favour.[4]

By 1575 Dering needed all the physical comforts that these pious matrons could lavish on him in return. His illness was approaching its last stage and his letters to Mrs. Killigrew are scattered with refer-ences to his symptoms, described as only a devout puritan could des-cribe them, and with thanks for the medicines with which she plied him. 'Touching my disease, I did suddainly cough and spit much blood, so that when with much forcing my selfe I refrained, it ratteled in my throat as if I had bin a dying. Next day in the like sort I did, and once since the taking of these medicines for the stay-ing of it. It is nowe staied, but I feele a great stopping of my wind and muche provocation to cough, which if I did I shuld spit blood as before.' But, he wrote, 'I see the goodnes of God such towardes mee as (I thanke God) except sinne I weigh not all the world a feather, and with as glad a minde I spitte blood (I trust) as cleare spittle. To those that love God all things are for the best. He hath a hard hart that beleeveth not this . . . The Lord blesse us all, that we make our bodies shake and not our bodies us.'[5] With similar

---

1 MS. Dering C1/1 fol. 7ᵛ reads 'fearefull'.
2 *GCL*, Sig. C 6.
3 Thomas Fuller, *The History of the Worthies of England*, 1662, ii. 85-6.
4 *GCL*, Sigs. A6-B3, C1ᵛ-2ᵛ.
5 Dering to Mrs. Killigrew, 25 July 1575, *GCL*, Sig. C4.

homilies on his lips he died a year later at Thobie Priory in Essex, on 26 June 1576, in a stylized death-bed scene, surrounded by preachers and others who set down his last words. One of the preachers standing by told him prophetically: 'It is for thee a great blessing that thou shalt depart in peace and goe from many troubles that our bretheren shall beare and see.'[1]

At the outset I said that Dering was the archetypal puritan divine. It was his posthumous treatment that led me to describe him in that way. By his early and affecting death, Dering became the first of the puritan saints. His death-bed utterances were preserved, and memorial verses were composed, one elegant set by Thomas Norton, the translator of the *Institutes* and a great House of Commons man.[2] His engraved portrait appears with those of Foxe, John More of Norwich and Perkins in Holland's *Herwologia Anglica*[3] and he was one of the very few Elizabethan divines to be thought worthy of inclusion in that related work of Protestant hagiology, Fuller's *Abel redevivus*.[4] His letters of spiritual counsel must have been one of the first of such collections to be made. And he was the first of the many puritan divines to have their collected works posthumously published.[5] We will leave the last word to that busy propagandist John Field, to whom we owe so many of the essential materials for the history of the early puritans, and who was responsible for gathering together Dering's letters and other writings as we have them in the collected *Workes*.[6] 'One day', he told Dering's widow, 'the Lord

[1] 'M. Dering's words spoken on his death-bed at Toby, the 26 of June 1576', attached to *Godly private prayers* in *Workes*, Sig. I4v.

[2] Ibid., Sigs. Kv-K2; Dering MS. C1/2.

[3] Henry Holland, *Herwologia Anglica*, 1620; see the frontispiece to this lecture.

[4] First edn., 1651, pp. 341-2; William Nichols's edn., 1867, ii. 38-40. Fuller's account of Dering consist of little but the death-bed speeches, taken from Dering's *Workes*.

[5] The first edition was printed by Richard Schilders in Middelburg in 1590 under the half-title *Maister Derings Workes*. For an account of the contents of this first edition, see Appendix 1 below. Schilders was identified as the printer of several of Dering's writings in 1590 by R. B. McKerrow & F. S. Ferguson, *Title-page Borders Used in England and Scotland, 1485-1640*, Bibliographical Socy., 1932, App. no. 4.

[6] See my 'John Field and Elizabethan Puritanism', cited above. The evidence for Field as the editor of Dering's *Works* exists in the preface to his edition of John Knox's *Notable and comfortable exposition . . . upon . . . the tentations of Christ* of which he had obtained the MS. from Knox's old friend and Dering's widow, by that time (1583) the wife of Richard Prowse of Exeter: 'I keepe also by me many of the writings, labors and letters of that worthy and godly man's, your late and deare husband, M. EDWARD DERING (whom I name even for honor's sake) and gather them in dayly as I can get them of his and my good friendes.' (Knox, *Works*, ed. David Laing,

may give opportunitie, that as he liveth still by those notable readings of his in Poules Church, so he may live in his other writings, and all may thorowly see what a man also he was, and what a losse we received when God tooke him from amongst us.'[1]

---

iv. Edinburgh, 1864, 92-3.) There is also the evidence of Field's initials to the epistle printed with the *Sermon preached before the Queenes Maiestie* in its earliest editions and with the *Two godly sermons* in the collected *Workes*. An anonymous epistle set before the *XXVII lectures or readinges upon part of* . . . *Hebrues*, dated 24 Nov. 1576, which appears in all editions, is in Field's style and may be ascribed to him with fair confidence. Field died in 1588, two years before Schilders printed the first omnibus collection of the *Works*. But the puritan publishing committee of which Field had been the inspiration continued its activities after his death, and Schilders was its printer after Robert Waldegrave had retreated to Scotland in 1589.

[1] Knox. *Works,* iv. 93.

A List of Dering's Works in Chronological Order[1]

1. *A sparing restraint of many lavishe untruthes which M. Doctor Harding doth chalenge in the first article of my lorde of Sarisburies replie.* 1568 (6725). Not reprinted. Dedicatory epistle addressed to Thomas Wootton Esq. dated 2 April 1568.

2. A collection of household prayers composed for the use of the duke of Norfolk by Dering and Edward Hansbie. B.M., MS. Landowne 388, no. 14, fols. 320-42. Not published. Dated 13 September 1569 in an epistle dedicating the collection to Norfolk. Prefaced by Dering with these verses:

> Lyve longe: but live to God on hie,
> for lyfe in worldelie wealthe
> Is nought but deathe: then live to die,
> for lyfe in Christe is helthe.

3. *A sermon preached at the Tower of London the 11 day of December 1569.* Possibly four edns. in 1570 (6694, 6694a, 6695-6); further edns. 1584, 1589 (6697-8).

4. *A sermon preached before the Queenes Maiestie the 25 day of Februarie . . . 1569(/70).* Three edns. in 1570 (?) (6699, 6699b, 6700); further edns. 1575 (?) (6701, copies in Dr. Williams's Library and Folger Shakespeare Library), 1578, 1584, 1586, 1589, 1593, 1596, 1600, 1603 (6702-10). 6699b and 6701, printed by J. Awdely, and apparently these edns. only, are prefaced with an undated 'Epistle to the Christian Reader' signed I(ohn) F(ield).

5. These two sermons were reprinted as *Two godly sermons* in an edn. of 1586 (?) (6732) and by Richard Schilders of Middelburg for inclusion in the *Workes* of 1590 (6733). These edns. are prefaced by Field's epistle, first printed with no. 4.

6. *A brief and necessary instruction, verye needefull to bee knowen of all householders.* Composed largely by John More, but more strongly associated with Dering's name and prefaced by him with an epistle dated 'from my chamber' 22 April 1572. Edns. of 1572, 1583, 1597 (6679-81). In 1583 the Tonbridge schoolmaster, John Stockwood, published an edn. of the catechism with 'the prooves of the Scripture for everie poynt of the sayd Catechsime' added, 'according as they were noted in the Margin by the first Authors' (6711). Further edns. 1583, 1584, 1587, 1588, 1595

---

[1] The numbers in brackets are the entry-numbers from Pollard and Redgrave's *Short-Title Catalogue*, supplemented from the catalogue cards of the Folger Shakespeare Library, Washington D.C.

(6712-15a). (I believe that the last three edns. cited will prove to be of this version although I have been unable to inspect them.)

7. *Godly private praiers for housholders to meditate upon and to saye in theyr families.* Edns. of 1576, 1580, 1581, 1585 (?), 1590, 1624 (6685-90). In the 1597 edn. of the *Workes* the collection of *Godly private prayers* was greatly augmented. Some but not all of the subsequent combined edns. of the prayers with the catechism include the full 1597 collection of prayers.

There were many edns. of the catechism printed with the godly prayers, the first (apparently) in 1577 (*A bryefe and necessary catechisme or instruction,* B.M. press-mark 3932.a.l. (2), not in *S.T.C.*); and others in 1582, 1597, 1603, 1606, 1610, 1614, 1617, 1620, 1625, 1627, 1631 (6711, 6716-17, 6682, 6718-24). Many have the half-title *A short catechisme for housholders . . . with godly private prayers annexed thereunto.* The edns. of 1603, 1614, 1617 and 1625 say of the catechism 'first made by Maister Moore'.

8. 'Of the viseble Churche, how it may be knowne.' 1572? Kent Archives Office, MS. Dering U 350 C1/2, first 11 un-numbered folios. Not published.

9. *A lecture or exposition upon a part of the v. chapter of the Epistle to the Hebrues. Set forth as it was read in Paules Church in London, the vi of December 1573 (recte 1572?).* Dedicated by Dering 'to his very loving friend Mayster M. F.' First edn. 1573 (6691, a copy in Dr. Williams's Library); further edns. 1574, 1583 (6692-3).

10. *XXVII lectures or readings upon part of the Epistle written to the Hebrues.* First edn. 1576 (6726). Prefaced with an unsigned 'Epistle to the Christian Reader' (by John Field?) dated 24 November 1576. Further edns. 1577, 1578, 1583, 1590 (2) (6727-31).

11. *Certaine godly and comfortable letters full of Christian consolation.* Printed by Schilders in Middelburg, 1590.[1]

Collected Works:

1590. *Maister Derings Workes* (6676, printed by Schilders[2]). Contains nos. 5, 10, 6, 7 in that order.

1597. *M. Derings Workes. More at large then ever hath heere-to-fore been printed in any one volume* (6677, printed by James Roberts for Paule Linley and John Flasket). Contains nos. 4, 3, 10, 11, 6, 7 in that order. The *Godly private prayers* include 26 pages of prayers not previously

---

[1] Not listed in *S.T.C.* But a copy in the Cambridge University Library (press-mark Syn. 8. 59. 42) is noted by McKerrow and Ferguson, op. cit., App. 4.

[2] Ibid.

printed. The *Sermon preached before the Queenes Maiestie* is prefaced with Field's undated epistle and with 'M. Derings owne Preface to her Maiestie', evidently written to accompany the *Lectures on Hebrews*, but here printed for the first time. The volume ends with 'Certaine godly speeches uttered by Master Dering, a little before his death, with a prayer which he used before his Lectures' and T(homas) N(orton)'s elegiac verses on Dering.

1614. (6678). This edn., printed by Edward Griffin for Edward Blount, is identical with the 1597 edn. except that the *Catechisme, Godly private prayers* and godly speeches are bound between Field's epistle and Dering's epistle to the queen.

APPENDIX NO. 2

A List of Dering's Extant Letters in Chronological Order

1570   To Sir William Cecil, March; B.M., MS. Lansdowne 12, fol. 98.
To Archbishop Parker, Latin, 5 Sept.; B.M., MS. Stowe 743, no. 1, fols. 1-2.
To Cecil, 18 Nov.; MS. Lansdowne 12, fols. 190-91ᵛ.
To Richard Dering Esq., 19 Dec.; *GCL*,[1] Sigs. A 3-4.

1572   To Burghley, Latin, 24 March; P.R.O., S.P. 12/85/75.
To Burghley, 5 April; MS. Lansdowne 15, fols. 154-5.
To the duke of Norfolk, no day or month; *GCL*, Sigs. D 3-E 2ᵛ.
To Norfolk, 1 June; B.M., MS. Add. 33271, fols. 40ᵛ-1ʳ.

1573   To Burghley, 28 Sept.; MS. Lansdowne 17, fol. 195.
To Burghley, 3 Nov.; ibid., fols. 197-200ᵛ.
To the Council, 27 Nov.; ibid., fols. 203-4.
To Richard Dering Esq., 24 Dec.; *GCL*, Sigs. A 4-5ᵛ.

1574   To Richard Dering (early in the year?); Kent Archives Office, MS. Dering U 350 C1/1, fols. 3ᵛ-4ᵛ.
To Thomas Brent Gent., 6 Nov. 1574; MS. Dering U 350 C1/2.

1575   To Mrs. Catherine Killigrew, 10 Jan.; *GCL*, Sigs. C 5ᵛ-6.
To Mrs. Killigrew, 28 Feb.; ibid., Sig. C 3.
To Mrs. Kiligrew, 25 July; ibid., Sig. C 4.
To Mrs. Killigrew, 14 Aug.; ibid., Sig. C 4ᵛ.

1576   To Lady Mary Mildmay, 10 Jan.; ibid., Sigs. C 8ᵛ-D 3.

Undated Letters

To John Dering Esq.; *GCL*, Sigs. A 5-6.
To Mrs. Mary Honywood; ibid., Sigs. A 6-B 3.
5 letters to Mrs. Barret of Bray; ibid., Sigs. B 3ᵛ-C 1ᵛ.
To Mrs. Honywood, 19 April, no year; ibid., Sigs. C 1ᵛ-2ᵛ.
To Lady Elizabeth Golding; ibid., Sig. C 7.
To Lord Abergavenny; MS. Dering U 350 C1/2.
To Mrs. Anne Locke, (1572?); ibid.

---

[1] This signifies the edn. of the *Godly and comfortable letters* bound in the *Workes* of 1597.

12

THE 'NOTT CONFORMYTYE' OF THE
YOUNG JOHN WHITGIFT

Cambridge University in the early 1570s, according to John Strype,[1] 'ran now much divided into two factions, whereof the younger sort, which were the majority, was much for innovations, and such were followers of Cartwright's principles; which the graver sort, especially the Heads, laboured to restrain'. It has been pointed out that the differences of age between 'grave' conformists and 'rash' non-conformists in the Cambridge of Cartwright and Whitgift were not so obvious and extreme as the authorities of the time liked to pretend.[2] John Whitgift as master of Trinity and vice-chancellor was no more than thirty-eight; his opponent, Thomas Cartwright, was perhaps three years younger; and most of Cartwright's supporters were in their late twenties. Yet such seemingly small differences in seniority were not without significance in the hot-house of university politics and religious faction, especially when the 'seniors' were themselves such comparatively young men. Only four years before he set himself against the Cambridge Puritans as the very personification of authority and Anglican discipline, Whitgift, as fellow of Peterhouse and Lady Margaret professor of divinity, was openly sympathetic to the party of younger dons who were refusing to wear the surplices and square caps required by their own statutes and the ordinances of the Church.

When Cecil made Whitgift master of Trinity, in 1567, the future archbishop was still regarded with suspicion in some quarters as a favourer of the 'precisians'. 'For God sayk, ryght honorable,' he told his patron a week or two before his election, 'lett ytt be iugged what I am by my doenges and nott by the report of those who do nott to me as they wolde themselfes be donne unto. As towching my nott conformytye, which ys one thing layd against me, I dare be iugged by my lord of Canterberrye hys Grace, your Honor, or my Lorde of London, or Master Deane of Yorke, who knoweth more of my mynde in that matter then any man doth besyde. I never incorragyd any to withstand the Quenes Maiestyes lawes in thatt behalfe, but I bothe have and doo, by all meanes I can, seke to perswade men to conforme them selfes. For yt greavyth me that any man

---

[1] John Strype, *Whitgift*, Oxford 1822, i. 50–1.
[2] H. C. Porter, *Reformation and Reaction in Tudor Cambridge*, Cambridge 1958, 213–15.

showld cease frome preaching for the use of these thinges, beyng of them selfes indifferent.'[1] When Whitgift's biographers have taken note of this letter they have accepted it as a sufficient vindication of his record in this respect.[2] But surely this elaborate self-justification arouses rather than silences our curiosity. What had been the true extent of Whitgift's 'nott conformytye'?

A document which links Whitgift obliquely with the Cambridge non-conformists has been known since Strype's day. This is a letter to Cecil, as chancellor of the university, dated 26 November 1565, begging him not to enforce the vestiarian regulations on tender consciences. The signatories were Whitgift, as Lady Margaret professor of divinity, the regius professor, Matthew Hutton, master of Pembroke (the 'Master Deane of Yorke' of Whitgift's letter to Cecil) and three other heads of houses, Richard Longworth of St. John's, Roger Kelke of Magdalene and Robert Beaumont, master of Trinity and until lately vice-chancellor.[3] 'Singular to relate,' wrote Dixon, 'Whitgift thus enters history in the cause of Nonconformity.'[4] I believe that this letter and the motives of its subscribers deserve close consideration if we are to understand the critical turn taken in the affairs of the Church of England in this winter of 1565–6. The irregularity of this appeal by 'men of reputation' stirred Cecil to unusual anger, and Beaumont was obliged to explain why he and his collaborators had resorted to such a procedure. He told Cecil that two letters had been drawn up in the university, one of them addressed to the queen and the other to himself, which 'many not of the gravest sorte' were intending to subscribe. The tone of these letters would certainly have brought down the heavy displeasure of the queen upon the whole university. So Beaumont and the other heads and Whitgift had persuaded the younger men to set their letters aside in favour of the more moderate document which they had composed and signed. 'Nowe the facte being misliked I am sory for it.'[5]

Cambridge at this moment was divided between those seniors who felt no compunction in enforcing the demands of authority—Dr. Andrew Perne, master of Peterhouse and Richard Curteys, president of St. John's,

---

[1] Whitgift to Cecil, 17 June 1567: P.R.O., S.P. 12/43/8; printed, Whitgift, *Works*, ed. J. Ayre (Parker Soc., Cambridge 1853), iii. 597–8.

[2] For example, P. M. Dawley, *John Whitgift and the Reformation*, London 1955, 74–5.

[3] The letter is printed in Strype's *Parker*, Oxford 1821, iii. App. no. XXXIX, 125–6. Strype's reference is '*MSS. penes me*', but I have been unable to trace the original document. The operative sentence runs as follows: 'Qua quidem in re, cum nobiscum ipsi quotidie recordamur, quanta sit apud nos et piorum et eruditorum multitudo, qui testimonio conscientiae usum omnem ornatus hujusmodi sibi illegitimum ducant, et quorum discessu (si vis edicti urgeat) omnino est periculum, ne Academia nostra orba fuerit: nostri esse officii putamus imprimis, ut ea conditione fratrum ac nostratium tibi patefacta, vehementer a tua prudentia per literas contendamus, ut pro ea tum fide, tum gratia, quam apud serenissimam regiam Majestatem obtines, ad remittendam promulgationem ejusmodi, teipsum intercessorem interponas.'

[4] R. W. Dixon, *History of the Church of England from the Abolition of the Roman Jurisdiction*, Oxford 1878–1902, vi. 68.

[5] Beaumont to Cecil, 6 December 1565: P.R.O., S.P. 12/38/10 (1).

most conspicuously—and a party of younger puritan dons, leading their scholars in truculent defiance. But the letter of 26 November identifies a middle party (Beaumont, Longworth, Hutton, Kelke and Whitgift), whose sympathies were strongly engaged by the non-conformists, but who were not regardless of their duty to lawfully established authority. Perhaps their motives were not entirely disinterested. Before the new statutes of 1570 altered the constitution of the university, senior men were tempted to defer, perhaps too readily, to the opinion of the younger regent masters. Whitgift in particular, as Lady Margaret professor, seems to have been a popular figure with the younger element. Sir George Paule, his secretary and biographer, speaks of the throngs of students, young and old, at his divinity lectures, and even he preserves the tradition that 'many of the precise Faction were his daily Auditors'.[1] Perhaps this first-hand knowledge of the temptations of 'popularity' and 'singularity' facing the divinity lecturer in a university predominantly of young men influenced Whitgift when he later framed the new statutes which placed power securely in the hands of the heads of colleges. Yet, whatever their motives, the desire of these men to tender the consciences of their precise brethren had hitherto maintained a bridge between the two diverging parties in the university, and in the Church of England, which was in a shaky condition by the later months of 1565.

Dr. Beaumont of Trinity has left us a clear statement of the conflict of sympathy and duty which all of this group seem to have experienced. As an old member of the English congregation in Geneva in Mary's reign, he was forced to defend himself against an outbreak of rumours that, in his zeal to enforce conformity, he had reverted to the ways of popery.[2] He wrote at length to his countryman and sometime fellow-exile, 'Father' Anthony Gilby, in Leicestershire, making clear his own distaste for the surplice and square cap, but pleading his inevitable duty to the magistrate in an indifferent matter:

'I weare only the square cappe and surplesse, wherby I so litle seke the pleasing of man that I have both to our High Chancellowr and other Honourable spoken and written that we may be freed from them. I do not remember that I have alledged to any man at any tyme th'argument of obedience, although being throughly examined it will not so easily be wiped away as some thinke . . . Have I sett up my bristles against any for not wearing these nedelesse raggs? I deprive none, I punishe none that refuse them . . . Indede, I can hardly escape th' execution of the decree made with the Queen's authority when the tyme of deprivation cometh, althoughe I shold do it with much grief of harte; and in the mean tyme will seke and procure their release if it possibly may be. For myne owne parte, desirous to teache our ignorant bretheren so long as I may, I weare the cappe and surplesse, the which if I refused to do I coulde not be suffered

[1] G. Paule, Life of John Whitgift, 2nd. ed., London 1699, 7.
[2] See my Letters of Thomas Wood, Puritan, 1566–1577 (Bulletin of the Institute of Historical Research, Special Supplement no. 5, November 1960), 24–5. See above, 106-7.

to preache. I wishe with many mo godly bretheren that they may spedely be taken awaye; the which sholde shortly be brought to passe if I were the publike person for suche matters lawfullie awthorised. But nowe my hands are tyed . . . '.[1]

Up to this point Beaumont had deprived no-one for refusing the surplice and was doubtful of the legality of doing so,[2] but he had called for prudence in a university sermon as early as the end of October: 'I reprehended the rashe and unlawfull attemptes of them which being private menn wolde by making publike reformation thrust themselves into th'office of the Magistrate.'[3] Hutton, too, had preached in similar terms, 'to represse the fonde dealing of rashe yong men in framing suche groundes and argumentes as they are not hable to prove'.[4]

This, we may presume, approximated to Whitgift's view of the matter —a view, it must be said, quite unlike that of the mere disciplinarians, of whom he himself would become the most notable representative in later life. And, in the opinion of the watch-dogs of authority, Whitgift remained a dangerous man for some weeks after Cecil's angry rejection of the *démarche* of 26 November. Archbishop Parker wrote darkly on 8 December of 'a fewe Catylyns, who be suffrance wil enfect the holl,'[5] and five days later: 'I see ther is strange deling amongest the wiser sort. Men be men . . . '.[6] Most of our information over the next few weeks comes from Cecil's old college of St. John's, where non-conformity was most strongly rooted, and where Longworth, the master, was openly partial to the puritan faction led by the college lecturer in divinity, William Fulke, which was opposed by the president, Richard Curteys.[7] On 12 December Curteys, who was striving to restore order in the college while Longworth was held in London to account for his stewardship, advised Cecil to confide only in 'such as be cleare in the matter', and warned him that one or two of the heads were still supporting the non-conformists 'and sho[w] so much favor as thei well darre'. There follows this obscure statement: 'The Masters drift is thought to be to bringe all thinges to my Lord of Ely, and then that Mr. Whitgifte shall have a great stroke in them, who is suspected to be scarce indifferent.'[8] The syntax of this passage is so impenetrable that if there were not more unmistakable evidence of Whitgift's non-conformity (in the letter printed below) we might be

[1] Cambridge University Library MS. Mm.1.43 (Baker 32), pp. 427–30; there are extensive quotations from this letter in Porter, op. cit., 115–18.

[2] See John Welles to Cecil, 20 January 1565 (16): 'It is demanded of Mr. Beamont, who ys verie deligent in observinge the order prescribed by your Honour, by what authoritie he can (for not weringe of a surples) deprive anye man of his lyvinge': P.R.O., S.P. 12/39/14.

[3] Beaumont to Cecil, 6 December 1565: P.R.O., S.P. 12/38/10 (1).

[4] Ibid.

[5] Parker to Cecil, 8 December 1565: B.M. MS. Lansdowne 8, fol. 144; printed in *Correspondence of Matthew Parker*, ed. J. Bruce (Parker Soc., Cambridge 1853), 245–6.

[6] Parker to Cecil, 13 December 1565: B.M. MS. Lansdowne 8, fol. 146.

[7] The fullest account of these troubles is in Porter, op. cit., 119–35.

[8] P.R.O., S.P. 12/38/11.

tempted to ignore it. But it clearly implies that Whitgift, who was chaplain to bishop Cox of Ely, was not 'cleare in the matter'. This was not the first time that Curteys had warned Cecil that the Puritans of St. John's hoped to be supported by their visitor, bishop Cox. On 1 December he had asked Cecil to see to it that Cox should clarify his position,[1] and it was alleged that Longworth had suppressed the bishop's disciplinary letters already written to the college. On 13 December Curteys's messengers brought back from Cecil three letters, one for the vice-chancellor, one for Curteys himself and one for Cox, all calling for the speedy restoration of order in St. John's.[2] Cox's letter was only to be sent to him if Curteys felt unable to deal with the situation unaided. But Curteys seems to have lost no time in invoking the bishop's authority. For, two days later, Cox addressed a homily on the subject of conformity to another college of which he was visitor, Peterhouse.[3] But, so far as he knew, 'none of Peterhouse was of that disorder'.

That vicar of Bray,[4] Andrew Perne, master of Peterhouse, knew better. On 11 January—a month after this rapid exchange of letters—he sent archbishop Parker an informal report on the state of the university in the letter which is here printed for the first time. Beaumont and Whitgift and their friends had done the best they could to keep surplices out of Peterhouse, but the sharp letters of Parker, Cecil and Cox had 'brokyn the wilfull disorderid that are wise in their owne conceites'. Yet they were careful to be out of town on holy days so that none should see them wear 'that that thaye have so mutche raylyd a genst'. Whitgift had sworn 'that he had rather have spent xl[li] [£40] then for to have had surplesis in Peter howse, but nayther he nor any of his will lose in dede vi[d] for the weringe of a surples, as sume of them reportithe, but will rather weare iii surplesis'. Dr. Perne was at the first Whitgift's kindly patron and at the last his pensionary, and I know of no other evidence that relations between them were ever strained. But it was an intrinsically odd relationship, and even without this letter we should have known that their views were very divergent.

Cecil was expected to arrive in Cambridge on the very day that Perne wrote to Parker, but greater affairs of state seem to have prevented him. He sent instead his chaplain, who had to dispose otherwise of the doe which bishop Cox prudently sent for his entertainment. One purpose of this chaplain's visit was to collect the names of likely men who could be attached to the service of Cecil and other magnates, and who would make

[1] P.R.O., S.P. 12/38/1.

[2] Drafts of these letters in the hand of Cecil's secretary and amended in Cecil's own hand are in P.R.O., S.P. 12/38/13. Strype (*Parker*, iii. 128–31) used copies of the letters now in the Inner Temple Library (MS. Petyt 538/37, no. 20, fol. 55).

[3] Quoted by Strype (*Annals*, Oxford 1824, I. ii. 159) from a copy in MS. Petyt 538/37, no. 20, fol. 55.

[4] He was vice-chancellor in Mary's reign when the remains of Bucer and Fagius were exhumed and burned and, again, when their names were restored to honour under Elizabeth.

fitting recipients in the future of the patronage which Cecil effectively dispensed. The chaplain reported that he could find no man 'of such yeares and gravitie as you would have abowt my Lordes', and that Curtèys of St. John's was so discouraged that he intended to leave the university for Sir Henry Cheney's service. 'There be divers yong men in thuniversitie, learned and honest, the which would gladlye serve your Honour, wyth whom I will talke concernynge that matter whan I know your further pleasure.'[1] Within a week something had been said to Curteys to persuade him to reconsider his plans and to stick to Cecil.[2] Before the year's end he was dean of Chichester, and this led on to the bishopric of Chichester three years later.

Is it too much to presume that Whitgift was among the learned and honest young men who were spotted and attached during this January visit, and with even more fruitful consequences? In the following year his career began in earnest, when he became regius professor, a royal chaplain, and master in rapid succession of Pembroke and Trinity. When he heard that Cecil intended to place him in Trinity College (his own phrase), Whitgift acknowledged that 'the preferment that I have, what so ever yt ys, I have yet by youre Honor hys meanes, and therefore I owe my self holye unto you'. 'So oft as I doo remember youre singuler goodnes towardes me (ryght Honorable) and earnest desyer to doo me good, I can not butt mervelously lawde and prase my mercyfull God, and gyve moste umble and harty thangkes unto your Honor, for what or who am I, that you showld be so carefull for me?'[3] Three years later Whitgift was still regarded somewhat wistfully as a lost leader by those who had chosen the other path. 'Dr. Whitgifte is a man whome I have lovyd,' wrote Edward Dering of Christ's, 'but yet he is a man, and God hathe suffred [him] to fall intoe greate infirmities. So froward a minde against Mr. Cartwright and other sutche bewrayethe a conscience that is full of sicknes. His affections ruled him and not his learninge when he framed his cogitations to gett moe statutes.'[4]

In the earliest years of Elizabeth's reign, to an extent still often under-estimated, there was a firm front maintained among English Protestants which was, by the standards which later prevailed in the Church of England, a puritan front. But the events of the winter of 1565-6 forced all 'men of reputation' to face the responsibilities of their positions and set them on new paths from which there was no turning back, and which soon carried them some distance from their 'precise brethren'. For Whitgift's career, these months were decisive. From his reluctant conclusion that no-one should relinquish his power to do good in the Church for the surplice and cap, 'being of themselves indifferent', flowed the ever-

---

[1] John Welles to Cecil, 20 January 1565(/6): P.R.O., S.P. 12/39/14.
[2] Curteys to Cecil, 28 January 1565(/6): P.R.O., S.P. 12/39/19.
[3] Whitgift to Cecil, 17 June 1567: P.R.O., S.P. 12/43/8.
[4] Dering to Cecil, 18 November 1570: B.M. MS. Lansdowne 12, fol. 190ᵛ; printed, Strype, *Parker*, iii. 22.

broadening stream of his devotion to the Church and to its royal governor; and, one is bound to add, the equally generous flow of his preferments.

As for Whitgift's future opponent, Thomas Cartwright, there is no doubt that he was already established as the leader of the puritan faction in Trinity. He was wise enough to leave the scene of action for Ireland in December 1565, to become chaplain to archbishop Loftus of Armagh and, for this reason, his biographer, Dr. Scott Pearson, thought that there was nothing to connect him with the vestiarian controversy.[1] Yet Dr. Beaumont assured Cecil on 12 December that he hoped 'in shorte tyme so to refourme the inordinate walkers of Trinitie Colledge (specially nowe when Mr. Cartwright goeth into Irelande) that muche lesse faulte shalbe founde then presently there maye'.[2] By January 1566 the lines were drawn.

APPENDIX

Dr. Andrew Perne, master of Peterhouse, to Matthew Parker, archbishop of Canterbury, 11 January 1565 (/6). Holograph. Lambeth Palace Library MS. 2002, fol. 119.

[Lambeth Palace Library MS. 2002 is a volume of personal papers of the Elizabethan archbishops of Canterbury, entitled, in a hand which I think is archbishop Bancroft's, 'Transactions .touching Matters Ecclesiastical in the Queen's time'. In 1634 this collection was listed as an unbound bundle of papers, Bundle 'P', but with the contents in the same order, on Shelf 32 of archbishop Laud's 'paper study' (Bodleian Library, MS. Tanner 88, no. 2, pp. 84–5.) Almost all the papers in the volume are individually described in this list of 1634, except for Dr. Perne's letter and two other letters which are described as 'diverse letters'. This bundle was among the papers which were taken from Lambeth and passed into Selden's possession during the Interregnum. After an extended migration of three centuries it has recently been restored to Lambeth Palace Library, with other Selden MSS. which can also be identified from the 1634 list of Laud's papers. In the late seventeenth or early eighteenth century this and other papers in the collection now restored to Lambeth were seen and transcribed by the non-juror, George Harbin, and his copy survives in British Museum MS. Additional 29546, fols. 59v–60r.

Besides the points discussed above, Perne's letter casts light on the translation of the Bishops' Bible, and tends to confirm the puritan jibe that 'the chaplaynes traviled, and the Bishopes brought forthe'.[3] It also enlivens our knowledge of Dr. Caius, recently described as of a 'quiet, retiring, inoffensive demeanour'.[4]

My thanks are due to his Grace, the archbishop of Canterbury, and the Trustees of Lambeth Palace Library for permission to print this letter.]

'Yowr Gracis letters were sent to me beinge at Elye, sines what tyme I dyd heare of no messenger before this tyme. Ther was as mutche procuryd agenst surplesis in Peterhowse by Mr. D. Bewmont and Mr. Whitgyvet and thers as thaye cowlde possible, but yowr Grac and Mr. Secretarie,[5] thankes be to God, have brokyn the wilfull disorderid that are wise in their owne conceites. Mr.

---

[1] A. F. Scott Pearson, *Thomas Cartwright and Elizabethan Puritanism, 1535–1603*, Cambridge 1925, 19–20.   [2] P.R.O., S.P. 12/38/10.

[3] This was a marginal comment in a pirated translation of Parker's official biography, the *Matthaeus*, printed in 1574 (at Heidelberg?) under the title, *The life off the 70 archbishope off Canterbury presentlye sittinge Englished*. It occurs at Sig. Ciir.

[4] M. H. Curtis, *Oxford and Cambridge in Transition, 1558–1642*, Oxford 1959, 168.

[5] Cecil.

Secretarie dyd wright a letter to my Lord of Elye, wherin amonge other thinges he dyd chardge him with to mutche softenes and bearinge in this matter. But as yowr Grace dyd see he dyd wright a verie rownde letter to us of Peter howse, wherebye thaye that before bare them sel[fes] of him and his sayinges in this matter are compellyd for to relent. But yet do thaye get them selfes owte of the towne on the hallydaye that thaye sholde not be sene to weare that that thaye have so mutche raylyd a genst. Mr. Whitgyvt saythe in wordes that he had rather have spent xl[li] then for to have had surplesis in Peter howse, but nayther he nor any of his will lose in dede vi[d] for the weringe of a surples, as sume of them reportithe, but will rather weare iii surplesis. My Lorde of Elye dothe diligentlye lawbor a bowte the translatinge of the Actes of the Apostiles and Sayncte Powle to the Romanes, as I thinke, by yowr Gracis appoyntment. He have bestowid Mr. Andrewe Denes prebende at Elye upon Mr. Bell his chappeline. And his parsonadge of Downame he have gyven it to Mr. Thomas Aywarde, your Gracis chapeline,[1] hoo dothe helpe my Lorde well in his sayd translation. For I do tak him to be better lernyd in the Greke tonge than ayther my Lorde or any of his chaplines. Yowr Grace might do well to gyve my Lorde thankes for the bestowinge of this benefice upon yowr Gracis chapeline. Yowr Grace knowithe best what to be done. As I do well lyke Mr. Doctor Caius good zeale towardes byldinge up the wales of his colledge, so do I mislyke his ondistrete[2] severitie a genst his felowes, wherby thaye be great[ly] discoradgyd from ther lerninge, the whiche ought to be the ende of his other byldinge. Yet I do thinke no thinge more requisite this daye than prudent severitie in furderinge of vertewe and lerninge. But to use it as he dothe in callinge his felowes boyes, knaves, beggers, openlye, and strivinge to put them in to the stockes, expellinge more felowes in one yer then all the colledgis in Cambridge, makyng statutes dayelye upon private matters, whiche he will change shortlye after, wherbye he bringe him self, his colledge and statutes in contempte.[3] I shall moste humblye desyer yowr Grace to pardon me that I dyd wishe so often and ernestlye for Mr. John Parkers returninge to Cambridge, the whiche I dyd it of good will, thinkyng that it wolde have bene mutche for his furderinge in learninge, and I trustyd and wisshid no hinderance to ayther his good disposition to vertewe and godlynes, nor impayringe of his helthe of his bodye.[4]

[1] Andrew Deane was a fellow of Gonville Hall from 1532 to 1547 and later of Corpus Christi (Parker's college). He held the sixth prebendal stall at Ely and the rectory of Downham from 1559 until his death on 16 December 1565. John Bell was a fellow of Peterhouse in 1554, university preacher in 1567, master of Jesus from 1579 to 1585 and vice-chancellor 1582–3. He held his prebend at Ely from 1566 until he resigned on becoming dean of Ely in 1589. (J. A. Venn, *Alumni Cantabrigienses*, Cambridge I. ii. 1922*, 25, I. i. 128; J. Le Neve, *Fasti Ecclesiae Anglicanae*, Oxford 1854, 359–60.) Nothing seems to be known about Thomas Aywarde (Hayward?), and he is not in the register of either university.   [2] I.e. 'undiscreet'.

[3] The quarrel between Dr. Caius and a faction of the fellows of Gonville and Caius College and the efforts of Parker and Cecil to resolve it are documented in P.R.O., S.P. 12/38/26, 39/4, 5 and 7, and in *Correspondence of Matthew Parker*, 248–50. The affair is discussed by Dr. John Venn in his biographical sketch of *John Caius*, Cambridge 1910, 22–7.

[4] John Parker matriculated a fellow-commoner of Peterhouse in 1562. There is no record of his residence after 1565, or that he took a degree. He was later married to a daughter of bishop Cox. His father provided him with offices in the administration of the diocese of Canterbury. In 1570 Parker was told by the puritan, Edward Dering: 'Againe your sonnes . . . I would that they should be more moderate in their apparell; let them use honest and comely clothes, leaving gawdy garmentes to others.' (J. A. Venn, op. cit., I. iii. (1924), 306; T. A. Walker, *A Biographical Register of Peterhouse Men*, i. (Cambridge 1927) 226; V. J. K. Brook, *A Life of Archbishop Parker*, Oxford 1962, 342; B.M. MS. Stowe 743, fol. 6[v]).

* *Cantabrigienses*, Cambridge 1922–47, I. ii. 25, I. i. 128.

Wherefore my truste and humble desyer is that yowr G[race] will take my rudenes in good parte, proceedinge of good will. We do loke for Mr. Secretarie to cume this daye to Cambridge. I praye Allmightye God longe to preserve yowr Grace in honorable prosperitie with all yowr godly familye. From Peterhowse, the xi daye of Januarie 1565.

Yowr Gracis daylye orator, Andrewe Perne.

[Endorsed in Perne's hand: 'To the moste reverende father in God, my Lorde of Canterberie his Grace, these be deliverid at his howse at Lambithe.']

Note (1983): William Williams was not Thomas Wood's son-in-law (p. 205) but his brother-in-law. See p. 47, above.

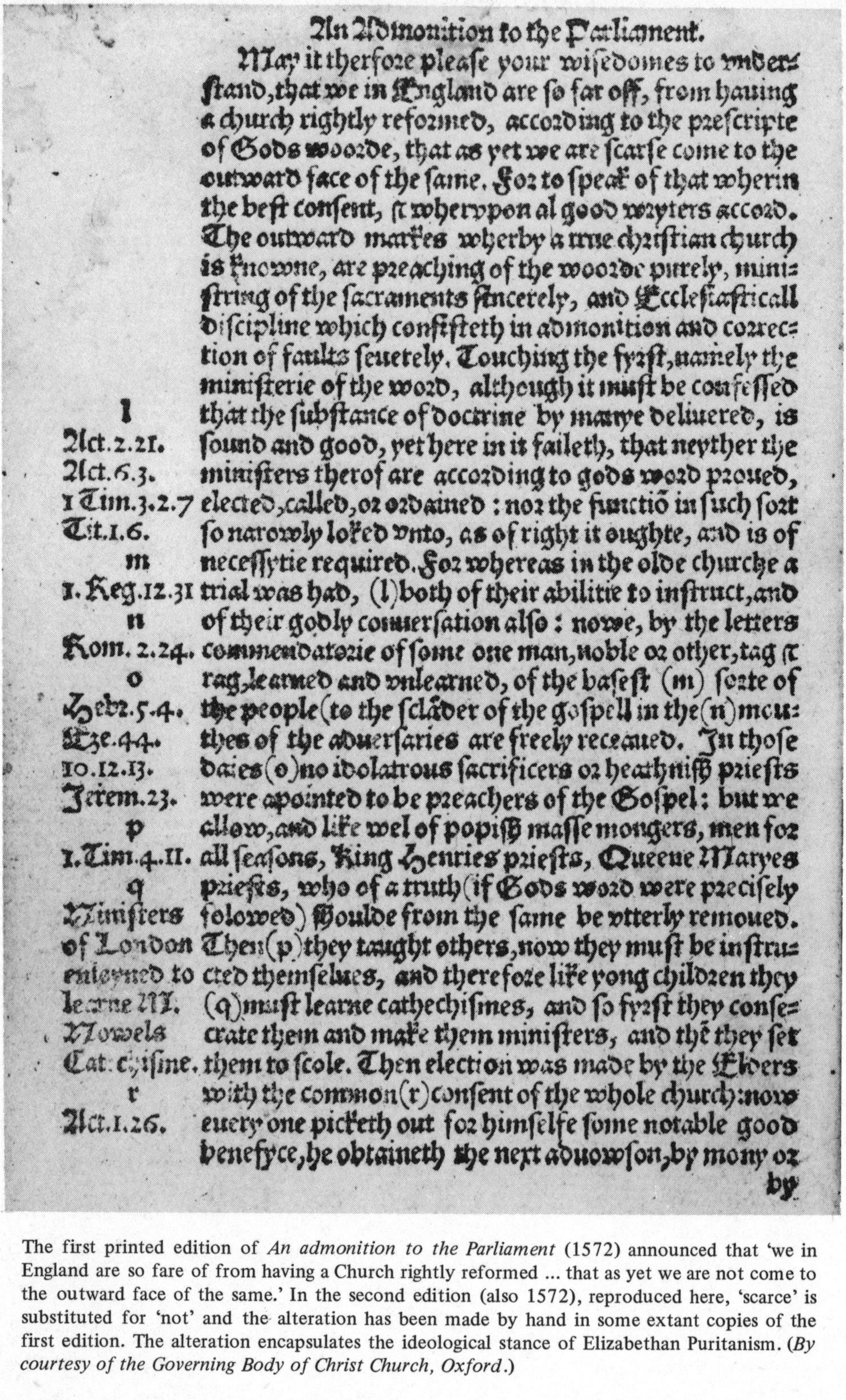

May it therfore please your wisedomes to vnder-
stand, that we in England are so far off, from hauing
a church rightly reformed, according to the prescripte
of Gods woorde, that as yet we are scarse come to the
outward face of the same. For to speak of that wherin
the best consent, & wherypon al good writers accord.
The outward markes wherby a true christian church
is knowne, are preaching of the woorde purely, mini-
string of the sacraments sincerely, and Ecclesiasticall
discipline which consisteth in admonition and correction of faults seuerely. Touching the first, namely the
ministerie of the word, although it must be confessed
that the substance of doctrine by manye deliuered, is
sound and good, yet here in it faileth, that neyther the
ministers therof are according to gods word proued,
elected, called, or ordained: nor the functiõ in such sort
so narowly loked vnto, as of right it oughte, and is of
necessytie required. For whereas in the olde churche a
trial was had, (l)both of their abilitie to instruct, and
of their godly conuersation also: nowe, by the letters
commendatorie of some one man, noble or other, tag &
rag, learned and vnlearned, of the basest (m) sorte of
the people (to the sclaader of the gospell in the(n)mou-
thes of the aduersaries are freely receaued. In those
daies (o)no idolatrous sacrificers or heathnish priests
were apointed to be preachers of the Gospel: but we
allow, and like wel of popish masse mongers, men for
all seasons, King Henries priests, Queene Maryes
priests, who of a truth (if Gods word were precisely
folowed) shoulde from the same be vtterly remoued.
Then(p)they taught others, now they must be instructed themselues, and therefore like yong children they
(q)must learne cathechismes, and so first they consecrate them and make them ministers, and then they set
them to scole. Then election was made by the Elders
with the common(r)consent of the whole church:now
euery one picketh out for himselfe some notable good
benefyce, he obtaineth the next aduowson, by mony or
by

Marginal references (left column):

1

Act.2.21.

Act.6.3.

I Tim.3.2.7

Tit.1.6.

m

I.Reg.12.31

n

Rom.2.24.

o

Heb.5.4.

Eze.44.

10.12.13.

Ierem.23.

p

I.Tim.4.11.

q

Ministers
of London
enioyned to
learne III.
Nowels
Catechisme.

r

Act.1.26.

The first printed edition of *An admonition to the Parliament* (1572) announced that 'we in England are so fare of from having a Church rightly reformed ... that as yet we are not come to the outward face of the same.' In the second edition (also 1572), reproduced here, 'scarce' is substituted for 'not' and the alteration has been made by hand in some extant copies of the first edition. The alteration encapsulates the ideological stance of Elizabethan Puritanism. (*By courtesy of the Governing Body of Christ Church, Oxford.*)

13

JOHN FIELD AND ELIZABETHAN PURITANISM

THE STORY of John Field is that of a man who led a movement which failed, and whose role was largely anonymous or clandestine. Hence he is so little known to Elizabethan historiography that it was possible for a succession of writers, mistaking the evidence of a single document, to style him 'minister of Wandsworth', which he never was,[1] and for a modern authority to dismiss him as 'a London preacher',[2] which, though true, is as adequate a description of Field as to say that Francis Place was a Charing Cross tailor. For, during the 1570s and 1580s, Field's influence on the evolving puritan movement was constant and sometimes decisive; and a study of his career reveals the strength and the weakness—as well as the inherent conflicts—of the reformist sector of the Elizabethan Church.

His cause was the further reformation of the Church of England according to the presbyterian platform: the establishment of 'pure' —that is, non-liturgical—worship, and of a reformed ministry and discipline. Field and his contemporaries could not know that the measures for the settlement of religion undertaken by Elizabeth and her early parliaments and convocations embodied a final form of constitution for the Church of England or that they determined the place of the English Church in divided western Christendom. A reformed doctrinal confession had been grafted on to a Church which had renounced the Roman obedience (but preserved, within the limits imposed by the act of supremacy, a Catholic ministry and order), and which was bound by the act of uniformity to the

---

[1] e.g. P. Heylyn, *Aerius Redivivus* (1670), 273; Athony à Wood, *Athenae Oxonienses* (1813), i, 535.

[2] W. H. Frere, *The English Church in the Reigns of Elizabeth and James I, 1558– 1625*, 179.

use of a liturgy which was essentially Catholic, although accommodated in some places to Protestant doctrines. Our sense of the
inevitability of these arrangements has given us too rigid a
conception of an Elizabethan Church 'Settlement' and obscured
until recently its partly circumstantial origins.[1] Yet few Englishmen
and no sincere Protestant could have regarded as 'settled' a
Church reformed in doctrine but only partly in ceremonies and
not at all in discipline. The concept of an insular Anglicanism,
Reformed and Catholic, had not been generally assimilated, even
at the end of the reign. By Field it was attacked as 'a certain kind
of religion, framed out of man's own brain and fantasy, far worse
than that of popery (if worse may be), patched and pieced out of
theirs and ours together'.[2]

Field was one of the extreme puritans who laboured confidently
to complete what they regarded as an interim settlement by
making a clean sweep of all the 'popish dregs' yet remaining in
the Church. Besides the displacement of bishops by a hierarchy of
presbyterian synods, and of liturgical worship by an austere form
of public prayer resembling the Scottish 'Book of Common
Order', their schemes, to be successful, would have necessitated
far-reaching changes in the structure of politics and society which
neither the Queen nor the majority of her subjects desired. Field
was the man chiefly responsible for devising the means by which
this handful of fanatics proposed to accomplish what would have
been the most drastic revolution in English history. Its agencies
were to be pulpit and press, patronage, suit and petition, and
parliament. The campaign was managed by a disciplined organization which not only conducted the public agitation for reform
but privately practised presbyterianism within its own membership. Field's importance as the instigator and co-ordinator of much
of this activity was recognized shortly after his death by Richard
Bancroft, later archbishop of Canterbury, who in 1593 publicly
exposed the pattern of puritan subversion from the letters and
papers of the puritans themselves:

This John Field ... whilst he lived was a great and chief man amongst
the brethren of London, and one to whom the managing of the discipline

[1] J. E. Neale, 'The Elizabethan Acts of Supremacy and Uniformity' (*E.H.R.*
lxv), 304–32; *Elizabeth I and her Parliaments, 1559–1581*, 51–84.
[2] Field to Anthony Gilby, 4 Aug. 1572: Camb. Univ. Library MS. Mm.1.43
(Baker 32), pp. 442–3. This collection will be subsequently referred to as Baker
MS. 32.

(for the outward practice of it) was especially by the rest committed. So as all the letters that were directed from the brethren of other places, to have this or that referred to the London assemblies, were for the most part directed to him.[1]

Although the cause failed, its effect was not entirely lost. The pamphleteering, the national agitation organized in a great public cause, the appeal to parliament and the early connection between that appeal and the claim to free speech in the house of commons: all pointed forward to the puritan revolution of the seventeenth century.[2]

Field's origins and early history are obscure. By the evidence of an ordination certificate which appears to be his, he was born in London in 1545. He was at Oxford in the 'sixties, and later referred to the Jesuit John Howlet, who entered Exeter College in 1564, as 'a scholar in my time';[3] but the details of his university career are indistinguishable from those of his contemporaries of the same names.[4] He was perhaps the John Field who proceeded B.A. in 1564 and M.A. in 1567.[5] His ordination certificate describes him as a Bachelor of Arts of Christ Church. On 25 March 1566 Field was ordained priest by Bishop Grindal of London.[6] About a year before, he had secured as patron the earl of Warwick,[7] the elder brother of the earl of Leicester, a circumstance which perhaps facilitated his ordination at the uncanonical age of twenty-one.

The weeks which followed may well have had a decisive influence on the genesis of his militant puritan outlook. The day after his ordination, thirty-seven London ministers—the first significant and organized group of nonconformists—were suspended at Lambeth for their refusal to wear the vestments prescribed by the Prayer Book rubric and Archbishop Parker's

---

[1] R. Bancroft, *A survay of the pretended holy discipline* (1593), 369.

[2] P. Collinson, 'The Puritan Classical Movement in the Reign of Elizabeth I' (Lond. Univ. Ph.D. thesis, 1957).

[3] J. Field, *A caveat for Parsons* (1581), epistle.   [4] A. Wood, *Athenae*, i, 535.

[5] *Register of the University of Oxford*, ed. C. W. Boase and Andrew Clark, ii (3), 255.

[6] Ordinations register, bishop of London, 1550–77 (London Guildhall Lib. MS. 9535/1) f. 124*b*. I owe this reference to Dr. H. G. Owen.

[7] Caspar Olevian, trans. J. Field, *An exposition of the symbol of the apostles* (1581), dedication to Warwick; petition from the parishioners of St. Mary Aldermary to Leicester, 1585: *A Seconde Parte of a Register, Being a Calendar of Manuscripts under that title intended for publication by the Puritans about 1593*, ed. A. Peel, i, 135 (misdated).

'Advertisements'.[1] Their vacant pulpits were at once supplied by young and unbeneficed preachers who had not at first been called upon to conform. But these 'godly young men', among whom Field was surely numbered, were shortly afterwards cited before the archbishop and silenced, whereupon Field seems to have returned to Oxford.[2] In January 1567 we have the first letter from his hand: an elegant Latin epistle written to John Foxe, the martyrologist, from Broadgates Hall. Evidently he was much influenced at this time by Laurence Humphrey, the puritan president of Magdalen and a leader of the anti-vestiarian movement.[3] By the spring of 1568 Field had returned to London and after preaching for some time in the church of Holy Trinity, Minories, he became curate of the neighbouring parish of St. Giles, Cripplegate.[4] He is named in the parish books as minister in 1570, when he was living 'at Goodman Swanne's without Cripplegate'.[5] By then he was married (nothing is known of his wife Joan) and his seven children were subsequently baptized in the parish of St. Giles: among them Theophilus (who was to become a Laudian Bishop of St. Davids), in 1574, and Nathan, the future dramatist, in 1587, only a few months before his father's death.[6] By November 1571 Field had his own house in Grub Street, where John Foxe came to live at about the same time.[7]

The neighbourhood of Cripplegate and the Minories was a hot-bed of puritanism and even of sectarianism. As a royal peculiar, the Minories church was exempt from the bishop's jurisdiction, and the parishioners themselves appointed and supported their ministers and preachers, who were always radical puritans.[8] Stow tells us that the first puritans, 'unspotted Lambs of the Lord . . . kept their church in the Minories, without Aldgate',[9] and the

[1] M. M. Knappen, *Tudor Puritanism*, 196–7.

[2] Thomas Wood to William Cecil, 29 March 1566: Herts. Rec. Off. Gorhambury MS. viii/B/143 f. 2b; *Correspondence of Matthew Parker* (ed. John Bruce, Parker Soc.), 278.

[3] Field to Foxe, 26 Jan. 1567: B.M. Harl. MSS. 416 f. 185.

[4] H. G. Owen, 'The London Parish Clergy in the Reign of Elizabeth I' (Lond. Univ. Ph.D. thesis, 1957), 519, 611.

[5] Francis Hall to Field, 13 Sept. 1569: B.M. Harl. MSS. 416 f. 189.

[6] R. F. Brinkley, *Nathan Field, the Actor-Playwright* (Yale Studies in English, lxxvii), 2–3, 7.

[7] Field to Anthony Gilby, 22 Nov. 1571: Baker MS. 32 p. 445; *D.N.B.s.v.* Foxe.

[8] E. M. Tomlinson, *A History of the Minories, London*; Owen, loc. cit. 517–24.

[9] *Three Fifteenth Century Chronicles* (ed. J. Gairdner, Camd. Soc. N.S. xxviii), 143.

names of those who preached there in 1569 and 1570 are sufficient to establish a connection between the parish and the separatism of those Londoners who, already partially estranged from their parish churches, were meeting in Plumbers' Hall and other places to use the forms of prayer of Knox's Geneva congregation and of the 'privy churches' of Mary's days.[1] Among the preachers of this semi-sectarian connection, Field began, not later than 1570, to attend regular meetings which seem to have been intentionally modelled on the *classis*, or local conference of ministers of reformed church order. Twenty years later, an erstwhile member of the group named the preachers who in about 1570 had been 'of the brotherhood', 'stood so much upon reformation', and met twice a week in their houses by rotation: they had all at some time preached in the Minories. Field and a young curate of All Hallows, Honey Lane, named Thomas Wilcox were the conveners of the group.[2] This London conference was to have an unbroken existence at least until Field's death in 1588, and with strengthened membership would provide the nerve-centre for a presbyterian movement extending into most of the English counties south of the Trent.

It was almost certainly this group which in the summer of 1572, and towards the end of the parliamentary session of that year, launched the anonymous *Admonition to the Parliament*, the first popular manifesto of English presbyterianism.[3] Field and Wilcox of Honey Lane were the authors: Wilcox contributed the trenchant 'Admonition' itself, Field the more scathing and brilliant 'View of popish abuses yet remaining in the English Church' appended to it, while Field seems to have been the manager of the whole enterprise.[4] These two tracts advanced far beyond the rather superficial objections which until then had been voiced against the Queen's Church. The mere excising of a vestments rubric—the 'shells and chippings of Poperie'[5]—was not enough. 'We in England are so far off from having a Church rightly reformed, according to the prescript of God's word, that as yet we

---

[1] A. Peel, *The First Congregational Churches, 1567–81*; C. Burrage, *Early English Dissenters*, i, 79–93; ii, 9–18; Owen, loc. cit. 521; Tomlinson, op. cit. 166, 220.

[2] Deposition of Thomas Edmunds, 13 Oct. 1591: Star Chamber 5 A 49/34; Owen, loc. cit. 518–19.

[3] Repr. in *Puritan Manifestoes* (ed. W. H. Frere and C. E. Douglas, Church Hist. Soc. 1907, repr. 1954), 5–55.

[4] A. F. Scott Pearson, *Thomas Cartwright and Elizabethan Puritanism*, 59; *Seconde Parte of Register*, i, 89.

[5] Field to Gilby, 22 Nov. 1571: Baker MS. 32 p. 445.

are not[1] come to the outward face of the same.'[2] The very foundations of a Reformed Church, a 'sincere' ministry and ecclesiastical discipline in the Calvinist sense, were yet to be laid. Two years earlier Thomas Cartwright, the theorist of the presbyterian movement, had said much the same in the polite Latin of the Lady Margaret divinity lectures in Cambridge.[3] Yet, by the degree of popular interest and official displeasure which it aroused, the 'Admonition', rather than Cartwright's lectures, may be said to have launched the presbyterian attack on the Elizabethan Settlement. In mid-June 1572 Field and Wilcox were arrested and in October they were sentenced to a year's imprisonment. In their confinement they entertained a stream of visitors of the ultra-Protestant faction and overnight became popular heroes.[4]

Field and Wilcox gave the signal for a succession of presbyterian manifestoes. The 'Admonition' had been largely a destructive document, anti-anglican rather than positively presbyterian, although founded upon certain Calvinist principles as to the nature of the Church. The elaboration of a presbyterian constitution for the English Church was left to other tracts which appeared from clandestine and foreign presses between 1572 and 1577: the anonymous *Second Admonition*, the *Ecclesiasticae disciplinae . . . explicatio* of Walter Travers, which Cartwright translated as *A full and plain declaration of ecclesiastical discipline*, and Cartwright's own salvoes in the Admonition Controversy with John Whitgift.[5] Although it is often stated that puritanism entered its 'presbyterian phase' in 1572, the 'Admonition' was a product of circumstance, reflecting the exasperated mood of Field and his immediate circle more than a general swing to presbyterianism in the puritan movement. After the dissolution of the parliament of 1571 Field, with some older puritan leaders, had been subjected to special examination by the High Commissioners, perhaps with the aim of uncovering the organization behind the campaign for moderate puritan reform which had been launched in that session. Required to signify his assent to the disputed ceremonies specifically, as well as to the Prayer Book and Thirty-Nine Articles, Field had joined

[1] In 2nd edn. 'scarce'.   [2] *Puritan Manifestoes*, 9.
[3] Scott Pearson, op. cit. 26–30.
[4] Inner Temple Lib. Petyt MS. 538/47 f. 481; Bishop Sandys to Burghley, 5 Aug. 1573: B.M. Lansd. 17 no. 43 ff. 96–97.
[5] *The Works of John Whitgift* (ed. J. Ayre, Parker Soc., 3 vols.); D. J. McGinn, *The Admonition Controversy* (Rutgers Studies in English, v).

with others in offering 'a kind of agreement' to the bishop of London. This peace proposal included a polite refusal to wear the vestments which led to Field's suspension from preaching. By January 1572 he was reduced to school-teaching, to his sorrow and vexation:

I sigh and sob daily unto God that I may have a lawful entrance to teach the flock of Christ. . . . And I await when the Lord will give me a place, a flock, a people to teach. I study for it and employ my whole travail unto it; and nothing is more grievous unto me than that, through the over-much tyranny of those that should be my encouragers, I am compelled instead to teach children, so that I cannot employ myself wholly unto that which I am bent most earnestly.[1]

Field's bitter and doctrinaire opposition to bishops dated from this time. Early in 1572 he was adopted by the parishioners of the Minories as their curate,[2] but it is unlikely that he obtained a licence to serve there. The last hope for Field, as for other inflexible nonconformists, lay in a bill debated in the house of commons in May 1572 which would have authorized the bishops to licence nonconformist deviations from the Prayer Book.[3] It was the failure of this attempt to exclude the puritan ministry from the operation of the act of uniformity which had provoked the printing of the 'Admonition', a declaration of war, not against the Queen, who was really responsible, but against the bishops who were her instruments in enforcing conformity. For the next eight years Field held no licence to preach. Indeed, the occasions on which he preached in parish churches were hardly more than incidents in the career as a revolutionary on which he now embarked with a zeal violent even for a Calvinist of the first generation. Admitting sole responsibility for the 'bitterness of the style' in the 'Admonition', he told Archbishop Parker's chaplain: 'As God hath his Moses, so he hath his Elijah. . . . It is no time to blanch, nor to sew cushions under men's elbows, or to flatter them in their sins.'[4]

Wilcox, for his part, was no Elijah. Most of his published works were concerned with the cultivation of individual piety and show him to have been one of the first of the puritan pastoral casuists.[5] He corresponded copiously with his many patrons, and more

[1] *Parker Corresp.* 381–82; *Seconde Parte of Register,* i, 82; Field to Gilby, 10 Jan. 1572: Baker MS. 32 p. 447.   [2] Tomlinson, op. cit. 220.
[3] Neale, *Elizabeth and Parliament, 1559–81,* 297–304.
[4] *Seconde Parte of Register,* i, 89.
[5] *The works of . . . Mr. Thomas Willcockes,* ed. John Burgess (1624).

especially with their wives, but we are told that his letters contained
'little but godly, plain and necessary exhortations for the exercise
of godliness'.[1] Ten years after their collaboration in the 'Admonition', Field led the London conference in debarring Wilcox from
preaching and in witholding his stipend, penalties for some
undisclosed moral offence. The friendship ended in mutual
recriminations, Wilcox suggesting that he 'had perhaps concealed
as great infirmities of Field's 'and Field rebuking him for despising
the censure of the brethren. 'If God hath made you an instrument
to seek for the advancement of Christ's sceptre', Field told him,
'kiss it your self and be subject unto it.'[2] Field was as careful as
Wilcox to make friends among the influential Protestant gentry,
but he did this less as a spiritual physician than as one with his eye
to the main chance. From prison he sent collections of the first and
second 'Admonitions' and other pamphlets to ladies of his
acquaintance, each inscribed with eight lines of doggerel, which
began:

> Read and peruse this little book,
> with prayer to the Lord
> That all may yield that therein look
> to truth with one accord.[3]

Later he was to present a copy of another of his works to the
foundress of Sidney Sussex College with the inscription: 'To the
right honourable and my very good Lady the Countess of Sussex:
stand fast: truth shall prevail.'[4]

Propaganda and organization: these revolutionary arts were
instinctive to Field and from the early 'seventies he was to use them
to construct from the somewhat incoherent dissent of the puritan
clergy a purposeful and militant movement. As a propagandist, he
had served his apprenticeship in collecting information for Foxe's
Acts and Monuments;[5] by 1571 he had his own connections with
the press and his own methods of procuring inflammatory material

[1] The 17th-century puritan antiquary Roger Morrice's 'Chronological Account
of Eminent Persons', Dr. Williams's Library, Morrice MS. ii. 417 (2 & 4),
517 (4), 617 (2 & 4).

[2] R. Bancroft, *Daungerous positions and proceedings* (1593), 118–19.

[3] R. Hooker, *Works*, ed. Keble, Church and Paget, i, 152 *n*; F. Paget, *Introduction
to the Fifth Book of Hooker's . . . Ecclesiastical Polity*, 47–48.

[4] Philippe de Mornay du Plessis, trans. Field, *Treatise of the Church* (1579): B.M.
C.60.b.2.

[5] Below, 354.

for publication. He informed 'Father' Anthony Gilby of Ashby-de-la-Zouch, a revered puritan of the older generation, that 'had there not been wiser men' than he, he would have printed one of Gilby's pamphlets which had come into his possession, together with a tract of Thomas Sampson's authorship: 'Howbeit, upon the advice of the brethren it is stayed.' Two months later, he told Gilby of his own unsolicited translation of another of Gilby's tracts from Latin into English, presumably for publication: 'I hope you will not be angry with Mr. Wood for sending it unto me, since it is yet at your commandment.'[1] In later years, Field was not always so scrupulous.

His letters to Gilby show that in 1572 Field was urging the puritan leaders to unite more closely in a formal system of conferences approximating to the synods of presbyterian organization. In August he wrote from prison, appealing to Gilby to consider how best to defend the cause against the repression of the bishops. His own remedy was that 'as of late there was a conference, so it might again be renewed, everyone submitting their judgement to the mighty word of God'; and that this conference should prepare a formal doctrinal statement. 'The same I write to you,' Field added suggestively, 'I write to others.'[2] His intention was that Gilby and his other correspondents should communicate these letters to the conferences of preachers in their own districts. Most puritan ministers were already organized in the local associations for the exercise of 'prophesying' which, with episcopal approval, had been set up in many market towns in the early years of the reign and by the early 'seventies were to be found in most of the dioceses of the province of Canterbury.

The principal function of a prophesying was to educate a preaching ministry through the agency of the better clergy of the district. The main proceedings consisted of sermons preached on a select text by three or four of the company under the presidency of a moderator, and before the other members of the exercise and, in most cases, a lay audience. But the public preaching was followed by private 'censure' and conference among the ministers alone, and that by a dinner where there might be some discussion of matters of common interest. This part of the day's proceedings enabled the ministers of an area roughly equivalent to the rural

---

[1] Field to Gilby, 22 Nov. 1571, 10 Jan. 1572: Baker MS. 32 pp. 445, 447.
[2] 4 Aug. 1572: ibid. pp. 443-4.

deanery to play some part in the government of their churches. The prophesyings, derived from continental experiments in church order, introduced some element of Reformed discipline into the over-centralized episcopal government of the Elizabethan Church. Most of the exercises, in fact, owed their existence to the initiative of local puritan leaders and some became platforms for the dissemination of puritan propaganda. Yet few of these associations were presbyterian or even tended towards presbyterianism. Their orders were sanctioned by the bishops, who in some dioceses bound the whole clergy to attendance and invested permanent moderators with powers of discipline. Where these moderators exercised the bishop's delegated authority, the prophesyings were an experiment in reformed or 'reduced' episcopacy and not a presbyterian conspiracy. Their leaders had no reason to share Field's doctrinaire hostility to bishops. Field's main task after the publication of the 'Admonition 'was to win support for the cause of extremism in these moderate circles.

The leaders of early Elizabethan dissent accepted a reformed episcopacy as a legitimate form of church order and believed that only a difference in inessentials divided them from those who held authority in the Church. Laurence Humphrey, Thomas Sampson, Thomas Lever, Anthony Gilby, these 'fathers' of English Reform had been the contemporaries and friends of some of the bishops both at the universities and in exile. They represented an early and more latitudinarian stage in the Reformation, while the 'Admonition' spoke for a less tolerant generation which followed Theodore Beza's Geneva in proclaiming new dogmas, especially on the question of church government.[1] Bancroft was probably mistaken, therefore, when he reported that the decision to publish the 'Admonition' had been taken at a conference held in London in May 1572 and attended by Gilby, Sampson and Lever.[2] It is more likely that a conference with this representation concerned itself only with the bill to obtain toleration for nonconformity which was brought before parliament that month, and that it was the failure of this moderate programme which gave the extremists their opportunity. What is certain is that the 'Admonition' and the conduct of the presbyterian faction were alike condemned by

---

[1] N. F. Sykes, *New Priest, Old Presbyter*, 42–44; G. Donaldson, 'The Relations between the English and Scottish Presbyterian Movements to 1604' (Lond. Univ. Ph.D. thesis, 1938), ch.i.　　　[2] *Survay of the discipline*, 54.

most of the older puritan leaders, including Humphrey and Sampson. Thomas Norton, their representative in the early Elizabethan parliaments, speaks for them all: 'Surely the book was fond, and with unreasonableness and unseasonableness hath hindered much good and done much hurt.'[1] These veterans now lost their claim to march in the van of the reformist movement. Field and his friends led what was essentially a new puritan movement, which attracted many of the young men now entering the ministry from the expanding universities, and especially from Cambridge, where the doctrines of Cartwright had become the watchword for a younger generation in revolt.

Conscious of the youthfulness prevailing in the presbyterian faction and of its isolation from what was still the main stream of the reformist movement, Field exerted himself to recruit some at least of the older men. In a letter to Gilby of August 1572 he condemns the bishops in violent terms and contrasts 'our misery, their cruelty, our religion, their superstition, our duty, their negligence'. For too long the godly have exercised restraint 'for hope of amendment in some and peace with all'. Now that the bankruptcy of this policy stands revealed, they must speak the truth fearlessly. Conferences must be organized to maintain unity —a presbyterian unity—on the questions in controversy. 'For otherwise it cannot but come to pass that our churches by mutual dissentions shall be quite overthrown.'[2] Having ranged all bishops with Antichrist and concluded that the established Church lacked even the 'outward face' of a Reformed Church, Field followed a consistent course in calling for a formal presbyterian organization of the puritan churches. At this time he proposed to translate the 'Admonition' into Latin and to circulate it among the conferences for subscription, and with Wilcox he did compose and distribute a private 'Confession of Faith'.[3] Dissuaded in 1572 from the perilous step of making this a public declaration of the faith of the puritan churches, in 1574 the London presbyterians still cherished the idea of a 'confession of our faith, that it may well appear to the world what we are in deed'.[4] Futher evidence of the same trend may be seen in Field's ratification of the 'order of Wandsworth', the

[1] Norton to John Whitgift, 20 Oct. 1572: Inner Temple Lib. Petyt MS. 538/38 f. 65.
[2] 4 Aug. 1572: Baker MS. 32 pp. 443–4.
[3] Ibid.; *A parte of a register* (1593), 528 sqq.
[4] Laurence Tomson to Gilby, 4 April 1574: Baker MS. 32 p. 448.

precise nature of which remains obscure, but which must imply
the establishment of some kind of local presbyterian organization.[1] In some churches puritan ministers were encouraged by
Field and others of the London conference to seek appointment
by the processes of congregational election and presbyterian
ordination.[2]

Yet Field was no separatist and had no intention of calling out
a gathered church of the godly few. Only a national Reformation,
imposed by law on the whole Church, could satisfy him. It follows
that his renunciation of the established discipline of the Church
could only be justified by an early triumph of the presbyterian
cause. This was not an unreasonable expectation in 1573, when
Field and Wilcox were 'esteemed as gods' by the London popu-
lace[3] and a popular lampoon, written at about this time, implored
Matthew Parker that 'as Augustine was the first, so Matthew might
be the last' archbishop of Canterbury.[4] Field had powerful friends,
even among privy councillors,[5] and it was with difficulty that the
archbishop persuaded the council to issue a proclamation calling
for obedience to the established order and prohibiting possession
of the 'Admonition' and other presbyterian tracts.[6] Even then,
scarcely a pamphlet was surrendered, although the tracts were in
the hands of many London merchants and country gentlemen.[7]
The truth was that episcopacy had few defenders.

It was the Queen, in spite of optimistic puritan rumours to the
contrary,[8] who set herself resolutely against the anti-episcopal
drift. A further proclamation in October 1573, in which Elizabeth's
hand is clearly discernible, castigated bishops and magistrates for
their negligence in suppressing nonconformity.[9] This was followed

---

[1] Bancroft, *Daungerous positions*, 67; cf. Scott Pearson, *Cartwright*, 74–82;
Collinson, 'Classical Movement', 140–3.

[2] *Seconde Parte of Register*, ii, 69–70.

[3] Bishop Sandys to Burghley, 5 Aug. 1573: B.M. Lansd. 17 no. 43 ff. 96–97.

[4] Part of the title of *The life of the 70th Archbishop of Canterbury presentlye sitting
Englished* (1574), ascr. to John Stubbs.

[5] *Seconde Parte of Register*, i, 91; Sandys to Burghley, 30 April 1573: *Puritan
Manifestoes*, app. iii, 153.

[6] R. Steele, *Tudor and Stuart Proclamations*, i, no. 687; cf. Inner Temple Lib.
Petyt MS. 538/47 f. 479.

[7] Sandys to Burghley, 2 July 1573: *Puritan Manifestoes*, app. v, 154–5; list of
Norfolk gentlemen in possession of the tracts: Camb. Univ. Lib. MS. Ee.ii.34
no. 4, f. 3.

[8] Laurence Tomson to Gilby, 19 May 1573: Baker MS. 32 p. 448.

[9] Steele, *Proclamations*, no. 689.

by council action: special commissions were set up to make a general enquiry into puritan disobedience, and to require subscription from suspected persons to articles defining the law of the Church on the questions in controversy.[1] The proceedings which followed delayed the development of English presbyterianism by ten years. In many dioceses puritan preachers were deprived or suspended, and in Northamptonshire the moderators of the prophesying were forced to leave the county. In London many puritans gave way and subscribed, while the recalcitrants, clergy and laity, were sent to prison, where at least four had died before April 1574.[2] Cartwright escaped a warrant for his arrest by fleeing to the Palatinate.[3]

Nothing is known about Field during these critical months. On 2 October 1572 he and Wilcox had been sentenced to a year's imprisonment by the lord mayor and aldermen of London. 'Sundry letters from noblemen'—Leicester and Warwick—had secured their removal from Newgate to Archdeacon Mullins's house, but in June 1573 they were threatened with banishment under the act of uniformity and in October they were informed that their release was impossible without special order from the council.[4] Yet by the end of the year Wilcox was free; in December he visited puritan centres in the midlands and by early February was back in his own house in London.[5] Of Field there is no trace, no letters, no published works, no evidence that he was preaching: he reappears only in July 1575, at the burning of two Dutch anabaptists in Smithfield.[6] In the winter of 1573–74, Gilby received his London news from Wilcox, so that Field may have been lying low in the country or have even joined Cartwright abroad. In 1574 some major manifestoes of English presbyterianism appeared from Michael Schirat's press at Heidelberg, and Field, rather than Cartwright, was the man to supervise the printing.[7] He was later

---

[1] *Acts of P. C.* 1571–75, 140, 171; *Seconde Parte of Register*, i, 93–97.

[2] Collinson, 'Classical Movement', 160–72.

[3] Scott Pearson, *Cartwright*, 121.

[4] *Seconde Parte of Register*, i. 91; *Puritan Manifestoes*, 153; *Acts of P. C.* 1571–75, 90, 93; Inner Temple Lib. Petyt MS. 538/47 f. 480.

[5] Wilcox to Gilby, 21 Dec. 1573, 2 Feb. 1574; Baker MS. 32 pp. 441, 439.

[6] *Seconde Parte of Register*, i, 105; John Stow, *Annales* (1631), 680.

[7] Scott Pearson, *Cartwright*, 135–47; A. F. Johnson, 'Books Printed at Heidelberg for Thomas Cartwright' (*Library*, 5th ser. ii), 284–6; P. Collinson, 'The Authorship of *A Brieff Discours off the Troubles Begonne at Franckford*' (*Journ. Eccles. Hist.* ix), 188–208.

to translate a collection of divinity lectures by a Heidelberg doctor, Caspar Olevian, the only work of his published in England.[1]

By 1577 Field was back in his 'poor house in Grub Street',[2] when Bishop Aylmer complained that he was preaching 'God knows what' in private houses. Aylmer recommended that with Wilcox and other notorious puritans he should be exiled to the 'barbarous countries' of the north midlands, there to wear out his zeal on the papists.[3] If the bishop's advice had been taken, Elizabethan dissent might have had a very different history. But Field remained in London, doubtless protected by his powerful friends.

The London presbyterian conference was still active and claimed a final authority among all the puritan conferences in deciding questions of doctrine and conscience. In 1577 it clashed with Cartwright himself. Under the influence of the liberal Calvinism of the Palatinate, Cartwright had begun to teach that it was better to conform and wear the vestments than to be deprived of the liberty to preach doctrine which he would state publicly in his *Rest of the second reply* against Whitgift. But for Field and other members of the London conference this was the thin end of a dangerous wedge. Strengthened by the presence of deprived ministers from Norfolk and Northamptonshire, they had written for Cartwright's opinion on the matter, but when they received it they at once condemned him for setting himself 'against the Church and the brethren'.[4] In the following year, the London conference was drawn into the plans of a group of puritan government officials for establishing Calvinist orders in the congregation of the Merchant Adventurers at Antwerp. Henry Killigrew and William Davison followed the correct presbyterian procedure in communicating their need of a preacher to the conference, and it was Field who canvassed and nominated suitable candidates. Eventually, Walter Travers was appointed and later he received a presbyterian ordination in the Netherlands. In 1580, when he returned to take up a lectureship at the Temple and to rejoin the London conference, his place was taken by Cartwright. The Antwerp congregation

[1] *An exposition of the symbole of the Apostles . . . gathered out of the catechising sermons of Gasper Olevian Trevir* (1581).

[2] Jean de l'Espine, trans. Field, *An excellent treatise of christian righteousness* (1578), epistle, dated 2 Nov. 1577.

[3] John Strype, *Historical Collections . . . of John Aylmer*, 36–37.

[4] *Parte of a register*, 401–8; *Seconde Parte of Register*, i, 136–43.

later exerted some influence on the development of presbyterianism in England itself.[1]

As secretary of the London conference, Field was the natural intermediary between 'the brethren of England' and Calvinist leaders in other states. In July 1582—a difficult time for presbyterians north of the Border—he wrote to assure John Davidson, a leader of the extreme presbyterian group in Scotland, of the concern of the English puritans. A similar message arrived from the Huguenots at La Rochelle. A few months later, Davidson told Field: 'It is no small comfort, brother, (as ye and I have divers times spoken in conference) to brethren of one nation to understand the state of the brethren in other nations; and therefore let us practise it as occasion will serve.' His letter offered the help of the Scottish Church in procuring a petition from the king and the general assembly to Elizabeth on behalf of the English puritans, a suggestion which was 'liked by the brethren in England'.[2] Such episodes remind us that, in its origins at least, English puritanism, far from being the insular phenomenon which it is sometimes represented, was part of an international revolutionary movement. Bancroft reports that the puritans made regular collections of money 'for their brethren that travail for them beyond the seas' —probably in France—and delivered them to Field and to Richard Culverwell, a mercer of Thames Street, who had many links with the French Protestants.[3]

Although the London conference continued and maintained links with 'the brethren' in the country and overseas, the presbyterian element in the puritan movement was almost wholly submerged in the years after 1574. Parker's repression of the presbyterians culminated in the exposure of what turned out to be a wholly bogus puritan 'conspiracy' and there was a revulsion of feeling against the archbishop in the privy council. In 1575 Parker was succeeded by Edmund Grindal, an old Marian exile who was sympathetic to all but the most divisive puritans. This was the period of closest co-operation between the bishops and the puritan

[1] S.P. 15/23/442 and S.P. 15/25/68, 71, 74, 78, 98, 116, 117; B.M. Add. MSS. 6394; Scott Pearson, *Cartwright*, 171–87; *D.N.B. s.v.* Travers.

[2] 1 Jan. 1583: R.M. Gillon, *John Davidson of Prestonpans*, 262–3; cf. Donaldson, 'Presbyterian Movements', 157–9, 295–6.

[3] *Tracts Ascribed to Richard Bancroft* ed. A. Peel, p. xxix; Culverwell's will, P.C.C. 9 Windsor.

clergy in the prophesyings. In Grindal's early years, the air was full of projects for the adaptation of episcopacy to reformed ideas. At the same time, the growing menace of Counter-Reformation Catholicism had strengthened the plea of the moderates for unity among loyal Protestants at any price: according to Thomas Norton, bishops and puritan preachers were agreed to 'join together against the papists, the enemies of God and of her Majesty, and not spend themselves in civil wars of the Church of God'.[1] The origins of English presbyterianism had been largely shaped by circumstances, and the movement lost ground at a time when most nonconformists enjoyed 'a goodly space of quietness'.[2]

Field appeared to adapt himself to the prevailing atmosphere. Doubtless he shared the common view that the danger of Catholic subversion now overshadowed even the evils of English prelacy: moreover, the bishops would not gain from a crusade against popery, while the puritans could hardly lose. To assault the 'Bishop of Rome' and his agents was obliquely to attack the English prelates, who in common opinion made a poor contribution to Zion's defence in comparison with the godly preachers. There is no reason to suppose that Field ever abandoned the extreme views which he had expressed in 1572—the 'Admonition' was reprinted in 1578—but in the later 'seventies he devoted his main energies to translating from French works of Protestant apology in that language. These were published with dedications addressed to some of the great patrons of English Reform which stridently called for a more forthright Protestant policy and the elimination of all papists and sectaries. In 1577 Field dedicated his translation of Jean de l'Espine's *Excellent treatise of christian righteousness* to Lady Elizabeth Tyrwhit, once the Queen's governess and perhaps still an influential lady at court. The year 1579 saw the printing of two collections of Calvin's sermons, one dedicated to the earl and countess of Bedford and the other to the earl of Huntingdon.[3] In the same year appeared a translation of Philippe de Mornay's *Treatise of the church* with a dedication to Leicester and an epistle directly appealing to the earl to lead an anti-Catholic crusade: it was the immediate occasion of Robert Parsons's *Brief discourse why Catholics*

---

[1] *Seconde Parte of Register*, i, 190–1.
[2] Josias Nicholls, *The plea of the innocent* (1602), 9–10.
[3] *Thirteene sermons entreating of the free election of God in Jacob, and of reprobation in Esau; Foure sermons, with a briefe exposition of the lxxvii psalme.*

refuse to go to church (1580), a manifesto of Catholic recusancy prefaced with an epistle to the Queen which included a personal attack on Field, 'a strange brainsick fellow, whom Newgate possessed for a long time for his fantastical opinions'.[1] In this epistle Parsons argued that the puritans were a greater danger to the peace and unity of the kingdom than the papists; he provoked more than one puritan reply, including a savage attack from Field on the 'crafty underminings' of 'these parasitical papists' in his *Caveat for Parsons*, published in 1581 and also dedicated to Leicester. In the same year, Field presented Leicester's brother and his own patron, the earl of Warwick, with his translation of Olevian's Heidelberg sermons, and in the preface renewed his attacks. In September 1581 he acted as notary for the disputations in the Tower with the Jesuit Edmund Campion, and subsequently edited the official account of these conferences.[2]

Field's new respectability had won its reward in July 1579, when Leicester successfully petitioned the university of Oxford to grant him a licence to preach. Lord Norris and Sir Francis Knollys, on whose behalf Leicester had written to Oxford, had hopes of placing Field in a town lectureship at Henley.[3] But, in spite of Aylmer's continued hostility, he does not appear to have left London. In 1580 he preached in the church of St. Martin Orgar,[4] and by the following year he had become the parish lecturer of St. Mary Aldermary, where he remained until his suspension in 1585. In November 1581 he declared his gratitude to Leicester, 'since not only I but the whole Church do owe thankfulness unto you as the instrument both of my peace and liberty and of the poor blessing it enjoyeth by my preaching'.[5] But it was not only papists who angered Field, and he went on to rebuke Leicester for patronizing stage-plays: during his time at the Aldermary, too, he took advantage of an accident in a Paris Garden bear-pit to

---

[1] *Brief discourse*, Sig. F vi.

[2] *A true reporte of the disputation . . . held in the Tower of London with Ed. Campion, Iesuite, the last of August, 1581*, and *The three last dayes conference held in the Tower with Edmund Campion Jesuite, the 18.23 and 27 of September 1581 . . .*, published together, 1583.

[3] *Reg. Univ. Oxford*, ii (1), 149; Eleanor Rosenberg, *Leicester, Patron of Letters*, 253.

[4] St. Martin Orgar vestry minutes and churchwardens' accounts (London Guildhall Lib. MS. 959/1) f. 44b. I owe this reference to Dr. H. G. Owen.

[5] 25 Nov. 1581: Brinkley, *Nathan Field*, 148–9.

denounce the growing popularity of the Southwark plays and shows on the Sabbath.[1]

Prolific author and translator though Field was, the works which appeared under his own name probably represent the least part of his propagandist activity at this time. As he wrote in the preface to a posthumous translation by a fellow-minister: 'I am easily drawn . . . to put to my helping hand in the furtherance of any profitable work. . . . And this is the cause that this godly work . . . was by me egged forward to be published to all that fear God.'[2] Field was an inveterate collector and publisher of anything which he thought might help the cause or 'profit the whole Church of God'. When papers of John Knox were lent to him, after Knox's death, by Mrs. Anne Prouze of Exeter, who as Mrs. Locke had been a close friend of the Scottish reformer, he promptly published a sermon which he found among them and only informed the owner by way of a dedicatory epistle. In this he declared that no private person had the right to reserve the common heritage of the whole Church and begged Mrs. Prouze to supply him with any other Knoxiana which she might still possess or could procure from others.[3] He was especially anxious to trace Knox's letters, which contained 'an whole History of the churches where he lived'. Perhaps we owe it to Field's persistence that there was preserved the famous correspondence from Knox to Mrs. Locke which casts so much light both on the character of the writer and on the history of the Scottish Reformation. Anne Locke's second husband had been Edward Dering, a popular preacher who had died of tuberculosis in 1576 at the height of his fame.[4] Field informed his widow that he preserved 'many of the writings, labours and letters of that worthy and godly man . . . and gather them in daily, as I can get them of his and my good friends:'[5] hoping that they would increase the posthumous reputation which Dering already enjoyed through his celebrated sermons on the Book of Hebrews. Dering's surviving works were constantly reprinted, both separately and in collections.[6] Two of these tracts have prefaces which

[1] *A godly exhortation, by occasion of the late iudgement of God, shewed at Paris-garden, the thirteenth day of Ianuarie* (1581).

[2] Peter Viret, trans. John Brooke, *A faithfull and familiar exposition upon the prayer of our Lorde* (1582), epistle.

[3] Knox, *Works*, ed. D. Laing, iv, 91–94.

[4] Scott Pearson, *Cartwright*, 82–83, 115–17; Kent County Rec. Off. Dering MS. C1/1, 2.

[5] Knox, *Works*, iv, 92–93.　　　　[6] S.T.C. 6676–6733.

seem to be of Field's writing,[1] and it may well be that he was the editor of the collected works of Dering as we have them in late Elizabethan editions.[2]

We shall never know how many anonymous and posthumous writings were 'egged forward' to the press by Field, but we can be certain that he had a hand in most, if not all, of the many tracts printed by Robert Waldegrave, the puritan printer *par excellence*, which are of the nature of presbyterian party manifestoes.[3] We know that it was Field who by some means got hold of Beza's letter to Lord Glamis in denunciation of diocesan episcopacy, and published it in 1580 as *The judgement of a most reverend and learned man from beyond the seas concerning a threefold order of bishops*.[4] Of another important presbyterian tract, the *Brief and plain declaration*, written by William Fulke in the early 'seventies, but only printed in 1584 by Waldegrave, Matthew Sutcliffe wrote: 'When John Field contrary to his mind did publish the pamphlet called *The learned discourse*, [Fulke] was offended with him, and if he had lived would have confuted the same himself.'[5] Where a manuscript which he edited had no direct bearing on the puritan cause, or had been written years before, it was Field's practice to couple it with a topical preface, carrying the familiar appeal for further reformation. He chose the eve of a parliament—whether the session of 1571 or 1581 is not clear—to publish Dering's *Sermon preached before the Queen's Majesty*, in order, as he explains in the preface, 'that things amiss may be reformed, and true religion sincerely advanced, and against this time especially, because that a Parliament is instant and at hand; wherein . . . known abuses shall be removed and many unprofitable strifes ended'.[6]

Besides what he actually put through the press, Field was responsible for amassing the 'register' of evidences of the puritan controversy which today forms our most important source for the

---

[1] *A sermon preached before the Queenes Majestie,* epistle attached to undated edns. (*S.T.C.* 6699b, 6701) and as one of *Two godly sermons* (1590 and later edns.), initialled 'I.F.'; *XXVII lectures or readings upon part of . . . Hebrews* (1576 and later edns.).

[2] Cf. edns. of ?1590, 1597, 1614, *S.T.C.* 6676–8; C. H. Cooper, *Athenae Cant.* i, 357.

[3] W. J. Couper, *Robert Waldegrave, King's Printer for Scotland*; W. Pierce, *An Historical Introduction to the Marprelate Tracts.*

[4] Donaldson, 'Presbyterian Movements', 154.

[5] Scott Pearson, *Cartwright*, 273.

[6] Epistle to an undated edn., initialled 'I.F.'

history of the movement.[1] Among the resolutions sent down to the conferences from a general presbyterian assembly held in London in the winter of 1586–87 were instructions that cases of the oppression of the bishops and their officers 'especially towards the ministers' were to be 'registered and gathered'.[2] This was no new procedure in 1587, as the copious material in the register from about 1565 shows. There are altogether some two hundred and fifty documents in the register, amounting in manuscript to six hundred and fifty closely-written folios and in print to five hundred and fifty-four pages. They span the years 1565–89 and represent almost every county where puritan preachers were to be found: a striking memorial to the extent and efficiency of the Elizabethan presbyterian organization. We have the testimony of a member of the London conference that it was Field who kept this 'register of all acts and proceedings in his day'.[3] Some of the items are addressed to him or bear his endorsement,[4] and there is evidence that he was the compiler of a contemporary catalogue of the register which survives.[5] Field's project of a register of the sufferings of the puritans was an imitation of Foxe's *Acts and Monuments*, which was a history of 'great persecutions and horrible troubles . . . gathered and collected' from the original sources with which the successive editions of the 'Book of Martyrs' were inflated. Field had begun his literary career as one of Foxe's assistants in tracing information, and it was no doubt in this school that he had learned both the value of such material as propaganda and the technique of collecting it through an organized chain of correspondents.[6] The *Brief discourse of the troubles begun at Frankfort* was the first puritan work in the same vein, and Field almost certainly took a leading part in gathering and publishing these original records of the

---

[1] Partly printed, by Schilders at Middelburg or Waldegrave at Edinburgh ?1593, as *A parte of a register . . . written by divers godly and learned in our time, which . . . desire the reformation of our Church in discipline and ceremonies*; largely remaining in MS. as 'The seconde parte of a register' and 'Old loose papers', Dr. Williams's Library, MSS. Morrice A and B, and calendared as *A Seconde Parte of a Register*, ed. A. Peel (1915).

[2] *The Presbyterian Movement in the Reign of Queen Elizabeth as Illustrated by the Minute Book of the Dedham Classis, 1582–1589* (ed. R. G. Usher, Camden Soc. 3rd ser. viii), 92–93.

[3] Deposition of Thomas Edmunds: Star Chamber 5 A 49/34.

[4] *Seconde Parte of Register*, i, 219; ii, 219, 238, 239.

[5] B.M. Harl. MSS. 360 ff. 86b, 87b.

[6] Francis Hall to Field, 13 Sept. 1569, endorsed by Foxe: B.M. Harl. MSS. 416 f. 185; cf. J. F. Mozley, *John Foxe and his Book*, 141.

troubles of the Marian exile.[1] The project was continued in the puritan historical register. 'If it will anything help the common cause, I pray you then, use your discretion', wrote an East Anglian puritan in sending Field an account of his troubles.[2] Many of the documents in the register were circulated in manuscript to support the claims of puritan petitions and bills: there is evidence that they were passed from hand to hand in the house of commons itself.[3] It may have been Field's intention to publish a puritan 'Book of Martyrs' from the material in the register, but it was not until five years after his death that a selection of the documents appeared from a foreign press as *A part of a register*, while the bulk of the collection has remained unprinted.

In the first of the Marprelate Tracts, Martin warns the prelates that he keeps 'a register' of their misdeeds. 'You shall not call one honest man before you, but I will get his examination . . . and publish it. . . . Secondly all the books that I have in store already of your doings shall be published.'[4] Although Field was dead before the first of these brilliant libels appeared, and although serious puritan opinion condemned the tracts for their frivolity, Martin's warning indicates that his plan of campaign closely resembled that of Field's register. Moreover we are told by a contemporary witness that *The Epistle*, the first of the tracts, was written from 'some such notes as were found in Master Field's study',[5] while John Udall of Kingston admitted having shown part of the same tract to Field.[6] While the extent of Field's implication in the Marprelate affair will never be known, there is no doubt that Martin was born from a tradition of puritan libelling which Field had done much to establish and which derived in part from the appeal to history of the *Acts and Monuments* and the register, and in part from the polemic of the *Admonition to the Parliament*.

The 'goodly space of quietness' which had marked Grindal's early years ended with the succession in September 1583 of John Whitgift, who in the early years of the presbyterian movement

[1] P. Collinson in *Journ. Eccles. Hist.* ix, 199–201. *See above*, 202-4.
[2] Dr. Williams's Library, MS. Morrice B 11 f. 91*b*.
[3] J. E. Neale, *Elizabeth and Parliament, 1584–1601*, 229–30; cf. the private papers of an Elizabethan puritan M.P., Sir Edward Lewkenor: B.M. Add. MSS. 38492.
[4] *The Marprelate Tracts*, ed. W. Pierce, 81–82.
[5] E. Arber, *An Introductory Sketch to the Martin Marprelate Controversy*, 94.
[6] B.M. Harl. MSS. 7042 f. 4*b*.

had made himself the champion of Anglicanism against the puritan challenge. Acting on royal instructions, he now initiated an energetic campaign for conformity. The whole clergy were required to subscribe their assent to the Royal Supremacy, to the Prayer Book as containing 'nothing in it contrary to the word of God' and to the Thirty-Nine Articles as 'agreeable to the word of God'.[1] No puritan could conscientiously fulfil the second of these requirements and some approached the other two with misgivings. The penalty for non-subscription was suspension from the ministry and ultimately, for incumbents, deprivation of their livings. This challenge stimulated afresh the extremist, anti-episcopal wing of the puritan movement and Field emerged, from the comparative retirement of the past ten years, to lead it.

The *modus vivendi* between bishops and puritan preachers which had marked the Grindalian episode had been under fire from both sides in the years immediately before Whitgift's elevation. In 1576 the exercises of prophesying were suppressed by the Queen's order and the archbishop who rose in courageous defence of them placed under suspension.[2] This setback was followed within a few years by the deaths of most of the 'fellow-travelling' bishops of Grindal's outlook and the rise of a new generation of prelates who shared Whitgift's abhorrence of puritanism. In some dioceses the bishops were still willing to wink at the prophesyings under another name, but elsewhere the puritan conferences were forced to become voluntary and unauthorized associations. Unlike the prophesyings, their orders were presbyterian[3] and their meetings secret. In East Anglia, where bishops Freke of Norwich and Aylmer of London aligned themselves with factions hostile to puritan preaching, every puritan was faced with the constant threat of silencing or deprivation. In 1582, extraordinary conventions of preachers were held at the churches of leading puritan ministers—John Knewstub's Cockfield in Suffolk and Richard Rogers's Wethersfield over the Essex border—and at Cambridge.[4] These and perhaps other meetings of a similar character elsewhere led to the establishment of clandestine conferences resembling the presbyterian *classes*, in

---

[1] J. Strype, *The Life and Acts of John Whitgift*, i, 229–32.

[2] *The Remains of Edmund Grindal* (ed. W. Nicholson, Parker Soc.), 376–90.

[3] Cf. the Norwich orders drawn up during the vacancy of the see in 1575: J. Browne, *History of Congregationalism in Norfolk and Suffolk*, 18–20.

[4] Bancroft, *Daungerous positions*, pp. 112–13; Essex Rec. Off. Quarter Sessions Rolls 84/34, 43.

which the puritan ministers of convenient circuits met monthly to discuss their troubles and to regulate the affairs of their churches. The minute-book of one such conference, formed by the preachers in the neighbourhood of Dedham in Essex, has survived and sheds much light on the development of this practical presbyterian movement.

It was at about this time, apparently, that the London conference began to make definite plans for the establishment of a working system of presbyterian assemblies.[1] The East Anglian leaders informed Field of developments in their country and may even have taken their instructions from him. Of the secret meeting at Cockfield, a Suffolk preacher wrote: 'I hope all things were so proceeded in as you your self would like of. . . . I suppose before this time some of the company have told you by word; for that was permitted unto you.'[2] It was Field who suggested a general meeting to follow at Cambridge, and in Suffolk it was thought that this might 'easily be brought to pass, if you at London shall so think well of it, and we here may understand your mind'.[3] It may have already been regular practice, as it certainly was a year or two later, to hold synods at the two universities in July, at the time of the graduation ceremonies—at Stourbridge Fair time (September), too, at Cambridge—and a general assembly in London during the days of the St. Bartholomew Fair. These occasions provided cover for the unusually large assemblies of puritan ministers. In this way the *classes*, synods and assemblies of a presbyterian Church of England were already roughly sketched out. Yet it took Whitgift's general assault on nonconformity to stir this embryonic organism fully into life. Field's correspondence with the country leaders had grown occasional: when he wrote to Gilby in February 1581, some of his London news was more than a year old.[4] In the summer of 1583 an Antwerp correspondent congratulated Field on the establishment of presbyterian assemblies, but added: 'I will tell you that which is true: you have begun this course too late.'[5] Field himself confessed to the ministers of the Dedham conference that he had been 'strongly drawn of late not to be so careful, diligent and zealous in God's causes as I was wont; this unhappy time of looseness and liberty gaining upon me and

[1] Deposition of Thomas Edmunds: Star Chamber 5 A 49/34.
[2] Oliver Pig to Field, 16 May 1582: Bancroft, *Daungerous positions*, 112–13.
[3] Ibid.   [4] Field to Gilby, 28 Feb. 1581: Baker MS. 32 p. 446.
[5] Bancroft, *Daungerous positions*, 73.

choking those good things which I thank God I was wont to feel in greater measure'. But conference and correspondence became an urgent necessity after October 1583. While Edmund Chapman of Dedham urged Field to call a 'general conference for unity', Field told Chapman: 'You are wise to consider by advice and by joining together how to strengthen your hands in this work. The Lord direct both you and us, that we may fight a good fight and finish with joy. Amen.'[1]

'This work,' this 'good fight': Field's attitude to the subscription struggle was characteristic and exceptional. Most moderate puritans looked no further than their own parishes, where they hoped to occupy their pulpits quietly and to be allowed the discreet use of some nonconformist practices. Faced with the test of subscription, they at first refused, but hoped that they would later be permitted to make a modified, conditional subscription and that the tolerance of earlier years would return. These hopes were well-founded, for a policy found few defenders which silenced hundreds of zealous preachers at the very time when the country stood in mortal danger of Catholic subversion. In the later months of 1584, Whitgift was forced by the pressure of opinion in the council and the court to give way, and to allow the majority of the ministers to subscribe with reservations. Of three to four hundred non-subscribers, only a fraction were deprived of their livings or permanently suspended from preaching.[2] These were, as Whitgift himself termed them, the ring-leaders,[3] whom the general demand for subscription had served to identify, and who were now singled out and called up to the High Commission to answer to a new schedule of inquisitorial articles.[4] Field himself, who had somehow contrived to continue as lecturer at the Aldermary throughout 1584, was suspended by the High Commissioners on 4 March 1585,[5] and so far as we know never preached openly again. In 1586 he was included in the puritan register in a short list of ministers and preachers who still stood suspended or deprived.[6]

For as long as the issue was uncertain, Field seems to have been

---

[1] *Dedham Minute Book*, 95–96.
[2] Collinson, 'Classical Movement', 419–34, 457–62.
[3] Whitgift to Burghley, 29 May 1584: B.M. Lansd. 42 no. 43 f. 105.
[4] Strype, *Whitgift*, iii, app. iv, 81–87.
[5] *Seconde Parte of Register*, i, 283–4; the two petitions from parishioners to Leicester of the same time (ibid. 135, 284) are misdated by the editor.
[6] Ibid. ii, 262.

as determined as the archbishop himself that the outcome should not be a return to latitudinarian tolerance, partly because such a settlement would isolate the presbyterian minority from the more numerous moderates, but also perhaps because he saw in the archbishop's extreme demands an opportunity to discredit the bishops once for all. Subscription would certainly be refused by hundreds of clergy who were no fanatical opponents of episcopacy but who habitually omitted parts of the Prayer Book or ignored its rubrics. If these ministers continued to resist even a modified subscription, a general revulsion of Protestant opinion against Whitgift and his suffragans might follow, opening the way for the overthrow of episcopacy itself. If, on the other hand, the ministers subscribed, even with reservations, it might later be claimed, even against the presbyterians—as in fact it was by 1585 —that they had abandoned their position. 'I am sure the greater part, yea even of your forwardest men, subscribed.'[1]

By early December 1583 Field had prepared a statement on the unlawfulness of subscription of which a version was probably sent out to the conferences. Like other tracts in circulation at the same time it listed the particular errors in the Prayer Book, but unlike them it insisted more on the generally Catholic spirit of the Anglican liturgy; so that, even if every fault were explained away or excepted, the 'general inconveniences' of the book remained insurmountable. The liturgy by its length alone left little time for preaching—and on that subject Field professed to find 'a deep silence throughout the whole book'—while to subscribe to the threefold, Catholic ministry of the Ordinal, which was contained within the Prayer Book, was plainly impossible. Field concluded that the most tolerable of conditional subscriptions was 'vain and frivolous. . . . Might we not as well and better subscribe to Æsop's fables?' He warned the bishops 'to take heed whereunto they urge us' and the people 'to consider that we have cause to refuse and admonish our fellow ministers to beware of subscription'.[2]

This was not the attitude of most non-subscribers. Indeed, Chapman of Dedham confessed 'some dislike of both parties for

[1] John Udall, *The State of the Church of England*, ed. E. Arber, 21; cf. the preface to Thomas Rogers, *The English creed* (1587).

[2] Three versions of Field's views are extant: S.P. 12/164/11; Dr. Williams's Library, MS. Morrice B 11 ff. 94–96, printed in part, *Seconde Parte of Register*, i. 284–6; and 'the general inconveniences of the Book of Common Prayer', ibid. i, 256–7.

their hot and violent manner of proceeding, either seeking by all means to conquer and deface the other'.[1] While the puritan ministers throughout the province of Canterbury searched for a common policy and circulated a variety of forms of answer to the articles,[2] the great influence of the London conference was exerted to persuade them to refuse subscription in any form. When a group of Sussex non-subscribers, who came to Lambeth to present their case in December 1583, were inclined between one day and the next to withdraw their conditional subscription, bishop Young of Rochester remarked: 'It seemeth they have been with some in London since they went hence. If I were as you, I would not care with how few such I were acquainted.'[3] In the early months of 1584, while most of the puritan ministry still resisted subscription, Whitgift complained of a conspiracy in their 'disordered flocking together ... from divers places and gadding from one to another', which argued 'some hope of encouragement and of prevailing'.[4] Petitions to the archbishop and the council from the suspended ministers and from groups of gentlemen on their behalf flowed into London, closely followed by delegations of the ministers and their patrons. Field was doubtless active in engineering much of this agitation, as in spreading the rumour that the cause of subscription would soon be abandoned, which, complained Whitgift, 'is spread abroad in every place, and is the only cause why many forbear to subscribe'.[5] A group of Lincolnshire ministers who were pressed by their archdeacon to subscribe replied that they had heard in London that they would be restored to their pulpits without subscribing. The archdeacon reported that many of them held copies of a letter from Field to the corresponding secretary of the movement in Lincolnshire, exhorting them to 'stand stoutly to the cause, affirming the same not to be theirs but the Lord's'. Those who had already subscribed were told that they had 'made a breach' and henceforth would be 'branded men' who would do no good in the Church.[6] Field may have written in these terms

[1] To Thomas Cartwright, 4 Nov. 1584: *Dedham Minute Book*, 81.

[2] The puritan register alone contains over twenty forms of answers and limited subscription and the papers of the Dedham conference many more.

[3] Dr. Williams's Library, MS. Morrice B 11 f. 46b.

[4] To the privy council, 4 Feb. 1584: Inner Temple Lib. Petyt MS. 538/52 f. 8–10b.

[5] To Sir Christopher Hatton, 9 May 1584: B.M. Add. MSS. 15891 f. 123.

[6] John Barefoot, archdeacon of Lincoln, to Whitgift, 1 June 1584: Hist. MSS. Com. *Bath*, ii, 24–26.

to every county. 'Weaklings, led by the masters of that faction,' was a Lichfield prebendary's opinion of the non-subscribers.[1]

There is no knowing what the outcome for the Church of England might have been had parliament met in the early months of 1584, with hundreds of pulpits silenced, the radical Protestant gentry in an uproar, and everyone at court, with the exception of Sir Christopher Hatton and the Queen herself, opposed to Whitgift's policy.[2] By the time parliament was called in November, the archbishop had lowered his demands and the majority of non-subscribers had been re-admitted to their charges upon some form of limited subscription: a settlement which Field had striven unsuccessfully to prevent. But even so, this parliament was bombarded with petitions for the relief of the small number of preachers who still stood suspended, and for the reformation of the ministry. These petitions were accompanied by the first instalments of a great 'survey of the ministry' on which the puritan conferences in many counties were now engaged.[3] The survey was an examination of the Church, parish by parish, which set out to prove how many of the clergy were unfitted for their callings, and so to strengthen the plea for more preaching and less persecution of the godly ministers. The Commons, spurred on by letters from the country conferences,[4] were wholly in sympathy with this clamour and sent up the substance of the puritan complaints to the house of lords in a grand petition of sixteen clauses. The effect of this was to demand the abandonment of the archbishop's attempt to reduce the Church to conformity and the adoption of a familiar programme of moderate puritan reform, which had already been rejected on more than one former occasion. But as always, these efforts were made futile by the personal intervention of the Queen, who stated plainly that 'as she found it at her first coming in', so she intended to maintain the state ecclesiastical.[5]

The large number of puritan gentlemen who sat in this parliament—many of them for shires[6]—and the enthusiasm with which

[1] Herts. Rec. Off., Gorhambury MS. VIII/B/143 f. 45.

[2] Cf. Whitgift to the Queen, 12 April 1584 (B.M. Cotton MSS. Vespasian C XIV. ii. f. 224) and to Hatton, 9 May 1584 (B.M. Add. MSS. 15891 f. 123).

[3] Most of the surveys are preserved in the puritan register: *Seconde Parte of Register*, ii, 88–184.

[4] Examples are in B.M. Add. MSS. 38492 ff. 37–38*b*, 68–69.

[5] Neale, *Elizabeth and Parliament, 1584–1601,* 75.

[6] R. C. Gabriel, 'Members of the House of Commons, 1586–87' (Lond. Univ. M.A. thesis, 1954), 10, 18–19.

they received the puritan petitions are no doubt a measure of the fears and passions aroused at a climax in the cold war against the Counter-Reformation. But we must also recognize in the composition and humour of this parliament the fruit of activity by the organized puritan movement, and especially by Field and the London conference. We have little means of judging to what extent organized puritanism had been capable of influencing the parliamentary elections of 1584. Yet on the eve of the next parliament the Dedham conference advised Field to take note of the boroughs which were represented in the house of commons and to use his best means to secure the election of godly members who would advance God's cause. 'Confer amongst yourselves how it may best be compassed. You are placed in the highest place of the Church and land to that end.'[1] When parliament assembled in November 1584 the conferences held fasts and prayer meetings, timed according to Field's directions, and sent up representatives to a general assembly for which the London conference provided the venue.[2] Thomas Fuller reports (without stating his evidence) that these delegates attended 'all day at the door of the Parliament House, and some part of the night in the chambers of the Parliament men, effectually soliciting their business with them'.[3] The correspondence of the puritan conferences shows that there were two sessions of the assembly, one before and the other after Christmas, corresponding to the two sessions of this parliament.

The object of the petitions before the parliament of 1584 was to make the Church safe for puritans and to promote a learned, preaching ministry. There is no reason to suppose that more than a small minority of the puritans were such fanatical presbyterians as to hazard the failure of this moderate programme on a presbyterian bill overturning the entire ecclesiastical establishment. When a presbyterian Member, Dr. Peter Turner, tried to procure the reading of the Geneva 'Form of Prayers' and an enacting bill, he found almost no support from a House which a few days later gave its full backing to the petition of sixteen clauses. Field and the London conference, with some of the Scottish presbyterian leaders then in England, were probably behind this move, but it was

---

[1] *Dedham Minute Book*, 58.
[2] Ibid. 40–42; Bancroft, *Daungerous positions*, 75; *Survay of the pretended holy discipline*, 366.
[3] *Church History of Britain* (1845), v, 83.

certainly not endorsed by the country conferences. On the eve of the next parliament, Dedham was concerned because some of the London brethren proposed to demand 'a full reformation and to accept of none if they had not all', and decided to advise London that a moderate reformation should be accepted if it were offered.[1] There were many in the Dedham conference who held that presbyterian discipline was not an essential mark of the Church, that prelacy was not necessarily 'antichristian', and that the ministers were bound to offer a 'reconciliation' to the bishops and to accept their government, if only to preserve the unity of the Church. The only practical alternative to a *modus vivendi* with the bishops, they pointed out, would be to 'erect discipline, which we desire, that we may proceed by the order thereof appointed and laid out by the word of God'.[2]

To 'erect discipline', that is, to set up presbyterian church government secretly, within the Church of England: this was the 'grand design'—to use Fuller's phrase—with which Field and other presbyterian leaders were now increasingly occupied. Their first concern was to prepare a constitution to be approved by the puritan assemblies, a 'book of discipline', such as already defined the systems of church order of other Calvinist churches. But to compose such a document and to have it subscribed would bring the puritan churches to the brink of separation from the established Church. Behind this new and critical development lay the influence of a score of leading Scottish presbyterians, including Andrew and James Melville and John Davidson, who were refugees in England from an episcopalian reaction north of the Border. Soon after their arrival in London in June 1584 some of these Scottish ministers had conferred with English puritan leaders,[3] and during July others of them visited the two universities and took part in the usual puritan synods of that month. The secretary of the Oxford conference, Edward Gellibrand of Magdalen, informed Field of profitable meetings in which the delegates had discussed how far they should wait for the state to take the initiative in establishing a presbyterian reformation—an obvious reference to the English, as well as to the Scottish situation.[4] Some of the Scots,

[1] *Dedham Minute Book*, 59.

[2] Ibid. 81, 97–98; John Rylands Lib., English MS. 874 ff. 33–34.

[3] Donaldson, 'Presbyterians Movements', 183.

[4] James Melville, *Autobiography and diary* (Wodrow Soc.), 219; Bancroft, *Daungerous positions*, 73–74.

including James Melville and Davidson, spent the winter of 1584–85 in London, and they no doubt influenced the general assembly which was meeting at the same time. One of the offences for which Field was suspended from preaching in March 1585 was resorting 'to the Scottish ministers, being three of them, and sometimes they come to his house'.[1]

The first draft of the English book of discipline may be found in the book which Dr. Turner proffered to parliament in December 1584. This was the Geneva liturgy, extensively revised and recently reprinted by Waldegrave,[2] which contained the form of government for a single congregation, John Knox's at Geneva. But Field and his friends had pasted in the back cover a loose leaf,[3] which briefly defined a polity of conferences and synods and so adapted the book to the needs of a national presbyterian Church. Turner's book provided the basis for the full-scale book of discipline on which the theorists of English presbyterianism were now engaged. The authors of the *Disciplina Ecclesiae*[4] or, as the seventeenth century knew it, the *Directory of Church-government*,[5] were Walter Travers and, probably, Thomas Cartwright. Field's function was to hasten the work, to inform the conferences of its progress, and finally to send out copies of the completed text. By July 1585 the first draft must have been complete, for Field told Travers that he wanted it 'read over with as much speed as could be', so that instructions could be given to the conferences for putting it in practice.[6] This suggests that Field had already received requests like that from Suffolk, which asked him for 'the several grounds and demonstrations for the holy discipline, which we are sure you have in readiness'.[7] Field told Travers that if the brethren agreed to circulate the conferences with fair copies of the discipline and instructions for action, he would 'wholly employ' himself in that service.[8] In November, Gellibrand of Oxford sent Field an urgent request for the book. But meanwhile it must have been agreed

[1] *Seconde Parte of Register*, i, 284.

[2] W. D. Maxwell, *John Knox's Genevan Service Book*, 75; Bancroft, *A sermon preached at Paules Crosse* (1589), 62.   [3] An example is in B.M. C. III. b. 6.

[4] In two parts: *Disciplina ecclesiae sacra Dei verba descripta* and *Disciplina synodica ex ecclesiarum quae eam ex verbo Dei instaurarunt usu synodis atque libris de eadem re scriptis collecta, et ad certa quaedam capita redacta;* printed, F. Paget, *Introduction to the Fifth Book of Hooker's Ecclesiastical Polity*.

[5] Eng. trans. with this title, 1644; repr. in facsimile by P. Lorimer, 1872.

[6] Bancroft, *Daungerous positions*, 76.   [7] Bancroft, *Survay of the discipline*, 366.

[8] *Daungerous positions*, 76.

that Travers should revise the text. In January 1586 Gellibrand was again asking Field to send him the discipline, 'which Master Travers promised to make perfect, when it is finished. We will put it in practice and try men's minds therein as we may.'[1]

In the event, repeated revisions of the discipline seem to have delayed its dispersal until early in 1587, when copies were distributed from a general assembly which had sat in London to direct the puritan campaign in the parliament of 1586–87.[2] Attached to the book of discipline was a form of subscription to its contents, probably composed by Field.[3] The conferences were to subscribe the discipline 'as agreeable to God's Word', if necessary with the exception of doubtful points; to promise to work for its establishment by petition to the Queen, privy council and parliament 'and by other lawful and convenient means to further and advance' it; and to undertake to practise it, so far as the law of the land and the 'peace of our present state of our Church may suffer and not enforce to the contrary', a safeguarding clause on which the issue of a prosecution would later depend. In particular, the ministers were to promise to follow a uniform order in their preaching and ministry—presumably an approximation to the Geneva liturgy—and to observe the discipline in convening the conferences and assemblies of the Church: meeting every six weeks in local *classes* of not more than ten members, every half year in provincial synods and at the general assembly annually, at parliament time, and on any other occasion when it might be summoned.

The welcome accorded to the book of discipline varied from county to county. In some places, the puritans seem to have subscribed the articles of approbation and, where meetings of the ministers had hitherto followed no formal order, to have distributed themselves in *classes* of the prescribed size and set up provincial synods. In Northamptonshire, for example, the ministers divided themselves between three conferences, which sent delegates to a provincial meeting in Northampton.[4] Yet when a general assembly met in Cambridge in September 1587, most conferences had sent no reply to the London articles, while others

---

[1] Ibid.

[2] Collinson, 'Classical Movement', 561–9, 577–8.

[3] Versions in *Dedham Minute Book*, 92–93 and Lambeth Palace Lib. MS. 113; fragments in B.M. Harl. MSS. 6849 f. 222 and Star Chamber 5 A 49/34.

[4] Bancroft, *Daungerous positions*, 76; deposition of John Johnson: Star Chamber 5 A 49/34.

had registered doubts, and all action was deferred.[1] The Dedham conference repeatedly put off consideration of the book, having already ruled before they received it that to subscribe their opinion in such a matter was 'not safe in any respect'.[2] There is no evidence for the frequently quoted statement of Daniel Neal that there were five hundred subscribers to the book of discipline. The probability is that it was rejected or indefinitely deferred by the majority of the members of the conference movement. A decision of the Cambridge assembly of September 1587 to circulate a printed text[3] was never implemented, and the book was still undergoing revision at assemblies which met in London and at Cambridge in 1589.[4] Field's attempt to impose a presbyterian uniformity on English puritanism had plainly failed.

Although it is sometimes stated that the book of discipline was 'prepared for Parliament',[5] there is no evidence that the puritans ever contemplated putting the presbyterian system before parliament in such a systematic and detailed form. In spite of the limiting clauses which were inserted in the articles of approbation to preserve a shadow of legality, there is no doubt that the discipline was intended for immediate practice. Nevertheless, there was one final attempt to employ the authority of parliament to establish a presbyterian Church of England. A new parliament met at the end of 1586, and in November petitions for the relief of suspended preachers and for the reform of the ministry once more came into London from many counties. The survey of the ministry, complete for at least thirteen counties or portions of counties, was summarized and attached to a massive 'General Supplication'.[6] A general assembly met in London and presumably communicated these documents to sympathetic Members of the house of commons.[7]

Under cover of this barrage, the presbyterian leaders intended once more to bring the Geneva 'Form of Prayers', newly revised, before parliament. On this occasion, they had the assistance of a

[1] John Strype, *Annals of . . . Queen Elizabeth's Happy Reign* (Oxford, 1824), iii (2), 477–9.

[2] *Dedham Minute Book*, 61–67; John Rylands Lib. English MS. 874 f. 10b.

[3] Strype, *Annals*, iii (2), 478.

[4] Depositions of Thomas Stone, Thomas Barber, William Perkins: Star Chamber 5 A 49/34.

[5] P. J. Hughes, *The Reformation in England*, iii, 202.

[6] *Seconde Parte of Register*, ii, 70–87.

[7] *Dedham Minute Book*, 60–61, 92–93, 98.

small organized party within the House. Five Members, including Peter Wentworth, were later stated to have made plans before parliament met for preferring the Geneva liturgy and a bill to establish it, preparations in which Field and others of the clerical party must surely have shared. The great matter of Mary queen of Scots prevented any action before Christmas, but on 27 February Anthony Cope, one of the group of five, rose to bring before the attention of the House the 'Form of Prayers'[1] and an enacting bill, which, if carried, would have authorized the Geneva liturgy as the only legal prayer book of the Church of England.[2] More than that: the bill proposed to make 'utterly void and of none effect' all 'former laws, customs, statutes, ordinances or constitutions' which in any way defined the religious practice or ecclesiastical organization of England. Cope's collaborators followed him in speaking to this drastic measure. It says much for the extremes to which Protestant feeling was running on the eve of the Armada, and something, too, for the lobbying by presbyterians inside and outside parliament, that the Commons heard these speeches out and, in calling for the bill to be read, overrode the Speaker himself. At this moment the Queen acted. She confiscated both the documents then before the House and Turner's bill and book of 1585, thus provoking Wentworth's celebrated oration on the privileges of the house of commons. Cope and his fellow-conspirators were committed to custody, and three privy councillors were charged to make set speeches in the House against presbyterianism.

These events proved once and for all that, so long as Elizabeth lived, the most masterly tactics which Field and his parliamentary friends could devise would not achieve the establishment of presbyterianism by public authority. It was doubtless at the close of this parliament that Field told a wavering brother: 'Tush, Mr. Edmunds, hold your peace. Seeing we cannot compass these things by suit nor dispute, it is the multitude and people that must bring the discipline to pass which we desire.'[3] All hope now rested on the covert practice of presbyterianism: these were the months when the book of discipline was circulated to the conferences.

A general assembly at Cambridge in September 1587 came

---

[1] A revised text printed by Richard Schilders in Middelburg in 1586.
[2] *Seconde Parte of Register*, ii. 212–15; for partly corrected text: S.P. 12/199/2.
[3] Deposition of Thomas Edmunds: Star Chamber 5 A 49/34.

within a hair's breadth of advocating separatism, when it decided
to refer to the conferences and to other reformed churches overseas the motions that the brethren should cease to communicate
with unlearned ministers, should withold recognition from the
bishops and repudiate the unlawful episcopal discipline, and should
base their ministries on the true, presbyterian discipline.[1] At a
synod in Warwickshire in the spring of 1588 it was ruled that 'the
faithful' ought not to communicate with unlearned ministers;
that since the calling of bishops was unlawful, the godly could not
be ordained by them or accept deprivation from them unless
'compelled by . . . civil force'; and that the discipline was to be
taught to the people and that 'men of better understanding' were
to be persuaded to embrace and practice it 'so far as they shall be
well able, with the peace of the Church'.[2] In Northamptonshire,
some ministers renounced their orders and received a new ordination from the brethren of the conferences.[3] Presbyterian elderships
were secretly established in some parishes.[4]

Unless the Church of the Elizabethan Settlement was no true
Church, these decisions were a denial of all that the puritans had
hitherto stood for. The hope of a national reformation was now
abandoned for a sectarian separation. Field had said that 'the people'
were to bring the discipline in. But how many presbyterians were
there among the people of England? Presbyterianism could not hope
to stand unless it stood united with its discipline strengthened by the
authority of the civil magistrate. Only a minority, even of the
puritan ministers, would follow the extremists in their complete
renunciation of the ministry and discipline of the Establishment.
Richard Rogers of Wethersfield, certainly one of the hotter spirits,
noted in his diary 'the variety of opinions' about church government among the learned, confessing his own 'unsettledness therein', and later observed that the question of communicating with
unlearned ministers 'doth still spread further undissolved'.[5] And
now, while the puritans floundered in perplexity 'and men's minds

[1] Strype, *Annals*, iii (2), 477–9.
[2] Bancroft's translation of the *Acta* of this synod: B.M. Harl. MSS. 6866 f.
321*b*; *Daungerous positions*, 86–87; cf. the examinations of participants: Star
Chamber 5 A 56/1.
[3] B.M. Harl. MSS. 6849 ff. 220, 222*b*; Star Chamber 5 A 56/1, 27/33; Bancroft,
Daungerous positions, 113–14.
[4] Collinson, 'Classical Movement', 710–16.
[5] *Two Elizabethan Puritan Diaries*, ed. M. M. Knappen, 98–99.

wavered this way and that way',[1] the political tide turned decisively against them.

The great patrons of puritanism were dead or dying; the defeat of the Armada had for the time allayed those extravagant fears of popery which had sheltered the puritans for so long; while the mischievous libels of Martin Marprelate disgraced the whole puritan cause and gave its enemies their opportunity. Confident of the Queen's favour, Whitgift, Hatton and, among the High Commissioners, Richard Cosin and Hatton's chaplain, Richard Bancroft, now undertook the systematic exposure and repression of organized puritanism. One by one, in 1589 and 1590, the known ring-leaders of the movement were examined before the High Commissioners and their studies searched for incriminating evidence. Among the papers which fell into the hands of the authorities were some at least from Field's files, including at least fifty letters from more than twenty correspondents in the country conferences, which Bancroft later used in his published exposures of presbyterian subversion. The register, however, escaped Bancroft's vigilance. The evidence gathered by these means was employed in the prosecution of nine ministers, including Cartwright, first before the High Commission and then in the Star Chamber, the aim being to prove judicially that the presbyterian movement had been seditious in manner and intent. Although it was clear by 1592 that this exemplary prosecution had failed in its main purpose, its effect was to drive the organized puritan movement so far underground that only occasional glimpses of it can be caught in the decade before its revival at the accession of James I. Many puritans were driven into the congregationalist separatism of the Barrowist movement, while many more conformed and reserved themselves 'to a better time.'[2] Very few found the presbyterian position of the 'church within the Church' to be any longer tenable.

Whether the course of events would have been the same if John Field had remained at the centre of the organization is a matter for mere speculation, for Field was buried at St. Giles, Cripplegate, on 26 March 1588.[3] There are very few references to him in puritan documents for some months before that, and we may guess that illness had removed him from active leadership of the movement

[1] Nicholls, *The plea of the innocent*, 31–32.
[2] Ibid. 35.
[3] Brinkley, *Nathan Field*, 5.

even earlier.[1] With the death of Field, the London conference ceased to give the decisive lead which had always been the mainspring of the presbyterian movement. When the Northamptonshire conference suggested preparing a new survey of the ministry for the parliament of 1589, Walter Travers, who had taken Field's place as London corresponding secretary, 'seemed nothing to mislike' the suggestion but thought that there was too little time to complete the survey before parliament met.[2] What if Field had lived? There are some hints, such as the impatient remark to Thomas Edmunds already quoted, and the possibility of a connection with Martin Marprelate, that in the last year of his life, Field was moving into a more extreme position out of exasperation with the repeated failure of the puritans to make any headway in parliament. Like some in the midlands, he may well have come to the conclusion that an established Reformed Church of England was no longer realizable. It is at least possible that he was about to use his remarkable powers of organization to lead out a presbyterian secession from the Church on a larger scale than the sectarian separation of the Brownists and Barrowists.

John Field was one of the most brilliant revolutionaries in an age of revolution, although neither his own generation nor posterity has appreciated the scope and significance of his career. In a state with the political structure of a France or a Scotland, and perhaps even in England under any sovereign but Elizabeth, he might have emerged as one of the statesmen of sixteenth-century Calvinism: the Melville, or even the Knox, of a thoroughgoing English Reformation.

---

[1] His will was made on 1 Feb. 1588: P.C.C. 38 Rutland.
[2] Deposition of John Johnson: Star Chamber 5 A 49/34 f. 8.

14

THE DOWNFALL OF ARCHBISHOP GRINDAL
AND ITS PLACE IN ELIZABETHAN
POLITICAL AND ECCLESIASTICAL HISTORY

If Queen Elizabeth had not been thwarted, her second archbishop of Canterbury would have been the first and indeed the only primate of all England to have been deprived of his great office by judicial process, little more than a year after she had placed him in it.[1] The year was 1577. Saved from annihilation by powerful friends and by the forbidding prospect of unexplored legal terrain, Archbishop Edmund Grindal remained sequestered and suspended from many of his functions for the remainder of his days. Writing about this episode on a previous occasion, I reached for a somewhat strained analogy. In France, in 1572, events had forced another queen into the desperate steps which precipitated the Massacre of St Bartholomew. 'With her surer grasp, Elizabeth merely kept an archbishop in limbo.'[2] The hyperbole was intended to suggest that Grindal's downfall deserves more than the incidental mention it has received in the historical literature, even that it had a certain centrality among the critical choices confronting the Elizabethan régime in the late 1570s.

Grindal has no place in the three volumes and the thousand pages of Conyers Read's *Sir Francis Walsingham and the Policy of Queen Elizabeth*.[3] And if his troubles were given a couple of pages in the same author's *Lord Burghley and Queen Elizabeth*,[4] no connection was made with more salient political questions. Not that Read was insensitive to the interrelation of mid-Elizabethan public issues. 'A half-hundred threads of policy were so knotted and joined that the pulling of any one meant the displacement of all the rest . . . Everything reacted upon everything else.'[5] But whereas Read was disposed to trust that the threads of policy were in good hands, capable of disentangling them, this essay will tend towards Professor Charles Wilson's more recent impression of strange and tortuous dealings, 'a subject of oriental deviousness'[6]: a story not so much of policy as of its absence, or of the neutralization of policy through deep antitheses. By these same antipathies Archbishop Grindal too was neutralized.

We begin with Grindal's two reputations: on the one hand his standing among his contemporaries and immediate posterity; on the other, and in striking conflict, the verdict of history. The annalists' obituary notices were of 'a right famous and worthy prelate.'[7] But if historians for long found little significance in Grindal's disgrace it was because they believed Grindal himself to have been insignificant, rather infamous than famous. His predecessor, Parker, and his successor, Whitgift, while never beyond criticism, have always commanded respect. But Creighton's assessment of Grindal in the *Dictionary of National Biography* was of a weak man, 'infirm of purpose'. Sir Sidney Lee supposed that he 'feebly temporised with dissent',[8] Bishop Frere complained of his 'natural incapacity for government',[9] Gwatkin attributed the elevation of such an unsuitable primate to 'some passing turn of policy',[10] and a modern author has called it 'a mistake'.[11] The misreading of character implied in all these judgments can be traced to the ecclesiastical and political bitterness of the seventeenth century and its aftermath. Thomas Fuller, albeit in a charitable rather than bitter spirit, began the tradition of misrepresentation by casting Grindal as 'our English Eli', blind and broken-hearted at his death. Like Eli who indulged his wicked sons he was accused as a father of the Church for 'too much conniving at the factious disturbers thereof.'[12] For mid-seventeenth century puritans, the heirs of the 'factious disturbers', Grindal provided a stick with which to strike the unacceptable face of prelacy. Milton called him 'the best' of the Elizabethan bishops[13] and William Prynne praised him, and only him, as 'a grave and pious man', while censuring Parker and Whitgift as 'over pontifical and princely'.[14] After two revolutions, and in the unparalleled rancour of public life in the reign of Anne, this archbishop who was revered by puritan nonconformity became a whipping-boy for the high-flying churchman Dr Sacheverell in his notorious political sermon, *The perils of false brethren*. Intending his attack for the archbishop of the day, Thomas Tenison, Sacheverell selected Grindal for denunciation as 'that false son of the Church', 'a perfidious prelate' who was to blame for what he called 'the first plantation of dissenters'.[15]

To the present generation of historians (including more than one contributor to this volume), Grindal's advanced protestantism and moderate churchmanship no longer appear scandalous. The 'Grindalian' tradition is even acknowledged to have been nearly central to the post-Reformation Church of England, long after Grindal's own disgrace. This may constitute the third of his reputations. But the measure has yet to be taken of Grindal's stature, not only as a symbol of moderation and of pastoral excellence but as an effective governor, remembered by the annalist Sir John Hayward as 'a man famous, whilst he lived, for his deep judgment, both in learning and affairs of the world', and as a man of 'magnanimous courage'.[16] When Parker was known to be dying, Alexander Nowell, the Dean of St Paul's, advised William Cecil, Lord Burghley, that the archbishop's place should be 'furnished with a man of great government' and that Grindal, then Archbishop of York, was the man 'of the greatest wisdom and ability to govern, and unto whom the other bishops with best contentation would submit themself [sic].'[17] Burghley needed no prompting[18] and Grindal would later acknowledge him as the 'principal procurer' of all his preferments.[19] Ninety-eight letters are still extant which Grindal addressed to this great patron, most of them in the 1560s when he was Bishop of London and Cecil Secretary of State.[20] They are what the age knew as 'familiar letters', tossed off in the writer's own hand, without deference or artifice, and mostly concerning urgent matters of public policy. Since not even Archbishop Parker was as businesslike in his dealings with Mr Secretary they imply that Grindal rather than his metropolitan was the ecclesiastical counterpart of Cecil in the early Elizabethan régime. This is no more than a hunch, since we have lost all but a few of the records of the Ecclesiastical Commission which was Grindal's principal sphere of activity, and which might have clinched the matter.

Insofar as the translation of such a man to Canterbury aroused partisan expectations among 'forward' protestants it may have been a difficult matter to expedite with the queen. It was not until late November 1575 that Burghley was able to confirm the choice which he himself had made six months earlier: 'I think assuredly her Majesty will have your grace come to this province of Canterbury to take care thereof, and that now, at this Parliament.'[21] Another month was then lost in what may have been more than procedural delays before the congé d'élire was at last signed, on Christmas Eve. But Grindal's appointment was also welcomed as bringing an effective hand to the Church's helm after a period of uncertain and uncreative government. Parker in his declining years was an aged man, and his treatment by the Court would have discouraged the most resolute of prelates. But it implied a kind of abdication and an alarming lack of restraint for Parker to draft a letter to Burghley which ran: 'If I had not been so much bound to the mother [Queen Anne Boleyn] I would not so soon have granted to serve the daughter in this place. And if I had not well trusted to have died ere this time, your honours should have sent thrice for me before I would have returned from Cambridge.'[22] It is not recorded that in his even greater extremity Grindal openly regretted having consented to his promotion, although in 1575, as he paused over his reply to Burghley, he confessed to 'many conflicts with myself about that matter.'[23]

The hopefulness but also the delicacy of the circumstances surrounding the transition from Parker to Grindal are conveyed in a letter which, although without signature in the fugitive copy which survives, seems to emanate from a high source and conveyed to Grindal the news of the signing of his congé d'élire:

It is greatly hoped for by the godly and well-affected of this realm that your lordship will prove a profitable instrument in that calling; especially in removing the corruptions in the Court of Faculties, which is one of the greatest abuses that remain in this Church of England. For that it is determined that Parliament should hold at the day prefixed, I could wish your lordship to repair hither with as convenient speed as ye may, to the end that there may be some consultation had with some of your brethren how some parts of those Romish dregs remaining in [the Church?],[24] offensive to the godly, may be removed. I know it will be hard for you to do that good that you and your brethren desire. Herein I had rather declare unto your lordship at your repair hither frankly by mouth what I think than to commit the same to letters.[25]

The implication is that matters which historians have associated with 'puritanism' were of interest to the writer, who seems to have been a councillor, and were assumed to have the support of Grindal and other bishops as well.

Illness delayed Grindal's arrival in London until a matter of days before the 1576 Parliament met, and this must have restricted the process of discreet consultation which had been proposed.[26] Nevertheless, the intense interest in the reform of the ministry and discipline of the Church evidenced in this Parliament suggests a broader and more influential constituency than the radical puritan network which Sir John Neale thought he could discern at work. After all, the committee which presented the queen with Parliament's petition for 'supply and reformation of these great wants and grievous abuses' consisted of six privy councillors. But Elizabeth deflected this powerful initiative in the direction of the clergy in Convocation, where she seems to have ensured that the measures for the improvement of the clergy contained in the Canons of 1576 would be of such a limited and conservative character as to earn even from Sir Walter Mildmay (Grindal's anonymous correspondent?) the comment that they were 'little or nothing to the purpose.'[27] Meanwhile the efforts of Grindal and his episcopal colleagues in the House of Lords to stiffen the laws against popish recusancy were nullified, almost certainly by royal intervention.[28]

Grindal's correspondent had drawn particular attention to the archbishop's Court of Faculties, an institution which supplied a variety of dispensations from the constraints of the canon law and which embarrassed many protestants by its evident continuity with pre-Reformation procedures.[29] After the prorogation of Parliament the Privy Council took order, either on its own initiative or that of the archbishop, for the curtailment of the activities of the Faculty Office. Some classes of licence were to be abolished altogether 'as not agreeable to Christian religion in the opinion of the Lords of the Council'. These included dispensations for holding three or more benefices in plurality and for ordination at less than the canonical age, and licences to marry without the calling of banns. Others, considered more tolerable, were to continue, but with the fees differently distributed.[30] In a memorandum justifying the full restitution of the temporalities of the see it was said that Parker had had occasions of wealth 'the possibilities whereof are now taken away',[31] and a predictive statement of income anticipated that with the projected reform the proceeds of the Faculty Office would drop from £60 to £30 a year:[32] a token reduction in a total revenue of more than £3,000 a year[33] but significant as a symbol of intent. There is no evidence that the queen had any part in these transactions or would have approved of them.

In the same late spring of 1576 Grindal called for reports on the state of his remaining courts: the Court of Arches, the Court of Audience, and the Prerogative Court of Canterbury. He received from one of the learned civilians and judges the advice that 'in your grace's Court of Audience, as in all other your courts, so things be out of order that few things be as they should be.'[34]

Enough has been said to suggest that Grindal was expected to effect reforms which would be radical but which it would be inappropriate to label, still less to dismiss, as 'puritan', since they enjoyed solid governmental support. But it was in the nature of things that little had been accomplished when Grindal found himself administratively paralyzed. This happened, after all, only 16 months after his appointment. And Dr Aubrey had found diagnosis of the ills of the courts spiritual an easier matter than the prescription of a cure: 'I am not so able to advertise your grace how to remedy the disease of these delays as to make them known to you.'[35] Recent work on the Prerogative Court of Canterbury, the seat of the archbishop's testamentary jurisdiction, confirms that 'Grindal's projected reforms did not materialize.'[36]

Grindal's troubles began when a cloud the size of a man's hand appeared in the summer sky of 1576: disquieting reports from Northamptonshire and Warwickshire concerning the meetings for preaching and instruction known as prophesyings, to which the archbishop was alerted from the Court, and which he at once referred to the diocesan bishops concerned.[37] There had been trouble over the prophesyings before which had blown over. This time Grindal's awkward conscience would ensure that the matter would come to a head. Macaulay's schoolboy, if he still exists, knows that the prophesyings were the cause of Grindal's disgrace. But the prophesyings themselves are often misunderstood, thanks to the ambiguities surrounding the terms 'prophet', 'prophecy', 'prophesying'.[38] They had nothing to do with ecstatic utterance, nor were they necessarily disorderly or anti-hierarchical. They were meetings in large and centrally located churches under strict moderation, where, in place of the usual sermon, two or three ministers took their turns to expound the text, in the presence of their brethren, and before a lay audience drawn from the surrounding country. They embodied an element of what is

nowadays called 'continuing education' and compensated for the deficiencies
of the clergy. Institutions like these, taking their name from certain matters
discussed by St Paul with the Corinthians, were part of the common resources
of the Reformed churches at a primitive stage of their consolidation. They
were all but domesticated in many parts of England, including the diocese of
Canterbury, in Parker's time. But they were never above controversy and
sometimes they were the scene of open disputes or worse scandals. When the
queen heard of their existence, which was perhaps not often, they aroused her
displeasure. In 1576 unfavourable reports were said to have reached the Court
from 'sundry of the bishops and sundry also of her justices of circuit.' Leicester,
Walsingham and Burghley all wrote urgently to Grindal about the disorders
in the Midlands and on 12 June he was summoned to Court.[39]

What transpired on that occasion we do not know, but Grindal was soon
trying to protect the prophesyings both from puritan abuse and from the
unfriendly attentions of the Court. He gathered reports from most of the
bishops of the province, many of them favourable to the practice.[40] Materials
were collected for a scholarly treatise on the subject, 'Tractatus de exercitiis',
which survive and have recently been restored to the Library of Lambeth
Palace.[41] And finally Grindal composed his 'Orders for the reformation of
abuses about the learned exercises and conferences among ministers of the
Church.'[42]

There followed a famous set piece of Tudor history: another summons to
Court and a painful interview with the queen in which Grindal was instructed
to transmit an order to the bishops putting down the prophesyings and 'abridging' the number of preachers; the archbishop, denied the right of verbal
expostulation, shaken but resolute, returning home to write his 'book'
to the queen, just over four hundred years ago, on 8 December 1576.[43]
In this manifesto of more than 6,000 words Grindal defended preaching as
the mainstay not only of faith but of civil order as well ('where preaching
wanteth, obedience faileth') and, after offering the fruits of his investigations
into prophesying ('only backward men in religion do fret against it'), came
to that measured but defiant statement in which he withheld the assent of
his conscience from the queen's policy and refused to transmit her command:

> I am forced, with all humility, and yet plainly, to profess that I cannot
> with safe conscience, and without the offence of the majesty of God,
> give my assent to the suppressing of the said exercises: much less can I
> send out any injunctions for the utter and universal subversion of the
> same. . . If it be your Majesty's pleasure, for this or any other cause, to
> remove me out of this place, I will with all humility yield thereunto,
> and render again to your Majesty that I received of the same. . . Bear
> with me, I beseech you Madam, if I choose rather to offend against your
> earthly Majesty than to offend the heavenly majestey of God.

One historian of the Elizabethan Church called this famous letter 'a particular piece of characteristically puritan crankiness'.[44] But Strype was moved by the passage just quoted to exclaim: 'O episcopus vere apostolicus!'[45] Fuller in the seventeenth century was no less appreciative: 'What could be written with more spirit and less animosity? more humility and less dejection? I see a lamb in his own can be a lion in God and the Church's cause.'[46] But it was gratuitous to end the letter with a peroration composed from the rhetoric of St Ambrose in his celebrated epistles to the emperors Theodosius and Valentinian.[47] For the admonitions of Ambrose echoed a polity foreign to Tudor England, when a bishop could confidently refuse entry to his church to the agents of a still partly alien imperial power.[48] And perhaps there was no need to write at all. As the Dutch divine and man of affairs Loiseleur de Villiers wrote in another connection, three years later: 'I cannot refrain from saying that the way to pacify kings is not to oppose them, or announce by writings, signatures or remarks that one does not approve their doings. It is necessary to be humble, or at least to hold one's tongue. You know why I say this and there is no need of longer discourse.'[49]

But it is by no means clear that the offending letter was the sole or immediate cause of calamity. More than a week after the Earl of Leicester had taken it to Court (and was that a friendly office or not?) there was no royal response. Perhaps the queen had not yet seen the letter. But Leicester and Burghley knew the contents and proposed a compromise. Would Grindal consent to the exclusion from the prophesyings of the lay audience? Grindal could see no reason why the people should not benefit and so closed off this way of escape.[50] As spring approached he was transacting business as usual.[51] In late February Burghley sought to prevent a second confrontation with Elizabeth: 'I could be content your coming to speech with her Majesty were delayed a little longer, and to that end I wish my lord of Leicester were your intercessor, to excuse your absence by reason of your sickness. This I wish for your respects. And yet I refer the order to yourself.'[52] Grindal may never have gone to Court again, as a free agent. By May political efforts to avert disaster had failed. Royal letters went out to the bishops, directly ordering the suppression of the prophesyings, a command obeyed in Grindal's own diocese and peculiars.[53] Soon afterwards the archbishop was sequestered and confined to Lambeth House. The order was apparently made by the Council, after Grindal had made a personal appearance and, in spite of persuasion, had refused to make a perceptible retraction, 'a second offence of disobedience, greater than the first.'[54] The text of the order of sequestration has not survived and its terms are uncertain.

Worse was intended. The queen now called in question the validity of the patents of appointment held by the archbishop's principal officers 'in this time of sequestration' and instructed two ecclesiastical lawyers, Dr Lewyn and Dr Dale, to prepare the ground with the principal law officers of the Crown for the archbishop's deprivation.[55] In mid-July, after seven weeks of confinement, Grindal told a correspondent, probably Leicester: 'I never in all my life numbered days so precisely as I do now, being afore this time never called to answer in any place of judgment.'[56]

If Camden is to be trusted, it is not surprising that Leicester's mediation had failed to save the archbishop since the true author of his misfortune was none other than the earl himself. The root of the matter concerned the marital affairs of Leicester's Italian physician, Giulio Borgarucci, a man with a grudge against Grindal for denying him the means to make an irregular marriage.[57] This story appeared in print as early as 1584, in the notorious libel known to history as *Leicester's Commonwealth*, and variants of it occur in early historical memoirs of the reign and in Fuller's *Church History*, where we find the added suggestion that Leicester had covetous designs on Lambeth House, as Ahab had for Naboth's vineyard. In Peter Heylyn's *Aerius Redivivus* this became Leicester's prime motive.[58] One might discount these rumours from a tainted source but for a letter which 'Dr Julio' sent to Leicester, four days before Grindal addressed himself to the queen in December 1576. This is full of complaints at the frustration of his marriage, directed against the archbishop in person, Grindal having sworn, as Julio's lawyers had reported, that 'I should never obtain this gentlewoman I have married, nor enjoy her.'[59] And when Burghley and Walsingham later discussed the queen's intention to deprive the archbishop Burghley revealed that it was Julio who had instructed an eminent lawyer on what should be done. 'So as I see that he was more of her Majesty's Council than two or three that are of present council.'[60] We cannot remove all traces of ambiguity from Leicester's role in the affair. The rumour was already current that he had furthered the archbishop's troubles.[61] The puritan jungle telegraph was humming with damaging reports about his responsibility for the betrayal of the Midland prophesyings, as well as about his 'ungodly life', which the earl was bound to treat seriously.[62] But Leicester easily aroused mistrust and unpopularity. Camden's hostility is known to have flawed an otherwise impeccable judgment.[63] Ostensibly, Leicester, the chief hope of the forward protestant cause, went out of his way to help Grindal.

So what of Dr Julio? If Julio was Leicester's physician and intimate[64] he was also the queen's physician, and of her chamber.[65] Elizabeth herself became the archbishop's relentless adversary, and we may have no need of the hypothesis that she was influenced against him by some other party or parties: which is not to deny that Grindal's disgrace was welcome to all those at Court who were hostile to his progressive protestantism. There remains the possibility that the affair in its innerness was an episode in the upward progress of the particular favourite of the hour, Christopher Hatton. Hatton too was part of the Italian connection. In 1573 Julio had attended him on a journey to the Spa, just as he later accompanied Leicester to the waters at Buxton.[66] As the patron of Aylmer and Bancroft and the supporter of Whitgift there can be no doubt of

Hatton's political involvement with the rise of a conservative, even reactionary churchmanship which Grindal's fall facilitated.[67] And it is possible that this ecclesiastical strategy was adopted with the intention of outflanking Leicester. Yet there is no positive evidence to link Hatton with Grindal's disgrace, apart from a comment attached to a copy of the archbishop's 'book to the queen' to the effect that in ordering the prophesyings to be put down the queen had been 'moved by Hatton and some other'.[68] This endorsement may not date from 1577 and Hatton, as the enemy of radical puritans, was a natural object of suspicions which may or may not have been well founded. What is documented is that Hatton intervened with the queen on Grindal's behalf in the spring of 1578. It remains possible that it was Hatton's earlier responsibility for the archbishop's discomfiture which invested this initiative with the peculiar importance evidently attached to it.[69]

Clearly Grindal's fall was not the simple consequence of his formal refusal to transmit the queen's order against the prophesyings. So far we have introduced evidence which may seem to trivialize the affair by dissolving it into personal and courtly intrigues. But the struggle of factions and interests in the mid-Elizabethan Court was not at all trivial, connected as it was to events which made these years 'a political and military watershed in European history'.[70] Edmund Spenser had some poetic intuition of Grindal's place in the critical political decisions of the time, which he expressed among the cryptic allegories of The Shepheardes Calender:

> He is a shepheard great in gree
> but hath bene long ypent . . .
>
> Ah good *Algrin*, his hap was ill,
> but shall be better in time.[71]

Modern Spenser scholarship claims to have cracked the ciphers and to have made explicit the integration of politics, religion and art in Spenser's poetic rhetoric, especially in its bearing on the Alençon courtship of 1579.[72] But the ecclesiastical crisis of 1577 has yet to be plausibly located in the matrix of contemporary political events.

Let us briefly recall the state of the world, as it appeared to some English eyes, in 1577 and 1578. What Dr Simon Adams has called 'the protestant cause',[73] the cause of 'political puritanism', was espoused by many near to the centre of affairs, including most of those royal servants conducting diplomacy in the sensitive spheres of France, Scotland and, above all, the Netherlands. Their ideology expressed itself in passionate, but by no means irrational, responses to every new turn in international affairs. The queen and the realm were in danger. Their only firm friends were those 'of the religion': in the Netherlands the Prince of Orange above all, who was to be sustained at all costs. Papists were dangerous and deceitful. Policy towards native catholics

and in the Netherlands must take account of the ultimate ambition of the
Spaniards to overcome England. The reluctance of their mistress to read these
signs of the times, her readiness to listen to bad advice, her endless procrastina-
tions, were sources of frustration frequently vented in semi-private diplomatic
correspondence.

Here is a selection of the commonplaces contained in memoranda and letters
from the period of the Pacification of Ghent and its aftermath: 'The present
quiet her Majesty now enjoyeth cannot long continue.' (From 'a brief discourse laying forth the uncertainty of her Majesty's present peace and quietness'.[74]) 'And never will I think that ever any perfect or assured amity will be
amongst any that are divided in religion. The queen's Majesty may perhaps
mislike my plain writing in these matters after so bold a manner.' (Dr Thomas
Wilson to Sir Francis Walsingham, April 1577, in the weeks after the conclusion of the 'perpetual edict' between the Estates and Don John of Austria.[75])
And as Wilson wrote to the queen herself, in June of the same year: 'This is my
belief, not to believe' – that is, not to believe papists.[76] In September, with
Elizabeth's resolution to support Orange fading and with the Archduke
Matthias appearing on the Belgian horizon, Sir Nicholas Bacon, a relatively
conservative observer, plucked up the courage to memorialize his mistress to
the same effect: 'I see no way so sure for your Majesty as to keep the Prince of
Orange in heart and life.' 'Most gracious sovereign, I have been so unquieted
with these things.'[77]

In January 1578 the army of the Estates was defeated at Gembloux and
according to Charles Wilson the English government scuttled back to perform
another set of strange diplomatic quadrilles.[78] Yet what Walsingham reported to Randolph on 20 February was that 'we are now here in daily and
earnest consultation what is best to be done, in which generally I see all my
lords inclined to one course for her Majesty's safety, if it please God to incline
herself to embrace and follow the same.'[79] This course was not to do nothing.
Two days later Henry Killigrew wrote to William Davison: 'The Lord give us
grace to do that may be to his glory, our own surety and the help of our
friends and good neighbours in time.'[80] But in April he wrote: 'Her Majesty
hath some that do mar more in a day than all her godly councillors and servants
can persuade in a week.'[81] We may spare ourselves the longueurs and dis-
tresses of the spring and summer of 1578, culminating in the counter-productive
Walsingham–Cobham mission of August: a story which pains Professor Wilson
in the telling and which had the principal protagonist, Walsingham, writing by
September: 'God send me well to return and I will hereafter take my leave of
foreign service.'[82]

This sketch adds nothing to the dense narratives contained in Conyers
Read's *Walsingham* and his *Burghley*. But nowadays the strength and broadness
of base of the protestant cause appears more impressive than it did to Read,
who was over-attracted to the symmetrical model of a Privy Council split

between conservative and radical wings, and who attributed too conservative a consistency to Burghley.[83] And from the standpoint of modern scholarship Read made too little of Leicester.

We return to Archbishop Grindal, whose fate was not a wholly separate issue but an aspect, by no means peripheral, of the contention between conservative and progressive forces at Court. It would be too much to claim that the oscillations in Grindal's fortunes corresponded exactly to every barometric variation in the protestant cause. But they can be read as a rough index of the way things were going, a windsock as it were.

This is the significance with which the matter was invested in a letter written to Secretary Wilson by Sir Francis Knollys in January 1578. After general reflections on the familiar theme of vigilance and on the difficulty of conscientiously performing the office of a councillor to a mistress so careless of her safety and so open to false counsel, Knollys comes to particulars:

> The avoiding of her Majesty's danger doth consist in the preventing of the conquest of the Low Countries betimes; secondly, in the preventing of the revolt of Scotland from her Majesty's devotion unto the French and the Queen of Scots; and thirdly, in the timely preventing of the contemptuous growing of the disobedient papists here in England.

'And also', he added, 'if her Majesty will be safe, she must comfort the hearts of those that be her most faithful subjects, even for conscience sake.' And then, in what serves as the rhetorical climax of the discourse: 'But if the bishop of Canterbury shall be deprived, then up starts the pride and practice of the papists. And then King Richard the Second's men will flock into Court apace and will show themselves in their colours.'[84] 'King Richard the Second's men' we must take for the antitypes of Knollys himself, with his robust, protestant plain speaking:[85] smooth-tongued flatterers and 'parasites' who would conceal the truth and bring all to confusion.

In the previous summer of 1577, when the queen had first revealed her radical intention against Grindal, Walsingham conveyed the news to Burghley in a letter which accompanied a discouraging despatch from overseas: 'Her Majesty seemeth to be greatly perplexed with this news. But yet it worketh not that effect, to make her stay her proceedings against the archbishop (which at this time, howsoever he hath offended, were in true policy most requisite), a matter that doth greatly grieve as many as truly love her Majesty.' Details were added of the preliminary steps towards deprivation already taken. 'Thus my good lord you see how we proceed still in making war against God: whose ire we should rather seek to appease that he may keep the wars that most apparently approach towards us from us. God open her Majesty's eyes that she may both see her peril and acknowledge from whence the true remedy is to be sought.' Burghley's response was an echo ('these proceedings cannot but irritate our merciful God') and contained the news of Dr Julio's machinations.

'I think the persons appointed to consult for the deprivation of the archbishop shall be much troubled to find a precedent.'[86]

This was as much as to admit that Burghley, and presumably other councillors, would do all in their power to shelter Grindal from deprivation. It seems significant that the rare glimpses of their efforts which are revealed from time to time occur for the most part in State Papers Foreign, in correspondence with William Davison, the dedicated puritan who had replaced Wilson as ambassador in the Netherlands in July 1577.

On 8 August Davison's cousin and Grindal's secretary, Edward Cheke, reported that he was in daily attendance at Court 'about my lord's business', where he was assured by Leicester and Hatton that it would 'take end very shortly.' 'The queen hath been so troubled with matters of the Low Countries and for the relieving of the protestants in France as it hath [been] the only let of my lord's cause.'[87] A fortnight later Killigrew assured Davison that Grindal had been released from strict confinement,[88] and in mid-September Cheke confirmed that his master had enjoyed 'some enlargement' and that the queen was 'well pacified'.[89] From now onwards the archbishop was free to commute between Lambeth and his manor at Croydon. (There seems to have been no question of a retreat into his diocese, as with other disgraced bishops in earlier times. Indeed one may search in vain for any positive local evidence that Grindal so much as visited Canterbury during his archiepiscopate.[90]) At this point Cheke was optimistic: 'I am now almost despatched from my long travail, for before I go home from the Court I am surely promised to have my lord's liberty.'[91] This was at a time when it appeared likely that Elizabeth would strike the hot iron and intervene in the Netherlands. The same letter from Cheke reported that Leicester was to lead an expedition. 'This is his full determination, but yet unknown unto her Highness, neither shall she be acquainted with it until she be fully resolved to send, which will not be until the Prince of Orange send back again . . . My lord of Leicester is the most desirous to go the chief of this journey that ever you heard of, and doth labour it both by his own policy and by favour of all his friends.'

In October Grindal formally requested the Council to 'be means for me to her Majesty to receive me again into her gracious favour', and acknowledged his particular debt to Leicester, 'who hath from the beginning most carefully and painfully travailed for me to her Majesty.'[92] In November he was 'put in assured hope of liberty.' But then 'a sudden contrary tempest' arose, and at the end of that month he was summoned to appear before the Council, meeting in Star Chamber.[93]

From a remarkable account of what followed, almost certainly composed by Sir Walter Mildmay and surviving among his papers,[94] it appears that the queen had informed the Privy Council that her pleasure was that on his appearance Grindal should either confess his fault or 'receive his deprivation'. When the Council gathered in the Star Chamber on the last two days of

November the judges were also present and the court was in some sense empowered to 'hear and determine' the cause. But before the appointed day the lords of the Council were said to have met 'all together' at the house of the lord keeper, Sir Nicholas Bacon, to consider the implications of the queen's instructions. Mildmay suggested to his colleagues that they indicated a 'very strange course' for which the Council had received no formal commission and which would involve it in actions beyond its jurisdiction. He asked what would follow if the archbishop were to appear 'and stiffly maintain his doings', 'the people addicted to the matter as they were.' It was decided to send Mildmay himself and Sir Ralph Sadler to sound the archbishop out, while Burghley wrote to advise him on how to conduct himself at the expected hearing in Star Chamber, and on the terms of his submission.[95] But Grindal told the two councillors in uncharacteristically spirited language that before he would yield 'he would be torn in pieces with horses', and he entrusted to Mildmay his own form of submission which avoided any acknowledgment of guilt.[96]

It was fortunate that illness prevented Grindal from making his appearance in the Star Chamber on either of the two days appointed, whereupon Lord Keeper Bacon announced in a short speech that it was thought inexpedient and by the queen inadmissible to proceed against the archbishop in his absence.[97] In December Cheke resigned himself to waiting until the following term for a decision.[98] In at least three collections of Bacon's speeches there survives an oration intended for use in the Star Chamber, a stern sermon of public rebuke to be addressed to the archbishop.[99] It is not clear whether this was prepared for the hearing of late November and never delivered, or whether it belongs to a subsequent occasion. But since Mildmay conflates elements of both of Bacon's speeches in his account of what transpired on 30 November and suggests that this was the end of the matter ('from that time forward he remained in his house as prisoner, continuing in his opinion') it seems most likely that Grindal never did confront a tribunal charged, however dubiously, with power to deprive him.[100]

The queen was not pleased. In Burghley's absence from Court it seems to have fallen to Mildmay to draft a memorandum 'touching the archbishop of Canterbury in the matter of the exercises', containing arguments which may have been intended to justify his deprivation.[101] This was dated 22 January. On the following day Wilson reported to Burghley: 'Her Majesty is much offended with the archbishop and disliketh our darings for dealing with him so at large, whom her Highness would have deprived for his contempt committed.' Wilson had advised the queen that the deprivation of an archbishop could not be so easily arranged, especially since Grindal was likely to contest the matter. He hoped that on his return Burghley would succeed in persuading her of the advantages of an arranged resignation, a course 'more safe, more easy, and as honourable as the other.'[102] A week later Killigrew reported: 'The bishop of Canterbury is now more likely to be deprived than *at the first*.'[103] But then, a month later: 'There is hope that the bishop of Canterbury shall do better and better daily', coupled with the news that it was resolved to send Leicester over the North Sea with ten thousand men. 'I would this were a true prognostication.'[104]

At this point Sir Christopher Hatton, newly knighted and preferred to Knollys's old office of vice-chamberlain, became the man upon whose good offices Grindal's reinstatement appeared to depend. On 7 March 1578 Bishop Cox of Ely wrote to a correspondent who could only have been Bishop Aylmer of London, and among other matters asked whether 'by any means we may possibly help our brother', meaning Grindal. 'Ye know the man to be wise, zealous and godly.' His own efforts in this regard had failed. But if Mr Vice-Chamberlain 'could by any prudent means mitigate and assuage her Majesty's displeasure I am persuaded that he should do God high honour and her Majesty good service, and deserve at the hands of those that be zealous and godly infinite thanks and win their hearts for ever.'[105] This was to suggest that Hatton should look for new friends in preserves which were traditionally Leicester's. Two months later, on 2 May, Grindal, in a letter which had no other purpose, thanked Hatton profusely for his 'continual, honourable, and most friendly cares and travails for me, by the which, as also by your sundry comfortable messages at divers times sent unto me, I am brought into an assured hope by your good means to recover her Majesty's grace and favour in time convenient.' Although Hatton's efforts had not yet taken effect, 'yet do I think myself especially bounden to give you most hearty thanks, and that in as ample manner as if I presently enjoyed the fruition of the end of my suit.' The letter suggests that Hatton's intervention was particularly significant. For one thing he was able to exploit a very special relationship with the queen. For another (and this is to speculate) if it was the case that he had initially shared the queen's hostile reaction to the arch-bishop's letter, or had even provoked her into it, his preparedness to help at this juncture would be all the more likely to succeed. Grindal was more deferential and submissive in this letter than in any other statement he made during this crisis in his affairs.[106] All to no avail. Later in the month the Earl of Huntingdon reported to the Dean of York that the archbishop had been on the point of delivery 'by the good means of Mr Vice-Chamberlain' when reports of a factious puritan sermon conveyed to the queen by Arch-bishop Sandys of York and Bishop Barnes of Durham were so inflated as 'to make a stay of his deliverance.'[107]

After this the archbishop's cause dragged inconclusively on. Twice in the early months of 1580 he renewed his petition to the Privy Council 'to be means' to the queen for his liberty and restitution.'[108] His health was now broken beyond repair and he was losing his sight.[109] By the New Year of 1583 even the queen's displeasure must have mellowed, for she gave him a 'standing cup', apparently her first gift since the original year of his archiepiscopate.[110] In the following July he forestalled the arrangements at last concluded for his resignation[111] by dying, still in office. He was honourably buried.[112] We need not pursue the details of the story beyond the summer of 1578, for by then the archbishop's cause had reached a kind of plateau. In 1579 the storm over the proposed French marriage shifted attention to another quarter and to a different kind of martyr to the protestant cause, John Stubbs, author of *The gaping gulf*.[113]

An instructive aspect of Grindal's sequestration was the support which he never ceased to enjoy in high places. In public utterance, as in the speeches which Bacon prepared for his appearances before the Council, the archbishop might be reprimanded for his extreme insubordination. Yet surely Bacon gave the game away when he told the company in Star Chamber: 'Some no doubt are apt enough to marvel why her Majesty should so proceed against him. But if it were as well known to you as to my lords here present what reasons her Highness hath to lead her hereunto, I should not need so many words in this matter.'[114] This reflection of public concern is reminiscent of Camden's description of the crowd at John Stubbs's immolation: 'The multitude standing about was altogether silent, either out of horror at this new and unwonted punishment, or else out of pity towards the man, being of the most honest and unblameable report, or else out of hatred of the marriage, which most people perceived would be the overthrow of religion.'[115]

Among the bishops Grindal had but one enemy: Richard Barnes of Durham, a churchman whom he held in contempt as a venal careerist.[116] In February 1578, with the archbishop poised on the brink of deprivation, Barnes found it necessary to defend himself to Burghley against reports that he did not have 'a good mind' to Grindal, and to explain why on a visit to London he had avoided a call at Lambeth.[117] Even conservative bishops such as Cox, Aylmer and Whitgift did nothing to worsen the archbishop's predicament. Cox indeed made use of what he presumed to be a still privileged position to intercede with the queen and Burghley,[118] and, as we have seen, indirectly with Hatton. But it is perhaps significant that in 1580 Whitgift and his ally, Piers of Salisbury, took the initiative in commending to Grindal a form of total retraction and submission,[119] and that three years later Piers was involved in the arrangements for his resignation.[120] In 1581 Convocation and 12 of the bishops presented the queen with formal addresses in favour of their primate's restitution.[121] Admittedly the suspension of the metropolitan was sufficiently prejudicial to the hierarchy as a whole to elicit a united response, almost regardless of the merits of the case. But the absence, or concealment, of any desire to profit from the archbishop's eclipse is nevertheless impressive.

Clearly the sympathetic concern of the protestant nation was firmly engaged on Grindal's behalf. On the other side stood the queen herself and, one must suppose, 'King Richard the Second's men', whose identity one may guess at. They may have included, among privy councillors, Sir James Croft and the Earl of Sussex; and, beyond the Council, the connection of catholics and crypto-catholics of the Court who would later show their hand in the struggle over the French marriage: Lord Henry Howard, Lord Paget, Charles Arundel, Sir Edward Stafford, and the Earl of Oxford, until he was detached from his unsuitable friends by his father-in-law, Burghley.[122] Whether Hatton should be included in their company, at least in the inception of the archbishop's troubles, must remain an open question. Like any account of courtly intrigue, the picture retains its areas of shade and its indefinite outlines.

Finally, what was the state of the Church of England while its senior pastor was under a cloud? This essay has hitherto avoided definition of the legal and administrative intricacies of a suspension from office which was never total, was not set out in any document which survives, and which was not consistently enforced. The relevant facts are in the archiepiscopal Register.[123] As soon as Grindal had been sequestered, in late May 1577, such formal documents as licences for schoolmasters, letters dimissory (vouching for candidates for ordination in another diocese) or commissions to institute to benefices in vacant sees were not only issued by Dr Thomas Yale, as official principal and vicar general, but in his name, rather than that of the archbishop.[124] In November, when Yale took to his deathbed, the Privy Council authorized Grindal to appoint 'two sufficient persons' to take his place. Grindal accordingly issued his own commission to Dr William Drury and Dr Lawrence Hussey.[125] But on 20 January he was informed by Thomas Wilson, as Secretary, that their places as vicars general were to be taken by Dr William Aubrey and Dr William Clark. Aubrey had been nominated by the queen, Clark by the Council, and they were to occupy jointly during royal pleasure the office described at one point in the Register as 'the vicarageship of the archiepiscopal see of Canterbury'. From September 1581 Aubrey appears to have acted alone in the execution of this office.[126]

Among the mandates issued as a matter of course by Aubrey and Clark were commissions to conduct the metropolitan visitation of the various sees. But on 20 January 1583 Grindal inexplicably issued in his own name the commission to visit Lichfield Cathedral.[127] (It was at this time that the queen had favoured him with a New Year's gift.) As for the exercise of his more properly spiritual, episcopal functions, these never seem to have been inhibited by his sequestration. He took part in the consecration of bishops in March 1578, August 1579, September 1580 and September 1581, and mandates to confirm the elections of bishops and for their installation continued to be issued in the archbishop's own name.[128] Moreover, whenever directly instructed to do so by the Council Grindal continued to take a variety of administrative actions, such as the forwarding to the other bishops of royal briefs for charitable collections in aid of distressed individuals or communities, the ordering of enquiries into popish recusancy, and the transmitting of an order of the Council requiring unbeneficed preachers to celebrate communion.[129] On one such occasion he was required to act 'notwithstanding your present sequestration.'[130] In 1579 Grindal was active and authoritative in arbitrating in a major dispute between the cathedral chapter of Canterbury and Queen's College, Cambridge, and in 1581 in efforts to pacify the warring factions in Merton College, Oxford.[131] But such traditional primatial responsibilities as the presidency of Convocation and the appointing of court preachers were assumed by the bishop of London, who also seems to have presided over the Ecclesiastical Commission.[132] In the Parliament of 1581 Archbishop Sandys of York took precedence, although Whitgift of Worcester made an impression which implies that his eventual promotion to Canterbury was already anticipated.[133]

It would require a better sense of the relations between the person of the archbishop and the administrative machinery operated in his name than ecclesiastical historians can yet command to judge how damaging was the absence of personal direction over a period of six years, from the diocese of Canterbury, from the vacant sees, and from the province at large. A memorandum listing 'inconveniences by the sequestration of the archbishop of Canterbury'[134] noted that the processes which normally went out over his name and title would be 'less esteemed' and their validity even doubted when these were lacking. The absence of the archbishop from Convocation was 'a new precedent of dangerous and doubtful sequel.' In vacant sees the archbishop was accustomed to arbitrate personally in major disputes, 'which now he cannot do.' The metropolitan visitation was likely to be ineffective and to leave many dioceses unreformed. The credit and authority of the archbishop were lost to the Ecclesiastical Commission. And

> where as well the bishops and other of the clergy as also of the laity throughout the whole province were wont to resort to the archbishop to consult with him and have his direction in matters of great weight, whereby many controversies and occasions of strife and slander within their dioceses were cut off, although there do arise many like occasions daily, yet there lacketh the authority of the same archbishop for the appeasing thereof.

It was at this personal and political level that the effective headlessness of the Church proved most damaging. Almost half the sees in England seem to have been shaken by storms or scandals of one kind or another between 1575 and 1583. In Sussex and in Norfolk and Suffolk there were major political contests between the bishops and the ruling gentry, and although Bishop Curteys of Chichester was at odds with a conservative, even catholic gentry and Bishop Freke of Norwich with puritans, the two 'country causes' were otherwise of the same order: in both cases the bishop over-reached his political strength in taking on the leaders of local government. The case of Bishop Curteys was a minor reflection of Grindal's greater tragedy: suspension from office, precipitating his death in 1582.[135] Bishop Cox of Ely was being hounded by Lord North and Sir Christopher Hatton and was in serious danger of enforced resignation.[136] Scory of Hereford, who called his diocese a 'purgatory', was under suspicion for 'certain matters of very foul disorder'.[137] Robinson of Bangor had to defend himself against the charge of being a papist[138] and his brother Middleton of St Davids was already linked with the colourful list of crimes which would eventually lead to his degradation.[139] Lichfield witnessed a battle royal for the chancellorship between Dr Becon and Dr Babington, with the ring held by the venal Bishop Overton in a diocese described by Whitgift of Worcester as 'in sundry parts . . . out of frame'.[140] In the north, Archbishop Sandys was in conflict with the lord president, Huntingdon, and with the deans of both York and Durham, Hutton and Whittingham. Then in 1582 came the scandal, juicy if contrived, of the archbishop and the landlord's wife, in an inn at Doncaster.[141] 1580 saw a general enquiry into the wastage of timber in episcopal parks and woods, which exposed many of the bishops as opportunists in estate management.[142]

Above all there was the major scandal of a tripartite delapidations suit involving the senior members of the hierarchy, the two archbishops and the bishop of London, which arose in the first instance from a bitter dispute about the financial affairs of the diocese of London between Sandys and his successor, Aylmer.[143] This quarrel was invested with more than ordinary venom, Sandys writing of Aylmer: 'Coloured covetousness, an envious heart covered with the cloak of dissimulation will, when opportunity serveth, show forth itself.' 'So soon as the bishop of York had holpen him on with his rochet, he was transformed and showed himself in his own nature.'[144]

In retrospect the state of the Church and of religion in the time of Grindal's addled archiepiscopate was both applauded and deplored. The Kentish puritan, Josias Nicholls, recalling that this was a season when preaching ministers were not molested, thought it 'a golden time, full of godly fruit'.[145] But Whitgift's secretary and biographer, Sir George Paule, wrote of 'that crazy state of the Church (for so it was at this archbishop's [Whitgift's] first coming and a long time after'.[146]) Readers who have come thus far will concede that Paule discovered the *mot juste* in 'crazy'.

The contention of this essay has been that Archbishop Grindal's troubles were coherent with the struggle over Elizabethan policy, especially foreign policy. But an almost contradictory argument is equally valid. Once Grindal had written the offending letter and for this and any other contributory causes had incurred the queen's displeasure he became a liability for protestant politicians and it was an important objective of their policy to save him from the worst consequences of his action. But it was no part of policy that Grindal should have written such an undiplomatic letter in the first place and we may be sure that it was without political advice that he put impolitic pen to paper. Policy, even protestant policy, would say: 'It is necessary to be humble, or at least to hold one's tongue.' Grindal represents not political puritanism but that sturdy strain in reformed protestantism which rediscovered the difference between religion and politics and for which 'policy' was almost a term of abuse.[147] In another century and another polity Grindal's 'puritanism' might have been compatible with 'deep judgment' and 'the greatest wisdom and ability to govern'. In Elizabethan England these things were plainly incompatible, and there was a certain inevitability about the archbishop's political extinction.

1. Archbishop William Sancroft's deprivation in 1690 was by Act of Parliament.
2. *The Elizabethan Puritan Movement* (1967), 200.
3. 1925.
4. 1960.
5. *Sir Francis Walsingham*, II, 1.
6. *Queen Elizabeth and the Revolt of the Netherlands* (1970), 2.
7. Thomas Rogers, *The Catholic Doctrine of the Church of England* (1607), ed. J. J. S. Perowne (Parker Soc., 1854), 9.
8. *Cambridge Modern History*, III (1907), 341.
9. W. H. Frere, *The English Church in the Reigns of Elizabeth and James I* (1904), 19.
10. H. M. Gwatkin, *Church and State in England to the Death of Queen Anne* (1917), 255.
11. P. A. Welsby, *George Abbot the Unwanted Archbishop 1562–1633* (1962), 1.
12. Thomas Fuller, *The Church History of Britain*, V (1845), 58.
13. *Of reformation, touching church-discipline in England* (1641), 15.

14. *The antipathie of the English lordly prelacie both to royall monarchy and civil unity* (1641), 147–9.

15. *The tryal of Dr Henry Sacheverell* (1710). For the context, see Geoffrey Holmes, *The Trial of Doctor Sacheverell* (1973); and for the relevance of the Sacheverell affair for the publication of John Strype's *Life of Grindal* see Cecile Zinberg, 'The usable dissenting past: John Strype and Elizabethan puritanism', in *The Dissenting Tradition*, ed. C. R. Cole and M. E. Moody (Athens, Ohio, 1975), 123–39.

16. *Annals of the First Four Years of the Reign of Queen Elizabeth*, ed. J. Bruce (Camden Soc., O.S. vii, 1840), 89.

17. Nowell to Burghley, 16 May 1575: PRO, SP 12/103/49. See also the Earl of Huntingdon's commendation of Grindal to Burghley, 24 June 1575: BL, Lansdowne MS. 20, no. 50, f.130.

18. Burghley to Sir Francis Walsingham, 15 May 1575: PRO, SP 12/103/48.

19. Grindal to Burghley, 27 February 1583: BL, Lansdowne MS. 37, no. 23, f.50.

20. With two exceptions the letters are in BL, Lansdowne MSS. and PRO, State Papers Domestic (SP 12), in roughly equal proportions. A letter of 3 August 1564 is in BL, Add. MS. 35831, no. 86, f.184 and another of 25 November 1575 in Inner Temple Library, Petyt MS. 538/47, no. 267, f.502. Of the 98 letters, 61 are printed, in whole or part, in *The Remains of Edmund Grindal*, ed. W. Nicholson (Parker Soc., 1843; hereafter cited as *Remains*), and occupy 82 of the 484 pages of *Remains*.

21. Burghley to Grindal (holograph), 25 November 1575: Inner Temple Library, Petyt MS. 538/47, no. 267, f.502.

22. A letter neither signed, nor addressed, nor dated, but in Parker's hand: BL, Lansdowne MS. 15, no. 34, f.66. Parker appears to apologize for this outburst in a letter to Burghley, endorsed 6 October 1572: *ibid.*, no. 43, f.84.

23. Grindal to Burghley, 10 December 1575: BL, Lansdowne MS. 20, no. 69, f.168.

24. Blank in the MS.

25. PRO, SP 59/19, f.248v. The item is numbered '983' from its old location in SP 70/141 (see *Calendar of State Papers, Foreign*, 1575–7, 468–9), from where it was transferred to State Papers, Scotland and the Borders.

26. The minutes of the dean and chapter of Canterbury record the awarding of additional expenses to the dean, who had travelled to London to pay his respects to the archbishop and to present the certificate of his election, 'by reason of attending and waiting for the coming of the said archbishop from York, which happened by reason the said archbishop was stayed by sickness.' (Cathedral Archives and Library, Canterbury, MS. Y.11.3, Chapter Acta, f.93; Misc. Accounts 41, accounts for 1576.)

27. J. E. Neale, *Elizabeth I and her Parliaments, 1559–1581* (1953), 349–53; Collinson, *op. cit.*, 161–3. The canons of 1576 are printed in *Synodalia*, ed. E. Cardwell, I (1842), 132–8.

28. F. X. Walker, 'The implementation of the Elizabethan statutes against recusants, 1581–1603' (unpublished Ph.D. thesis, London University, 1961), 36–118.

29. See *Faculty Office Registers, 1534–1549*, ed. D. S. Chambers (1966).

30. There is one copy of these orders in BL, Lansdowne MS. 23, no. 61, f.127 and two further copies in PRO, SP 12/129/25, 26. Two of these copies bear the names of

nine privy councillors: Bacon, Burghley, Lincoln, Sussex, Arundel, Bedford, Knollys, Croft and Mildmay. The last section of the orders is unaccountably dated in the first SP 12 copy '13 January 1578'.

31. PRO, SP 12/107/41.

32. *Ibid.*, SP 15/24/72.

33. Canterbury was variously valued at about the time of Grindal's translation at £3,093 18s. 8d. (BL, Lansdowne MS. 21, no. 20, f.40) and £3,453 1 8s. 8d. (*ibid.*, Lansdowne MS. 23, no. 60, fos. 125–6).

34. A substantial collection of reports in Inner Temple Library, Petyt MS. 538/54, fos. 265–71, 282r, 284: partly printed, J. Strype, *Life of Grindal* (1821 edn), 300–9. One of a group of related papers, concerning a dispute about precedence between the archbishop's leading officials (Petyt MS. 538/54, fos. 7–11, 16–18, 21–2, 23–5, 64–7) is dated 3 May 1576 (not 23 May as in Strype, *op. cit.*, 309). Further copies of many of these documents are in Bodl., Tanner MS. 280.

35. Memorandum of Dr William Aubrey, 30 April 1576: Inner Temple Library, Petyt MS. 538/54, fos. 268–71.

36. C. Kitching, 'The Prerogative Court of Canterbury from Warham to Whitgift', in *Continuity and Change: Personnel and Administration of the Church in England, 1500–1642*, ed. R. O'Day and F. Heal (1976), 191, 207.

37. Grindal to Burghley, 10 June 1576: BL, Lansdowne MS. 23, no. 4, f.7; further references and documentation in my *Letters of Thomas Wood, Puritan, 1566–1577*, *BIHR*, special supplement 5 (1960), XVIII–XIX, 9–24. *See above*, 60-1, 91-106.

38. See my attempts to remove misunderstandings in *Elizabethan Puritan Movement*, 168–76; and in 'Lectures by combination: structures and characteristics of church life in seventeenth-century England', *BIHR*, XLVIII (1975), 198–9. *See below*, 483-4.

39. Sir Nicholas Bacon's speech to Grindal in Council: BL, Harleian MS. 5176, f.95; Grindal to Burghley, 10 June 1576: BL, Lansdowne MS. 23, no. 4, f.7.

40. Lambeth Palace Library, MS. 2003, fos. 1–34; eighteenth-century copies of most of these with a letter from the Bishop of Gloucester, not otherwise extant, in BL, Add. MS. 29546, fos. 36–57; extracts from the correspondence in Lambeth Palace Library, MS. 2003, fos. 35–6, and in BL, Add. MS. 21565, f.26, adding information from four letters no longer extant; imperfect transcripts of much of the material from the Lambeth MSS. in S. E. Lehmberg, 'Archbishop Grindal and the prophesyings', *Historical Magazine of the Protestant Episcopal Church*, XXXIV (1965), 87–145.

41. Lambeth Palace Library, MS. 2014, fos. 72–80, MS. 2007, fos. 126–44; further material relating to the *tractatus* recently recovered by Lambeth Palace Library is in MS. 2872, fos. 10–11.

42. BL, Lansdowne MS. 109, no. 2, fos. 3, 5.

43. The contemporary fame of the letter is reflected in the many copies which survive: e.g., in BL, Add. MSS. 22587, 33271, Harleian MS. 1877 (imperfect and dated 12 November 1578), Lambeth Palace Library MS. 595, Bodl., Tanner MS. 79, Queen's College Oxford, MS. 292, Northamptonshire Record Office, Fitzwilliam of Milton Papers, F.(M).P.54. The text in *Remains* is taken from BL, Lansdowne MS. 23, no. 12, fos. 24–9, which is endorsed by Burghley 'December 20th 1576', a dating repeated in other copies. The copy in the Morrice MSS. in Dr Williams's Library (*Seconde Parte of a Register*, ed. A. Peel, 1915, I, 135) is dated

'the 10th of December 1576'. The correct date is inferred from Grindal's letter to Burghley of 16 December (*Remains*, 391).

44. Frere, *op. cit.*, 192.

45. *Remains*, 387.

46. *Op. cit.*, IV, 454.

47. Among the books bequeathed by Grindal at his death to the Queen's College Oxford and still extant is his copy of the Erasmian text of the *Opera* of St Ambrose in the Basle edition of 1538. The passages from the Epistles of Ambrose which are quoted in the letter to the queen are extensively annotated in Grindal's hand.

48. 'The palace belongs to the emperor, the churches to the bishop.' (*Early Latin Theology*, ed. S. L. Greenslade, Library of Christian Classics, V, 1956, 178–81.)

49. *Calendar of State Papers, Foreign*, 1578–80, 99–100.

50. Letters to Burghley, 16, 17 December 1576: *Remains*, 391–2.

51. See, for example, Grindal's letter to the Earl of Sussex, 30 January 1576(/7), enclosing a list of Lenten preachers for the Court: BL, Harleian MS. 6992, no. 34, f.69. Grindal's Register records no abnormalities before late May 1577. The earliest commission issued in the name of the vicar general, Dr Yale, is dated 1 June 1577. (Lambeth Palace Library, Grindal's Register, f.406.)

52. Burghley to Grindal (holograph), 23 February 1576(/7): Lambeth Palace Library, MS. 2003, f.39.

53. BL, Lansdowne MS. 25, no. 44, fos. 92–3 contains two alternative drafts of royal letters to the bishops, one of them addressed to the bishop of Lincoln and endorsed 'Aprill 1577. A minute of a letter to be written from her Majesty to the bishops concerning the exercise of prophetie.' BL, Lansdowne MS. 25, no. 44 (3), fos. 94–5 is a draft of a different letter, the one actually despatched, annotated by Burghley and endorsed in his hand: '7 Maii 1577. The queen's Majesty's letter to the bishops to stay of all rites in the Church not warranted by law.' A fair copy of this version in BL, Cotton MS. Cleopatra F. II, f.289 is printed by Strype (574–6) and in *Remains* (467–9). A copy bearing the queen's signet and received and endorsed by Whitgift as bishop of Worcester is in Lambeth Palace Library, MS. 2003, fos. 40–1. That the royal command was obeyed in Grindal's own diocese and peculiars is asserted in the form of submission prepared for him by bishops Whitgift and Piers (See 385 below).

54. This is the most likely reconstruction of events, by inference from Bacon's speech to Grindal in Council on a later occasion (BL, Harleian MS. 5176, f.95).

55. Walsingham to Burghley, 31 May 1577: PRO, SP 12/113/17.

56. Grindal to Leicester (?), 13 July 1577: Lambeth Palace Library, MS. 2004, f.1. The reference to 'mediation' in this letter suggests that it was intended for Leicester rather than Burghley, who did not publicly make himself Grindal's advocate.

57. William Camden, *History of the most renowned and victorious princess Elizabeth* (1688 edn), 287–8.

58. *The copie of a leter wryten by a master of arte of Cambrige* (1584), 26–7; John Harington, *A briefe view of the state of the Church of England* (1608) (1653 edn), 6–7; Fuller, *op. cit.*, IV, 455; Peter Heylyn, *Aerius Redevivus* (1672), 248. The impediment to Julio's marriage seems to have been that the lady was previously married, or contracted, and that the parties were related within the prohibited

degrees of affinity. The case had been before the bishop of London, the Master of the Rolls and the High Commission since 1573 (Strype, *op. cit.*, 333–6). The author of *Leicester's Commonwealth* (*The copie of a leter*) and Fuller confusingly suggest that it was Julio himself who was already married.

59. Giulio Borgarucci to Leicester, 4 December 1576: BL, Cotton MS. Titus B.VII, f.36. I owe this reference to Mr D. C. Peck, late of Ohio State University.

60. Burghley to Walsingham, 31 May 1577: BL, Add. MS. 5935, f.68. This is a late (eighteenth-century?) copy of a letter not otherwise extant.

61. Bishop Richard Barnes of Durham to Burghley, 11 February 1577(/8): BL, Lansdowne MS. 25, no. 78, fos. 161–2.

62. See my *Letters of Thomas Wood, op. cit. See above*, 45-107.

63. H. R. Trevor-Roper, *Queen Elizabeth's First Historian: William Camden and the Beginnings of English 'Civil History'* (1971).

64. On 25 June 1578 Leicester wrote to Burghley from Buxton: 'My lord, having so convenient a messenger as Mr Dr Julio . . .' (BL, Harleian MS. 6992, no. 51, f.102.)

65. *Calendar of State Papers, Venetian*, 1558–1580, 545.

66. H. Nicolas, *Memoirs of Life and Times of Christopher Hatton, K.G.* (1847), 24.

67. Collinson, *Elizabethan Puritan Movement*, 193–4, 201, 245, 259, 282, 312–14.

68. *HMC*, Hastings MSS., I, 433. I have not seen the original of this document, which is in the Huntington Library.

69. See p. 52 below.

70. Wilson, *op. cit.*, 43.

71. *The Shepheardes Calender* (1579), f.29v.

72. J. J. Higgenson, *Spenser's 'Shepheardes Calender' in Relation to Contemporary Affairs* (New York, 1912); E. Greenlaw, 'The Shepheards Calender', *Publications of the Modern Language Association of America*, XXVI (1911), 419–51; P. E. McLane, *Spenser's Shepheardes Calender A Study in Elizabethan Allegory* (Notre Dame, 1961), esp. 140–57.

73. I quote from the title of S. L. Adams's Oxford D. Phil. thesis of 1973, 'The protestant cause: religious alliance with the west European Calvinist communities as a political issue in England, 1585–1630'.

74. PRO, SP 12/108/82.

75. PRO, SP 70/144/1164.

76. PRO, SP 70/145/1242.

77. PRO, SP 12/115/24. See Robert Tittler, *Nicholas Bacon: The Making of a Tudor Statesman* (1976), 168–86.

78. *Op. cit.*, 49.

79. BL, Harleian MS. 6992, no. 48, f.95.

80. PRO, SP 15/35/74.

81. PRO, SP 15/25/79.

82. Wilson, *op. cit.*, 70.

83. Conyers Read, 'Walsingham and Burghley in Queen Elizabeth's Privy Council', *EHR*, XXVIII (1913), 34.

84. Knollys to Wilson, 9 January 1577(/8); BL, Harleian MS. 6992, no. 44, f.89.

85. W. D. J. Cargill Thompson, 'Sir Francis Knollys' campaign against the *Jure Divino* theory of episcopacy', in Cole and Moody, *op. cit.*, 39–77.

86. Walsingham to Burghley, 31 May 1577; PRO, SP 12/113/17. Burghley to Walsingham, 31 May 1577; BL, Add. MS. 5935, f.68. Since both letters bear the same date and both parties seem to have been at Court, it may be that only the need to convey the ambassadorial report to Burghley with accompanying comments led to the committing to paper of highly confidential matters and reflections which might otherwise have been confined to word of mouth.

87. PRO, SP 15/25/30.

88. PRO, SP 83/2/43.

89. PRO, SP 15/25/35.

90. My own investigations have covered the city and dean and chapter archives which survive for this period and which are preserved in the Cathedral Archives and Library, Canterbury.

91. PRO, SP 15/25/35.

92. Grindal to the Privy Council, 24 October 1577; PRO, SP 12/117/9.

93. Grindal to Matthew Hutton, Dean of York, 2 December 1577; *Remains*, 394–5.

94. Northamptonshire RO, Fitzwilliam of Milton Papers, F. (M).P.70. This MS. contains three items, wholly or partly in Mildmay's hand. They are a memorandum (item c) headed: 'The occasion whereupon the displeasure grew from the queen's Majesty to the Archbishop of Canterbury'; an account (item a) of proceedings in the Star Chamber on 30 November 1577; and notes for a memorandum (item b) headed 'Touching the Archbishop of Canterbury in the matter of the exercises. 22 January 1577(/8)'. These documents are discussed by Stanford E. Lehmberg, *Sir Walter Mildmay and Tudor Government* (Austin, Texas, 1964), 148–53, but without specific reference to the meeting at Bacon's house.

95. Strype, *op. cit.*, 348–50.

96. Copies in BL, Cotton MS. Cleopatra F.2, f.273 (whence printed by Strype, *op. cit.*, 350–2), endorsed '29 No[vember] 1577. The request of the Archbishop of Canterbury to my lords of the Privy Council'; and in BL, Lansdowne MS. 25, no. 79, fos. 163–4, endorsed: 'The humble submission of Edmund Archbishop of Canterbury to the lords of her Majesty's Privy Council in the Star Chamber. Touching the exercise of prophesying. Sent by Sir Walter Mildmay.' A nearly illegible date follows which has been (mistakenly) read as 3 March 1577(/8). Both copies bear Grindal's signature.

97. Copies of Bacon's speech in BL, Harleian MS. 398, f.12; and in Folger Shakespeare Library, MS. V.a.197, f.19. A somewhat fuller version of what Bacon reportedly said is in Northamptonshire RO, F.(M).P.70a.

98. PRO, SP 15/25/50.

99. BL, Harleian MS. 5176, f.95 (whence printed, *Remains*, 471–3); Harleian MS. 36, no. 55, f.391; Huntington Library, MS. EL 2579, fos. 59–60r. A passage, purportedly from the Huntington Library copy of this speech and quoted by Tittler in his study of Bacon (*op. cit.*, 172), in fact occurs in Mildmay's account of the transactions in the Star Chamber of 30 November 1577. (Northamptonshire RO, F.(M).P.70.a.)

100. *Ibid.*

101. Northamptonshire RO, F.(M).P.70.b. From the form of this paper it is clear that it cannot be read as Lehmberg reads it (*op. cit.*, 153), as an expression of Mildmay's private views.

102. PRO, SP 12/122/15.
103. Henry Killigrew to William Davison, 29 January 1578; PRO, SP 15/25/71. The
letter has been damaged by damp and uncertainty persists about the reading of
the words italicized after prolonged scrutiny under ultraviolet light.
104. Killigrew to Davison, 22 February 1577(/8); PRO, SP 15/25/74.
105. Gonville and Caius College Cambridge, MS. 30/53, f.53.
106. The letter is printed verbatim by H. Nicolas from BL, Add. MS. 15891, f.30:
op. cit., 52–3.
107. Huntingdon to Matthew Hutton, 20 May 1578: *The Correspondence of Dr Matthew
Hutton*, ed. J. Raines (Surtees Soc., XVII, 1843), 59–60.
108. BL, Cotton MS. Vespasian F. XII, f.192.
109. The archbishop's physical degeneration may be traced through the following
letters: Grindal to Hutton, 2 December 1577 and 18 February 1579: *Remains*,
394–6; Grindal to Leicester, 15 August 1581: PRO, SP 12/150/5; Grindal to
Walsingham, 7 July 1582: PRO, SP 12/154/61; Grindal to Burghley, 30 January
1583: BL, Lansdowne MS. 37, no. 17, f.36.
110. The cup is mentioned in Grindal's will: Strype, *op. cit.*, 601.
111. The draft of the formal instrument of resignation is in PRO, SP 12/160/31. The
negotiations over its terms are documented in Grindal's letters to Burghley,
30 January, 9 February, 27 February, 12 April 1583, in BL, Lansdowne MSS. 37
and 38; printed, *Remains*, 397–403.
112. See 'Things prepared at the funeral of Edmund Grindal Archbishop of
Canterbury, who died on Saturday 6 July 1583', PRO, SP 14/89/6; and 'The
proceedings in the church at Croydon at the burial of the Archbishop of
Canterbury, 1583, Lammas Day [1 August]', Bodl., Ashmolean MS. 817, f.25.
113. *John Stubbs's Gaping Gulf with Letters and Other Relevant Documents*, ed. L. E. Berry
(Charlottesville, Va., 1968).
114. BL, Harleian MS. 398, f.12.
115. Quoted, Berry, *op. cit.*, xi.
116. The deterioration of their relations can be documented from Grindal's time as
archbishop of York. On 28 April 1577 he told Dean Hutton of York: 'If I had had
any special credit when Durham and Carlisle were bestowed some had not sped so
well. But blame yourself and Sir Thomas Gargrave. Ye two commended him to
be rid of him and now Simon is as good as Peter.' (*Hutton Correspondence*, 56–7.)
Barnes was in turn suffragan bishop of Nottingham, bishop of Carlisle and
bishop of Durham.
117. Barnes to Burghley, 11 February 1577(/8): BL, Lansdowne MS. 25, no. 78,
fos. 161–2.
118. Cox to Burghley, 12 June 1577: BL, Lansdowne MS. 25, no. 29, f.61; Cox to the
queen, 8 June 1577, 8 January 1577(/8): Gonville and Caius College, MS. 30/53,
fos. 50, 43.
119. Endorsed 'A form of submission devised and sent by the Bishops of Sarum and
Worcester 21 January 1580', BL, Add. MS. 32091, f.22. Strype (*op. cit.*, 403–4)
printed another version of this document which lacked the endorsement. His
assumption that Grindal actually made such a submission is unsupported.
120. Grindal to Burghley, 30 January 1583: BL, Lansdowne MS. 37, no. 17, f.36.
Whitgift's secretary and first biographer Sir George Paule is the source of the

tradition that his master 'utterly refused' to accept the primacy *per resignationem* and 'besought pardon in not accepting thereof upon any condition whatsoever in the lifetime of the other'. (*Life of Whitgift*, 1699 edn, 35.) Piers's involvement in the arrangements for Grindal's resignation must place this matter in some doubt.

121. Convocation engaged for this purpose the celebrated eloquence of Dr Toby Matthew, the future archbishop of York. Bodl., MS. Top Oxon. c. 5 contains Matthew's 'oratio' to the upper house on this occasion (pp. 1–7) and (pp. 45–7) the 'supplicatio' prepared by Matthew and subscribed: 'Serenissimae tuae maiestatis observantissimi episcopi, decani, archidiaconi et reliqui ministri ecclesiae Anglicanae presenti hoc synodo congregati'. Another copy is in BL, Sloane MS. 1710, fos. 106v–7r. The text in Wilkins's *Concilia* (IV, 295) is taken from Fuller, *op. cit.*, I.ix.120. The bishops' letter is in Bodl., MS. e. Museo. 55, no. 1, f.3.

122. Identified with the aid of J. Bossy, 'English catholics and the French marriage, 1577–81', *Recusant History*, v (1959), 2–16; and of an as yet unpublished paper by my colleague Dr P. R. Roberts on the political background to the publication of *Leicester's Commonwealth* which he kindly allowed me to read.

123. In Lambeth Palace Library.

124. The earliest commission issued in Yale's name (to visit the diocese of Salisbury with the archdeaconry of Dorset) is dated 1 June 1577 (Grindal's Register, f.406).

125. Privy Council to Grindal, 7 November 1577: *ibid.*, f.157v. The original patent of appointment of Drury and Hussey is in Lambeth Palace Library, Cartae Misc. XII/52.

126. Grindal's Register, fos. 167, 159v, 239v, 244v.

127. *Ibid.*, f.140. The original commission is in Lambeth Palace Library, Cartae Misc. II/79. All but one of the subsequent documents connected with this visitation were issued in the name of Dr Aubrey (Register, fos. 141–3).

128. *Ibid.*, fos. 48, 49, 53, 54, 58v, 59v, 64v, 66r, 70v, 71v, 77.

129. Examples in Register, fos. 158, 164, 171v, 176, 191, 193–5, 198v–9r, 206, 234, 235, 236v–7. For evidence of Grindal's participation in the enquiry into recusancy of October–November 1577, see *APC*, 1577–8, 87–8; PRO, SP 12/117/9, 14.

130. Register, f.234.

131. BL, Add. MS. 32092, fos. 13–21; Register, fos. 591–8.

132. Strype, *op. cit.*, 382; Wilkins, *Concilia*, IV, 292; Bishop Aylmer to the Earl of Sussex (as lord chamberlain), 27 January 1577(/8): BL, Harleian MS. 6992, no. 46, f.92. For an account of Aylmer's activities at this time, see H. G. Owen, 'The London parish clergy in the reign of Elizabeth I' (unpublished Ph.D. thesis, London University, 1957), 540–52; and John Strype, *Life of Aylmer* (1821 edn), esp. 60–4.

133. Collinson, *Elizabethan Puritan Movement*, 205–7.

134. Copies in Bodl., Tanner MS. 280, f.330v, Inner Temple Library, Petyt MS. 538/54, f.278.

135. For Bishop Curteys and his troubles see R. B. Manning, *Religion and Society in Elizabethan Sussex* (1969), 91–125. The controversy between Bishop Freke of Norwich and a faction of Norfolk gentry is documented in PRO, SP 12/126 and SP 15/25. See A. H. Smith, *County and Court: Government and Politics in Norfolk*,

1558–1603 (1974), 210–25. Bishop Freke's subsequent struggle with the puritan J.P.s of Suffolk is described in detail in my unpublished London University Ph.D. thesis, 'The puritan classical movement in the reign of Elizabeth I' (1957), 881–929, which is followed by J. S. Cockburn, *A History of English Assizes, 1558–1714* (1972), 199–206.

136. Walsingham sent Burghley on 8 December 1575 details of 'the principal matters wherewith the Bishop of Ely is to be charged', agreeing with Burghley's opinion that the penalty should 'light upon him and not upon the see'. (BL, Harleian MS. 6992, no. 16, f.31.) A page of Burghley's rough memoranda (PRO, SP 12/136/10) bears a note: 'Bishop of Ely resignation'. The account of Cox in F. O. White, *Lives of the Elizabethan Bishops* (1898), 78–95, may now be compared with the unpublished Cambridge University Ph.D. theses by G. L. Blackman, 'The career and influence of Bishop Richard Cox, 1547–1581' (1953) and F. Heal, 'The bishops of Ely and their diocese during the Reformation period: c. 1515–1600' (1972).

137. Privy Council memorandum to the archbishop of Canterbury 'concerning the Bishop of Hereford', June 1583: BL, Egerton MS. 3048, fos. 207v–8. Cf. White, *op. cit.,* 13–19.

138. Robinson to Walsingham, 28 May 1582: PRO, SP 12/153/66.

139. White, *op. cit.,* 251–9; R. E. Head, *Royal Supremacy and the Trials of Bishops* (1962), 23–8.

140. Documentation in PRO, SP 12/158/1, 22, 22 II, 38, 41. Becon, whose chequered career took him from Freke's Norwich through Curteys's Chichester to Overton's Lichfield had this to say about the bishops: 'Having such experience of bishops as I have . . . I had rather live a poor student in St Johns, where I was brought up, than to enjoy their lordships' palaces.' (SP 12/158/41.)

141. Compare the account in White, *op. cit.,* 97–108 and *DNB*, Sandys, Edwin, with the modern unpublished theses by I. P. Ellis, 'Edwin Sandys and the Settlement of religion in England, 1558–88' (unpublished B. Litt. thesis, Oxford University, 1962) and S. Storer, 'The life and times of Edwin Sandys, archbishop of York' (unpublished M.Phil. thesis, London University, 1973).

142. The bishops' certificates, detailing the felling of timber on their estates, are in PRO, SP 12/136 and 137.

143. Cause papers and summaries in PRO, SP 12/112/45 I, 131/22, 137/39, 54, 55, 149/17–27. Letters from Sandys to Walsingham, 30 April 1577: SP 12/112/45; Sandys to Walsingham and Aylmer to Walsingham, April–June 1579: SP 12/130/39, 131/14, 21.

144. PRO, SP 12/112/45, 45 I.

145. Josias Nicholls, *The plea of the innocent* (1602), 9–10. For Nicholls, see P. Clark, 'Josias Nicholls and religious radicalism, 1553–1639', *Journal of Ecclesiastical History*, XXVIII (1977), 135–50.

146. Paule, *op. cit.,* 82.

147. Dr Peter Lake of Clare College helped me to see this point by his comments when I read a paper at Professor Hurstfield's evening seminar at the Institute of Historical Research. It is pleasant to have occasion to record the latest of very many debts incurred around this table in the England Room, where I first met Joel Hurstfield in October 1952.

Robert Dudley, Earl of Leicester
(*National Portrait Gallery*)

15

CRANBROOK AND THE FLETCHERS
POPULAR AND UNPOPULAR RELIGION
IN THE KENTISH WEALD

In 1579 the churchwardens of Cranbrook returned a formal complaint against
their vicar, Richard Fletcher, who had settled in the Wealden township early in
the reign of Elizabeth and was to die there in 1586. Fletcher was the progenitor
of a remarkable family: the father of the Richard Fletcher who ended his days
as bishop of London and so the grandfather of the dramatist John Fletcher,
eternally linked with Francis Beaumont. There was also a younger son, Dr Giles
Fletcher, a distinguished civilian who served on an embassy to Muscovy and
wrote one of the earliest and least diplomatic accounts of Russia in English and
much else besides, including some verse. Giles Fletcher's sons were not insignificant literary figures: Giles Fletcher the younger, and Phineas Fletcher.
Since both the vicar of Cranbrook's sons married local girls, there was Cranbrook blood flowing in these talented veins. In comparison with his descendants,
Richard Fletcher the elder is almost unknown to history, even to the extent of
being sometimes confused with his son and namesake.[1] But he was a familiar
and even commanding presence in the Kentish Weald for a quarter of a century,
appearing constantly in the act books of the archdeacon's court[2] as the moving
force behind the detection of sexual crimes and other transgressions, publishing
sentences of excommunication and more occasionally certifying the due
performance of penance. These are doubtless but a selection of the scenes from
a busy clerical life, an energetic round of preaching, treating wounded consciences, investigating sin, composing quarrels and making some of his own.
Never before in almost twenty years had Fletcher himself been cited to appear
in court.

The terms of the presentment were enigmatic: 'We present Mr Fletcher for
that he preached that there were some of his paryshe that dyd sweare they would
not come unto the church untyll such thinges were brought to passe that they
had devysed.' This amounted to a charge that the vicar had defamed his parishioners as schismatics. On two successive court days Fletcher failed to appear.
The innerness of the matter, which will become apparent in the course of this
essay, may at first have eluded the archdeacon's officers. But on the third
occasion, when Fletcher was again contumacious, the judge used his discretion
to dismiss the case *ex certis causis* and no more was heard of it.[3] But whereas the
interest of the court was not sustained, it will be seen that Fletcher's unhappy
experience with his flock will open a path into a fruitful exploration of the uncertain terrain lying between two kinds of religion in Tudor England. Historians

1 The confusion occurs in John Strype, *Ecclesiastical Memorials* (Oxford, 1822), vol. ii, part
I, pp. 402–3; and more recently in Roger B. Manning, *Religion and Society in Elizabethan
Sussex* (Leicester, 1969), p. 76n.
2 A principal source for this essay: CALC, in the series X.1–10.
3 CALC, X.2.2, fol. 58r.

of the English Reformation have long been concerned to understand the nature of the interface between the officially inspired Reformation of the national Church and what might be called the local and unofficial Reformation, with its ancient Lollard roots. And since no living historian has contributed more to our knowledge of these aspects of Reformation principle and practice than A. G. Dickens, it is appropriate that they should be investigated on this occasion. Another and related area of persistent interest concerns the bifurcation of English Protestantism towards, on the one hand, those conservative religious sentiments which approximated to our understanding of Anglicanism, and on the other through a transitional Puritanism to the Dissent of the later seventeenth century. The microcosm of Cranbrook, more especially in the time of the Fletchers, will serve to particularize both these large questions and to shed some light on them.

In this period Cranbrook was one of the largest parishes in Kent and possibly the most populous of all. Measuring eight miles by six it contained in 1557 three hundred households and 1,500 communicants. Forty years later there were said to be at least 2,000 communicants; in 1640 the vicar wrote of his labours among 'above 2000 soules'.[4] All these people, many of them dispersed in the distinct hamlets of Milkhouse Street (or Sissinghurst), Golford, Hartley, Glassenbury and Flishinghurst, as well as in isolated farms and cottages in the Wealden 'dens', were served by a single parish church, 'the cathedral of the Weald', the only subsidiary chapel of ease at Milkhouse having been suppressed in 1548.[5] Some parishioners must have lived as far as five miles from the church along by-roads which, even in the eighteenth century, were 'very bad in winter' and in summer 'offensive and painful'.[6] In the late sixteenth century it was the custom of the parish to stagger the obligatory Easter communion over the weeks between Easter and Whitsun and not to certify the archdeacon of absentees until this season was past.[7] When plague came to the district in 1597, those dying in the outlying hamlets were buried at their doors with no attempt made to carry them into Cranbrook.[8] Modern social historians have begun to ask whether such an entity as Cranbrook was a community at all, or in what sense it was a community.[9] Alexander Dence, the town's chief benefactor in the six-

---

4 *Archdeacon Harpsfield's Visitation, 1557*, ed. W. Sharp and L. E. Whatmore, Catholic Record Society, vols xlv, xlvi (1950, 1961), pp. 182–3; CALC, X.3.5, fol. 133ᵛ; Robert Abbot to Sir Edward Dering, 15 March 1640, BL, MS Stowe 184, fols 47–8.
5 C. C. R. Pile, *The Chapel of Holy Trinity Milkhouse*, Cranbrook Notes & Records no. 1 (n.p., 1951).
6 Edward Hasted, *History of Kent* (1972 edn), vol. vii, p. 91.
7 In 1592 the newly-installed vicar, William Eddy, presented the churchwardens for reporting this custom to him (CALC, X.3.5, fol. 133ᵛ). The dates for the purchase of bread and wine given in the churchwardens' accounts suggest staggering of the Easter communion in some years (KAO, P/100/5/1, fols 63ᵛ, 76, 78, 102ᵛ).
8 KAO, TR/1042/5 (typescript of earliest Cranbrook registers, without foliation or pagination).
9 Alan Macfarlane et al., *Reconstructing Historical Communities* (Cambridge, 1977).

teenth century, may have pondered the same question when he provided in his will for an annual Christmas dinner at the inns and taverns 'for all the honeste howseholders and fermors of the towne and parishe', explaining that he did not have in mind the rich or the poor, for whom he had made other provision.[10]

Much of this inflated population was sustained, directly or indirectly, by the industry which produced Cranbrook's famous and 'durable broad cloths with very good mixtures and perfect colours.'[11] It was a population as unstable and fluctuating as the cloth trade itself, the great variety of surnames in the parish registers[12] and much other circumstantial evidence suggesting that people were for ever coming and going. 535 individuals, presented in the archdeacon's court between 1560 and 1607, shared 369 surnames, while 283 of these family names occur once only in the presentments. And only fifty-one parishioners were cited on more than one occasion within these dates. The historian who studies the history of a parish in such flux over a period of a century may well wonder whether or in what sense he is contemplating the 'same' community. On the other hand, the leading clothing families show little variation throughout the sixteenth and early seventeenth centuries. At the end of this period, as at the beginning, the parish vestry was dominated by the names of Hendly, Dence, Sheaffe, Sharpy, Courthope, Cuchman, Brickenden and Hovenden, these wealthy clothiers yielding precedence only to the parish gentry, the Bakers of Sissinghurst and the Roberts family of Glassenbury. The bearers of these names dined together at the George, had ground broken for them inside the parish church, and formed a self-defining and self-perpetuating oligarchy. It was the custom for each churchwarden, at the end of his first year of office, to recruit the colleague with whom he would serve for his second year, 'with the consent of the parishioners'.[13]

Historians cannot agree whether to attribute the persistent reputation of places like Cranbrook for religious dissent to intractable geographical and demographical conditions, inimical to the pastoral interests of the established Church, or to some intangible, but sympathetic, connection between radical religion and the manufacture of cloth.[14] Both explanations are generalizations

---

10 PRO, PROB/11/56/20.
11 J. Philpot, *Villare Cantianum or Kent Surveyed and Illustrated* (1659), p. 98, quoted by Peter Clark in *English Provincial Society from the Reformation to the Revolution: Religion, Politics and Society in Kent, 1500–1640* (Hassocks, 1977), p. 463n. See C. C. R. Pile, *Cranbrook Broadcloth and the Clothiers*, Cranbrook Notes & Records no. 2 (n.p., 1951); C. W. Chalklin, *Seventeenth-Century Kent: A Social and Economic History* (1965), pp. 116–23.
12 KAO, TR/1042/5.
13 KAO, P/100/5/1.
14 Alan Everitt, 'Nonconformity in Country Parishes', in *Land, Church and People: Essays Presented to Professor H. P. R. Finberg*, ed. Joan Thirsk, *Agricultural History Review*, vol. xviii supplement (Reading, 1970); J. F. Davis, 'Lollard Survival and the Textile Industry in the South-East of England', *Studies in Church History*, vol. iii, ed. G. J. Cuming (Leiden, 1966), pp. 191–201.

which cannot help very much in understanding the religious history of a particular place. What is certain is that no later than the 1420s the Kentish Weald became a breeding-ground for Lollard heresy. The credit for this is usually given to the priest William Whyte who fled from Kent to Norwich and was burned there in 1428.[15] But for all that is known, anti-catholic and specifically anti-sacramentarian sentiment in the region may have had older, indigenous origins. Archbishop Warham's investigations of 1511 – the so-called *magna abiurata*[16] – uncovered a long-established heretical tradition in the clothing towns of Tenterden, Cranbrook and Benenden. Four inhabitants of Cranbrook were interrogated, among whom William Baker confessed how after 'communication ageynst pilgrimages and worshipping of sayntes and of offeryngs' he had altered his intention to offer money to the rood of grace 'and went not thyder but gave his offeryng to a poore man.' Villagers assisting the ecclesiastical judges in their enquiries identified the arch-heretic of the region as William Carder, a Tenterden weaver, who for many years had pursued his cryptic apostolate with ones and twos, sometimes at home, sometimes at alehouses or in church, communicating the doctrine that the sacrament of the altar was 'very bread and not Christ's body' and that the other sacraments were 'nothing profitable' for man's soul. It was forty years since Carder's mother had fled from Tenterden for fear of these opinions, and twenty since Carder had spoken of them to John Grebill of Tenterden as he sat at his loom, reading from 'a book of two evangelists'.

When, in 1511, William Baker of Cranbrook declared of St Matthew's Gospel that 'it was pitie that it might not be knowen openly', Richard Harman, a native of Cranbrook, may have already been living in Antwerp, where he later became William Tyndale's associate and factor, helping, as Queen Anne Boleyn later testified, 'both with his gooddis and pollicie . . . to the settynge forthe of the Newe Testamente in Englisshe.'[17] When Harman's papers were searched in 1528 they were found to include letters of pious exhortation from two Cranbrook men, one of them a clothier, both 'consernyng the New Testament in Yngliche.'[18] Perhaps they were carried to Antwerp by Thomas Hitton who,

15 J. A. F. Thomson, *The Later Lollards 1414–1520* (Oxford, 1965), pp. 173–6; *Heresy Trials in the Diocese of Norwich, 1428–31*, ed. Norman P. Tanner (1977), Camden ser. 4, vol. xx, passim.
16 Lambeth Palace Library, Archbishop Warham's Register, fols 159ʳ–75ᵛ. See Thomson, op. cit., pp. 186–91, and Thomson's critique of Foxe's use of Warham's Register for his account of these trials, 'John Foxe and Some Sources for Lollard History: Notes for a Critical Appraisal', *Studies in Church History*, vol. ii, ed. G. J. Cuming (1965), pp. 251–7.
17 Quoted in *The Complete Works of St. Thomas More*, ed. Louis A. Schuster et al. (New Haven and London, 1973), vol. viii, p. 1182n. 'Robert Necton's Confession' (*Letters and Papers of the Reign of Henry VIII*, vol. iv, 4030) establishes that Simon Fish sold New Testaments which he received 'from one Harmonde, an Englishman beyond sea.'
18 *The Letters of Sir John Hackett 1526–1534*, ed. E. F. Rogers, Archives of British History and Culture vols i and ii (Morgantown, 1971), pp. 173–7, 207. I am grateful to Dr A. C. Duke of Southampton University for this reference.

after visiting his 'holy congregaccyons' in 'dyvers corners and luskes lanes', was taken at Gravesend in 1530 and burned at Maidstone. It provoked Sir Thomas More beyond measure that Hitton supplanted St Polycarp in the calendar published by the Protestant exiles as the new 'St Thomas of Kent'.[19] Nine years later a royal commission of enquiry into the sacramentarian heresy specified three localities: Calais, Bristol – and Cranbrook parish.[20]

'Sacramentarianism' (the denial of Christ's bodily presence in the sacrament of the altar) was still a touchstone of vernacular heresy in Kent in the 1550s, when once again the Wealden townships were of particular interest to the tribunal charged with the extirpation of heresy in the diocese of Canterbury.[21] At Cranbrook the vicar was enjoined not to bury any parishioner who had failed to confess or receive the sacrament and not to administer communion to any who refused to creep to the cross on Good Friday. Every household was to be represented, week by week, at procession and litany on Wednesdays and Fridays.[22] The town was to win notoriety in local Protestant folklore not for its two martyrs, William Hopper and William Lowick,[23] but as the place where many suspect persons were sent for questioning by Sir John Baker and other justices and detention in the room above the south porch of the church, 'Baker's Jail'.[24] The history of the Marian persecution in Kent, like the story of the Bristol martyrs,[25] suggests that as late as the mid-sixteenth century popular heresy, was expressed in categories which ostensibly owed very little to the new Protestant theologians. Far from assuming that dissenting circles readily submitted to the intellectual and pastoral leadership of university-trained divines, Dr J. F. Davis suggests that the academic reformers were themselves susceptible to popular heretical traditions, and particularly responsive to traditional Lollard sacramentarianism.[26]

Consequently, it is a question to what extent the Marian martyrs in Kent had embraced the officially-endorsed Edwardine doctrine, or were heretics in a more

19 *Complete Works of More*, vol. viii, pp. 13–16, 684, 1207, 1216; *The Acts and Monuments of John Foxe*, ed. G. Townsend and S. R. Cattley (8 vols, London, 1837–40) (hereafter, *A & M*), vol. viii, pp. 712–15. Peter Clark (op. cit., p. 34) calls Hitton 'the Maidstone curate'. But he is described in the signification of his relaxation to the secular arm (PRO, C/85/25/23) as 'Thomas Hitton laicus', and by his own confession he had lived 'by the joiner's craft' (*Works of More*, vol. viii, p. 15).
20 Lambeth Palace Library, Archbishop Cranmer's Register, fol. 68ʳ. I owe this reference to Mr K. G. Powell.
21 J. F. Davis, 'Heresy and the Reformation in the South-East of England: 1520–1559' (unpublished Oxford D.Phil. thesis, 1966), pp. 67–8, 153–4, 433. I am indebted to Dr Davis's account of Kentish 'neo-Lollardy' and grateful for permission to cite his thesis.
22 *Archdeacon Harpsfield's Visitation*, pp. 182–3.
23 *A & M*, vol. viii, pp. 322, 326.
24 *Archdeacon Harpsfield's Visitation*, pp. 127, 129, 132, 177; William Tarbutt, *Annals of Cranbrook Church*, vol. i (Cranbrook, 1870), pp. 11–14.
25 K. G. Powell, *The Marian Martyrs and the Reformation in Bristol* (Bristol, 1972).
26 Davis, 'Heresy and the Reformation', pp. 445–50.

fundamental sense, or at least eclectic in their beliefs. Elizabethan Protestants, and John Foxe in particular, scouted the possibility that any of the martyrs could have been deviant from the godly Protestant consensus. Foxe was told that at Maidstone the turncoat curate John Day had been forced to confess, on the doorstep of his favourite alehouse, that he had lied shamelessly in condemning those who had died at Maidstone as 'heretykes most damnabelle', who had denied the divinity of Christ and the doctrine of the Trinity.[27] But there is evidence in documents which were in Foxe's own files that some of the Kentish martyrs were indeed heretics in precisely the sense that Day had alleged.[28] Such embarrassments were glossed over by the martyrologist with the formula: 'To these articles what their answers were likewise needeth here no great rehearsal, seeing they all agreed together, though not in the same form of words, yet in much like effect of purposes.'[29]

But perhaps the nature of the beliefs entertained in the village conventicles was less significant than the existence of the conventicles themselves, with their sense of brotherhood and their insistence on primary moral and social virtues to the extent of shunning those who were morally offensive. John Fishcock of Headcorn, seven miles from Cranbrook, one who 'had a good iudgemente of the Trynytie' and condemned 'yvill opynyon therein', told his judges that 'if there be anny that is a brother whiche is an adulterer, a fornicator, an extorcioner, a worshipper of images, he thought not to eate nor drinck with him, nether yet salute him.' John Plume of Lenham 'beynge emonge the congregation' had often heard it affirmed as a general doctrine that 'they oughte not to salute a synner or a man whome they knowe not.'[30] What John Philpot of Tenterden called, in contradistinction to the Catholic Church, 'Christ's congregation',[31] was no abstract theological principle but a social reality and a matter of intense experience. In a letter to Mrs Roberts, a gentlewoman of Hawkhurst included in Foxe's tally of near-martyrs, Richard Woodman, an iron-maker of Warbleton in Sussex, saluted 'all our brethren and sisters that are around about you', 'all the people of the household of God', 'all others of God's elect': 'Now is the Lord come with his fan in his hand, to try the wheat from the chaff.'[32]

Richard Fletcher was not a native of Kent,[33] but as a staunch Edwardine

27 BL, MS Harl. 416, fols 123-4.

28 Examinations of William Prowtynge of Thornham, John Syms of Brenchley and Robert Kynge of (East) Peckham; BL, MS Harl. 421, fols 94-5.

29 A & M, vol. viii, p. 300. See Davis, 'Heresy and the Reformation', pp. 423-4, Thomson, loc. cit., pp. 251-7.

30 BL, MS Harl. 421, fols 101, 103, 134ᵛ.

31 Ibid., fol. 92.

32 A & M, vol. viii, pp. 374-7.

33 His origins are problematical. His funerary monument (inscription in Tarbutt, op. cit., vol. ii (1873), p. 17) describes him as 'ex Eboracensi Provincia' and further states that he was ordained by bishop Ridley of London (confirmed by Strype from Ridley's Register, Ecclesiastical Memorials, vol. ii, part I, pp. 402-3) and served in his diocese. His son Giles was born at Watford in 1549 and he was vicar of Bishop's Stortford from 1551 until he was deprived in 1555,

Protestant he may have evaded the Marian persecution by concealing himself in the close, wooded country of the Weald. This is implied by his ability to supply Foxe with information about the troubles of Edmund Allin, the miller of Frittenden.[34] It is more certain that in June 1555,[35] in company with his son Richard, then a young boy of perhaps nine, he witnessed the burning at Dartford of the linen-weaver Christopher Wade, and, more than twenty years later, communicated to Foxe one of the most vividly circumstantial of all the narratives in the *Acts and Monuments*, with its details of fruiterers coming with horse-loads of cherries to sell to the crowd and the victim clad in a 'fair long white shirt from his wife', 'standing in a pitchbarrel'.[36] If only it was possible to measure the distance in mentality between the Cambridge graduate and Bishop Ridley's ordinand and the linen-weaver of Dartford! Perhaps the gap was far from unbridgeable? Foxe's brief account of the interrogation of Wade and the bricklayer Nicholas Hall suggests that Hall was the more radical and eclectic of the two; while according to Fletcher's narrative Wade died exhorting the people 'to embrace the doctrine of the gospel preached in King Edward's days.'[37] No doubt Fletcher's subsequent reputation with the godly fraternity rested on his known fidelity in the years of trial. According to the funerary monument erected in Cranbrook church by his sons, he had himself suffered hardship and imprisonment, 'adversa multa et vincula'.[38] As late as the 1570s, he was a vocal critic of John Day, the turncoat curate of Maidstone.[39]

With the renewed Protestant ascendancy under Elizabeth, the relationship between the dissenting Protestant minority and the parish churches was dramatically altered. Dr Peter Clark has found 'little evidence of any popular backlash in Kent against the Marian persecutors.'[40] To be sure, the martyrs were of less interest to most of their contemporaries than they were to Foxe, or to the contributors to this volume. At Cranbrook, the churchwardens reported, laconically, that 'one Hopper' had been burned and 'dyvers other imprisoned whose names we know not.'[41] But Dr Clark perhaps underestimates the

---

presumably as a married priest. But his son Richard was admitted in 1569 to one of archbishop Parker's Norfolk fellowships at Corpus Christi College, Cambridge, and was styled 'Norfolciensis' (*DNB*, art. Fletcher).

34 *A & M*, vol. viii, pp. 320–5. On the other hand Foxe was not in possession of this information in 1563. William Fuller reported in the seventeenth century that bishop Richard Fletcher was born in Cranbrook *c.* 1546. But the statement is unsupported.

35 Foxe's dating is corrected from the original signification of relaxation to the secular arm, which relates to Christopher Wade, Nicholas Hall and Margery Polleye (PRO, C/85/144/33).

36 *A & M*, vol. vii, pp. 319–21.

37 Ibid., pp. 318, 320. Davis however ('Heresy and the Reformation', pp. 291–4) regards both Foxe's summary of the examination and Fletcher's account of Wade's attachment to Edwardian orthodoxy as somewhat suspect.

38 Tarbutt, op. cit., vol. ii, p. 17.

39 DWL, MS Morrice B II, fol. 22[r].

40 Clark, op. cit., p. 151.

41 CALC, X.1.2, fol. 32[v].

strength of feeling which found expression in some parishes. At Littlebourne, near Canterbury, and at Maidstone, there were formal complaints against clergy who had defamed the martyrs in their preaching.[42] At Elmstead, near Wye, the wardens objected to their vicar as 'an open enemy to Godes worde' and begged the archdeacon: 'The Lorde move you by some meanes to rydd hym from us.'[43] Here and in other parishes there were clashes between Protestants and 'the enemyes of God', 'Kayne's children', when the rood-lofts were removed. At Throwleigh the ancients of the parish ordered a man to be present at the pulling down of the rood-loft 'for that he was an accuser in Queen Marys tyme.'[44] Ministers were denounced for failing to preach against popery, or in line with sound Protestant doctrine.[45] At Bethersden, the churchwardens thought it in order to present their vicar for preaching at Tenterden that 'yt was not lawfull for us to use the servyce used at Geneva', and that it was no more lawful to follow the Genevan church than the Roman church.[46] A lone Anglican voice crying in the wind!

But at Cranbrook, with the resignation (deprivation?) of the Marian vicar and the admission in October 1561 of Richard Fletcher,[47] Protestants had cause for satisfaction rather than complaint. Until this late date there had probably been no experience of a genuine Protestant ministry in the parish, and not much experience of a resident vicar. From 1534 until 1554 the incumbent had been Hugh Price, notable as the founder of Jesus College, Oxford, but also as a pluralist who was represented at Cranbrook by curates.[48] This tradition of absenteeism was not incompatible with a vigorous parish life, an active vestry and sacrificial expenditure on the fabric of the church and its goods, which suggests the continuing vitality of traditional Catholic sentiment. In 1530 eighty-eight parishioners had contributed £370 to the rebuilding of the south

42 CALC, X.1.2, fol. 9ᵛ; BL, MS Harl. 421, fol. 123ʳ.

43 CALC, X.1.2, fols 27ʳ–8ᵛ.

44 CALC, X.1.3, fol. 133ᵛ; another case, ibid., fol. 155ᵛ.

45 At Preston iuxta Faversham (CALC, X.1.2, fol. 42ᵛ) and Boughton Mallarde (X.1.3, fol. 68ᵛ).

46 CALC, X.1.2, fo. 34.

47 Various dates are given by local historians for the commencement of Fletcher's ministry at Cranbrook. There is no doubt that he was collated by archbishop Parker on 17 October 1561; *Registrum Matthei Parker*, ed. W. H. Frere, Canterbury and York Society (Oxford, 1928–33), p. 784. This is inconsistent with the details on Fletcher's funerary monument where it is stated that at the time of his death in February 1585(/6) he had had charge of the church for 26 years and 7 months (Tarbutt, op. cit., vol. ii, pp. 17–18). This is either a mistake or Fletcher had served as a curate before his collation. But in 1560 there was another curate, Robert Foster, who is mentioned in the churchwardens' accounts (KAO, P/100/5/1, fol. 11ᵛ) and for whom letters dimissory for ordination to the priesthood were issued on 2 June of that year, describing him as of Cranbrook (*Registrum Matthei Parker*, p. 346).

48 A. B. Emden, *A Biographical Register of the University of Oxford A.D. 1501 to 1540* (Oxford, 1974), p. 462. Dr Price was noted as non-resident from 1550 to 1554 in the earliest surviving visitation call books for this period (CALC, Z.3.6, fols 13, 40, 60, 76ᵛ). Three curates came and went within these four years.

aisle.[49] Consequently Dr Clark can identify Cranbrook (which he will soon call 'the Puritan town of Cranbrook') as 'an old Lollard centre' and (on the evidence of late Henrician will preambles) a 'major conservative stronghold'.[50] But now the outward symbols of religious conservatism were promptly erased. Before Fletcher's arrival, the rood-loft had been taken down and the altars removed (in accordance with the Injunctions), and a great quantity of Catholic ornaments and furniture sold or otherwise disposed of. In Fletcher's first year there was payment to the painter 'for blottynge owt of the ymagrye in the glass wyndowes.'[51]

Dr Clark has suggested that, once such external matters had been dealt with, the Protestant ascendancy in Elizabethan Kent became identified with 'ethical radicalism' and 'a growing preoccupation with social control', popery having proved 'something of a paper tiger'.[52] The criminal or 'office' business of the court of the archdeacon of Canterbury bears him out, with its copious documentation of a crusade against sin, and sin as defined by respectable Protestant opinion. It was sufficient to be 'a common minstrel' to be presented,[53] since as professional musicians[54] the minstrels played on Sundays in houses or inns where there might be 'half a hundred of youth', 'drinkyng of syder' or 'a firkyn of beere', 'fydling, pyping, and as we suspect dauncing' and perhaps outnumbering the people in church.[55] From Cranbrook, for example, Walter Mascall was presented in 1570 for 'keepynge daunsynge in his house apon the sabothe day whereby the people be styrred to wantonnes.'[56] In the 1560s and 1570s (but not thereafter) there were also many presentments from Wealden parishes for various forms of witchcraft and sorcery, most involving *maleficium*, but others not remote from vestigial Catholicism, as when Henry Clegate of Headcorn confessed that he helped bewitched people and cattle by repeating prayers and the creed, as he had been taught to do years before by a neighbouring priest and by his mother.[57]

For Dr Clark, such cases indicate that Protestantism was expressing itself

---

49 KAO, P/100/5/1, fol. 5. See also the inventory of church goods of 1509 (ibid., fols 1–2* printed in *Archaeologia Cantiana*, vol. xli, pp. 57–68) and the list of subsequent benefactions (P/100/5/1, fols 3ᵛ–6).
50 Clark, op. cit., pp. 30–1, 59, 62, 151.
51 KAO, P/100/5/1, fol. 10.
52 Clark, op. cit., pp. 157, 149, 152.
53 Examples in CALC, X.1.7, fol. 47ᵛ, X.1.12, fol. 136ᵛ.
54 There is a reference in 1581 to 'Henry Newman beinge a mynstrell . . . and his ii parteners' (CALC, X.1.14, fol. 44) and another to the hiring of minstrels 'to come to Ashford to play' and to 'divers' sharing in the payment of their wages (X.2.2, fol. 26ᵛ).
55 Details drawn from cases from Molash 1575 (CALC, X.1.12, fol. 151ᵛ) and Cranbrook 1606 (X.4.11, fol. 7ᵛ). It was the minister of Warden in Sheppey who complained in 1576 that 'John Herne the mynstrell . . . had more with hym then I had at the churche.' (X.1.13, fol. 80ᵛ.)
56 CALC, X.1.10, fol. 11.
57 *Acta* in Archbishop Parker's metropolitan visitation; CALC, X.8.5, fol. 72.

in an onslaught on the mores of a 'Third World' of the poor and spiritually
ignorant, a world of 'the charmist, the church absenter and the tramp' – 'non-
respectable society'. But the alluring 'Third World' analogy can be deceptive.
By identifying Protestantism with advancing wealth and respectability it posits
a polarity of culture which did not yet exist, as if only the poor and disreputable
enjoyed a drink, or the children of the poor a romp on Sundays.[58] Likewise, it
diverts attention from the fact that a high percentage of the sins which concerned the parochial and archidiaconal authorities were of a sexual nature:
fornication, whoredom, adultery – 'incontinence' in all its forms. Such moral
failings have rarely been confined to one social class. It must have been with
respect to sexual transgression, and in measure as they were socially discriminatory in proceeding against it, that the new disciplines approximated to 'social
control'.

Richard Fletcher's reign at Cranbrook began in a confrontation with unsympathetic elements in the town which was worthy of Geneva itself in its lack
of respect for persons. Within weeks of his coming, the wife of Alexander Dence
was presented as a noisy 'contemner of prests and ministers' and 'a talker in the
church'. Alexander Dence would become the greatest of the town's benefactors
when he wrote his will in 1573. But it was a conservative will which retained in
its preamble the old kyries. Dence himself was presented on this same occasion
for keeping suspicious company with the wife of another man of property,
Stephen Sharpy, who at his death disposed of no less than seventeen houses.
The suspicious goings-on had occurred in the house of Bartholomew Hendly,
another man of substance, whose wife, 'an evell woman from her youth', was
herself presented for 'bawdry'.[59] It was not every day that a Dence or a Sharpy
or a Hendly was called to account for such matters.[60] In May 1562 a number of
parishioners of lesser rank were brought to book as 'receivers of naughty and
evil persons' and 'maintainers of evil rule'. One of these, a widow, was also
accused of 'charminge, in measuring and fealing of sycke persons and telling
howe things lost should be founde againe.'[61] In the following year the bawdy
court (to use its popular name) met exceptionally in Cranbrook itself, as it did
in other Wealden parishes, and in addition to the vicar and churchwardens,
forty-two parishioners from the elite of the town were cited, with the intention
that they should be sworn, and present any of their neighbours who had

58 Clark, op. cit., especially pp. 152, 180. See also Dr Clark's essay in Donald Pennington and
Keith Thomas (eds), *Puritans and Revolutionaries: Essays in Seventeenth-Century History
presented to Christopher Hill* (Oxford, 1978), pp. 47–72. These remarks are intended to engage
with the concept of 'the reform of popular culture' launched by Dr Peter Burke in *Popular
Culture in Early Modern Europe* (1978).
59 CALC, X.1.3, fol. 74ᵛ. Dence's will in PRO, PROB/11/56/20.
60 Walter Hendly, gentleman, was presented for adultery in 1597 (CALC, X.4.3, fol. 100ᵛ).
Simon Dence was accused of fathering a bastard in 1605 but the case lapsed for lack of evidence
(X.4.8, fol. 160). I know of no other cases involving these names.
61 CALC, X.1.4, fols 94ᵛ–6ᵛ.

offended within the terms of the visitation articles. The fact that only Fletcher, one churchwarden and nine other parishioners appeared doubtless reduced the value of this ambitious experiment. But Fletcher personally accused four of his flock of drunkenness, one of them being also 'a great swerer and blasphemer of God's name.' And he denounced a servant boy in the employ of one of the richest inhabitants, Richard Taylor,[62] 'for swearing together with other boys being and lyinge together on a night determyned who should or could best or most swear by the name of God.'[63] (The prize was later won by an older person, Alexander Warley, who appeared in court to answer for such blasphemous oaths as 'by the flesh of God, by the guttes of God.'[64])

It should not of course be thought that the vicar was solely responsible for bringing such matters to the attention of the authorities. Normally bills of presentment were drawn up by the churchwardens with the consent of the sidesmen and in response to articles published in the archdeacon's visitation. The detection of Mrs Dence's loquacity, for example, would have been prompted by some such question as 'whether there be enye that walketh, talketh or slepeth in tyme of divine service or sermon?'; and of the drunkards and swearers by the question 'whither ther be eny notorious dronkardes, great swearers or common skowldes and disquieters of ther neighboures?'[65] But the response to such questions, and with it the whole tone of the parish, depended to an immeasurable extent on the minister's interpretation of his pastoral functions. In the eighteen months before Fletcher's arrival there were only five presentments from Cranbrook. Within the next seven months there were thirty, all concerned with immoral or irreligious behaviour.

With the stabilization of the Protestant settlement, Fletcher continued to meet occasional defiance from certain intractable parishioners,[66] who may indeed have been provoked by his naming individuals from the pulpit, a practice known as 'personal preaching'.[67] But the detection of sin soon settled into a routine of which the outstanding and by no means unusual feature was passive non-compliance with ecclesiastical authority. The facts are best stated as statistics (see Tables 1 and 2). From Table 2 it will be seen that of all those parties cited, two-thirds, 66%, failed to appear in court. But of those cited under

62 Taylor himself, 'old Richard Taylor', 'a very riche and a welthy man' and a septuagenarian bachelor, was repeatedly presented for failure to pay his assessment towards parish expenses and was suspected of usury (CALC, X.1.5, fol. 168ᵛ, X.1.9, fol. 76ᵛ, X.1.11, fol. 68ʳ).
63 Details of the extraordinary 1563 visitation in CALC, X.1.5, fols 168ʳ–9ʳ. Seven other Wealden parishes were given the same special treatment: Benenden, Biddenden, Goudhurst, Hawkhurst, Headcorn, Rolvenden and Sandhurst. The court spent half a day in each parish.
64 CALC, X.1.11, fol. 67.
65 Articles in the visitation of exempt parishes by the archbishop's commissary, 1564; preserved in CALC, X.8.2, fol. 28.
66 Particularly in 1570; CALC, X.1.10, fols 11, 74.
67 Suggested by episodes in 1570, 1575, 1580; CALC, X.1.10, fol. 11; DWL, MS Morrice B II, fol. 22ʳ; CALC, X.2.2, fol. 58.

TABLE I

Topical analysis of office cases from the parish of Cranbrook
in the corrective jurisdiction of the
Archdeacon of Canterbury, 1560–1607

Incontinence as evidenced by bridal pregnancy	All other sexual and marital offences	Other disorderly offences against religion and morality
50	307	69
Working or trading on Sabbath or holidays	Non-attendance at church	Failure to receive communion
19	14	114
Usury	Failure to pay 'cesses', 'scots' or other dues	Catholic Recusancy
2	38	4*
Conduct symptomatic of Puritanism	Offences against ecclesiastical order and abuse of office	Stands Excommunicate
4†	52	44
TOTAL 717		

* Two individuals only: Mary Baker, wife of John Baker Esq., of Sissinghurst, and her maid servant.

† Only two individuals were presented under this heading in the entire history of the parish from 1560 to 1640: Robert Holden (on three counts) in 1585, and Peter Walker, servant to Richard Jorden, clothier, in 1591.

NOTE The record is not necessarily complete. There are apparent gaps in the series of act books covering the Deanery of Charing in 1569 and 1573 and there may be other omissions, less readily detected.

the category of 'All Other Sexual and Marital Offences', no less than 211 of 257, or 82%, proved contumacious. An even higher level of contumacy could be demonstrated if only one sex were counted, for in cases of simple fornication the man sometimes appeared and attempted to clear his name, or render satisfaction, but the unmarried woman almost never. On the other hand, of those cited to answer a charge of incontinence as evidenced by bridal pregnancy, 50% thought it in their interest to appear in court, usually to attest a contract of marriage undertaken before carnal knowledge took place. Presentments for bridal pregnancy increased towards the end of the period covered in these tables, outnumbering the presentments for all other sexual offences in 1592 and in 1606, when there were no less than twenty presentments under this heading. These presentments may reflect social anxiety in a time of economic hardship rather than any sense of moral outrage. For this reason the figures have been given up to 1607, by which date they suggest a new pattern, and a secular progression from

TABLE 2
Procedural analysis of cases, 1560–1607

Presentments	Citations	Individual cited appears in court or certifies to the satisfaction of the court
637	602	179
Respondent denies matter objected or objects to form or terms of citation	Respondent dismissed summarily	Respondent dismissed with monition
25	76	33
Respondent required to undergo purgation	Purgation successful	Court imposes penance
21	11	43
Court is certified that penance performed according to the schedule	Penance commuted	Individual cited fails to appear and is contumacious
28	2	396
Poena reservata in proximo	*In poena excommunicationis in scriptis*	Sentence of excommunication pronounced and recorded
44	25	328
Court is certified that sentence of excommunication has been denounced in parish church	Excommunication for cause other than contumacy	Excommunicate is subsequently absolved
230	2	44*
General pardon or *indulgentia regia* claimed	Court applies for writ *de excommunicato capiendo*	Case transferred to another court
5	10	7
Proceedings terminated by death of individual presented and/or cited		
10		

* The record of the court is likely to be incomplete. Many of those excommunicated may have removed themselves, for that or other reasons, to other parishes or jurisdictions. But many inhabitants of Cranbrook may have found it possible to live in a state of semi-permanent excommunication. In some instances excommunicate persons applied for absolution after an interval of as much as eight years. Not all these applications were successful. Many excommunications may have lapsed informally, with the passage of time. It is not known whether excommunicates were regularly denounced every six months, as the Canons required.

the urgent reformism personified by Fletcher in early Elizabethan days to the routinized procedures found in 1606: 'We the churchwardens . . . do presente for incontinent living before the time of their marriages as manifestly doth appear by publique fame . . .', followed by a list of names.[68]

Fletcher coped as best he could with what might seem to have been an intolerable disciplinary situation. Denunciations of those excommunicated for contumacy must have punctuated Morning Prayer with the same frequency as the calling of banns of marriage. The performance of public penance followed by the vicar's certificate to the archdeacon's court that it had been done penitently, according to the schedule, was a more occasional spectacle which may have been seen less than twenty times in Fletcher's twenty-four years in the parish. This is all that is normally seen of Fletcher's pastoral activity in the archdeaconry act books. But in 1566 the registrar made an unusually full record of a curious case which shows him briefly in a different light. Mrs Walter, the wife of the vicar of the neighbouring parish of Goudhurst, married for twenty years with seven children, was persuaded that the village tailor, whom she had been 'moved inwardly to love', was her husband before God. Following the advice of St James to seek wisdom of God, she resorted to prayer, whereupon it was revealed to her that the tailor 'in tyme to come' should be her husband. Either she took her problem to the vicar of Cranbrook or, more probably, the initiative lay with him, since it was a notorious fact that Mrs Walter was estranged from her husband. Either way here is a glimpse of Fletcher in the role of marriage-guidance counsellor, sixteenth-century style.[69]

Clearly to refer to 'Puritan Cranbrook' is not to suggest that the whole town reverberated with psalm-singing and godliness. Nor was morality and attendance at sermons enforced with the same credible sanctions which the magistrates employed in communities of a comparable size which were corporate towns – such as Rye, a subject to be discussed later in this essay. Early in the seventeenth century it was still a place where the barbers and butchers plied their trade on a Sunday morning.[70] When Paul Baines, the famous Puritan divine, married into the clothing family of Sheaffe, as Richard Fletcher junior had done before him, he found that Mrs Sheaffe, his wife's sister, and others of her family, spent their time playing cards 'and such like games'. Baines (whose only recreation was chess) converted his sister-in-law from her habits by preaching against them in a public sermon. ('It might not have been so well if he had spoken to her in private.'[71]) The visitation of the plague in 1597 was attributed by the vicar, William Eddy, to the sins of the town, especially 'that vice of drunkenness which did abownd heere', and to the recent deaths of 'many honest and good men and

68 CALC, X.4.11, fol. 4ᵛ.
69 CALC, X.1.8, fols 119ʳ–20ᵛ.
70 In 1606: CALC, X.4.11, fols 52ᵛ–3ᵛ, 64ʳ, 72ʳ; 1611: X.5.5, fols 49ʳ, 51ʳ; 1620: X.6.7, fol. 37.
71 'The Life of Master Paul Baines', in Samuel Clark, *Lives of Thirty-Two English Divines* (1673), pp. 23–4.

women'. But what distressed him most was that God's judgement, far from driving people to repentance, had hardened them in their sins, a conventional parsonical complaint.[72] But the historian can discover for himself that, of 122 Elizabethan and early Jacobean wills made by Cranbrook inhabitants, only eight include professions of faith (or 'religious preambles') which breathe an authentic and personal spirit of Calvinist piety.[73] This is less remarkable than it may seem since, until his own death in 1597, nearly all wills were drawn up by the parish clerk, Laurence Weller, and shared an identical preamble.[74]

What is more notable is that, with the exception of the generous and imaginative will made by Alexander Dence, only three out of 122 testators in this community of fluid and disposable wealth made any religious or charitable bequests whatsoever apart from the common form gift of a few shillings for distribution to the poor, sometimes in the form of bread.[75] This is not to count the prosperous carrier who left sixpence each to Canterbury Cathedral and the parish church, who was either a pleasant man, or anticlerical, or more probably both.[76] It should not be forgotten that the inhabitants of Cranbrook in their lifetimes were regularly and heavily assessed by the vestrymen for a variety of public expenses, from the two shillings paid annually to the man who whipped the dogs out of church to charges for repair of the fabric, payment of clerk, sexton and schoolmaster and the relief of the poor.[77] This for Cranbrook was the orderly, rational alternative to voluntary charity rather than a redirection of the philanthropic impulse of the kind imagined by Professor W. K. Jordan.[78] But for the present purpose, the important fact is that only two testators left sums of money to select groups of godly preachers, a practice much commoner in the clothing towns of the Essex–Suffolk border than in Cranbrook.[79] Only ten Cranbrook testators made provision for a funeral sermon, an institution with less appeal than the sociable 'drinking' paid for in many wills, 'for my neighbours',

72 KAO, TR/1042/5.
73 I have examined 85 wills proved in the archdeacon's court (KAO, PRC 17/36–60), 8 proved in the consistory court (KAO, PRC 32/30–39) and 29 proved in the Prerogative Court of Canterbury (PRO, PROB 11).
74 'First and principally I commend my soul to Almighty God my creator, saviour and redeemer, trusting and assuredly and steadfastly believing to be saved by and through the death and bloodshedding of our Lord and Saviour Jesus Christ.'
75 This would appear to have been a secularization of the pre-Reformation common form of leaving small sums to the high altar in respect of 'tithes neglygently forgotten' and other sums for 'alms deeds'. All these provisions invariably occur immediately after the religious preamble.
76 The carrier was Thomas Hollandes, who otherwise disposed of £60 and 'six of my best horses with the furniture belonging to them.' (KAO, PRC 17/47/400.)
77 KAO, P/100/5/1, passim.
78 W. K. Jordan, *Philanthropy in England, 1480–1660* (1959), and *Social Institutions in Kent 1480–1660: A Study of the Changing Pattern of Social Aspirations, Archaeologia Cantiana* (Ashford, 1961), vol. lxxv.
79 For the two testators, see p. 191. References to Suffolk wills will be found in my essay 'Magistracy and Ministry: A Suffolk Miniature', in R. Buick Knox (ed.), *Reformation Conformity and Dissent: Essays in Honour of Geoffrey Nuttall* (1977), p. 77. *See below, p. 452.*

or for 'them which go to church with me on the day of my burial' – the old 'good fellowship' rather than the new puritanism. To continue: out of 138 Cranbrook probate inventories covering the years 1565 to 1612 only twenty mention a Bible among the contents of the household.[80] Nine of the households possessing Bibles also had some other books, and five more inventories mention books other than the Bible. Admittedly this evidence is less than decisive, since Bibles and other books might have been given away by will, as when Elizabeth Jorden, after a distinctly Calvinist profession of faith, found a home for her 'whole booke of Martyrs'.[81] Richard Fletcher's own inventory values only the books 'lefte ungeven away'.[82] But the wills add only two more households which contained Bibles. If only 17% of modern English homes boasted a television set we should conclude that viewing was a sub-cultural activity. So no doubt was the pursuit of godliness in Cranbrook. Bibles are sometimes owned and never read. One of the twenty-two Bibles belonged to a man who in the year before his death was in trouble for allowing dancing in his house on the Sabbath and for calling the vicar a knave when he denounced him from the pulpit.[83]

So Cranbrook was Puritan merely in the sense that it contained a Puritan minority, in some measure set apart if only by the pastoral failure to correct and convert the rest of the community. It cannot be shown, and may not be worth asking, whether this minority was associated with a particular socio-economic group. It is an interesting suggestion that the tendency to Puritan exclusivism in late-Elizabethan Kent articulated the resentful alienation of 'small respectable folk' from hardening local oligarchies,[84] but it would be hard to demonstrate that this was the case in Cranbrook. To be sure, there is little evidence linking Puritanism especially with the wealthy clothiers, the customers of the mercer William Ruck whose shop contained hundreds of pounds worth of such merchandise as gloves, ribbons, silk buttons, drinking glasses, currants, raisins and playing cards.[85] Like Alexander Dence's Christmas diners, it is likely that Cranbrook's godly inhabitants were neither very rich nor very poor.

At first the godly may have depended upon Fletcher for inspiration, and later it would be conceded by a Puritan critic that some had assigned 'a great part of their conversion' to his teaching.[86] But if so their affections were increasingly alienated towards a godlier, or at least more radical style of discourse, still represented in early-Elizabethan Kent by itinerant preachers, following

80 The inventories are in KAO, PRC 10/1–33.
81 KAO, PRC 32/39/146. Mary Sheaffe, widow, mother-in-law to Dr Giles Fletcher and so the grandmother of Giles and Phineas Fletcher, left 'my Booke of Marters in two volumes' in her will of 1609 (PRC 17/58/375).
82 KAO, PRC 10/15, fols 172ᵛ–3ʳ.
83 Walter Mascall's inventory (4 May 1571) is in KAO, PRC 10/5, fol. 180, and his presentment in court in 1570 in CALC, X.1.10, fol. 11ʳ.
84 Clark, op. cit., pp. 177–8.
85 KAO, PRC 10/25, fols 233ʳ–5ᵛ.
86 DWL, MS Morrice B II, fol. 18ᵛ.

in the steps of the Marian martyr John Bland, and perhaps supported by some of the gentry.[87] In 1661 it would be said that 'the wild of Kent is a receptacle for distressed running parsons.'[88] So it was perhaps in 1561. In that year a preacher called Thompson aroused conservative opposition in both Cranbrook and Frittenden, which in Cranbrook was offered by the formidable Mrs Dence.[89] Another preacher was a blind man called Dawes, of whom the historian catches a glimpse as he entered Headcorn, 'comyng through the streat with dyvers honest men with hym.' Dawes preached in many parishes on working days, and one Headcorn man thought it 'a shame that he is suffered soe to goe about a-preachinge.'[90] When Mr Ridley preached at Goudhurst in 1562 he had to compete with dancing at the market cross.[91] In Cranbrook such sporadic and irregular preaching later gave place to a weekly sermon on Saturdays, market day, and offered not by Fletcher but by the preachers of the surrounding country taking their turns: the device known in the early seventeenth century as a 'lecture by combination'.[92]

Towards 1580 numbers of godly preachers were settling down in the Wealden parishes, where they formed a brotherhood if not a *classis* of 'the ministers of Kent', soon to resist archbishop Whitgift and conformity in 1584.[93] Two of the more notable members of the group were Josias Nicholls, minister of the tiny parish of Eastwell from 1580 (72 communicants compared with Cranbrook's 2,000!)[94] and George Ely, vicar of Tenterden from 1571. The kind of ministry which was now almost the norm in such places is implied in the description accorded to the vicar of Benenden, never a member of the Puritan group, in a formal document, the inventory of his possessions: 'mynister and preacher of the worde to the congregation at Benenden.'[95]

Fletcher was not part of the brotherhood. Whether he would wish to have been is not known. But he was a conformable man and the practice in Cranbrook church was Protestant rather than Puritan. The surplice seems to have been worn throughout the 1560s and 1570s,[96] and communion was received kneeling,

87 Clark, op. cit., pp. 151–2. For Bland, see *A & M*, vol. vii, pp. 287–306. See also Davis, 'Heresy and the Reformation', p. 426.
88 *Victoria County History of Kent*, vol. ii, ed. William Page (1926), p. 100.
89 CALC, X.1.3, fol. 75ᵛ; X.1.4, fol. 86ᵛ.
90 CALC, X.1.9, fol. 66.   91 CALC, X.8.5, fol. 104.
92 KAO, P/100/5/1, fol. 58ᵛ; Thomas Wotton to Sir Francis Walsingham, 3 May 1579, *Thomas Wotton's Letter-Book 1574–1586*, ed. G. Eland (1960), pp. 24–5. Cf. P. Collinson, 'Lectures by Combination: Structures and Characteristics of Church Life in 17th-Century England', *Bulletin of the Institute of Historical Research*, vol. xlviii (1975), pp. 182–213.
93 Patrick Collinson, *The Elizabethan Puritan Movement* (1967), pp. 249–72. Documents in *The Seconde Parte of a Register*, ed. Albert Peel (Cambridge, 1915), vol. i, nos 132, 149, 150.
94 Peter Clark, 'Josias Nicholls and Religious Radicalism 1553–1639', *Journal of Ecclesiastical History*, vol. xxviii (1977), pp. 133–50.
95 Marten Sanders, who died in 1585: KAO, PRC 10/15, fols 120–1.
96 There are several references in the churchwardens' accounts to the making, washing and repairing of surplices (KAO, P/100/5/1).

in the chancel.[97] The organs were repaired, not destroyed.[98] This is no more than was to be expected of a client and perhaps a friend of archbishop Parker, who also became his son's patron.[99] Thanks to Parker, Fletcher was able to become a pluralist. In 1566 he was collated to the rectory of Smarden, a parish ten miles to the east of Cranbrook, and a better living.[100] In the words of a Puritan critic, there was no need for the vicar to complain of hard times, now that he had two strings to his bow and had 'put two haycockes into one.'[101]

So Fletcher was no Puritan. But between 1575 and 1585 he employed, in succession, three curate-preachers who were. Their presence may have been due to circumstances not entirely within his control in the form of financial and other inducements and pressures from the godly element in the surrounding country, some gentry included, who may have promised support for preachers of whom they approved.[102] For two at least of the three were already men of some notoriety. There is clear evidence of this element of voluntary support in the case of John Strowd, the first of a trinity to arrive on the scene. Strowd, a deprived minister on the run from the West Country, was one of the operators of the clandestine Puritan press of the early 1570s, and he arrived with recent experience of the Presbyterian church settlement in the Channel Islands.[103] Strowd was followed by Thomas Ely (or Hely), who first appeared as Fletcher's curate at Smarden: perhaps the brother of George Ely of Tenterden, and possibly the same man who, as minister of Warbleton, was later a leading Sussex nonconformist.[104] And last but far from least there came to Cranbrook the most erudite of the Puritan divines of his generation, the young prodigy Dudley Fenner, who arrived in 1583 to become a spokesman for 'the ministers of

97 'Payd for mattes to laye in the quyre to knele on', 1563; 'Payd for 12 yardes of mattynge for the communyon place', 1564 (KAO, P/100/5/1, fols 20ᵛ–23ʳ).
98 Ibid., fol. 23. But in 1568 the parish received 36s 8d for the sale of 75 organ pipes (ibid., fol. 34).
99 DNB, art. Fletcher.
100 Registrum Matthei Parker, p. 825.
101 DWL, MS Morrice B II, fol. 24ᵛ.
102 Fletcher seems to have employed an assistant curate from time to time. A will of 1566 was witnessed by 'Henry Wybarne, curatt of Cranbroke' (KAO, PRC 17/39/313). If Henry Wybarne was by any chance the brother of the well-known Puritan Percival Wiburn, at this time a prebendary of Rochester, this may add to the score of radical Cranbrook curates.
103 Seconde Parte of a Register, vol. i, pp. 112–14; A. F. Scott Pearson, Thomas Cartwright and Elizabethan Puritanism 1535–1603 (Cambridge, 1925), pp. 87, 110–13. Strowd's recent visit to Guernsey is hinted at by both Richard Fletcher the younger and Thomas Good in DWL, MS Morrice B II, fols 9ᵛ, 22ʳ.
104 Ely's presence in Cranbrook has not previously been noticed. His curacies at Smarden (1576–7) and Cranbrook (1579–80) are recorded in the archdeaconry call books: CALC, Z.7.1, fols 14, 41ᵛ, 62ᵛ, 79ᵛ, 255; X.2.3, fols 32ᵛ, 67ᵛ, 103ᵛ. On Thomas Hely of Warbleton, see Seconde Parte of a Register, vol. i, pp. 209–20; and Manning, Religion and Society in Elizabethan Sussex, op. cit., pp. 201, 209n, 211. There was also Nathaniel Ely, son of George and later a preacher at Biddenden. He is mentioned in Cranbrook wills of 1582 and 1600 (KAO, PRC 17/44/40, 52/44.)

Kent' in their confrontations with archbishop Whitgift.[105] That Fletcher himself was not in this special sense a 'minister of Kent' is suggested by two Cranbrook wills of 1579–80. Both testators left sums of money to select preachers. Peter Courthope, a clothier employing four weavers, provided £20 for distribution among nine preachers, including Ely of Tenterden and Josias Nicholls and 'Mr Strowd'. The widow Rose Austen similarly remembered six preachers, including Nicholls and Mr Ely of Tenterden and 'Mr Ely of Crane-brooke, minister.'[106]

John Strowd was a provocation by his mere presence. His activities as a clandestine Puritan printer had made him well known to the ecclesiastical courts in both London and Rochester. But this did nothing to damage his reputation in the upper Medway valley and the Weald where he was regarded with great admiration by a cross-section of 'the country', including several ranking gentry, Walter Roberts of Cranbrook among them.[107] His arrival in Cranbrook as a kind of refugee from his previous base at Yalding in the diocese of Rochester (where Josias Nicholls replaced him) rapidly brought to a head the uneasy relations between Fletcher and a party in his parish. The story has to be disentangled from thousands of words of spirited but rancorous rhetoric exchanged between one of Strowd's protagonists, the Cranbrook schoolmaster Thomas Good, and Fletcher's son, the future bishop.[108]

According to Good, who was 'a special party' to bring him in, Strowd's arrival (probably in late May 1575) was initially welcome to Fletcher as 'a mutuall healpe', paid for by others. But since Strowd was still under excommunication, it seems more likely, as Fletcher's son alleged, that he thrust himself in with the encouragement of his local supporters. Strowd had undertaken not to preach in another man's charge without his good will but then in contempt of Fletcher's attempt to deny him the pulpit preached in his absence, twice on one day. Good could not see why Strowd should have held back 'for a froward man's fantasies'. One of the churchwardens had said 'we will have him to preach', and someone else remarked: 'The vicar of Cranbrook proposeth but God disposeth.' If Fletcher's son is to be believed, Strowd's doctrine was sufficiently inflammatory and 'popular'. Those who were not sent of the Spirit should never do good in the ministry. The bishops would be called gracious lords 'but you may call them ungracious knaves'. 'It is said credibelly in the countrie that he hathe preched that it is no greater a sinne to steal a horse on

105 DNB, art. Fenner.
106 KAO, PRC 32/34/64, PRC 17/44/134.
107 Seconde Parte of a Register, vol. i, pp. 114–16.
108 The controversy occupies fols 6–25 in DWL, MS Morrice B II and is calendared by Peel in Seconde Parte of a Register, vol. i, pp. 116–20. It consists, in order, of 'Evill coherences not without some errours gathered out of Mr Fletchers sonnes sermon made July 27th 1575'; 'An answere made by Mr Fletcher of Rye'; 'The answere unto a certayne pryvie reply of invective of Mr Fletcher of Rie'; and, finally, five tables prepared by Good, extracting 'scoffs' and uncharitable speeches from Fletcher's reply.

Munday then to sell him in fayre on the Sunday; that it is as ill to play at games as shooting's, bowlings on Sundaye as to lye with your neybors wiffe on Monday.' Strowd was also active on another front in what Fletcher junior called conventicles. 'It is a common thinge now for every pragmaticall prentice to have in his hand and mouthe the government and reformation of the Churche. And he that in exercise can speak thereof, that is the man. Every artificer must be a reformer and a teacher, forgetting their state thei stand in bothe to be taught and to be reformed.' But Good insisted that what Fletcher called conventicles were 'honest and lawfull convencions', and some of the 'pragmaticall prentices' weighty clothiers. 'Your eyes dasill by tooting on Cranbrooke clothiers colours.'

On 12 June the vicar mounted his pulpit to preach of the necessity and dignity of church ceremonies and of obedience to the law. When, in his usual style, he attacked Strowd by name, there were 'open challenges' from the congregation, and one man was removed by the constable and subsequently punished by the magistrate, Sir Richard Baker. Good was present with his scholars, making notes ('pens walking at sermons'), and thought the interruptions an excusable disorder since Fletcher's defence of ceremonies had wounded tender consciences by repudiating the sound doctrine which he himself had delivered in the past. He had 'run headlong, to the eversion of many consciences, unless God's spirit prevent them'. That amounted to a declaration that Fletcher's revisionism threatened to drive the godly into separation.

On 27 July Fletcher's son was recruited to preach in his father's defence and 'for the staying or appeasing of error, dyvysyon or schism'. Richard Fletcher the younger had assisted his father in the Cranbrook ministry in the past but, since September 1574, he had been fully employed as preacher and minister of Rye,[109] a parish no less populous and demanding than Cranbrook.[110] He agreed with Thomas Good on one thing at least. There was schism, or the threat of schism, in his father's parish. But he attributed this to ingratitude and to Strowd's alienation of the people who had 'gone back from their first love' with 'great alteracion and hartburninge', making 'a new circumcision against their ancient and sufficient pastor'. Strowd was 'one of Austen's puritans' (the first

109 The likelihood is that Richard Fletcher the younger assisted his father between his marriage in Cranbrook in May 1573 and his engagement by the town of Rye in September 1574. Some books inaccurately describe Fletcher as vicar of Rye. The true situation was one of some complexity. In Fletcher's time the vicarage was leased and the fruits were a matter of litigation and for a time sequestered. Attempts by the mayor and jurats and by the bishop of Chichester to resolve this impasse were not successful. Fletcher was in receipt of some benefit from the fruits of the vicarage and of a further 'augmentation' or 'benevolence' from the town of £10, £5 of which was paid by the churchwardens and £5 by the town chamberlain. His normal style was 'preacher[or minister] of the word of God in the church at Rye' (ESRO, RYE MSS 47/12/6, 11 and 22/10; RYE MS 1/4, fols 171^v, 186^r, 252^v, 340; RYE MS 147/2; RYE MS 60/9, fols 54^r, 47^r).

110 There were alleged to be 1,800 or 1,900 communicants in June 1580 (ESRO, RYE MS 47/22/10).

recorded use of the word 'puritan' in the context of Cranbrook), his religion the disliking of religion. The usual charges of Anabaptism and Familism were thrown in for good measure. Pens walked at this sermon too, and a bitter exchange ensued between the younger Fletcher and Good, in which other issues made their appearance. Fletcher made the half-hearted charge that Strowd, the 'printing preacher', might be operating a press somewhere in the parish. Good retorted that Cranbrook, as a clothing town, was full of presses, 'but they will not nor cannot print'. At a time of worsening trade for the town the vicar was said to have pressed his claim to tithe and other dues with callous disregard of any interest but his own. 'His tythes must not faile howsoever the worlde goeth.' But Fletcher claimed that his father was more reasonable in his demands than his predecessors, and told Good that he was the unworthiest schoolmaster that had ever been seen in Cranbrook,[111] neglecting his scholars for religious agitation. True enough, Good would later be presented in the archdeacon's court for not using 'such diligence in teachyng as ought to be', and was duly admonished.[112] The controversy came to its climax when Strowd was again inhibited from preaching, by the archbishop of Canterbury. This caused great dismay in the country and widespread petitioning which was perhaps encouraged by the fact that the archbishop was now (1576) Edmund Grindal. According to a document subscribed by twelve ministers and 138 of their people, headed by Ely of Tenterden, 'our beloved neighbours of Cranebrooke' joined in with a testimonial to Strowd's worthiness. Naturally their vicar's signature is not to be found in this roll-call of the godly of the Weald and the Medway, which included twenty names of quality.[113] Strowd remained in Cranbrook as a private person, and was buried as a plague victim in October 1582.[114] No doubt he continued to be found in private 'exercises', and perhaps some were more willing to hear him in their homes than to be present at the public sermons in the parish church. Was this why Fletcher brought Thomas Ely over from Smarden in 1579, the same year in which he publicly accused some of his people of staying away from church?

111 There has been some discussion about the date when Cranbrook first acquired a school, given the complications arising from the application of bequests left by William Lynch (1539) and Alexander Dence (1574), although it is known that eventually the town enjoyed a grammar school and (the intention of Dence) a school for reading and writing in English. (Jordan, *Social Institutions in Kent*, pp. 80–1; Clark, op. cit., p. 444n.) There are references to the schoolmaster's wages in the churchwardens' accounts from 1564 (KAO, P/100/5/1, fol. 24) and in 1566 the effects were valued of Michael Halsall 'scole-master, late of Cranebrook' (KAO, PRC 10/1, fols 167–8).
112 CALC, X.2.4, fol. 53ʳ.
113 *Seconde Parte of a Register*, vol. i, pp. 114–16; DWL, MS Morrice B II, fol. 5ʳ. Clark discusses the significance of the names of some of Strowd's more notable supporters (op. cit., pp. 151–2, 165–6).
114 Strowd was named in Peter Courthope's will of 20 November 1579 (KAO, PRC 32/34/64) but not as a minister and not as 'of Cranbrook'. The John Strowd buried in October 1582 (KAO, TR/1042/5) was presumably the preacher, although he is not so described.

Thomas Good struck a shrewd blow when he told the younger Fletcher that in preaching against Reformation 'you speak against yorselfe.' For Fletcher's background, like his father's, was impeccably Protestant. Some historians, not too nice about terms, might call it Puritan. He had rallied to the defence of his father, not of some abstract 'Anglicanism', and not all of his invective against Good was in the currency of a Whitgift or a Bancroft. Some was drawn, no doubt with cunning, from the Puritans' own mint. It was good Presbyterian doctrine that the bond between a pastor and his flock was all but indissoluble. So Fletcher could state that unlike Strowd he 'drew noe love or lykinge of people from their pastor but preached it, maynteyned it.' In his Cranbrook sermon he admitted the existence of 'hurtfull ceremonys', even 'corruptions', while denying to private men the liberty to cut themselves off from a church where the word was truly preached and the sacraments duly administered.

In Rye the Protestant settlement had been enthusiastically enforced. The church had long since been whitewashed and adorned with Scripture texts, 'the great organs' in their turn 'taken asunder'.[115] Fletcher's predecessor as 'preacher of the word of God within the church of Rye' was John Philpot, a leading nonconformist in the London vestiarian troubles of 1566.[116] Still preserved in Rye church is a collection of sermons on the Decalogue, traditionally attributed to Fletcher, which are forthright in their condemnation of ecclesiastical imagery:[117] 'For surely if idolatry it selfe as a most execrable thinge be forbidden then all occasions and means leading thereunto are likewise prohibited and what stronger provocation to that spirituall whoredome then erecting images in the place of Godes worship and therfore without doubt the meaning of the Commaundment is to bind the Chirche from all such snares and allurements to sinne.' They were a scandal to 'the simple sort' and to 'them that cary idolatrous mindes'. With the same *topos* from 1 Corinthians in mind,[118] Good accused the Fletchers of wounding poor men's consciences with the defence of ceremonies admitted to be 'hurtful'.

Whether or not these sermons were preached by Fletcher,[119] they reflect the uncompromising Protestantism in which he participated as minister of Rye. Like his father he devoted himself with energy to the promotion of a godly order

115 ESRO, RYE MS 147/1, fols 162ᵛ, 165ᵛ, 211ʳ.

116 ESRO, RYE MS 1/4, fol. 186ʳ. On Philpot, see Collinson, op. cit., pp. 77–8, 82.

117 I am most grateful to the vicar of Rye, the Rev. Canon J. E. R. Williams, for allowing me to examine and partially transcribe the contents of this small paper book (5 inches by 3 inches) without cover, title, date or foliation and written in an Elizabethan hand. It was sight of this object in a display case in St Mary's church in Rye in February 1974 which first prompted the questions which have led to the writing of this essay.

118 John S. Coolidge, *The Pauline Renaissance in England: Puritanism and the Bible* (Oxford, 1970), especially chapter 2.

119 There is nothing in the MS itself to connect them with Fletcher. The only dateable reference is to 'this sickness of plague' which may refer to either of the terrible visitations of 1563 and 1579–80.

in what was often a disorderly seaport town.[120] Soon after returning from battle with the Cranbrook Puritans, he was invested with 'jurisdiction ecclesiastical' in Rye for 'the ponishment of synne and wickedness' and the securing of 'suche a civill and vertuous order of lyvinge as the worde of God dayly taught unto us doth require.' The effect of this arrangement, negotiated between the mayor and jurats and the bishop of Chichester, Richard Curteys,[121] was to unify civil and ecclesiastical government in the town. The correction of 'ill rule' was sometimes a matter for Fletcher by virtue of his own, delegated authority, but on other occasions he sat with the civil magistrates in a tribunal which resembled Elizabethan ecclesiastical commissions in its dual character but which presumably conformed to civil procedures and offered no threat to the secular magistracy.[122]

Thus fortified, Fletcher engaged with irreligion and disorder, and like his father met with his share of defiance: from the ruder sort in the taverns and market place, where one John Bennett with 'other reproches' inaccurately declared that he was as good a man as Mr Fletcher since his father was a butcher and Mr Fletcher's a weaver; and more insidiously in the 'indirect and sinester' approaches made to the bishop by Richard Abbot, a powerful and dangerous man living outside the town's liberties and jurisdiction and allegedly a maintainer of 'roges, incontinent persons, theves, pirates and all such lyke skumme of the world.'[123] So Fletcher was too distracted to give much thought to Cranbrook. His children were being born in quick succession: Nathaniel (1575), Theophilus (1577) (godly names both!), Elizabeth (1578) and the dramatist John (1579).[124] And in 1579 and 1580 he exercised joint responsibility with the magistrates for the enforcement of measures against the plague which, for the second time in a generation, carried off as much as a quarter of the town's population.[125] Not

120 There was a particularly spectacular occurrence of 'ill rule' in the town on the night of 26 September 1575 when among other acts of wanton destruction the lattice was torn down from Thomas Edolfe's window and deposited in the vicarage garden (ESRO, RYE MS 1/4, fols 214ᵛ–15ᵛ).
121 For the career of Curteys, see Manning, op. cit., passim.
122 Mayor and jurats of Rye to the bishop of Chichester, 20 September 1575; bishop to mayor and jurats, 26 September 1575; decision of the mayor and jurats to draw up 'an instrument in wrytinge' to be sent to the bishop, and draft of the 'instrument', 10 October 1575; mayor and jurats to bishop, 16 October 1575. (ESRO, RYE MS 47/12/5, 6; RYE MS 1/4, fol. 215ᵛ; RYE MS. 47/12/11ᵛ, 11ʳ). The letters but not the draft 'instrument' are printed in Historical Manuscripts Commission 13th Report, Appendix IV, pp. 45–7. Cf. the letter written by bishop Parkhurst of Norwich to the bailiffs of Yarmouth, 12 November 1572, granting them 'that aucthoritie I may to punishe synne . . . All that I and you with all my officers can do is to litle, synne doth so much abound and punishment therof is so slack.' But Parkhurst required the rights of his comissary to be respected. (The Letter Book of John Parkhurst 1571-5, ed. R. A. Houlbrooke, Norfolk Record Society (1975), vol. xliii, p. 215.)
123 ESRO, RYE MSS 47/12/29b and 47/13.
124 ESRO, PAR 467/1/1/2, fols 12ᵛ, 21ʳ, 24ᵛ, 28ᵛ.
125 ESRO, RYE MS 1/4, fols 309ᵛ–10ʳ, 310ʳ–11ᵛ, 323ᵛ; RYE MS 47/22/3. 562 were buried in August–October 1563 and 627 between November 1579 and October 1580 (ESRO, PAR 467/1/1/1 and 2).

long after these terrible events Fletcher was gone, to reap his reward in a brilliant ecclesiastical career which, as dean of Peterborough, found him on the scaffold with Mary Stuart in February 1587; and took him from there in rapid order to the bishoprics of Bristol, Worcester and London. His last days drew out sadly in the Queen's displeasure at his second, unsuitable marriage and came to an end suddenly and incongruously, 'taking tobacco in his chair, saying to his man that stood by him, whom he loved very well, *Oh boy, I die.*' So departed at the age of about fifty the boy who in June 1555 had been obliged to watch Christopher Wade burn until 'altogether roasted'. Sir John Harington's epitaph was that 'he could preach well and could speak boldly, and yet keep *decorum*. He knew what pleased the Queen, and would adventure on that though that offended others.'[126]

It would be an oversimplification to imply that the events at Cranbrook in 1575 converted the future bishop and his father out of primitive Protestantism into a kind of Anglicanism. They were a step in that direction, but in the ten years of life remaining to him the relations of Richard Fletcher with the godly of his parish were neither broken off nor tidily resolved. In 1579, as already indicated, there were complaints against him for denouncing 'some of his paryshe that dyd sweare they would not come unto the church untyll such thinges were brought to passe that they had devysed.'[127] But from his side there was no attempt to make a case against the Puritans in the archdeacon's court. 'Such thinges' probably included the abandonment of the hated surplice; and by 1582 Fletcher seems to have worn it no longer.[128] It was only now that Foxe received Fletcher's account of the martyrdom of Wade.[129] Was the vicar of Cranbrooke concerned to hold his place in 'the English Protestant tradition', or to remind Foxe's readers in Kent that Wade's dying words were an endorsement of prayer-book religion? Some kind of *modus vivendi* with the Puritan preachers in the parish must have been achieved. They too were never presented for any offence, and if there were unseemly scuffles around the pulpit they were not made public. Fenner might seem to have been a formidable threat, with his precocious intellect, glowing reputation and private means.[130] But there is some

126 *DNB*, art. Fletcher; F. O. White, *Lives of the Elizabethan Bishops* (1898), pp. 308–16; John Harington, *A briefe view of the state of the Church of England* (written 1608, published 1653), pp. 29–32; *A & M*, vol. vii, p. 321.

127 CALC, X.2.2, fol. 58ᵣ.

128 In December 1582 the churchwardens reported: 'The mynister weareth no surples' (CALC, X.2.4, fol. 52ᵛ).

129 The account of Wade's martyrdom appeared in *Acts and Monuments* for the first time in 1583 (pp. 1679–80), authenticated by 'Spectatores presentes, Richardus Fletcher pater, nunc Minister Ecclesiae Crambroke (*sic*); Richardus Fletcher filius, Minister Ecclesiae Riensis.' It must therefore have been communicated between the setting up of the 1576 edition, when Foxe still had 'no full certaintie when [Wade] suffered' (p. 1591), and the departure of Richard Fletcher the younger from Rye, apparently late in 1580 or in 1581.

130 According to a source quoted in the *DNB* (art. Fenner) he was 'heire of great possessions'. His personal contribution to the relief of Geneva in a collection organized in the diocese of

evidence that he employed these talents for the healing of old sores. When Reginald Scot, author of *The discoverie of witchcraft*, accused Fenner of making 'broile and contention' in Cranbrook he was told: 'If there were broile and contention in Cranbrooke he found it there and made it not, but rather he pacified some contentions and dislikinges which he found among them.'[131] Unless it was a later hand which embellished the entry, Fletcher described Fenner in an obituary notice in the parish register as 'a most worthy preacher'.[132] Dr Clark suggests that the basis of peaceful coexistence may have been that Fenner had unchallenged control of the Saturday lecture.[133] No doubt this market day occasion was a rallying ground for the Cranbrook saints, and for their friends living beyond the parish within riding distance.

It was Fenner who introduced to Cranbrook, without any apparent resistance from the vicar, the still novel and outlandish practice of baptizing with peculiar names. The apparent intention was to underline baptism as a true separation from the world and to God and his Church by the use of a name having 'some godly signification for that worke.'[134] The new fashion was first seen in March 1583 with the baptism of Joyagaine Netter and Fromabove Hendly (surnames of quality in the town), and continued at the end of the year with the christening of Fenner's own daughter Morefruit, sister of Freegift, who, having been brought to Cranbrook, died there in September 1583. Two years later, Faintnot Fenner was baptized; and in August 1588 Wellabroad Fenner was buried, after her father's death in voluntary exile in the Netherlands.[135] Only when Fletcher was almost on his deathbed was a Cranbrook man presented in the archdeacon's court for participating in the naming of John Bigge's son Smallhope.[136]

Canterbury in 1583 was £4. This was the largest contribution by any individual cleric with the exception of the archbishop himself and the archdeacon, and was surpassed by only five secular magnates (PRO, S.P. 12/161/21).

131 DWL, MS Morrice B I, fol. 426ᵛ. 'The defense of the mynisters of Kent' is calendared in *Seconde Parte of a Register*, vol. i, pp. 230–41.

132 The entry reads: 'Faint not Fenner, daughter of D. F. Concional. (*sic*) Digniss.' The surviving copy of the register for this period was made by William Eddy in 1598 (Tarbutt, op. cit., vol. ii, pp. 15, 20.)

133 Clark, op. cit., pp. 439–40n, following KAO, P/100/5/1, fol. 58ᵛ.

134 As Dr Tyacke has suggested, Fenner was most probably the inventor of a practice for which he supplied the rationale in *The whole doctrine of the sacramentes* (Middelburg, 1588), sig. C2, and *The order of householde* (Middelburg, 1588), sig. F5ᵛ: Nicholas Tyacke, 'Popular Puritan Mentality in Late Elizabethan England', in *The English Commonwealth 1547–1640*, ed. Peter Clark, Alan G. R. Smith and Nicholas Tyacke (Leicester, 1979). But if, as seems likely to me, Thomas Ely of Cranbrook and Thomas Hely of Warbleton in Sussex were one and the same, it is a curious and perhaps significant circumstance that Ely preceded Fenner at Cranbrook before proceeding to Warbleton where, as Tyacke has shown, more than half the children baptized between 1587 and 1590 received peculiar Puritan names. Since Fenner himself was apparently of Wealden stock, it strengthens the possibility that the notion of names with 'godly signification', like primitive sacramentarianism, was nurtured in the popular rather than highly educated mind.

135 KAO, TR/1042/5.

136 CALC, X.2.4, fol. 274. I am happy to report that the unfortunately-named Smallhope was

Smallhope Bigge was the fifth child to be given such a name, and there would be twenty more in the next nineteen years of whom the archdeacon would take no cognizance. Among them, the six children of Thomas Starr made their own little procession to the font: Comfort, Nostrength, Moregift, Mercy, Suretrust, and Standwell. Comfort Starr grew up to be a physician who later emigrated from Ashford to Massachusetts where he died in 1659, leaving to his son 'my large Book of Martyrs'. Other Starrs remained in Kent, and when in 1669 a later Comfort Starr preached in Cranbrook, this too was an echo of its Elizabethan past.[137]

Dr Tyacke has shown that the historian can use the evidence of peculiar baptismal names to identify and evaluate the distinctive Puritan element in the parishes where they occur.[138] The fact that relatively few Cranbrook children were made to suffer such names, compared with the mass movement in some Sussex villages, could suggest that the Puritan presence in the parish was neither large nor influential, but may only mean that successive vicars discouraged a practice which in any case was somewhat peripheral to the Puritan mainstream. Other fragments of evidence enable scholars to form vivid impressions of individuals, but not to measure, still less to characterize, the religious and social phenomenon which was Cranbrook Puritanism. The Reignold Lovell who christened his children Thankful and Faithful, buried them in the plague of 1597 and then named another Faithful in 1599,[139] was presumably the 'Lovell of Cranbrook', 'a good honest poore silly puritane', who aroused the admiration of a Kentish cousin of the diarist John Manningham. ' "O" said shee, "he goes to the ground when he talks in Divinitie with a preacher." '[140] Robert Holden, who was Smallhope Bigge's godfather, refused to let his wife be churched and often said of his own son that he would grow up to be a bishop, 'bycause that every day after dynner he will fall asleepe.'[141] But for a chance presentment, perhaps motivated by private circumstances still unknown, nothing would have been recorded of this man's obstinate but whimsical mind. There are no Puritan signals in the will which the parish clerk Laurence Weller wrote for Robert Holden, yeoman, in 1594,[142] unlike the clothier Richard Jorden's will, made a year later, which included an unusual prayer 'for the restauration of the churche instituted by the apostles of our Lord Jesus Christe

alive and well in 1615, when he was appointed executor to Richard Busse, clothier (KAO, PRC 17/60/85).
137 KAO, TR/1042/5; B. P. Starr, *A History of the Starr Family of New England* (Hartford, Conn., 1879), p. vii; G. F. Nuttall, 'Dissenting Churches in Kent Before 1700', *JEH*, vol. xiv (1963), p. 188.
138 Tyacke, loc. cit.
139 KAO, TR/1042/5.
140 *The Diary of John Manningham of the Middle Temple, 1602–1603*, ed. R. P. Sorlien (Hanover, New Hampshire, 1976), p. 44.
141 CALC, X.2.4, fol. 274.
142 PRO, PROB 11/91/17.

and prescribed in the word of God.'[143] Presbyterian in their prejudices some of the Cranbrook godly certainly were; Strowd and Fenner had seen to that.

But were some of them also schismatics, as the Fletchers had insinuated? Were such people even 'hereditary separatists', as Dr Clark has suggested?[144] This to be sure is the crucial question on which it is easier to adopt a position before, rather than after, undertaking grassroots research. On the one hand, there is the evidence of Strowd's conventicling, which seems to have amounted to the household religion familiar to students of Puritanism in other localities.[145] Were these gatherings separatist in their tendency by associating people otherwise unrelated for purposes which were not shared or tolerated by the majority? Or, on the contrary, did they relate to the given circumstances of settlement and kinship? If with further research it proved possible to place the Cranbrook puritans on the map it might emerge that they were concentrated in some of the outlying hamlets of the parish. It would be useful to know where Strowd lived, and Fenner. When a will like Rose Austen's is found to contain bequests to neighbouring preachers it can be assumed that this widow woman was in the habit of 'gadding to sermons' and that she had shared in the select society of the godly-minded. Yet, in the manner of widows, Mrs Austen also found room in her will for numerous kinsfolk, sharing twenty-two surnames.[146] No social shunning on her part. In his Presbyterian will Richard Jorden renounced, as might be expected from a man of his opinions, all the 'heretikes and scismatickes of this age', including, specifically, the Brownists.[147] But when it is discovered that in 1591 Jorden's servant Peter Taylor 'woulde by no perswasion come into the church' for a service which included the sacrament of baptism, but 'in contempt and ill example to others and dishonour to God made his refusall'.[148] Knowledge of Cranbrook's Baptist future poses a question. Nevertheless on the evidence available it is not possible to state that household religion in this community went beyond what a later vicar referred to approvingly in 1639 as 'the private communion of saints', in the same breath as he condemned the separatists of that later generation.[149]

'Private communion' may well have had a long ancestry in Cranbrook. There is an odour of it, a distinctly feminine odour, in the *obiter dicta* in which the vicar William Eddy indulged as he copied out the parish registers in 1598.

143 PRO, PROB 11/87/15.
144 Clark, op. cit., p. 177. Clark gives a generalized impression of widespread and rampant separatism in Kent at the turn of the sixteenth and seventeenth centuries. Reviewing *English Provincial Society* in the *Times Literary Supplement* (1.9.78), Professor Alan Everitt raised a cautious eyebrow.
145 Collinson, op. cit., pp. 372–82.
146 KAO, PRC 17/44/134.
147 PRO, PROB 11/87/15.
148 CALC, X.3.8, fol. 95ʳ.
149 Robert Abbot, *A trial of our church-forsakers. Or, a meditation tending to still the passions of unquiet Brownists* (1639), sig. aᵛ.

Most of his people were incorrigibly sinful. But this had been 'a good woman' and that 'a godly and good woman'. Bridget Sheaparde, a gentlewoman who boarded at the vicarage until her premature death, was 'a mayden and most godlie'.[150] Eddy wrote her will and placed in her mouth this touching Calvinist affirmation: 'Jesus Christ, in whome amongst many other daughters in Israell [God] hath elected mee before the foundation of the world unto eternall lyfe and salvation.'[151] Yet like Fletcher before him, and like his successor Robert Abbot, Eddy would have found schism, a separation of these saints, as grievous to bear as wickedness and vice.

If ever favourable conditions obtained for an outbreak of formalized separation in Elizabethan Cranbrook, it was in the five years before Eddy became vicar in 1591. Archbishop Whitgift's policies had driven Dudley Fenner not only away from Cranbrook but out of England, and he was soon to die in Middelburg. The godly were orphaned. Nationally the reaction against Puritanism intensified; the cause of further Reformation was blighted and in London the consequent frustration led to a new separatist movement associated with the leadership of Henry Barrow and John Greenwood. After Richard Fletcher's death there was a reversion in Cranbrook to an impoverished pastoral situation. There were two brief incumbencies,[152] long periods of non-residence, the neglect of basic parochial duties and sometimes only the clerk or the sexton to read the services, or to bury the dead.[153] And with the hungry nineties there was more than spiritual deprivation to contend with. If separatism was a natural growth in areas of scattered settlement and pastoral neglect, still more if it is read as the expression of harsh and unsettling economic conditions, it might have been expected to flourish in this decade among a people sensitized by a generation of intensive Puritan indoctrination. Yet there is no reason to suppose that it did. Separatism in the proper sense of the gathering and covenanting of a separated people to form a new kind of church was a rare phenomenon before the mid-seventeenth century. Apart from any other favourable circumstances, it may

150 KAO, TR/1042/5.
151 KAO, PRC 17/52/44.
152 Robert Rhodes, 1586–90, and Richard Mulcaster, 1590–1, probably regarded Cranbrook more as a benefice than as a cure. Rhodes, who had been president of St John's College, Cambridge, was intermittently resident and in his will remembered 'the poorer sort that live nearest the vicarage' as well as an otherwise unknown curate, Mr Allen (PRO, PROB 11/75/21. See also CALC, X.2.4, fols 295, 307, 333, 346, 374, 379ʳ). The distinguished schoolmaster and educational theorist Richard Mulcaster was almost wholly non-resident, for which he was cited, but failed to appear to answer the charge on thirteen successive occasions. His resignation was perhaps enforced (CALC, X.3.5, fols 39ᵛ, 40, 47ᵛ–8ʳ, 50, 133ᵛ). William Eddy seems to have been a curate in the parish from as early as May 1586 and in November 1587 married a local girl. He was collated to the vicarage late in 1591 and remained until his death in 1616 (CALC, X.2.4, fol. 295, X.3.5, fol. 83ᵛ; Tarbutt, op. cit., vol. iii, pp. 16–21).
153 CALC, X.3.5, fols 39, 40, 47ᵛ–8ʳ, 133ᵛ. Griffith Bishop, the sexton, presented for churching women and burying the dead, appeared on 6 October 1590 to say that 'some four tymes at the request of Mr Moncaster their vicar in his absence' he had performed these offices.

have required a species of charismatic leadership which was lacking in Cranbrook in the 1590s, to overcome the strong inhibitions which held the separating urge in check.

The origins of the Dissent – Independent, and above all Baptist – for which Cranbrook was later noted,[154] are to be found in the 1630s, under the pressure of royal and episcopal policies which provoked a more profound alienation of the godly than any of the events of Elizabeth's reign. The beginnings can be observed through the eyes of Robert Abbot, vicar from 1616 until 1643,[155] whose experience replicated that of Richard Fletcher sixty years before but surpassed it in personal bitterness. Abbot was a divine in the moderate Calvinist tradition which his patron and namesake archbishop Abbot promoted in the Church at large. In his earlier years he was fiercely anti-Catholic and content to be known as 'preacher of God's word at Cranbrook.'[156] As a pastor he was earnest, warning his fellow ministers: 'We dwell like men under a Frigid Zone, our parishes Friezeland, our people frozen into the mud of the world and dregges of sinne; and will you not be hissing hot in spirit ?'[157] He was exceptionally well-disposed to his flock, dedicating a published sermon in Pauline terms to 'my deare and loving parishioners . . . my brethren beloved and longed for, my ioy and my crowne.'[158] Where Fletcher might have denounced sin indifferently, Abbot could beg that a parishioner might be excused the trauma of public penance: 'I would willingly winne him by more gentle courses if I may.'[159] He stayed with an attempted suicide in the three days that it took her to die, persuading her into a repentant state of mind.[160]

But with Abbot's affection for his people went a sense of professional, clerical dignity which was typical of his generation, and a growing devotion to the institutional Church as 'my deare mother, the much honored, holy and blessed Church of England.' In the conditions prevailing in the diocese of Canterbury under William Laud's government, his unconcealed respect for the established polity of the Church won him the name of 'bishop's creature', with a pope in his belly. 'I have loved the godly, as such, though I have hated their indiscretions, as well as my owne . . . Onely, this is the truth, I have loved the Church of God amongst us, and the whole government ecclesiastical and

---

154 Hasted (op. cit., vol. vii, pp. 92–3) reported in the mid-eighteenth century that of some 3,000 inhabitants 'a great part' were dissenters and attached to five distinct religious societies. See C. C. R. Pile, *Dissenting Congregations in Cranbrook*, Cranbrook Notes and Records no. 5 (n.p., 1953). The facts relating to the formation of the earliest dissenting churches in Kent are supplied by Nuttall, loc. cit.
155 *DNB*, art. Abbot.
156 See Abbot's sermons *The danger of popery* (1625) and *Bee thankfull London* (1626).
157 Abbot, *Davids desires* (1623), sig. *₊*3.
158 Ibid., sig. A6.
159 CALC, X. 6.7, letter from Abbot to the archdeacon's official, 13 June 1621, loose between fols 35 and 36.
160 Ibid., fol. 185ᵛ.

temporal.' It was a fatal conflict of loves. 'I have loved and desired to spend and
to be spent, though the more I love the lesse I am loved of some few.'[161] The
schism which ensued was portrayed in letters to the parliamentarian Sir Edward
Dering whose views on all matters Abbot was glad to share. 'They stick not
onely at our bishops, service and ceremonies, but at our Church. They would
have every particular congregation to be independent, and neither to be kept
in order by rules given by king, bishops, councels or synods.'[162] This was a
more serious matter than the old private communion of saints, and it prefigured
the formation of a gathered and covenanted church which followed in 1648.[163]
These people were proud to call themselves separatists, glorying in the Biblical
resonances of the word 'separate', but Abbot unhesitatingly labelled them
'Brownists'. As he wrote in 1639: 'It is no small charge to unchurch a church,
to unminister a ministry, and to unworship a worship.'[164] The probability is
that this drastic course was not followed in Cranbrook before the stressful
decade which preceded the Civil War. The sequel, the history of Cranbrook
nonconformity, enjoys only superficial continuity with earlier traditions of
dissent. Separate, in the sense of different, Cranbrook's 'hotter sort of protestants' may have always been. Separated they were not, until the 1640s.

This essay should end with a comment on the 'popular and unpopular
religion' of its title. What was 'popular religion' in sixteenth- and seventeenth-
century Kent? According to current usage it must be looked for in Dr Clark's
'Third World'. It has been demonstrated that, among the majority, Protestant
and Puritan religion never enjoyed popularity. But there was a sense in which the
religion of the godly was also 'popular': it was held against John Strowd that his
preaching was seasoned 'to please the people'.[165] And to these people nothing
could be more unpopular than the fatal, recidivist tendency of clerics like
Fletcher and Abbot to align themselves with some of the more unpopular
features of the established Church. In matters of religion, 'popular' and 'unpopular' are relative terms, and deceptive.

161 Abbot, *Trial of our church-forsakers*, sigs A8ᵛ, A6ᵛ. The circumstances are discussed by
Clark, op. cit., pp. 364, 386; and by Alan Everitt, *The Community of Kent and the Great Rebellion*
(Leicester, 1966), pp. 86–7.
162 Abbot to Dering, 15 March 1640; BL, MS Stowe 184, fols 27–30. Further letters, 5 July,
3 October 1641; ibid., fols 43–4, 47–8.
163 Nuttall, loc. cit., p. 182.
164 Abbot, *Trial of our church-forsakers*, sig. a2ʳ.
165 DWL, MS Morrice B II, fol. 10ᵛ.

16

THE BEGINNINGS OF ENGLISH SABBATARIANISM

THIS communication summarises the findings of an enquiry into the origins of English Sabbatarianism at the turn of the sixteenth and seventeenth centuries.[1] Two aspects of this movement have seemed to merit fresh investigation: the sources of English Sabbatarian notions and the circumstances in which the Sabbath became a major controversial issue in the Church of England, dividing the puritan Nonconformists from the representatives of authority.

Sabbatarianism, for the purpose of this discussion, is defined as something more than a certain ethical and social attitude to the use of Sunday: it implies the doctrinal assertion that the fourth commandment is not an obsolete ceremonial law of the Jews but a perpetual, moral law, binding on Christians; in other words, that the Christian observance of Sunday has its basis not in ecclesiastical tradition but in the decalogue. The more important propositions of the Sabbatarians are that the Sabbath derives from the creation and so antedates both man's fall and the Mosaic law, although its use was defined in the decalogue; that the hallowing of the Lord's day in place of the Sabbath was of apostolic or even divine appointment, and more than an ecclesiastical convention; so that the Sabbath is still in force in this altered form, commemorating the second creation in Christ's resurrection, and robbed only of some of its ceremonial detail; that the whole day should be kept holy and devoted to the public and private exercise of religion; and that this

---

[1] I am indebted to Mr Ian Breward of Manchester University who has read this communication since it was delivered at Cambridge and has made some useful suggestions which I have incorporated. I have also benefitted from the comments of Mr Basil Hall on the occasion when the communication was read.

precludes all otherwise lawful recreations and pastimes as well as the work of one's calling, unlawful games and mere idleness.

This doctrine had long been as it were assumed in much that was indignantly said about the misuse of Sunday in sermons and tracts in the style of Philip Stubbes's *Anatomy of abuses*. Among the more notable complaints were the sermons preached at Paul's Cross by John Stockwood and Thomas White,[1] Humphrey Roberts's *An earnest complaint of divers vain, wicked and abused exercises practised on the Saboth day* (1572) and John Northbrooke's *A treatise wherein dicing, dancing, vain plays or enterludes with other idle pastimes etc. commonly used on the Sabbath are reproved* (1577?). The dogma was implied by the Sabbatarian bye-laws enacted by many corporate towns[2] and by the attempts of the House of Commons to legislate against Sabbath-breakers.[3] As early as 1573 one hears reported from the Kentish weald the kind of saying which would be a stereotype of anti-puritan satire thirty years later: 'It is said crediblelly in the countrie that he hathe preched that it is no greater a sinne to steal a horse on Munday then to sell him in fayre on the Sunday; that it is as ill to play at games as shoutinge, bowlinge on Sundaye as to lye with your neyghbor's wiffe on Munday.'[4] But the biblical authority for these attempts to regulate the Englishman's Sunday was uncertain, and it was only in the last fifteen years of the century that this practical Sabbatarianism received a dogmatic rationale, when English divines began to discuss the fourth commandment with some theological detachment and to publish whole works on its doctrine. The attention they paid to the Sabbath reflected a growing interest among puritan preachers and theologians with questions of ethics, which is suggested by the increased attention paid to the ten commandments both in catechisms and sermons, a trend discernible equally on the continent and in this country. It was in the course of catechising or delivering catechising sermons on the

[1] Stockwood, *A sermon preached at Paules Crosse on Barthelmew day, being the 24 of August 1578* and *A very fruitefull sermon preached at Paules Cross the tenth of May last*, 1579; White, *A sermon preached at Pawles Crosse on Sunday the thirde of November in the time of the plague*, 1578.

[2] W. B. Whitaker, *Sunday in Tudor and Stuart Times*, 1933, 37-44, collects some of the evidence.

[3] J. E. Neale, *Elizabeth I and her Parliaments, 1584-1601*, 1957, 58-60.

[4] The writer is Richard Fletcher (later bishop of London and father of the dramatist) attacking John Stroud, schoolmaster, hedge-priest and printer of Cranbrook; (Dr Williams's Library, MS Morrice B II, f. 9ᵛ).

doctrine of the decalogue that preachers were forced to examine their conception of the Sabbath.

The rigorism of the Sabbath doctrine might seem to make it a natural emphasis of puritan religion. But it was originally no part of protestant teaching, even in its more radical forms, to bind Christians to the literal observance of the fourth commandment. Tyndale taught that 'we be lords over the Saboth; and may yet change it into the Monday, or any other day, as we see need. Neither needed we any holy day at all, if the people might be taught without it.' [1] And when the official 'Homily of the Place and Time of Prayer' threatened Sabbath-breakers with the dire penalty of the Hebrew who gathered sticks on that day, it was a Puritan who protested that this was to confound 'our Sunday with the Jewes' Sabaoth . . . which doctrine is superstitious.' [2]

The first extensively argued, dogmatic assertion that the fourth commandment is morally and perpetually binding was published in 1595, *The doctrine of the Sabbath*[1] by the Suffolk puritan divine, sometime fellow of Peterhouse and rector of Norton, Dr Nicholas Bownd.[3] Within twelve years at least seven further treatments of the topic appeared from the press.[4] Perhaps the most extreme view was that expressed in Dod and Cleaver's *Exposition upon the ten commandments* which had nineteen editions between 1603 and 1635; 'For goe through the whole commandement, what one word in all of it hath any note of ceremony, what reason savours of any special thing to the Jewes, that the commandement should be tyed onely to them?' Mary Magdalene did well not to buy ointment for anointing the body of Christ on the Sabbath. Those who break the

---

[1] *An answer to Sir Thomas More's dialogue, the supper of the Lord*, Parker Soc. Cambridge 1850, 97-8.

[2] Dr Williams's Library, MS Morrice B I, p. 339.

[3] A second, expanded edition appeared in 1606 under the title *Sabbathum veteris et novi testamenti ; or the true doctrine of the Sabbath*.

[4] Richard Greenham, *A treatise of the Sabbath*, first printed 1599; George Estey, *An exposition uppon the tenne commaundements*, 1603; John Dod and Robert Cleaver, *A treatise or exposition upon the ten commandements*, 1603; George Widley, *The doctrine of the Sabbath*, 1604; *Three posicions concerninge the aucthoritie of the Lordes daye*, printed 1606 but not extant, see Arber's *Stationers' Register*, III, 146; John Sprint, *Propositions tending to proove the necessarie use of the christian Sabbaoth or Lords day*, 1607; *Master Bonner upon the Sabaoth*, 1608 but not extant, see Arber, III, 172. In the same period a more conservative point of view was represented by Robert Lowe's *Effigatio veri Sabbathismi*, 1605.

Sabbath will suffer 'all curses and wretchednesses.' Those who observe it 'shall thrive in the Lord's house and in religion and in other worldlie matters, so farre as may stand with true prosperitie.' [1] These publications presumably reflect much attention paid to the Sabbath in the pulpits. But what survives from the press suggests that there was a lull in controversy before the topic was revived by James I's *Book of Sports* in 1618.

It has been thought that this fairly novel teaching, so much in vogue in the early seventeenth century, was an original invention of the English puritan divines. We learn from the *Oxford Dictionary of the Christian Church* that 'in its more rigorous form [Sabbatarianism] is a peculiar development of the English and Scottish Reformation, being unknown on the Continent even among Calvinists.' And M. M. Knappen hazarded the statement that the doctrine was 'the first and perhaps the only important English contribution to the development of Reformed theology in the first century of its history.'[2] These assumptions require some qualification, at least with respect to the theology of Sabbatarianism.

Certainly Sabbatarianism was no part of the teaching of the proto-reformers, if one excepts the eccentric Andreas Karlstadt.[3] The earliest protestant teaching, equally in its Lutheran and Reformed expressions, relegated a literal Sabbath to the obsolete ceremonial law of the Jews and subjected the fourth commandment to a tropological exegesis.[4] It is also true that the Sabbath received an emphasis in English protestant religion which was unknown on the continent except in the Netherlands; and that the Sabbatarianism of Dutch Calvinists owed something to English influence. But to describe English Sabbatarianism as a wholly insular phenomenon is to ignore the probable influence of a number of continental Reformed theologians of the second generation who were well-known to Bownd and other English Sabbatarians. One might add that this question of the Sabbath seems to exemplify the insularity of puritan studies, the general failure to place English puritan

[1] Edition of 1603, ff. 62^v, 78^v, 90^v, 91^r.

[2] *Tudor Puritanism*, Chicago 1939, 442.

[3] See his *Von dem Sabbat und gebotten Feyertagen*, Jena 1524; discussed by Professor Gordon Rupp in 'Andreas Karlstadt and Reformation Puritanism,' *JTS*, n.s. x (1959), 308-26.

[4] There are useful extracts and summaries of the teaching of the reformers in Robert Cox, *The Literature of the Sabbath Question*, 2 vols. Edinburgh 1865.

theology in its European Reformed setting. The doctrine of the Sabbath, with its emphasis on obligation, was consistent with the theology of the covenant, teaching the necessity in the economy of salvation for faithfulness on either side of the compact between God and man. Covenant theology was not, as it has been represented, the independent fabrication of English puritan theologians but derived from the theological tradition of the Zwinglian reformation in Zurich, transmitted in part to the whole family of Reformed churches in the doctrinal *consensus* of the mid-sixteenth century.[1]

Among continental Reformed theologians of what may be loosely called the second generation one finds the view rather widely expressed that the fourth commandment is partly moral, partly ceremonial, and that an essential part of its moral content is that one set day—some would say, one day in seven—is to be reserved for God's worship and service. This belief is joined logically to the view that the Sabbath is older than Moses and belongs to the natural law, observed by man in his innocence. This teaching amounts to the recognition of a literal Sabbath and it represents an important modification of the purely figurative treatment of the Sabbath in the earliest Reformation writings. The way was prepared not only in Zurich but by both Melancthon and Calvin when they emphasised the third use of the law, to instruct the Christian in a life of virtue. The teaching that the Sabbath is natural, universal and moral occurs in Bullinger[2] and hence in the Anglo-Zuricher, John Hooper[3]; embedded in Bullinger's *Decades*, which from 1587 were required reading for all clergy below the status of Master of Arts,[4] it must have been familiar in late Elizabethan England. A positive view of the Sabbath, understood as the reservation of one day in seven for the service of God, received equal emphasis in Strasbourg, or so one gathers from Martin Bucer's later, English writings. In the *De regno Christi* Bucer taught that 'nos unum in septimana diem consecrare religionibus debemus' and that 'dies

[1] Jens G. Møller, 'The Beginnings of Puritan Covenant Theology,' in *JEH*, XIV (1963), 46–67.

[2] *Decades*, Parker Soc. Cambridge 1849, I, 253–67.

[3] 'A declaration of the x holie commaundements' in *Early Writings*, Parker Soc. Cambridge 1843, 337–51.

[4] Lambeth Palace, Registrum Whitgift, I, f. 131.

dominicus ab apostolis creditur in locum sabbati esse substitutus.' [1] As in so many other matters, Bucer's thought here seems to have been seminal. The same doctrine was upheld by Peter Martyr in his *Commonplaces* and in his lectures on Genesis given at Strasbourg and heard by many exiles from Marian England.[2] Similar views were evidently entertained by Theodore Beza[3] and by Zacaharias Ursinus of Heidelberg, although in his *Summe of christian religion* Ursinus denies that the Sabbath was pre-Mosaic or that it possesses *predominantly* the characteristics of a moral law.[4] Ursinus's view was propagated in England by the master of Tonbridge School, John Stockwood,[5] and it also became known through the Heidelberg Catechism composed by Ursinus and Caspar Olevianus.[6]

In the 1580s the Reformed theologians of what can best be called in the usage of the time 'high Germany' were thus enlarging on a well-established tradition when they emphasised the perpetual, moral attributes of the Sabbath rather than its significance as a type or figure. Their doctrine, if not identical with English Sabbatarianism, approximated to it and provided it with a dogmatic springboard. It would appear significant that all these divines were Hebraists. Two founders of the Reformed orthodoxy of the Palatinate, Emmanuel Tremellius and Hieronymus Zanchius (Giralomo Zanchi) of Heidelberg and Neustadt, both by origin Italians, were disciples of Peter Martyr, but more narrowly biblicist and not so well-grounded in patristics as their master.[7] Both, incidentally, had strong English connections: Tremellius was Hebrew professor at Cambridge in Edward's reign and Zanchius was a close friend of Archbishop Grindal. The sense given to a number of texts, together with the critical notes supplied in Tremellius's translation of the

[1] *De Regno Christi*, lib. I cap. xi; in *Opera Latina*, xv, ed. François Wendel, Paris 1955, 80-4.
[2] *The common places of the most famous and renowned divine Doctor Peter Martyr*, tr. Anthony Marten, 1583, 374-7; *In primum librum Mosis . . . commentarii*, Zurich 1569, ff. 8ᵛ-9. For a contrary, anti-Sabbatarian point of view, see the *Common places* of Wolfgang Musculus, tr. John Man, 1563, ff. 60-70.
[3] See the annotations to his New Testament. These notes (for example on such texts as 1 Cor. xvi, 2 and Rev. i, 10) were familiar to English Puritans in Laurence Tomson's translation and were cited by Bownd.
[4] *The summe of christian religion*, 1645, 575-81.
[5] *A verie profitable and necessarie discourse concerning the observation and keeping of the Sabboth day*, 1584.
[6] See A. S. Thelwall's 1850 edn., 86.
[7] Joseph C. McLelland, *The Visible Words of God*, Edinburgh 1957, 267-71.

Old Testament from the Hebrew and of the New Testament from the Syriac, tended to encourage a serious attitude to the Sabbath, while the whole great project fostered a more sympathetic understanding of the old law and of the judaic roots of the Christian religion. The influence of the Tremellius Bible was extensive for, when Henry Middleton printed a London edition in 1580,[1] it supplied a need in England, as elsewhere, for a Latin Bible of unimpeachable Reformed orthodoxy. In the following year a pious and cultured Suffolk gentlewoman, Frances Jermyn, bequeathed copies to a group of neighbouring preachers in this county where the intellectual system of Sabbatarianism was soon to make its first controversial appearance.[2] Within two years a Suffolk minister was referring to Tremellius's note on a text in Exodus in debating the Sabbath with his fellow-ministers,[3] and Nicholas Bownd on several occasions refers to his renderings of the text.

Franciscus Junius of Heidelberg and later of Leyden—François du Jon the elder—co-editor of the Tremellius Bible, taught in his sermons on Genesis, printed in 1589, that the substance of the fourth commandment was natural, and that for this reason it found itself in the decalogue. The Lord's day was substituted for the Jewish Sabbath 'Christi facto, exemplo institutoque Apostolorum et Ecclesiae veteris observatione constantissima et Scriptura teste. . . . Inepte faciunt qui observationem diei dominici ex traditione, non ex Scriptura sacra in Ecclesia perdurare asserunt, ut hominum traditiones his adminiculis (si Deo placet) statuminent.' [4] Zanchius expounded the fourth commandment at great length[5] in a systematic exegesis of the decalogue, emphasising the perpetual and moral character of the law that there should be one certain day in the week set aside for God's service: 'Secunda causa, ob quam Sabbatum institutum fuit, est: ut status dies esset, quo ad legem audiendam et

---

[1] *Testamenti veteris Biblia Sacra sive libri canonici . . . Latini recens ex Hebraeo facti . . . quibus etiam adjunximus novi Testamenti libros ex sermone Syriaco . . . in Latinum conversos.*

[2] Will of Frances Jermyn, Bury and West Suffolk Record Office, Register of Sudbury Wills, vol. 34.

[3] John Rylands Library, Rylands English MS 874 (papers of the Dedham puritan conference) f. 240: 'Therefore the word here doth not signify anie type but a common signe as Tremellius also speaketh of it, Exodus 31.'

[4] Πρωτοκτισια, *seu creationis a Deo factae . . . praelectiones Francisci Iunii,* Heidelberg 1589, 64; in *Opera theologica Francisci Iunii Biturigis,* Geneva 1613, I, col. 28.

[5] The fourth commandment takes up 206 of the 641 columns devoted to the decalogue in the Geneva edition of the *Opera.*

ceremonias peragendas conveniret populus. . . . Et propter hanc causam; quia non est umbra aut figura, sicut prima, non est abrogatum Sabbatum.'[1] The same doctrine is stated more emphatically by a Zürich theologian, Joannes Wolphius. In his *Chronologia*, printed in 1585, he asserted that the Sabbath was 'in paradyso ante hominis lapsum institutum ad cultum Dei, et in decalogo, qua nihil ceremoniale, nihil typicum et abrogandum continet, praeceptum est.' As for the new Sabbath, it was appointed by Christ and the apostles.[2] Here, in the orthodoxy of Heidelberg and Zürich, defined in the last quarter of the sixteenth century, there was a perceptible development towards Sabbatarianism, in dogma if not in homiletical application, at the same time as the question came under agitation in England.

In Geneva in the same years there seems to have been a slight trend in the same direction, although its strength is not easy to determine. Beza related the observance of Sunday to the decalogue and beyond that to the seventh day of the creation in the annotations to his New Testament, but I am not aware that he laid any emphasis on the Sabbath in his systematic expositions of doctrine; while Lambert Daneau (Danaeus) treated the Sabbath figuratively in an analysis of the decalogue in his influential treatise on Christian ethics.[3] But among the *Propositions and principles of divinitie* propounded by students of the Geneva Academy, which were translated by the Welsh puritan extremist, John Penry, and printed in Edinburgh in 1591 by Robert Waldegrave, there are a number of strong Sabbatarian propositions, defended, it is interesting to note, by a Netherlander—none other than Jan Utenbogaert.[4]

---

[1] '*De decalogo*' in *Operum theologicorum D. Hieronymi Zanchii, tomus quartus*, Geneva 1613, col. 855. See also a number of passages tending to confirm the pre-Mosaic status of the sabbath in Zanchius's voluminous *De operibus Dei intra spacium sex dierum creatis opus*, 2nd. ed., Hanover 1597.

[2] *Chronologia, sive de tempore et eius mutationibus ecclesiasticis tractatio theologica*, Zurich 1585, 91-7.

[3] *Ethices christianae libri tres: in quibus . . . atque etiam legis divinae sive decalogi explicatio*, Geneva 1577; see Paul de Félice, *Lambert Daneau*, Paris 1881, 173 ff. I have been unable to consult the *Ethices* at first hand, but I have deduced its teaching on the Sabbath from the English Sabbatarian writers.

[4] These 'principles upon the fourth commandement' include the statements that the fourth commandment was established 'in the verie creation of the world'; that it was placed by our Lord Himself among the number of those that are moral and perpetual and that the apostles appointed the new Sabbath in place of the old in memory of the resurrection; 'the observance therefore of this Lord's day is not to be accounted as an

English Sabbatarianism was elaborated in full awareness of the progress of the question in learned circles overseas. When the Sabbath was debated in the Dedham conference in 1584,[1] reference was made to Bullinger, Martyr, Tremellius, Beza and Danaeus. Bownd made extensive use of Junius and Wolphius as well as of Bullinger and Martyr in the first edition of his *Doctrine of the Sabbath* (1595). By 1606, when the official onslaught on his teaching demanded some learned reinforcement of the argument, Bownd had become acquainted with Zanchius's voluminous lectures, and included in his second edition lengthy quotations from *De decalogo* and *De operibus Dei*. These authors were not necessarily unknown to other Sabbatarians who wrote more economically, or whose doctrine is known only from notes taken from their sermons by their hearers. Indeed, a Gloucestershire minister, John Sprint, in his *Propositions tending to proove the necessarie use of the christian Sabbaoth* is another English writer who claims to be in agreement with Martyr, Beza, Ursinus, Junius, Zanchius and Wolphius.

It would not be helpful to suggest that English Sabbatarianism was entirely derived from these continental sources, and there is certainly insufficient evidence to support such a contention. The use which the Sabbatarian divines made of their learned contemporaries was as opportunist as their pillaging of the Fathers for proof-texts: a speaker in the Dedham conference in 1584, and Bownd in 1595, both made use of an argument from Danaeus's *Ethices* that the fourth commandment should be placed first in the table 'because it is most ancient,' although Danaeus was not in other respects a Sabbatarian. The present writer would be the first to grant that theology was only one component of Sabbatarianism. Social factors characteristic of the English—and Scottish— scene must account for the widespread application of doctrines which were stated in Germany but never greatly emphasised or formative of social behaviour. But the familiarity of many of the Elizabethan country clergymen with theological works printed in Germany and Switzerland in the last twenty years of the sixteenth century and never printed in this country is in itself notable. It is clear that the theological climate in which the English Sabbatarian

indifferent thing, but as an Apostolical tradition to be perpetually observed.' (*Propositions and principles*, 78-82.)

[1] See 439, below.

doctrines were elaborated was anything but insular. Renewed investigation of the reception of continental Reformed theology in this country seems to be called for if we are to relate the definition of English puritan orthodoxy—not merely on the Sabbath question, but over the whole concept of the covenant to which it was related— to European theological development as a whole.

It is only possible here to outline the circumstances in which the Sabbath became a controversial issue in the English Church. The Sabbath was energetically discussed in Cambridge and in the conferences of preaching ministers in the neighbouring county of Suffolk from the early 'eighties onwards. The Suffolk ministry, insofar as it was learned, was a Cambridge ministry. Of some eighty or so Suffolk ministers of this generation who for one reason or another may be reckoned Puritans, more than fifty were resident in the university in the decade 1565-75, thirty of them at one college, St John's.[1] In Cambridge, early in 1586, John Smith, a graduate of Christ's who was soon to be beneficed in Suffolk, was examined by the vice-chancellor for implying in a sermon that the Christian Sabbath was of twenty-four hours' duration and that it was violated by any activity which was neither of religion nor of necessity. No more than a year before this, Lancelot Andrewes, still in his puritan phase,[2] had asserted the essentials of Sabbatarianism in his catechising sermons on the decalogue preached in Pembroke Hall on Saturday and Sunday afternoons.[3] We are told that these sermons were heard by 'divers,' not only out of other colleges in the university but also out of the country, and that 'many hundreds of copies passed from hand to hand.'[4] Rather earlier Andrewes had taken part in weekly conferences with other puritan students of his generation,[5] including at least three who were later celebrated preachers in East Anglia, Ezekiel Culverwell, John Knewstub and

[1] See my unpublished London Ph.D. thesis 'The Puritan Classical Movement in the Reign of Elizabeth I', 1957, 126.

[2] John Strype, *Annals*, Oxford 1824, III, pt i. 496-7.

[3] M. M. Knappen, 'The Early Puritanism of Lancelot Andrewes,' *Church History*, II, (1933), 95-104.

[4] Printed in garbled form in *The pattern of catechisticall doctrine*, 1630; in John Jackson's improved ed., *The morall law expounded*, 1642; and in a further ed. under that title prepared from Andrewes's own notes but 'doctored' to conform to Laudian doctrine, 1650.

[5] Isaacson's 'Life of Andrewes' in *Two Answers to Cardinal Perron*, ed. J. Bliss, Lib. of Anglo-Catholic Theology, Oxford 1854, vi; Jackson's preface to *The morall law expounded*, Sig. A 3ᵛ.

John Carter.[1] Another of Andrewes's puritan friends was the famous Richard Greenham of Dry Drayton. Greenham was a fellow of Pembroke Hall when Andrewes matriculated in 1571, and Thomas Fuller, whose father knew Greenham, tells us that 'if Greenham gained any learning by Andrews, Andrews lost no religion by Greenham.'[2] Greenham was Bownd's step-father,[3] and he himself had written a treatise on the Sabbath which circulated in manuscript and was known to Bownd before he embarked on his own work on the subject.[4] It was printed posthumously in 1599 and Fuller says that 'no book in that age made greater impression on people's practice.'[5] Perhaps Greenham was the original source of the doctrine of the Christian Sabbath in this country; his famous household at Dry Drayton was certainly a nursery of English Reformed casuistry.

As we know from the minutes and other papers of a conference of preaching ministers which met monthly in the neighbourhood of Dedham on the Essex-Suffolk borders,[6] the Sabbath was under debate among the Suffolk ministers as early as 1582—in fact the question was raised at the first meeting of the Dedham conference on 3 December of that year, and discussion went on sporadically until 1585.[7] As in other districts, the problem tended to rear its head when sermons were delivered on the decalogue. It was while filling his place in a series of sermons devoted to the ten commandments in 1586 that Bownd made known his views on the subject and was persuaded by his brethren to put them into print.[8]

Bownd wrote of the Sabbath that 'I doe not thinke that there is any one poynt of our religion that is so in controversie among the

---

[1] Life of Carter in Samuel Clarke, *A collection of the lives of ten eminent divines*, 1662.

[2] *Church History of Britain*, ed. J. S. Brewer, Oxford 1845, V, 191.

[3] Knappen, *Tudor Puritanism*, 450.

[4] See Bownd's preface (1595), Sig. A 3.

[5] *Church History of Britain*, V, 193.

[6] John Rylands Library, Rylands English MS 874; the minutes and some of the other papers were edited by R. G. Usher, *The Presbyterian Movement in the Reign of Queen Elizabeth*, Camden Soc. 3rd. ser. VIII, 1905.

[7] *Presbyterian Movement*, 27-8, 30-3, 35, 47.

[8] In a dedicatory epistle to his 'Christian Readers', dated 27 June 1595, Bownd explained that 'about nine yeeres since I was solicited to publish my sermons upon the tenne commaundements by certaine of my godly brethren, auditors then of the same.' (Sig. A 3.) Other references in the work suggest that the whole course of sermons was not handled by Bownd: e.g. 'surely to speake of the true manner of worship-

learned of all sortes . . . wherein many friendes doe disagree.'[1] The
papers of the Dedham conference confirm that the Sabbath was a
question which divided those who otherwise regarded themselves
as brethren. The early debates on the subject were left unconcluded
'till further conference of brethren in other places might be
required.' In June 1583 it was agreed to 'crave the judgementes of
some godly men in Cambridge,' while members of the conference
were invited to dispute the matter scholastically, giving in their
reasons to Dr Richard Crick, the preacher at East Bergholt. Crick
was not a Sabbatarian, and during the ensuing twelve months he
conducted a vigorous and sophisticated debate with the chief
defender of the Sabbath in the conference, Henry Sandes, pastor of
Boxford. Boxford was on the way to Bury St Edmunds from
Dedham, and Sandes combined membership of the Dedham
conference with attendance at a meeting of ministers in West
Suffolk which probably included Nicholas Bownd. He argued that
the Church had no liberty to alter the Christian Sabbath; that it was
'a natural day' since 'the busynes of the Sabboth . . . will take up all
the tyme'; and that the breaking of the Sabbath would be requited
with the same punishment as blaspheming the name of God. Crick
opposed these arguments with assertions that 'to thinke one tyme
more holie then another is to observe tymes'; that if the Sabbath
were moral, the day could not have been changed or the rest in any
way relaxed, since 'nothing prohibited in the morall lawe is dispensed
with by God'; and that 'if any writer affirmeth yt necessarie to have
the resurrection of our Savyour only remembered by a daie, it is
more then I knowe'; he believed that Bullinger and Martyr and all
other writers taught that the observance of Sunday was an
ecclesiastical convention.[2]

The Sabbath was not an issue which united all the forward
ministry or which could serve to identify them as a party, any more
than the presbyterian doctrine of church order had served that
function. How then did Sabbatarianism establish itself as one of the
main planks of the seventeenth-century puritan platform? Largely,
no doubt, through the growing success of the Sabbatarian doctrine,

ing God doth not properly belong to this place, it was sufficiently opened unto us in the
second commandement' (165).

[1] *Doctrine of the Sabbath*, 30.

[2] Sandes's and Crick's arguments are lengthy and occupy ff. 15 (237)-25 (247) of
Rylands English MS 874; they have not been printed.

which seems to have carried all before it in puritan circles in the reign of James I. But initially the identification of Sabbatarianism with presbyterian Puritanism was effected in an attack from the opposite camp akin to the literary 'smear campaign' by which Richard Bancroft had implicated the whole cause of further reformation with presbyterian extremism.[1] This campaign was conducted by one of Bancroft's chaplains, Thomas Rogers, rector of Horringer in Suffolk, a neighbour of Bownd but an Oxford man, and perhaps for that reason isolated from the godly fellowship of the preaching ministers. In 1590 Rogers complained in a letter to the archdeacon of Sudbury, John Still,[2] of his 'shameful seclusion' from the regular Monday 'exercise'[3] of preachers at Bury. This seems to have been the penalty for a sermon against Laurence Chaderton's notorious presbyterian sermon on the twelfth chapter of Romans which Roger had preached in the exercise and at once printed.[4] He was also blamed for a provocative attack on a fellow-minister, Miles Moss,[5] a Bury preacher and later rector of Combs. Moss had published what Rogers took to be defamatory words against himself in the preface to a catechism which had commented unfavourably on the excessive quantity of books published in their own time and 'such as disturbe the Church.' It was not surprising that Rogers was sensitive to an attack of this nature. The *Short-Title Catalogue* and Anthony à Wood between them list twelve of his original works and eleven translations,[6] eighteen of which had been published by 1590.

[1] See his *Daungerous positions* and *Survay of the pretended holy discipline*, 1593.

[2] The letter, dated 8 June (1590?) survives on the fly-leaf of Roger's own annotated copy of his pamphlet against Miles Moss, *Miles Christianus*, 1590 (B.M., press-mark 4103.bbb.26).

[3] The catalogue of Dawson Turner's MSS, sold by Messrs Puttick and Simpson on 6 June 1859, describes (p. 61) a volume of 'Ecclesiastical Miscellanies' (originally a Selden MS) which included 'articles drawen according to the verie thoughts of the classical brethren for the wel-managing of theire Mondaie exercise at Burie' and 'a Narrative of an Exercise or Disputation, held, apparently, amongst certain ministers assembled at Bury St. Edmunds, 1st April 1590.' I am indebted to Dr A. H. Smith of Homerton Training College for this reference.

[4] *A sermon upon the 6.7. and 8. verses of the 12 chapter of S. Paules Epistle unto the Romanes . . . made to the confutation of another sermon*, 1590.

[5] *Miles Christianus, or a just apologie of all necessarie writings and writers*, 1590.

[6] Roger's translation of the *Imitatio Christi* had fourteen editions between 1580 and 1640. He translated mystical works ascribed to St Augustine and several works by contemporary Lutheran divines.

They are the product of a learned, diverse but ambitious church-man, an inveterate controversialist who had already ranged himself with the opponents of the godly preachers in the preface to his commentary on the thirty-nine articles, *The English Creed*.[1] Few divines of his generation had so strong a conviction of the catholicity of the reformed Church of England[2] or such loyalty to the implic-ations of the Act of Supremacy. But neither this, nor a sedulous approach to numerous influential patrons[3] and the enjoyment of Sir Christopher Hatton's and Bancroft's active patronage brought the preferment he sought, and he died rector of Horringer.

When Bownd published his Sabbatarian doctrines in 1595, Rogers sensed an opportunity to uphold Anglican orthodoxy against a new-fangled notion and at the same time to avenge himself on the Suffolk ministers and recommend himself to those in authority. 'It is a comfort unto my soul,' he wrote 'and will be till my dying hour, that I have been the man and the means that these sabbatarian errors and impieties are brought into light and know-ledge of the state.'[4] He preached a sermon in Bury on 10 December 1599 in which the doctrine that 'we Christians of the Church of England ar bound to keepe the Sabbath day' was described as 'antichristian and unsound.' With characteristic Erastianism he preferred to call Sundays 'the Queen's dayes.' 'Those which hold that opinion against which he himself preched he called Saba-tarians and dominicans.'[5] I know of no earlier use of the label 'Sabbatarian' to describe those of Bownd's persuasion. At this time Archbishop Whitgift called in the remaining copies of Bownd's book and Lord Chief Justice Popham at the Bury assizes in 1600 forbade any more copies to be published. Rogers claimed the credit

---

[1] *The English Creede, consenting with the true, auncient, catholique and apostolique Church*, 1585.

[2] Norman F. Sykes, *Old Priest, New Presbyter*, Cambridge 1956, 59–60.

[3] Besides his acknowledged patrons, Hatton and Bancroft, Rogers dedicated his works at various times to the queen, Dr Thomas Wilson, Sir Francis Walsingham, Sir Thomas Bromley, the countess of Sussex, Archbishop Grindal, Bishops Aylmer and Ravis of London, Bishop Scambler of Norwich and Henry Blagge and Thomas Poley esquires, two Suffolk justices.

[4] *The faith, doctrine and religion . . . of England*, 1607, edited by the Parker Society as *The Catholic Doctrine of the Church of England*, Cambridge 1854, 20.

[5] Brief notes of the sermon survive among the papers of Sir Edward Lewkenor of Denham, Suffolk; B.M. Add. MS 38492, f. 104.

for both these actions.[1] Later he announced in the preface to a new edition of his *English Creed* that the Sabbatarian teaching represented a new and subtle manoeuvre by the Presbyterians: in their efforts to supplant episcopal government with the presbyterian discipline, 'from an odd corner and after a new fashion' they had assaulted the Church with 'their sabbath speculations' which Rogers calls presbyterian 'more than either kingly or popely,'[2] ignoring, if he was aware of it, that there were Presbyterians in Suffolk, like Dr Crick, who shared his own anti-Sabbatarian views. Anthony à Wood reports that Rogers's attacks provoked the puritan party 'so far to be enraged as maliciously to asperse and blemish him. Whereupon he wrote a vindication of himself in MS., now in the hands of a near relation of his'.[3]

Thomas Fuller records that the suppression of Bownd's book increased its sale and stimulated a market for the second edition; 'and scarce any comment, catechism, or controversy was set forth by the stricter divines, wherein this doctrine (the diamond in this ring) was not largely pressed and proved; so that, as one saith, "the sabbath itself had no rest".'[4] But Rogers's ingenious insinuation that Sabbatarianism was a new and cunning attempt at subversion of the established order by the Presbyterians was exploited by Peter Heylyn and repeated by Fuller and Jeremy Collier in their church histories,[5] and so established itself as a plausible if not a sufficient account of the origins of English Sabbatarianism.

[1] *The Catholic Doctrine*, 20.

[2] Ibid. 18.

[3] Ibid. ix.

[4] *Church History of Britain*, v, 218-19.

[5] Ibid. v, 216-17; Heylyn, *History of the Sabbath*, 1636, II, 249-56; Collier, *An Ecclesiastical History of Great Britain*, ed. Thomas Lathbury, 1852, VII, 190-2.

The tomb of Sir Edward Lewkenor in the tiny parish church of Denham, Suffolk. 'Not good' is Sir Nikolaus Pevsner's terse comment in *The Buildings of England*. Nevertheless there is no better representation of the values of early seventeenth-century godly magistracy. Lewkenor kneels as if to lead the devotions of his wife Susan, who predeceased him by one day in October 1605, and their six surviving children. The eldest, Sir Edward Lewkenor the younger, presumably provided this ostentatious monument but later deemed the money laid out on funeral expenses 'of all others worst bestowed'. (*By courtesy of the Reverend John Bridgen and the Parochial Church Council of St. Mary's church, Denham, Suffolk.*)

17

MAGISTRACY AND MINISTRY
A SUFFOLK MINIATURE

'OH THE heavenly harmony and sweet amitie that then was amongst you from the highest to the lowest! The magistrates and the ministers imbracing and seconding one another, and the common people affording due reverence and obedience to them both.'[1] Our text is provided by William Burton, a Norwich minister forced into a kind of exile as the price of an intemperate sermon,[2] looking back on the halcyon Elizabethan days when Norwich was as kind to its preachers as it was famous for its government. This essay is about not Norwich but a small corner of Suffolk, although a certain reciprocity links Burton's 'religious and famous citie' to what Bishop Hall called 'that sweet and civil county of Suffolk, near to St Edmunds Bury'.[3] For if Elizabethan Norwich provides the paradigm of urban puritanism, Suffolk was the pattern of rural England under puritan government. And the subject is not 'the common people' either. Burton's faith in the willing subordination of their kind was no more than a rhetorical convention, a *topos* which can be contradicted with more rhetoric from the same mouth.[4] On this occasion we shall look no further than 'magistracy and ministry', the 'imbracing and seconding'.

The intention will be modestly descriptive, but descriptive

[1] Burton, William, *Seven dialogues both pithie and profitable,* 1606, Sig. A2.

[2] Burton, William, *A sermon preched in the cathedrall church in Norwich the xxi day of September 1589 . . . and published to the satisfying of some which took offence thereat,* n.d.

[3] *Works of Joseph Hall,* ed. Wynter, P., 1863, I, xxv.

[4] In his 1589 *Sermon* (Sig. D4v) Burton complained of the 'discourteous dealing' of the Norwich citizenry, 'whose hearts runne after covetousnes', and who hear the preacher 'for a fashion' but go home to jest their 'bellyesfull'.

of particular circumstances which have almost never been described, as an offering to a scholar who delights in particularities, especially those of place. The miniature is composed of fragments, restored to a frame which itself has to be reassembled from a variety of fugitive sources. Puritan Suffolk is one of those worlds we have lost, together with almost all record of its civil administration, many important ecclesiastical sources, especially those relating to the two archdeaconries, and all but a few materials of a more intimate character: that is to say, letters and diaries.[5]

If a world of understanding is to be discovered in a grain of sand it will be found to consist in our *leitmotiv* of 'magistracy and ministry'. The equal and reciprocal value of civil office and ecclesiastical office was a matter on which John Calvin was insistent, and the magistrates and ministers of Elizabethan and Jacobean Suffolk were never more Calvinist than in their understanding that these roles stood in equal need of each other, and the christian commonwealth of both. Historians have seemed reluctant to admit even the possibility of such a working mutuality, perhaps because the topic of 'church and state' has trained us to look for instability and ceaseless competition for the upper hand. Thus what Eugène Choisy identified as the 'double régime' of Calvin's Geneva[6] has been depicted as not only a theocracy but a one-sided clerical dictatorship to which an equally extreme 'Erastianism' has been seen as a realizable, even inevitable alternative. As for the English Reformation, it is fashionable to interpret it as a process of assertion of the laity against the clergy. Elizabethan puritanism is represented as a clerical backlash, its ideology, according to Professor Michael Walzer, entirely a clerical creation. 'The ministers were forced to act on their own.' Then in the early seventeenth century, as Walzer would have it, their alienation was alleviated, thanks to some improvement in the social standing of the more celebrated puritan clergy.[7]

---

[5] In gathering the fragments that remain, mostly in national collections, the essential tool is W. A. Copinger's remarkable publication *The County of Suffolk. Its History as Disclosed by Existing Records and other Documents, being Materials for the History of Suffolk*, 5 vols., 1904–6.

[6] *La théocratie à Génève au temps de Calvin*, Geneva 1897.

[7] *The Revolution of the Saints: A Study in the Origins of Radical Politics*, 1966, esp. 114–17, 135–40.

It is questionable whether these oscillations were as clearly visible in actuality as they appear in Walzer's model. It may be that the perfect mutuality of Calvinist theory was unattainable in any real world, but so were the stark alternatives of pure Presbyterianism or unadulterated Erastianism. To understand the relationships which in fact obtained between the puritan ministry and the governing class it may be the beginning of wisdom to recollect the principles to which lip service, at least, was paid.

We begin with what was said in Suffolk about this matter. In 1618 the famous Samuel Ward of Ipswich delivered an assize sermon at Bury St Edmunds which went through at least four editions as *Jethros justice of peace*.[8] In the dedication to Francis Bacon, a lord chancellor of Suffolk stock, Ward noted that the ills of the body politic were likely to arise from faults in 'magistracy and ministery', which he calls its principal lights, 'these two opticke peeces'.[9] The biblical figure of Jethro, prince and priest, was the archetype of both. The 'principall scope of magistracy in God's intention' was to promote his glory and to countenance the gospel and its professors. And 'what is our office that are ministers, but as God's trumpets and drummers to encourage, hearten and put life in these that fight his battles and doe his work' It is interesting that Ward should underline these reflections by referring to the advice given to Edward VI by the reformer Martin Bucer in a book by then all but forgotten, *De Regno Christi*. For, as had been noted in Elizabeth's reign, 'he that concludes that to have the Church governed by meet pastors and ministers taketh away the authority of christian magistrates is by Bucer sufficiently confuted'.[10]

Walzer would regard Ward as representative of a less isolated and alienated generation of preachers. So compare *Jethros Justice of Peace* with *The doctrine of superioritie and subiection*, a catechism on the fifth commandment[11] based on

---

[8] *STC* (revised) numbers, 25046–25048, 5.

[9] *Jethros justice of peace*, 1618, Sig. A3, pp. 1, 27, 34.

[10] Ibid., pp. 1, 7; Brit. Libr., MS. Lansdowne 18, fols. 55–6.

[11] *STC* 20337; edited (in 1609) by Robert Allen, a Suffolk minister and prolific author who moved to London after deprivation of his living. The book bears a further commendation from the leading London puritan minister, Stephen Egerton.

sermons preached by Robert Pricke, minister of the Suffolk village of Denham for more than thirty years until his death in 1608, one of the figures who will compose this miniature. The fifth commandment was the foundation of all subordination, private and public. Public superiority was exercised by both magistrates and ministers. The office of magistrate concerned principally religion and godliness and only secondarily the civil estate. He was to 'call and cause to be chosen learned and fit ministers' and to 'inforce and compell' the faithful performance of their duties, defending the worthy and if need be deposing the unworthy. Clerical immunity from such procedures was held to be 'a cursed devise of Antichrist'. As for the people, they were to be constrained by the magistrate to attend and submit themselves to the ministry of the word. 'Take away the magistrate and there would remain no outward worship of God.' But the minister was possessed not only of a ministry but also of his own ecclesiastical government, which included the power to excommunicate. No practical limits were placed on the obedience owed to magistrates and ministers. The subject was to pay willingly 'all such taxes, customes, subsidies and other such paiments as are levied, commanded and imposed' (not freely voted!). And the ministers were to be loved, 'not coldly nor feebly but most fervently and aboundantly'. 'Whosoever doth despise the minister (which is the Ambassador of God) despiseth and contemneth God himself and Jesus Christ, which is a fearful and execrable thing.'[12] We will look in vain within these commonplaces for any suspicion that the two 'optic pieces' could fail to see eye to eye (set in the same head they must have looked out at the world together) except in a negative form of the *topos* already heard from William Burton: 'If magistrates and ministers agree not and the people reverence and love them both, what can come of it?'[13] A tradition of radical dissent and non-conformity was the most unintended of consequences to follow from such a doctrine.

At this point we may put away the mirror or, as we have to

---

[12] *The doctrine of superioritie,* Sigs. B8, C7–8, D1, 5v–6, E2, 6v, F1, 3v.

[13] George Estey, preacher of Bury St Edmunds, to an unnamed correspondent, 14th April 1599; Brit. Libr., MS. Add. 24191, fols. 40–1.

say nowadays, the model, and turn to reality, for the preachers were dealing not with some unattainable ideal but with what was actually the case within local experience. In Elizabethan and Jacobean Suffolk there may have been a closer approximation to the type of a godly commonwealth than in any part of England at any time: closer than anything achieved in the years of ostensible puritan triumph, which was also a time of confusion and division. The mutually supportive alliance of magistracy and ministry was first consolidated in Suffolk in the 1570s, when a generation of ministers who would make their names as preachers, writers and contenders in the cause of reformation began to settle in the rural parishes where many would spend the rest of their days, extending into the first, second and even third decades of the following century. Robert Walsh was at Little Waldingfield from no later than 1573 until his death and notable funeral[14] in 1605. Boxford was the home of Henry Sandes from the early eighties until 1626. John Carter ministered at Bramford for thirty-four years, from 1583 until 1617, and then for a further eighteen years at Belsted. These were famous names, in their time and place. John Knewstub, the most famous and the acknowledged president of the Suffolk preachers, was rector of Cockfield for as many years as Elizabeth was queen of England, from 1579 until 1624. And at Denham, the setting for our miniature, the succession of father and son in the ministry ensured a pastoral continuity of sixty years. These vital details provide the rough confining dates of what might be called the primitive puritan commonwealth in Suffolk, from about 1580 to about 1630.

Also arising from the 1570s, a fervent and public-spirited Calvinist piety begins to appear as the most conspicuous attribute of a number of gentlemen entering upon their inheritances and starting careers on the Commission of the Peace. To name the two who were among the magistrates as Knewstub was among the ministers: Sir John Higham inherited Barrow from his popish father, Sir Clement, in 1570, and his ally Sir Robert Jermyn of Rushbrooke succeeded his father Sir Ambrose Jermyn in 1577. The two shared office

[14] *Winthrop Papers,* I. *1498–1628,* Massachusetts Historical Society, 1929, 89, 153.

as deputy lieutenants in 1585 and as knights of the shire in the parliament of the following year, and they shared the disgrace of being temporarily put out of the Commission of the Peace as the penalty of their puritanism.[15] In the reign of James I their pre-eminence was inherited by the 'eminently religious'[16] Sir Nathaniel Barnardiston of Kedington, reputedly the richest man in Suffolk.[17] Without fuller evidence we are left with the problem of the chicken and the egg. Should the conversion of Suffolk be attributed to the gentlemen who brought in the preachers and were their patrons, Jermyn in no less than ten livings,[18] or to the preachers who won over the gentry? Or should we look to various fundamental characteristics of the county with its 'exceptionally advanced' economy?[19] The preaching ministers were not settled on the light soils of the eastern parts of Suffolk, nor in Ipswich, where the parochial tithes were alienated and the churches served by curates on starvation wages. Their employment was in the affluent townships, on the intensively-farmed corn and dairy lands around Bury St Edmunds, and in the clothing belt which ran down the valley of the Stour, along the Essex border.[20] It was not a new thing for religion to benefit from the prosperity of this region: witness many famous churches of cathedral-like proportions.

When Robert Reyce composed his 'Breviary of Suffolk' in 1618 he listed 'a learned ministry' first among the 'commodities' of his native country, before 'clothing', 'the aire', 'the evenness of the country', 'the soyle'. The then bishop of Norwich was quoted as saying that no bishop in Europe had so grave, learned and judicious a ministry, 'especially in this county'.[21]

---

[15] Collinson, P., 'The Puritan Classical Movement in the Reign of Elizabeth I', unpublished London Ph.D. thesis, 1957, ch. 9.

[16] Clarke, Samuel, *Lives of sundry eminent persons,* 1683, 106.

[17] Everitt, Alan, *Suffolk and the Great Rebellion 1640–1660,* Suffolk Record Society, III. 1960, 16 and *passim.*

[18] Brit. Libr., MS. Harley 4626, fols. 324–46; Seckford Library Woodbridge, V.B. Redstone's transcript of 'Inductionum Liber Redivivus', an eighteenth-century copy of Induction Registers for the Archdeaconry of Sudbury, 1537–1641.

[19] Everitt, op. cit., 17.

[20] The distribution is indicated on one of the maps and in the accompanying list appended to my 'Puritan Classical Movement'.

[21] *Suffolk in the XVIIth Century: the Breviary of Suffolk by Robert Reyce 1618,* ed. Hervey, Lord Francis, 1902, 21f.

The Suffolk clergy were indeed a remarkable society, one of the first groups of English clergy to have realized the reformed ideal of the pastoral ministry, and to have achieved it in concert, as 'brethren and fellow ministers', 'the reverend, wise and godly learned fathers and brethren'.[22] Most of the first generation had been contemporaries at Cambridge, no less than thirty at St Johns,[23] where Knewstub was twice a candidate for the mastership.[24] (Their sons favoured Emmanuel.) They were inveterate attenders of one another's sermons, especially at the administrative centre of Bury St Edmunds, with its regular Monday combination lecture [25] and its 'then famous school', from which Knewstub sent the young Richard Sibbes to Cambridge – to St Johns, not Emmanuel.[26] Many of them were comfortably off and died possessed of silver and pewter, four-poster beds and feather bedding, and sizeable libraries.[27] They bred large families and baptized their children with biblical names, the inevitable Sarahs and Susans, the more occasional (and surprising) 'Rabshakeh'.[28] But Knewstub was a bachelor, admired for his 'contentation in a sol life'.[29] Many wrote books, in which there is sometimes evidence of familiarity with recent theological literature from the Continent, as well as with the Tremellius Bible, the most scholarly of the Reformation

---

[22] Phrases from the dedicatory epistles to works by Nicholas Bownd: *The holy exercise of fasting*, 1604, Sig. ¶3; *The doctrine of the sabbath*, 1595, Sig. A3.

[23] Evidence summarized in my 'Puritan Classical Movement', 123–6 and Appendix B.

[24] Thomas Ithel to Lord Burghley, 3 June 1577, P.R.O., S.P. 12/114/5; twenty-two fellows of St John's to Burghley, 15 December 1595, Brit. Libr., MS. Lansdowne 79, fol. 156.

[25] Collinson, P., 'Lectures by Combination: Structures and Characteristics of Church Life in 17th-Century England', *Bulletin of the Institute of Historical Research*, XLVIII. November 1975, 191–5. *See below*, 476-80.

[26] Bedell, William, 'Life and Death of William Bedell', *Two Biographies of William Bedell*, ed. Shuckburgh, E. S., Cambridge 1902, 15; *DNB.*, art. Sibbes.

[27] Among a number of Suffolk clerical wills consulted particular reference is intended to those of William Browne of Culford (ob. 1607) and Reginald Whitfield of Barrow (ob. 1608); P.R.O., P.C.C. wills 23 Huddlestone, 79 Dorset.

[28] These remarks are based on the examination of parish register transcripts in the Ipswich Public Library. Thomas Jeffray of Depden fathered fourteen children: Sarah, Elizabeth, Lydia, Ann, Priscilla, two Thomases, Martha, Josias, Dionisius, Rabshakeh, Samuel, Phoebe and Esther; Richard Dow of Stratford St Mary ten: Dameris, Daniel, Mary, Elizabeth, Susan, Barjonah, Amy, Robashry, Sarah and Abijah.

[29] By Richard Rogers of Wethersfield in his diary in a passage bearing the marginal, note 'the example of mr knew [stubs]': *Two Elizabethan Puritan Diaries*, ed. Knappen M. M., American Society of Church History, 1933, 95.

versions.[30] Learning like the cloth industry was widely dispersed in this countryside. One Suffolk author explained that it was life in a small village which provided the leisure to study and write, and he published a 1,000-page book on *The doctrine of the gospel* so that the world should know 'what those things are which the faithful ministers of Jesus Christ doe beate their wittes about, and wherein they spend themselves among their severall flockes and charges'.[31]

Original ways were found of expressing appreciation of the ministers. When Nicholas Chaplin of Chelsworth made his will he provided for pairs of winter gloves to be given to ten preachers, Knewstub being named first. Sir Robert Jermyn's sister left copies of the Tremellius Bible, again to ten ministers, Knewstub on this occcasion ranking second. The godly among the minor gentry and rising clothiers seem almost as a matter of course to have left sums of £5 or 40s. to groups of preachers, headed by Knewstub: as Thomas Gale, clothier of Edwardstone, puts it, 'for that I have receyved manye spirituall benefits to the singuler comforte of my soule by the prechinge of certaine godlie prechers hereafter named'.[32]

The major gentry, such of them as Knewstub addressed as 'those gentlemen in Suffolke whom the true worship of God hath made right worshipful',[33] provided a more political support, standing shoulder to shoulder with the ministers as occasion required, against a hostile bishops and his officers, or even against the assize judges.[34] There was a set piece at the summer assize of 1582 when 'fourteen of the principal men out of Suffolk', seven of them knights, waited on the judges at their lodging to ask for greater forbearance to be

[30] Collinson, P., 'The Beginners of English Sabbatarianism', *Studies in Church History*, I. ed. Dugmore, C. W. and Duggan, C., 1964, 212–15. *See above*, 434-7.

[31] Allen, Robert, *The doctrine of the gospel by a plaine and familiar interpretation of the particular points or articles thereof*, 1606, Sig. *4-5.

[32] Muskett, J. J., *Suffolk Manorial Families*, III. iii. Exeter 1911, 82; Suffolk Record Office (Bury St Edmunds), Register of Sudbury Wills, vol. 34, fol. 284v; ibid., vol. 37, fol. 125. Cf. the wills of Martha Higham (see p. 81 below), Joan Barflet of Boxford (Register of Sudbury Wills, vol. 39, fol. 166), Robert Gurdon, Esq., of Assington (Muskett, *Suffolk Manorial Families*, I. Exeter 1900, 278–9), Edward Appleton, gentleman of Edwardstone (ibid., 324).

[33] *An aunsweare unto certayne assertions tending to maintaine the church of Rome to be the true and catholique church*, 1579, dedicatory epistle to the gentlemen of Suffolk.

[34] Cockburn, J. S., *A History of English Assizes 1558-1714*, Cambridge 1972, 199–206, following pp. 881–929 of my 'Puritan Classical Movement'.

shown to non-conformist ministers 'for our sakes'.[35] Such stray records of administration as survive suggest that it was permeated with religion. An act of bigamy was described by Jermyn and Higham and other justices as 'quite contrary unto the worde of God and the lawes of the realme', a matter 'offensyve unto all good men who with sorrowful hart lament the lyke precedent in a christian commonwealth'.[36]

Towards 1580 the solidarity of godly magistracy and ministry in Suffolk was already well enough established to be satirized. The preacher's sermon must on no account touch on the social sins of the gentry, rack-renting, enclosure, oppression of the poor, but must be confined to attacks on the constitution of the Church. The sermon ended, 'the chief gentleman in the place begynnynge with a gronynge, but yet with a lowde voyce crieth most religiously, *Amen*. And then the whole companye of that sect followe. *Amen. Amen.*' This was from the future Archbishop Bancroft's poison pen.[37] But forty years later a preacher of the country was denounced as a 'turbulent spirit' after a sermon at the Clare lecture in which he castigated hypocrisy even among 'our greatest professors', some of whom said Amen to every petition but once out of the church took their own highway to Hell as usurers, 'extreme landlords' and reluctant tithers. The preacher wished to defend property, but not an absolute property. 'Though thy goods be thine, yet are they not so thine, but that the poore have a letter of attorny from God to have to their use as well as thy selfe.' Was it the preacher's 'Christian Socialism' or his scandalous aspersions which went down so badly at the lecture which Sir Nathaniel Barnardiston regularly frequented?[38]

According to Professor Alan Everitt, the Suffolk gentry were surprisingly uncultured, 'absolutely impervious to new ideas', comparing in this respect unfavourably with their Kentish counterparts.[39] Perhaps so. Calvinism may have had a progressively narrowing effect on some. Yet the earliest

[35] Lord North to Lord Burghley, 13 February 1583, Brit. Libr., MS. Harley 6993, no. 33, fol. 61.
[36] Brit. Libr., MS. Harley 286, fol. 22.
[37] *Tracts Ascribed to Richard Bancroft*, ed. Peel, Albert, Cambridge 1953, 71–3.
[38] Carter, Bezaleel, *Christ his last will and John his legacy*, 1621, 71–3, 86.
[39] Op. cit., 19.

madrigals to be printed in England were first performed in Rushbrooke Hall and were dedicated to Sir Robert Jermyn's daughters by the composer, George Kirbye, who was Jermyn's music master.[40]

Within this setting we come to our miniature, set in the village of Denham, not far from Bury St Edmunds, the home of the Lewkenor family and of their ministers, Robert Pricke alias Oldmayne and his son Timothy.[41] A more celebrated partnership was that of Sir Natheniel Barnardiston, 'top-branch of the Suffolk cedars' in the days of James I, and his minister Samuel Fairclough, which came to fruition in the Long Parliament. Of this alliance it was noted, in a variant of our now familiar *leitmotiv*, 'that the magistracy and ministry joined both together, and concurred in all things for promoting of true piety and godliness'.[42] Sir Nathaniel was thirteenth in succession in a Suffolk pedigree which runs from the reign of Richard I to modern times. But the Lewkenors of Denham came and went in three generations, their time in Suffolk coinciding exactly with our primitive puritan commonwealth, from the early seventies when Edward Lewkenor took up his residence in the county to 1634, when his grandson died without a male heir at the age of twenty-one.

To visit Denham[43] is to be given the doubtless deceptive impression that the sixty years of the Lewkenors were the only eventful years in its history. Certainly this was the only period when it knew a seigneurial presence. The small, cheaply-built manor house is still there, close to a tiny church, reconstructed and given a tower in the nineteenth century but otherwise the same modest chapel which the Lewkenors knew, not one of Suffolk's village cathedrals. The parish was

[40] Kirbye, George, *The first set of English madrigalls to 4.5. and 6. voyces*, 1597.

[41] A principal source for what follows is an (unnumbered) volume in the series of 'Suffolk Green Books' edited by the Suffolk antiquary S. H. A. Hervey: *Denham Parish Registers 1539–1850, with Historical Notes and Notices*, Bury St Edmunds 1904.

[42] Lives of Fairclough and Barnardiston in Clarke, op. cit. This alliance is a centre-piece of the Yale doctoral dissertation by Mr Kenneth W. Shipps, 'Lay Patronage of East Anglian Puritan Clerics in Pre-Revolutionary England', 1971. I am grateful to Mr Shipps for allowing me to read a revised version of this work, intended for publication.

[43] I am greatly indebted to Mr Paul Stannard of the Parochial Church Council of Denham who in August 1976, in the vacancy of the cure, introduced me to the church and its monuments, and allowed me to consult the documents in the church safe.

scarcely a parish, its tithes being appropriated in the past to St Osyth Priory and later to the lay landlords who succeeded the monks in ownership of the manor of Abbots Denham. The chaplains and curates who served the place before the time of the Lewkenors and Prickes are mostly unknown, even by name. In 1591 a gentlewoman living in the village willed twenty shillings for the repair of the stools in the church, which gives some impression of the accommodation which it provided.[44] At the north-east corner there is a mortuary chapel, containing two very immodest tombs, the only objects in view to have cost a lot of money. The older of the two bears a fulsome Latin inscription which announces that Sir Edward Lewkenor, who had served at Court and in almost every parliament for thirty years, was to be praised 'chiefly' for bringing the preaching of the gospel into this tiny community: *Inter caeteras autem justi praeconii causas, haec maxime duxit et sempiterna memoria digna quod ejus opera in perexiguam hanc villam obscuramque evangelii praedicatio est introducta, cujus luce et beneficio ad extremum vitae terminum fruebatur.*[45] We may suspect that it was not so much the 'town' as his family and household and indeed his own personal life which Lewkenor sought to enrich by sustaining a godly ministry on his doorstep. The place was and is too small to support much of a congregational life. What we confront at Denham is an example of the very personal values and priorities to which that famous East Anglian worthy John Stubbs gave expression when in middle life he resolved to settle down and 'give continually some time to an ordinary and standing exercise of the word'.[46]

The Denham ministry was provided by Robert Pricke, from no later than 1577 and perhaps earlier, until 1608, and then for a further thirty years by his son Timothy. The older Pricke is described by the younger as 'a right grave devine and learned clerke', but there is no record of him at either university and he was probably of very local origin, Robert and John Pricke, carpenters, being assessed in the nearby village of Barrow in the subsidy of 1568. Still preserved in

[44] Hervey, 114–15.
[45] Ibid., 74–5.
[46] John Stubbs to Michael Hicks, 22 July 1581, Strype, John, *Annals of the Reformation*, Oxford, II. ii, 305.

Denham church is the parish register which Pricke began to keep and to make up retrospectively in 1599. Under the record of his son's baptism in 1577 he entered a curious antiquarian fable in explanation of the alias of Oldmayne. Oldmayne was said to have been the original family name, traceable to the twelfth century. The name of Pricke was acquired from a Suffolk man of that name who had reared an orphaned ancestor in Henry VII's days. Much of this entry has been erased, perhaps by Timothy, who used the name of Oldmayne and may have objected to this inventive piece of family history. Professor Everitt has commented on the indifference of even the greatest in Suffolk to such trifles. In his later years Timothy was well-connected among the spiritual brotherhood of East Anglia. His sister married the famous Richard Blackerby who had ministered to the Lewkenors for a time and whose own daughter later married Samuel Fairclough. In the account of Blackerby published in Clarke's *Lives* it is said that the alias 'Oldman' was assumed by Robert Pricke to escape the Marian persecution. Perhaps neither tale contains the true explanation for this curious alias, the only one known to me among the Elizabethan clergy. In his sixty-first year, the last of his life, it was a matter of wonder to Timothy that he had spent almost all his days in the obscurity of Denham: 'This towne, which now affordeth me my being, formerly afforded mee my first breath.'[47]

The principal credit for making this little corner a place of evangelical enlightenment may belong to neither Prickes nor Lewkenors but to Lewkenor's mother-in-law, Martha Higham. Martha was a Jermyn, married to Thomas Higham of Higham, so that she was an aunt of Sir Robert Jermyn and a cousin by marriage of Sir John Higham, to whom she bequeathed her husband's ring. The last thirty-five years of her life were spent in widowhood, mostly at Denham, where she acquired the formerly monastic property of Abbots Denham, apparently from the Howards, joined it to her husband's manor of Denham, and built a house. Her religious persuasion is left in no doubt by her will, proved in 1593. Apart from the almost

[47] Hervey, pp. 53, 116–19, 268–78, 246; *Suffolk in 1568: Being the Return for a Subsidy Granted in 1566,* Suffolk Green Books XII. Bury St Edmunds 1909, 257.

customary legacies to eleven preachers, headed by Knewstub, there are some very personal features, suggestive of concern for the religious future of Denham. Her Geneva Bible was left to the church, for the use of the parishioners. She endowed a scholarship at Emmanuel on condition that in due course it should be awarded to Timothy Pricke: which came to pass. And in place of an annuity of forty shillings, previously allowed to his father, she left the sum of £40 to provide a parsonage: a house which still exists. Presumably Pricke had previously lived in the manor house, and we may suspect a relationship of spiritual intimacy between Pricke and Mrs Higham of the kind which so often grew between a pious gentlewoman and her chaplain.[48]

Edward Lewkenor was not a native. He belonged to a large and ramified Sussex family with a persistent talent for marrying its sons to heiresses.[49] It was through such a match, with Susan, one of the two daughters and co-heirs of the Highams, that he came to Suffolk, round about 1570. In his lifetime he built up an estate of middling size, through his marriage, by subsequent conveyance from Martha Higham, and by purchases from his sister-in-law Ann Higham and her husband, Thomas Clere of Norfolk, and from Thomas Howard, Earl of Suffolk. In addition he held the manor of Kingston Bowsey in Sussex which was inherited from his father, Edward Lewkenor, groom porter in the court of Edward VI and in the following reign a conspirator who died in the Tower. Lewkenor was to fill one of the Sussex livings in his gift with Samuel Norden, who became the most militant of the puritan ministers in that county, and another with the no less radical Christopher Goldsmith. With lands valued (in the artificial terms of an inquisition post mortem) at a little less than £100 at the time of his death Lewkenor was not the richest of the Suffolk gentry. The house which Mrs Higham had built on a moated site beside Denham church was an unpretentious structure of lath and plaster of only four bays, which found no difficulty in becoming a

---

[48] Hervey, 93–100, 192–5.
[49] Mousley, Joyce E., 'Sussex Country Gentry in the Reign of Elizabeth', unpublished London Ph.D. thesis 1955, 575, 578.

simple farmhouse after the passing of the Lewkenors, and which owes its present brick façade to the nineteenth century.[50]

Lewkenor's distinction arose from what the sixteenth century knew as 'virtue', learning, public-spiritedness – and religion. He entered St John's College late in Mary's reign, matriculated after the lifting of his father's attainder, and took his degree in 1561. He was then a fellow of the college for two years before going on to the Middle Temple, surely one of very few eldest sons of the gentry to have held a fellowship. (A cousin and namesake, a minor Latin poet, was a fellow of St Johns at the same time and went on to an academic career in Oxford.[51]) Lewkenor was perhaps not active in Suffolk affairs until his later years and may not have been a J.P. until 1592. It was as a 'parliament man of mark', John Chamberlain's description,[52] that he was somewhat famous, sitting for every parliament from 1571 until his death in 1605, with the exception of the session of 1601.[53]

In the parliaments of 1584, 1586 and 1589, when the campaign to reform the Church and the ministry reached a crescendo, and again in 1593, Lewkenor sat for the Essex borough of Maldon, a town under strong puritan influence,[54] where the recorder was an old room-mate from the Inner Temple, James Morice, himself an outspoken puritan M.P. There can be no doubt that Lewkenor's regular presence in the House of Commons was the result of inner motives and external persuasion of the kind to which Peter Wentworth referred elusively in one of his speeches.[55] He was there as a puritan, to advance the cause, and although he was a committee man rather than an orator, much of his recorded activity was in matters of religion. In 1587 he was one of a select group

[50] Wills, inquisitions post mortem and other information in Hervey, pp. 86–93, 101–7, 128–38, 198–258, 298–300; Loades, D. M., *Two Tudor Conspiracies,* Cambridge 1963, 232–3. For Norden and Goldsmith, see Manning, R. B., *Religion and Society in Elizabethan Sussex,* Leicester 1969, pp. 212–13, 215–16 and Babbage, S. B., *Puritanism and Richard Bancroft,* 1962, 192–6.

[51] Venn, J. and J. A., *Alumni Cantabrigienses,* I. iii, Cambridge 1924, 82; Cooper, C. H. and T., *Athenae Cantabrigienses,* I. 1858, 251.

[52] Winwood, Ralph, *Memorials,* 1725, II. 141.

[53] I am indebted to the History of Parliament Trust for making available information on Lewkenor's parliamentary career.

[54] See many references in my *The Elizabethan Puritan Movement,* 1967.

[55] Neale, J. E., *Elizabeth I and her Parliaments, 1559–1581,* 1953, 181–4.

of puritans who spoke in support of the extreme measures contained in Anthony Cope's presbyterian 'bill and book', and he was among those sent to the Tower, where his father had died thirty years before, apparently for his part in quasi-conspiratorial meetings associated with this initiative. In one parliamentary speech he referred bitterly to the bishops as 'rather deformers than reformers'.[56]

In 1910 the British Museum acquired among the Townshend MSS. a collection of Lewkenor's papers preserved through the marriage of his great-granddaughter to the first Viscount Townshend. This is now MS. Additional 38492 and comprises a unique file of the working parliamentary papers of an Elizabethan and Jacobean puritan M.P. All sixty-five items relate in one way or another to religion; and all but thirteen are connected with the national campaign for further reformation. No less than forty belong to the first two years of James's reign: to the Hampton Court Conference and (the vast majority) to the issues of conformity and subscription as they impinged on James's first parliament, where Lewkenor, now knighted, once again represented Maldon. This was a replay of the struggle waged twenty years earlier at the time of the subscription crisis provoked by Archbishop Whitgift, and a few papers of major interest relate to 1584. They include a survey of the state of the ministry in the home country of Sussex, addressed from there by a relation to 'his verie good cousin Mr Edward Lewkenor', which Lewkenor is known to have tabled in the House of Commons,[57] and an account of the troubles of the godly people of the Suffolk village of Lawshall, the kind of propaganda which may have circulated from hand to hand in the House.[58] A brief account of the second day of the Hampton Court Conference is addressed: 'To mi veri loveing and wel beloved husband sur Edward Lewkenor att mistres quarles in rumforde geve thes with spede.'[59]

[56] Neale, J. E., *Elizabeth I and her Parliaments, 1584–1601*, 1957, 145–65, 66.

[57] Brit. Libr., MS. Add. 38492, no. 50, fol. 91; D'Ewes, Simonds, *The Journals of all the Parliaments During the Reign of Queen Elizabeth*, 1682, 349.

[58] MS. Add. 38492, no. 63, fols. 107–8. See Neale, *Elizabeth I and her Parliaments, 1584–1601*, 229–30.

[59] MS. Add. 38492, no. 44, fol. 81. The Lewkenors' daughter Hester was married to Robert Quarles Esq. of Romford, Essex.

In the relations between Lewkenor and his minister, Robert Pricke, we encounter an institution subtly different from 'magistracy and ministry' and one with which historians of early modern society are more conversant: the nexus of gentleman and chaplain, patron and protegée. Whereas magistracy and ministry may imply formal parity, this was an intrinsically unequal relationship. And since Denham was a wholly impropriate parish, a 'donative' cure, Pricke lacked even the financial independence of a rector or vicar. He was said to have been the first curate of the parish for two hundred years to have enjoyed the tithes in full,[60] and we know that he received an additional annuity from Mrs Higham, but all this was of mere grace and favour. Yet there is no reason to suppose that Pricke's bearing towards his patron was servile or excessively deferential, and every indication that each acknowledged the integrity of the other in his proper sphere.

The evidence is in MS. Additional 38492. Among the contents is the draft of a petition to the bishop's chancellor, perhaps in the name of several gentlemen, asking for the restoration of Pricke's preaching licence, probably to be dated in 1584, the 'woeful year of subscription'.[61] Scribbled on the back of another document is a list of nine 'books borrowed of Mr Lewkn[or]', doubtless by Pricke. All the titles are theological, and they include William Fulke's sermons on the Apocalypse and works by Beza, Danaeus and Pierre du Moulin.[62] There is a letter from Pricke to Lewkenor, written on 22 February 1585, in the midst of a parliament which was critical for the puritan cause:

> Sir, although it was not so necessarie for mee to write to you at this tyme, considering the abundance of meanes where you nowe remayne, your owne sufficiencie without mee, and my smale skill in anything which in that honorable assemblie where dailie you are might anything availe you. Yet for the dutie which in many respectes I owe unto your w[orship] I could not staie but write a fewe lines.

[60] Noted in the parish register in the entry relating to Timothy Oldmayne's funeral: Hervey, 53.
[61] No. 38, fol. 70.
[62] No. 39, fol. 101v.

Fervent exhortation follows, sharpened by fear that 'sin' may frustrate the godly endeavours of Lewkenor and other godly members:

> We cease not here in our smale measure to lift up our unworthie eies and handes toward the god of heaven both in confessing of our sinnes and striving with his majestie by humble requestes for all necessarie blessing upon you and the rest of your worthie yokefellowes in the service of Jesus Christ. . . . Ah sir that I could further you any waies, I wold by the grace of God be willing to the uttermost of my power.[63]

Another 'brotherly caveat to the godlye zealous and wyse gentlemen of the parlament house' evidently came from the same pen and belongs to the same circumstances. Pricke searches his heart for the reason why the expectations of the godly have so far been disappointed.

> Then my harte melted with fear and I thought, Oh sinn, sinn, sinn, that thou shouldest soe take from us the favour of God, that in soe fitt a tyme and place, under soe godlye and christian a queen, such godlye zealous and wyse men should have theyre tongs cleve to the roof of theyr mouthes, and be destitute of all power to promote soe worthye, weightye, so nedfull a cause. . . . Consider whether the lettinge passe of this occasion be not in some respect to denye Christe and to be ashamed of him before men.[64]

Here was a prolepsis of the working partnership between Samuel Fairclough and Sir Nathaniel Barnardiston in the early days of the Long Parliament, nearly sixty years later.

In the summer of 1605 there was sickness in Cambridge and fear of the plague. Lewkenor's two sons, both at Emmanuel, were called home to escape the infection and with them came the son of a neighbour. This boy contracted smallpox and Lewkenor and his wife were infected. Lady Susan died on 5 October and Sir Edward on the following day.[65] The double tragedy made a profound impression.

---

[63] No. 37, fols. 68–9.
[64] No. 22, fols. 37–8.
[65] This story can be disentangled from the opening verses of the *Threnodia*, referred to below.

Robert Pricke's funeral sermon, an early example of a still
new genre, was preached not long before his own demise and
posthumously published by the Suffolk preacher and author
Robert Allen.[66] The sermon is notable for its structure
deriving from the 'new puritanism' of covenant theology and
providing many proofs that both Lewkenor and his wife
were 'effectually called'. In addition a copious volume of
elegiac verse appeared from the press, a *Threnodia* in Greek,
Latin, Hebrew and English, to which many Cambridge
luminaries contributed, including the regius professor of
Greek and two future and famous bishops, William Bedell
and Joseph Hall.[67]

And in the mortuary chapel purposely constructed a truly
monstrous tomb was erected: a table with six classical columns
in mock porphyry, bearing a canopy with massive armorial
achievements. Under the canopy, in life-size effigy, Sir
Edward and Lady Susan are found kneeling on cushions in
attitudes of strongly-marked devotion, their six surviving
children in rows behind them. The heir, Sir Edward the
younger, seems to have more than proved his filial piety both
by assembling the versifiers of the *Threnodia* and by providing
this monument. Aesthetically, there is as much to object to
in the one as in the other. Both verge on the grotesque. But
the historian cannot pass by with the terse 'not good' of Sir
Nikolaus Pevsner.[68] For one thing, the ostentation speaks
volumes. At a rough guess the tomb must have cost more
than the family home was worth. And the heavy expenditure
is a puzzle, for no tomb would be erected for the son, who
was said to have deemed the money laid out on funeral
expenses 'of all other worst bestowed'.[69] Perhaps this was his
rueful conclusion, after his father's obsequies. But what the
tomb was meant to say it still says very loudly. Whoever

[66] *A verie godlie and learned sermon, treating of mans mortalitie and of the estate both of his
bodie and soule after death,* 1608.

[67] *Threnodia in obitum D. Edovardi Lewkenor equitis & D. Susannae coniugis charissimae.
Funerall verses upon the death of the right worshipfull Sir Edward Lewkenor knight and Madame
Susan his lady. With deaths apologie and a reioynder to the same,* 1606.

[68] *Suffolk,* The Buildings of England, 1961, 168–9.

[69] Oldmayne, Timothy, *Gods rebuke in taking from us . . . Sir Edward Lewkenor knight,*
1619, p. 3. Copies of this sermon are scarce and I am indebted to the Trustees of Dr
Williams's Library for my sight of it.

makes his way to Denham will enrich his reading about puritanism by seeing the thing itself, in convincing and concrete representation.

Only twelve years later came the second Lewkenor funeral at Denham. Sir Edward the younger died unseasonably on May Day 1618, in the midst of his year as sheriff, and at the early age of thirty-two. This time there were two orations, the funeral sermon proper preached by Timothy Oldmayne, entitled *God's rebuke in taking from us that worthy and honourable gentleman Sir Edward Lewkenor,* and a sermon volunteered at nearby Cavenham 'upon a lecture day' by Bezaleel Carter, whom Sir Edward had presented to the living.[70] Tragedy continued to stalk the Suffolk Lewkenors. In 1634 the third of the line, aged only twenty-one, succumbed to the same disease which had killed his grandparents. Timothy Oldmayne preached yet another funeral sermon[71] and the widow erected a second prestigious tomb, this one a chaste creation of marble in impeccable taste.[72] In both sermon and monumental inscription much was made of the fact that with this young man's death the race of Lewkenors at Denham was extinguished, although an unmarried sister would continue to live in the village until her death in 1679. The inheritance had by then passed to the Townshends through the marriage of a daughter who was an infant of three months at the time of her father's death. When this daughter herself died as Mary, Lady Townshend, in 1672, she left £100 for the purchase of property, the rent from which was to provide for the apprenticing to useful trades of poor orphans born in Denham.[73] The safe in Denham church contains the crumbling indentures of apprenticeship of children who benefited from this charity in the eighteenth century, and I am told that the fund is still administered to make token contributions to some of the

[70] *The wise king and the learned judge: in a sermon out of the 10 verse of the 2 psalme: lamenting the death and proposing the example of Sir Edward Lewkenor, a religious gentleman,* 1618. The biblical reference is to the Geneva version: 'Be wise now therefore ye Kings: be learned ye Judges of the earth'.

[71] *Lifes brevitie and deaths debility. Evidently declared in a sermon preched at the funerall of that hopeful and vertuous yong gentleman Edward Lewkenor esquire, etc. In whose death is ended the name of that renowned family of the Lewkenors in Suffolke,* 1636.

[72] Hervey, 75–6, 243–4.

[73] Ibid., 259–61, 305–6.

young people who go out into the world from Denham. This
is the last lingering touch of the charitable puritan piety
which was kindled in this village, four hundred years ago.

Finally we turn to the four Lewkenor funeral sermons, not
only to satisfy Geoffrey Nuttall's known predilection for this
form of literature, but because in themselves they provide a
cameo of puritan magistracy in harmonious concert with
puritan ministry. In all three generations the preachers discovered a consistent and experienced godliness. Sir Edward
and Lady Susan 'accompted all things in the world but drosse'
in comparison with Christ. Constant attention was paid to the
ministry of the word and devotion was shown to the ministers.
Sir Edward the younger was never known to be absent from
church when he was at home, morning or evening. He
presided over prayers in his family two or three times a day,
with reading and a psalm and 'repetition' on the days of
exercise, conceiving the prayer himself when no minister was
present. His parents 'loved most dearelie the ministerie of the
word and ministers thereof . . . with no lesse reverence and
tender affection than naturall children doe their naturall
parents, of whom they are bred and begotten'. Of the grandson it was noted that in his regard for faithful and diligent
ministers he honoured the elder as fathers and the younger as
brethren. Sir Edward the younger is said by Bezaleel Carter
to have purchased advowsons with which to promote godly
ministers. Both Sir Edwards were paragons of philanthropy,
which with the younger became an institution. A special
building was erected alongside the house (still standing in the
nineteenth century) in which the poor were fed daily and 'with
more large provision than ordinarie' on three days in the week,
and there was an annual distribution of clothing to the destitute of the surrounding villages, as many sets as there were
years to the benefactor's life. As for public reputations, Robert
Pricke, who had preached on *The doctrine of superioritie,* presented his patron as a model magistrate, with the 'very special
grace' of being known to utterly reject all bribes and rewards.

Thus far the sermons contribute to a stereotype, an
important part of the integrated ideology of 'the Country',
which was set up against not only the corrupt values of 'the

Court' but also in opposition to the mindless vanities of mere rusticity. 'He cannot be a gentleman which loveth not a dogge.'[74] The half-brother of Francis Bacon, the Suffolk gentleman Edward Bacon, was told by an Ipswich preacher: 'Many be the allurements that mighte tie your affection to the glittering delights of this present world: yet have you learned . . . to trample under your feete the vaine glorie thereof and not to spende your witte and your studie and your revenewes upon haukes and dogges and gawdish apparell.'[75] Samuel Ward of Ipswich, or his publisher, made a similar point more economically in an illustrated title page to one of his sermons. A booted and spurred foot, an open Bible and a mailed fist grasping a lance confront a stockinged leg with fashionable shoe, cards, dice and a hand holding an elaborate glass and a smoking pipe of tobacco.[76] Fortunately the characterization of Sir Edward Lewkenor the younger partially escapes the 'pious panegyric'[77] and suggests a more human complexity. There was piety, to be sure, and 'such a piercing insight into points of doctrine'. But we learn that relations with the tenantry were not always harmonious, that he died in debt, and that 'he carried himself like a gentleman in all respects whatsoever, whether you regard his apparell, his attendance, and lastly his pleasure, keeping as he best liked both hawkes and hounds, as well he might'.[78]

We owe to Timothy Oldmayne this fleeting impression of a puritan magistrate whose humanity was generous and approachable, who 'knew right well to put a difference between the use and the abuse'. To Timothy, whose whole existence was involved in the Lewkenors, we allow the final say:

Foure generations of your honourable *Family* have I seene here upon the *Stage*, successively acting their several *Parts*. . . . But now alas the *Theater* is wholy empted, and all the *Actors* quite gone, the *Stage* hourely expected to be pulled down; and if it

[74] Northbrooke, John, *Spiritus est vicarius Christi in terra*, 1579, fol. 39.
[75] *The lectures of Samuel Bird of Ipswidge upon the 11 chapter of the epistle unto the Hebrewes*, Cambridge 1598, Epistle.
[76] *Woe to drunkards*, 1627 edn.
[77] Stauffer, Donald A., *English Biography Before 1700*, Cambridge Mass. 1930, 71.
[78] Oldmayne, *Gods rebuke*, 11–13, 32–3, 36–7.

stand yet little hope that ever our eyes shall see such *Actors* any more upon it, to play their parts so commendable, as those *Antients* did.[79]

Timothy himself would soon be gone, three or four years before the onset of what used to be called the Puritan Revolution.

18

LECTURES BY COMBINATION
STRUCTURES AND CHARACTERISTICS OF CHURCH LIFE IN 17TH-CENTURY ENGLAND

OF ALL the facets of English religious life in the decades preceding the Civil Wars, the institution of lectureships may seem to stand least in need of further attention, still less of any fundamental reappraisal. Dr. Christopher Hill has given persuasive currency[1] to a modern version of the Laudian charge that the 'ratsbane of lecturing'[2] was both symptom and cause of a radical undermining of the established order of the Church of England.[3] Dr. Paul Seaver has devoted a substantial monograph to *The Puritan Lectureships* (mainly in London), viewed as an aspect of *The Politics of Religious Dissent, 1560–1662*.[4] And Professor Mark Curtis has conflated the modern theory of revolutions with Hobbes to discover in the puritan lecturers copy-book examples of the 'alienated intellectual' in early Stuart society.[5] In 1659 a defender of established religion, Immanuel Bourne, reproached a Quaker opponent for disregarding the lecturing tradition:

If your eyes be not blind, or your ears deaf, and refuse to hear, you might hear and know that many godly Ministers do preach in Market-Towns and many other places freely, witness weekly Lectures, and monthly Exercises, in which commonly two Ministers joyn together, and preach to the great comfort of Christian souls, whose hearts God moveth to attend at wisdoms gates: this is the practice in *London*, in *Derby-shire* where I lived, and is in *Leicester-shire* where I now live, and in *Lincoln-shire*, and *Rutlandshire, Northamptonshire*, and in many other places: and this I have known near this fifty year, and have Preached my self in many places . . .[6]

Surely no modern student of the seventeenth century need fear a similar charge of wilful blindness with respect to lectures and lecturers.

[1] J. E. C. Hill, *Society and Puritanism in Pre-Revolutionary England* (1964), in particular contains extensive discussion.

[2] The phrase was used by Clement Corbet, Bishop Wren's chancellor, in a letter extracted in Bodleian Library, MS. Tanner 68 fo. 2.

[3] Wren himself may be quoted in a (draft) letter to Corbet(?), 27 May 1636: 'And here I must be bold to say playnely, the breach of that unity and uniformity in the Church of England hath bin principally caused or occasioned by lectures and lecturers'. (*Ibid.*, fo. 92.)

[4] P. Seaver, *The Puritan Lectureships: the Politics of Religious Dissent, 1560–1662* (Stanford, 1970).

[5] M. Curtis, 'The alienated intellectuals of early Stuart England', *Past and Present*, xxiii (1962), repr. in *Crisis in Europe, 1560–1660*, ed. T. Aston (1965), pp. 295–316, esp. pp. 308–11.

[6] Immanuel Bourne, 'Some animadversions upon Anthony Piersons great case of tythes', in *A defence and justification of ministers maintenance by tythes* (1659), pp. 123–4. I owe this reference to Dr. M. R. O'Day.

Yet closer investigation, which at first need not go beyond Bourne's reminiscences, suggests that while historians have had their eye on lectures, the eye has caught a distorted image, thrown out of proportion by the polemics of the age, and perhaps even more by that familiar medium of distortion: knowledge of what was to happen after 1640 to a society which we know as 'pre-revolutionary England'. The lectures have been noticed for their subversive potential and, in consequence, have attracted less attention than the subversives, the lecturers themselves, understood as unbeneficed stipendiary preachers, aliens in the Church to which (in Christopher Hill's words) 'they ostensibly belonged', 'freelance clergy', even 'an anti-clergy'.[1] Much has been made, again following a strong seventeenth-century lead, of the financial ties between the lecturers and their lay employers, which apparently made them answerable to interests hostile to the Church.[2] Lectureships, in short, have been studied as an aspect of opposition and even as an element of revolution. For Seaver, any evidence that a parliamentary borough maintained a controlling interest in a town lectureship tends to confirm the view that 'the major towns had turned their backs on the Established Church, and by implication the Crown, long before loyalty to the Crown itself came into question'.[3] Yet it may be noticed that the point intended by Bourne was that lectures were commonly given free of payment by ministers who far from being stipendiaries may well have been beneficed parish clergy. Moreover Bourne was at pains to insist on the normality and long usage of such practices, time out of mind, from the early years of James I through to the years of Civil War and ecclesiastical disruption, without apparent discontinuity.

Bourne's reference to 'weekly lectures and monthly exercises' suggests a certain looseness and fluidity of expression which is general to the documents of the period and may account for the elusiveness of the topic in the modern literature. What are called weekly lectures are best distinguished by a term in common use by the early years of Charles I but not, perhaps, much earlier: combination lectures or lectures 'by combination'. By mid-century a biographer was in no danger of being misunderstood when he described a certain divine as having been 'one in a combination': 'He was one in a combination at Dedington in Oxfordshire; and for some time he kept a lecture alone at Stratford upon Avon in Warwickshire every week'.[4] But elsewhere, and especially in the north of England, the term 'exercise' was attached and had a special meaning in relation to a similar institution. A combination lecture or exercise was a device for a regular provision of preaching, typically in a market town and weekly, on market day, or once a month. The 'com-

---

[1] Hill, pp. 79, 80.

[2] Clement Corbet again: 'The layicke contribution and support hath made the ecclesiasticke persons and cerimonies wagg and dance after their pipe from whom they receive the livelihood, which is stopt or runnes as the Levytes popularise'. (Bodl. Libr., MS. Tanner 68 fo. 2.)

[3] Seaver, p. 90.

[4] Samuel Clarke, *The lives of thirty-two English divines* (1667), p. 320.

bination' was a panel of ministers, as few as three or four or as many as twenty or more, with the figure of thirteen often preferred, most of whom would be incumbents of churches within the natural catchment area of the preaching centre or within the same deanery. The members preached by rotation (quarterly, where the combination was of thirteen) in order of age or of academic seniority. Others of the combination would often be present, and the sermon would sometimes be followed by conference among the ministers, before or in the course of a dinner paid for by the magistrates of the town or by the preachers themselves. These clerical gatherings were not unlike those associated with episcopal visitations and with synods, but they were more frequent and regular and were characterized by a distinctive element of voluntary adherence and commitment.

Combination lectures are recognized by Hill and other writers as one of several types of lecture, but recognition has not led to informed discussion. Hill mentions them only once or twice and Seaver devotes only three of his 400 pages to the subject,[1] while Curtis misunderstands the matter so radically as to assume that more than seventy 'lecturers' named in a survey of market town lectures in Jacobean Lincolnshire must have been unbeneficed stipendiaries, candidates for the ranks of the alienated intellectuals.[2] The neglect of combination lectures cannot be regarded as trivial, for nothing was more typical of the reformed Church of England as it came to maturity in the reign of James I. Indeed, this article may lead to the conclusion that lectures by combination were so characteristic of the Anglicanism of this epoch, of its settled life as much as of its tensions and divisions, and above all perhaps in their often successful containment of conflict, that there will be something at fault with any account of the Jacobean Church which overlooks them, or which treats the institution of lecturing too exclusively in the categories of opposition and disruption.

It is first necessary to trace a genealogy in order to establish a number of points of contact and assimilation, as well as certain primary distinctions, between this and other forms of preaching 'exercise' and other expressions of clerical collegiality. On the face of it, the combination lecture may appear a simple convenience for securing regular sermons which could not otherwise be obtained. Towns without an acceptable preacher among the parish clergy (a common enough experience in the sixteenth century, given the depleted value of urban livings) might appoint a salaried preacher, or might resort to some alternative course, such as paying for sermons offered by visiting preachers. The initiative would lie with ardent protestant elements within the governing oligarchy or, in the case of small towns without effective independence, with some of the surrounding gentry. Alternatively, and this was common in London especially, a lectureship might be established within

---

[1] Seaver, pp. 84–7.

[2] Curtis, p. 310. The error is followed by Hill (p. 85) and compounded by Peter King in his article 'Bishop Wren and the suppression of the Norwich lecturers' (*Historical Journal*, xi (1968), 245n) which refers to 'the 70 lecturers in the diocese of York in 1614'.

a particular parish, by the action of the vestry or through the benevolence of an interested party or parties.[1] At its lowest, the combination was a means of acquiring a 'constant lecture' on the cheap. When Bishop Davenant of Salisbury consulted the corporation of Reading about the 'setlinge of a lecturer', the alternatives were considered of a lecture assigned to one man 'at charge' and to 'divers neighbour ministers within the deanery, gratis'. To a man, the members voted for settling it 'upon divers, gratis'.[2] Bishop Richard Corbet's satirical description of a lecture at Daventry contains the comment: 'We all had Preachers wages, *Thankes* and *Wine*'.[3] Typically it was the larger and wealthier town which would hire a preacher of its own, hopefully an ornament and a magnet.

Two East Anglian examples illustrate the alternatives open to the sponsors of a preaching ministry, and the nature of the sponsorship. In 1579 in Thetford, a poor and undistinguished borough, orders were taken 'for the coming of the prechers upon the Saterday every fortnight'. The 'preachers of the countrie' were appointed to preach 'of their free wyll', but the burgesses were to take it in turns to entertain the preacher to dinner. Some years later the sermon was on a Thursday and the entertainment was at the mayor's expense, at an inn called The Christopher. By then attempts to fund a permanent preacher by obtaining a neighbouring benefice for the use of the town or by raising the money by public subscription had failed. So much for the formal record.[4] But there was more here than meets the eye. The royal progress in Norfolk and Suffolk in 1578 had alerted the privy council to irregularities in the government of Thetford which led to the appointment of a number of Suffolk J.P.s to look into the town's affairs. These were gentlemen reliable in religion whose account of the Thetford factions discriminated between 'a syde of godlye and honest men' and 'an other parte ... frowardlye inclyned ... to overthrowe every good and honest purpose', 'the badde sort of people in the towne'. The mayor ('very cold in the cause of religion') was said to have resisted pressure to procure a preacher, 'being oftentimes thereunto required', although some inhabitants had promised contributions and the bishop his 'furtheraunce'. When the visiting preachers came he absented himself 'upon lyght causes'. When 'the badde sort' presented their side of the story to the council, both the mayor and the coroner were obliged to make their marks on the certificate.[5]

---

[1] Seaver, *passim*; H. G. Owen, 'Lecturers and lectureships in Tudor London', *Church Quarterly Review*, clxii (1961), 63–76.

[2] *Reading Records*, ed. J. M. Guilding (4 vols., 1892–6), ii. 250.

[3] *Poems of Richard Corbett*, ed. J. A. W. Bennett and H. R. Trevor-Roper (Oxford, 1959), pp. 32–3.

[4] Hist. MSS. Comm., *Various Collections*, vii. 134, 140–2; supplemented with material from the original town books kindly supplied by Miss N. M. Fuidge. Memoranda of Bishop Wren of *c.* 1636 include this note: 'At Thetford the sermon of Sir Richard Fulmarshes foundation altred from afternoone to forenoon. Stet.' (Bodl. Libr., MS. Tanner 68 fo. 209.)

[5] Extensive documentation of the Thetford dispute in Public Record Office, S.P. 12/155/11, 11(II), 11(III), 63, 67, 68; also S.P. 12/138/27.

Contrast this case with that of Ipswich, a wealthy town and a cradle of the Reformation. As early as 1551 the borough records refer to 'the common preacher of the towne'. ('Common', 'ordinary' or 'general' preacher were the terms in Ipswich, never 'lecturer'.) In 1560 the office was revived at an annual salary of £20, soon increased to forty marks. When the first Elizabethan preacher died in 1576 the salary was raised to £50 for his successor, and in the following year it was resolved to support two preachers, at a combined cost of £113. But this proved ambitious and the salaries were later reduced. They depended upon supposedly voluntary contributions, although the bailiffs had power to assess those who refused to pay their share and were even prepared to distrain their goods and to go to law. From time to time the preachers were appointed by patent and a rate levied to cover their wages, but this procedure enjoyed no consensus and the money was always hard to collect. Some of the preachers appointed were drawn away by other opportunities while others were in danger for nonconformity. The only entirely successful appointment was that of the famous Samuel Ward who came to Ipswich in 1605 and survived some dangerous passages, including the ecclesiastical disturbances occasioned by Bishop Wren, to die in office in 1639. Evidently the 'ordinary preacher' of a town like Ipswich was expected to be its principal pastor in a manner reminiscent of the Swiss Reformation. He was bound to preach three times a week, and in 1575 it was said that he should also visit the sick and comfort distressed consciences.[1]

The device of supplying pulpits by means of a roster was no puritan novelty but commended itself wherever there was a call for a regular sermon but no corresponding endowment. The protestantization of cathedrals, such as York Minster in the time of the Edwardian Archbishop Holgate, often involved a statute requiring the dignitaries and prebendaries to preach 'in their course',[2] although such orders were less necessary where, as in

[1] There are numerous entries in N. Bacon's *The Annals of Ipswiche*, ed. W. H. Richardson (Ipswich, 1884), pp. 235–374, and in J. Wodderspoon, *Memorials of the Ancient Town of Ipswich* (Ipswich, 1850), pp. 366–77. The original records (Ipswich & East Suffolk Record Office, Ipswich Borough Records) are more copious. See many entries in the Great Court Book, 1572–1643 and in the Assembly Books covering this period. A 'Book of Enrolments of Apprenticeship, Indentures and Rate Assessments, 1571–1651' includes a number of assessments of the governing body and the inhabitants of parishes for the preachers' wages (in addition to the assessments made to raise the wages paid to the curates of the parish churches under 13 Eliz. I c. 24). From 1585 some of the Treasurer's Accounts record receipts of the very variable sums 'receyved of the collectors for the prechers wages', parish by parish. British Library, Stowe MS. 881 contains a detailed account of the sums delivered to the treasurer by the collectors in 1587–8.

[2] *Visitation Articles and Injunctions of the Period of the Reformation*, ed. W. H. Frere (3 vols., Alcuin Club Collections xiv–xvi, 1910), ii. 312–14; cf. Horne's injunctions for Winchester Cathedral, 1562, Guest's injunctions for Rochester Cathedral, 1565, and Grindal's injunctions for York Cathedral, 1572, *ibid.*, iii. 134–5, 152, 352–4; and the order taken by Grindal in his primary visitation of St. Paul's in 1561, Guildhall Library, Corporation of London, MS. 9537/2 fo. 15.

London at St. Paul's, there was an endowed cathedral lectureship.[1] The
famous sermons preached outside St. Paul's, at Paul's Cross,[2] were also
maintained by preachers 'in their turns', although in this case there was no
roster, it being the function of the bishop of London to look where he could
to ensure a regular supply, one of the least enviable of his responsibilities.[3]
At Norwich, too, there was a tradition of preaching outside the cathedral in
the 'common preaching place', known as the Green Yard, an area furnished
with a covered pulpit, sheltered seating for persons of consequence, and
benches for the common people, who paid a penny or a halfpenny for their
places, which was also the practice at Paul's Cross. But the Green Yard
sermons had no endowment while the cathedral statutes which required
the clergy to preach in turn on Sunday mornings were often disregarded. In
about 1620 a number of Norfolk gentlemen financed 'combination sermons'
to be preached on Sunday afternoons, in the Green Yard. In 1636 Bishop
Wren was regularly in touch with his chancellor on the appointment of
'Green Yard preachers' and on their 'allowance'. It became the custom for
the bishops of Norwich to roster the preachers at the biennial diocesan
synods, from among the Suffolk clergy in the summer, and from the
Norfolk clergy in the winter.[4]

If combination sermons were no more than a mechanism to supply
regular sermons little more would need to be said about their origins. But
in some towns, such as Bury St. Edmunds and Leicester, there was both
a resident preaching ministry, even a town preacher, and a combination
lecture provided by neighbouring ministers besides. This suggests some
other purpose and motive, an interest in the associational character of the
combination, as imparting some element of collegiality to its members. To
appreciate the force and significance of this motive it is necessary to refer
to the prophesyings of Elizabethan days, the forerunners of the combination
lectures and exercises of early Stuart England.[5]

---

[1] Discussed by Seaver, pp. 76–9, who regards cathedral lectureships as a 'collateral
family and a parallel development'.

[2] M. McClure, *The Paul's Cross Sermons, 1534–1642* (Toronto, 1958).

[3] Bishop Ridley charged the future Archbishop Parker to take his day at the Cross
'as ye will answer for the contrary on [sic] to Almighty God, at your own peril',
while 'leaving at this time to charge you with answering for the contrary to the King
and his council'. (*Correspondence of Matthew Parker* (Parker Soc., Cambridge,
1853), p. 45.) But in his primary visitation of 1561 Bishop Grindal established an
'ordo in concionibus habendis ad divi Pauli crucem' which imposed an obligation
on the dean, archdeacons and other dignitaries and on certain of the prebendaries to
preach at the Cross 'ab episcopo Londinenso cum menstrua premonitione assig-
nandis', or to find a substitute, or to pay a fine into a scholarship fund. (Guildhall
Libr., Corporation of London, MS. 9537/2 fo. 15.)

[4] F. Blomefield and C. Parkin, *History of Norfolk* (11 vols., 1805–10), iv. 23, 565;
*Extracts from the Two Earliest Minute Books of the Dean and Chapter of Norwich
Cathedral, 1566–1649*, ed. J. F. Williams and B. Cozens-Hardy (Norfolk Record
Soc., xxiv, 1953), pp. 7, 16; Bishop Wren's notes of letters to his chancellor, Bodl.
Libr., MS. Rawlinson C 368 fos. 3, 6, 10.

[5] P. Collinson, *The Elizabethan Puritan Movement* (1967), pp. 169–76.

An 'exercise of prophecy' was a kind of public conference in the form of two or three sermons, preached in succession on the same text, approached in the course of systematic exposition of some part of Scripture or of some commonplaces in divinity by a company of ministers meeting under a moderator, to whom it fell to summarize and wind up proceedings. Afterwards there was formal 'censure' both of the doctrine preached and of the lives and faults of the members in the context of a conference private to the ministers. As large assemblies, asserting the social ascendancy of protestantism, the prophesyings attracted hostility and were more than once denounced at court. In 1577 they came under the queen's personal and immediate ban, after Archbishop Grindal had declined to convey to his suffragans an order for their suppression.

Prophesying was itself pluralistic in its origins.[1] The name derived from continental practice (and ultimately from St. Paul in 1 Corinthians 14). *Prophezei*, as pioneered in Zürich, was progenitive in many reformed churches of the *kirchenconventen* or *colloques* which served the dual and associated purposes of promoting concord in doctrine and providing machinery for discipline. From these evolved in their turn the *classes* and synods of mature Calvinism. In Elizabethan puritan circles a similar progression can be observed. No doubt English practice was directly imitative. At Southam in Warwickshire an early Elizabethan incumbent was the faithful Swiss associate of Bishop Latimer, Augustine Bernher,[2] and later there was at Southam an exercise 'which of all other without comparison was esteemed the best in this realm'.[3] It was the doings at Southam which directly occasioned the reverse of 1577. Less influential for English practice, in spite of the assumptions of some writers, was the more popular form of congregational prophesying described in the early church orders of François Lambert (for Hesse) and John à Lasco. In English puritan circles prophesying as dialogue was replaced by 'repetition', a process of inculcation.

The Elizabethan prophesyings were also extensions or elaborations of the orders made at various levels of authority in the Church for the further education of the unlearned, non-graduate clergy.[4] At their simplest, these

---

[1] A fuller account of these origins will be found in my unpublished London Ph.D. thesis, 'The puritan classical movement in the reign of Elizabeth I' (1957), pp. 175–96.

[2] It was from Southam that Bernher introduced his 1562 edition of certain of Latimer's sermons. (*Sermons by Hugh Latimer*, ed. G. E. Corrie (Parker Soc., Cambridge, 1844), pp. 311–25.) Dr. O'Day drew my attention to Bernher's connection with Southam.

[3] *Letters of Thomas Wood, Puritan, 1566–77*, ed. P. Collinson (Bull. Inst. Hist. Research, Special Supplement v, 1960), p. 17. *See above*, p. 99.

[4] The evolution of these orders can be traced from Bishop Hooper's practice in the diocese of Gloucester in 1550 (*Later Writings* (Parker Soc., Cambridge, 1852), pp. 131–2) through the Royal Injunctions of 1559 and Archbishop Parker's Advertisements of 1566 (*Visitation Articles and Injunctions*, iii. 13–14, 178) and the Canons of 1571 (E. Cardwell, *Synodalia* (2 vols., Oxford, 1842), i. 117) to the orders made by Bishop Cooper of Lincoln in the 1570s which appear to have been seminal;

orders, the responsibility, primarily, of the archdeacons, provided for the performance of written tasks, 'exercises'. But arrangements for the invigilation and correction of the work presupposed a coming together which in some jurisdictions, notably in London under its first Elizabethan archdeacon, John Mullins, and in the diocese of Durham under Bishop Barnes, was institutionalized into a regular quasi-synodal meeting, lasting two or three days.[1] In the archdeaconry of St. Albans the exercise of prophesying grew directly out of a similar arrangement, and in Essex, Kent and the diocese of Lincoln the oversight of written tasks was provided for within the framework of prophesying.[2] Such an 'exercise' was essentially a school of preaching, which the unlearned were bound to attend,[3] under the authority of perpetual moderators, and where they might hope to advance their gifts. Other prophesyings approximated to the model of a more or less voluntary and equal association of established preachers in which the office of moderator circulated among the whole company.[4] No doubt the secular movement was towards the freer and more equal society, as clerical standards rose and as the proportion of non-graduates and non-preachers diminished.

The suppression of the prophesyings led, in institutional terms, to a process of fission. One consequence, outside the scope of this enquiry, was the emergence in the fifteen-eighties of clandestine conferences, not associated with any common preaching enterprise, and resembling the *classes* and synods of Calvinist church order.[5] On the other hand, assemblies resem-

---

(*Elizabethan Episcopal Administration*, ed. W. P. M. Kennedy (3 vols., Alcuin Club Collections xxv–xxvii, 1924), ii. 45–6; *The State of the Church in the Diocese of Lincoln*, ed. C. W. Foster (Lincoln Record Soc., xxiii, 1926), pp. xix–xxi). In 1584 Archbishop Whitgift promised the house of commons to 'devise some kinde of exercise . . . more private', a promise fulfilled in 'Certaine orders for the increase of learning in the unlearned sort of ministers', promulgated in 1585 and perfected by Convocation in 1587 as 'Certaine orders for the better increase of learning in the inferior ministers and for more diligent preaching and catechising'. (Inner Temple Library, MS. Petyt 538/38, fo. 79; *Records of the Old Archdeaconry of St. Albans*, ed. H. R. Wilton Hall (St. Albans and Herts. Archit. & Archaeol. Soc., 1908), pp. 21, 45, 49–50; *The State of the Church*, p. xx; J. Strype, *Life of Whitgift* (3 vols., Oxford, 1822), iii. 194–6.)

[1] Mullins's practice described in a letter to Bishop Sandys, 1576, Lambeth Palace Libr., MS. 2003 fos. 23–4; for Barnes's orders, *The Injunctions and Other Ecclesiastical Proceedings of Richard Barnes, Bishop of Durham* (Surtees Soc., xxii, 1850), pp. 70–97 and *Elizabethan Episcopal Administration*, ii. 75.

[2] For the practice in Essex and St. Albans archdeaconries, letters from Archdeacons Walker and Kemp to Sandys, July 1576, Lambeth Palace Libr., MS. 2003 fos. 12–13, 16–19; for the practice in Kent, Cathedral Archives and Library, Canterbury, MS. Z.5.1, fos. 166v–167, 169v–171; for the Lincoln practice, Lambeth Palace Libr., MS. 2007 fos. 106–9.

[3] E.g. by Cooper of Lincoln (*Lincoln Episcopal Records in the Time of Thomas Cooper*, ed. C. W. Foster (Lincoln Record Soc., ii, 1912), p. 114) and by Scambler of Peterborough (Brit. Libr., Lansdowne MS. 21 no. 2 fo. 4).

[4] Especially the Norwich order of 1575, *sede vacante*; printed, John Browne, *History of Congregationalism in Norfolk and Suffolk* (1877), pp. 18–20.

[5] Collinson, *Elizabethan Puritan Movement*, pp. 222–39, 291–329; *The Presbyterian Movement in the Reign of Queen Elizabeth*, ed. R. G. Usher (Camden 3rd ser., viii, 1905).

bling the prophesyings to the extent that a number of sermons were preached on the same occasion continued to be held under the name of fasts. These were observed on occasions, without the regularity of the prophesyings or, for that matter, of the fasts held at Westminster and in the country in the years of the Long Parliament. Fasts, too, were diverse in origin, owing something to the international practice of the reformed churches, something to official orders requiring solemn days of prayer and preaching in response to a visitation of the plague or other evidence of divine displeasure.[1] One of their peculiarities was that they seem as a matter of course to have involved the offering of money for some religious or charitable purpose.[2] In a number of centres associated with prophesying in the fifteen-seventies, among them Southam,[3] fasts were held in subsequent decades. Invariably they are indicative of advanced, radical puritanism. They were unauthorized, and after 1604 the appointing of such occasions was clearly reserved to the bishop, under Canon 72. It was said of Thomas Taylor of Reading, who died in 1632, that he was noted for 'keeping fasts among the godly of the place, which in those daies was something a dangerous exercise'.[4] But in some areas, notably in the north-west, the puritans learned to hold their fasts on the Church holy days, when large assemblies would arouse less suspicion.[5]

With fasts and the rich variety of other occasions for assembly exploited by the puritans, days of thanksgiving, days of conference, general communions and funerals, this essay is not concerned. Nor does it deal with the many lectures and weekday sermons offered by individual preachers, whether as beneficed clergy or as stipendiary lecturers, or more casually by itinerant 'running lecturers'. That is another and sufficiently extensive topic, explored by Dr. Hill, Dr. Seaver, and the authorities on the Feoffees for the Purchase of Impropriations.[6] Our interest is restricted to the exercises and lectures by combination which also survived from the débâcle of 1577.

Moderate reformers or even those, like Francis Bacon, who merely favoured 'the peace of the Church', sometimes expressed the hope that meetings of ministers for conference and exercise, without a popular

---

[1] Collinson, 'Puritan classical movement', pp. 323-46.

[2] E.g., it was charged against Samuel Greenaway that as curate of Tibbenham in Norfolk in 1584 he had 'appoynted solemne fastes for reformation to be had etc. and gathered mony of such as came to the sermons of other townes, which he bestowed as pleased himselfe'. (Norfolk & Norwich Record Office, Norfolk & Norwich Archaeol. Soc. MSS., MS. Frere K.12(A).)

[3] M. R. O'Day, 'Clerical patronage and recruitment in England in the Elizabethan and early Stuart periods, with special reference to the diocese of Coventry and Lichfield', unpublished London Ph.D. thesis (1972), p. 315. I am grateful to Dr. O'Day for permission to cite her thesis.

[4] S. Clarke, The lives of two and twenty English divines (1660), p. 158.

[5] S. Clarke, The lives of sundry eminent persons in this later age (1683), p. 63.

[6] Isabel M. Calder, Activities of the Puritan Faction of the Church of England, 1625-33 (1957); E. W. Kirby, 'The lay feoffees: a study in militant Puritanism', Journal of Modern History, xiv (1942), 1-25.

auditory, might escape proscription,[1] and the view was sometimes taken that such meetings were not in fact disallowed in the queen's letter. Such was the plea of the ministers who were prosecuted in the High Commission and the Star Chamber in 1590–1 for holding classical assemblies, and who alleged that conferences 'were allowed by many bishops within their dioceses and to our knowledge never disallowed or forbidden by any'; 'as namely in the dioceses of Litchfield and Coventrie and of Chichester', Thomas Cartwright assured Archbishop Whitgift.[2] As in the past, these conferences were associated with public preaching, but with this difference, that after 1577 the congregation was confronted by a single preacher rather than by the panel of the prophesying.

Meanwhile the northern province (which in any case was not touched by the royal ban of 1577) was the scene of an independent development, commencing only in 1583. The initiative of certain 'preachers of the diocese of Chester', among them the veteran publicist Christopher Goodman, assisted by the privy council and not resisted by the bishop of Chester, led to the introduction of monthly exercises in the 'middle town' of every deanery throughout that extensive diocese, thirteen centres in all.[3] The form of these proceedings was a sermon *ad clerum*, followed by 'exercise', the learned sort speaking, the mean sort taking notes, and last of all a sermon for the people. Attendance was general, and enforced.[4] Within the next twenty years, regular exercises, perhaps of a more informal kind, spread to other parts of the North.[5] When the Canons of 1604 brought such practices under regulation (in Canon 72) what were called 'meetings for sermons, commonly termed by some prophecies or exercises, in market-towns, or other places' were not absolutely forbidden, as they must have been in any document to which Queen Elizabeth would have put her name, but were subordinated to 'the license and direction of the bishop of the diocese first obtained and had under his hand and seal'.[6]

From one of the most thriving scenes of early seventeenth-century religious life, the country which Bishop Joseph Hall called 'that sweet and

---

[1] Francis Bacon, 'An Advertisement Touching the Controversies of the Church of England', in *Letters and Life of Francis Bacon*, ed. J. Spedding (7 vols., 1861–74), i. 88; Bishop Cox to Burghley, 12 June 1577, Brit. Libr., Lansd. MS. 25 no. 29 fo. 61; Thomas Norton in his 'Devices' of 1581, Brit. Libr., Add. MS. 48023 fo. 56.

[2] Brit. Libr., Add. MS. 48064 fos. 102, 221v; Lansd. MS. 72 no. 49 fo. 138. For the trial which formed the context for this plea, see Collinson, *Elizabethan Puritan Movement*, pp. 403–31.

[3] Chester (Bangor, Chester & Wirral deaneries), Macclesfield (Macclesfield deanery), Nantwich (Nantwich & Malpas deaneries), Northwich (Fordham & Middlewich deaneries), Prescot (Warrington deanery), Bury (Manchester deanery), Padiham (Blackburn deanery), Preston (Amondersham & Leyland deaneries), Richmond (Richmond deanery), Bedale (Catterick deanery), Egremont (Copeland deanery), Kendal (Kendal deanery) and Ulverston (Furness deanery).

[4] R. C. Richardson, *Puritanism in North-West England: a Regional Study of the Diocese of Chester to 1642* (Manchester, 1972), pp. 65–9; Collinson, 'Puritan classical movement', pp. 265–9.

[5] Below, pp. 201–2.   [6] Cardwell, *Synodalia*, i. 287–8.

civil county of Suffolk, near to St. Edmunds Bury',[1] evidence survives to
confirm the substantial continuity of prophesying, exercise and combination
lecture throughout the years from 1572 to 1636. In the latter year, Bishop
Matthew Wren confirmed and regulated, according to Laudian ecclesiastical
practice, the two single lectures preached at Bury on Wednesday and Friday
(the one in St. Mary's, the other in St. James's church) and a lecture conducted on Monday, market day, by 'a combination of neighbouring divines'.
In consenting to the combination lecture, Wren 'allowed' fifty 'choise
divines inhabiting within that archdeaconry', upon stringent conditions
which, or so he reported, were 'joyfully and duely performed'.[2] In the
sixteen-twenties another bishop, Samuel Harsnet, had taken similar steps
to regulate the Monday combination lecture, insisting that it be confined to
'these preachers by us named and allowed'.[3] The rhythm of Monday, Wednesday and Friday lectures was evidently one of long continuance, and it
seems plausible to derive the Monday lecture from 'the godlye exercise of
expounding the scriptures by the way of prophecie' which Bishop Parkhurst
had allowed at Bury in 1573, upon the request of 'sundrye godly and well
learned persons, aswell of the clergie as other wies'.[4] Soon after this the
exercises throughout the diocese were called in question,[5] and three years
later came the general order for their suppression. The years which followed
witnessed religious divisions and disturbances in Bury, when Parkhurst's
successor, Edmund Freke, came into confrontation with the preachers
and puritan gentry of West Suffolk. With the assize judges opposing the
preachers and their supporters (who could count on support from the
privy council, however) this grew to a major 'country cause' to which,
for a time, the preaching ministry in Bury succumbed altogether.[6]

Yet in the aftermath of this affair we find Bishop Freke referring to 'the
moderators of the exercise within each deanerye by us lately appoynted'.[7]

[1] *The Works of Joseph Hall*, ed. P. Wynter (10 vols., Oxford, 1863), i, p. xxviii.

[2] Wren's 'account touching the roiall instructions', 7 Dec. 1636, P.R.O., S.P.
16/337/19. Wren referred to his action in answering the 16th art. of impeachment
in 1641 (C. Wren, *Parentalia* (1750), p. 100) and Archbishop Laud also alluded to
the Bury exercise in answering the articles of impeachment against himself (*Works
of William Laud* (7 vols., Oxford, 1847–60), iv. 301). The activities of Wren's commissioners in Bury in Apr. 1636 are further documented in Bodl. Libr., MS. Tanner
68 fos. 41, 43, 45, 92 and in MS. Tanner 92 fo. 9v.

[3] Bodl. Libr., MS. Tanner 137 fo. 3, endorsed without date by Wren: 'Orders
prescribed by Bishop Harsnett to the lecturers at Bury St. Edmunds'. Harsnet was
bishop of Norwich from 1619 to 1628.

[4] Cambridge University Library, MS. Ee.11.34 fo. 106.

[5] A brief account in Collinson, *Elizabethan Puritan Movement*, pp. 191–2 and the
full story in Collinson, 'Puritan classical movement', pp. 201–7. See also Dr. R.
Houlbrooke's forthcoming edn. of Parkhurst's letter book (Cambridge Univ. Libr.,
MS. Ee.11.34) in the Norfolk Record Soc. series.

[6] Collinson, 'Puritan classical movement', pp. 881–929, followed by J. S. Cockburn, *A History of English Assizes 1558–1714* (Cambridge, 1972), pp. 199–206.

[7] Freke to the archdeacon of Sudbury, 6 Jan. 1583(/4?); no longer extant but
printed, *Suffolk Institute of Archaeol. & Natural Hist. Proc.*, ii (1859), 40. The
reference to 'moderators' is incidental to the main purpose of the letter, which

In the absence of any context for this statement one can only assume that it has to do with the 'exercises' for the further education of the unlearned clergy, although 'moderator' is a term otherwise unknown in this connection. However, it appears probable that from the mid fifteen-eighties, at the latest, there was a regular preaching exercise with conference, held at Bury St. Edmunds on Mondays. A number of printed works published in 1590, 1593 and 1603 had their origin in sermons preached in the Bury exercise,[1] and to this list should no doubt be added the first edition of a famous work on the Sabbath by Nicholas Bownd, rector of Norton, six miles from Bury, which he tells us arose from a course of sermons on the Ten Commandments delivered in about 1586.[2]

There is fugitive evidence from 1590 concerning another Suffolk minister, Thomas Rogers,[3] rector of Horringer (Horningsheath), some two miles from Bury, the most prolific author among the Suffolk clergy of his generation, but an Oxford man and a conformist, at odds with his puritanical Cambridge neighbours. In that year Rogers complained to Archdeacon John Still of Sudbury of 'that shamefull (as themselves cal it) secluding me from the Berie exercise' and of complaints against himself to the bishop from 'no lesse than ten of the chiefest ministers of the faction in Suffolk'.[4] Such was the consequence of a sermon preached by Rogers, probably while taking his turn in the exercise, which attacked a notorious presbyterian sermon ascribed to Laurence Chaderton, and which was subsequently published.[5] It is no doubt with the same episode that we should link certain 'articles drawen according to the verie thoughts of the classical brethren for the wel-managing of theire Mondaie exercise at Burie', and a 'narrative' of

concerns an enquiry into 'unsound' schoolmasters and the education of the children of recusants required by the bishop of London in response to an order from the privy council to the archbishop of Canterbury.

[1] Below, pp. 495–11

[2] N. Bownd, *The doctrine of the sabbath plainely layde forth* (1595). An epistle 'to the godlie and christian readers, and namely to the reverend, wise and godly learned fathers and brethren, ministers and preachers of the gospell' refers to 'when as about nine yeeres since' the author was solicited to publish his sermons 'by certeine of my godly brethren, auditors then of the same'. (Sig. A3.)

[3] Best known as author of *The English creede* (1585), revised in 1607 as *The Faith, doctrine and religion professed and protected in the realm of England* and republished by the Parker Soc. as *The Catholic Doctrine of the Church of England* (Cambridge, 1854). His writings are discussed in P. Collinson, 'The beginnings of English Sabbatarianism', *Studies in Church History*, i, ed. C. W. Dugmore and C. Duggan (1964). *See above*, pp. 441-3.

[4] Rogers published in 1590 a pamphlet called *Miles christianus* which attacked another Suffolk minister, Miles Mosse, for remarks in the preface to a published catechism (no longer extant) which complained of the multiplicity of modern writings, and which Rogers may have thought detrimental to himself. The Brit. Libr. copy of this tract (C.124.c.7, reclassified from 4108.bbb.26) is interleaved and contains much additional matter in MS., apparently in Rogers's hand, together with the draft of a letter to the archdeacon of Sudbury, 8 June (1590 ?), from which this information comes.

[5] T. Rogers, *A sermon . . . made to the confutation of another sermon* (1590).

an 'exercise or disputation' held among certain ministers on 1 April 1590, a Sunday.[1] Nothing daunted, Rogers returned to the attack against his puritan brethren in a sermon on 10 December 1599 in which the word 'Sabbatarian' was used, perhaps for the very first time.[2] December 10 was a Monday, which makes it likely that this calculated attack on the new Sabbatarianism was made in the same forum which had served Nicholas Bownd to introduce the doctrine thirteen years before.

In the later fifteen-nineties the town preacher of Bury St. Edmunds was a youthful prodigy, George Estey. It is likely that some at least of the *Certaine godly and learned expositions* of Estey, published posthumously in 1603, were first heard in the Bury exercise. After Estey's premature death, the position of 'public preacher' was offered to Joseph Hall, the future bishop of Exeter,[3] but upon his declining it passed to one of the most distinguished scholars and divines of the coming age, the future bishop of Kilmore, William Bedell. In October 1604 we find Bedell informing a correspondent of what he had said 'in some meetings where by the cheife of our company I have been enforced to take the place of the respondent'. When Bishop Jegon regulated the weekly sermons or exercises in various market towns of the diocese in 1609, it was provided that 'the minister in everye towne, if he be a preacher' was to be 'first and cheefe'. For Bury we find the entry: 'Mr Bedle and 12 others'.[4] Eleven years later, Sir Simonds D'Ewes recorded an early departure for his Suffolk home on a Monday morning in May in order to take in Bury *en route*.

My kind friend Mr Gibson, pastor of Kediton, was the forenoon to preach at Bury St Edmunds in the same county (it being his course in a weekly exercise held there by divers country ministers on the Monday or market-day).[5]

Twelve years later still in 1632, midway between the attempts of Bishop Harsnet and Bishop Wren to bring the Bury lecture into line, there was a minor crisis in the affairs of the exercise which reveals something of its inner life. A 'Mr Catlin' (no doubt Zachary Catelyn, vicar of Thurston, four miles from Bury) preceded his sermon on Shrove Monday with a proposal that 'the ministers of the combination' should meet 'to consulte

---

[1] These are titles of certain 'Ecclesiastical Miscellanies', a Selden MS. offered for sale by Messrs. Puttick & Simpson, 6 June 1859, the present location of which is unknown. I owe this information from the sale catalogue to Dr. A. Hassell Smith. Rogers was Archbishop Bancroft's chaplain and the titles are reminiscent of Bancroft's own polemical style. Bancroft had earlier preached in Bury against the puritans. (*Tracts Ascribed to Richard Bancroft*, ed. A. Peel (Cambridge, 1953), pp. 71–3.)

[2] Brit. Libr., Add. MS. 38492 fo. 104. For the calculation, see the preface to Rogers, *The Catholic Doctrine of the Church of England*, pp. 17–20.

[3] Hall, *Works*, p. xxxiii.

[4] *A True Relation of the Life and Death of . . . William Bedell*, ed. T. W. Jones (Camden new ser., iv, 1872), pp. 6–23; Bedell to Samuel Ward, 16 Oct. 1604, Bodl. Libr., MS. Tanner 75 fos. 126–7; *The Registrum Vagum of Anthony Harison*, i, ed. T. F. Barton (Norfolk Record Soc., xxxii, 1963), p. 97.

[5] *The Autobiography and Correspondence of Sir Simonds D'Ewes*, ed. J. O. Halliwell (2 vols., 1845), i. 142.

of the making of the combination, that those ministers that wold
doe good might be put in seasonably for it'. Apparently Catelyn had been
obliged to preach '*ex improviso*' after 'a newe-come minister' had been put
in first in the combination, but had declined 'to goe before the graver
preachers', leaving the day unprovided for. Catelyn hoped that by filling
the gap he could be relieved from his ordinary turn, but this had been
disallowed.[1] This suggests that conference among the ministers was no
longer as regular as it had been, and that some of the spirit of voluntary
enthusiasm had evaporated, perhaps as the consequence of Bishop Harsnet's
intervention. At Christmas 1635, as Bishop Wren reported, the combination
lapsed of itself, and only began again after a formal approach to himself.[2]

The happy accidents which have preserved some sort of continuous
record for the Bury exercise cannot be matched for any other centre. But
a broadly consistent picture of continuity and growth will emerge from a
listing of the known centres of prophesying in the fifteen-seventies, followed
by a tally of market towns where some record survives of combination
lectures in the early decades of the following century. Prophesying had
been established in a majority of dioceses in the southern province, although
absent from most parts of the province of York, and from Wales, and unknown, at least to the authorities, in the dioceses of Ely and Salisbury; while
for the dioceses of Bristol, Oxford and Worcester we have no information.
Prophesyings are known to have flourished in Nottinghamshire; in several
market towns of Lincolnshire, including Grantham; at Stamford, Leicester,
Ashby-de-la-Zouch, Northampton, Oundle, Oakham and Uppingham, and
at Huntingdon; at Coventry and Southam; at Shrewsbury; at Bedford; at
Aylesbury, Welwyn, St. Albans and other centres in Hertfordshire and
Buckinghamshire; at Norwich, Holt, Wiveton and Fakenham in Norfolk;
at Bury St. Edmunds and Eye in Suffolk; at Colchester, Chelmsford,
Horndon-on-the-Hill, Maldon, Brentwood and Rochford in Essex; on a
deanery basis in the diocese of Canterbury and also in the diocese of
Rochester, in Surrey, Sussex and Devon; in two places in the diocese of
Gloucester; briefly, at two or three places in the diocese of Hereford; and
for a time at Bruton, in Somerset.[3]

---

[1] *Diary of John Rous, Incumbent of Santon Downham, Suffolk, 1625–42*, ed. M. A.
E. Green (Camden Soc., lxvi, 1856), pp. 68–9.

[2] P.R.O., S.P. 16/337/19; Wren, p. 100.

[3] Evidence collected in Collinson, *Elizabethan Puritan Movement*, pp. 171–6, and
in 'Puritan classical movement', pp. 182–201. The most important source is a collection of episcopal letters (together with reports to the bishop of London from four
archdeacons) prompted by Archbishop Grindal in 1576. (Lambeth Palace Libr.,
MS. 2003 fos. 1–34; 18th-cent. copies of most of these with a letter from the
bishop of Gloucester, not otherwise preserved, in Brit. Libr., Add. MS. 29546 fos.
36–57; extracts from the correspondence in Lambeth Palace Libr., MS. 2003 fos.
35–6 and in Brit. Libr., MS. Add. 21565 fo. 26, adding information from four letters
no longer extant.) Orders from Bishop Cooper's diocese of Lincoln for Bedford and
Hertfordshire are in Lambeth Palace Libr., MS. 2007 fos. 106–9 and for Buckinghamshire in Cambridge Univ. Libr., MS. Ff. 5.14 fo. 85. Most but not all of the

It appears unlikely that Bury St. Edmunds can have been the only town in East Anglia to perpetuate the traditions of the prophesying in an exercise or combination lecture. Between 1606 and 1614 Bishop Jegon of Norwich employed the procedure assumed by the 72nd Canon by giving formal allowance to sermons or exercises to be held weekly or fortnightly on market days in nine centres of the diocese: in Norfolk, at North Walsham, Diss, Wighton, Fakenham and Hingham; and in Suffolk at Bungay, Framlingham and Botesdale, as well as at Bury. This cannot all have been virgin soil. From North Walsham, Fakenham and Hingham there is evidence of local pressure to which the bishop responded, and there are reports of earlier activity at Fakenham and also at Wiveton, in an area much affected by the patronage of the puritan Nathaniel Bacon, son of Sir Nicholas. From one of these letters there is a reminder that even in Jacobean England the prime justification for a combination lecture could be the famine of preaching and consequent ignorance, for around Swaffham the people were said to be 'more rude then easilie will be believed to be of those that have been brought up in more civil places, the greater part of them utterlie destitute of teaching ministers'. Jegon and his officers favoured a uniform order which associated with each exercise the minister of the leading town as 'first and cheefe', with twelve other preachers, imposing a quarterly obligation on each. The documents list the names of the thirteen preachers for North Walsham, the thirteen for Fakenham, six for Hingham, fifteen for Botesdale and nineteen for Framlingham.[1] How long these arrangements continued is uncertain. From D'Ewes we hear in 1631 of 'a constant lecture of neighbouring min-

Lambeth documents have been printed, but with serious errors of transcription, in S.E. Lehmberg, 'Archbishop Grindal and the Prophesyings', *Historical Magazine of the Protestant Episcopal Church*, xxiv (1965), 100–1. The orders for the exercises in Grindal's own diocese (but set up in Archbishop Parker's time and perhaps suppressed by Parker before his death) are recorded in Henry Sutton's Precedent and Formula Book (Canterbury Cathedral Archives, MS. Z.5.1), together with 'the order of our prophisyenge at Aye' (i.e. Eye) (fo. 166) which is otherwise unknown and a copy of the order for Buckinghamshire. They are: 'Artycles agreed uppon by the mynysters of the deanryes of Sandwiche and others for due or orderle exercise or conference to be hadd emongeste them' (fos. 166–7), 'Certen articles agreed uppon by the ministers of the deaneryes of Ospringe and Sittingbourne', dated 22 May 1572 (fo. 169v), seven articles headed 'Decanat. Sandwich' (fo. 170) containing orders for a monthly exercise in Sandwich and subscribed on 19 May 1572 by 15 ministers, and 'Certen agrementes agreed uppon by all the ministers within the deaneryes of Lympne and Charinge', dated 7 May 1572 and bearing 24 names with titles and benefices (fos. 170v–171). I am indebted to Mr. P. A. Clark who drew this MS. to my attention.

[1] *Registrum Vagum*, i. 96–103. There is an undated letter to a bishop of Norwich among Nathaniel Bacon's papers from 9 ministers of the neighbourhood of Stiffkey. It refers to an exercise of preaching continued in Wiveton for 15 years and 'mayntayned by severall ministers dwelling thereabouts'. It requests allowance for 'the like exercise to be erected upon the Tuesday as before at Bynham or Langham'. Biographical evidence seems to place it between 1596 and 1603, in the time of Bishop Redman. (*The Official Papers of Sir Nathaniel Bacon*, ed. H. W. Saunders (Camden 3rd ser., xxvi, 1915), pp. 189–90.)

isters' at Lavenham, held weekly on Tuesday, market day.[1] Yet when Bishop Wren applied pressure to the lectures in the diocese of Norwich five years later nothing more was heard of Lavenham, and apart from Bury the only survivals from Bishop Jegon's time were the lectures at Diss, and less certainly, at North Walsham and Bungay. On the other hand, Wren contended with a more recently established combination lecture at New Buckenham, and commended his new orders for Bury as a model to petitioners at Haverhill and Debenham in Suffolk and East Harling and Wymondham in Norfolk, which implies some activity of this kind at these centres before his arrival on the scene. At Ixworth in Suffolk there was a lecture 'started up by Sir William Spring within these four years', which appears to have been a combination lecture. Archbishop Laud later reported, perhaps inaccurately or incompletely, that Wren had reduced the lectures in his diocese to those 'performed by conformable and neighbouring divines' at Wymondham, North Walsham, East Harling, Norwich, Lynn and Bungay.[2]

From the Midlands there is evidence of a persistent tradition of preaching exercises in an area overlapping the common borders of Leicestershire, Derbyshire and Staffordshire. The ministers at Ashby-de-la-Zouch, a famous puritan centre secure under the wing of the Hastings family, had protested at the suppression of the prophesyings,[3] and stray evidence from the later fifteen-nineties of continuing exercises in this vicinity comes as no surprise.[4] The great names in this country in the early years of the seventeenth century were those of Arthur Hildersham and William Bradshaw, who are said to have been the principal upholders of the 'two famous exercises' at Burton-on-Trent and Repton, and of the continuing exercise at Ashby.[5] Burton and Repton lay within the jurisdiction of the bishop of Coventry and Lichfield, and the exercises consequently benefited from the easy government of Bishop William Overton, whose friendship could be bought with a present of venison, and who had been in the diocese for almost thirty years when he died in 1609. When Richard Neile became the diocesan in 1611 the Burton and Repton exercises were put down, at least

[1] *Autobiography of Sir Simonds D'Ewes*, ii. 31.

[2] This conflates much information, not entirely consistent, in the Tanner MSS. in Bodl. Libr., and especially in MS. Tanner 68; also Wren's notes of his correspondence in Bodl. Libr., MS. Rawlinson C 368; Wren's 'account touching the roiall instructions', P.R.O., S.P. 16/337/19; Laud's accounts to the king for 1636 and 1637, in *Works*, v. 340, 350; and Wren's answers to the articles of impeachment, *Parentalia*, pp. 100–1. Mention is found in these sources of single lectures at Beccles, Bury St. Edmunds, Cockfield, East Bergholt, Ipswich, Middleton, Walpole, Westleton, Wickham Market and Woodbridge in Suffolk, and at Lynn, Norwich, Thetford and Yarmouth in Norfolk.

[3] Brit. Libr., Add. MS. 27632 fos. 47–51.

[4] The evidence is in the pamphlets conveying the controversy surrounding the activities of the puritan exorcist, John Darrell (below, p. 489). See esp. S. Harsnet, *A discovery of the fraudulent practises of John Darrel* (1599), pp. 2, 270–1.

[5] Life of Hildersham in S. Clarke, *A generall martyrologie* (1651), pp. 377–8; Thomas Gataker's Life of Bradshaw in Clarke, *Lives of two and twenty English divines*, p. 66. The Darrell literature contains a reference to 'the common exercise' held on Mondays at Burton (Harsnet, pp. 270–1).

for the time being.[1] Neile passed on to Lincoln, and two years later he instructed the officers who conducted his primary visitation to make particular enquiries about the 'public lectures' in that diocese.

In due course Neile was informed[2] about a total of ten lectures of the combination type: in Lincolnshire, at Grantham, Market Rasen, Lowth, Grimsby, Alford and Horncastle; and in other parts of the diocese at Leicester, Huntingdon, Berkhampstead and Aylesbury. The report includes in addition a remarkable account of the single-handed ministry at Boston of that 'extraordinary Paraclete that could not erre', the young John Cotton. The names of the ministers supplying the Lincolnshire lectures (only) were given: seventy-two in all.[3] It is likely that most if not all of these exercises were long-established. In 1590 Thomas Cartwright had informed Whitgift that 'in Lincolne diocese sermons were appointed as I have heard to be made by divers ministers in sundry market townes, . . . by which occasion the ministers did usually meet and conferre together'.[4] Some of the lectures had come under suspicion in the time of Neile's predecessor, Bishop Barlow, when the Huntingdon lecture had been suppressed,[5] and a suit for a new lecture at Sleaford disallowed. The monthly Leicester lecture, which was questioned under Barlow, was said at that time, 1611, to have continued for forty years and more. It survived both Barlow and Neile, for in 1618 a sermon was published which had been preached at 'the ordinary monthly lecture' in that year.[6]

Given the strong tradition of Elizabethan puritanism in Northamptonshire,[7] and the classical meetings kept for some time around Northampton, Kettering and Daventry, one would expect to find evidence of combination lectures in this county. The lecture at Daventry, satirized in famous verses by Bishop Corbet,[8] was probably a lecture of this type. At Kettering there was certainly a combination lecture, where the future Archbishop John Williams took his turn when still a Northamptonshire rector in the second

[1] So much is clear from the Life of Hildersham.

[2] Copies of the report in Cambridge Univ. Libr., MS. Baumgartner 8 fos. 220–2 and in Lincoln, Dean & Chapter MS. A 4/3/43, from where printed in *Associated Architectural Societies Reports & Papers*, xvi (1881), 31–54.

[3] Grantham 14; Market Rasen 7; Lowth 12; Grimsby 9; Alford 12; Horncastle 20. One lecturer (David Allen) was a member of three combinations.

[4] Brit. Libr., Add. MS. 48064 fo. 221v.

[5] Its place was taken in later years by a single lecture. See Thomas Beard's remarks in the dedication to the mayor, aldermen and burgesses of Huntingdon of the 1631 edn. of his *Theatre of gods iudgements* and Laud's account of his province for 1633, *Works*, v. 321.

[6] *Records of the Borough of Leicester, 1603–88*, ed. H. Stocks (Cambridge, 1923), p. 115; A.Cade, *Saint Paules agonie. A sermon preached at Leicester at the ordinary monthly lecture* (1618). I am grateful to Canon G. J. Cuming for drawing my attention to this sermon.

[7] Recently explored in the unpublished London Ph.D. thesis by William Sheils, 'The Puritans in church and politics in the diocese of Peterborough, 1570–1610' (1974).

[8] *Poems of Richard Corbett*, pp. 32–3.

decade of the century,[1] and which was later associated with the literary works of three members of the combination, Robert Bolton, Joseph Bentham and Nicholas Estwick.[2] This circle enjoyed the patronage of a leading county family, the Montagues, but by January 1637 the lecture had nevertheless been suppressed and Bishop Dee of Peterborough wrote to Lord Montague explaining as man to man why he could not be an active agent for its revival.[3] In Rutland, an exercise which still flourished at Oakham in 1583, perhaps with the participation of most of the preachers of the county,[4] was succeeded in the sixteen-twenties by a single lecture preached by Jeremiah Whitaker, who was also 'a principal prop to hold up some other lectures in the neighbourhood'.[5] In 1589–90, Bishop Howland of Peterborough bound both clergy and lay people to attend the continuing exercise at Oundle, an episode not easy to square with what is otherwise known of episcopal policies in this period.[6] Even at Peterborough itself, where the episcopal presence had maintained an unexceptional conformity over the years,[7] there was a regular combination, in 1629 if in no other year.[8] And at Brackley, in the same diocese, and as late as 1639, the bishop responded to a petition of the inhabitants by promulgating orders for a tightly regulated combination of fifteen named ministers.[9]

In neighbouring Oxfordshire, the town of Banbury (a byword for puritanism) had a lecture associated with famous divines, including John Dod of Hanwell, William Whateley, first preacher and then vicar of Banbury, Robert Cleaver, rector of Drayton until his deprivation in 1606 and death in 1609, Henry Scudder his successor, and Robert Harris, Dod's successor at Hanwell and later Master of Trinity College, Oxford. Harris belonged to another combination at Deddington, six miles to the south of Banbury.[10]

Elsewhere in the southern province, scattered references may be gathered.

[1] J. Hacket, *Scrinia Resarata* (1693), pt. I, p. 34.
[2] Below, pp. 211–12.
[3] Hist. MSS. Comm., *Buccleuch MSS. (Montagu House)*, i. 275.
[4] T. Gibson, *A fruitful sermon preched at Occham in the county of Rutland, the second of November 1583* (1584). This was a sermon preached *ad clerum* which taught the doctrine that non-preaching ministers were no ministers at all, and on that account was 'in the country where I dwell, openly slaundered and evill spoken of'. (Sig. A 6.) See also these words (Sigs. C 5v–6): 'Amongst us, and such others as use this place, and such like places, there is difference, everye one of us have not the like measure. . . . To you that have any measure of these gifts, which the Lord requireth in his ministers, to you (I say) . . .'.
[5] First as schoolmaster of Oakham then as rector of Stretton. See Life of Whitaker in Clarke, *Lives of thirty-two English divines*, p. 265, and its source in Whitaker's funeral sermon, S. Ashe, *Living loves betwixt Christ and dying christians* (1654), pp. 50–6.
[6] Sheils, pp. 197–9. I am grateful to Dr. Sheils for permission to cite his thesis.
[7] Noted at several points in Dr. Sheils's thesis.
[8] *Peterborough Local Administration, 1541–1689*, ed. W. T. Mellows (Northants. Record Soc., x, 1937), pp. 55–6.
[9] W. Prynne, *Canterburies doome* (1646), pp. 378–80.
[10] Clarke, *A generall martyrologie*, p. 405; Clarke, *Lives of thirty-two English divines*, p. 320.

In Laud's time there was a combination lecture every Saturday at Ashford in Kent, another ancient puritan centre.[1] There were combination lectures at Guildford and at Dorking,[2] and at Kingston-on-Thames, where some time after 1628 Dr. Edmund Staunton set up a weekly lecture 'which was supplyed, in their turns, by as eminent ministers as those parts of England did afford'.[3] It looks as if a combination lecture was established in Reading, Laud's home town, in 1629, at the instance at least in part of Bishop Davenant of Salisbury.[4] At Marlborough in Wiltshire the thirteen preachers 'for the Satterdaye Lecture' were nominated in 1627.[5] Seven years later, Laud noted: 'The kinges instructions not observed by the lecturers at Marleburgh'.[6] Still further to the west, in Somerset, Bishop Pierce of Bath and Wells was charged at his impeachment in 1642 with having suppressed market town lectures, some of them maintained voluntarily by 'neighbour ministers', which had been in uninterrupted existence for thirty, forty, or even fifty years. These included the 'ancient weekly lecture' at Bath, habitually attended by the nobility and other strangers who resorted to Bath in spring and autumn for the sake of their health. There was also a lecture at Bridgewater, dating from Elizabeth's reign. In other Somerset parishes there were preaching exercises on the days of revels and church-ales, regarded as a provocation by those who supported these 'heathenish' festivals.[7] Bishop Pierce was also said to have threatened with suspension preachers who took their turns at lectures in neighbouring dioceses, most probably in Gloucestershire, where Bishop Godfrey Goodman for reasons of his own is known to have adopted a complacent policy towards the lectures, as Miles Smith had done before him.[8]

For the northern province the evidence is more impressive still, suggesting that in the reign of James I the preaching exercises were the central institutions of an emergent religious life, tending to presbyterianism or to independency, or to some polity combining elements of both, but for the time being contained within the diocesan organization of the Church. This is the picture conveyed by the rich biographical material which was one product, especially in Lancashire, of the puritan cultivation of conscience. From

[1] Prynne, p. 373.

[2] It was reported in 1635 that of a number of ministers suspended for refusing to read the Book of Sports, all were 'lecturers of Guilford' and some were 'lecturers of Dorking'. (Prynne, p. 151.)

[3] Clarke, Lives of sundry eminent persons, p. 162.

[4] Reading Records, ii. 250.

[5] The names occur on a page in the marriage register. (Wiltshire Parish Registers: Marriages, ed. W. P. W. Phillimore and J. Sadler, ii (1906), p. 72.) I owe this reference to Mrs. A. Wall.

[6] P.R.O., S.P. 16/260/90.

[7] Articles of accusation and impeachment ... against William Pierce ... Bishop of Bath and Wells (1642), pp. 3–5; Prynne, pp. 128–48; Laud, Works, v. 319, 325, 330, 334. For a political analysis of the church-ales controversy in Somerset, see T. G. Barnes, 'County politics and a Puritan cause célèbre: Somerset churchales, 1633', Foyal Hist. Soc. Trans., 5th ser., ix (1959), 103–22.

[8] Laud, Works, v. 330; P. Heylyn, Cyprianus Anglicus (1668), p. 65.

these lives and other evidence it is clear that the tradition of monthly exercise widely established in the diocese of Chester in the fifteen-eighties continued far into the seventeenth century on a rather more voluntary basis, especially in south-east Lancashire, at towns such as Manchester, Blackburn, Bolton and Warrington. At Congleton, in Cheshire, the borough accounts for the sixteen-thirties record payments in connection with 'exercise days', and there are similar entries from Frodsham. Liverpool successfully petitioned the bishop of Chester for a monthly combination lecture in 1629.[1]

In 1594 there was an exercise at Northallerton, in the North Riding of Yorkshire, which struggled to maintain its separate existence against the rival attractions of Richmond, one of the centres for exercise in Chester diocese. There was also an exercise at Barnard Castle in 1593. The evidence is of the most elusive kind, but suggestive of the exercise movement spreading beyond the archdeaconry of Richmond into neighbouring jurisdictions. For Barnard Castle was in the diocese of Durham and Northallerton in the diocese of York, as was the deanery of Craven where there is also evidence of exercises in 1593.

There can be little doubt that the promotion of the preaching ministry in these unlikely environments was due principally to the Elizabethan earl of Huntingdon, Lord President of the Council in the North, and to other puritan magnates.[2] Early in the next century, if not before, monthly exercises became established in a number of centres in the West Riding, which seem to have been built up with the assistance of visiting Lancashire preachers. Copious notes survive of the many sermons preached by forty-eight or more preachers at Halifax, Leeds, Pudsey and neighbouring places between 1609 and 1629.[3] These suggest a very different kind of exercise from the

[1] *Oliver Heywood's Life of John Angier of Denton*, ed. E. Axon (Chetham Soc., new ser., xcvii, 1937), pp. 54–5; W. Hinde, *A faithfull remonstrance of the holy life and happy death of John Bruen* (1641), pp. 100–1; Richardson, pp. 66–9; R.W. Dunning in *History of Congleton* (Manchester, 1970), p. 221; G. Chandler, *Liverpool under Charles I* (1965), p. 158. Supporting material in Lives of John Ball and of Richard Rothwell in Clarke, *A generall martyrologie* and in Clarke's own Life and that of Richard Mather in Clarke, *Lives of sundry eminent persons*.

[2] For Northallerton and Richmond, Francis Kaye to the earl of Huntingdon, 7 Feb. 1595, Huntington Library, Hastings MSS., MS. H.A. 8012. I owe this reference to Dr. Claire Cross. For Barnard Castle, Thomas Wilson's transcript of Archbishop Tobie Mathew's Diary, Minster Library, York, p. 38. For Craven, R. A. Marchant, *Puritans and the Church Courts in the Diocese of York* (1960), pp. 31, 213. For background, see Claire Cross, *The Puritan Earl* (1966).

[3] Brit. Libr., Add. MSS. 4933A, 4933B. This is a large (416 fos. in all) and confused collection of sermon notes in various hands, including some from the 1650s and 1660s. The only discussion of this material and of the West Riding exercises is in the unpublished London Ph.D. thesis of J. A. Newton, 'Puritanism in the diocese of York (excluding Nottinghamshire) 1603–40' (1955), pp. 218–38, and more briefly in his 'The Yorkshire Puritan movement, 1603–40', *Congregational Hist. Soc. Trans.*, xix (1960–4), 3, 14–15. See also Marchant, pp. 30–1. The sermon notes were once part of the library of the Leeds antiquary Ralph Thoresby, who was also responsible for preserving and drawing the attention of John Strype to the account of the lectures in Lincoln diocese in 1614; (above, p. 198).

uniform order for the diocese of Chester of the fifteen-eighties: an elastic, voluntary institution, moving from chapelry to chapelry, sometimes devoted to a coherent course of expository sermons, sometimes not, with a second afternoon sermon, doubtless following on a substantial dinner. These crabbed and all but illegible pages are, or ought to be, among the most precious records of northern religious culture. Although there is less to show for them, there were certainly exercises in the East Riding as well,[1] and there is reason to suspect a distinct organization in the Sheffield district.[2] All this seems to have been tolerated by Archbishop Tobie Matthew, an inveterate preacher himself, who occasionally preached at the Nottinghamshire exercises held at Nottingham, Mansfield and Retford, which seem to have continued without a break from the days of Archbishop Grindal.[3]

It cannot be claimed that this tally is complete. Indeed, the fortuitous survival of much of the evidence makes it highly improbable that it should be so. Without doubt further references to combination lectures both known and as yet unknown remain to be uncovered.[4] On the present showing, they are more likely to turn up in odd and unexpected places (a stray leaf in a parish register, the draft of a letter improbably preserved, the accounts of a careful borough treasurer) than in the major and familiar classes of ecclesiastical record, such as visitation *detecta* and *comperta* or the act books of the ecclesiastical courts. The topic belongs to the gamblers and the fishermen among historical researchers, rather than to the systematic student. This is methodologically instructive. No ecclesiastical historian should foster the illusion that the diocesan muniment room furnishes an objective, faithful portrait of the Church as it was. It is altogether possible that important, perhaps the more important features may be missing from the formal record.

Many bishops have already been named in the course of this survey, and it will be clear that lectures by combination met with more episcopal encouragement than discouragement. When Grindal had sounded the opinions of his suffragans on the prophesyings in 1576, eight or nine out of fifteen whose replies are known had expressed in varying degrees their approval.[5] Bishop Alley, the first Elizabethan bishop of Exeter, and like

[1] Newton, 'Puritanism in the diocese of York', pp. 234–6; Marchant, p. 31.

[2] Newton, 'Puritanism in the diocese of York', pp. 236–8.

[3] Transcript of Archbishop Mathew's Diary, pp. 85, 92, 105 and *passim*; Marchant, pp. 17–18, 134–6.

[4] Needless to say the searches of the present author, who is more at home in Elizabethan than in 17th-century sources, have been less than exhaustive. I shall be a grateful recipient of any information which will add to my tally of combination lectures.

[5] Information in Lambeth Palace Libr., MS. 2003 fos. 1–36; Brit. Libr., Add. MS. 29546 fo. 56; Add. MS. 21565 fo. 26. The approving bishops were Bentham of Coventry and Lichfield, Berkeley of Bath and Wells, Bradbridge of Exeter, Cheyney of Gloucester, Cooper of Lincoln, Curteys of Chichester, Pierce of Rochester and Sandys of London. Cox of Ely, Ghest of Salisbury, Hughes of St. Asaph and Scory of Hereford expressed hostile opinions, while Davyes of St. Davids and Robinson

Matthew a bishop who enjoyed preaching, was said to have been 'a furtherer therein', who 'tooke paynes to travell in the work himselfe', and his successor claimed to have followed this example, and to have taken the part of moderator 'if I be nighe to the place'.[1] In Sussex the exercises seem to have been introduced by Richard Curteys, bishop of Chichester from 1570. Curteys was himself the moderator for the western deaneries,[2] and was publicly congratulated by the entire preaching ministry of his diocese as *'dux gregis*, geving good example unto the rest'.[3] This 'Grindalian' interpretation of episcopal responsibilities did not simply lapse after 1577. In much the same manner Archbishop Matthew took his turn in the Nottinghamshire exercises, as the future Archbishop Williams did at Kettering. It was said in 1642 that some bishops of Bath and Wells had done the same in their diocese,[4] which sounds like a reference to John Still, a good friend to the preaching ministry in Suffolk when still archdeacon of Sudbury, and bishop of the diocese from 1593 until 1608; to his successor, James Montague, who as the brother of Lord Montague of Boughton came of puritan stock and was the first Master of the puritan foundation of Sidney Sussex College; and to the third bishop in a Calvinist succession, Arthur Lake, diocesan from 1616 to 1626.

Bishop Hall of Exeter spoke of 'willingly giving way to orthodox and peaceable lectures', and Bishop Dee of Peterborough remarked, 'while they deport themselves peaceably and conformably, I rest contented':[5] these were more typical of episcopal attitudes than the inveterate hostility of a few. Bishop Jegon of Norwich seems to have actively promoted the market town lectures and to have preserved the niceties in addressing himself to the preachers: 'I have presumed upon my credit with you to name you 13 to assist that exercise, every man once a quarter'.[6] According to Heylyn, Archbishop Abbot was 'alwaies favourable' to the lecturers.[7]

The minority of bishops who were committed to something like a vendetta against lectures included Samuel Harsnet, bishop of Norwich and

---

of Bangor were indifferent. There is doubt about the views of Horne of Winchester whose letter is not extant, but who is variously reported in Grindal's notes as 'Episcopus Winton. per privatas litteras approbat' and 'Contra'. The sees of Bristol, Oxford and Worcester were vacant, and no replies are recorded from Blethin of Llandaff, Freke of Norwich and Scambler of Peterborough.

[1] Lambeth Palace Libr., MS. 2003 fo. 40.

[2] *Ibid.*, fo. 50.

[3] R. Curteys, *An exposition of certayne words of S. Paule to the Romaynes* (1577), Epistle signed 'in Sussex 16 December 1576' by 'your beloved in the Lord, the preachers of the dyocesse of Chichester', 42 names in all. Much of this preface is reprinted in *Sussex Archaeological Collections*, x. 52–8, and it is discussed in R. B. Manning, *Religion and Society in Elizabethan Sussex* (Leicester, 1969), pp. 63–4.

[4] *Articles of impeachment against William Pierce*, pp. 3–5. Dr. N. R. N. Tyacke suggested to me that the reference was perhaps primarily to Bishop Lake.

[5] Hall, *Works*, i, p. xlvi; Hist. MSS. Comm., *Buccleuch MSS.* (*Montagu House*), i. 275.

[6] *Registrum Vagum*, i. 100.

[7] Heylyn, p. 201.

briefly archbishop of York. As chaplain to Archbishop Bancroft, Harsnet had been active in the exposure of the alleged fraudulence of the puritan exorcist John Darrell, who had used exercises of prayer and fasting to treat cases of supposed demoniac possession in Nottingham, Burton-on-Trent and Lancashire.[1] The episode left its mark in a curious passage of the 72nd Canon of 1604 which links 'meetings for sermons, commonly termed by some prophesies or exercises' with attempts 'upon any pretence whatsoever, either of possession or obsession, by fasting and prayer, to cast out any devil or devils'.[2] It was in the terms, and generally only in the terms of this Canon, incorporating this bizarre element, that market town lectures were enquired into by the Jacobean bishops in their visitation articles. As bishop of Norwich in the sixteen-twenties, Harsnet seems to have led the way in developing a policy against stipendiary lecturers and their connection with corporate towns, a policy which aroused approving echoes from James I.[3] In 1622 the king wrote a letter to Harsnet which the bishop himself (or Laud ?) had no doubt inspired, which denounced the stipendiary system and instructed him to set aside the 'sole lecturers' and to replace them with 'five or six or more grave learned men, conformable preachers, having benefices with cure of soules'. Special arrangements were proposed for Ipswich, to end the reign of Samuel Ward, although Ward was spoken of with respect as 'a man endued with many good parts of learning and understanding'. A further letter to the bailiffs and burgesses of Ipswich required Ward to cease his lecture and Sunday sermons and provided for his salary to be divided among 'the ministers that shalbe nominated by the bishops [sic]'. Although the borough records establish receipt of the letter and its referral to legal counsel there is no reason to suppose that this order was carried out.[4] But at the prorogation of the 1624 parliament, the king commended Harsnet's suppression of 'popular lecturers'.[5]

In the Midlands, Richard Neile, the true father of the 'Laudian' or Arminian faction, was feared by the puritans while still bishop of Rochester. 'Bishop Neal was the man, whom all the pious, as well private men as

---

[1] K. Thomas, *Religion and the Decline of Magic* (1971), pp. 483–6, refers to previous accounts and concisely supersedes them. In London, too, there was an episode of exorcism by prayer and fasting in Nov. 1602 which was observed by Bancroft and Harsnet and which led to some arrests. It was reported in J. Swan, *A true and briefe report of Mary Glovers vexation* (1603), which speaks of 'the strange works of God in these our dayes' 'and namely at *Northwich*, at *Woolwich*, at *Nottingham*, at *Burton*, at *Colchester*, in *London*, in *Lankashire* and further off (as I heere) in *Kent* and in *Sussex*' (p. 70). Since Colchester was Harsnet's native town, this may shed some light on his close study of these phenomena.

[2] Cardwell, *Synodalia*, i. 288.

[3] James's reflections on lecturers in the Directions Concerning Preachers of 1622 are well known: '. . . a new body severed from the ancient clergy of England, as being neither parsons, vicars, nor curates'. (E. Cardwell, *Documentary Annals* (2 vols., Oxford, 1844), ii. 203.) If Heylyn is to be believed (p. 97), the voice was the voice of James, but the hand was the hand of William Laud.

[4] Bodl. Libr., MS. Tanner 265 fo. 28; *Dict. Nat. Biog.*, art. Samuel Ward.

[5] Seaver, p. 115.

ministers, in these parts mis-doubted would do the most mischief'.[1] As
bishop of Coventry and Lichfield, Neile exploited the embarrassing and, so
to speak, homœopathic connection of the heretic Edward Wightman (the
last man to be burned in England for heresy) with the Burton exercise,
Hildersham having preached in the exercise against Wightman's doctrine
of psychopannychism. Both the Burton and the Repton exercise were
suppressed.[2] Three years later in 1614, Neile was bishop of Lincoln, and
his call for information on the market town lectures in his new diocese
implies that he had in mind a general liquidation. One of his visitation
articles gave a hard interpretation to Canon 72 tending to exclude all possibility of legitimacy from the exercises:

Whether hath your minister presumed to appoint or hold any meetings for sermons,
commonly tearmed by some, prophesies or exercises in market townes, or other
places, or hath hee attempted upon any pretence whatsoever, eyther of possession
or obsession, by fasting and prayer to cast out any devil or devils ?[3]

But although as archbishop of York Neile was later reported by Laud to
have suppressed 'divers monthly lectures, with a fast and a moderator',[4]
his officers did not recommend draconian measures for the diocese of Lincoln
and there is no reason to suppose that he resorted to them. Of the Berkhampstead lecture he was told: 'This lecture, I never heard but wel of it'. It was
reported from among the graver and more learned ministers of the diocese
that there was no desire for 'the utter extinguishing of the lectures', which
would 'make a clamour in the countrey, as though your Lordship were an
enemie to the preaching of the gospell'. What was rather called for was a
series of salutary reforms.

For like as factious and schismaticall preaching hath broke down the walls of our
church-discipline; soe it is to be hoped that the godly sermons of orthodoxall and
conformable preachers may build them up againe.[5]

This advice was a sign of changing conditions in the Church, for such a
remedy could not have been advocated in Elizabethan days, when few of
the 'graver and learneder' could be relied upon to be 'conformable', and
when outright repression was often the only weapon in the hands of Whitgift
or Bancroft.

In 1629 the policy which had been commended to Neile in 1614 and which
Harsnet seems to have followed in Norwich became prescriptive for the
Church of England as a whole. In that year Harsnet, newly translated to
York, came together with Laud, still bishop of London, to draft 'certain
considerations' which, with a few amendments, are known to history as the

---

[1] Thomas Gataker's Life of Bradshaw, Clarke, Lives of two and twenty English
divines, p. 61.
[2] Life of Hildersham, Clarke, A generall martyrologie, pp. 377–9.
[3] Articles to be enquired of within the diocesse of Lincolne (1614).
[4] Laud, Works, v. 320.
[5] Assoc. Archit. Socs. Repts. & Papers, xvi. 44–7.

'royal instructions' to which Charles I put his name in the month of December.[1] The fifth of these contained a number of articles concerning lectures which implemented what had been proposed in Lincoln fifteen years before. Afternoon sermons were to be turned into simple sessions of catechizing. Every bishop was to take care that all lecturers were to read divine service in surplice and hood before the lecture. And when a lecture was set up in a market town it was to be read 'by a company of grave and orthodox divines near adjoining and in the same diocese', who were to preach in gowns according to their academic degrees, not in cloaks 'as too many do use'. When a corporation maintained a single lecturer, he was not to be suffered to preach until he had declared his willingness to take a living with cure of souls in the same town. The instructions were reissued in 1634, when they were tightened to require that the members of the 'company' should be *of* the same diocese.

The combination lecture, always with 'grave', 'orthodox', 'conformable' connotations, now became the Laudian salve for a running sore. After 1629 bishops' visitation articles naturally reflected the instructions, and enquired in these terms after the existence and conduct of lectures. Before 1629 few such questionnaires ventured beyond Canon 72 and Canon 56, which required stipendiary preachers and lecturers to read divine service and minister the sacraments at least twice a year. After 1633 information about lectures and lecturers figured prominently in Archbishop Laud's annual accounts to the king of the state of his province.[2] But few of the surviving articles[3] display the personal and informed concern with the subject reflected in Matthew Wren's notorious articles for Norwich of 1636, still less the near-paranoia suggested by the articles of his successor, Richard Montagu (called by the *Dictionary of National Biography* 'controversialist and bishop', in that order), which include a detailed analysis of 'the course and humour of lecturing' in the manner of a pamphleteer, a curiosity among such documents.[4] Even Neile's articles for York in 1633 were terse on the subject, while Montagu's Chichester articles of 1637 were restricted to Canons 56 and 72, which is hardly surprising, since they repeat word for word his articles for his primary visitation of 1628, before the royal instructions were issued.

It has already been shown by others that it was no part of Wren's strategy

[1] Heylyn, pp. 199–200; *Historical Collections*, ed. J. Rushworth (8 vols., 1721–2), ii. 7, 30; Laud, *Works*, v. 307–9; Cardwell, *Documentary Annals*, ii. 230.

[2] Laud, *Works*, v. 317–60.

[3] This is based upon examination of the following visitation articles in the British Library: Chester 1634 (Bridgeman); Chichester 1628, 1637 (Montagu), 1638 (Duppa); Ely 1638 (Wren); Exeter 1638 (Hall); Hereford 1634 (Lindsell), 1635 (Wren); Lincoln 1614 (Neile), 1618 (Mountaigne), 1622, 1630 & 1631, 1635, 1641 (Williams); London 1621 (Mountaigne); Norwich 1619 (Overall), 1620, 1627 (Harsnet), 1629 (White), 1636 (Wren), 1638 (Montagu); Peterborough 1623 (Dove), 1631 (Pierce), 1633 (Lindsell); Salisbury 1614 (Cotton), 1616 (Abbot), 1633 (Davenant); Winchester 1636, 1639 (Carle); Worcester 1626, 1632 (Thornborough); York 1607 (Mathew); and of Archbishop Laud's Metropolitical Articles, 163–.

[4] *Articles to be inquired of within the dioces of Norwich* (1636); *Articles of enquiry and direction for the dioces of Norwich* (1638).

to extirpate the lectures in Norfolk and Suffolk.[1] He continued Harsnet's policy, in effect, in circumstances of greater political exposure. Evidently the plan was to reform the ancient combination of Bury St. Edmunds (as Harsnet had done before him) and to commend this model to other towns. In the neighbouring diocese of London a similar policy was implemented by Laud's officers. In 1629, with the retirement from Chelmsford of the redoubtable Thomas Hooker, the authorities attempted to substitute a combination of fifteen beneficed ministers living within five miles of the town, a device tried once before, in the two years before Hooker's arrival in Chelmsford in 1626.[2] Pierce followed the same tack in Somerset. There was ambiguity in this policy, Pierce being variously credited with both putting down and setting up combination lectures.[3] But evidently the imposed 'orthodox' combination was a different creature from its predecessors. It required the unwelcome (and in many places, unheard of) appurtenances of ceremonial conformity: surplices and hoods,[4] the full Prayer Book service before the lecture. And when Wren appointed a combination of fifty lecturers to man the Monday lecture in Bury he had something different in mind from the collegiality and conference of the past. This was no more than a roster to ensure that every Monday a minister would present himself from somewhere in the archdeaconry to take his annual turn.

Above all, the Laudian policy ignored the delicate reciprocity of local and diocesan interest which Bishop Jegon had been so careful to observe in East Anglia. When Laud's commissary in Essex signed up the ministers around Chelmsford in 1629 there was dismay and from one of those appointed a flat refusal to take part in such 'a no-whit desired combination of preachers',

putt upon and (as some saye) thrust upon them, without any desires one their part, signifyed eyther to our reverend diocesan, as was fittest, or to us. We are most of us very unwillinge, as who forsee both the disrespect of us that will follow upon it, and (verie likely) the small successe of our preching to a people nothing desiringe it.[5]

From the Laudian standpoint, such complaints reflected the affliction of 'popularity' which the new policies were designed to lift from off the backs of the clergy.

If the Laudian combination was devised as a bulwark of 'orthodoxy' in the Arminian sense, it is not apparent that the combination lectures and

[1] D. W. Boorman, 'The administrative and disciplinary problems of the Church on the eve of the Civil War in the light of the extant records of the dioceses of Norwich and Ely under Bishop Wren', unpublished Oxford B. Litt. thesis (1959), pp. 98–108; King, Historical Journal, xi. 237–54. I am grateful to Mr. Boorman for permission to consult his thesis.

[2] P.R.O., S.P. 16/142/113, 144/36, 151/45, 152/16, 160/66, 161/54.

[3] Articles of impeachment against William Pierce, pp. 3–5; Laud, Works, v. 325, 334.

[4] Described as 'a thing not used before in that diocesse' (Norwich) in Articles of impeachment . . . against Matthew Wren (1641), p. 8.

[5] Jeffrye Watts, rector of Great Leighs, to Dr. Arthur Duck, 11 Feb. 1630, P.R.O., S.P. 16/160/66. The whole affair is treated in Harold Smith, The Ecclesiastical History of Essex under the Long Parliament and Commonwealth (Colchester, n.d. [1933]), pp. 30, 33–4.

exercises of earlier years were markedly unorthodox, according to the more widely accepted standards of the time, or necessarily tended towards that radical subversion of the Church which we have been taught to associate with lectures and lecturing. The true character of these institutions is more likely to be conveyed by the scholarly letters which William Bedell, public preacher of Bury St. Edmunds, wrote through the years to his friend Dr. Samuel Ward, Master of Sidney Sussex.[1] They reflect the tone of a clergy whom the Suffolk antiquary Robert Reyce called 'religious, grave, reverend and learned', quoting Bishop Jegon as often saying that no bishop in England, no, none in Europe, had so learned and judicious a ministry.[2] But Bedell was an Emmanuel man, William Perkins's pupil and the purchaser of his library. While still at Cambridge, he shared with Thomas Gataker a design for preaching in the neglected villages around Cambridge.[3] His lifelong correspondent kept what we know as a 'puritan diary'.[4] Reyce, for that matter, was a decided puritan.[5] When Wren's commissioners visited Bury in 1636 the physical arrangements in the two churches were entirely coherent with the godly preaching ministry: a 'mountainous reading desk', blocking the entrance to the chancel, the chancel itself full of seating which ran 'all the waie under the east window', high pews in the middle aisle, a pulpit halfway down the nave. And the reception of the preaching was consistent with Bancroft's satirical account of a Bury sermon of more than half a century before:

The deep, passionate, trembling, quavering, singultive twang, which crept into the brestes of the thirsty auditory and was received *bibulis auribus*; the weomens sighes and the mens hauchins [i.e. hawkings] shewed it.[6]

But however distasteful such things may have been for Laudian visitors and however un-Anglican they may appear to us, they had not hitherto been thought incompatible with what one writer called 'the sound, solid and substantial truths taught and defended by the ancient and modern worthies; and the infallible and undeniable truth of God's word'.[7]

The most common cause of trouble in an exercise was not any suspicion that the enterprise in its entirety was schismatical, but the introduction of

[1] Scattered through vols. 71–5 and 290 of the Tanner MSS. in Bodl. Libr. This Samuel Ward is not to be confused with Samuel Ward of Ipswich.

[2] *Suffolk in the XVIIth Century. The Breviary of Suffolk by Robert Reyce, 1618*, ed. Lord Francis Hervey (1902), p. 21.

[3] *True Relation of the Life of Bedell*, pp. 1–7; S. Ashe, *Gray hayres crowned with grace* (1654), p. 45.

[4] *Two Elizabethan Puritan Diaries by Richard Rogers and Samuel Ward*, ed. M. M. Knappen (American Soc. of Church History, Studies in Church History, ii, Chicago, 1933).

[5] *Winthrop Papers* (5 vols., Massachusetts Hist. Soc., 1929–47), ii. 127–32.

[6] Orders made at Bury 2 Apr. 1636, and letter from Thomas Goad to Wren, 5 Apr. 1636; Bodl. Libr., MS. Tanner 68 fos. 41, 43, 54. Cf. *Tracts Ascribed to Bancroft*, pp. 71–3: 'The cheif gentleman in the place begnnynge with a gronynge, but yet with a lowde voyce crieth most religiously, Amen'.

[7] J. Bentham, *The christian conflict* (1635), pp. 147–8.

novel doctrine by one member of the combination, leading to public controversy of the kind stirred up by Thomas Rogers's Bury sermon of 1590. Publicly to confute the doctrine of another preacher was a liberty carefully restricted by Canon 53.[1] Thus, the circumstances in which the Leicester lecture was 'questioned' arose when 'some received disgrace in a conference they held after their lecture'.[2] Bishop Jegon was told by a senior clergyman, sponsor of a revived exercise in the Fakenham area where there had been trouble in the past:

Wee are noe way encombred with buisie boddies to sowe the seedes of schisme emonge us to the unioynting of the peace of the ecclesiasticall boddie: and noe sooner shall a coale of that fire bee kindled but wee shall doe our best by way of complaint to your honour or your chancellour utterlie to extinguish it.[3]

One should not expect to encounter the courtly style of preaching or Arminian theology in the setting of a combination lecture. The tone would be Calvinist and, in a broad sense, puritan. *Per contra*, from Bancroft and Harsnet to Neile and Laud, efforts to curtail the lectures or to alter their character were always identified with the theological reaction against Calvinism. From the biassed, Arminian account of the Lincoln visitors, it appears that some of the clergy either excluded themselves or felt themselves to have been excluded, while one of the more 'popular' and radical preachers was a member of no less than three lectures, an 'apostolick man', although no graduate. But although the word 'factious' is employed, it is nowhere suggested that the Lincolnshire combinations are in themselves factions, and it would be a mistake to regard such societies as deeply alienated cells of extreme puritanism. Members of the Rutland exercise could be incensed by the puritan doctrine that non-preachers were no true ministers.[4] The Bury exercise could accommodate such a notorious apologist for conformity as Thomas Rogers. Many years later a leading light of the Kettering lecture, Joseph Bentham, a puritan in his divinity, would become an ardent royalist who suffered ejection from his living in 1643 and published at the Restoration *The right of kings by scripture*, a treatise 'penned when our martyr-king was living, but low'.[5] Simple polarities belong in the textbooks, not in the real world of the seventeenth-century Church. 'Innovation' in the religious parlance of the sixteen-thirties was more likely than not to mean Arminian innovation, 'orthodoxy' Calvinism rather than its opposite.[6]

[1] This was a matter regularly enquired of at visitations. See, e.g., Bishop Abbot's Articles for Salisbury, 1616: ' Item, whether hath there been any publique opposition betwixt precher and precher in your church or chappell, touching any sermons of doctrine . . . ?'

[2] *Assoc. Archit. Socs. Repts. & Papers*, xvi. 44.

[3] *Registrum Vagum*, i. 99.

[4] Gibson, *A fruitful sermon*, Sig. A6.

[5] *The right of kings by scripture . . . By Joseph Bentham, once again rector of the church of Boughton in Northamptonshire* (1661), Sig. A2.

[6] The categories and judgements of this paragraph owe much to Nicholas Tyacke, 'Puritanism, Arminianism and Counter-Revolution', in *The Origins of the English Civil War*, ed. C. S. R. Russell (1973), pp. 119–43.

The question, what kind of sermons, what kind of doctrine was handled in the combination lectures, is hardly worth putting, since the answer would have to be as wide as the scope of Jacobean preaching itself. Whatever was preached was preached in the market town lectures: exposition, doctrine, 'instructions' and 'uses', little that was sensational or political, little that was likely to fall foul of ecclesiastical censorship. Apparently the themes of moral and 'practical' divinity predominated: the Decalogue, the life of the Christian, the guidance of conscience. Since the attendance was of some distinction, including ministers of the combination, instructed 'private' Christians and patrons, the address was often *ad clerum* and designed to instruct and, doubtless, to impress such an auditory. Anthony Cade's sermon in the Leicester lecture in 1618 was given a running headline by an optimistic publisher as 'a very feeling and moving sermon', but, as the author explains:

The concourse of many learned ministers at an ordinary monthly lecture . . . whereunto now also resorted . . . many learned judicious gentlemen required matter of more then ordinary worth and learning. To satisfie whom, if I have layd the grounds of my sermon more schoole-like then thou thinkest fitte for the country, beare with mee, now thou knowest the occasion.[1]

Not much reading between the lines is needed to appreciate the likely utility of combination lectures as a means of establishing reputations and pursuing preferment. It seems to have been a common practice for the chapelries of Lancashire to pick their ministers from the offering at the exercise,[2] and what chapelries did in Lancashire patrons may have done elsewhere.

Combination lectures seem to have been of some significance for promoting and supplying the religious book trade. In the later years of Elizabeth's reign, the erudite Suffolk clergy, students of the Tremellius Bible and well read in the best modern theologians,[3] were prolific writers, and several of their works seem to have owed their origin to the Bury exercise. Nicholas Bownd's *Doctrine of the sabbath* arose from a course of sermons on the Decalogue. Rogers's *Sermon upon the 6.7. and 8. verses of the 12 chapter of . . . Romanes* seems to have been preached in the exercise.[4] *The arraignment and conviction of usurie* by the Bury preacher Miles Mosse was delivered in Bury as six sermons, on 19 March, 23 April, 7 May, 4 and 18 June and 2 July 1593. These were all Mondays, so that there can be no doubt that the forum was the exercise. In his final section, Mosse exhorts his fellow ministers to 'lift up their voices as trumpets, and tell the people of this sinne'.

---

[1] Cade, *Saint Paules agonie*, Sig. A4v. One section of the sermon begins (p. 32): 'Reverend men and brethren . . .'.

[2] *Oliver Heywood's Life of Angier*, pp. 54–5.

[3] The learning of the Suffolk preachers is discussed in my 'The beginnings of English Sabbatarianism', pp. 215–21. Bownd's *Doctrine of the sabbath* in its second, 1606 edn. (*Sabbathum veteris et novi testamenti*) cites 93 sources apart from the Bible, including the principal Fathers and modern theologians, but very few English writers.

[4] Above, pp. 478-9.

In his preface he felt bound to explain that his 'recital of authors' (157 are listed) should not be ascribed to 'pride or affectation of vaine glorie'.[1] George Estey's copious and posthumous 'expositions', including yet another treatment of the Ten Commandments, must all have originated in one or other of the Bury lectures.[2]

In later years, the Kettering lecture was associated with a small spate of publications, inspired by the notable ministry of its chief adornment, Robert Bolton, rector of Boughton. Of Bolton's own works two of the most considerable, *Some generall directions for a comfortable walking with God*[3] and *Instructions for a right comforting afflicted consciences*[4] were 'delivered in the lecture at Kettering', as were two substantial works of Bolton's successor, Joseph Bentham, *The societie of saints*[5] and *The christian conflict*.[6] Three of these works were dedicated to the patron of both the authors, Lord Montague, or to members of his family, and Bentham speaks of Montague's 'not only often but usual and ordinary frequenting' of the Kettering lecture, and of the fraternal association in the enterprise of himself with Bolton and Nicholas Estwick, rector of Warkton, who preached Bolton's funeral sermon.[7] The numerous and best-selling works[8] of the Banbury preachers, Dod, Cleaver, Whateley, Scudder and Harris, make no overt reference to any shared enterprise of preaching,[9] but it seems plausible to connect this copious output with the mutual pressures of a fraternity, and Dod and Cleaver were the most successful co-authors of the century. Combinations were far from being the only occasions which brought the clergy together to hear a sermon and which led to benevolent pressure to publish. Printed versions of the sermons preached at assizes and visitations commonly had the same midwives. But combination lectures led, as assize sermons could not, to lengthy and systematic treatments of major questions in divinity. Moreover the

---

[1] M. Mosse, *The arraignment and conviction of usurie* (1595), Sig. B6, pp. 33, 58, 89, 112, 138, 170. Mosse tells the reader (p. 8): 'I have been called foorth and required to this busines, not onely of many of the common sort of men . . . but also most of the brethren about me, and some even of the best gifts and account have exhorted me to begin, and encouraged me to continue this argument and treatise of usurie'.

[2] G. Estey, *A most sweete and comfortable exposition upon the tenne commaundements and upon the 51. Psalme* (1602); included with five other works in *Certaine godly and learned expositions upon divers parts of scripture* (1603).

[3] Edns. in 1625, 1626, 1630, 1634, 1638, and in *Works*, 1641.

[4] Edns. in 1631, 1635, 1638, and in *Works*.

[5] Edns. in [1630] and 1636.   [6] 1635.

[7] Bentham, *The christian conflict*, Sigs. A2v, A5; Bentham, *The societie of the saints* (1630 edn.), Sig. ¶2v; N. Estwick, *A learned and godly sermon* (edns. 1633, 1635, 1639). I am grateful to Dr. Tyacke for alerting me to the importance of the Kettering lectures.

[8] In S.T.C. (Pollard and Redgrave), 6935–79, 5378–92, 25296–324, 22116–22, 12816–56; and in Wing H 868–79.

[9] On the contrary, the enormously successful *Plaine and familiar exposition* of chs. i–ii and ix–xx of Proverbs, published and republished in parts (S.T.C. 6954–66, 5390) and abridged by Cleaver (S.T.C. 5378) was undertaken when Dod and Cleaver were both under suspension from preaching and had taken refuge in Northamptonshire.

fraternal association of the clergy, institutionalized in the preaching combination, was in itself an important factor in stimulating the vast outpourings
of the religious press.

As other writers have not been slow to notice, the value of market town
lectures for the market towns was even more pragmatic and, in part at least,
commercial. Bishop Wren's complaint has been often quoted. In Suffolk
'not a market, or a bowling green, or an ordinarie' (eating establishment)
could stand without a lecture.[1] When the ministers around Chelmsford
resisted efforts to draft them into a contrived combination they protested
that their non-compliance should not be taken to imply lack of respect for
their market town.[2] It could be thought inappropriate that a place which was
not a market town but 'private' should aspire to enjoy a lecture.[3] These
were some of the local interests which, with the willing co-operation of the
lecturers themselves, led to the initiatives which seem to have been indispensable for the success of a combination lecture and which Laudian
bishops disregarded at their peril.

This enquiry has stopped short of 1640, although there is a continuing
story to be told.[4] It has established the prevalence of the lecture by combination in the Jacobean Church, casting doubt on Dr. Seaver's claim (made on
the untypical basis of London) that 'there can be little doubt that the parish
lecture in one form or another was the most common variety of lecture in
England'.[5] The combination lecture seems to have been significant, not
as a threat to the very being of the Church, but as an element in its cohesion
and common life. In the most unspecific and non-partisan sense, the
character of the institution was presbyterian, and knowledge of the strength
of this tradition in Lancashire makes the orderly progression to a working
system of *classes* in that county in the sixteen-forties in no way mysterious.[6]
But since the combination lectures endured for so long within diocesan
structures, 'collegiality' may prove a better term than 'presbyterianism' to
connote their character and tendency. Some exercises were doubtless more
radical and 'alien' than others, but the institution in its total setting was
more typical of the Church of this epoch than of alienation from it. It was,
to be sure, a Church consolidated by local loyalties, it was not characterized
by ardent or even willing conformity to its public formularies, and non-
parochial patterns of religious life were developing in a manner threatening
to some of its fundamental structures. But it was a Church still largely
intact and sure of its integrity.

[1] P.R.O., S.P. 16/337/19.

[2] P.R.O., S.P. 16/160/66.

[3] One reason why Bishop Wren looked askance at a request to continue the lecture
at East Bergholt was that the place was 'no market town'. (P.R.O., S.P. 16/337/19.)

[4] Dr. Claire Cross has written of 'The Church in England 1646–1660': 'Historians
. . . are only just beginning to examine in critical detail Church life as it was actually
lived in England at this time'. (*The Interregnum: the Quest for Settlement, 1646–1660*,
ed. G. E. Aylmer (1972), p. 99.)

[5] Seaver, p. 88.

[6] Often observed, most recently by Richardson, pp. 66–7.

Viewed from another and still relatively untested angle,[1] lectures by combination were relevant to developments in the clerical profession, and even to the emergence of a new sense of professionalism, which is apparent as much in the voluntary impulse of exercise, conference and combination as in the ill-judged Laudian attempt to grasp for the clergy an unnatural and unattainable degree of ecclesiastical independence. In short, lecturing as practised in the combinations may have had effects quite opposite to those often alleged. It favoured the enhanced dignity and advancement of the beneficed, parochial clergy of seventeenth-century England, on whose labours these lectures very largely depended.

There can be no better way to conclude than by quoting the arguments for combination lectures put in the diocese of Norwich in the reign of James I, pointing as they do to several social and religious realities which Laudian churchmen and modern historians have united in neglecting.

1. First, the propagation of the Ghospell and edefieng of the church.
2. Incouraging of the meaner sorte of preachers.
3. Exciting of sluggards to the studie of divinitie by means whereof their owne parishes also shallbe the better served.
4. Increase of love and acquaintance amongst preachers.
5. Increase of religion and learning, by meetinges and conference.
6. Varietie will more delighte the people's attention.
7. Advauncement to the clergie man, when their guiftes shalbe knowne.
8. People wanting preachers shall or maye be there taught.
9. Benefit also to the inhabitauntes for their markett by concurse of people.[2]

---

[1] Dr. O'Day is pioneering the study of the 17th-century clergy, not only in the ecclesiastical setting, but as a part of the history of the professions in the early modern period.

[2] *Registrum Vagum*, i. 97.

19

'A MAGAZINE OF RELIGIOUS PATTERNS'
AN ERASMIAN TOPIC TRANSPOSED IN
ENGLISH PROTESTANTISM

I N his *Paraclesis* or *Adhortatio ad christianae philosophiae studium*
Erasmus of Rotterdam proposed a famous anti-scholastic definition of the theologian:

To me he is truly a theologian who teaches not by skill with
intricate syllogisms but by a disposition of mind, by the very
expression and eyes . . .
In this kind of philosophy, located as it is more truly in the
disposition of the mind than in syllogisms, life means more than
debate, inspiration is preferable to erudition, transformation is a
more important matter than intellectual comprehension. Only a
very few can be learned, but all can be Christian, all can be
devout, and—I shall boldly add—all can be theologians.[1]

In the context of this preface to the new testament the model was the
supremely Christian life, 'the speaking, healing, dying, rising Christ
himself'. Elsewhere, Erasmus sketched a portrait of exemplary
Christian character as he had witnessed it at first hand, among his
contemporaries. In response to a correspondent whom he judged to
be in search of 'some eminent pattern of religion' he described the
obscure Jehan Vitrier, 'a man unknown to the world but famous
and renowned in the kingdom of Christ', as a foil, in the manner of
Plutarch, for the more celebrated John Colet. Of Vitrier Erasmus
said that 'in truth his whole life was nothing else than one continual
sermon'; of Colet that 'nothing could divert him from the pursuit of
a gospel life.'[2]

---

[1] [Desiderius Erasmus, *Christian Humanism and the Reformation: Selected Writings*, ed
John C.] Olin (New York 1965) pp 92–106. The Latin text of the *Paraclesis* has been
reproduced in facsimile in Desiderius Erasmus, *Prefaces to the Fathers, the New Testament,
on Study*, ed Robert Peters (Menston 1970) pp 116–21.

[2] Letter to Jodocus Jonas on Vitrier and Colet, 13 June 1521, *Opus Epistolarum Des.
Erasmi Roterodami*, 4 ed, P. S. Allen and H. M. Allen (Oxford 1922) pp 507–27;
English translation by J. H. Lupton in *The Lives of Jehan Vitrier and John Colet* (London
1883), reprinted, Olin, pp 164–91. See Peter G. Bietenholz, *History and Biography in
the Work of Erasmus of Rotterdam*, *Travaux d'humanisme et renaissance* 87 (Geneva 1966).

Erasmus's 'practical divinity' was transposed in English religious life after and well beyond the protestant reformation. The most distinct echoes were returned from as far away as the third quarter of the seventeenth century when the appetite for exemplary Christian biography was not to be satisfied with a mere couple of lives such as Erasmus had composed for his friend Jodocus Jonas (although the sketch of Colet was put into print at that time[3]) but called forth 'living effigies' by the score, published in voluminous folios of many hundreds of pages, not to mention at least as many (well over two hundred) spiritual autobiographies.[4] 'The nature of man is more apt to be guided by *Examples* than by *Precepts*.' That is not Erasmus but the puritan divine Edmund Calamy, commending Samuel Clarke's *Marrow of ecclesiastical historie*. 'These... did not reason but run.' That is Clarke himself, introducing the second part of the *Marrow, The lives of many eminent christians*. 'A Magazeen of religious patterns' is Thomas Fuller's typically spicy term for the celebrated collection of the lives and deaths of modern divines known as *Abel redivivus*.[5] Fuller and Clarke, opposites in churchmanship and literary style, found the field of ecclesiastical biography (and the market for it) expansive enough to contain them both.[6] It is the 'magazeens' published over the name of Clarke, actor-manager in a considerable collaborative enterprise, which provide the centrepiece for this paper.[7]

It would be rash to claim a distinctly Erasmian parentage for this literature. Others have struck that reef and there are now warning buoys

[3] As an appendix to the edition by Thomas Smith of *A sermon ... made to the convocation at S. Pauls church in London by John Colet D.D. .... writ an hundred and fiftie years since* (Cambridge 1661); doubtless the source of the *Life* of Colet in *The lives of thirty-two English divines*, appended to Samuel Clarke, *A general martyrologie* (London 1677).

[4] [Owen C.] Watkins, [*The Puritan Experience*] (London 1972).

[5] *Abel redivivus. Or, the dead yet speaking. The Lives and deaths of the modern divines. Written by severall able and learned men* (London 1651).

[6] Fuller wrote of 'Master Samuel Clarke, with whose pen mine never did, nor never shall interfere.' Like the flocks of Jacob and Laban their styles were 'set more than a Months journey asunder.' Quoted [William] Haller, [*The Rise of Puritanism*] (ed New York 1957) p 107.

[7] *The marrow [of ecclesiastical historie]* (London 1650, 2 ed 1654, 3 ed in 2 pts 1675); [*The*] *second part of the marrow* (bk 1 1650, bk 2 1652); *A generall martyrologie* (London 1651, 2 ed 1660, 3 ed 1677); *The lives of two and twenty English divines* (London 1660); [*A collection of the lives of*] *ten eminent divines* [... *and of some other eminent christians*] (London 1662); *The lives and deaths of such worthies* (London 1665); [*The lives of the*] *thirty-two English divines* (London 1667, another ed 1677); [*The*] *lives and deaths of most of those eminent persons* (London 1675); [*The*] *lives of sundry eminent persons* (London 1683). On the collaborative aspect, see the *Life* of Thomas Hill, who died in 1653: 'He was a great friend to the publication of the lives of godly and eminent ministers and christians.' *Thirty-two English divines* (1677 ed) p 234.

in position—'beware "influence studies" '[8] 'avoid "Erasmianism" '[9]
—which only a clumsy navigator could fail to notice. Since Erasmus
was not so much an originator as the distiller of elements of received
and even perennial wisdom, his influence cannot be isolated. In 1561 a
London preacher published an abridgement of a celebrated Erasmian
text, the *Enchiridion*, without knowing what it was: 'And as I know
not the author thereof, no more found I any title or name given unto
the book.'[10] This scarcely credible episode can serve as a symbol of the
insidious rather than overt means whereby Erasmian values may have
continued to colour the religion of English protestants.

The argument will rather be that in English protestantism, and even
in the unlikely setting of puritanism, the notion that Christian truth
was more persuasive mirrored in the particularities of human
existence than argued in dogmatic abstractions, which is an Erasmian
but not a peculiarly Erasmian idea, was persistent; and that when this
principle was applied to the recorded observation of particular lives it
carried with it at least some taste for those classical virtues which were
at a premium in Erasmus's 'philosophy of Christ', if only through
the continued reception of a rhetorical tradition which furnished the
models, categories and vocabulary for any large-scale undertaking in
biography.

But first it is necessary to state a paradox. Erasmus was a man of
letters. Yet the *Paraclesis* seems to say that life is more than learning,
and perhaps more to be valued even than literature. The only concrete examples it provides of a true theologian are a weaver or common
labourer. It is character which counts, expressed as much in the
disposition of a man's face and eyes as in words. But the *Paraclesis*
is the preface to a book, the new testament. The notion that life and not
literature is the best of schools is itself a literary and pedagogical
conceit. It is eloquence which can catch the life and convey its value

[8] Quentin Skinner, 'The Limits of Historical Explanations', *Philosophy* 41 (London 1966)
pp 199–215; Quentin Skinner, 'Meaning and Understanding in the History of Ideas',
History and Theory 8 (Middletown, Conn., 1969) pp 3–53.

[9] Reviewing J. K. McConica, *English Humanists and Reformation Politics under Henry VIII
and Edward VI* (Oxford 1965), which somewhat overstates the influence of
'Erasmianism', A. G. Dickens wrote in *History* 52 (1967) pp 77–8: 'After all, what
educated man did not know at least some of the writings of Erasmus? Who had not
breathed atmospheres subtly perfumed by his ubiquitous presence?' G. R. Elton wrote in
HJ 10 (1967) pp 137–8: 'People did not read Erasmus . . . and say with a sudden
inspiration: indeed, indeed, this is what we will do.'

[10] *Elizabethan Puritanism,* ed L. J. Trinterud, Library of Protestant Thought (Oxford 1971)
pp 19–39.

more transparently than the life itself. We cannot improve on the hyperbole which the *Paraclesis* itself contains: the new testament renders Christ 'so fully present that you would see less if you gazed upon Him with your very eyes.'[11]

As historians we must take these words on trust and apply them to the lives of English protestants in the century after the reformation. For if these lives had not been turned into a literature—*Lives* in another sense—we should not be able to see them at all. What we see is what the writers permit us to see, and perhaps more than was originally there. The full ambiguity inherent in the very word 'life' appears to have been missed by one of the greatest of literary historians, the late William Haller. The question may be asked whether in his book *The Rise of Puritanism*[12] Haller was recording the rise of puritanism or the rise of a puritan literature, including puritan biography. Between 1570 and 1643, while their plans to reorganise the church were checked, the puritans are said by Haller to have 'devoted themselves to the production of a literature'. It is only as they appear in that literature that they begin, as it were, to exist. Haller's account of the 'physicians of the soul' and 'the spiritual brotherhood', celebrated chapter headings in *The Rise of Puritanism*,[13] describes those puritan divines who achieved 'full expression in writing' and draws heavily on Clarke's *Lives*. The earliest of these biographies belong to men born in Elizabeth's reign who came to maturity in the time of James I. This was not the first generation of puritanism, still less of the protestantism with which it was in so many ways continuous. But Haller, while not fully satisfying our curiosity as to why such a literature came into existence when it did, seems to be incurious himself about puritanism before it received 'full expression in writing'. The consequence is to make an unnatural separation between puritanism and its protestant roots. And there is no mention of John Foxe, to whom Haller later devoted years of study.[14]

The Erasmian ambiguity suggests that there are two themes to be

---

[11] Olin p 106.

[12] First published 1938; Harper Torchbooks, New York 1957.

[13] Haller, caps 1 and 2.

[14] Haller told me in conversation in 1953 that he supposed that he was the only person who had seen every page of every edition of Foxe's *Acts and Monuments*. In *Foxe's Book of Martyrs and the Elect Nation* (London 1963) he identified (p 207) the Marian martyr John Bradford as 'a prototype of all the physicians of the soul who would presently be undertaking the spiritual direction of more and more of Elizabeth's subjects', and developed the point.

pursued within the scope of this paper. There is first the possibility that in the English reformation life itself in the sense of character was more persuasive than doctrine, or than anything put into writing, except for the English bible. There is then the theme of the persuasiveness of the recorded life, published biography, chronologically secondary to and dependent upon the first.

There is not very much than can or needs to be said about the first and more elusive of these topics. Paradoxically, the evidence that the wisdom of the *Paraclesis* was received and applied in the English reformation would have to be looked for in the absence of positive documentary record. It hardly needs to be argued that protestant Christianity in its original propagation was preached as much or more by example as by doctrine, in the old cliché caught rather than taught. It was not theological expertise or originality which made Thomas Bilney, in Foxe's phrase, 'the first framer of [Cambridge] university in the knowledge of Christ.'[15] But the documentary and literary bias of historians tends to let this almost self-evident fact go by default. There are some leads in the career of the Alsatian reformer Martin Bucer which can serve to develop this point. When Peter Martyr Vermigli first shared Bucer's household in Strasbourg he described it to his old friends in Lucca in a letter which was later well enough known to readers of his correspondence in English:

> Beholde, welbeloved brethren, in our age, Bishopes upon the earth, or rather in the Church of Christ, which be trulie holie. This is the office of a pastor, this is that bishoplike dignitie described by Paul in the Epistles unto Timothie and Titus. It delighteth me much to read this kinde of description in those Epistles, but it pleaseth me a great deale more to see with the eyes the patternes themselves.[16]

In Edwardian Cambridge Bucer maintained another model establishment which must have impressed in much the same way the future

---

[15] E. G. Rupp, *Studies in the Making of the English Protestant Tradition* (Cambridge 1966 ed) p 22.

[16] *Martyrs divine epistles*, bound with *The common places of Peter Martyr*, tr Anthonie Marten (London 1583) pp 62–3; whence printed in G. C. Gorham, *Gleanings of a Few Scattered Ears During the Reformation in England* (London 1857) pp 19–27; original Latin text in *Petri Martyri epistolae theologicae*, appended to *Loci communes* (London 1583) p 1071. Reference was made to the letter by S.T. (Samuel Torshell of Bunbury, Cheshire) in a funeral sermon of 1639, 'Gods esteeme of the death of his saints', in *The house of mourning* (1640). (See p 522 below.)

leaders of the English church who were his friends.[17] The influence of Bucer on the English reformation has been learnedly discussed,[18] but with difficulty once the discussion moves beyond his death and the matter of his proven contribution to prayer book revision. For very few of Bucer's writings were ever published in England, and even the great volume of *Scripta Anglicana* printed at Basle in 1577 does not appear to have been widely read. Bucer's prolixity was notorious. It is not unlikely that the more profound influence was of a personal character, exerted on the lives of English churchmen such as John Bradford and Edmund Grindal with whom the great reformer had been intimate. Both Bradford and Grindal would later appeal to the memory of Bucer's living impact on their generation, not to anything in print.[19]

The Elizabethan puritan vision of a church rightly reformed was a reflection not only of abstract ecclesiology but also of much human and social experience, mediated in 'the meetings of the godly' and in ministerial confraternity and conference. A frequent observation in the seventeenth-century biographies that many lit their lamps from this or that celebrated divine was to turn this into a cliché. But we can meet it fresh and at first hand in such Elizabethan sources as the minutes and other papers of the so-called Dedham *classis*[20] or the diary of the Essex minister Richard Rogers.[21] Rogers's sense of inadequacy was both aroused and in some measure allayed by the compelling example of the brethren whom he had cause to admire. 'No smalle helpe herto was our whetting on one the other who being 4 daies together communicated many things together.'[22]

We turn from real life to the mirror held up to life by religious

[17] 'Formula vivendi praescripta familiae suae a M. Bucero et propria manu revisa', Corpus Christi College Cambridge MS 418 pp 627–33; printed and discussed, François Wendel, 'Un document inédit sur le sejour de Bucer en Angleterre', *Revue d'histoire et de philosophie réligieuses* 34 (Strasbourg 1954) pp 223–33.

[18] A. E. Harvey, *Martin Bucer in England* (Marburg 1906); Constantin Hopf (Hope), *Martin Bucer in England* (Oxford 1946); Herbert Vogt, *Martin Bucer und die Kirche von England* (Inaugural dissertation, Westfälischen Wilhelm-Universität zu Münster 1966).

[19] Patrick Collinson, 'The Reformer and the Archbishop; Martin Bucer and an English Bucerian', *JRH* 6 (1971) pp 305–30.

[20] John Rylands Library, Rylands English MS 874; partially and imperfectly published in R. G. Usher, *The Presbyterian Movement in the Reign of Queen Elizabeth, CSer,* 3 ser 8 (1905).

[21] Original in Dr Williams's Library; partially printed in *Two Elizabethan Puritan Diaries,* ed M. M. Knappen, American Society of Church History (Chicago 1933).

[22] Knappen p 64. Compare the passage (p 95) in which Rogers takes to heart the exemplary life of John Knewstub, rector of Cockfield, Suffolk, headed: 'The example of Mr Knew[stubs]'.

biography. In the whole sweep of English religious history from the beginnings of the reformation to the Glorious Revolution there were two major episodes of edifying protestant biography, the one represented by the *Acts and Monuments* of John Foxe, a massive undertaking begun in 1554 and substantially complete by 1570, the other dominated by the biographical tomes published by Clarke and Fuller between 1650 and 1683. To identify Foxe as a biographer is to defy the convention which separates martyrology from the experimental vein of autobiography, and even biography. But Foxe, and more especially some of the independent sources which Foxe, like Clarke, ingested, was no less a biographer for being a martyrologist, both in respect paid to certain ethical conventions in the biographical tradition and in the attention paid to individuality and even idiosyncracy of character. As for Clarke, he was as much martyrologist as biographer, author of a *General martyrologie* which incorporated a potted version of Foxe and brought it up to date. But if we can distinguish between martyrology and biography with Clarke it is biography (or hagiography) which predominates. He was at pains to insist that the divines of the seventeenth century were in some sense themselves martyrs, but this served as little more than a polite fiction to bring these moderns within the scope of ecclesiastical history in the Eusebian tradition. So between Foxe and Clarke there was continuity, acknowledged in the congratulatory messages which accompanied Clarke's ambitious ventures: 'On our English Martyrs and Martyrologers, Master FOX and Master CLARKE'.[23]

But between Foxe and Clarke there also lies a chasm of eighty years, separating the definitive edition of *Acts and Monuments* from the earliest of Clarke's compilations, and a narrower gap of some forty years between the last events chronicled by Foxe and the first of Clarke's lives. Clarke's attempt to bridge the gap with sketchy accounts[23a] of the Elizabethans only draws attention to it. So far as their careers and reputations can be reconstructed from a variety of scattered sources, such Elizabethan divines as John More of Norwich, Percival Wiburn of Northampton, Eusebius Paget, Dudley Fenner, Thomas Wilcox the Londoner were as famous in their generation, at least locally, as Gouge or Sibbes or Preston in the next.[24] It is by no

---

[23] [*A*] *general martyrologie* (London 1677 ed) Sigs C2 –4 .

[23a] These resemble in length the mini-biographies of modern authors found in successive editions of Bale's *Catalogus* which I distinguish from 'edifying' biography.

[24] Patrick Collinson, *The Elizabethan Puritan Movement* (London 1967).

means clear that they were deficient in 'practical divinity' or untried as 'physicians of the soul'. Foxe himself was no mean practitioner.[25] But they were not the authors of books devoted to these matters, nor did they provide the subjects for biographies exemplifying their personal and pastoral attainments. We should not forget the memoir of Foxe himself, written in 1611 by his son Simeon, who deplored the recent neglect of biography which had robbed 'of their future memory these great men whose labours have won for us the blessings we enjoy.' But this did not see the light of day until 1641, when it was appended to the edition of *Acts and Monuments* of that year.[26]

Why was the biographical genre so slow to revive and mature? The keen interest in living examples which Foxe both expressed and aroused had not expired. In 1576 a letter-writer could easily turn his hand to a Foxeian character sketch: 'But now I will tell yow of a good byshope indeed. There is not far from Asheby a pore town called Mesham; the most parte there are colliers. They have had one Peter Eglesall, a grave and godly man, to their minister . . .' And so we proceed with the colourful detail of 'two aun016ent old men above three-score years a pece', riding with their preacher to the bishop to assure him that they would still have been ignorant and obstinate papists if it had not been for his ministrations and example.[27] The more militant and organised of the Elizabethan puritans continued and extended Foxe's history through the 'registering' of the troubles of their party, including biographical and autobiographical narratives. But these materials were assembled for a narrowly polemical, even political purpose. They remained for the most part in manuscript and were without literary impact.[28] Throughout the Elizabethan period and its immediate sequel the only steps taken to perpetuate the memory of a deceased divine of note, and that somewhat rarely, was to promote the posthumous publication of his writings.[29] And even then, when the

[25] J. F. Mozley, *John Foxe and his Book* (London 1940) pp 105-7.

[26] *Ibid*, pp 1-11. The Latin version of the *Life* is in BL MS Lansdowne 388.

[27] *Letters of Thomas Wood, Puritan, 1566-1577*, ed Patrick Collinson, *BIHR* Special Supplement 5 (1960) pp 20-1. *See above*, 102-3.

[28] Partially published in *A parte of a register* (n.p. 1593?); the remainder, comprising part of the Morrice MSS in Dr Williams's Library, calendared in Albert Peel (ed) *The Seconde Parte of a Register* 2 vols (Cambridge 1915). See my 'John Field and Elizabethan Puritanism', in *Elizabethan Government and Society*, ed S. T. Bindoff, J. Hurstfield, C. H. Williams (London 1961) pp 127-62. *See above*, pp. 335-70.

[29] The prototype was perhaps John Day's publication *The worckes of T. Becon, whiche he hath hytherto made and published*, 3 pts (London 1560-4). The *Works* of William Perkins were published posthumously in eds of 1597, 1600, 1603, 1605, 1609 and 1613, this

collected *Works* of such a model Christian and divine as Edward Dering were printed (in 1590, 1597 and 1614) no information about his life was included. It was left to Holland in his *Herωologia anglica* of 1620 to publish (alongside a portrait of Foxe) a sensitive engraving of Dering which would presumably have been available to his editors if there had been sufficient interest in the personality of the original to have employed it. This was forty-four years after Dering's premature death.[30]

Literary historians will tell us that biography is more of a seventeenth-century than a sixteenth-century phenomenon.[31] This is a reminder that the question is broader than the scope of this occasion but the statement is too circular to provide an explanation. A more satisfactory if partial answer to our problem may be that for the three generations which intervened between the Elizabethan settlement and the puritan commonwealth the bible and Foxe between them entirely satisfied the demand for edifying biographical history. Foxe was their Plutarch. He was read not once but repeatedly, and devotionally. Ignatius Jourdain, mayor of Exeter in the 1620s (and we know this from Clarke) read Foxe seven times over, and the bible above twenty times.[32] Clarke's *Lives* contain examples of references to episodes in Foxe so cryptic as to suggest that a knowledge of the context could be assumed, as with scripture itself.[33] So the missing generation was hidden in the long shadow cast by the *Book of Martyrs*. Although for the Elizabethans this was nearly contemporary history, the new dispensation had a distancing effect, and this sense of distance could not be experienced with respect to the Elizabethan and Jacobean saints

---

last the definitive three volume edition, several times reissued. Richard Greenham's *Works* were published in 1599 and were in their fifth edition by 1612. *The works of that late divine Mr T. Wilcocks* were published in 1624. Wilcox had died in 1608.

[30] [Patrick] Collinson, *A Mirror of Elizabethan Puritanism: [the Life and Letters of 'Godly Master Dering']*, Friends of Dr Williams's Library 17th Lecture 1963 . *Above*, 289 ff.

[31] 'Even biography was an undeveloped art during the reign of the first Elizabeth.': Margaret Bottrall, *Every Man a Phoenix: Studies in Seventeenth-Century Autobiography* (London 1958) p 1.

[32] *Ten eminent divines* p 453.

[33] 'If the Word will not prevaile, the Cross will come, and make a *Hooper*, and a *Ridley* imbrace one another.' (*Ten eminent divines* p 260.) The reference is to the letter from bishop Ridley to bishop Hooper, written from prison in 1555, John Foxe, *Acts and Monuments*, ed S. R. Cattley, 6 (London 1838) pp 642–3. In a codicil to his will made in 1636 Robert Harris told his wife: 'You shall find the substance of that I would say to you printed in the Book of *Martyrs* vol. 2 p. 1744, to wit in John Careless his letter to his wife: keep the Book and often read the letter.' (*Ten eminent divines* p 322.)

themselves until after the 1640s, another watershed. Then again in substantial tomes which physically matched the *Book of Martyrs* the reader would encounter the 'ancients', 'the good old puritans of England'. Of the Suffolk preacher John Carter and his wife it was said that their clothing was 'of the old fashion', so that visitors came away saying that they had seen 'Adam and Eve, or some of the old Patriarchs'. Of William Gouge it was noted that 'towards his latter end' he did 'much resemble the Picture that is usually made for *Moses*. Certainly he was the exact *Effiges* of *Moses* his spirit.' Robert Harris, master of Trinity College Oxford in the interregnum, 'much bewayled the vast difference both in garb and practice betwixt new and old professors' and Richard Blackerby's biographer thought that he would have been amazed if he could have lived beyond the restoration to see 'the professors' garbs' in the wealthier congregations.[34] To be canonised the old puritan way had to be historicised, and to historicise it was to canonise it.

Further reasons for the late flowering of puritan biography will suggest themselves if we dismember the *Lives* into their component sources.[35] The most material were funeral sermons. Others included prefaces to books containing biographical information, spiritual letters, diaries, and collections of sayings on matters of conscience, preserved in the conventional form of 'To one who asked him . . . he said . . .'[36] The sayings were readily converted into improving and diverting anecdotes which influence the somewhat episodic rhythm of many of the lives. Here is an example from the life of John Carter:

> There dwelled in that Parish a Tanner, that was a very godly man, and one that had much familiar society with Mr *Carter*. This man as he was very busie in Tawing of a Hide with all his might, not so much as turning his head aside any way: Mr *Carter* coming by accidentally, came softly behinde him, and merrily gave him a

[34] *Ibid* pp 7–8, 114–15, 316; *Lives of sundry eminent persons* p 64.

[35] Haller, pp 100–6.

[36] The sayings of Richard Greenham were celebrated. *Godly instructions for the due examination and direction of all men* was printed in 1598 and *Short rules sent to a gentlewoman* in 1621. John Rylands Library, Rylands English MS 524 contains a large collection of Greenham's sayings, apparently recorded by Arthur Hildersham. Ignatius Jourdain's biographer records: 'There is a somewhat like saying of Mr Greenhams, and possibly Mr Jurdaine might borrow it thence, it suiting so well the temper of his spirit.' (*Ten eminent divines* p 481.) In 1659 Samuel Clarke published *Golden apples. Or, seasonable and serious counsel from the sanctuary to the rulers of the earth, held forth in the resolution of sundry questions, and cases of conscience about divisions, schisms, heresies, and the tolleration of them, gathered from the writings of twenty divines.*

little clap on the back: the man started, and looking behinde him suddenly, blushed, and said, Sir, I am ashamed that you should find me thus: To whom Mr *Carter* replied, *Let Christ when he comes finde me so doing:* What (said the man) doing thus? *Yes* (said Mr *Carter* to him) *faithfully performing the Duties of my Calling.*[37]

All these were available to Clarke either as raw materials or, more commonly, in the form of finished biographies, some of them written or even published somewhat earlier in the century by such polished hagiographers as Thomas Gataker, others prompted by the advertise-ments which Clarke inserted in successive volumes: 'I intend not . . . to sit downe here, but to make some further progress in writing the lives of others of Gods Worthies: Wherefore my request is to all such as can furnish me with materials for the continuance of the blessed Memorials of their deceased friends, and for the publick good, and utility of the Church, to send them in to me . . .'[38]

Of these sources only the spiritual letters seem to have been deliber-ately preserved from as early as the middle years of Elizabeth.[39] Biographical prefaces were a novelty of the early seventeenth century and themselves reflective of heightened biographical interest. The clue to the problem must lie in the funeral sermons on the one hand and in the collected sayings of notable 'physicians of the soul' and diaries on the other. The sayings were a by-product of the pastoral art of resolving cases of conscience, and although this art was practised from the earliest years of the reformation it was only with the turn of the century that the theology of conscience, puritan casuistry, became systematised as a pastoral science and in the literature which began with Perkins's pioneering *Cases of conscience* and culminated in Baxter's *Christian directory.*[40] The recording of case-book morality was but one

---

[37] *Ten eminent divines* pp 11–12.

[38] *Second part of the marrow* (1675 ed) Sig A2v.

[39] Examples are Edward Dering's *Certaine godly and comfortable letters*, printed in 1590 and also extant in manuscript in Kent Archive Office, MSS Dering U 350 C/1 and 2; and Thomas Wilcox's *A profitable, and comfortable letter for afflicted consciences: written and sent . . . 1582* (London 1584?) and *Large letters. Three in number, for the instruction of such, as are distressed in conscience* (London 1589). A large collection of Wilcox's spiritual letters was still extant in manuscript in the late seventeenth century and is described in Dr Williams's Library MS Morrice I pp 617(2), (4).

[40] [I.] Breward, ['William Perkins and the Origins of Puritan Casuistry'], in *Faith and a Good Conscience: (Papers Read at the Puritan and Reformed Studies Conference, 18th–19th December 1962)*] (London 1963) pp 5–17; *The Work of William Perkins*, ed I. Breward, *Courtenay Library of Reformation Classics* 3 (Appleford, Abingdon 1970).

manifestation of the growth of a system of practical divinity in which the developed tradition of biography eventually took its own place: a programme to satisfy the desire expressed by Francis Bacon 'that a man may be warranted in his particular actions, whether they be lawful or not.'[41] It was the discipline of self-warranting by means of regular self-examination which produced the puritan diary. But while these sources sometimes yielded invaluable information, directly or indirectly, they were not determinative of the structure or intention of the biographies.

Published funeral sermons, which connected more directly with the biographies, made their appearance at about the same time as the earliest literature of puritan casuistry, and only became a staple of the book trade in the second and third decades of the seventeenth century. The funeral sermon was another sign of a quickened interest in individual conduct and in exemplary models. But as something of a cuckoo in the protestant nest it had a delayed domestication in the puritan tradition: a matter to be explored in the second part of this paper.

II

Protestant and puritan biography served two major as well as any number of subsidiary purposes. The merits of the exemplary life were a recommendation of the faith in which the life was pursued and triumphantly concluded. This was a theological purpose and, often, more crudely a partisan purpose, butressing protestantism against catholicism, as in Foxe, or puritan orthodoxy against sectarianism, as in Clarke. But there was also a practical and ethical purpose, within the economy of casuistry: the conscience of the dead available for the instruction of the living. 'We must eye them for imitation. We must look upon the best, and the best in the best.'[42] Either way the emphasis was on character, active in rational moral choice. Of the divine Samuel Crook we learn that his entire life was 'but one continued commentary upon his doctrine, and an exemplary sermon consisting of living words, or of words translated into works.'[43] Of Robert Harris: 'He lived religion, while many only make it the subject of their discourses.'[44] Of Julines Herring: 'His sermons, preched in the congre-

---

[41] Quoted, Breward, *The Work of William Perkins*, p 61.
[42] *Ten eminent divines* Sig A3r.
[43] *Ibid* p 30.
[44] *Ibid* p 303.

gation, were printed in his conversation.'[45] It must have been an assumption of this as of any protestant discourse that (to quote Perkins) 'all actions that please God must be done in faith' and have their ground in the word of God.[46] But there was often no occasion or means to spell this out, so that the stress appears in practice to fall the other way, life validating faith.

Since its descriptive content is more ethical than theological it is not surprising that this literature contains many reminders of the Erasmian 'philosophy of Christ', or rather of older voices underlying Erasmus. Somewhere not far away is the moral framework of Plutarch and the general currency of classical ethics in their Aristotelian formulation, so essential to Plutarch. The remainder of this paper will advance the thesis that the ethics of protestant and puritan biography were the ethics of Aristotle transposed, a surprising discovery if we regard Aristotelian man and Pauline man as opposites; by no means startling if we remind ourselves of the classical education which was still a necessary acquisition for divines as for any other educated persons, and of the diffusion of classical literature in translation.[47] Since Sir George Paule in writing his *Life of Whitgift* of 1611 chose Plutarch, Suetonius and Tacitus for his models, it was natural that he should make moderation and restraint the leading motifs of Whitgift's character and of his conduct of ecclesiastical affairs. The fact that Whitgift was 'choleric' and quick-tempered was too notorious to be concealed, but had somehow or other to be squared with the general reputation of a 'grave and prudent' archbishop.[48]

These influences were not absent even from the character studies in Foxe's *Book of Martyrs*.[49] At first sight this looks unlikely. What more certain to smother the Aristotelian mean than the smoky fires of Smithfield? What could be more extreme and in an inverted sense violent than to offer one's body to be burned, rather than to recant and reach a reasonable accommodation with the authorities? But whereas the issue of conscience which took the martyrs to the stake was a moral absolute and according to Aristotle's own reasoning no occasion

---

[45] *Thirty-two English divines* p 164.
[46] Quoted, Breward, *Faith and a Good Conscience*, p 11.
[47] H. S. Bennett, *English Books and Readers 1558 to 1603* (Cambridge 1965) cap 4.
[48] George Paule, *The life of John Whitgift* (London 1699 ed) pp 82, 90, 108–9. Compare [D. A.] Stauffer, [*English Biography before 1700*] (Cambridge, Mass., 1930) p 67.
[49] I follow the Townsend-Cattley ed of [*The Acts and Monuments of John*] Foxe, 8 vols (London 1837–41).

for applying the ethics of mediocrity,[50] on their long way to the fire
these confessors had many opportunities to pursue the golden mean.
According to the Foxeian narratives they were men and women of
dispassionate moderation, temperate in speech, given to no extremes
of behaviour, even in their utter extremity. Even Julius Palmer,[51]
a prototypal Angry Young Man, always espousing the minority
opinion, is said to have been 'of manners courteous without curiosity,
of countenance cheerful without high looks, of speech pleasant without
affectation.'[52] It is always the persecutors who fall into passions and
furies: 'in the midst of his rage'—'the prolocutor in his ruff . . . how
stoutly he stood'; and of the deaths of the persecutors: 'he desperately
died'—'and so most miserably died'—'his horrible end'.[53] The martyrs
are even physically appealing, thanks no doubt to a sensibly moderate
diet. Hugh Latimer in his worn-out clothes and with halting gait is
affectionately drawn as a decent old man who knows how to take care
of himself.[54] In the gruesome appendix which relates the miserable
fates of the persecutors in the manner of Lactantius there is a tale of how
years later divine judgement fell upon a certain ploughman for
gossiping about Latimer, whom he had seen burned, and for saying
'in despite' that he had teeth like a horse. In the same hour his son
hanged himself, not far away.[55]

Some of the martyrs are 'merry' and jest all the way to the stake.
(We may recall that Sir Thomas More, who had been that way
before, could 'see the humorous side of martyrdom', Chambers's
comment[55a] on the famous 'mocks' with which he mounted the
scaffold.) Thomas Rogers, woken betimes to 'break the ice' as the first
of the martyrs says: 'Then if it be so I need not tie my points.'[56] In
similar circumstances the portly Rowland Taylor hugs the pillar in his
chamber and tells his cell-mate: 'O master Bradford, what a notable
sway I should give if I were hanged!' And then on the way to burn in
Suffolk he cracks his grisly joke about cheating the worms in Hadleigh
churchyard of their expected 'jolly feeding' upon his 'great carcase'.[57]

---

[50] W. F. R. Hardie, *Aristotle's Ethical Theory* (Oxford 1968) cap 7.
[51] This narrative was reproduced as a discrete biography, 'The Life of Mr Julines Palmer',
in Clarke's *General martyrologie* pp 475–81.
[52] Foxe, 8 p 202.
[53] *Ibid* pp 629, 633, 635, 637.
[54] See many passages in the account of Ridley and Latimer, *Ibid*, 7 pp 406–583.
[55] *Ibid*, 8 p 641.
[55a] R. W. Chambers, *Thomas More* (London 1938) p 347.
[56] Foxe, 6 p 609.
[57] *Ibid* pp 700, 696.

The fisherman Rawlins White of Cardiff, a kind of Grandpa Moses of the persecution, settles himself down at the stake to listen to the sermon to be preached before the faggots are lit, makes two stays for his elbows with a little straw, leans forward and gives 'good ear and attention'.[58] There is room for a little book on 'The Wit and Wisdom of the Marian Martyrs'.

These were all aspects of classical *apatheia*. Once in the flames there were further opportunities for the display of a kind of heroic indifference. Bishop Hooper washed his hands in the fire as though it had been in cold water.[59] Rogers was 'nothing moved' by the sorrowful sight of his wife and eleven children: that is to say, nothing moved from his purpose.[60] Bishop Ferrar said that if he were seen once to stir in the pains of burning no more credit should be given to his doctrine. 'And as he said, so he right well performed the same; for so patiently he stood, that he never moved.'[61] But this was not the unnatural *apatheia* of stoicism for which Plutarch found that he had no use.[62] The Marian martyrs felt pain but were not overcome or deterred by it. Theirs was a true Aristotelian courage, midway between cowardice and temerity. The point of it all, no doubt, was to vindicate the protestant religion. Seven thousand people were present not just to see Hooper die but to observe 'his behaviour towards death', and the question for them was the question which Foxe intended to resolve for his readers: did he die in true faith?[63] Nevertheless, the manner of recording these transactions has the power to suggest, for this reader at least, that these were also victories of character and for humanity.

In the world of Samuel Clarke, a century later, we are still in the thick of the Aristotelian virtues. And since Clarke wrote hack biographies of the likes of Alexander the Great, Pompey and Tamburlaine, it is a Plutarchan world too. 'Plutarcha cede', suggested one of his well-wishers in congratulatory verses prefacing one of his collections.[64] The qualities most often admired in the spiritual biographies are humility, modesty, and, once again, a sure instinct for the safe sure middle way, expressed in a wide variety of clichés.

[58] *Ibid* 7 p 32.
[59] *Ibid*, 6 p 611.
[60] *Ibid* p 612.
[61] *Ibid*, 7 p 26.
[62] D. A. Russell, *Plutarch* (London 1973) pp 84–5; Alan Wardman, *Plutarch's Lives* (London 1974) pp 107–8.
[63] Foxe, 7 p 656.
[64] *Second part of the marrow*, Sig B.

Samuel Crook was 'grave without austerity, pleasant without levity, courteous without dissembling . . . seldome the first speaker although he was best able to speak'.[65] John Carter 'never made Feasts, yet always had wholsome full and liberal Diet in his house.' 'He had a sharp wit, and was sweet, milde, affable, and pleasant in his conversation; yet were there not any of his most facetious passages, that did not savour of holiness.'[66] Thomas Gataker was commended for 'that low esteem he had of his own gifts', 'his freedome from ambition of outward advantages', 'his meek conversation with, and condescention to the meanest christians.'[67] Richard Capel was a 'constant and stable man . . . set up a sure Sea-mark.'[68] Robert Harris was 'grave without affectation, pleasant without levity';[69] Herbert Palmer 'neither wastfull nor covetous'.[70] Mrs Jane Ratcliff was 'a woman of a well composed spirit, discreetly advised'. As for humility, she had 'got it so by heart that there was no need of Art to make profession or ostentation of it.'[71]

A particular aspect of the restraint described in the *Lives* suggests a close parallel with the Erasmian evaluation of academic learning. As in the late medieval devotionist tradition to which Erasmus had given fresh expression, a consistent polemic was trained against the vanity of useless knowledge. Typically the divines of the biographies showed outstanding promise in their university careers. They were the ablest disputants, the best linguists, the 'choicest ornaments' of their colleges. But learning was never a source of pride. The model divine was 'one that did not vainly encrease his Liberary for ostentation but chose books for use.'[72] Knowledge of ancient languages was applied 'only upon necessary occasions, not for ostentation, to amuse . . . but for the more full, and clear opening of the Text.'[73] By a kind of 'holy Alchimy'[74] learning, having been acquired, had in a sense to be lost again, or at least lost to view, in the plain preaching of 'solid and savoury truths' to 'poor simple people that never knew what Religion meant.'[75] Of Robert Harris it was said that 'his chiefest Learning lay where he made

---

[65] *Ten eminent divines* p 44.
[66] *Ibid* p 8.
[67] *Ibid* pp 148–9.
[68] *Ibid* p 258.
[69] *Ibid* p 305.
[70] *Thirty-two English divines* p 200.
[71] *Ten eminent divines* pp 419, 443.
[72] *Ibid* p 156.
[73] *Ibid* p 27.
[74] *Ibid*.
[75] *Thirty-two English divines* p 177.

least shew of it in publick', and that he had 'learned to cancel his Art'.[76] If these reports are placed alongside the published output of some earlier writers in the puritan tradition they illuminate a situation which might otherwise appear problematical. The Elizabethan Edward Dering was reported to be the best Greek scholar of his time in Cambridge, but little enough of this learning obtrudes in his sermons and biblical commentaries, although they contain a denunciation of others who 'use the pulpit like a philosopher's chaire.'[77] Perkins in his *Art of prophesy* recalled the proverb: 'Artis etiam est celare artem.'[78]

Among the many saints enshrined in Clarke there appears but one extremist, the only life to resemble Malvolio or to approximate to the popular stereotype of later nonconformity. This was Ignatius Jourdain, a substantial merchant of Exeter, mayor and MP. Jourdain is described as 'for his temper . . . a man of a raised zeal, and *heroicall* spirit, one of those rare examples which the Lord giveth the world now, and then, and therefore his actions are not to be measured by an ordinary standard.' He was a man of exceptional and humourless severity, a relentless punisher of sin with the whip and the stocks, and the un-successful promoter of a law to punish adultery with death. When he moved this bill on the floor of the house of commons the members cried: 'Commit it, Mr Jourdain, commit it; upon which a great laughter was occasioned; whereupon he presently said unto them (in a zealous manner like himself) *Do you laugh when a man speaks for God's honor, and glory?* Upon which there was a more than ordinary silence in the House.'[79] Admittedly a 'private Christian' needed some exceptional, even 'heroical' quality to achieve canonisation, having none of the professional advantages of the divine. But even in this company Mr Jourdain, 'the wonder and *Phoenix* of his age', was the exception to prove the rule of 'mediocrity'.

There were historical and polemical reasons for the stress on moderation in Clarke. His divines all without exception espoused what may be called orthodox puritan opinions, in terms still a shade anachronistic for the times in which they lived, presbyterians or moderate episcopal men, rarely independents and certainly never

---

[76] *Ten eminent divines* pp 310–11.
[77] Collinson, *A Mirror of Elizabethan Puritanism*, pp 4–6.
[78] Quoted, Watkins p 7. I am indebted to Mr John Morgan of Cambridge University for alerting me to this theme.
[79] *Ten eminent divines* pp 480–1, 464, 477.

sectaries. When Simeon Ashe and John Wall wrote a commendatory epistle for one of Clarke's earliest ventures, in December 1649, they expressed interest in the further publication of the 'characters' of such as Preston, Sibbes, Dod and Hildersham who all their lives had 'kept a due distance from *Brownistical* separatism and were zealously affected towards the *Presbyterial* Government of the Church.'[80] Clarke himself might well complain of the odium cast upon some of the subjects of his *Lives*, 'as though they were Fanaticks, Anabaptists, . . . enemies to the State, Traytors, etc.'[81] In the circumstances of the 1650s, and even more after 1662, it became all the more desirable to insist on the general moderation of these worthies and on their detestation of schism. The life of Hildersham disclosed that he had been called 'the *Hammer* of Schismatickes'.[82] Clarke's own father, a minister in Warwickshire, was said to have 'mightily confuted' and 'reclaimed' Brownists, as far back as the 1580s.[83] Edmund Staunton called separatism 'England's in-curable wound', but would always converse and communicate with those that 'were sound in the vitals of christian religion'.[84] 'Moderation' therefore was a keynote struck for a purpose, but the conventions of biography made it a particularly suitable polemical medium.

These discoveries may appear commonplace. The admirable qualities displayed by the puritan saints were not very distinct from those associated with Christian perfection in almost any age. That the biographies should make much of the 'catholic' moderation of the presbyterians is no more than we should expect. But the most striking feature of this literature has still to be mentioned. It is the fact that the conventional virtues of the godly life were represented as indeed virtues, not so noticeably the work of grace as inherent properties and achievements of human character, a suitable subject for admiration and even for eulogy. To recognise this is to see seventeenth-century religious biography in a new light and to link it very closely to the classical biographical tradition.

This will sound like heresy to anyone who supposes that the inevitable centrepiece of puritan biography was a story of the con-version of a naturally vicious and abandoned sinner, and to readers of Haller's *Rise of Puritanism* in particular. According to Haller, the

---

[80] *Lives and deaths of most of those eminent persons*, Sig dv.
[81] *Ten eminent divines*, Sig A4r.
[82] *Thirty-two English divines* p 120.
[83] *Ibid* p 129.
[84] *Lives of sundry eminent persons* p 170.

pattern to which the life of the elect was supposed to conform required an account of a sinful state 'from which the soul destined to be saved was called and after terrific struggle converted'; followed by the chronicle of a lifelong struggle against temptation, especially the temptation to despair: and culminating in a deathbed scene, 'one last terrific bout with Satan and then triumph and glory forever after.' Summaries follow of three of the *Lives* which conform more or less to this model and Haller concludes his analysis: 'We need not further multiply illustrations.'[85]

What the reader will not suspect is that in the majority of the lives chronicled by Clarke there is no mention of conversion at all, only casual references to a calling by grace, and little enough about a life-long struggle to prove that calling. Although too much should not be made of this, it may be significant that two out of Haller's three con-version narratives, as well as other accounts of conversion which he did not mention, had their origins in Lancashire and neighbouring Cheshire.[86] For the north-west was a region polarised between the old and new faiths, where the pilgrimage of a puritan saint was more than likely to begin with conversion of, so to speak, a primary order, from one religion to the other. It is also from Lancashire that one of the most remarkable stories comes of the last 'terrific bout' with Satan, on the deathbed. The story was told because the Lancashire catholics had spread a tale of the failure of protestant faith *in extremis*.[87] These were special cases and the framework of reference was not that of interior spirituality. Narratives of conversion and of the dealings of God and Satan with the Christian, seen as it were from the inside, derive from the personal testimonies made by the members of gathered congrega-tions as the condition of their admission, a procedure alien to the ecclesiology and practice of more 'orthodox' puritans.[88] Clarke's

[85] Haller pp 108–11.
[86] Conversion is a significant element in the following Lancashire and Cheshire lives: Robert Bolton (*Lives and deaths of most of those eminent persons*), Richard Rothwell (*Thirty-two English divines*), these two included by Haller among his examples, John Ball (*Lives of thirty-two English divines*), Richard Mather (*Lives of sundry eminent persons*) and John Bruen Esq of Bruen Stapleford, Cheshire (William Hinde, *A faithfull remonstrance of the holy life and happy death of John Bruen* (London 1641) and in *Second part of the marrow*). Haller's third example, Samuel Fairclough, born at Haverhill in Suffolk, provides the most elaborate conversion narrative outside of the north-west.
[87] The story comes from *A brief discourse of the christian life and death of Mistris Katherine Brettargh*. (See p 521 below.)
[88] Watkins pp 29–30. But non-sectarian puritans sometimes required a form of public renewal of baptismal vows as a condition of admission to the Lord's Supper. (See the *Life* of Samuel Fairclough in *Lives of sundry eminent persons* p 169.) Mrs Elizabeth

Lives have little to do with this interior world, known to us from the puritan diary and the spiritual autobiography into which it fed. The world of Bunyan is not the world of Samuel Clarke.

It would be foolish to suggest that Clarke's *Lives* indicate any theological divergence from the fundamentals of puritan religion, that they were not in some sense governed by the doctrines of covenanted grace, assurance and sanctification which were so incessantly expounded from the pulpit and in countless publications. But the doctrines were not explicitly taught in the biographies. If the godly were twice-born their biographers often neglect to mention the fact and proceed for much of their space to delineate the admirable intellectual and moral qualities with which the saints would appear to have been endowed from birth. The account of the early life of Herbert Palmer, a moderate presbyterian member of the Westminster Assembly, may be cited, not because its features are necessarily typical, but because it offsets the impression left by Haller. Palmer, we are told, 'had excellent natural parts, both intellectual and moral', and enjoyed 'the happiness of a prudent and pious eduction'. From his infancy he was 'addicted to the study both of religion and learning'. 'The *Symptomes* of Grace and Piety began betimes to put themselves forth to the view and observation of others, as soon almost as the exercise and use of reason; so that we may not without good ground esteem him sanctified from the Womb.' When little more than five years old he read the story of Joseph and wept. From a child he intended himself for the ministry and would not be deterred. In a lengthy biography of twelve thousand words, Palmer proves to be faultless, and in ways which could hardly be more puritanical. All this was presumptively the work of grace, but the emphasis is wholly on Palmer's faithfulness to God, not on what God may have wrought in him. He was 'subservient to the glory of God', maintained 'an even walking with God', 'wholly laid himself out for God', 'zealous and tenacious in things that concerned God's glory.'[89]

To sum up the impression gained from our survey of the world of Samuel Clarke: It was an encomiastic world, and this is not surprising, since the proper origins of this literature lay not in the internalised

---

Wilkinson, no separatist, composed a lengthy 'narrative' of 'God's gracious dealing with her soul' and sent it to Dr Robert Harris in order to give account of herself before admission to the Lord's Supper. But this was in the unusual circumstance of her regular parochial ministry being interrupted. (*Ten eminent divines* pp 515–24.)

[89] *Thirty-two English divines* pp 183–201.

doubts and fears of the tender conscience but in the public encomium. The most fruitful and influential source for the puritan biography was the funeral sermon, which I have already dubbed the cuckoo in the protestant nest. This specimen had hatched from the dubious egg of the classical panegyric, which was not laid by Luther or Calvin, nor yet by St Paul. So to the funeral sermon, as the heart of the matter, we finally come.

Originally not only funeral sermons but even the barest forms of prayers at burial were rejected, at least by the more extreme and austere of the early puritans. It was said that burial of the dead was an office belonging to every Christian and a 'surcharge' on the ministry. The *Admonition to the parliament* of 1572 compared funeral sermons to popish trentals 'whereout spring many abuses, and therfore in the best reformed churches, are removed.'[90] Since there was evidence even in the liturgy of the English congregation which had worshipped in Geneva in Mary's reign that this was not so,[91] a discussion followed between John Whitgift and Thomas Cartwright in the course of the mammoth engagement known nowadays as 'the Admonition Controversy'.[92] Under pressure, Cartwright shifted from an absolute objection to funeral sermons as superstitious in implication and socially discriminatory to the concession that it was desirable that notable men should have their public commendation, but that this should take the form of a civil oration and should not be confused with the office of preaching. Both Cartwright and the separatist Henry Barrow plausibly derived the funeral sermon from the burial orations of heathen orators, Cartwright remarking that the Christian oratory of Gregory Nazianzus 'savoured of the manner of Athens, where he was brought up.'[93]

But the godly laity, while deploring such popish funeral customs

---

[90] *An admonition of the Parliament* (London 1572), in *Puritan Manifestoes*, ed W. H. Frere and C. E. Douglas (London 1954 ed) p 28; *Seconde Parte of a Register*, 1 pp 132, 259, 2 p 45; *The Writings of Henry Barrow 1587–1590*, ed Leland H. Carlson, E[lizabethan] N[onconformist] T[exts] 3 (London 1962) pp 459–62; *The Writings of Henry Barrow 1590–1591*, ed Leland H. Carlson, ENT 5 (1966) p 83.

[91] W. D. Maxwell, *John Knox's Genevan Service Book* (London 1931) pp 56–7, 161–4. Variations in the Genevan tradition with respect to the burial service can be traced through *The Book of Common Order of the Church of Scotland*, ed G. W. Sprott (London 1901) p 80, *The Middelburgh Prayer-Book* (Middleburgh 1586) in *Reliquiae Liturgicae* 1, ed Peter Hall (Bath 1847) p 69, and *A directory for the publique worship of God* (London 1644) pp 73–4.

[92] *The Works of John Whitgift*, ed J. Ayre, PS (1851) 1 pp 250–1, 3 pp 361–80.

[93] *Works of Whitgift*, 3 p 375.

as the giving of blacks and the ringing of bells, commonly provided in their wills for a sermon to be preached at their burial.[94] Such sermons were doubtless a nearly universal institution in the Elizabethan church and social pressure soon made a general stand against them a peculiarity of some separatists. As for the funerals of notable preachers, these became occasions for triumphalism, with six brethren of the ministry to carry the bier, a memorable sermon, a large congregation, and lavish entertainment.[95] Nevertheless, individuals retained serious reservations, not on account of any inference of superstition, but for fear of flattery. Alas! Those who revealed that scruple ran the risk of having it added to their other virtues in the panegyric which was certain to follow their demise whether they desired it or not. Samuel Ward, 'the glory of Ipswich', came to John Carter's funeral with his mourning gown, ready to preach to the large congregation assembled, only to be told by Carter's children that their father had charged them 'and that upon his blessing' that there should be no sermon. 'For it may give occasion to speak some good of me that I deserve not and so false things may be uttered in the pulpit.' Ward went away disappointed, but preached his funeral sermon on the next lecture day at Ipswich 'to the great satisfaction of the whole Auditory. *Gloria fugentes sequitur.*'[96] The wealthy and munificent Richard Fishburne towards his end 'did divers times . . . grate upon the abuse of this custome of over-spicing the dead in large commendation' and begged his minister, Nathaniel Shute, to include nothing personal in his funeral sermon. He might have saved his breath. Shute could not disappoint 'the common expectation', and having told this story which only served to prove Fishburne's modesty, he then proceeded to speak of him to the length of twenty-one pages of text, specifying the large amounts bestowed on various charities, to the last penny.[97]

Once again life, or, in this case, death, anticipated the appearance of

---

[94] See, for example, the will of Basil Fielding, a Warwickshire gentleman (ob. 1584) which required that 'at the daie of my burriall a godly sermon be made by some godly learned man, moving the people to prayse God for his mercies bestowed on me in my lyfe and the contynuance thereof to my deathe, and for his comforte and victorye of faythe in a christian lief, and he to have for his paynes sixe shillings eight pence.' (PRO P.C.C. Will Registers Brudenell 5.)

[95] See accounts of the Suffolk funeral of Robert Walsh of Little Waldingfield in 1605 in *Winthrop Papers* I *1498–1628*, Massachusetts Historical Society (1929) pp 89, 153; and of the Chelsea funeral of William Bradshaw, in *Thirty-two English divines* p 51.

[96] *Ten eminent divines* p 20.

[97] [Nathaniel] Shute, *Corona charitatis. [The crowne of charitie]* (London 1626) pp 25–46.

a literature. Up to the end of Elizabeth's reign almost the only funeral sermons thought suitable for publication commemorated members of the nobility and notable gentry, and they appeared with plain and formal titles. All others were allowed to waste their sweetness on the desert air. But in 1602 a little book was published which pointed to a new literary fashion and perhaps even initiated it. This was *Deaths advantage little regarded*, containing the two funeral sermons preached at the burial near Liverpool of a lady remarkable only for her religion, Mrs Katherine Brettergh, together with an account of her life.[98] Mrs Brettergh was a young person of twenty-two at the time of her death, married but two years, and she was the sister of John Bruen, a Cheshire squire who would later provide the subject for one of the earliest and most elaborate of puritan biographies.[99] *Deaths advantage* proved to be a best-seller and went into its fifth edition by 1617. From the beginning of James's reign there was a steady flow of published funeral sermons honouring the memories of divines and notable 'private Christians'. A peak was reached in 1619 with at least eleven such publications,[100] and some preachers, such as Thomas Gataker, began to acquire a special reputation not only as funeral preachers but as the authors of funeral sermons. The floodgates were not yet opened as they would be with the general torrent of publication in the forties and fifties. By a rough count there were some seventy separate funeral sermons printed between 1600 and 1640 which survive,[101] a tally which must surely have

---

[98] *Deaths advantage little regarded, and the soules solace against sorrow. Preched in two funerall sermons at Childwal in Lancashire at the buriall of Mistris Katherine Brettargh the third of Iune 1601.* The preachers were William Harrison and William Leigh. The institution of two sermons, separated by dinner, seems to have been a north-country custom— see my article 'Lectures by Combination: Structures and Characteristics of Church Life in the 17th-Century England', *BIHR* 48 (1975) pp 201–2. The second sermon is followed by a separate title: *A brief discourse of the christian life and death of Mistris Katherine Brettargh.* There is also an engraved portrait of the lady. *See above*, 486-7.

[99] William Hinde, *A faithful remonstrance of the holy life and happy death of John Bruen of Bruen-Stapleford in the county of Chester, Esquire* (London 1641); reprinted in *Second part of the marrow* pp 80–104.

[100] John Barlow, *The joy of the upright man*; John Barlow, *The true guide to glory*; Samuel Crooke, *Death subdued. Or, the death of death* (for Queen Anne); Stephen Denison, *The monument, or tombe-stone* (for Mrs Elizabeth Juxon); Thomas Gataker, *The benefit of a good name and a good end*; Thomas Gataker, *Pauls desire of dissolution and deaths advantage* (for Mrs Rebekka Crisp); Timothy Oldmayne, *Gods rebuke in taking from us Sir E. Lewkenor* (of Denham, Suffolk); John Preston, *The patriarchs portion* (for Sir T. Reynell); John Preston, *A sermon preached at the funeral of Mr Arthur Upton Esquire in Devon*; William Sclater, *Three sermons* (including a funeral sermon).

[101] This figure has been arrived at after a cursory perusal of *STC* and investigations in the British Library, Dr Williams's Library and the library of New College, London (shortly before its dispersion). I am particularly grateful to the librarian of New

been exceeded in the following twenty years. But in 1640 itself there
was a kind of apotheosis with the publication of an ambitious folio
volume containing no less than forty-seven funeral sermons, *The house
of mourning*.[102] By this time the convention of curious titles was for-
malised: *Deliverance from the king of feares. Or, Freedom from the feare of
death; The destruction of the destroyer. Or, The overthrowe of the last
enemie; Sinnes stipend and gods munificence.*

But the preachers still assumed a defensive tone and sometimes
paraded ancient authorities to justify their enterprise: not so much the
epistle to the Hebrews ('and these all having obtained a good report
through faith') as Cicero, Seneca, Pliny, Basil and Gregory Nazianzus,
a great standby.[103] Moreover among the puritans a strict convention
required that what was termed the 'testimony' or 'commendation'
should be detached from the sermon proper, so partly meeting
Cartwright's requirement that epideictic oratory should not imper-
sonate preaching.[104] There were habitual ways of marking the transition from the sermon to what was no doubt often regarded as the
major business: 'And now brethren beloved and longed for (I say
now) that I have finished my course, ended the text, and closed up the
booke, give me leave a little to turne me to the dead . . .'[105] 'Thus much
of my text. Give mee leave to adde a fewe words about the particular
occasion of this our meeting.'[106] 'And so I fall downe from the text to
the occasion.'[107] The change of gear was sometimes a further occasion

College, the Reverend Dr G. F. Nuttall, for his kindness in enabling me to look into
the remarkable collection of some 1900 funeral sermons amassed in the last century
by Mr Charles Godwin of Bath and among the holdings of that Library.

[102] *Threnoikos. The house of mourning. Delivered in XLVII sermons, preached at funeralls
of divers faithfull servants of Christ. By Daniel Featly Richard Sibbs Martin Day Thomas
Taylor and other reverend divines* (London 1640). However the subject of this collection
is mortality. Few of the preachers and fewer still of the deceased are identified and the
motive of 'memorial' or 'testimonial' is largely absent.

[103] See especially the epistles to two of Thomas Gataker's publications: *Two funeral
sermons much of one and the same subiect: to wit, the benefit of death* (London 1620);
The decease of Lazarus Christs friend (for Mr John Parker) (London 1640). There are
quotations from Nazianzus in I.F., *A sermon preched at Ashby de la Zouch* (for
Elizabeth, countess of Huntingdon) (London 1635).

[104] See, for example, [Robert] Harris, in his funeral sermon for Sir Anthony Cope of
Hanwell, *Samuels funeral* (London 1618) Sig A4: 'Onely I could wish that our age
would distinguish betwixt funerall orations and funeral sermons, as former ages have
done, and not confound so different things.'

[105] William Leigh, *The soules solace against sorrow*, with *Deaths advantage*, p 69.

[106] Nicolas Guy, *Pieties pillar. Or, a sermon preched at the funerall of Mistresse Elizabeth
Gouge* (London 1626) p 37.

[107] Shute, *Corona charitatis*, p 24.

for critical reflection on the common abuse of flattery: 'I professe first to you, that I have often greved at the licentiousnesse of my brethren in this kind.'[108] Alternatively the 'testimony' could be wholly separated from the sermon and published as a separate item, or as a preface.[109] With Mrs Brettergh it appears as a freestanding biography with separate title page: *A brief discourse of the christian life and death of Mistris Brettargh*. Such a 'relation' or 'true narration' was sometimes contributed by a husband or other relative of the deceased,[110] reminding us of how close we are to the 'testimony' of the funerary inscription, still with us in an attenuated form. Puritan funerary monuments were sometimes expressive of a triumphalism strangely out of keeping with the humility with which the godly dead had been credited in life.[111]

Haller knew that the funeral sermon and more especially its testimonial 'lean-to' fed into puritan biography,[112] but he was insensitive to the implications of this parentage when he represented the *Lives* as typically stories of conversion and spiritual struggle. Detached from the sermon, or only loosely associated with it as a kind of 'use' or application of the text, the testimony was not only free to become in essence an encomium in the classical manner: it was almost obliged to assume this shape for want of any other model to follow. Reformed theology was an accidental, not a substantial element in these orations. Consequently the preachers were sometimes conscious of stepping well outside their proper role into unfamiliar and uncongenial territory. Robert Harris began his testimony to his patron, Sir Anthony Cope of Hanwell, by explaining that 'as I never flattered him living, so I will not deifie him (as the Heathens did their Patrons) being dead. He had his wants, his faults, nor did wee concurre in all opinions.' But

---

108 Richard Stock, *The churches lamentation for the losse of the godly* (for Lord John Harrington) (London 1614) p 61.

109 See, for example, [Thomas] Wilson, *Christs farewell [to Jerusalem and last prophesie]* (for Dr Colfe, sub-dean of Canterbury) (London 1614) Sig A4.

110 See, for example, the 'short relation' added by the husband of Mrs Mary Gunter to the funeral sermon preached by Thomas Taylor, *The pilgrims profession* (London 1633). From a much earlier date one may recall a similar office performed for his wife by the moralist Philip Stubbs: *A chrystal glass for christian women. Containing a most excellent discourse of the godly life and death of Mrs Katherine Stubs, who departed this life in Burton upon Trent in Staffordshire the 14th December* (London 1591). The fame of Stubbs suggests that he may have set the fashion followed a decade later with the elaborate commemoration of Mrs Brettergh.

111 I may refer to my remarks on the tomb of Sir Edward Lewkenor of Denham, Suffolk (ob. 1605) in my essay 'Magistracy and Ministry: a Suffolk Miniature', to be published in 1977 as part of a *Festschrift* for Geoffrey Nuttall. *See above*, pp. 445-66.

112 Haller pp 101-2.

this was no way out of a classic *circulus vitiosus*. Harris had achieved only a subtler brand of flattery. In life when he had preached sharply against his patron's sins Cope would say: 'Goe on, spare us not . . .' What could be worthier of praise and imitation than that?[113]

Most funeral preachers were not over-subtle in their eulogies. In the words of Donald Stauffer, who was not appreciative of this grossly repetitious, heavily stylised rhetoric, 'they damned with great praise.'[114] 'An anniversary to his fame' is a phrase which appears in one title.[115] A wealthy London merchant is 'a man of a thousand'.[116] Of a twelve-year old girl it is said: 'She hath deserved praise, having not onely done vertuously, but exceeded all others of her sexe and age.'[117] Goodness is the sovereign word. 'I say but this, God's Church in him hath lost a good Minister, this Parish a good Pastor, his Wife a good Husband, Schollers a good Patron, the poore a good friend, and we all a good neighbour.'[118] 'He was first bonus vir, secondly bonus Christianus, thirdly bonus Theologus, fourthly bonus Pastor,'[119] The question asked of old 'Why callest thou me good?' seems for the purpose of these occasions to have been forgotten; and with it that other question 'What has Athens to do with Jerusalem?'

Allow me to admit that when this paper was first proposed the inclusion of 'Erasmian' in the title was little more than a ploy, a wedding garment to preserve the puritans of the seventeenth century from being cast into outer darkness from a feast dedicated to 'Renaissance and Renewal'. But after all there has turned out to be something in it. In his *Paraclesis* Erasmus put his own rhetorical question which has always been at hand throughout this discussion: 'Moreover what else is the philosophy of Christ, which He himself calls a rebirth [*renascentia*], than the restoration of human nature, originally well formed?'[120] But knowing Erasmus, as we must all feel that we do, a little, he would surely have been disconcerted by the volume of the response which has been measured in this paper: too indigestible to be a truly 'godly feast'. In a sense only one pattern for living was needed. And if living

---

[113] Harris, *Samuells funerall*, Sig A4ᵛ.
[114] Stauffer p 89.
[115] Shute, *Corona charitatis*.
[116] Gataker, *The decease of Lazarus*, p 33.
[117] John Bryan, *The vertuous daughter* (Mistress Cicely Puckering, ob. 1636) (London 1640) p 10.
[118] Richard Pecke, *Christs watch word. Occasioned on the funerall of the truly reverend M. Laurence Bodley* (London 1635) p 1.
[119] Wilson, *Christs farewell*, Sig A5.
[120] Olin p 100.

examples were called for, two or three were sufficient: not a whole 'magazeen of religious patterns'. Erasmus would probably wish to be exempted from parentage of what has turned out to be a chapter in *The Rise of Moralism*,[121] a somewhat depressing foretaste of the routinisation of the puritan spirit which lay in the future. It was, after all, in the future that the literature reviewed in my paper was to do its work. My copy of Clarke's *Marrow of ecclesiastical history*, picked up in the Charing Cross Road in 1961, carries the inscription: 'Mary Estwicks book given her by old Mr Williams of Peldon which she give to Elizabeth Estwick after her Death'; and in a nineteenth-century hand 'M. Hudson's Book'.[122]

---

[121] I quote from the title of the book by C. F. Allison, *The Rise of Moralism. The Proclamation of the Gospel from Hooker to Baxter* (New York 1966).

[122] I am indebted to my colleague Miss Marion O'Connor for a number of helpful comments on this paper.

THE
MARROW
OF
Eclesiastical History,

CONTAINED IN

The LIVES of one hundred
forty eight FATHERS, SCHOOLMEN,
first REFORMERS, and MODERN DIVINES
which have flourished in the Church since Christ's
time to this present Age :

Faithfully collected, and orderly disposed according to the
CENTURIES wherein they lived :

Together

With the Lively Effigies of most of the eminentest of
them cut in COPPER.

The second Edition enlarged in most of the Lives, with the addition of
nine Lives which were not in the Former.

By SAMUEL CLARK Pastor of *Bennet Fink, London.*

*Ut qui præceptis non accendimur, saltem exemplis incitemur, atq, in appetitu Rectitudinis,
nil sibi mens nostra difficile æstimet quod perfectè peragi ab aliis videt* Greg. Mag. l. 9 c. 43.
Wherefore seeing we are compassed about with so great a cloud of witnesses, let us lay
aside every weight, and the sin which doth so easily beset us, and let us run with
patience the race which is set before us, *Heb. 12. 1.*

London, Printed for *T. V.* and are to be sold by *William Roybould*
at the *Unicorn* in *Pauls-Church-yard,* 1654.

SAMUEL CLARK'S *MARROW OF ECCLESIASTICAL HISTORY* (1654). This copy,
purchased in the Charing Cross Road in 1961, bears an inscription which points evocatively
towards the long historical legacy of the godly people: 'Mary Estwicks book given her by Old
Mr Williams of Peldon which she give to Elizabeth Estwick after her death'; and, in a
nineteenth-century hand, 'M. Hudson's Book'.

20

TOWARDS A BROADER UNDERSTANDING
OF THE EARLY DISSENTING TRADITION

THE STRATEGY OF THIS ESSAY[1] can be expressed in geometrical terms, as one of dimension. The origins of the dissenting tradition have received from religious, denominationally committed historians (and also, although this lies beyond the scope of this paper, from historians of early American culture) an excessively vertical, or linear treatment. Questions of genealogy, concerning the descent of religious bodies and systems, have prevailed. *A Genetic Study*, the subtitle of the late Professor Perry Miller's book *Orthodoxy in Massachusetts*,[2] is a label which can be widely applied to the literature. The present study is set in another dimension and explores some of the horizontal and lateral relationships of early protestant dissent. It treats the eighty years from the Elizabethan Settlement to the Long Parliament for this purpose, as historians often do for other legitimate purposes, as if they were a unity, and with more respect for regularities and consistent features than for events and developments. Politics are not forgotten but for reasons of economy disregarded, and so is the earthquake which immediately followed the period under review. Sometimes it may be helpful to share the ignorance of the early seventeenth century, few of whose inhabitants could have suspected that they were living in "Pre-Revolutionary England."[3]

The genealogical approach so apparent in much of the historiography of early Dissent owes something to the nature of the task, something to the way in which it has been tackled. If the story is told on a chronological plan, the historian is driven down a tunnel which shuts out any expansive views on either side. This tunnel is the separatist tradition, nearly continuous from the second or third decade of the reign of Queen Elizabeth I, a tradition of renouncing all communion with the Church of England in order to form, as might be said in the 1970s, an alternative church. Something may be said about the first generation of Protestants, and even about their Lollard antecedents, but the story is assumed to have its proper beginnings with Elizabethan Puritanism, treated as the matrix of Dissent and migration. A recent writer remarks: "The English Reformation and Elizabethan Puritanism belong to the prehistory of Dissent; its own history begins with the Separatists."[4] The story detaches itself from the matrix with the earliest episodes of Separatism and Near-Separatism in London in the 1560s, and ten years later with the gathered church and the writings of Robert Browne and Robert Harrison. Separatism is now stuck with the brand name of Brownism, because of Browne's later defection a cause of grave embarrassment; as John Waddington wrote in 1869: "No educated Congregationalist can feel flattered by the ecclesiastical genealogy that takes its rise from Robert Browne."[5] The next two decades bring the reorganization of London Separatism under the leadership of Henry Barrow and John Greenwood, the martyrdom of Barrow and Greenwood and also of John Penry, the exodus to Holland, the long and controversial rule of Francis Johnson. The scene is now set for three or four decades in Amsterdam, Leyden and Rotterdam, and the themes are the troubled affairs of the Amsterdam church and its offshoots, the new elements entering from the East Midlands under Robinson and Smith, the rancorous relations between these groups and other nonseparated churches serving the needs of Englishmen overseas on, so to speak, legitimate business: an ecclesiastical Balkans of baffling diversity. Later still the story moves again, to New England, and to the search for true church principles by brethren in three countries. And all this is but the curtain-raiser to the properly denominational history which begins in the 1640s. Inevitably, the historian who follows this course closely and with an eye to every turn of persuasion or argument makes his own separation from the mainstream of English religious life in these decades. It is the contention of what follows that the broader context is as much a part of the early dissenting tradition as the annals of the Separatists.

It is not the purpose of this essay to enter into denunciation of denominational history, least of all at a time when the past as a system of values and in the shape of denominational and connexional archives is at serious risk from modern indifference. The soundness of the best denominational scholarship, as well as its inestimable value for the life of the churches, needs no emphasis. Nor do its more perverse characteristics.[6] It may be taken as read that denominational history, indeed ecclesiastical history itself, derives from martyrology and has been given to robust apologetic (as Benjamin Brook told his readers in 1813: ". . . the contents of these volumes tend to expose the evils of bigotry and persecution"[7]); that it is engaged history, committed to the buttressing of contested positions in the internal or external affairs of the churches; and that it has tended to foster an illusion of continuity between the past and the historian's present, so that the nineteenth century is assumed in the seventeenth, and the millenarianism which conditioned so much seventeenth-century perception becomes an embarrassment, rarely mentioned and perhaps not even noticed.

But a further critical point connects more directly with the present argument and will stand some elaboration. As the writing of denominational history became more professional and critical, from the late nineteenth century onwards, so its angle of vision was narrowed rather than extended. Waddington had written exuberantly of the *Track of the Hidden Church,* and of the light of congregational principles gleaming forth in unexpected ways.[8] He managed to write 700 pages of his *Congregational History* before he reached the reign of Elizabeth, expansive history on the scale of John Foxe's Book of Martyrs, adapting indeed a perspective and vision which were Foxe's to a denominational purpose. But the American scholar H. M. Dexter, who inaugurated the modern, critical study of congregationalist history, was not tempted to predate Independency. He derived it from its perceptible historical roots, which for him were literary roots: it was *The Congregationalism of the Last Three Hundred Years As Seen In Its Literature.*[9] (The astonishing Bibliography of 7250 items remains indispensable.) The process of scholarly contraction continued with another American classic, Williston Walker's *Creeds and Platforms of Congregationalism* (1893), which handled its subject as an intellectual system, pure and simple: in effect, "a Congregationalist is one who accepts the tenets of Congregationalism."[10]

In the first half of this century, the religious historians of early dissent continued with increasing sophistication and precision to investigate the descent of their church principles. Their writings reflect on the one hand a heightened denominational awareness and the formalising of inter-church relations, and, on the other, the prevailing and, as someone has said, still "majestically narrow" ways of Anglo-Saxon historians, the sovereignty of constitutional studies, dealing with the descent of political institutions on a basis of the rigorous study of the public records. Champlin Burrage and Albert Peel, the two leading scholars in this field, were at home in the great manuscript collections, compensating for Dexter's pronounced literary bias,[11] and Peel was one who knew the Elizabethan religious scene from the inside. But Peel was also a devoted servant of his church, who paid due attention to the somewhat scholastic question: "Who were the first Congregationalists?"[12] His bequest was the great series of Elizabethan Nonconformist Texts which Professor Carlson carries on his shoulders, and which we honor in this volume.[13] By establishing the complete canon of the earliest separatist printed literature, these volumes have brought refinement and reinforcement to an established historical school: witness the distinct advances registered in Dr B. R. White's recent review of the whole question.[14]

Meanwhile, in the United States, the great Perry Miller had complicated the genealogy by denying that the New England way of Congregationalism, the orthodoxy of Massachusetts, stemmed from the separatist tradition, as mediated through the New Plymouth Colony. It was John Cotton who first wrote, in 1648, of "the line of the Pedigree of the Independents in New-England,"[15] and Miller returned to something close to Cotton's account of the matter in deriving the pedigree from a distinct body of thought which, as he believed, proved of crucial importance among the various streams converging on the "single pool of New England orthodoxy," a source in its turn of English Independency. This, according to Miller, was the philosophy of "Non-Separating Congregationalism", of which more presently. This thesis, stated in *Orthodoxy in Massachusetts*, was contributory to the grander design of the book called *The New England Mind*, which asserted the majestic coherence of American puritan thought.[16] Miller never doubted that the early history of American culture was implicit in its literature, and it has taken a later generation of New England historians to point out (in the words of one of them) that "the history of the New England mind is not the history of New England."[17]

Evidently much of the scholarship we have considered, including the best of it, runs the risk of incurring strictures of the kind expressed by Lucien Fèbvre in a famous article of 1929 on the origins of the French Reformation, entitled "Une question mal posée."[18] In that article Fèbvre attacked a century of historians for their fixation on questions of a highly specific nature, while neglecting the deeper springs of cultural change. He ended with the demand that the words "specificité, priorité, nationalité" be erased from the historian's vocabulary. Transferred to the history of early English Dissent, such a programme would be too drastic, and would lead to some slipshod history.[19] Nor is it clear that questions of this order are necessarily "mal posée." But they are not the only questions. Dr. White evidently aspires to encompass "the whole story," and the final chapter of his book is called "The Significance of the English Separatist Tradition."[20] But 'significance' means its significance for the further evolution of nonconformist churchmanship. It is as if the historian of the fashionable subject of witchcraft in Tudor and Stuart England were to discuss its significance exclusively in terms of what the witchcraft tradition and the subsequent practice of witchcraft may owe to the witches of the seventeenth century. (No doubt such a work is even now in progress.)[21] The sociologist Dr. Bryan Wilson, who specializes in religious sects, regards them as isolated, model structures which may prove relevant to our understanding of the wider society to which they relate.[22] But the sects of the seventeenth century are approached by some denominational historians, not for what they may tell us about the Church and the society from which they came out, nor even, in that deceptive phrase, "for their own sake," or in the mountaineer's words, "because they are there," but for their value for denominational posterity, an entirely legitimate, but restricted motive.[23]

The escape-hatch from the critical prolegomenon to the main body of this essay is provided by Perry Miller's famous Non-Separating Congregationalists. These were a number of writers, William Bradshaw, William Ames, Paul Baynes, Robert Parker, and also, in his own distinctive vein, Henry Jacob, all flourishing in the first two or three decades of the seventeenth century, all ambiguously and eclectically related to the Church of England on the one hand, and to the churches of the separation overseas on the other.[24] Our knowledge of their opinions comes partly from manifestoes calling for further reformation as they conceived of it, such as Bradshaw's celebrated pamphlet *English Puritanisme containeing the maine opinions of the rigidest sort of those that are called puritans in the realme of England*;[25] partly from works of systematic divinity or casuistry, aimed at a European audience, notably from the pen of the internationally recognised Ames;[26] partly from polemical exchanges with John Robinson of Leyden and other Separatists.[27] Secondarily, in the 1630s, with the apparent conversion of John Cotton to these views at about the time of his emigration and that of Thomas Hooker, the line of non-separatist thought broadened to nourish the polity of the New England churches: the work of "a sort of second generation to the Ames-Bradshaw group" according to Miller.[28]

The Non-Separating Congregationalists apparently participated in many essential positions of Independency which had been discovered by the Separatists or which would be disclosed in the future by those of the Congregational Way. As Bradshaw wrote in *English Puritanisme*: "They hould and maintaine that every Companie, Congregation or Assemblie of men,[29] ordinarilie ioyning together in[30] the true worship of God, is a true visible church of Christ, and that the same title is improperlie attributed to any other Convocations,[31] Synods, Societies, combinations, or assemblies whatsoever."[32] ("Touching the outward forme," wrote Ames, there were "so many visible Churches as there are distinct congregations.")[33] "Joyning together" implied "a special bond among themselves . . . a covenant, either expresse or implicite, wherby believers doe particularly bind themselves to performe all those duties, both toward God and one towards another, which pertain to the respect and edification of the Church."[34] In most of these writings, the germ of a major principle of Independency appears, which in the future would distinguish those of the Congregational Way as much from Presbyterianism as from Prelacy: there may be and even ought to be synods, "convocations . . . voluntarily confederate," able to assist the local congregation with "counsel," "advice", "support." But synods can have no power to overrule or "rule imperiously" the churches, which must not suffer a "subordination," says Jacob, "or surely not a subjection."[35] Significantly, *English Puritanisme* has nothing to say on the subject of synods.

In spite of notions apparently incompatible with a national and hierarchical religious establishment, these writers condemned the path taken by the Separatists. As a casuist, Ames granted the rationality of choosing as between true churches "the purest as farre as we are able," but he found "grievous discommodities" in any "rash departure" from the English Church, which was a true church by the only valid criterion: true faith.[36] His close friend Bradshaw wrote on *The unreasonablenesse of the separation*.[37] Jacob's position was more rigid, since by 1616 when he formed at Southwark what is traditionally claimed as the first properly congregational church on English soil[38] (genealogy again!) he taught that Christians were bound in conscience to join themselves to "Christ's true, visible, political Church" in the form of "a free congregation of visible Christians," and to forsake other bodies which were "polities of men's mere devising." But Jacob and his congregation were willing to communicate with the English parish congregations so long as no assent was implied to human traditions and abuses, and to acknowledge that among these congregations were "many true, visible, yea politicall churches in some degree and in some respect," although their validity could be said to rest curiously and perhaps transiently on their ignorance of these truths.[39]

Some of Jacob's tracts and Ames against Robinson rest the case for non-separation not on the Church of England as an undifferentiated whole but on those godly elements in the Church and on the more "forward" preachers, "the true members of our best assemblies,"[40] in John Winthrop's words, "the faithfull in England (whom we account the Churches)";[41] and specifically on the agreement that was held to exist among these undoubtedly sound Christians to assemble and worship without constraint. This was what Ames had in mind when he wrote that a church covenant might be implicit rather than explicit. In subsequent New England writing it was taken for granted that although the covenant was a necessary ground for the Church's existence, such a covenant could and often did exist implicitly in England.[42] Ames had reminded Robinson of the "many exercises of religion in England" where none were present by constraint, and where the Prayer Book did "not so much as appeare."[43] Similarly, it could be alleged that wherever there was some element of agreement and mutual consent between the minister and his people, a valid ministry was present which was not prejudiced by the "accidents" of episcopal ordination and institution, or by the patron's rights in presentation, an argument with extensive background in the counsels of Elizabethan Puritanism;[44] as Bradshaw put it: "Soe that they are onely in aequivocation, and name, or Metaphorically, Priestes and Deacons: But really Pastors and Teachers."[45] If all ecclesiastical organization outside the congregation was merely civil, it could be acknowledged civilly, without harm to essentials. The English parishes were "entyre spirituall bodies though civilly combined into a diocesan government."[46] The majority of ministers migrating to Massachusetts after 1630 appear to have been impressed with such arguments as these. To their own satisfaction, they were making not "a separation (rigidly taken) but a lawfull secession, or a heavenly translation from corrupt to more pure churches." The Laudian regime had now made it, in terms of Ames's casuistry, less inconvenient to go than to stay. But this was a considered alternative to setting up "private separated churches" inside England, while "to make the *English* Churches, and their Ministries, and their Worship, and their Professors, either nullities or Anti-Christian" was said by Cotton from New England to be "a witnesse not onely beyond the truth, but against the Truth of the Lord Jesus and his word of Truth."[47]

The argument of *Orthodoxy in Massachusetts*, and for that matter the whole of Perry Miller's stately intellectual edifice, has taken some hard knocks. Since his death, the New England Way has been disassembled by a generation of revisionists for whom the acceptable word is "pluralistic," the damning word "monolithic."[48] Some time ago now, from the other side of the Atlantic, Dr. Geoffrey Nuttall, in the manner of Voltaire on the Holy Roman Empire, doubted whether the Non-Separating Congregationalist group was a "group," or truly "congregationalist," or "nonseparating," pointing out that "semiseparatist" was a preferable term, used by contemporaries.[49] Moreover it can be shown that Perry Miller's understanding, or rather misunderstanding, of puritan ecclesiology, whether separatist, or semiseparatist or nonseparatist, was vitiated (the word is hardly too strong) by a radical misapprehension of the puritan doctrine of covenanted grace, so that he imagined, against all the evidence, that the purpose of a church covenant was to restrict membership of the visible church to a minority of the proven elect, in order to achieve physical identity with the church invisible; whereas the true intention was to confine membership to the visibly worthy, that is, to "saints visible to the eyes of rational charity."[50]

Given that mistake near the heart of the matter, the Non-Separating Congregationalists (so-called) were bound to appeal perversely ingenious, so that Miller rejected their argument, except as a piece of casuistry, never ceasing to denigrate the "glaring inconsistency" of this "prize bit of circumlocution," this "abstruse point," this "adroit subterfuge," the fruit of a "labyrinthine process of . . . reasoning"—which, however, deceived no one. Of course, Miller was concerned only with the value of the argument as intellectual currency, and even so it is odd that such a "cobweb of sophistry" should have been credited with parentage of what he otherwise calls "the majesty and coherence of Puritan thinking."[51] It did not occur to him that affairs within the Church of England could have remotely resembled the account of them given or implied by Jacob and Ames. This essay seeks to rehabilitate the apparently shaky mainstay of a discredited thesis, and to put flesh and blood on the nonseparatist case as not merely intellectually consistent but corresponding in some degree to the experience of Puritans remaining unseparated in the Church of England. That a scholar of Perry Miller's stature should find such a proposition incredible points in the first place to the neglect of the grass-roots, manuscript evidence, and in the second to some inappropriate perspectives in relation to the Elizabethan and Jacobean Church and to the place of Puritanism within it.

These perspectives, widely shared, include some misunderstanding of how the Puritans related to the established church structures, coupled with a tendency to underestimate the extent to which the Church and society were affected by puritan practice and influence; failure to recognize the strong inbuilt tendency towards Independency in puritan circles; and reluctance to acknowledge the strength and forcefulness of Puritanism as a lay and popular movement. These complaints apply to much of the literature, but not, it must be said, to the books of the Master of Balliol, Christopher Hill,[52] which neglect none of these points, although they are turned by Hill to purposes rather different from those of the religious historian.

On the issue of definition and relationship, Puritanism is too often treated in contradistinction to Anglicanism or conformism as Nonconformity and minority opposition, which is to say that it is defined negatively, with respect to supposed norms, and peripherally, in relation to a supposed center. Of course Puritanism often embraced a nonconformist resistance to some Anglican ceremonies, or even a more general rejection of Anglican worship and polity, and there could be little point in denying that it was as a protest against the policy of the Elizabethan Church that it acquired identity in the first place. But it is also possible, and by the early decades of the seventeenth century preferable, to consider Puritanism as embodying the mainstream of English Protestantism, to which some of the distinctive institutions and ordinances of the established Church (loyalty to which was widely and usefully characterized as "formalism") were not so much opposed as irrelevant.[53] Some Jacobean and Caroline Puritans were not nonconformists at all in their response to what one of them called "things of small matter, not touching matter but manner, not substance but Ceremonyes, not piety but pollity, not devocton (sic) but decency, not conscience but Comelynesse,"[54] and yet as in Richard Baxter's youthful experience, contemporaries called them Puritans and had no doubt what they meant by it: a "singular" style of life.[55] Baxter's family were alienated from their neighbors, and the fact that they were called Puritans expressed their alienation, but it is nevertheless a mistake to interpret Puritanism too exclusively in terms of *anomie*.[56] At least it is necessary to decide what the Puritans were alienated from. In towns dominated by puritan oligarchs and in a Church widely infiltrated with puritan religion, often with the connivance of those in authority, it is not clear that Puritanism could always be equated with rejection of the *status quo*.

It is above all necessary to recognize that Puritanism expressed an evolved but still in some vital respects primitive and fresh Protestantism which, perhaps because of the peculiar conditions obtaining in the English Church, retained its free, popular and expansive impulse for longer than might otherwise have been expected. With the Puritans we are still in the full flush of the Reformation, not in some post-Reformation atmosphere of orthodoxy or unorthodoxy, and we are seeing the first fruits of a protestant preaching which was an appealing novelty in some regions as much as a century after the Reformation, nationally, is held in the textbooks to have occurred.[57] At no point is it possible to distinguish absolutely between Puritanism and, so to speak, mere Protestantism. This is not to deny that much of what we can recognize as Anglicanism was equally emergent in these decades, and was also legitimately derived from the Reformation. But as Dr. Tyacke has rightly insisted,[58] it was the high Anglicanism of the time, Arminian doctrine and Laudian formalism, which appeared strange and novel in the 1630s, whereas what we take for Puritanism would have been widely equated with orthodoxy. In 1641 a clerical writer remarked that he had been a minister for thirty years "when innovations were not thought of," and there can be no doubt that the innovations he had in mind were "innovations savouring of popery," for his experience had been in places "branded with the odious reproch of Puritanical rather than of Popish or formall." This was said in the context of a tract on the administration of the Communion which cites and approves "the ancient practice of the Church of England" of receiving in the chancel, seated around the table, and speaks of another very general custom to which the author takes exception only on practical grounds, of taking the bread and wine down to the people sitting in their pews.[59]

There is no satisfactory way in a single essay to justify claims for the widespread social entrenchment of Puritanism (in these senses) in Jacobean England. To some extent they must be taken on trust, as the impression of an extensive forager in the sources. In my *Elizabethan Puritan Movement* I tried to convey something of the gathering and expansive influence of a Puritanism which amounted to the continuing Reformation, clerical, popular and political, and I illustrated its progress particularly in East Anglia,

Essex and the Midlands.[60] For the early decades of the seventeenth century, the studies of Yorkshire by Dr. Newton and Dr. Marchant and of the other side of the Pennines by Dr. Richardson have demonstrated the great inroads made by puritan religion in regions which were not much affected before the end of the sixteenth century.[61] There is no need to go beyond the accessible biographies of puritan saints collected in the 1660s and 1670s by Samuel Clarke[62] to be impressed and widely informed about the religious lives and habits of those who called themselves sincere professors of religion and were spitefully called Puritans, and who grew up in the early years of the century. Like all improving and exemplary literature, these lives of divines and of eminent "private christians" must be read with discrimination.[63] They paint a rosy picture and are written within conventions of topic and language. The many implications of a mass movement are not to be trusted. The proportion of the total population which was Nonconformist in the late seventeenth century was small,[64] and earnest saints were perhaps never very numerous. Like John Foxe's martyrology, the stylized and specialized vocabulary must gloss over much variety of opinion and experience, as well as disguising a steady evolution towards a more spiritual and interior religion. Moreover the language of some of the biographies belongs to the fifties and sixties rather than to the twenties or thirties, which produces some subtle distortions. But when literary form criticism has done its worst, these narratives still contain invaluable information, especially on the corporate religious activities of the Puritans, which the manuscript sources tend to confirm and enrich. In skeletal essentials at least, an impressively homogeneous religious world is disclosed, suggesting that historians have been more imprecise in their delineations than is necessary.[65]

When Richard Baxter gave an account of his pastoral experience at Kidderminster in the 1650s,[66] most of the institutional forms which he described had been known in many parts of England for decades. It was these which structured the religious experience of the "choicest preachers and professors." A summary account of these well-established proceedings can be readily given. The professors, whose profession is frequently said to have arisen from some process of conversion (and it is in relation to conversion, in particular, that the conventions of the *Lives* may stand between us and reality), depended upon the ministrations of a godly preaching minister. Their lives revolved around the Sabbath, when the whole day was given up to religious exercises, normally with a sermon in the morning, after an abbreviated morning prayer, and a sermon linked with catechizing in the afternoon, with the interstices filled with other "exercises"; and around other sermons heard on at least one other day of the week. Where there was no acceptable preaching in their parish of residence, the godly went elsewhere, and this "gadding to sermons" in the Elizabethan phrase, "as doves to the(ir) windows,"[67] which is the Biblical cliché of the biographies, was practised even when the people had their own preacher, "young and old together," "in companies" or "troops," "wet and dry," "summer and winter," "came from far and went home late," are phrases which reverberate. Monthly communions also gathered the faithful from a wide catchment area, and when disciplinary tests were applied to exclude scandalous or ignorant parishioners from the sacrament the communion service itself became a powerful solvent of parochial religion and a symbol of a differently ordered Christian community.[68] When the godly enjoyed a preaching minister of their own, whether he held the benefice or occupied a salaried lectureship or a private position in some household, a close bond between pastor and people was often established. Even in the case of beneficed clergy, episcopal ordination and institution were sometimes regarded as mere civil procedures to be passed through, or even obstacles to be circumvented. The puritan patron often colluded in a measure of congregational election, sometimes inviting the assistance if not the actual presbyterian laying on of hands of other preaching ministers. Not infrequently the minister was directly supported, in whole or part, from the voluntary offerings of the flock, or by the patron's generosity.

The sermons which the godly heard were rehearsed afterwards in exercises of "repetition," when the notes made by schoolboys and others were brought into play. Repetition, conference, prayer and psalms occupied the interval between public exercises on the Sabbath, and metrical psalm-singing was employed on all occasions, even whilst walking or riding to church, which in itself was not a casual but a studied social and religious activity. In some places there were regular days of conference, held in the houses of "the chief godly" or more "eminent Christians." These "conventicles" (in the eyes of authority or of hostile neighbors) were apparently the groups from which open separation might, and on rare occasions and in unusual circumstances did, arise.[69] Repetition could take place in church, immediately after the sermon, or more privately in the minister's house or in some other household, where it would approximate to the normal family exercise of catechizing. It involved not only the answering of questions but the offering of "conceived" prayer by members of the group encouraged to "try their gift." It was a question whether women (often extraordinarily influential in these circles) might or might not offer prayer in these semi-public circumstances.[70]

In addition, the preaching ministers met on regular occasions, most typically to support the "lectures by combination" or (in a specialized use of the term) "exercises" maintained in market towns, or to attend regular courses of lectures given by some celebrated divine in his own church, these being often sermons *ad clerum*. A list of all the places where combination lectures were a regular institution would probably prove to be a gazeteer of prosperous market towns.[71] These exercises were descended from the learned but public preaching conferences of Elizabethan days known as "prophesyings."[72] Normally there would be no more than one sermon (in this way circumventing Queen Elizabeth's celebrated order inhibiting the prophesyings), but the whole company of preachers would be present, and they would afterwards dine together, by public expense at an inn or at one of the principal magistrate's houses, and would discuss with formality a question of divinity or some other matter of professional clerical concern. It does not take much imagination to conclude that these arrangements, rather than any formal diocesan and synodal machinery, represented the wider world of the Church beyond the parish for hundreds of clergy in the Calvinist tradition, although there were no rigid lines of segregation between these societies and the Church at large, and those who took part were not necessarily possessed of a divisively sectarian spirit. "Wee are noe waye encombred with buisie boddies to sowe the seedes of scisme emonge us to the unioynting of the peace of the ecclesiasticall boddie," wrote a Norfolk minister to the bishop of Norwich in requesting his allowance for an exercise at Swaffham, adding that the inhabitants of that town were "more rude than easilie will bee believed to be of those that have bene brought up in more civill places, the greater parte of them utterlie destitute of teaching ministers."[73]

The godly seem to have accompanied their own preachers to these exercises, and perhaps their own subsidiary meetings were dovetailed with those of the ministers, as in Baxter's Kidderminster. Already these comings and goings were regulated by a weekly and monthly calendar, in the manner of Free Churchmen and members of the Society of Friends ever since, a total departure from the saints' days and other holy days of the Church's year. Besides the familiar Sabbath, historians should take note of the fact that the exercise at Bury St. Edmunds was held weekly, on a Monday, from the time of Bishop Parkhurst in the 1560s until the coming of Bishop Wren in the 1630s led to its better "regulation." The exercise at Burton-on-Trent, for some reason known as a "famous" exercise, was also held on Mondays.[74] This looks more like the coming Nonconformity than Anglicanism, and so do the churchyards "barricaded with horses tyed to the outward rayles," as one writer puts it,[75] while their owners were at the lecture, a scene which points forward to the way of life of Strict Baptists in rural Suffolk (for example), where the chapels still provide accomodation for the horses and traps of the country people who would spend all Sunday there and bring their dinners, a hundred years ago and less.

In addition to these ordinary exercises, there would be extraordinary occasions for gathering: days of solemn humiliation and fasting, and days of thanksgiving. There were also funerals. In 1605 the funeral of Robert Walsh, a noted minister at Little Waldingfield in Suffolk, was a major event, with John Knewstub, doyen of the Suffolk preachers, delivering the sermon and heading the ministers who bore the coffin on their shoulders. John Winthrop noted the anniversary of the event in his almanac, immediately before the anniversary of the coronation of the king and queen.[76]

And that is really all that needs to be said, so far as concerns the external, corporate structures. As for the corresponding inner story, on the theological and spiritual plane, much more could be and has been written: the modern literature is copious. It remains only to add that whereas from time to time preaching exercises and especially market town lectures might be "suspected" and even "put down," they were as regularly raised up again,[77] and that it was only with the ascendancy of the Laudian bishops in the 1630s that this way of life was seriously disrupted. Before that it received some episcopal encouragement, most notably in Yorkshire and Nottinghamshire from Archbishop Tobie Mathew.[78] This and the security of puritan religion in many localities under the protection of landed gentry and urban oligarchs complicates any analysis of Puritanism in terms of opposition and *anomie*.

That this was a religion tending towards Independency and involuntary voluntarism is another suggestion to be offered on trust in an abbreviated discussion.[79] No doubt many of the clergy were in a general and no exclusive sense presbyterian in outlook, and whether presbyterian or moderate episcopalian or Erastian or indeterminate (all, with the exception of the last, more or less anachronistic labels before 1640), they would take the view that in a properly ordered Church there should be a parish ministry, supported from tithes and ministering to and exercising discipline over the entire population of resident and professed Christians. So much was assumed in the beginning, by the Elizabethan Puritans, and wherever local conditions were favorable a general reformation would be attempted on, so to speak, Genevan lines. As the Separatists repeatedly complained, the Puritans would still have the whole land to be the Church, and in the revolutionary circumstances of the 1640s, the old vision of a godly commonwealth was still bright and clear. But in the intervening years, as the expectation of further reform by public authority receded, and as puritan piety became progressively an interior matter, aspirations were inevitably introverted.[80] Everything attempted and accomplished was of a voluntary character, the result of a free collaboration of the godly. The theological achievement of the Puritans, from William Perkins onwards, can be roughly interpreted as the adaptation and domestication of Calvinism to fit the condition of voluntary Christians, whose independence of the ordered, disciplined life of the Church Calvin would have found strange and disturbing.

These points have often been noted as a late development, for example

by Christopher Hill. But it could be argued that inasmuch as the godly were
in some degree from the beginning a people apart, their situation had always
been one of *de facto* Independency, even if their conscious and deliberate
aims were at variance. As for matters of polity, the Elizabethan Puritans
may have tended towards Presbyterianism, offering to erect in the place of
bishops a hierarchy of synods on the French or Scottish or Dutch model.
The national leaders, Cartwright, Travers and Field, were no doubt full-
blooded Presbyterians, who advocated and even attempted to set up classical
and synodal structures. But some of the theoretical literature of the period
was reticent on the delicate question of how these structures were to be related to local churches, and it may be that whenever their own interests were
involved, most Elizabethan Puritans would have been reluctant to concede
to synods anything beyond the power to "counsel" and "advise" allowed
in later years by the Independents. They would have derived such powers
upwards, from the constituent congregations, and not downwards, from a
true ministerial and synodical hierarchy.[81]

These suggestions are supported by the unique records of the conference
of ministers which met in the 1580s in the Stour valley on the borders of
Essex and Suffolk, the so-called Dedham *classis*, although the importance
of these papers in this connection has been obscured by the wretched edition
made by R. G. Usher for the Royal Historical Society in 1905, which omits
some important documents and falsifies others. This conference (as it knew
itself), or some members of it, aspired to exercise a properly presbyterian
discipline over common church affairs, but signally failed to do so. They
were obliged to record differences and to shelve decisions on important
matters of doctrine and polity. The conference could not prevent the departure from some churches of ministers whom it thought should stay, and
it could do nothing to restrain another congregation from arbitrary behavior
towards its minister, beyond recording impotent words about "the people's
course in rejecting and receiving their pastors without counsel of others."
When instructed by a higher and representative assembly in London concerning its own membership, Dedham as a body failed to respond. "We
reverence our faithfull brethren at London with their gratyous advises . . .
yet being best privy in our conference, what inconveniences we see likely to
ensue . . . in our consultation we finde not motives sufficient to perswade
us . . . ," and so on. This letter was written six months after receipt of the
letter to which it was an answer.[82]

The Dedham papers suggest that the bond between pastor and people was
considered to be the firmest of all ecclesiastical ties. One member thought
the conjunction so near that "thone shuld not forsake thother no more then
man and wieff shuld", and another said: "Blame not the people for being
lothe to part with their pastor, for if I were of that church, I had as lieve

they shuldest pluck out myne eie as take from me my paster." This same brother, Richard Crick, no rustic but a Doctor of Divinity, uttered passionate words when the validity of his calling by his own people came into question, "being become now at length as jealous for the honor of the church [that is, for the honour of his own congregation] as any of you are for your owne."[83] This is evidence in itself for the forceful independence of the "professors" of the Stour valley, many of whom were substantial clothiers with business connections with Antwerp and other commercial centers. That the puritan laity, sometimes condescendingly called "simple gospellers" by the puritan clergy, were not a submissive following or captive audience but a vigorous source of initiative should cause no surprise. It was implicit in the Reformation itself, in its anticlericalism, which seems to have been a persistent force in English life, and in the direct access to unmediated religious knowledge and experience, offered by the English Bible in the popular Geneva version, which the godly carried with them to sermons.

Elizabethan anticlericalism assumed the form of sustained agitation against the nonpreaching, often scandalous clergy, in which the laity enthusiastically joined, both at the parliamentary level and locally, where the particular failings of particular clerics were lovingly "registered" to form part of a country-wide Survey of the Ministry.[84] There are many indications that it was the "simple gospellers" who objected most uncompromisingly to the surplice, the cross in baptism, and other celebrated dregs of Antichrist still entertained in the English Church.[85] Evidently antivestiarianism was the typical English form of that iconoclasm which students of the Continental Reformation recognize as a particularly significant expression of radical popular sentiment. When the puritan clergy spoke of the "offence" caused by such ceremonies they must be understood to speak precisely, in terms of the Pauline *topos* of the offense to the weaker brethren occasioned by the eating of meats offered to idols.[86] Sometimes the offense was taken beyond hope of satisfaction, and schism ensued. It was in this way, as likely as not, that Separatism was provoked in London in 1567 and in Norfolk in 1581, and threatened in other places. When Mr. Fletcher, vicar of Cranbrook in the Kentish Weald (grandfather of the dramatist) preached in defense of the ceremonies it was said that his credit was "almost broken in sunder." Some assigned their conversion to his teaching, "but these very parties do now also affirme" that he had "run headlong, to the eversion of many consciences, unless Gods spirite prevent them." "Eversion of conscience" implied nothing less than schism.[87]

It is probably a mistake to adopt a perspective which allows for the slow gestation of the religious capacity of lay Protestants, until its potential was at last realized after 1640. That potential was already perceptible a full century earlier, at least in parts of the South-East of England where Lollardy, that older dissenting tradition, still persisted.[88] In a county like Essex, or in the Weald, it is more plausible to suppose that the puritan clergy achieved success in bringing self-assertive lay religion under control, and in reducing to submissive and orthodox responses the strongly innate tendency to sectarianism and the heresy of free will. In the exceptionally rich archdeaconry records covering the county of Essex there are indications of the ferment beneath the surface: open-air preaching in the woods in one village, in another a conventicle gathered around the schoolmaster, its members keeping their children from baptism.[89] How lay initiative was simultaneously stimulated and tamed is suggested in a hostile account of Cranbrook in the 1570s: "It is a commone thing now for every pragmaticall prentise to have in his head and mouth the government and reformation of the Churche. And he that in exercise can speak thereoff, that is the man. Every artificer must be a reformer and teacher . . . ." An opponent corrects the record. For "artificers and pragmaticall prentises," read Cranbrook clothiers, men of substance.[90] One of these Cranbrook clothiers would become brother-in-law to Paul Baynes, who as a "Non-Separating Congregationalist" has already figured in this discussion.[19] (And Dr. Edmund Chapman, the leading figure in the Dedham Conference, was brother-in-law to a prominent clothier of the Stour valley.)[92]

Decades later another generation of artificers, the early Ranters and Quakers, recorded in their spiritual autobiographies the deadening effect of a routinised puritan religion which they had sought out in their youth, but which had brought them no nearer to valid experience. Laurence Clarkson aspired to pray in the exercise ("fain would I have been judged a professor with them, but wanted parts") and at length he succeeded, but his religious conceptions remained primitive and outside what pertained to his own condition. "My God was a grave, ancient, holy, old man, as I supposed, sat in Heaven in a chair of gold, but as for his nature I knew no more than a childe."[93] But this should be read as no more than a corrective to the evidence on the other side of the success of the preachers in arousing and nourishing a piety which was content to know and express itself in the categories of puritan orthodoxy, the type characterized in the mid-seventeenth-century sources as "plain godly," "solid old Christian." No doubt these successes were scored among the clothiers and their social equals and betters, with their dependents, rather than in the ranks of the "pragmaticall prentises" and "restless itinerant artisans," inhabitants of Christopher Hill's *World Turned Upside Down* and A. L. Morton's *World of the Ranters*.

Separatism, to return full circle, is normally understood as a rejection of the Church of England as a national and comprehensive establishment of religion, whereas the Puritans who did not separate are said to have been moved by veneration for the principle of the indivisible Church, conterminous with the Commonwealth, part of the Church Universal. This is not false, but it misses the point that the Separatists cut themselves off, not from some legal abstraction, but from fellowship with like-minded brethren within and yet not wholly of the Church of England. The literary controversies which served to define Separatism were conducted, not with the bishops or other official spokesmen for the establishment, but with fellow-puritans. What the Non-Separatists objected to on their side was not so much desertion of the national Church as the schism perpetrated against the best assemblies of England, the true Christians, the most forward preachers. Consequently the most prominent single issue was that of hearing, or not hearing, the godly and non-separated preachers, so that when John Robinson "came backe indeed the one halfe of the way" from Separatism,[94] the nature of his recantation was posthumously disclosed in a *Treatise on the lawfulnes of hearing of the ministers in the Church of England*.[95] The question on the side of the Separatists was whether the godly, by adhering to a Church which was a confused heap of good and bad, and by submitting themselves to the corrupt power of the bishops, had put themselves beyond public communion and even private fellowship. But on both sides there was reluctance to repudiate those suspected to be, as one writer puts it, "sound in the vitals of Christian religion."[96] So the debate was not primarily about the Church of England but about the status and credentials of the godly elements in the Church of England so long as they remained within it. Robinson was not at all incredulous in the face of the evidence cited by Ames of the practical possibility of realizing a kind of voluntary church life in the Church of England, short of separation. The Separatists had always acknowledged the "graces" enjoyed by the godly in the English church assemblies, and even their capacity to arouse faith.[97] The issue between Ames and Robinson was that Robinson insisted that all such voluntary undertakings were not public but private in nature, understanding "public" as meaning "by public authority," whereas Ames understood "public" to refer to any proceedings in a public place, involving more than individuals or single households, a highly significant distinction. Ames's argument, said Robinson, was "pretending to prove public communion upon private, . . . consisting of a continued equivocation in the terms, 'public licence,' 'government,' 'ministry,' and the like."[98]

So there was agreement between Separatists and Non-Separatists on the presence of substantial godly elements in the English Church which were characterised by apartness. That this godly party was socially apart is suggested by the "odious name" of puritan itself, and by a long tradition of vernacular antipuritan sentiment which is epitomized in Richard Baxter's autobiographical reflections, for example, in the resounding statement that "the warre was begun in our streets before the King and Parliament had any armies."[99] We have seen that the common life of the godly was to a great extent structured by the religious exercises which were distinctive of Puritanism, and which exerted a strong if unintended separatist pull. It was a way of life which contained within itself much casual and disorderly separatism, as the professors deserted their own ministers for other, more popular preachers, so that it was a recurrent cause for concern "that a pastor might have his own people."[100] When people trooped to John Rogers at Dedham saying "let's go to Dedham to get a little fire,"[101] church order of the most basic kind was at risk.

The theological rationale of this situation is clearer since the publication of John S. Coolidge's important study, *The Pauline Renaissance in England*. Penetrating the rich language pertaining to "edification" in St. Paul's understanding of the Church, and detecting the crucial connection between this concept and the theme of Christian liberty (for Coolidge this connection constitutes the key to "the whole mystery of Elizabethan Puritanism"), the Puritans thought of the Church as composed of lively stones, ever in building and constantly maintaining its life, as members of the body grew up in Christ by communicating their strength from one to the other. By contrast, and thanks to the Elizabethan polity, it was characteristic of Anglicanism to limit the meaning of edification to the imparting of instruction within an already established and completed, nonliving structure. Coolidge suggests that "it is not too much to say that the whole subtle but radical difference between the Puritan cast of mind and the conformist appears in their different way of understanding the verb 'to edify'." "The social order which results from the operation of the spirit of life is opposed not merely to disorder but, more significantly, to a non-living kind of order." Consequently it was no "abstruse point" for the Non-Separating Congregationalists to find the essence of the Church, not in the diocesan and parochial structures which outwardly and apparently constituted the Church of England, but in the instinctive resourcefulness of the godly in their free and willing coming together.[102]

Admittedly the Separatists were more consistent in their practical application of the Pauline theology, and Coolidge considers that "the vision of a living Church, planted and visible in England" in the course of time passed to them.[103] The Separatists could say with total confidence: "The matter of the building is people, joined together in the profession of the Gospel," and: "Neither lies our exception against any personal, or accidentary profanation of the temple, but against the faulty frame of it."[104] But the Non-Separatists did what they could to make the saints visible, and to give some tangible form to their private Christian experience, while not actually repudiating the public communion of national Church and parish. The form was inevitably the intensely fashionable form of a covenant, "covenanting," to quote Henry Jacob, "to live as members of a holy society together."[105]

It is well known that Richard Bernard, who drew back from the separation of the Scrooby-Gainsborough Pilgrims, entered into a "particular covenant" with about a hundred "voluntary professors" from a number of parishes around Worksop, "to watch over one another, to admonish one another, . . . and thereupon to receive the Lord's Supper";[106] and that John Cotton, with "some scores of godly persons" in Boston, "entered into a covenant with the Lord, in the purity of his worship," which Cotton later said was "defective, yet it was more then the Old Non-conformity."[107] It is not so well known that in 1588 Richard Rogers of Wethersfield in Essex, keeper of an early puritan diary,[108] associated "divers well-minded Christians," all of his own parish, "well nigh twentie persons" in a covenant, mutually to amend their course of living, and that their action and the text of the covenant itself were held up as an example to others in Rogers's best-selling *Seven treatises*, which appeared in editions of 1603, 1604, 1605, 1607, 1610, 1616, 1627 and 1630.[109] On a certain Sunday in 1616 John Winthrop of Groton in Suffolk, later of Massachusetts, "arose betymes, and read over the covenant of certaine Christians sett downe in Mr. Rogers booke." Within a few days he was constrained to acknowledge his own unfaithfulness and to renew his own covenant "of walking with my God, and watchinge my heart and wayes." Winthrop and what he calls his "company" were already covenanted to meet with a number of Suffolk preachers and their wives annually on September 17th, and every Friday "to be mindefull one of another in desiring God to grante the petitions that were made to him" on the occasion of that meeting.[110] "With him I covenanted", wrote Captain Roger Clap of his relations with his master in an Exeter household "famous" for religion.[111]

These covenants were not church covenants but belonged to the puritan experience of covenanted grace, an area quite remote at this time from any overt ecclesiological reference. It could even be said that they represent a pietistic retreat from the robust vision of Elizabethan Puritanism of a reformed Church and a godly social order. But as Edmund S. Morgan has argued, the puritan morphology of grace would eventually underlie a more profound and searching Separatism, when the New England churches would demand as the condition of membership something never required by the earlier Separatists: evidence of the saving work of Christ in the heart.[112] The nub of William Ames's objection to the Separatists was that they despised clear tokens of saving faith at work in the Church of England and approached a new doctrine of salvation by works in gathering separated churches of the visibly worthy. Covenanted groups within the Church of England were devoted, as the Separatists apparently were not, to a shared examination of the heart. It is significant that Rogers reports of his brethren in covenant that they "did as farre exceed the common sort of those that professe the gospell, as the common professors do exceed them in religion which know not the Gospell";[113] super-saints, in fact, but not so much in performance and worthiness as in their sorrowful recognition of how unsatisfactory their Christian profession had been. If the Separatists held together in their separation that blend of Pauline teaching on edification and Christian liberty, which was of the essence of Puritanism, these Non-Separatists clung more securely to the principal Pauline anchor of Protestantism itself: Justification by Only Faith.

The path of this argument may by now have clarified what was said at the outset about the need for a lateral or horizontal approach to early Dissent. The act of separation was momentous, carrying the actors to the far side of a profound theological, social and psychological divide. But it could arise almost circumstantially, or so it appears if considered in a wider context than one of creeds and platforms. The schism of the Separatists served only to formalise a *de facto* situation of advanced near-Separatism, and it draws attention to that more extensive phenomenon as the tip of an iceberg draws attention to the bulk beneath the surface. Once the wide extent of forms and degrees of sectarianism is recognised, interest may shift somewhat away from the significance of Dissent for the future, as the prophetic cause of lonely pioneers, and towards its meaning in the world of the early seventeenth century itself. The sociologist Bryan Wilson calls sects "catalysts," sometimes "crystallising in acute form social discontents and aspirations, and marking the moments of social structural collapse, and sometimes heralding, or even promoting, social regeneration."[114] How are such intriguing possibilities of a "socially transformative role" to be explored and tested in the case of early Dissent? What did it mean in early Stuart times to be a "virtual dissenter"?[115]

Local researches may reveal who the Separatists and semiseparatists and Puritans were, and establish (or fail to establish) a correlation with social status and occupation, and with differing rural and urban economies and patterns of human settlement. Professor Alan Everitt and others are pointing the way.[116] Postgraduate work recently completed or in progress will certainly invest our knowledge of Puritanism with greater social precision.[117] However, Puritanism will never lend itself very readily to the essentially statistical method of religious sociography. We are dealing with groups whose relation to the established Church was untidy and ambiguous, groups fuzzy at the edges, not with organized nonconformist bodies with formal church records and registers. Another method, at once more universal and more particular, will be to explore among personal and literary sources the meaning of puritan and dissenting experience in the context of family and community relations: literature and anthropology, rather than economics and agronomy.[118]

If one looks, simplistically perhaps, no further than the written page of puritan literature, letters, biographies, sermons, one is bound to notice how incessantly it harps on themes and analogies of human affection, on the fervent love which is to be found in the society of the godly. The conventions of this ardent language can be traced back at least as far as the Marian persecution, when John Bradford wrote from prison to his "dear hearts and dearlings in the Lord, . . . mine owne sweet heart in the Lord."[119] Dr. Richard Crick told his Dedham brethren in the 1580s that he had looked upon their backs with greater joy than he beheld the eyes of any other company, and that their faces were "as if I had seen the face of God."[120] By the seventeenth century, the *Lives* gathered by Clarke resound with confident reports of the intimacy enjoyed by this or that company of Christians. "Holy affections . . . were exceedingly kindled and kept alive in them." John Angier's people at Ringley in Lancashire were "kind and every way helpful." Baxter and his flock "took great delight in the company of each other."[121] To an impressive extent, puritan saints appear to have proved their calling by the faithful performance of social virtues, towards wives, husbands, children, servants, and members of the religious group in general.[122] A notable act of a notable Christian would not be to fast but to provide ample refreshment for the godly on a religious occasion. One comes to recognize stock situations: the pious matron whose anxious spiritual life is guided by the pastoral casuist with ardent encouragement, and who nurses the preacher when he is sick and attends his deathbed; the adolescent who finds religion when boarded out in another family.

Friendships so demanding and exclusive must have upset all kinds of other, pre-existent relationships. A common piece of invective in antipuritan literature was the accusation that puritan preaching divides communities previously at peace and destroys neighborhood and good fellowship.[123] Sometimes the Puritans cry foul and insist that they too pursue and hopefully promote a general social harmony,[124] but often the charge is admitted, although the blame is shifted to the enemy. Christ came to bring not peace but a sword. "Can yee put fire and water together but they will rumble?"[125] While the Elizabethan Puritans had earnestly sought the reform of whole towns and parishes, with "discipline" their watchword, the improving literature of the next century significantly warns the godly to make friends among their own kind, and to mistrust traditional ties, Dod and Cleaver instructing their readers not to rely on "carnall friends" but on "godly men, for they will proove our surest friends. Vicinitie and neighbourhood will faile, and alliance and kindred will faile, but grace and religion will never faile."[126] More tangibly, it is quite clear that the religious exercises which filled the leisure hours of godly professors literally took the place of what Baxter called "the old feastings and gossipings."[127] The old obligations to keep house and entertain were far from neglected, but they suffered a transference. Evidently the godly supplied one another with the love and mutual support which they might otherwise have looked for among kindred and neighbors. Samuel Clarke described how his own people in the Wirral of Cheshire "though living ten or twelve miles asunder, were as intimate and familiar as if they had been all of one houshold."[128]

When Robert Browne wrote of being "wholy bent . . . to search and find out the matters of the church," it is notable that his search went on in conversation, among friends. The principle of the gathered church was not a ratiocinative matter only but a truth apprehended among other "forward" Christians, or so one gathers from his *True and short declaration.* Disillusionment for Browne, as for many later "Brownists," such as the lapsed and excommunicated members of Francis Johnson's Amsterdam congregation, may have been at root the disappointment of soured and mutually destructive human relationships, the family at war.[129] Should the historian be too cautious to find in the eager quest for the true Church and in the tergiversations of Separatism evidence of social as well as ecclesiological yearnings? Of the secret, "privy" church of Protestants which gathered in Marian London, and which was an abiding inspiration to Separatists and Puritans alike, it was said by an early Elizabethan sectary: "That persecution grew so fast as that it brought many a hundred to know one another that never knew before; and we joined all with one heart and mind to serve God with pure hearts and minds according to his word."[130]

There are, or may be, dimensions of meaning to social puritanism which would far outrun the scope of this exploratory essay. Ever since the appearance of Max Weber's famous *Protestant Ethic and the Spirit of Capitalism* in 1904-5, the saints of the seventeenth century have been invested with an almost cosmic significance as in some sense the mediators of nothing less than the transition from traditional to modern society, the agents of rationalization. The vast literature erected upon and branching out from Weber,[131] stands in relation to this modest paper as Rohan, Gondor and Mordor stand in relation to the Hobbit's cosy Shire. But let it be observed, Hobbit-like, that modern students of Puritanism who continue to be prompted by Weber and, behind Weber, by Marx, are nowadays interested as much in the intimacies of family relations as in the strenuous spiritual warfare of the inner-worldly ascetic.[132] "Puritan zeal," Professor Michael Walzer recognizes, "was not a private passion" but "a highly collective emotion," the emotion of "oppositional" "masterless men," whose response to the alienating experience of disorder and anxiety was to reject traditional order and to begin the construction of a new order.[133] Christopher Hill sees Puritanism as a social as much as a religious force, fragmenting a society religiously constituted by state church and parish only to remold it by voluntary action. Puritan sects and groups were "united by community of interest rather than by geographical propinquity or corporate worship," but the components were, so to speak, molecules rather than atoms, families rather than individuals. Household religion is a major theme,[134] and the household is said to be the "essential unit" of puritan piety. In a variety of ways, this fact is made to connect with "the economic tension of the community in process of breaking up," which is "focussed upon the household in transition from a patriarchal unit of communal production to a capitalist form."[135]

However, Dr. John Bossy wonders whether the "traditional community," at least at the parish level, ever really existed. The true social forms of late medieval religion seem to have been not parochial but tribal, connections of natural or contrived kindred, acquired through blood, baptism or marriage. The unity of the geographical parish in both Protestant and Catholic countries was something strictly nonexistent, but striven for as an ideal. The despised figure of the alebench vicar, composing quarrels and promoting good fellowship, becomes transcendental, beating the bounds of the parish at Rogationtide more than a folk survival, the church ale something more than a binge to boost church funds.[136] If this is right, then the Puritans were describing a circle, retreating from the forced bonds of mere co-residence and neighborhood in order to lose their *anomie* in new and more relevant forms of those old ties of kindred which had ceased to count for very much by the seventeenth century.[137] Nothing could more beautifully illustrate the co-existence and tension of conservative and innovative elements which both Weber and R. H. Tawney,[138] from differing standpoints, saw as the enigma of Calvinism.

Inevitably the social forms described in the puritan literature of the early seventeenth century were transitional in their novelty and spontaneity. John Cotton taught that "the faith of the parent doth bring the Children and houshold of a Christian . . . under a Covenant of salvation, as well as the faith of *Abraham* brought his houshold of old under the same covenant."[139] A religion which set so much store by family could scarcely become the permanent cause of division within families, still less the ideology for some alternative society to which family ties would be a matter of indifference. Rather it became a major and perhaps dominant concern of puritan parents that their children should be seen to inherit the promises and to share with them in the covenant, not least when experience proved that the parental home was the hardest place of all in which to find religion for oneself.[140] On the subject of New England, and in the general context of an argument about the supposed declension of the American puritan spirit which is as old as Cotton Mather, Edmund S. Morgan has written vividly of the triumph of a "tribalism" which dried up the springs of authentic Puritanism. When the Puritans "allowed their children to usurp a higher place than God in their affections," and "when theology became the handmaid of genealogy, puritanism no longer deserved its name."[141] Whether the passing of what a mid-seventeenth-century writer called "the character of an Old English Puritan"[142] was something equally within the logic of the domestication of the puritan religious experience is a question hardly put as yet by English historians. But it is a question which belongs to the middle age of the dissenting tradition, not to its origins.

A certain distinguished historian of the Reformation has been heard to say that religious history is too important a matter to be left to the theologians. But it is too important to be left to the secularists either. Those who write from within the tradition, with theological awareness and spiritual sensitivity, have much the better chance of getting it right.[143] Unfortunately, ecclesiastical history, not alone among the ecclesiastical endeavors of modern times, has too often been characterised by a kind of self-esteem, a concern with identity, even and perhaps most of all when seeking to lose that identity in a wider and ecumenical future. The burden of this essay has been to argue that the subject of the historical identity of churches and religious movements, while important, is not exhaustive; or better, to argue that the question of identity is much wider than has sometimes been suspected.

NOTES

1. Adapted from a Special University Lecture in Theology delivered in the University of London on February 19, 1974.
2. *Orthodoxy in Massachusetts 1630-1650: A Genetic Study* (Cambridge, Massachusetts, 1933).
3. Cf. G. R. Elton, "A High Road to Civil War?," in *From the Renaissance to the Counter-Reformation: Essays in Honour of Garrett Mattingly*, ed. C. H. Carter (1966), 325-47. (London is the place of publication of all books cited unless otherwise stated.)
4. Stephen Mayor, *The Lords Supper in Early English Dissent* (1972), 29.
5. *Congregational History*, i. (1869), vi.
6. *See* a useful succession of papers in the *Baptist Quarterly*: E. G. Rupp, "The Importance of Denominational History," n.s. vol. 17 (1957-8), 312-19; Christopher Hill, "History and Denominational History," n.s. vol. 22 (1967-8), 65-71; B. R. White, "The Task of a Baptist Historian," *ibid.*, 398-408.
7. *Lives of the Puritans*, I (1813), xii.
8. Waddington published in Boston, Massachusetts, in 1863 a series of lectures under the title *1559-1620: Track of the Hidden Church, or the Springs of the Pilgrim Movement*.
9. New York (1879).
10. *See* Douglas Horton's Introduction to the Pilgrim Press edition, Boston, Massachusetts (1960).
11. In this respect Burrage's *The Early English Dissenters in the Light of Recent Research (1550-1641)*, 2 vols. (Cambridge, 1912), is the next major

landmark after Dexter, followed closely by Peel's *The Second Parte of a Register, Being a Calendar of Manuscripts under that Title intended for publication by the Puritans about 1593, and now in Dr. Williams's Library, London*, 2 vols. (Cambridge, 1915).

12. Especially in *The First Congregational Churches: New Light on Separatist Congregations in London, 1567-81* (Cambridge, 1920), and *The Brownists in Norwich and Norfolk About 1580* (Cambridge, 1920); and other papers in *Transactions of the Congregational Historical Society* and *The Congregational Quarterly*. See Norman F. Sykes's appreciation of Peel in the *Transactions*, vol. 17 (1952-5), 4-7.

13. It would be superfluous in this volume of all places to list the six volumes which have so far appeared, containing the works of Cartwright, Browne and Harrison, and Barrow and Greenwood, or the further volumes projected, which will contain the works of Penry and *A Parte of a register*. See the prospective statements by Peel and Carlson in the first volume, *Cartwrightiana* (1951), vi-x.

14. *The English Separatist Tradition: From the Marian Martyrs to the Pilgrim Fathers* (Oxford, 1971).

15. *The way of congregational churches cleared: in two treatises*, Wing C 6469 (1648), pt. I, 12.

16. *Orthodoxy in Massachusetts, op. cit.; The New England Mind: The Seventeenth Century* (Cambridge, Massachusetts, 1939); and *see* also especially "The Marrow of Puritan Divinity," in *Errand into the Wilderness* (Cambridge, Massachusetts), 1956.

17. Robert G. Pope, *The Half-Way Covenant: Church Membership in Puritan New England* (Princeton, 1969), 9.

18. "Une question mal posée: les origines de la réforme française et le problème générale des causes de la réforme" *Revue historique*, vol. 160, 1-73; reprinted, *Au coeur religieux du XVIe siècle* (Paris, 1957), 3-70.

19. As in I. B. Horst's *The Radical Brethren: Anabaptism and the English Reformation to 1558*, Bibliotheca Humanistica & Reformatorica ii (Nieuwkoop, 1972), which is critical of "the particularistic approach: an emphasis on the unique and the formulation of clear answers," while it is unable to provide convincing evidence for the existence and influence of a native Anabaptist movement in England. To be fair to Dr. Horst, who has not persuaded many of his reviewers, he shares with the present writer a desire to transfer attention from the separatist to the non-separatist tradition of Dissent, and would not perhaps quarrel with the judgment of John Cotton (*op. cit.*, pt. I, 3) who denied that there was "such correspondency between the *Germane* Anabaptism and the *English* Brownism, as to make Brownism a native branch of Anabaptism." This was in answer to the Scottish Presbyterian Robert Baylie who had found "the derivation of the one from the other . . . very rationall." (*A dissuasive from the errours of the time*, Wing B 456, 1645, 13.)

20. *Op. cit.*, xii, 160-9.

21. Cf. Donald Nugent, "The Renaissance And/of Witchcraft" *Church History*, vol. 40 (1971), 69-78.

22. *Religious Sects: A Sociological Study*, 1970; and *Sects and Society: A Sociological Study of Three Religious Groups in Britain* (1961), Introduction, 1-11.

23. *See* Perry Miller's remark that Dexter and Williston Walker saw the past

"primarily in reference to their own present." (*Orthodoxy in Massachusetts*, xv.) This is hardly true of Dr. White, but the shadow of the old tradition lingers.

24. *See* the *Dictionary of National Biography* for biographies of all five; and Samuel Clarke, *The lives of two and twenty English divines*, Wing C 4540, (1660), and *The lives of thirty-two English divines*, Wing C 4539 (1677), for lives of Bradshaw (by Thomas Gataker) and Baynes. On Ames see especially K. L. Sprunger, *The Learned Doctor William Ames: Dutch Backgrounds of English and American Puritanism* (Urbana, 1972).

25. STC 3516 ([Amsterdam?], 1605); translated and published by Ames in 1610 at Frankfurt as *Puritanismus Anglicanus* and consequently sometimes misattributed to Ames; the original version republished, but with significant textual variations, in 1640 (STC 3517) and 1641 (Wing B 4158); the 1605 and 1640 edns. reprinted in facsimile, with other works of Bradshaw and Introduction by R. C. Simmons, Gregg Int., Farnborough, 1972. *See* also Baynes, *The diocesans tryall*, STC 1640 (1621), also reprinted in facsimile, Gregg Int., (Farnborough, 1971); and Jacob, *Reasons taken out of Gods word and the best humane testimonies proving a necessitie of reforming our churches in England*, STC 14338 ([Middleburg?], 1604).

26. *Conscience with the power and cases thereof*, STC 552, n.p. (1639); *The marrow of sacred divinity*, (first English edn. 1638), Wing A 3000, (1642). See also Parker, *De politeia ecclesiastica Christi et hierarchica opposita libri tres*, (Frankfurt, 1616).

27. Bradshaw, *The unreasonablenesse of the separation made apparent*, STC 3532 (Dort, 1614), printed with and paginated in sequence with Ames, *A manuduction for Mr. Robinson, and such as consent with him in private communion, to lead them on to publick*; Ames, *A second manuduction for Mr. Robinson*, STC 556, n.p. (1615). Bradshaw reprinted in facsimile in *Puritanism and Separatism: A Collection of Works by William Bradshaw*, with Introduction by R. C. Simmons, Gregg Int., n.p. (1972). Ames's writings against Robinson are to be reprinted in facsimile in a volume of *Church Controversies* by Gregg Int.

28. *Orthodoxy in Massachusetts*, 105, generally supported by Cotton, *op. cit.*

29. 1640 edn. substitutes for "men" "true beleevers" and omits "ordinarilie."

30. 1640 inserts "according to the order of the Gospell" between "together" and "in."

31. 1640 has "Congregations."

32. 1605 edn., 5.

33. *Marrow of sacred divinity*, 157; cf. Jacob, *Reasons taken out of Gods word*, 22.

34. Ames, *Marrow of sacred divinity*, 157-9.

35. Jacob, *An attestation of many learned, godly and famous divines*, STC 14328 ([Middleburg], 1613), 100 seq.; Jacob, *A confession and protestation of the faith of certaine christians in England*, STC 14330, ([Middleburg?], 1616), Sig. B 2; Baynes, *op. cit.*, *passim*; Parker, *op. cit.*, 329. That English divines were generally suspect in foreign Reformed circles for such views is suggested by the history of the English *classis* in the Netherlands as recorded in the Boswell Papers in the British Library, MS. Add. 6394 (partly printed in Burrage, *op. cit.*, vol. 2, 260-91.) *See* R. P. Stearns, *Congregationalism in the Dutch Netherlands: The Rise and Fall of the English*

Congregational Classics, 1521-1535 (American Socy. of Church History Chicago, 1940) and Alice C. Carter, *The English Reformed Church in Amsterdam in the Seventeenth Century*, Pubns. of the Municipal Archives of Amsterdam, vol. 3 (1964).

36. *Conscience*, bk. IV, 61-4. Cf. Jacob, *A confession and protestation*, Sig. B 8: "Doubtless we ought to leave the worse societies and to enjoy one that is and may be sincere."

37. *See* above.

38. *See* Benjamin Stinton's "Repository of Divers Historical Matters" in the so-called "Gould Manuscript," printed, Burrage, *op. cit.*, vol. 2, 292-308, and critically discussed, *ibid.*, vol. 1. 336-56.

39. *Reasons taken out of Gods word*, 55; *A confession and protestation*; *A collection of sundry matters* ([Middleburg?], 1616); and the Gould MS. printed by Burrage, *op. cit.*, vol. 2, 292-308. Jacob's earlier writings, in which he is presumed (perhaps not altogether correctly) to be totally at odds with the Separatists, contain many anticipations of these positions. *See A defence of the churches and ministery of England*, STC 14335 (Middleburg, 1599), *A short treatise concerning the truenes of a pastorall calling in pastors made by praelates* (in continuous pagination with *A defence*), and the papers of 1603-5 printed by Burrage, *op. cit.*, vol. 2, 146-66; *see* also John van Rohr, "The Congregationalism of Henry Jacob," *Transactions of the Congregational Historical Society*, vol. 19, 107-22.

40. John Sprint, *Considerations*, quoted and refuted in Henry Ainsworth, *Counterpoyson*, STC 234 ([Amsterdam?], 1608), 54 seq. The Separatist Ainsworth engages with this argument as stated by Sprint, Richard Bernard and William Crashaw.

41. Quoted, Miller, *Orthodoxy in Massachusetts*, 151.

42. Thomas Hooker, *A survey of the summe of church-discipline*, Wing H 2658 (1648), pt. I, 47-8. Cf. John Allin and Thomas Shepard, *A defence of the answer*, Wing A 1036 (1648), 13: "Congregations in *England* are truly Churches having an implicite Covenant."

43. *A manuduction*, Sig. Q 4.

44. *See* "The Congregation and its Ministers," pt. VII chap. 1, 333-45 of my *The Elizabethan Puritan Movement*, (Berkeley, 1967); and *A collection of certain letters and conferences lately passed betwixt certaine preachers and two prisoners in the Fleet* (1590), in *The Writings of John Greenwood, 1587-1590*, ed. L. H. Carlson, Elizabethan Nonconformist Texts vol. 4 (1962), 175-262.

45. *Op. cit.*, Sig. B 1ᵛ.

46. Ames, *A second manuduction*, 34.

47. Quoted Miller, *Orthodoxy in Massachusetts*, 151. Cf. Cotton, *op. cit.*, pt. I, 14: "Neither was our departure from ['the Parishionall Congregations in *England*'] even in those evill times, a Separation from them as no Churches, but rather a Secession from the corruptions found amongst them, unto which also we must have been forced to conforme . . . unlesse wee had timely departed from them."

48. Michael McGiffert, "American Puritan Studies in the 1960s." *William & Mary Quarterly*, 3rd ser. vol. 27 (1970), 36-67, reviewing much of the literature of revision and reporting the private communications of scholars.

49. *Visible Saints: the Congregational Way, 1640-1660* (Oxford, 1957), 10-11.

50. Ames departs as far as can be imagined from Miller's assumptions when he writes: "It is also very probable that there is no such particular Church in which the profession of the true Faith flourisheth, but in the same also there are found some true believers . . . But those who are onely believers by profession, so long as they remaine in that society are members of that Church, as also of the catholick Church as touching the outward state, not touching the inward or essential state. I *John* 2:19. They went out from us, but they were not of us." (*Marrow of sacred divinity*, 158.) On Miller's misapprehensions in this area see especially John S. Coolidge, *The Pauline Renaissance in England: Puritanism and the Bible* (Oxford, 1970), 71-6, and this statement in particular: "The nature of [the semiseparatist] compromise has been misrepresented in after times because of the modern *idée fixe* concerning the place of the doctrine of predestination in radical Protestantism." On this issue of covenanted grace, *see* Jens G. Møller, "The Beginnings of Puritan Covenant Theology." *Journal of Ecclesiastical History*, vol. 14 (1963), 46-67, Richard L. Greaves, "The Origins and Development of English Covenant Thought." *The Historian*, vol. 31 (1968), 21-35 and references supplied, and the Introduction by Dr Ian Breward to his *The Work of Williams Perkins* (Courtenay Library of Reformation Classics, Abingdon, Berks., 1970).

51. *Orthodoxy in Massachusetts*, 83, 84, 88, 89, 92-6; Coolidge, *op. cit.*, 74 n.57.

52. Especially not to *Society and Puritanism in Pre-Revolutionary England* (1964).

53. Professor L. L. Schücking in his pioneering study *Die Puritanische Familie* (Leipzig, 1929) insisted with reason that a distinctive pattern of domestic piety became the common property of both "Anglicans" and "Puritans," that the essential dividing line was one between "saints" and the children of the world, and that "denominational" labels lacked significance. Yet he called his study *The Puritan Family*.

54. The will of Robert Moore of Guiseley, Yorkshire, a veteran Elizabethan Puritan (see *The Seconde Parte of a Register*, vol. 2, 234-8), proved in 1642, printed, R. A. Marchant, *Puritans and the Church Courts in the Diocese of York, 1560-1642* (1960), 212-14.

55. Richard Baxter, *Reliquiae Baxterianae*, Wing B 1370 (1696), 1-3.

56. The mistake is made, for example, by Professor Mark Curtis in his essay 'The Alienated Intellectuals of Early Stuart England', in *Crisis in Europe, 1560-1660*, ed. T. Aston (1965), 295-316; and in the broader context of Professor Michael Walzer's *The Revolution of the Saints: A Study in the Origins of Radical Politics* (Cambridge, Massachusetts, 1965). For a particular local example of the social realities argued for here, see Paul Slack, 'Religious Protest and Urban Authority: The Case of Henry Sherfield, Iconoclast, 1633' in *Schism, Heresy and Religious Protest, Studies in Church History*, vol. 9, ed. D. Baker (Cambridge, 1972), 295-302. The trial of Sherfield, puritan iconoclast but also Recorder of Salisbury, suggests that the puritan urban oligarchy was ground between upper and nether millstones in the years of Laud's ascendancy. 'But in his own local community, it was Sherfield who was the representative of authority and the guardian, so it seemed, of social order.' Cf. T. G. Barnes, 'County Politics and a Puritan Cause Célèbre: Somerset Churchales, 1633.' *Transactions of the Royal Historical Society*, 5th ser., vol. 9 (1959), 103-22.

57. Christopher Hill, 'Puritans and "the Dark Corners of the Land".' *Transactions of the Royal Historical Society*, 5th ser., vol. 13 (1963), 77-102.

58. N. Tyacke, 'Puritanism, Arminianism and Counter-Revolution,' in *The Origins of the English Civil War*, ed. Conrad Russell (1973).

59. Ephraim Udall, Το Πρέπιον ἐμχαριστιχὸν *i.e. Communion comlinesse. Wherein is discovered the conveniency of the peoples drawing neere to the table in the sight thereof when they recive the Lords Supper. With the great unfitnesse of receiving it in the pewes in London for the novelty of high and close pewes*, Wing U 13 (1641). Udall was the son of the celebrated Elizabethan puritan preacher and pamphleteer John Udall. He was curate of Teddington, Middlesex, from 1614, and rector of St Augustine's, Watling St., from 1634. Udall was known as a Puritan, but the argument of this tract, making a utilitarian case for greater 'comliness', signalled a shift towards moderation, made clearer in the anonymous publication of 1642, misattributed to Archbishop Ussher but apparently Udall's, *The bishop of Armaghes direction concerning the lyturgy, and episcopall government*, Wing U 4.

60. Jonathan Cape, London, and University of California Press, Berkeley, 1967. The case is more copiously stated in my unpublished University of London Ph.D. thesis of 1957, 'The Puritan Classical Movement in the Reign of Queen Elizabeth I'.

61. J. A. Newton, "Puritanism in the Diocese of York (Excluding Nottinghamshire) 1603-1640," unpublished London Ph.D. thesis, 1955; summarized, "The Yorkshire Puritan Movement, 1603-1640." *Transactions of the Congregational Historical Society*, vol. 19 (1960-64); Marchant, whose study includes Nottinghamshire, *op. cit.*; R. C. Richardson, *Puritanism in North-West England: A Regional Study of the Diocese of Chester to 1642* (Manchester, 1972).

62. *A generall martyrologie, containing a collection of all the greatest persecutions which have befallen the Church of Christ from the creation to our present times. Whereunto are added the lives of sundry modern divines* Wing C 4513 (1651); *The lives of two and twenty English divines*, Wing C 4540 (1660); *The lives of thirty-two English divines*, Wing C 4539 (1667); *The lives of sundry eminent persons in this later age*, Wing C 4538 (1683). To these add such other lives as William Hinde, *A faithful remonstrance of the holy life and happy death of John Bruen of Bruen-Stapleford in the County of Chester, Esquire*, Wing H 2063 (1641), the *Life of Adam Martindale Written by Himself*, ed. R. Parkinson, vol. 4 (Chetham Socy, 1845); *Oliver Heywood's Life of John Angier of Denton*, ed. E. Axon, (Chetham Socy., n.s. 97, 1937), and *The Rev. Oliver Heywood 1630-1702: His Autobiography, Diaries*, ed. J. H. Turner, 3 vols. (1882). Cotton Mather's biographies in *Magnalia Christi Americana* (Boston, Massachusetts, 1702), are another storehouse.

63. Professor William Haller's justly famous *The Rise of Puritanism* (New York, 1938), in its biographical portions a veritable *Clarke Revised*, is a little incautious in the extent to which it reflects its principal source.

64. Alan Everitt, "Nonconformity in Country Parishes," in *Land, Church, and People: Essays Presented to Professor H. P. R. Finberg*, ed. Joan Thirsk, *Agricultural History Review*, vol. 18, Supplement (Reading, 1970), 186-8.

65. "The essential pattern of the lives of the elect, the 'saints' or 'godly', was unmistakable." (L. L. Schücking, *The Puritan Family*, English edn. (1969),

57.) Clarke remains for these purposes a surprisingly neglected source. None of his collections appear in Schücking's Bibliography. However, Owen Watkins, *The Puritan Experience* (1972), is a distillation of Clarke and of the rich autobiographical literature of the age.

66. *Reliquiae Baxterianae*, 83-7.

67. Isaiah 60:8.

68. These phenomena are discussed on the basis of Elizabethan evidence in my *Elizabethan Puritan Movement*, pt. VII, chap. 4, "The Meetings of the Godly," 372-82, and in a paper contributed to the Past and Present Society Conference on Popular Religion, 1966, "The Godly: Aspects of Popular Protestantism in Elizabethan England" (privately circulated by Past and Present Society) which embodies many citations from the Act Books of the Archdeaconries of Colchester and Essex. The most striking and persistent case known to me of a parish split into puritan and antipuritan factions effectively out of communion with one another is provided by the Essex village of East Hanningfield. The evidence is in vols. 12-15 of the Act Books of the Archdeaconry of Essex, Essex Record Office, Chelmsford, and in British Library, MS. Add. 48064 (Yelverton 70), ff. 85-7. *See above*, 1-17.

69. Clearly established, for example, in the origins of Broadmead Baptist Church, Bristol. (*The Records of a Church of Christ Meeting in Broadmead Bristol, 1640-1687*, ed. E. B. Underhill, (Hanserd Knollys Socy., 1847.) The case has been most recently discussed by Dr. Claire Cross in "He-Goats Before the Flocks: A Note on the Part Played by Women in the Founding of Some Civil War Churches," in *Popular Belief and Practice, Studies in Church History*, vol. 8, ed. G. J. Cuming & D. Baker (Cambridge, 1972), 195-202.

70. The question was put in the Dedham Conference in 1584 "whether it were convenient a woman shuld pray having a better gift than her husband," but it was "omitted as not necessary to be handled." (*The Presbyterian Movement in the Reign of Queen Elizabeth*, ed. R. G. Usher, Camden Socy. 3rd ser. vol. 8 (1905), 35.) For the role of women, *see* Cross, *loc. cit.*, my "The Role of Women in the English Reformation Illustrated by the Life and Friendships of Anne Locke," *Studies in Church History*, ed. G. J. Cuming, vol. 2, 258-72 and Keith Thomas, "Women and the Civil War Sects" in *Crisis in Europe, op. cit.*, 317-40. *See above*, 273-87.

71. It is a pity that Dr. Paul S. Seaver provides no such list in his fundamental study *The Puritan Lectureships; The Politics of Religious Dissent, 1560-1662* (Stanford, 1970). Seaver is systematic only in relation to London and devotes no more than three pages (84-7) to the subject of lectures by combination. Among evidence still much neglected one may cite the correspondence with Bishop Jegon of Norwich relating to exercises in several Norfolk market towns (*The Registrum Vagum of Anthony Harrison*, pt. I, ed. T. F. Barton, Norfolk Record Socy, vol. 32 (1963), 96-103); the notes of many scores of sermons preached at the West Riding exercises held at Halifax and other centers (British Library, MSS. Add. 4933A, 4933B), discussed by Newton, *loc. cit.*, but not by Marchant, *op. cit.*, and apparently unknown to Seaver; and the Report made to Bishop Neile of the Primary Visitation of the diocese of Lincoln made on his behalf in 1614, which gives many details, including the panels of membership, of combination lectures in eleven centers (Aylesbury, Berkhamstead, Huntington,

Leicester, Grantham, Sleaford, Market Rasen, Lowth, Grimsby, Alford and Horncastle.) This last report exists in MS. copies in the Cambridge University Library (Baumgartner MS. 8, ff. 220-2), British Library (MS. Add. 5853, ff. 166ᵛ-8) and in Lincoln (Dean & Chapter MS. A4/3/43) from where printed, *Associated Architectural Societies Reports & Papers*, vol. 16, pt. 1 (1881), 31-54. Seaver makes no reference to it, and Professor Curtis (*loc. cit.*, 310) mistakes the c.70 clergy associated with these lectures for professional, salaried lecturers, an error perpetuated by Hill, *Society and Puritanism*, 85. For information on exercises in the diocese of Chester, *see* Richardson, *op. cit.*, 65-9. *See Wiltshire Parish Registers: Marriages*, vol. 2, ed. W. P. W. Phillimore (1906), 72 for the names of the thirteen ministers who maintained "the Saturday lecture" at Marlborough, Wiltshire. (I am indebted for this last reference to my colleague Mrs Alison Wall.)

72. Collinson, *op. cit.*, 168-76.
73. *Registrum Vagum*, pt. I, 98-9.
74. Seaver, *op. cit.*, 86; Collinson, *op. cit.*, 438; and my "The Beginnings of English Sabbatarianism," *Studies in Church History*, vol. 1, ed. C. W. Dugmore & C. Duggan (1964), 219. *See above*, 429-43.
75. Clarke, *Lives of sundry eminent persons*, 187.
76. *Winthrop Papers*, vol. 1 *1498-1628* (Massachusetts Historical Socy., 1929), 89, 153.
77. The preface to Thomas Beard's famous *Theatre of gods iudgements* (1631) (3rd) edn., thanks the magistrates of Huntingdon for their support "in the late business of the Lecture." Anthony Cade of Leicester in 1618 published a sermon preached at the Ordinary Monthly Lecture, "intermitted" by Bishop Barlow in 1611 and revived in 1614. (G. J. Cuming, "The Life and Works of Anthony Cade, B.D., Vicar of Billesdon, 1599-1639," *Transactions of the Leicestershire Archaeological & Historical Socy.*, vol. 45 (1969-70), 39-56.) In Bishop Neil's Visitation of 1614 the Huntingdon Lecture was said to have been "put down" by Bishop Barlow, the Leicester Lecture "questioned" in Barlow's time. "The cause was some received disgrace in a conference they held after their lecture. But I take it it was restored again."
78. Newton, *loc. cit.*, and Marchant, *op. cit.*, *passim*. Archbishop Mathew's Diary (which is in the form of a record of the sermons preached by him from 1583 until 1622, 1992 in all) records that he preached at Barnard Castle in 1593 "at the Exercise," when still dean of Durham. In August, 1609, as archbishop of York, he preached "at Mansfield Exercise," and in 1613 he preached at the Mansfield Exercise in July, the Nottingham Exercise in August, and the Retford Exercise in September. (Thomas Wilson's transcript of Archbishop Mathew's Diary, Minster Library, York, 38, 85, 92, 105.)
79. Extensively canvassed by Hill however, especially in *Society and Puritanism*.
80. Among a rich variety of literature see especially Watkins, *op. cit.*
81. Collinson, *Elizabethan Puritan Movement*, 107-8, 318-29. Although the evidence is not very explicit, I suspect that the counsels of the Elizabethan Puritans were as much divided by this issue as those of the French Calvinists. (R. M. Kingdon, *Geneva and the Consolidation of the French*

Protestant Movement, Travaux d'humanisme et renaissance, vol. 92 (Geneva), 1967.)

82. John Rylands Library, Manchester, Rylands English MS. 874; in part published in *The Presbyterian Movement, op. cit. See* my *Elizabethan Puritan Movement,* 222-31, 318-21.

83. *Presbyterian Movement,* 43-6; Rylands English MS. 874, f. 56. Cf. a remark of Thomas Carew, curate of Hatfield Peverel, Essex, and later in Ipswich: "The knot between pastor and people is not easily loosed." (*Seconde Parte of a Register,* vol. 2, 33.)

84. *Seconde Parte of a Register,* vol. 2, 88-184.

85. Collinson, *Elizabethan Puritan Movement,* 92-7.

86. Coolidge, *op. cit.,* 41-3.

87. Dr. Williams's Library, London, MS. Morrice B.11, ff. 17-18. The entire Cranbrook controversy of 1573 as recorded in this "Seconde Parte of a Register" manuscript (calendared, *Seconde Parte,* vol. 1, 116-20) is instructive in connection with the points made here.

88. The most recent discussion of the continuity of Lollardy and early Protestantism in these areas is in Dr. J. F. Davis's Oxford D.Phil. thesis "Heresy and the Reformation in the South-East of England, 1520-1559." (1968). Dr Davis identifies two major heartlands of late Lollardy and incipient reform (apart from London): a broad corridor of North Essex running from Colchester inland to Thaxted and from the Suffolk border south to Witham and Colchester (the country later covered by the Dedham Conference and sister conferences) and the Kentish Weald. (I am grateful to Dr. Davis for access to his thesis.)

89. Essex Record Office, Archdeaconry of Colchester Act Books, ACA 10, ff. 66-7^r; Archdeaconry of Essex Act Books, AEA 14, f. 148^r, AEA 15, ff. 273^v-4^v.

90. Dr Williams's Library, MS. Morrice B.II, ff. 8, 17^v.

91. C. C. R. Pile, *Dissenting Congregations in Cranbook* (Cranbrook and Sissinghurst Local History Socy., n.p., 1953), 4. Professor Alan Everitt associates the later strength of dissent in the Weald and similar areas with a forest rather than arable economy, and questions the often-asserted connection between the manufacture of cloth and dissent. The evidence from the Stour valley of Essex and Suffolk and from the Weald seems to favor very strongly the traditional association without damage to Professor Everitt's wider speculations. (*Loc. cit.,* 188-97.)

92. Collinson, *Elizabethan Puritan Movement,* 223.

93. Laurence Clarkson (Claxon), *The lost sheep found,* Wing C 4580 (1660), 5-6. Cf. George Whitehead in *Jacob found in a desert land,* Wing W 1936 (1656), 4: "For I was alwayes learning there, and could not know the Truth"; and Richard Farnworth in *The heart opened by Christ,* Wing F 485 (1654), p. 4: "And so likewise their Preaching became but as the telling of a Tale, or a boy that saith over his weeks work at the School, that he had learned all the week"; and Arise (Rhys) Evans, *An eccho to the voice from heaven,*Wing E 3457 (1652), 17: "For afore I looked upon the Scriptures as a History of things that passed in other Countreys, pertaining to other persons, but now I looked upon it as a mysterie to be opened at this time belonging also to us." On "Quaker Testimonies," *see* Watkins, *op. cit.,* 160-81 and his article, "Some Early Quaker Autobiographies." *Journal of the Friends Historical Socy.,* vol. 45 (1953), 65-74. For Clark-

son, *see* also Christopher Hill, *The World Turned Upside Down: Radical Ideas During the Puritan Revolution* (1972), 171-4 and A. L. Morton, *The World of the Ranters: Religious Radicalism in the English Revolution* (1970), 115-42.

94. Cotton, *op. cit.*, 8.

95. *Works of John Robinson*, ed. R. Ashton, vol. 3 (1851), 343-78.

96. Clarke, *Lives of sundry eminent persons*, 170. In c. 1580, for example, Robert Browne found Robert Harrison inhibited in the path to Separatism with regard to "M. Robardes, M. More, M. Deering and others [puritan preachers] whome he then did greatlie like off." (*A true and short declaration, Writings of Robert Harrison and Robert Browne*, ed. A. Peel & L. H. Carlson, Elizabethan Nonconformist Texts, vol. 2 [1953], 407-11.)

97. Robinson, *A iustification of separation from the Church of England*, STC 21109 ([Leyden?], 1610), 259.

98. Ames, *A manuduction*; Robinson, *A manumission to a manuduction*, STC 2111, n.p. (1615); Ames, *A second manuduction for Mr Robinson*; Robinson, *A treatise on the lawfulnesse of hearing of the ministers*, in *Works*, vol. 3, 361.

99. Richard Baxter, *A holy commonwealth*, Wing B 1281 (1659), 456-7.

100. A tract published in 1589, *Sophronistes: a dialogue, perswading the people to reverence and attend the ordinance of God in the ministerie of their owne pastors* (STC 22930), was written within the internal economy of puritan churchmanship. Cf. the troubles of one member of the Dedham Conference who was forced to seek a ruling "that a pastor should have his own people." (*Presbyterian Movement*, 30, 62.)

101. *Heywood's Life of Angier*, 50.

102. Coolidge, *op. cit.*, chap. 1 "Scriptural Authority" and chap. 2, "Christian Liberty and Edification," *passim*.

103. *Ibid.*, chap. 3, "Separation."

104. Ainsworth, *op. cit.*, 60; Robinson, *Works*, vol. 3, 72.

105. *The divine beginning*, Sig. A1.

106. *The Works of John Smith*, vol. 2, ed. W. T. Whitney (Cambridge, 1915), 335; *Robinson, Works*, vol. 2, 101. Cf. Richard Bernard, *Plaine evidences: the Church of England is apostolicall, the seperation schismaticall*, STC 1958 (1610).

107. Cotton, *op. cit.*, pt. I, 20. Said in answer to Robert Baylie (*op. cit.*, 55), who had alleged that in England Cotton had "minded no more then the old non-conformity."

108. Printed by M. M. Knappen in *Two Elizabethan Puritan Diaries* (American Socy. of Church History, Chicago, 1933), 51-102.

109. *Seven treatises, containing such directions as is gathered out of the holie scriptures*, STC 21215 (1603), ff. 477-95. The covenant is some 13,000 words in length. Rogers explains that it was entered into at a meeting, common enough in Essex, held in a private house "after some bodily repast and refreshing," and he is at pains to prove that the participants were "no Brownists, for they were diligent and ordinarie frequenters of publicke assemblies with the people of God," and that their meetings were not "conventicles, for the disturbing of the state of the Church and peace thereof; as many imagine that there can be no private fellowship among Christians, but it is to such ends: the contrary may be seen by their conference."

110. *Winthrop Papers*, vol. 1, 169, 199-201.

111. *Memoirs of Roger Clap*, Collections of the Dorchester Antiquarian & Historical Socy., vol. 1 (Boston, Massachusetts, 1844), 17.
112. *Visible Saints: The History of a Puritan Idea* (Ithaca, 1963).
113. *Seven treatises*, f. 477.
114. *Religious Sects*, 7.
115. John Berridge wrote to the countess of Huntingdon on April 25, 1777; "You say the Lord is sending many gospel labourers into the Church. True; and with a view, I think, of calling his people out of it . . . What has become of Mr Venn's Yorkshire flock?—what will become of his Yelling flock, or of my flocks, at our decease? or what will become of your students at your removal? *They are virtual Dissenters* now, and will be settled Dissenters then. And the same will happen to many, perhaps most, of Mr. Wesley's preachers at his death." (Quoted, Charles Smyth, *Simeon and Church Order* [Cambridge, 1940], 238-9.)
116. Everitt, *loc. cit.*, and in his *The Pattern of Rural Dissent: the Nineteenth Century*, Leicester University Department of Local History, 2nd ser. vol. 4 (Leicester, 1972). *See* also some fruitful suggestions from Everitt and Dr Joan Thirsk in *The Agrarian History of England and Wales*, vol. 4, *1500-1640* (Cambridge, 1967), esp. 111-12, 562-3. *See* also the studies of the early Quakers by Alan Cole ("The Social Origins of the Early Friends," *Journal of the Friends' Historical Socy.*, 48. [1957], 99-118) and R. T. Vann ("Quakerism and the Social Structure in the Interregnum." *Past and Present*, no. 43, [1969], 71-91.) Cf. Margaret Spufford, "The Social Status of Some Seventeenth-Century Rural Dissenters," in *Popular Belief and Practice, op. cit.*, 203-11.
117. *See* Richardson, *op. cit.*, chap. 1, "The Context and Distribution of Puritanism" (scil. in the diocese of Chester.) The forthcoming (London) doctoral study of Northamptonshire by Mr. W. J. Sheils of the Borthwick Institute of Historical Research, University of York, will undoubtedly break significant new ground in this respect.
118. Compare Alan MacFarlane, *The Family Life of Ralph Josselin, A Seventeenth-Century Clergyman: An Essay in Historical Anthropology* (Cambridge, 1970), with the criticism of E. P. Thompson (demanding, among other things, more sensitivity to literature) in "Anthropology and the Discipline of Historical Context." *Midland History*, vol. 1 (1971-2), 41-55.
119. John Foxe, *Acts and Monuments of the Church*, vol. 7, ed. S. R. Cattley (1838), 207-253 and many other such references; and in *Writings of John Bradford*, ed. Aubrey Townsend (Parker Socy., Cambridge, 1853).
120. John Rylands Library, Manchester, Rylands English MS. 874, f. 56. The reference is to Genesis 33.8, words spoken by Jacob to Esau, an appropriate *topos* in view of Crick's strained relations with his brethren when this letter was written.
121. Clarke, *Lives of sundry eminent persons*, 4; *Heywood's Life of Angier*, 56; *Reliquiae Baxterianae*, 85.
122. The title page of John Bunyan's *Christian behaviour* (1663), refers to "the Fruit of true Christianity, shewing the ground from whence they flow, in their Godlike order in the Duty of *Relations*, as *Husbands, Wives, Parents, Children, Masters, Servants*, etc." (Quoted, Schücking, *op. cit.*, 56-7.)
123. This element seems to be missing from a standard work on the subject, W. P. Holden, *Anti-Puritan Satire, 1572-1642*, (Yale Studies in English,

vol. 26 [New Haven, 1954]. Two Elizabethan *loci classici* for the argument, as reported by puritan pamphleteers, are *A dialogue concerning the strife of our church*, STC 6801 (1584) and George Gifford's *A briefe discourse of certaine points of the religion which is among the common sort of christians, which may bee termed the countrie divinitie*, STC 11845 (1581). *See* also "The defence of the mynisters of Kent" (1584) in *The Seconde Parte of a Register*, vol. 1, 230-41, which addresses itself to the charge that various preachers who are named have brought "deadly hatred and bitter division," "broile and contention" to their towns.

124. Richard Greenham of Dry Drayton was said to be "a great friend to, and promoter of peace and concord amongst his Neighbours and acquaintance, insomuch that if any had come to him who were at variance, he would either have made them friends himself, or if he could not prevail, he would have made use of other friends to reconcile them together, thereby to prevent their going to Law." (Clarke, *Lives of two and twenty English divines*, 15.)

125. Gifford, *op. cit.*, f. 46ᵛ.

126. John Dod and Robert Cleaver, *A plain and familiar exposition of the thirteenth and fourteenth chapters of the Proverbs of Salomon*, STC 6960 (1609), 119.

127. *Reliquiae Baxterianae*, 83.

128. Clarke, *Lives of sundry eminent persons*, 4-5. Mrs. Elizabeth Wilkinson "valued no friends like to those who were friends to her soul." (Clarke, *Lives of thirty-two English divines*, 420.)

129. *Writings of Harrison and Browne*, 397-429; George Johnson, *A discours of some troubles in the banished English Church at Amsterdam*, STC 14664 (Amsterdam, 1603); Christopher Lawne et al., *The prophane schisme of the Brownists or Separatists . . . discovered*, STC 15324 (1612).

130. Peter Lorimer, *John Knox and the Church of England* (1875), 300.

131. For critical surveys of the literature, and of the question, *see* P. Besnard, *Protestantisme et capitalisme: la controverse post-weberienne* (Paris, 1970); E. Fischoff, "The Story of a Controversy." *Social Forces*, vol. 2 (1944); H. Luethy, "Once Again: Calvinism and Capitalism," *Encounter*, vol. 22 (1964), 26-38; H. R. Trevor-Roper, "Religion, the Reformation and Social Change" in the volume of that title (1967); David Little, *Religion, Order and Law: A Study in Pre-Revolutionary England* (1969).

132. In addition to the literature reviewed here, cf. an important and fruitful line of research pursued by historians of seventeenth-century New England: Edmund S. Morgan, *The Puritan Family: Essays on Religion and Domestic Relations in Seventeenth-Century New England* (Boston Massachusetts 1944, revised edn., Harper Torchbooks, New York, 1966); John Demos, *A Little Commonwealth: Family Life in Plymouth Colony* (New York, 1970); Philip J. Greven Jr., *Four Generations: Population, Land and Family in Colonial Andover, Massachusetts* (Ithaca, 1970); and, more theological than "anthropological," Robert G. Pope, *The Half-Way Covenant: Church Membership in Puritan New England* (Princeton, 1969).

133. *The Revolution of the Saints, op. cit.;* and cf. Little, *op. cit.*

134. As it was more than forty years ago with Professor Schücking, who wrote of "the family theocracy" as "the nucleus of the Puritan way of life." (*Op. cit.*, xii, 56.)

135. *Society and Puritanism*, esp. chap. 12, "The Secularization of the Parish," chap. 13, "The Spiritualization of the Household," chap. 14, "Individuals and Communities."

136. "Blood and Baptism: Kinship, Community and Christianity in Western Europe from the Fourteenth to the Seventeenth Centuries" in *Sanctity and Secularity: the Church and the World, Studies in Church History*, vol. 10, ed. D. Baker (Oxford 1973), 129-43. Dr. Bossy continues along the line of an argument begun with his "The Counter-Reformation and the People of Catholic Europe." *Past and Present* no. 47 (1970), 56-68.

137. Macfarlane, *op. cit.*, pt. III, "The Social World: Family, Kin and Neighbours." 105-60.

138. *Religion and the Rise of Capitalism*, Holland Memorial Lectures (1922), 1926.

139. Quoted, Morgan, *The Puritan Family* (1966 edn), 135.

140. Both Morgan, *The Puritan Family*, and Pope, *op. cit.*, imply that here was the rub.

141. *The Puritan Family*, 185-6 and chap. 7, "Puritan Tribalism," *passim*.

142. The title of a tract by John Geree, published in 1646, Wing G 589.

143. When the lecture on which this essay is based was delivered, some reference was made at this point to the Rev. Dr. G. F. Nuttall, doyen of historians of the mature age of Dissent, who was present on that occasion. It is both seemly and salutary that a tribute to Dr. Nuttall should appear in this printed text, since his work is a constant reminder that there is more than one horizontal dimension to the study of religious history. Spiritual rather than merely sociological breadth and understanding are surely the least dispensable qualities in the religious historian, and always will be.

APPENDIX

A GAZETTEER OF COMBINATION LECTURES

At the time of writing 'Lectures by Combination' and 'Towards a Broader Understanding of the Early Dissenting Tradition' (1974), combination lectures were known to have been established in the following sixty-three places:

Berkshire: Reading
Buckinghamshire: Aylesbury
Cheshire: Congleton, Frodsham
Derbyshire: Repton
Durham: Barnard Castle
Hertfordshire: Berkhampstead
Huntingdonshire: Huntingdon
Kent: Ashford
Lancashire: Blackburn, Bolton, Liverpool, Warrington
Leicestershire: Ashby-de-la-Zouche, Leicester
Lincolnshire: Alford, Grantham, Grimsby, Horncastle, Louth, Market Rasen, Sleaford
Norfolk: Diss, Fakenham, Hingham, King's Lynn, North Walsham, Norwich, Swaffham, Wighton, Wiveton, Wymondham
Northamptonshire: Brackley, Daventry, Kettering, Oundle
Nottinghamshire: Mansfield, Nottingham, Retford
Oxfordshire: Banbury, Deddington
Rutland: Oakham
Somerset: Bath, Bridgwater
Staffordshire: Burton-on-Trent
Suffolk: Botesdale, Bungay, Bury St Edmunds, Debenham, Framlingham, Haverhill, Ixworth, Lavenham, New Buckenham
Surrey: Dorking, Guildford, Kingston-on-Thames
Wiltshire: Marlborough
Yorkshire: Halifax, Leeds, Northallerton, Pudsey, Richmond

In 'Lectures by Combination' I appealed for further information on the subject (p. 487 n.4). New evidence was communicated by four correspondents and still more was discovered in the course of my own researches. It is now possible to add a further twenty-two locations, making eighty-five in all. This is not likely to prove an exhaustive list:

Cheshire: Bowden, Budworth, Ince, Knutsford, Macclesfield, Motteram, Nantwich, Northwich, Tarporley, Tarvin. (Thomas Paget, preface to John Paget, *Defence of church government* [1641]. I owe this information to the Revd. Dr. G. F. Nuttall.)
Cornwall: Saltash. (Richard Carew, *Survey of Cornwall* [1602], pp. 112-13. I owe this information to Mr. Jonathan Vage.)
Herefordshire: Elton, Leominster, Wigmore. (British Library, MS. Loan 29/202, Harley Papers i. 1582-1629, fol. 238ʳ.) Leintwardine. (British Library, MS. Harley 7517, fols. 20-3. I owe this information to Mr. Jonathan Harris.)
Kent: Cranbrook. (*Thomas Wotton's Letter-Book 1574-1586*, ed. G. Eland [1960], pp. 24-5.)
Lancashire: Winwick. (John Ley, *Defensive doubts and reasons for refusall of the oath*, [1641], Sig. a4.)
Shropshire: Bishops Castle, Shrewsbury, Webley. (British Library, MS. Loan 29/202, Harley Papers i. 1582-1629, fol. 238ʳ.)
Somerset: Crewkerne. (Crewkerne Grammar School Account Book 1610-1744, Somerset Record Office. I owe this information to Dr. R.W. Dunning.)
Suffolk: Aldeburgh. (*Suffolk Committees for Scandalous Ministers, 1614-1646*, ed. Clive Holmes, Suffolk Records Society, xiii [Ipswich, 1970], p. 118.)

INDEX